- 3 Day Loan
- No Renewals

REPORTING
for the
MEDIA

el W. Drager
Hays

OXFORD
UNIVERSITY PRESS

8 Sampson Mews, Suite 204, Don Mills, Ontario M3C 0H5
www.oupcanada.com

Oxford University Press is a department of the University of Oxford.
It furthers the University's objective of excellence in research, scholarship,
and education by publishing worldwide in

Oxford   New York
Auckland   Cape Town   Dar es Salaam   Hong Kong   Karachi
Kuala Lumpur   Madrid   Melbourne   Mexico City   Nairobi
New Delhi   Shanghai   Taipei   Toronto

With offices in
Argentina   Austria   Brazil   Chile   Czech Republic   France   Greece
Guatemala   Hungary   Italy   Japan   Poland   Portugal   Singapore
South Korea   Switzerland   Thailand   Turkey   Ukraine   Vietnam

Oxford is a trade mark of Oxford University Press
in the UK and in certain other countries

Published in Canada by Oxford University Press

Library and Archives Canada Cataloguing in Publication
Reporting for the media / Fred Fedler . . . [et al.]. — 1st Cdn. ed. Includes index.
ISBN 978-0-19-543019-6
1. Reporters and reporting—Problems, exercises, etc. I. Fedler, Fred
PN4781.R46 2010   070.4'3   C2010-903394-9

Cover images (top to bottom): © iStockPhoto.com/fotosipsak, iStockPhoto.com/track5,
iStockPhoto.com/dsteller, iStockPhoto.com/dlewis33

Oxford University Press is committed to our environment. This book is printed on permanent
(acid-free) paper ∞.

Printed and bound in Canada

1 2 3 4 – 14 13 12 11

Brief Contents

Detailed Contents

Preface

Is journalism part of the social sciences or the humanities? Do journalists have more in common with sociologists, political scientists and economists or with poets, philosophers and artists? These questions may seem esoteric, but the answers describe what journalists do and suggest how they should be trained.

The subject matter of most news stories falls squarely within the domain of the social sciences: crime, the economy, government policies, social justice and international relations. Reporters must be familiar with those fields. Some reporters have studied law, economics or diplomacy. Yet the practice of journalism has more to do with the humanities than with the social sciences. Like novelists and playwrights, reporters are storytellers. Like poets and artists, they seek compelling, emotionally powerful images. So what does it take to be a reporter?

Good reporters need two characteristics:

1. They must be engaged in the world around them.
2. They must be articulate.

Reporters' engagement in the world refers to a high degree of curiosity about their beats and life in general. Good reporters feel empathy for the people who are the subjects of their stories.

Curiosity helps reporters generate story ideas and develop the stories assigned to them. Good stories emerge when reporters ask why things work as they do, what's wrong, what's right, and who makes a difference. The more sophisticated the questions reporters ask, the more sophisticated and interesting their stories will be. Curiosity leads reporters to ask about things others may not have considered newsworthy or interesting. The incurious reporter might have a parent who is facing a debilitating disease and see it only as a personal problem. The curious reporter in the same situation recognizes that many people are living with the same problem and looking for support, information and encouragement. From that recognition emerges a great story idea. The incurious reporter may watch the city council award contract after contract to the same company and not wonder why that happens. The curious reporter will ask why the contractor is so successful, whether that success carries over to competition for private sector projects, and what connections to the city council the contractor might have. From those questions emerges a prize-winning investigative project.

Reporters must be constantly curious, asking about the details of their beats. How do police work? What do they do at a crime scene? How do they handle interrogations? Reporters should ask such questions with no expectation that the answers will lead to stories. No reporter can predict what tidbit of information may help unravel a great story. But even if the information yields no story, it might lead to a fact or insight that helps the reporter understand and explain events to readers and viewers.

Being engaged also means having empathy for the sources and subjects of news stories. People in the news often confront highly emotional situations. The sources and subjects may be victims of crime or the relatives of a victim; they may be people who have lost loved ones in a plane crash; they may be athletes who have just suffered a defeat; or they may be community residents worried about how a proposed development might affect their property and their lives. A story about a knife attack by a male employee on a female supervisor is not just an antiseptic crime story or an exercise in deductive logic. It is a story about anger, frustration, betrayal, terror and humiliation. A reporter who cannot empathize with the people involved cannot truly understand their experiences or tell their stories.

To empathize does not require reporters to abandon objectivity and impartiality. Empathy differs from sympathy. Sympathy requires one to share the feelings of another or to express a mutual understanding. Empathy means projecting oneself into the situation of another so as to better understand the other person. Reporters who have empathy for others can understand them without abandoning their own critical faculties. Empathy is not just consistent with objectivity; it is indispensable for producing a truly objective and thorough story. If reporters cannot understand the emotional states of the people they write about or assess the emotional changes events inflict on sources, they will fail to report fully.

Reporters also need to be articulate. Being articulate involves combining at least two skills: the first is to use words effectively, selecting the appropriate words, using them correctly, and arranging them in grammatical sentences with proper punctuation. The other skill is the ability to organize the elements of the story—the facts, the quotations and the anecdotes—in a manner both informative and captivating. Reporters who understand grammar and diction can construct sentences that are clear and precise. The skilful writer knows that the following sentences mean very different things:

> She only said she loved him.
> She said she loved only him.

The skilful writer also knows that one of these sentences accuses the subject of a crime:

> Wanda sent her husband Bob to the store.
> Wanda sent her husband, Bob, to the store.

The first sentence uses "Bob" as an essential (or restrictive) modifier of "husband"; it means that Wanda has more than one husband and the one she sent to the store is named Bob. The sentence implies that Wanda has committed the crime of bigamy. The second sentence has commas before and after "Bob"; it makes it clear that Wanda has only one husband, whose name is Bob.

The ability to construct clear, correct sentences is fundamental. But a news story may contain nothing but clear, correct sentences and still be impossible to read because the writer has failed to organize the material. Readers crave organization; if they don't find it, they stop reading. A story that jumps from one topic to another and back to the first without any sense of direction will confuse readers and drive them elsewhere for information. Reporters need to know how to organize information so that its significance becomes clear. Usually, in news stories, this means placing the newest, most newsworthy information early in the story. But sometimes writers want to hold some particularly dramatic or poignant fact for the end of the story.

All of the skills one needs to become a great reporter—curiosity, empathy, a knowledge of grammar, and the ability to organize stories—are learned skills. Some people may learn them more easily than others, or some may develop one set of skills more than the others. But anybody who can handle college- or university-level course work can cultivate the skills of a professional reporter.

Today's journalism students may worry less about mastering the essentials of journalism than they do about the sea changes affecting media industries and the possibilities of gainful employment once they graduate. Having weathered industry changes—plenty of them—in our own careers, we believe that preoccupation would be a mistake. The dust will settle, and when it does, those who have mastered the skills will be the ones who help to reinvent and reinvigorate a profession that at its best serves the public interest without fear or favour. We have been at pains in this first Canadian edition of *Reporting for the Media* to address the issues on both counts, and we hope readers will find it a welcome addition to the existing literature.

A Note on the Text

This first Canadian edition of *Reporting for the Media* (a longtime staple south of the border, now in its ninth U.S. edition) adheres to the approach Fred Fedler developed when he created this textbook nearly 35 years ago. In adapting this book for the Canadian market, we have engaged in exhaustive "Canadianization" of the original text—for instance, replacing American stories and commentary with comparable Canadian copy. We set out to maintain the standard of scholarship of the original and to contribute to the tremendous growth in recent years of Canadian sources for journalism students, educators and scholars. The book's features include:

- Design: The design has been updated (with new photographs and illustrations) by the publisher, Oxford University Press, to add visual interest for a visually oriented generation.

- Authority: Each chapter opens with a quotation from a Canadian journalist, writer or commentator.

- Chapter features: Most chapters close with the following four features: Checklist (to briefly recap the chapter's main points for easy review); Writing Coach Box (for sustenance and inspiration); Suggested Readings and Useful Websites (for further study); and Exercises (to practise and reinforce the skills addressed in the chapter).

- Copy-editing symbols: A list of these symbols appears on the inside of the front cover.

- Four appendices:

Appendix A: Copy-Editing Practice
Appendix B: *The Canadian Press Stylebook* (a summary of the stylebook, expanded to include broadcast)
Appendix C: Rules for Forming Possessives (for handy reference to common errors)
Appendix D: Answer Key (for selected exercises).

- Flexibility: *Reporting for the Media* is intended to be flexible. Teachers can assign the chapters in almost any order. Moreover, the book contains enough exercises for faculty members to assign their favourites and then assign extra exercises for students who need more help. Some teachers use the book for two semesters (for basic and advanced reporting classes). It can be used in media writing classes generally and in those specific to newswriting and reporting. Faculty members who prefer to emphasize traditional print media can assign the chapters on public relations and writing for the broadcast media as optional readings.

- Realistic exercises and examples: The exercises in this book are devised to represent real-world situations, and the example stories are drawn from actual and current news copy in Canadian publications to engage Canadian students and reflect Canadian values and concerns. To add to the realism, many of the exercises contain ethical problems: profanities, sexist comments, the names of rape victims, bloody details, and other material that many editors would be reluctant to publish. Students completing these exercises will have to deal with the problems, and we hope their decisions will spark lively class discussion.

- Practical approach: Like previous U.S. editions, the first Canadian edition is concrete, not abstract or theoretical. Its tone is practical and realistic. Its language is readable: clear, concise, simple and direct. Because of the book's realism, students will encounter the types of problems and assignments they are likely to find when they graduate and take entry-level jobs with the media.

A Note of Thanks

The authors wish to thank Oxford University Press for a vision of Canadian journalism education and for the opportunity to create a text that we hope will prove useful to Canadian journalism students and educators. We would also like to thank the many Canadian journalists whose fine work is featured and referred to throughout the text.

About the Authors

Maxine Ruvinsky is an associate professor in the School of Journalism, Faculty of Arts, at Thompson Rivers University in Kamloops, British Columbia. A former print and wire service reporter, she spent two decades in the newspaper business, working for a variety of Canadian dailies and for the national wire service Canadian Press in Montreal, where she was born and raised. She has also worked as a freelance writer and a teacher of writing. Ruvinsky is the author of *Practical Grammar: A Canadian Writer's Resource* (Oxford University Press, 2nd edn., 2009) and *Investigative Reporting in Canada* (Oxford University Press, 2008). She is a member of the advisory board of the Canadian Centre for Investigative Reporting. She holds a bachelor of fine arts degree in music (classical guitar) from Concordia University in Montreal, a master's degree in communications from the University of Calgary, and a doctorate in comparative literature (the language and literature of the press) from McGill University. Her research interests include investigative, issues, and literary journalism; freelance writing, non-profit news, and the democratization of media; rhetorical analysis; and pedagogical and cultural studies.

Charles A. Hays is an assistant professor in the School of Journalism, Faculty of Arts, at Thompson Rivers University. During a career in U.S. broadcast journalism, Hays worked as a radio producer and reporter at Oregon Public Broadcasting, followed by a move to the Northern High Plains where he worked in South Dakota as a commercial television and radio reporter. He has been active as a freelance magazine writer and freelance broadcast correspondent for cbs Radio News. He has also worked as a network administrator and technology trainer for a regional online education co-operative. Hays holds a bachelor's degree in technical journalism and broadcasting from Oregon State University, a master's degree in journalism from South Dakota State University, and a doctorate in mass communications from the University of Iowa, where he held the Moeller Doctoral Fellowship in Mass Communication and won an award for his classroom teaching. His research interests include the social construction of identity through mass media, communicating science news to audiences in the North, and methods of educating new journalists to cope with converged newsrooms.

We are always open to your opinions and comments about our work. If you have a comment or suggestion, please write us:

Maxine Ruvinsky
School of Journalism
Thompson Rivers University
900 McGill Road, P.O. Box 3010
Kamloops, BC V2C 5N3
mruvinsky@tru.ca

Charles A. Hays
School of Journalism
Thompson Rivers University
900 McGill Road, P.O. Box 3010
Kamloops, BC V2C 5N3
chays@tru.ca

1

Journalism Today

Our conventional response to all media, namely that it is how they are used that counts, is the numb stance of the technological idiot.
— Marshall McLuhan, Canadian academic, 1964

"For the times, they are a-changin'," wrote songwriter Bob Dylan, expressing the hope for social change embraced by an idealistic vanguard of the sixties generation. As the times change, so must journalism and the news media. Technological innovations that allow greater opportunity for updating developing stories and for disseminating news and opinion to larger audiences are to be welcomed, but they can hardly substitute for knowledge and skill in journalism.

Digital journalism and convergence are realities in today's news industries. Editors are asking new journalists to come to their first jobs with the traditional newsgathering savvy but also with a larger set of skills in digital news photography and still-image editing, pagination (or electronic layout), advanced computer-assisted research, the creation of online news content, and an eye for shooting and editing video for online or broadcast use. Even at smaller papers, the journalists who write the stories are increasingly responsible beyond the writing process for multimedia production techniques like Final Cut Pro.

Journalists must continue to be experts in reporting and writing news with passion, accuracy and authority, but they are adding the tools of videographers (video photographers) and imographers (digital image photographers). They are putting their stories not only on one media platform but also across the various platforms of print, television and the Internet—combining text with visuals and multimedia. They are expanding their skills to create blogs and podcasts, which can be downloaded onto consumers' cellphones, iPods and BlackBerries, not to mention the digital technologies that will likely have arisen by the time this book sees print.

This chapter describes what is happening in the ever-changing world of news and what it means for journalism training.

TRADITIONAL MEDIA

The traditional media make up a strong industry. Revenues generally have been increasing even as traditional media lose market share and newspapers experience downturns (not only in Canada but worldwide). Now, media companies are turning more attention to the Internet as a means of regaining old audiences and attracting new audiences. The Newspaper Association Databank (NADbank), an organization that tracks Canadian readership and circulation, found that in 2007, 78 per cent of adults over 18 read a newspaper at least once a week, spending an average of 46 minutes on the weekday version and lingering over the weekend editions for an average of 84 minutes.

As traditional hard-copy newspapers look for ways to transit the digital divide with new business models for online delivery, television outlets are also feeling the effects of competition from the Internet and changing their formats and business plans. Magazines are looking for alternative ways to maintain readership. Radio is reinventing itself as iPods, portable podcasting, satellite radio, digital high definition (HD), Internet streaming, and phones for downloading increase in use. A 2005 review of NADbank and Statistics Canada survey data by the Canadian Newspaper Association found that the Internet has forced people to reprioritize how they spend their time with various media. On the other hand, studies of new and emerging forms of public media show what older studies of traditional media have shown: that people who interest themselves in news, while they may favour one source above others, still tend to access all available sources. Decades ago, studies showed that regular newspaper readers also took in news from broadcast media, magazines and books. Recent studies show that the heaviest Internet users are also the heaviest users of other media. In addition to accessing information online, they also read more newspapers, magazines and books, listen to more radio, and view more television than those who say they spend little time online. In his groundbreaking book *The Vanishing Newspaper: Saving Journalism in the Age of Information*, U.S. journalism scholar and computer-assisted reporting pioneer Philip Meyer argued convincingly for a link between quality journalism and the financial success of news enterprises. Create quality journalism, Meyer contends, and loyal audiences will follow. The availability of powerful new technologies can enhance the ability to deliver that quality journalism.

As more people turn to the Internet, they take control of what news they access as well as how and when. Only 20 years ago, news consumers were at the mercy of traditional news organizations. They had to wait until their daily newspaper was delivered to learn the latest news or turn on the television for daily scheduled newscasts or the radio for brief hourly updates. The advent of the Internet has opened the possibility for news readers and viewers to get news as it happens and see stories updated continually. At first, however, Web editors for traditional print and broadcast media were content with just getting something online. Web content was "shovelware"—copies of newspaper or broadcast stories on the Internet—for users to access at any time, but sites updated the news only once a day. The novelty of the Internet is long gone. Internet users are no longer satisfied with yesterday's news or even this morning's news: they want to know what's happening now. The traditional media must adapt or die.

Media managers are making earnest investments to become successful in digital journalism. At one time, owners and managers feared that online news would replace print news and hoped if they ignored the Internet, it would just go away. Initially, their hopes seemed justified. Half-hearted experiments in the 1970s and 1980s produced unenthusiastic users who did not return. Today, however, Internet technology is more user-friendly, and revenues are growing. Media managers are striving to become successful news providers online and increasingly expect new journalists signing on to their companies to have a corresponding spectrum of skills. Digital journalism is regarded less as a competitor and more as an important component, bringing in revenue and audiences.

As media managers try to find the best ways to present stories online while protecting copyright and remaining financially viable, they also are experimenting with new ways to share resources with other media partners.

CONVERGENCE

The Encarta World English Dictionary defines "convergence" as "coming together from different directions, especially a uniting or merging of groups." In journalism, this means the sharing of facilities, newsgathering resources, personnel or content.

Convergence can mean that one media owner brings together its different news organizations under one umbrella to share personnel and equipment; convergence can also refer to partnerships between owners of different media, such as newspapers and television stations or the Internet. For instance, a television reporter might receive a news tip and share it with the newspaper partner. Sometimes the print reporter will cover an event and write about it for the newspaper and then do a stand-up or oral report for the television station. In the aftermath of the September 11, 2001, terrorist attacks in the United States, many online news owners realized they needed partners to get breaking news and updated information online quickly. It is more common now for television sites to borrow text content or graphics from newspapers and for newspaper sites to borrow video from television stations. News wire services have a long-standing practice of requiring member newsrooms to share stories generated "in-house" in return for receiving wire reports from outside the areas they cover.

Proponents of convergence say that sharing sources enables news organizations to cover stories in greater depth. They maintain that if organizations share newsgathering and reporting resources instead of competing for the "scoop," their stories will be more accurate, comprehensive and thorough. Most supporters contend that news organizations will be able to concentrate on covering local issues in greater depth.

Critics of convergence say that sharing tips and material leads to less diversity in stories between media markets. They fear the competition-lowering effect of such a levelling of the playing field between news organizations that used to compete with each other but now co-operate. They argue that when news outlets do not compete with each other, there is no incentive to strive for excellence or fight for a larger share of the audience. Critics also maintain that organizations in some markets waste time and space by advertising for each other and referring audiences to allied newspapers or TV stations for more information on a story.

DIGITAL JOURNALISM

More than 330 million people worldwide actively use the Internet, and more than 1 billion use it occasionally. In Canada, approximately 65 per cent of all adults are online from either home or work. The percentage is higher in major metropolitan areas (up to about 80 per cent) and lower in rural areas where large distances and sparse populations mean high-speed broadband connections do not exist.

Most online news sites do not charge for subscriptions or for access to their content; their revenues depend on advertisers. As news sites cultivate loyal users, they can sell the number of users to advertisers—in the same way media have always enticed advertisers. If the content is dull or inaccurate, the number of users dwindles, and advertisers will go elsewhere. If revenues are limited, the site loses quality, more users turn away, and the downward spiral continues.

Newspaper and television stations are aware that people who actively look for news, particularly younger audiences, get a lot of their information from the Internet. Many users are comfortable with multimedia, posting to blogs and social media sites like Facebook and YouTube.

The Internet gives users quick access to up-to-date stories told through multiple media—text, graphics, photos, audio, video, and hyperlinks to other information. The story may begin with one medium and then be layered with other media that can tell parts of the story better. Some news organizations want their journalists to be mobile and multi-faceted. The prestigious American Poynter Institute for media studies offers a popular course called The Backpack Journalist to teach journalists how to cover a story at the scene by taking notes, shooting with a video camera, operating a tape recorder, using a digital camera, and then sending the materials by satellite phone or packaging it together with a laptop computer. Back in the newsroom, the reporter might hand all of the raw data to a technician who combines it for presentation in various media. Or the multimedia reporter will take the raw data gathered from the scene to write a print story or a television script, tell the story in a TV stand-up, create graphics, compose a photo gallery or slide show, announce the story with sound bites, or put together a video package for uploading to a news website. Many journalists write their stories in blogs, complete with

A journalist uses modern technology and equipment to work on her story.

audio and video, or prepare them for podcasts. Multimedia—or digital—journalism is becoming more prevalent because users are accessing text, video and audio from the Internet in increasing numbers.

Some of the forms of digital journalism are new, but the technology also is driving news organizations back to their roots in reporting local news. Instead of sitting at a desk, gathering information from the phone, emails and the Internet, mobile journalists ("mojos") rarely go into the office, instead spending their days in the communities they cover. They often post their stories directly to the Web from their laptop in their car or from a wifi hotspot. News organizations can assign their reporters to covering local news because they can subscribe to the Canadian Press or other news services for regional, national, and international coverage in the forms of text, photo slide shows with audio, online video, and interactive graphics (maps and charts).

CITIZEN JOURNALISM

As news organizations increase their use of the Web, they have begun to invite readers and viewers to participate in creating content. Many invite users to post additional information or corrections to reporters' stories and to join in story blogs. They also encourage readers to share their still images or videos of community happenings. As citizens participate more in the news process, the flow of news and information is controlled less by editors, who were accustomed to choosing the stories to be covered from among the many possible events and issues that occur in a community—the much touted "gatekeeper" role of the press. Some editors rely on citizens' participation (called "crowd sourcing" or "user-generated content") to augment the work of their limited numbers of reporters and photographers. With more participation and coverage, journalists and citizens feel more connected to the community and each other.

Local news sites that operate outside of corporate media are called citizen-media sites. Hundreds of citizen-media sites exist, some for-profit and others non-profit. Most citizen-media site operators say the value of their sites is in their provision of local information not found elsewhere and in the opportunities created for dialogue. Most also say they add to what local news media provide and help build connections to the community.

Site owners range from veteran journalists disillusioned with corporate media to individuals wanting to build community among citizens by providing a place for reporting on events deemed unimportant by local news organizations. The overriding objective for many citizen media sites is to provide news and information about the community that is being overlooked by established newspapers and broadcast stations. Most of these sites began as a place for citizens to post whatever they wanted, such as discussions, photos, calendar events, committee reports, public meetings, ruminations, personal observances and photos—news other than violent accidents and deaths. Many have evolved into professional examples of alternative media in the twenty-first century. In some cases, citizen media have pushed local news organizations to do a better job of covering more local news. In the case of national and international news coverage, the effects may be less salutary, with news "aggregators" disseminating reports created and paid for by more traditional media but not sharing in the costs of production.

HOW TO TRAIN JOURNALISTS
FOR THE TWENTY-FIRST CENTURY

Long before the advent of online communications, journalism schools hotly debated the best ways to train reporters, asking, for instance, whether they should emphasize critical thinking or production skills. On the one hand, many of today's J-schools offer core courses that drill the fundamentals of news judgment and gathering, writing, and organizing information in one type of medium, usually print. The idea is that once students understand the basics of good reporting skills, they can adapt stories to other media with added training in the different equipment and technology. On the other hand, some schools immediately introduce their students to the presentation of news on a variety of platforms. Students are taught how to operate audio equipment, digital cameras, video cameras and computer software for different types of online presentations. Assignments often consist of adapting the same story to print, audio, voice-over slide shows, video, stand-ups, video packages, online, and multimedia combined. Schools across the globe are trying to predict whether future journalists will be specialists in one medium or will need to have a broad general skill set that allows them work anywhere.

Many journalism educators maintain that the essential elements for journalists depend not on online gadgetry but rather on the traditional skills of critical thinking and storytelling along with quintessential human qualities like integrity and compassion. One researcher of digital journalism surveyed some 450 online managers and producers and found that the top requirements for story editing were news judgment and knowledge of grammar and style; requirements for content creation were the ability to report and write original stories and edit photos; and for attitudes and overall skills, the successful digital reporter needed to be detail-oriented, a good communicator, and able to multitask and learn new technologies.

The objective of this textbook is to act as a springboard, training students in the fundamentals of journalistic critical thinking, news judgment and writing. This includes gathering, organizing and presenting information across media professions and platforms. Once students are thoroughly educated and practised in the basics of print journalism, they can adapt their knowledge and expertise to all types of reporting for the media.

 ## Changing the Way We Think

In 2007, Roger LeBlanc, news editor of the *Guelph Mercury* in Guelph, Ont., penned a local column lauding mobile journalism as a way of remaining current and involving the community:

We're almost there. *The Mercury*'s website is finally starting to come together.

It wasn't all that long ago when the site offered mainly portions of the day's newspaper.

But now we're striving to create a website that provides just about everything you need to know about what's happening in Guelph and the surrounding area.

We've been taking baby steps, but the staff here have eagerly taken on the challenge to take longer and longer strides.

We've not only changed the look of the site, but we're also changing the way we think. Instead of having one deadline per day, GuelphMercury.com has many.

A key feature of the website is the news update section where we post items that just happened or are ongoing.

It's provided a great tool for us to remain timely and accurate. For instance, when a disaster strikes, details are in short supply. But the website can now offer good numbers and context as they become available.

We're also growing our multimedia content.

The website now has locally created videos, photo slide shows, documents related to the day's news and audio files.

Some of it is exclusive to the web, such as a video tribute to the late Ken Danby. And some enhances what's in the newspaper, as with podcasts of news conferences and speeches. For instance, you can now read about *The Mercury*'s last book club session or listen to it at home.

The website is also a tool to foster conversations.

Each week we feature an online question with the results posted on page A2 of Saturday's paper. This week we ask if you think Councillor Gloria Kovach should try to replace ousted Conservative candidate Brent Barr.

That topic is also under discussion in one of our blogs, From the Editors.

We now have five blogs in action, with our new city hall offering, 59 Carden Street, generating quite a bit of traffic.

I think the same will happen on our varsity sports blog, Big Man on Campus, as word spreads about reporter Greg Layson's take on University of Guelph sports.

For the past few months the big online hurdle has been learning how to master all the technology.

The software for blogs is super easy to navigate, but editing video and getting it online for people like me—who have spent their entire careers with newspapers—has taken some work and much patience.

But I've found most of the people in our field have seen this as an opportunity.

It's a way to try new things and tell your stories in ways we never dreamed we could 20 years ago.

The idea of a roving mobile journalist with a laptop, digital camera and BlackBerry filing news as it happens where it happens isn't science fiction, but science fact. With a solid website in place and a mindset to make the most of it, I don't think that model is far off here.

In the meantime, do take the time to surf over to GuelphMercury.com and see what we have to offer, from multimedia to movie listings, community events to ways to report corrections.

And keep an eye out in the newsprint edition for teasers that will point you to the website for related material.

It's a work in progress, but I think it's heading in the right direction.

2 Newswriting Style

Get to the point as directly as you can; never use a big word if a little one will do.
— **Emily Carr, Canadian artist and writer**

Newswriters have a challenging task. They must convey information, often complex information, to their readers and viewers. They have to tell a story by providing facts in a clear and concise manner, using simple language. Simplicity of language matters because newswriters are trying to reach readers and viewers whose capabilities and interests vary greatly. Some may have a high school diploma, whereas others may have a doctoral degree. Some may be fascinated by world events, but others may prefer to learn about the world of entertainment and celebrities. To communicate effectively to a mass audience, newswriters must learn to present information in a way that will allow almost everyone to read and understand it.

Newswriting style also demands that reporters present factual information succinctly and in an impartial or objective manner. Unlike some other forms of writing, the news story must fit the limited time and space available. Yet even short stories must contain enough information that readers can understand what has happened. Also, one of the basic principles of journalism is the separation of fact and opinion. Reporters and editors strive to keep opinions out of news stories. Beginners may find newswriting style awkward at first; however, once it is mastered, students will find it can help them be more clear and concise in all writing.

The first step to a well-written story is planning and preparation. Before writers attempt to construct a news story—or any other piece of writing—they identify the main idea they want to convey to their readers and the steps they must take to do so.

PREWRITING

Identifying the Central Point

Writing, whether about simple or complex topics, requires preparation and organization. The preparation begins even before the reporter starts gathering information, when the story is just an idea in the mind of the reporter, editor or producer. When reporters have gathered all the information they think they need for a story, they still face the task of organizing. The best way to do this, for long stories and short ones, is to write a central point and a brief outline.

A central point for a news story is a one- or two-sentence summary of what the story is about and why it is newsworthy. It is a statement of the topic—and more. Several stories may have the same topic, but the central point of each of those stories should be unique. If a jetliner crashed on landing at an airport, the next edition of the local paper probably would have several stories about the crash, each of which would have a unique central point. One story might have as its central point "Wind and rain made airport runways treacherous, but other jetliners made successful landings." That story would report on weather conditions at the airport and whether air traffic controllers and other pilots considered them to be severe. The central point for another story might be "The heroism of passengers and flight attendants saved the lives of dozens of people." That story would report what happened in the passenger cabin after the crash and how those who survived made it to safety. A third story's central point might be "Federal investigators have recovered the flight data recorders but will need days or weeks to figure out what caused the crash." That story would focus on what will likely happen in the investigation of the crash. Although each of these stories would be about the jetliner crash, each would have a distinct central point, and each would have only information relevant to that central point.

Good writers include a statement of the central point in each story. The central point may be in the first paragraph, called the "lead." Or it may be in a nut paragraph—called a "nut graf"—that follows a lead and tells an anecdote, describes a scene, or uses some other storytelling device to entice the reader into the story. By including the central point, writers clearly tell readers what they will learn from reading the entire story.

News stories may have many possible central points. Which one reporters use can depend on their news judgment and their estimation of what their audiences want to know. If a flamboyant head of a major corporation resigns when the business is forced to pay millions of dollars in damages after losing a lawsuit, the story for a local newspaper might focus on whether the company will have to eliminate jobs. A story in a financial newspaper might have as its central point the impact of the lawsuit on investors' confidence in the company. A newspaper that covers legal affairs might emphasize the failure of the company's courtroom strategy. Although these publications and their reporters would select different central points for their stories, each choice would be appropriate for the publication's audience.

Story Outlines

Reporters usually have a good idea what the central point of their stories will be even as they begin gathering the information. Often, however, unexpected information emerges that forces them to rethink the central point of the story. Therefore, reporters always review their notes and other materials they have gathered before they start writing. Reviewing assures reporters they have identified the most newsworthy central point and have the information they need to develop it. It also helps them decide what the major sections of their stories will be. A reporter who has covered a local resident's decision to run for mayor might write a central-point statement that says "Smith announces plans to run for mayor." The reporter then might decide that the story should have these major sections:

- why the candidate is running;
- what the candidate plans to do if elected;
- reaction to the candidate's announcement.

The central point and this brief outline of the major sections form the skeleton of the story. The reporter needs only to develop each section.

Once reporters have selected a central point and written a brief outline, they can go through their notes again to decide what information belongs where. Some reporters number passages according to what section of the story they relate to. Others use coloured pens or markers to indicate where to put particular facts, quotes or anecdotes. They discard information that does not fit in any of the sections.

Reporters who fail to identify a central point for a story or who lose sight of that central point risk writing stories that are incoherent and incomplete. Here's a story by a student reporter that lacks a central focus:

Cellphones have implanted themselves in society as the leading communication tool and toy. Many people use their phone to conduct business in a work environment while others use it as a constant contact system among friends either through text messaging or frequent calling. Students tend to do both, but some might say they use their phone more as a toy than a tool.

Text messaging has become the new trend in cellphone usage, according to Jennifer Mason, spokesperson for Cingular Wireless.

"We have seen a tremendous increase in the volume of text messaging over the past two years," Mason said. "I think that shows our customers find the service useful and economical. Our customers do not have to be tied to a computer to send a message to a family member or friend."

For many college and university students, text messaging is a more convenient way to contact someone than calling. When asking students around campus how often they send or receive messages, many responded that they send or receive 10 or more messages on a daily basis. Most said they use the messaging feature on their cellphone to communicate with people more often than actually calling.

This text-messaging trend has the possibility of creating problems in the classroom. Students are now able to participate in academic dishonesty or cheating on tests with relative ease because of this feature. The process of sending a message is simple and silent, making it a stealthy way to get the answer from a buddy who has taken the exam.

New technologies such as downloading games and music to a cellphone are incentives for students to use their phones more as a toy than a tool. The ability to purchase wallpapers, screensavers, and ring tones also has sparked interest among students nationwide. The fees are small, and the technologies are ever increasing, leading to more and more "playtime" on cellphones.

In 2005, an American university conducted a study of nearly 600 students on their cellphone-use tendencies. The average number of calls per day found by the study was 11. Students seem to talk most between the hours of 6 p.m. and midnight, most of the time in their own homes. The study also showed that female students tend to talk more often while driving their car and speak more frequently with immediate family members than do male students. Male students, on the other hand, tend to talk more often while on campus and with close friends than do females.

With these trends it is clear that students rely heavily on their cellphones both as a toy and a tool. Many students like to casually call their friends or family just to check up on them. Others use their phones to communicate with colleagues at work or school. Whatever the use, cellphones are a part of student life on campuses across the country and will be for years to come.

The lead identifies ways university students may use their cellphones; however, the story does not clearly and completely explain why or how students use their cellphones. Then the story jumps to how students may use their phones for cheating, but it does not address students or university officials to determine how prevalent the problem may be. Finally, the story addresses the issue regarding using a cellphone as a "toy." Yet the story fails to adequately address the issue, making only a few general comments about cellphones as toys used for "playtime." Although all of these issues may be part of the same topic, they belong in separate stories with distinct central points. The writer of this story lost track of the story's central point and failed to find enough information to develop one central point thoroughly.

The process of identifying a central point and story outline has been described here in the context of routine news stories, which may have fewer than 1,000 words. This same process can help writers of much longer pieces, such as multipart newspaper series, magazine articles, and books. Donald Barlett and James B. Steele, U.S. reporters who have produced a number of long investigative stories and books, say one of the keys to their success is organizing information. They spend months gathering documents and conducting interviews, all of which are filed by topic or name of individual, agency or corporation. Then they read the material several times because important issues and ideas often become clear only after time. Once they have an outline of the major sections of their piece, they start drafting the story section by section. Finally, they polish sections and spend most of their time working on leads and transitions between sections. Barlett and Steele's description of how they work confirms what most writers say: No one sits down and writes great stories. Writers must plan their work.

SIMPLIFY WORDS, SENTENCES AND PARAGRAPHS

George Orwell, in his classic essay "Politics and the English language," complained that too often writers replace simple verbs and appropriate nouns with complicated phrases. Such phrases tend to obscure facts and confuse the reader.

To simplify stories, avoid long, unfamiliar words. Whenever possible, substitute shorter and simpler words that convey the same meaning. Use the word "about" rather than "approximately," "build" rather than "construct," "call" rather than "summon," and "home" rather than "residence."

Also, use short sentences and short paragraphs. Rewrite long or awkward sentences and divide them into shorter ones that are easier to read and understand. Research has consistently found a strong correlation between readability and sentence length: the longer a sentence is, the more difficult it is to understand. One survey found that 75 per cent of readers were able to understand sentences containing an average of 20 words, but understanding dropped rapidly as the sentences became longer.

Sentence length often reveals the publication's intended audience. The sentences in comics contain an average of eight words, whereas the sentences in publications for the general public average 15 to 20 words. Publications with sentences averaging 20 to 30 words are much more difficult to understand, and they appeal to more specialized and better educated audiences. These publications include such magazines as *The Walrus*, *Harper's*, and scholarly, scientific or professional journals.

This does not mean that all stories should have nothing but short sentences. Too many short sentences strung together makes writing sound choppy. Long sentences, constructed and used with care, can be effective tools for the writer. Overuse of either long or very short sentences can make the writing awkward and difficult for the reader to comprehend.

Newswriters should write for the ear, listening to the natural rhythm, or flow, of the words and sentences they put on paper. They should test their stories by reading them aloud to themselves or to a friend. If the sentences sound awkward or inappropriate for a conversation with friends, the writer must rewrite them and be particularly careful to avoid complex phrases and long, awkward sentences.

The following three paragraphs written by Anne Hull of the *St. Petersburg (Fla.) Times* in a story about a teenager who pulled a gun on a female police officer illustrate the impact one can achieve by combining short and long sentences:

> The sound she heard from the gun would reverberate for months.
> Click.
> It was the same sound the key in the lock makes as the father comes home now to the empty apartment, greeted by the boy in the golden frame.

Notice the construction of those three paragraphs. One is the ultimate of brevity—only one word—and the other two sentences are 11 words and 29 words. The combination of the three sentences creates a vivid picture for the reader, as well as a rhythm that produces drama and touches the emotions.

Writing coaches routinely note that concise writing can be just as dramatic and have as much impact as long narrative passages. Many writers tend to overwrite when seeking drama or impact. Yet a few carefully selected words can better convey the story to readers.

Often, students tend to write sentences that are much too long. They are more likely to write sentences containing 40 or 50 words than sentences containing four or five. Yet short sentences are clearer and more forceful.

Edna Buchanan, who won a Pulitzer Prize when she was a police reporter for the *Miami Herald*, wrote in her best-selling book *The Corpse Had a Familiar Face*:

> Dozens of fires erupted at intersections. Firefighters were forced back by gunfire. Businesses and stores burned unchecked. "It's absolutely unreal," said Miami Fire Inspector George Bilberry. "They're burning down the whole north end of town."
> Late Sunday, 15 major blazes still raged out of control. Snipers fired rifles at rescue helicopters. The looting and burning went on for three days. Public schools were closed, and an 8 p.m.–6 a.m. curfew was established.

Buchanan's sentences average only 8.1 words. Several of her sentences contain only five or six words. The longest contains 11. Yet the writing is graphic and dramatic, letting the reader feel the tension of the scene.

Compare Buchanan's writing style with the following sentence taken from William L. Shirer's book *Gandhi: A Memoir*:

> Clever lawyer that he was, Jinnah took the independence that Gandhi had wrestled for India from the British by rousing the masses to non-violent struggle and used it to set up his own independent but shaky Moslem nation of Pakistan, destined, I believed then, to break up, as shortly happened when the eastern Bengali part, separated from the western part by a thousand miles of India's territory, broke away to form Bangladesh; destined eventually, I believed, to simply disappear.

Because of its length and complexity, this sentence is much more difficult to understand. It contains 80 words.

To make their newspapers more readable, many editors are demanding shorter stories with shorter sentences and simpler words.

Some critics have charged that newspapers' emphasis on simplicity makes their stories dull, yet the opposite is true. When stories are well-written, simplicity makes them clearer and more interesting. Well-written stories contain no distracting clutter; instead, they emphasize the most important facts and report those facts in a clear, forceful manner.

There's another important reason for using short sentences and short paragraphs in news stories. Newspapers are printed in small type, with narrow columns, on cheap paper. Long paragraphs—producing large, grey blocks of type—discourage readers. So reporters divide stories into bite-sized chunks that are easy to read and understand. Also, from a newspaper design standpoint, the white space left at the ends of paragraphs helps to brighten each page.

One way to keep sentences short, clear and conversational is to use the normal word order: subject, verb, object. Notice how much clearer and more concise the following sentence becomes when it uses this normal word order:

> Designing a new front page for the paper was undertaken by the publisher.
> REVISED: The publisher designed a new front page for the paper.

Also be certain the ideas in each sentence are related. If they are not, even short sentences can become confusing:

> Elected president of the student senate, he went to Parkdale Elementary School.
> Planning on being the first person in line for the concert, she bought her first car when she was 16.

Long introductory phrases and subordinate clauses overload sentences, making them more difficult to understand:

> Fighting the wildfire from two fronts to keep the flames from engulfing the entire town, firefighters decided to let the house burn.
> REVISED: Firefighters decided to let the house burn. They had been fighting the wildfire on two fronts to keep the flames from engulfing the entire town.

Sometimes beginners pack too many ideas into a single sentence:

> The mayor said he was happy that the city council had passed the resolution increasing the public library tax to provide more funds to expand the library's book collection, build a website, and add a new wing to house government documents, but the amount of the increase was not enough to do everything that has to be done because repairs are needed to the roof of the public library building and facilities must be improved for the disabled.
> REVISED: The mayor said he was happy that the city council had passed the resolution increasing the public library tax but added that the amount of the increase

is not enough to do everything that has to be done. The tax increase will provide funds to expand the library's book collection, build a website, and add a new wing to house government documents. Other work that needs to be done, the mayor said, includes repairs to the library's roof and improvements in facilities for the disabled.

Paragraph length, as well as sentence length, varies from publication to publication. A paragraph should demonstrate relationships between ideas. It is a means of making complicated material clear. Like the words that form sentences, the sentences that form paragraphs should flow together, logically combining similar thoughts or ideas. Paragraphs should not combine unrelated ideas. But ideas that are related or belong together should not be artificially separated just to create shorter paragraphs. If you needlessly separate ideas, you risk producing choppy writing. Skilled writers are able to connect related ideas and material in a logical sequence that flows smoothly throughout the story.

Eliminate Unnecessary Words

Unnecessary words confuse readers and make reading more difficult. Newswriters must eliminate unnecessary words yet retain enough detail to make their stories informative.

Most news organizations can publish or air only a fraction of the information they receive each day. An editor for a large newspaper once estimated that the paper received 1.25 million to 1.5 million words every day but had enough space to publish only one-tenth of that material. By writing concisely, reporters present readers with as much information as possible. Brevity also helps readers grasp the main idea of each story. Writers who use two or more words when only one is necessary waste time and space. Some words are almost always unnecessary: "that," "then," "currently," "now," and "presently," for example. Because some nouns and the verb tense tell when an action occurred—in the past, present or future—it is redundant to add a second word reiterating the time, such as "*past* history," "is *now*," and "*future* plans."

Notice how easily several unnecessary words can be deleted from the following sentences without changing their meaning:

> She was able to begin college classes her senior year in high school.
> REVISED: She began college classes her senior year in high school.
> At the present time he is planning to leave for Toronto at 3 p.m. in the afternoon next Thursday.
> REVISED: He plans to leave for Toronto at 3 p.m. Thursday.

Be especially careful to avoid phrases and sentences that are redundant—that unnecessarily repeat the same idea. The following phrases contain only two or three words, yet at least one—the word in italics—is unnecessary:

> *dead* body
> *exactly* identical
> hurry *up*
> *mutual* cooperation
> reason *why*
> *armed* gunman
> split *apart*
> *unexpected* surprise
> *past* experiences
> free *of charge*

Improving some redundant sentences requires more thought and effort:

> Deaths are extremely rare, with only one fatality occurring in every 663,000 cases.
> REVISED: One death occurs in every 663,000 cases.

Redundancy often arises because writers introduce a topic and then present some specific information about it. Usually, the more specific information is sufficient:

Trying to determine who was responsible for the burglary, police checked the door frame for fingerprints.

REVISED: Police checked the door frame for fingerprints.

Needless repetition is even more common in longer passages involving several sentences. Sentences appearing near the end of a paragraph should not repeat facts implied or mentioned earlier:

This is not the first elected office she has held in the city. She has been a city council member, a member of the library board, and a tax collector.

REVISED: She has been a city council member, a member of the library board, and a tax collector.

Quiz

Are you ready for a quiz? Do not rewrite the following redundant sentences; simply cross out the unnecessary words.

1. She was in a quick hurry and warned that, in the future, she will seek out textbooks that are sexist and demand that they be totally banned.
2. As it now stands, three separate members of the committee said they will try to prevent the city from closing down the park during the winter months.
3. His convertible was totally destroyed, and in order to obtain the money necessary to buy a new car, he now plans to ask a personal friend for a loan to help him along.
4. After police found the lifeless body, the medical doctor conducted an autopsy to determine the cause of death and concluded that the youth had been strangled to death.
5. In the past, he often met up with the students at the computer lab and, because of their future potential, invited them to attend the convention.
6. Based upon her previous experience as an architect, she warned the committee members that constructing the new hospital facility will be pretty expensive and suggested that they step in and seek more donors.
7. The two men were hunting in a wooded forest a total of 12 kilometres away from the nearest hospital in the region when both suffered severe bodily injuries.
8. Based upon several studies conducted in the past, he firmly believes that, when first started next year, the two programs should be very selective, similar in nature and conducted only in the morning hours.

Now count the number of words you eliminated—your score. The answers appear in Appendix D.

0–30: Amateur	Were you really trying?
31–40: Copy kid	Time to enrol in Newswriting 101.
41–50: Cub	You've still got a lot to learn.
51–60: Pro	You're getting there, but can do even better.
61+: Expert	Time to ask your boss for a raise or your teacher for an A.

REMAIN OBJECTIVE

Journalists should strive to be as impartial or "objective" as possible. Reporters are neutral observers, not advocates or participants. They provide the facts and details of the stories they report, not their own opinions about the facts and events. Journalists express their opinions only in editorials and commentaries, which usually appear in a section of the newspaper or a part of the news broadcast reserved for opinion. Sometimes, keeping fact and opinion separate is difficult.

When CBC reporter David Common wanted to tell the public about rising casualties among Canadian soldiers in Afghanistan, his patriotism was evident in the first few sentences of his blogged Kandahar Dispatch on October 1, 2007:

> I've just spent a few days on a thrilling and depressing story. My camera operator and I were embedded with an American medevac helicopter crew. They're a good, friendly, capable bunch of guys who welcomed us instantly.
>
> By far, the majority of the injured who are loaded into the back of their heaving Blackhawks are Canadians.
>
> That tells a tale now rarely talked about: a great many Canadian soldiers are being injured in Afghanistan. And we're not hearing about it.

Common was obviously affected emotionally by the story he was telling, but he employed his journalist's training to stick to the point and to relay information that he knew would affect other Canadians in a similar way. He did not try to persuade readers to feel as he did; he reported the telling facts with simple eloquence.

Following the September 11, 2001, terrorist attacks in the United States, some news reporters and television anchors there and in Canada began wearing their patriotism on their sleeves. Critics said that overt displays of patriotism were inconsistent with news organizations' obligation to separate news and opinion. Tasteful expressions of love of country, especially in a time of national crisis, do not necessarily conflict with a journalist's obligation to remain impartial, as long as the journalist continues to examine government policies with diligence and skepticism.

More difficult problems with objectivity arose during the Iraq War when print and television reporters accompanied American combat units. These embedded reporters spent weeks training, travelling, and sharing hardships with the men and women they covered. Gordon Dillow, a columnist for the *Orange County (Calif.) Register* who covered a marine company during the war, wrote in an article for the *Columbia Journalism Review*: "The biggest problem I faced as an embed with the Marine grunts was that I found myself doing what journalists are warned from J-school not to do: I found myself falling in love with my subject. I fell in love with 'my' Marines."

A reporter's tendency to identify with sources is natural, even in situations less extreme than combat, but good reporters strive to resist the temptation and to keep their stories free of opinion. When reporters inject their opinions into a story, they risk offending readers and viewers who may not want reporters telling them how to think. Reporters assume audience members are intelligent and capable of reaching their own conclusions about issues in the news.

One way reporters keep their opinions out of stories is to avoid loaded words, such as "demagogue," "extremist," "radical," "racist," "segregationist" and "zealot." Such words are often unnecessary and inaccurate. Many times, these loaded words state the obvious: that an argument was "heated," a rape "violent," or a death "unfortunate." Reporters can eliminate the opinions in some sentences simply by deleting a single adjective or adverb: "*alert* witness," "*famous* author," "*gala* reception," "*thoughtful* reply." Here are two more examples:

> The pricey tickets are available only at the door.
> REVISED: The tickets are available at the door.
> The tragic accident killed three people.
> REVISED: The accident killed three people.

Writers can avoid loaded words by reporting factual details as clearly and thoroughly as possible.

Entire sentences sometimes convey opinions, unsupported by facts. Good editors (and instructors) will eliminate these sentences. Often, deletion is the only way to correct the problem. Here are two examples:

> The candidate looks like a winner.
> Everyone is angry about the mayor's decision.

Newswriters can report the opinions expressed by other people—the sources for their stories—but must clearly attribute those opinions to the source. If reporters fail to provide the proper attribution, readers may think the reporters are expressing their own opinions or agreeing with the source:

> The family filed a lawsuit because the doctor failed to notice the injury.
> REVISED: The family's lawsuit charges that the doctor failed to notice the injury.

A single word expressing an opinion can infuriate readers. When a student was raped, a news story reported that she suffered cuts on her arms and hands but "was not seriously injured." An irate reader asked, "Since when is rape at knifepoint not enough violence to constitute serious injury?"

Avoid Stereotypical "-Isms"

Stereotyping occurs when a newswriter uses offensive, condescending or patronizing terms or phrases in describing other individuals, especially women, racial or religious minorities, the elderly or the disabled. Good newswriters are attuned to the "-isms"—racism, sexism, agism—that can appear in a story even unintentionally. They understand their audiences and the impact their words may have on some readers.

Racism

Reporters should avoid racial stereotypes. Further, they should mention a person's race, religion or ethnic background only when the fact is clearly relevant to a story. *The Canadian Press Stylebook* advises identifying a person "by race, colour, national origin, or immigration status only when it is truly pertinent" and providing a full description, "including but not limited to colour," only if "a person wanted by police is at large."

Sometimes students and even professionals report that a "black" or an "aboriginal" committed a crime, but usually the criminal's race is irrelevant to the story. Identifying a criminal by race when that is the only characteristic known is especially harmful because it casts suspicion on every member of the race. *The Canadian Press Stylebook* offers the following guidelines:

> The appearance of racial minorities in news reports should not be confined to accounts of cultural events, racial tension or crime. A Korean shopkeeper's reaction to a sales tax is just as valid as a Scottish stockbroker's. Include comments from various groups in matters of public interest such as federal taxes or national surveys on general topics.... [Race or ethnicity is pertinent] when it motivates an incident or when it helps explain the emotions of those in confrontation. Thus references to race and ethnic background are relevant in reports of racial controversy, immigration difficulties, language discussions and so on.

By that policy, the following description makes appropriate use of a person's race to describe a specific individual whom some readers might be able to identify:

> Witnesses said the bank robber was a white man, about 50 years old and six feet tall. He weighed about 250 pounds, was wearing a blue suit, and escaped on a Honda motorcycle.

Some stories demean Canada's First Nations peoples by using descriptive words or phrases that cast them in a negative light. Avoid such obviously stereotypical words as "wampum," "warpath," "tepee," "brave" and "squaw" and such offensive terms as "drunk," "irresponsible," "lazy" and "savage" in stories about aboriginal peoples—or members of any ethnic group.

Sexism

In the past, news stories mentioning women often emphasized their roles as wives, mothers, cooks, seamstresses, housekeepers and sex objects. During the 1960s and 1970s, women began to complain that such stereotypes are false and demeaning because women are human beings, not primarily housewives and sex objects.

More women than ever are employed and hold high positions of responsibility in public and private organizations—including news organizations. Unfortunately, stereotypical statements continue to appear in news stories because reporters sometimes do not think about the consequences of what they write. It is offensive and demeaning to women when a newswriter uses words or phrases that suggest women are inferior to men. The offensive remark can be something as simple as describing a woman's physical appearance but not that of her male counterpart.

A headline in the *National Post* announced, "Blonde Bombshell: Defection gives Grits vote edge." Critics said the hair colour of the female politician (Belinda Stronach) was irrelevant to the story and that few journalists would have mentioned the hair colour of a male politician defecting from one party to another. A special report on Japan in the *Globe and Mail* carried this headline: "Women as investors? Few will bother their pretty little heads." Critics objected to the bald portrayal of Japanese women as too stupid to invest. A headline in the *Toronto Star* said, "Women man top positions at Etobicoke public libraries"; some readers objected that the headline suggested it is unusual for women to achieve positions of importance.

More generally, many Canadian newspapers persist in describing how females depicted in news stories are dressed, even though their clothing is neither unusual nor relevant to their involvement in the news and reporters would not have described the attire of men in similar positions.

A story published by a campus newspaper referred to women as "chicks." Several female students and faculty members were outraged. They complained the word implies women are cute, little, fluffy and helpless.

Some advertisements still contain sexual stereotypes. Some radio ads have urged women to ask their husbands for money so they could shop at a certain clothing store. Other ads have urged mothers (not fathers) to take their children to a certain amusement park.

Although reporters are expected to avoid demeaning comments and sexist stereotypes, they sometimes have difficulty breaking old ways of thinking, especially the stereotypes they developed in childhood.

As a first step, avoid occupational terms that exclude women: "fireman," "mailman," "policeman" and "workman," for example. Journalists substitute "firefighter," "mail carrier" or "postal worker," "police officer" and "worker." Similarly, use the words "reporter" and "journalist" instead of "newsman."

Although some groups favour their use, *The Canadian Press Stylebook* recommends journalists avoid awkward or contrived words, such as "chairperson" and "spokesperson." Instead, the stylebook advises using neutral terms such as "chair" or "representative."

Also avoid using the words "female" and "woman" in places where you would not use the words "male" or "man" (for example, "woman doctor" or "female general"). Similarly, use unisex substitutes for words such as "authoress" (author), "actress" (actor), "aviatrix" (aviator), and "co-ed" (student).

Do not refer to women as "gals," "girls" or "ladies," and do not refer to them by their first names. News stories do not usually call men "boys" or refer to them by their first names—except in stories in which multiple members of the same family are quoted as sources and first names are necessary to clarify who is being quoted.

Other unacceptable practices include:

- Suggesting homemaking is not work.

- Identifying a woman solely by her relationship with a man—for example, as a man's wife, daughter or secretary.

■ Identifying a woman by her husband's name. The common practice is to identify a woman by her own name unless she insists on the use of her husband's name.

SEXIST: Mrs. Anthony Pedersen participated in the event.
REVISED: Elizabeth Pedersen participated in the event.

■ Describing a woman's hair, dress, voice, or figure when such characteristics are irrelevant to the story. To avoid problems, writers should ask themselves: Under the same circumstances, would I describe a man's physical characteristics or marital status? Mentioning a woman's marital status, especially if she is divorced, unless it is clearly relevant to your story. Even when a woman's marital status is relevant, it seldom belongs in the headline or the lead of the story.

Never assume everyone involved in a story is male, all people holding prestigious jobs are male, or most women are full-time homemakers. Be especially careful to avoid using the pronouns "he," "his" and "him" while referring to a typical Canadian or average person. Some readers will mistakenly assume that you are referring exclusively to men.

Writers try to avoid, however, the cumbersome and repetitive "he/she" or "he and/or she." The effort to rid the language of male bias or female stereotyping should never become so strained that it distracts readers. Writers employ a couple of techniques to avoid those cumbersome terms:

1. Substitute an article for the male pronouns "he" and "his":

A contractor must always consult his blueprints when building a house.
REVISED: A contractor must always consult the blueprints when building a house.

2. Substitute plural nouns and pronouns for male nouns and pronouns:

A soldier must train himself to be ready.
REVISED: Soldiers must train themselves to be ready.

Agism

Stereotypes of the elderly suggest that all older Canadians are lonely, inactive, unproductive, poor, passive, weak and sick. In fact, most are still active, and some continue to work into their late seventies. When asked to describe their health, a majority respond "good" to "excellent." Yet television programs often portray the elderly as eccentric, foolish, forgetful or feeble. Similarly, news stories often express surprise at older people buying a sports car, falling in love, or remaining alert, healthy, innovative and productive.

Avoid using derogatory terms such as "geezer" or "old fogy" when describing the elderly. Even words that don't generally carry negative connotations can be used offensively. For instance, using the word "spry" when describing elderly people gives the impression that they are unusually active for their age. A person's age should not be a factor in a story about an accomplishment—getting elected to office, winning an award, being employed in an unusual occupation, for example—unless it is relevant to the story. The election of a 70-year-old grandfather in a provincial election should not be treated any differently from the election of a 40-year-old father. Neither should appear in the headline or the lead of the story.

Avoid Stereotyping Other Groups

Individuals with physical or mental disabilities often are stereotyped as helpless, deficient, or unable to contribute to society. In fact, many physically and mentally disabled people lead active lives and contribute to society both professionally and personally. (Does the name Stephen Hawking ring a bell?) The terms "disabled" and "challenged" have replaced "handicapped." More acceptable is "person with a disability," "person who is blind," and so forth. Such phrasing emphasizes the individual before the condition.

Veterans' organizations have accused the media of portraying the men and women who served in wartime as violent and unstable. The media, critics explain, sometimes report that a person charged with a serious crime is a war veteran, regardless of the fact's relevance.

Religious groups also accuse the media of bias in the portrayal of members of their faiths. Muslims around the world complain that Western media often portray Muslims as terrorists or inherently violent people. Some Christian denominations are portrayed in the media as strange, different, or extremist in their beliefs. Reporters must be careful when covering members of different faiths that they do not stereotype all members of a particular faith because of the actions of a branch of that faith.

 ## Don't Write Like This

Here are examples of bad writing that came from statements made on insurance forms. Motorists attempted to summarize the details of their accidents in the fewest words possible:

- Coming home, I drove into the wrong house and collided with a tree I don't have.

- The other car collided with mine without warning of its intentions.

- I thought my window was down, but I found out it was up when I put my head through it.

- I collided with a stationary truck coming the other way.

- A truck backed through my windshield into my wife's face.

- The guy was all over the road. I had to swerve a number of times before I hit him.

- I pulled away from the side of the road, glanced at my mother-in-law, and headed over the embankment.

- In my attempt to kill a fly, I drove into a telephone pole.

- I had been shopping for plants all day and was on my way home. As I reached an intersection, a hedge sprang up, obscuring my vision, and I did not see the other car.

- I was on my way to the doctor with rear-end trouble when my universal joint gave way causing me to have engine trouble.

- I had been driving for 40 years when I fell asleep at the wheel and had an accident.

- My car was legally parked as it backed into another vehicle.

- The pedestrian had no idea which way to run, so I ran over him.

- A pedestrian hit me and went under my car.

- As I approached the intersection, a sign suddenly appeared in a place where no stop sign ever appeared before. I was unable to stop in time to avoid the accident.

- I was sure the old fellow would never make it to the other side of the road when I struck him.

- I saw a slow-moving, sad-faced old gentleman as he bounced off the roof of my car.

- I told police that I was not injured, but on removing my hat, I found that I had a fractured skull.

- An invisible car came out of nowhere, struck my car, and vanished.

- The indirect cause of the accident was a little guy in a small car with a big mouth. I was thrown from my car as it left the road. I was later found in a ditch by some stray cows.

- The telephone pole was approaching. I was attempting to swerve out of its way when it struck the front end.

- To avoid hitting the bumper on the car in front, I hit a pedestrian.

CHECKLIST FOR NEWSWRITING STYLE

As you begin to write stories, check to make sure you follow these guidelines:
1. Identify the central point of the story.
2. Prepare a brief outline of the three or four major parts of the story.
3. Use short, familiar words.
4. Use short sentences and short paragraphs.
5. Eliminate unnecessary words.
6. Avoid overloading sentences with unrelated ideas.
7. Use relatively simple sentences that follow normal word order: subject–verb–direct object.
8. Avoid statements of opinion.
9. Avoid stereotyping people by race, gender, age, ethnic group or religion.

 ## The Writing Coach

PART 1: FIFTEEN WAYS TO IMPROVE YOUR WRITING AND REPORTING
by Don Gibb, Ryerson University

1. Jot down a brief outline. Take two minutes to figure out the shape of your story: how to open, where to go next, then next and next…and how to end it.
2. Give your story a label—a word, a few words, or a sentence—that addresses the point or theme. Put it at the top of your screen to keep you on track. If someone hacked into a government computer system and stole the social insurance numbers of thousands of Canadians, maybe this is a story about "fear"—the fear of being vulnerable, the fear of easy access to personal information.
3. Pay attention to your lead. It should set the theme and be specific—not vague or general. Make it the last thing you review before you hand in your story. Often, trimming a word or adding a word can make it better.
4. Quotes should be short. Often, one sentence is enough, two is fine, but three can be too many. Paraphrase basic and routine information.
5. The nut graf is essential. It tells readers why you are writing the story and why they should care. It should appear early in the story—generally, the fourth paragraph.
6. Transitions help sew your story and interviews together. They help the flow and rhythm of a story. They help take readers from one place to another, from one time to another. Work on tying your story together with smooth transitions.
7. "Said" is a good word for attribution. Avoid using other attributive words incorrectly, such as "claim" and "explain."
8. Check and double-check every proper name (people, streets, companies, cities, etc.). Do this as you write, or flag everything to check later as part of your own editing before handing in your story.
9. Get business cards from contacts. They not only help you create a base of sources you might want to contact again, but they also contain work numbers, cellphone numbers, email addresses, and even home numbers. What a treasure chest!
10. Always ask followup questions. Never leave a topic until you understand the information or have gathered enough details to write clearly and coherently.
11. Ask the readers' questions. Those you cover have an agenda. You don't automatically ignore that agenda, but you need to show what impact it has on your readers. You can cover a story about federal civil servants on strike for higher wages, but you should also tell readers what impact the strike will have on their lives.
12. Be skeptical. Don't assume that everything everyone tells you is right. Double-check if you doubt the accuracy of information.

13. Give yourself time to read a hard copy of your story before you hand it in. A hard copy makes it easier to catch obvious errors you may miss on the screen.

14. Ask people for examples of things they are telling you about. It helps readers understand and visualize your story.

15. Make observation a regular part of your reporting. Write what you see in your notes. What you *see* as well as what people *tell* you is an important part of your reporting. It can often be more important, and writers shouldn't be afraid to use their observations prominently in their stories.

The touchstone for good newswriting is clarity, and it can be achieved by paying attention to the main elements of clear writing: simplicity, understanding, polishing and caring. Let's consider each in turn.

PART 2: FIND THE CLEAR PATH TO WRITING GLORY

by Joe Hight

Simplicity

Poor writers try to impress by being complex instead of simplifying their sentences and paragraphs. They fear that someone will ridicule them for being too simplistic.

But as U.S. journalist Paula LaRocque observed: "Good, clear writing is neither dumb nor over simple. And unclear writing (unless also written by the unintelligent) is self-indulgent if not arrogant. The truth is that the best writers are and always have been the clearest writers—from Winston Churchill to Albert Einstein to Carl Sagan. They've learned that knowledge isn't worth much if we can't convey it to others."

Simplicity means:

- using subject–verb–object order whenever possible;

- using active verbs;

- reducing complicated words into single-syllable or simple terms;

- using specific details instead of general terms, concrete instead of abstract;

- keeping sentences short but pacing them with a variety of lengths;

- avoiding long backed-in clauses that only delay the subject;

- not using too many statistics or too many prepositions, generally limiting them to no more than three per sentence.

Understanding

A religious song titled "Prayer of St. Francis" has the following verse in it: "To be understood as to understand." The line should become a theme for anyone writing a newspaper story.

In their *Secrets of Great Writing*, journalism professors Maureen A. Croteau and Wayne A. Worcester list understanding as one of their 20 tips: "You can't write what you don't understand. If you don't know what you're talking about, nobody else will either. You can parrot information, drop in some quotes and produce something that looks like a story. But if you don't understand what you're writing about, no one else will."

Understanding means:

- Translating jargon into terms that readers can understand. Avoid excessive use of bureaucratic terms, or explain those that must be used. Avoid clichés that limit understanding. Avoid journalese—writing that speaks in terms that only a journalist can understand.

- Using quotations that are understandable to readers. How many times have you read a quote that's filled with so many parentheses, clichés or jargon that it's difficult to understand? Most are from reporters who fail to clarify or paraphrase quotes that are incomprehensible. Many longer quotes seem to come from tape recorders. But tape recorders aren't the problem. The problem is reporters who are so worried about transcribing that they forget to translate.

- Limiting the use of acronyms, except those that are commonly used. The late writing coach Mary Goddard used to give this advice for anyone writing stories or headlines: "Would the first 10 people polled at a McDonald's know instantly what these letters stand for?"

Polishing

Most writers should know Ernest Hemingway's famous words: "Prose is architecture, not interior decoration." Or Mark Twain's: "The difference between the right word and the almost-right word is the difference between lightning and a lightning bug." Or William Strunk, Jr.'s: "Vigorous writing is concise. A sentence should contain no unnecessary words, a paragraph no unnecessary sentences, for the same reason that a drawing should have no unnecessary lines and a machine no unnecessary parts."

All of these quotes emphasize the need to draft, and then polish.
Polishing means:

- Ensuring names are spelled correctly, the math is correct, and the facts don't conflict. (Sure, good writers make mistakes, but they strive to avoid them.)

- Pruning words like the best hedge-trimmer. Searching for dangling or misplaced modifiers. Rewriting to prevent double meanings. Carefully trimming away the excess for a precise work.

- Eliminating the complex. Good reporters, especially those who are investigative, are storytellers who select what is understandable and throw out material that is trivial or can't be understood.

- Finding better ways to self-edit. Reading sentences out loud. Talking with other reporters about complicated sentences. Working with editors to trim and edit—and editors working with reporters.

Caring

This is the most important element in clear writing. Caring that you've done your best work and caring for the readers of that work.
Caring means:

- Using simplicity, understanding and polishing to create powerful writing.

- Seeking brevity so the readers get no more than what they need to read.

- Establishing a focus in the story. From the lead to the end, focus on organizing your story to provide information that the reader should know.

- Providing meaning. Donald Murray, an award-winning U.S. writing expert and columnist, distinguishes between a reporter and a writer. He says in *Writer in the Newsroom* that writers and reporters both have goals of accuracy, simplicity and clarity. But the writer reveals meaning between pieces of information. The writer "collects accurate, specific, revealing pieces of information and constructs each draft by building firm, logical patterns of meaning. The writer is master of the craft of reporting—and the craft of writing."

- Hard work. "Writing is hard work," author William Zinsser writes. "A clear sentence is no accident. Very few sentences come out right the first time, or even the third time. Remember this in moments of despair. If you find that writing is hard, it's because it is hard. It's one of the hardest things people do."

Hard but still doable. Canadian writer and critic Frank Davey had some comforting words for aspiring writers: "There is nothing that cannot be written. A maxim, told to myself, in the morning."

When combined, these elements—simplicity, understanding, polishing and caring—produce clarity in your work and outstanding stories.

 ## Correcting Wordy Phrases

It is easy to overwrite—use too many words when just one or two will do. Here are examples of wordy phrases and their more concise replacements.

WORDY PHRASE	REPLACEMENT
appoint to the post of	appoint
conduct an investigation into	investigate
rose to the defence of	defended
succeed in doing	do
came to a stop	stopped
devoured by flames	burned
shot to death	shot
have a need for	need
made contact with	met
proceeded to interrogate	interrogated
promoted to the rank of	promoted

SUGGESTED READINGS AND USEFUL WEBSITES

The Canadian Press Stylebook: A Guide for Writers and Editors. 2008. 15th edn. Toronto: The Canadian Press.

Cumming, Carman, and Catherine McKercher. 1994. *The Canadian Reporter: News Writing and Reporting*. Toronto: Harcourt Brace Canada.

McFarlane, J.A., and Warren Clements, eds. 2003. *The Globe and Mail Style Book: A Guide to Language and Usage*. 9th edn. Toronto: *The Globe and Mail*.

Jacobi, Peter. 1982. *Writing with Style: The News Story and the Feature*. Chicago: Lawrence Ragan Communications.

Plotnik, Arthur. 2007. *Spunk & Bite: A Writer's Guide to Bold Contemporary Style*. New York: Random House Reference.

Stepp, Carl Sessions. 2000. *The Magic and Craft of Media Writing*. Chicago: NTC Publishing.

Strunk, William, and E.B. White. 1999. *The Elements of Style*. 4th edn. White Plains, NY: Longman.

Yagoda, Ben. 2004. *The Sound on the Page: Style and Voice in Writing*. Toronto: HarperCollins Canada.

Zinsser, William K. 2006. *On Writing Well: The Classic Guide to Writing Nonfiction*. 30th anniversary edition. New York: HarperCollins.

Canadian Association of Journalists: www.caj.ca

Online project of the Canadian Journalism Foundation: www.j-source.ca; www.projetj.ca

EXERCISE 1   Newswriting Style

Discussion Questions

1. Imagine that you have just been named editor of your city's daily newspaper. Formulate a policy that specifies when your staff can report that a person is "adopted," "illegitimate," "receiving welfare," "gay" or an "ex-convict."

2. Imagine that your city's new mayor, elected today, had never met his father and did not even know his identity. He was raised by his mother, who never married. Would you report that fact while describing the new mayor? Why?

3. You are interviewing a source for a story, and the source uses an offensive stereotypical term about senior citizens. Would you print the word? Why?

4. Suppose a bank in your city today named a woman its president and she was the first woman to head a bank in your city. Should your local daily publish a story about her promotion that emphasized she was the first woman to hold such a position? Why? Would you publish similar stories when the first women are named to head a local college, a local hospital, and a local police department?

5. For one week, examine every story published on the front page of your local daily newspaper. Look for sentences or phrases that are not objective. Why is the sentence or phrase not objective? How would you rewrite it?

6. Think of your favourite television programs. How do the shows portray men? Women? Minorities? The elderly? Do the portrayals foster or break stereotypical images? Why?

7. For one week, examine every story published on the front page of your local daily newspaper. Circle words and phrases that you could replace with simpler ones. Do the simpler words and phrases change the meaning of the story? Why or why not?

CHAPTER 2

Being Concise

SECTION I: USING SIMPLE WORDS

Substitute simpler and more common words for each of these words.

1. obliterate	11. deceased
2. objective	12. cognizant
3. utilize	13. lacerations
4. negligent	14. presently
5. imbibe	15. stated
6. duplicate	16. manufacture
7. gargantuan	17. loathe
8. remainder	18. component
9. eccentric	19. obtain
10. abandon	20. relocate

SECTION II: AVOIDING REDUNDANT PHRASES

Do not rewrite the following phrases; simply cross out the unnecessary words.

1. totally destroyed	11. honest truth
2. concrete proposals	12. future plans
3. postponed until later	13. awkward predicament
4. freak accident	14. fully engulfed
5. seldom ever	15. lag behind
6. major breakthrough	16. write down
7. dead body	17. free of charge
8. qualified expert	18. maximum possible
9. dangerous weapon	19. foreseeable future
10. armed gunman	20. lose out

SECTION III: AVOIDING WORDY PHRASES

Use a single word to replace each of these phrases.

1. on the occasion of	11. due to the fact that
2. despite the fact that	12. exceeding the speed limit
3. at an earlier date	13. made the acquaintance of
4. is going to	14. stated the point that
5. tender his/her resignation	15. file a lawsuit against
6. united together in holy matrimony	16. be acquainted with
7. give instruction to	17. came to a stop
8. on account of	18. rose to the defence
9. was in possession of	19. draw to a close
10. register approval of	20. arrived at a decision

SECTION IV: ELIMINATING UNNECESSARY WORDS

Eliminate the unnecessary words from the following sentences. The sentences do not have to be rewritten; simply cross out the words that are not needed.

1.   The contractor did a totally complete job on the renovation.

2.   The candidates for mayor will conduct a poll of the residents.

3.   She said the new innovation would save the company money.

4.   He said the birthday party was an unexpected surprise.

5.   The police officer tried to calm down the accident victim.

SECTION V: REWRITING WORDY SENTENCES

Rewrite the following sentences, eliminating as many words as possible and correcting any other errors.

1.   The mayor said everyone had to co-operate together or someone would file a lawsuit against the city.

2.   It would appear that the new school mascot, which got a stamp of approval from alumni, will make an appearance at Saturday's game.

3.   As a matter of fact, some of the tickets were free of charge to the contest winners while other tickets cost the sum of $50 for handling fees.

4.   Police claimed the armed gunman was carrying a dangerous weapon when he entered the bank with the underlying purpose of robbing it.

5.   Local residents said they planned to evacuate in the event that the floodwaters reached the banks of the river and completely destroyed the town.

SECTION VI: SIMPLIFYING OVERLOADED SENTENCES

Rewrite the following sentences, shortening and simplifying them and correcting any other errors.

1.   Two university students, Jonathan Colson and Marie Parkinson, both seniors and both majoring in business in the Department of Economic Sciences, were driving south on Addison Drive during a thunderstorm when a tree, which was blown down by strong winds, fell across the road in front of them, and Colson swerved to avoid the tree before hitting a utility pole with his car and causing more than 10,000 people to lose electricity to their homes.

2.   Police officers chased the suspect, who had attempted to rob Robert Ames and his wife, Emily, of $3,500 in cash and jewellery that was in a small safe in their home, into the park where he tried to climb through the window of a childrens playhouse and got stuck in the window because his belt buckle caught on a protruding nail, and officers had to cut the man's belt in order to get him out of the window and charge him with robbery, burglary, and resisting arrest.

CHAPTER 2

EXERCISE 3   Newswriting Style

-Isms

SECTION I: AVOIDING SEXIST TITLES AND TERMS
Replace these words with ones that include both men and women.

1. deliveryman
2. layman
3. housewife
4. councilman
5. salesman
6. chairman
7. policeman
8. mailman
9. meter man
10. insurance man
11. repairman
12. factory man

SECTION II: AVOIDING EXCLUSIVELY MALE NOUNS AND PRONOUNS
Rewrite the following sentences, eliminating their use of male nouns and pronouns and correcting any other errors.

1. A policeman has to inspect his weapons before going on patrol.

2. The chairman said the company would need more manpower to complete the contract on time.

3. The councilman said it is a fact that the average man will not understand the ordinance.

4. Encounters with dogs can be a frightening experience for a mailman as he makes his rounds delivering mail to his customers each day.

5. A deliveryman provides his customers with a written receipt so that he has proof that he delivered the package.

SECTION III: AVOIDING STEREOTYPES
Rewrite the following sentences, avoiding stereotypical language and comments and correcting any other errors.

1. Jackson Smith, a spry 86-year-old resident of Greeley Court, is a real old-timer when it comes to cars because everyday he drives a 1936 Chevrolet coupe that he amazingly restored just last year.

2. The newsboy dropped the paper on the porch just as the petite housewife opened the front door.

3. As pressure from 20 men and 60 females protesting the club's policies increased, the spokesman for the club said it had reached a gentleman's agreement with the protesters.

4. Margaret Adams, an attractive woman dressed in a knee-length grey business suit and black high heel shoes, became the first woman president and chief executive officer of the male-dominated Hudson Industries.

5. The congressmen assembled in the capitol building along with Anita Martinez, a Hispanic female congressman from Arizona, to protest the new immigration bill.

EXERCISE 4   Newswriting Style

Review
Answer Key Provided: See Appendix D

SECTION I: REMAINING OBJECTIVE
Rewrite the following sentences, eliminating all their statements of opinion and correcting other errors.

1. The famous speaker, who truly will delight her audience, will discuss the relationship of economics and poverty at tonights interesting presentation.

2. In a startling discovery, police claimed to have identified the despicable man who attacked the poor, defenceless 65-year-old woman.

3. The handsome man was presented with the prestigious award for his efforts on behalf of the agency.

4. Theatre-goers are urged to buy their tickets, at a cost of only $20, early for the sensational community theatre production of *Cats*, which can look forward to a long run in the city.

5. Another important point was the boards decision to end the contract for water service with the company.

SECTION II: AVOIDING REDUNDANT PHRASES
Do not rewrite the following phrases; simply cross out the redundant words.

1. small in size
2. join together
3. general public
4. honest truth
5. acute crisis

6. fell down
7. lag behind
8. protrude out
9. resume again
10. usual custom

SECTION III: AVOIDING WORDY PHRASES
Substitute a single word for each of the following phrases.

1. raze to the ground
2. made contact with
3. bring to a conclusion
4. on a few occasions
5. for the reason that

6. made an escape
7. give encouragement to
8. file a lawsuit against
9. conducted an investigation of
10. summoned to the scene

SECTION IV: AVOIDING UNNECESSARY WORDS
Improve these sentences by crossing out the unnecessary words or revising them to eliminate wordiness.

1. The professor said she was acquainted with the author of the book on account of the fact they had made contact with each other years ago.

2. The university's board of directors wanted to postpone until later a decision on the project until the board received concrete proposals from the contractors.

3. The mayor said the physical size of the new development was not that large but it would have the maximum possible impact on the city's future plans.

4. Police have the belief that it was a freak accident that allowed the deadly poison to seep out of the tanker truck and cause the worst ever chemical spill in the country's history.

5. Firefighters responding to the scene of the house fire were confronted with a blazing inferno and succeeded in doing their best to contain the flames.

SECTION V: TESTING ALL YOUR SKILLS
Rewrite the following sentences, correcting all their errors.

1. Mike Deacosta, his wife, and their two children, Mark and Amy, were invited to the representatives reception along with several other local residents.

2. The police officer made it perfectly clear to the motorist that he had been exceeding the speed limit and would face the maximum possible fine if he did not locate his drivers licence presently.

3. Before a young child can begin school, they must be able to read and write their name.

4. The informative information was presented at this point in time because all the members of the board, including Chairman Maggy Baille, were present and accounted for

and would be able to vote on the proposal to increase contributions to the employees retirement accounts.

5. An attractive young brunette, Donna Moronesi, seems to be an unlikely candidate for the office, but she has surprisingly raised more than 1 million dollars before the campaign has even begun.

6. The politician extended his thanks and appreciation to those who had supported him because they had collaborated together to win the election.

7. He sustained the loss of his right eye and broke his leg in the unfortunate accident.

8. As a matter of fact, the mayor claimed she had already considered the attorneys proposal, but the terms of the agreement to settle with the bitter old man who filed a lawsuit against the city over the death of his dog which had been taken to the city pound was not in accordance with the best interests of the city and its local residents.

9. The attorney was in possession of evidence that helped the jury to arrive at a decision.

10. It was the consensus of opinion of the board and chairman Jane Abbott that the impetuous offer by the other company would be a hindrance to negotiating a fair and equitable contract with her employees on the grounds that the massive increase would create an acute crisis of confidence among the employees and change the ground rules of the negotiations.

3 | The Language of News

A journalist is not something which just happens. Like poets, they are born. They are marked by a kind of altruistic nosiness.

— Robertson Davies, Canadian novelist, poet and journalist, 1954

"It was really comic what happened to Paul today on his way to class," she said.

Actually the funny thing that happened to Paul was "comical," not "comic." The difference? "Comic" is a noun meaning a funny person, a comedian. "Comical" is an adjective meaning something funny. But then what about "tragic" and "tragical"? Do the same rules apply? No. The opposite is the case. "Tragical" is a noun meaning "the tragic element in art or life," whereas the word "tragic" is an adjective meaning "of or having to do with tragedy."

THE EFFECTIVENESS OF WORDS

Writers sometimes do not understand the words they use. Other times they fail to express their ideas clearly and precisely. In such cases, the sentences they write may state the obvious (or impossible), or they may carry unintended, often comical meanings. Consider these examples:

Gothic architecture is distinguished by flying buttocks.
The horror gender is a complex field to study.
Rural life is found mostly in the country.
That summer I finally got my leg operated on, and what a relief! It had been hanging over my head for years.

People expect more of journalists, who must master the English language. When news organizations hire a new reporter, they look for someone who understands and respects the language, knows spelling and grammar, possesses an extensive vocabulary, and writes in a clear and interesting manner. Even careful writers make mistakes, sometimes hilarious ones. But if the errors become too numerous, they can damage a news organization's credibility and force it to print or broadcast costly and embarrassing corrections.

The men and women who devote their lives to journalism develop a respect for the language. They value prose that is clear, concise and accurate. They strive to select the exact word needed to convey an idea, use the word properly, and place it in a sentence that is grammatically correct.

When a major event occurs, such as an attack on Canadian troops in Afghanistan or the proroguing of Parliament by the prime minister, dozens and sometimes hundreds of journalists rush to the scene, gather information, and then transmit it to the public. All journalists write about the same event, but some stories are much better than others. Why?

Some reporters are particularly adept at gathering the information needed to write exceptional stories. Other reporters produce exceptional stories because of their command of the English language. Their language is forceful, and their stories are written so clearly and simply that everyone can understand them. These reporters describe people, places and events involved in news stories and use quotations that enable the actors in their stories to speak directly to the public.

Skilled reporters can transform even routine events into front-page stories. A reporter who is unimaginative about or indifferent to a topic may write a three-paragraph story that because of its mediocre writing will not be used. Another reporter, excited by the same topic, may go beyond the superficial—ask more questions, uncover unusual developments, and inject colour into the story. The second reporter may write a 20- or 30-inch story about the topic that because of the reporter's command of language and excellent use of words gets published at the top of page 1.

BE PRECISE

To communicate effectively, reporters must be precise, particularly in their selection of words. The perfect choice makes a sentence forceful and interesting; imprecision creates confusion and misunderstanding.

Some words simply are inappropriate in news stories. Few editors or news directors permit the use of words such as "cop" or "kid" (they prefer the more formal and proper "police officer" and "child") or derogatory terms about a person's race or religion. News executives allow profanity only when it is essential to a story's meaning; even then, they refuse to publish the most offensive terms. They prefer the word "woman" to the archaic "lady." Some ban the use of contractions (isn't, can't, don't) except in direct quotations. Professional journalists also object to using nouns as verbs. They would not write that someone "authored" or "penned" a book, a city "headquartered" a company, or an event "impacted" a community. Nor would they allow a reporter to write that food prices were "upped," plans "finalized," or children "parented."

Some errors occur because the reporter is unaware of a word's exact meaning. Few journalists would report that a car "collided" with a tree, a "funeral service" was held, a gunman "executed" his victim, or a child "was drowned" in a lake. Why? Two objects collide only if both are moving; thus, a car can strike a tree but never "collide" with one. A funeral is a service; therefore, "funeral service" is redundant. "Executed" means put to death in accordance with a legally imposed sentence; therefore, only a state—never a murderer—can execute anyone. A report that a child "was drowned" would imply that someone held the child's head underwater until the victim died.

Such considerations are not trivial. Journalists who fail to use words correctly can confuse or irritate their audience, undermine their credibility, and cause their audience to question the accuracy of their stories. Thus, instructors will object when students use language that is sloppy and inaccurate.

Sloppy use of words can creep into anyone's writing. The word "epicentre," for example, means the point on the earth's surface directly above the source of an earthquake. "Epicentre" is often misused, however, as a synonym for "centre."

Another phrase that is often misused is "beg the question." Begging the question is a logical fallacy in which a person constructs an argument using the conclusion he or she wishes to prove as a premise. Here's an example of an argument that begs the question: "Capitalist economies allow the greatest room for the exercise of individual initiative. Therefore, business owners in capitalist societies have the most opportunity to profit from their initiative." The premise and the conclusion in this example are saying the same thing. When the phrase "beg the question" appears in news stories, however, it usually is used as a synonym for "raise the question" or "prompt the question."

When reporters fail to express ideas clearly and precisely, audiences can derive meanings different from the one intended. The unintended meaning may be difficult for the writer to detect. Double meanings in the following headlines, all of which appeared in newspapers, illustrate the problem:

Grandmother of eight makes hole in one
Two convicts evade noose, jury hung
Iraqi head seeks arms
War dims hope for peace
Dealers will hear car talk at noon
Miners refuse to work after death
Hospitals sued by 7 foot doctors

Although readers often consider the double meanings humorous, few editors or news directors are amused when such errors appear. Yet even the best news organizations occasionally make mistakes. Here is an example from the *New York Times*:

> The State Health Department is surveying hospitals around the state to ascertain whether women patients are being given Pap tests to determine if they have uterine cancer as required by law.

Confusion sometimes arises because words look or sound alike. For example, a story reported, "About 40 years ago, she left her native Cypress for New York City and set up a bakery on Ninth Avenue near 40th Street." Few people are born in trees, and an editor wondered, "Could that have been 'Cyprus'?"

College students often confuse words such as "buses" and "busses," "naval" and "navel," and "reckless" and "wreckless." The word "busses" refers to kisses, not the vehicles people ride in. A "navel" is a belly button, and some motorists drive "wrecks" but are convicted of "reckless" driving.

USE STRONG VERBS

Verbs can transform a drab sentence into an interesting—or even horrifying—one. Notice the impact of "ripped," "shattering," and "unleashing" in the lead paragraph from an Associated Press story by Marc Santora in 2007 about the bombing of a mosque in Iraq:

> SAMARRA, Iraq (AP)—It has been a year since Sunni insurgents ripped a hole in the glorious golden dome here of one of Iraq's most sacred Shiite shrines, shattering its 72,000 golden tiles and unleashing a tide of national sectarian bloodletting. Not a single brick of the mosque has been moved since.

Strong verbs like these help readers or listeners envision the events described in the stories—they paint a vivid picture for readers. The following sentences are also colourful, interesting and vivid. Why? Because the college students who wrote them used descriptive verbs:

> A cargo door *popped* open, *tearing* a hole in the plane's side. Eleven passengers *sucked* out of the hole *plunged* 30,000 feet to their deaths.
> A gunman *jumped* behind the customer service counter of a department store Monday, *grabbed* a handful of money—then *fled* on a bicycle.

By comparison, the following sentences are weak and bland, yet it is easy to improve them. Simply add a strong verb:

> The bodies were located by rescue workers shortly after 6 p.m.
> REVISED: Rescue workers found the bodies shortly after 6 p.m.
> A historic railroad bridge that was once the tallest and largest in the world was destroyed by strong thunderstorms that crossed the state Monday afternoon.
> REVISED: Blustery thunderstorms sweeping across the state Monday afternoon toppled a historic railroad bridge that was once the tallest and largest in the world.

Strong verbs describe one specific action. Weak verbs cover a number of different actions. The first sentence in the following example is vague and bland because it uses a weak verb. The last three use specific, descriptive verbs and are more informative:

> His brother got a personal computer.
> His brother bought a personal computer.
> His brother won a personal computer.
> His brother stole a personal computer.

Avoid the repeated use of forms of the verb "to be," such as "is," "are," "was," and "were." These verbs are overused, weak and dull—especially when a writer uses them in combination with a past participle to form a passive-voice verb, such as "was captured." Sentences using passive verbs are also wordier than those with active ones:

> It was discovered by the company's lawyers that the financial records were incorrect. (13 words)
> REVISED: Company lawyers discovered the financial records were incorrect. (8 words)
> The program was created by parents and students. (8 words)
> REVISED: Students and parents created the program. (6 words)
> The defendant was sentenced by the judge to 10 years in prison. (12 words)
> REVISED: The judge sentenced the defendant to 10 years in prison. (10 words)
> Police officers were summoned to the scene by a neighbour. (10 words)
> REVISED: A neighbour called the police. (5 words)

AVOIDING PROBLEMS IN YOUR WRITING

Good writing requires thought and hard work. Reporters have to think about the best words for conveying their ideas to their audience—and the best words may not be the first ones they write. That's where the hard work comes in—reporters have to edit their work. Editing and rewriting can help reporters find better words. The following sections identify problem areas writers should watch for.

Words to Avoid

Adjectives and Adverbs

Newswriters avoid adverbs and adjectives because they tend to be less forceful, specific and objective than nouns and verbs. William Strunk, Jr., and E.B. White, authors of the influential book *The Elements of Style*, wrote, "The adjective hasn't been built that can pull a weak or inaccurate noun out of a tight place."

Most adverbs and adjectives are unnecessary. They waste space by stating the obvious, and they may unintentionally inject a reporter's opinion into the story. If you write about a child's funeral, you do not have to comment that the mourners were "sad-faced," the scene "grim," and the parents "grief-stricken." Nor is there reason to report that an author is "famous," a witness "alert," or an accident "tragic."

Adverbs and adjectives in the following sentences editorialize. Rather than simply reporting the facts, they comment on those facts:

> It was not until Monday that university officials finally released the report.
> REVISED: University officials released the report Monday.
> Upon hearing about the frivolous lawsuit, the mayor made it quite clear that she plans to fight the outrageous complaint.
> REVISED: The mayor said she plans to fight the lawsuit.

The word "finally" in the first sentence implies that university officials were negligent and should have released the report sooner. Similarly, reporting the facts in the second story clearly and concisely eliminates the need for words like "frivolous" or "outrageous." And saying the mayor made something "clear" implies she is stating a fact, not an opinion.

Clichés

Clichés are words or phrases that writers have heard and copied over and over. Many are 200 or 300 years old—so old and overused that they have lost their original impact and meaning. Clichés no longer startle, amuse or interest the public. Because they eliminate the need for thought, clichés have been called the greatest labour-saving devices ever invented.

The news media can take a fresh phrase and overuse it so that it quickly becomes a cliché.

Journalists employ clichés when they lack the time or talent to find words more specific, descriptive or original. So a reporter under deadline pressure may say that a fire "swept through" a building, an explosion "rocked" a city, police officers gave a suspect a "spirited chase," or protesters were an "angry mob."

Other clichés exaggerate. Few people are really as "blind as a bat," "cool as a cucumber," "light as a feather," "neat as a pin," "straight as an arrow," "thin as a rail," or "white as a sheet."

You are likely to be so familiar with clichés that you can complete them after seeing just the first few words. Want to try? The final word is missing from the following clichés, yet you are likely to complete all 10:

a close brush with _____	has a nose for _____
a step in the right _____	last but not _____
could not believe her _____	left holding the _____
evidence of foul _____	lived to a ripe old _____
fell into the wrong _____	lying in a pool of _____

Political reporting is especially susceptible to clichés. It seems as though candidates always "test the waters" before "tossing their hats into the ring." Other candidates launch "whirlwind campaigns" and "hammer away" at their opponents, or they employ "spin doctors" to control unfavourable news. Some candidates "straddle the fence" on the "burning issues of the day." However, few "give up without a fight."

Some clichés are so closely associated with newswriting that they are called "journalese." The term identifies phrases reporters use to dramatize, exaggerate and sometimes distort the events they describe. In news stories, fires "rage," temperatures "soar," earthquakes "rumble," and people "vow." Rivers "go on a rampage." Third World countries are often "war-torn" or "much-troubled." Sometimes they are "oil-rich." Politicians who get into trouble are "scandal-plagued." If the scandal lasts long enough, reporters will create a name for it by tacking the suffix "-gate" to the appropriate noun. The practice alerts readers and listeners that a tale of scandal is about to unfold. (Historically, the term dates back to the famous Watergate scandal that forced a U.S. president from office in 1974.) For example, when the story of corruption and conflict of interest over former prime minister Jean Chrétien's involvement in a golf course in his hometown of Shawinigan, Que., the affair came to be known as "Shawinigate."

Journalese is common on sports pages. Sports reporters and copy editors fear overusing the word "won" to describe the outcomes of contests. Instead, especially in headlines, they report that one team "ambushed," "bombed," "flattened," "nipped," "outlasted," "scorched," "stunned," "thrashed" or "walloped" another. Sometimes a cliché can be twisted into a fresh expression or used in a surprising way. Such opportunities for the effective use of clichés are rare, but Canadian cultural icon Robert Fulford gave it a good go in an article entitled (tongue-in-cheek, of course) "Are clichés the Achilles' heel of our language? Or do they take one for the team, give 110% and keep us in the loop?" (*National Post*, February 20, 2007). Here's an excerpt:

Anyone who talks about writing, or writes about talking, makes a point of condemning dead phrases. These denunciations, while effective and sometimes eloquent, change nothing. The enemies of clichés come and go, but clichés persist.

Everyone seems to agree that clichés stifle writing and thinking. In politics they're downright dangerous. Vaclav Havel, hero of the Czech struggle against the Soviets, claims that clichés, by supporting accepted ways of thinking, encourage dictatorships: "The cliché organizes life; it expropriates people's identity; it becomes ruler, defence lawyer, judge and the law."

Thirty-five years ago Walter Ong, a great student of language, described the anti-cliché campaign in *Rhetoric, Romance, and Technology*: "Clichés have for many years now been hunted down mercilessly with a view to total extermination." More recently, Martin Amis expanded that metaphor in his book of essays, *The War against Cliché*. Ideally, he claimed, all writing opposes cliché, including clichés of the mind and heart. "When I dispraise, I am usually quoting clichés. When I praise, I am usually quoting the opposed qualities of freshness, energy and reverberation of voice."

But if you open a newspaper, or watch the TV news, you're likely to be told that wolves are appearing in sheep's clothing, someone is killing someone else with kindness, fools aren't suffered gladly, X is a poster child for Y, and today's fast-paced society is causing widespread stress.

Meanwhile, some helpful soul will explain (as if it had been discovered recently) that most of an iceberg lies below the water, out of sight, like certain problems. Expressions like these fill the air around us. Just the other night on TV I heard it said that some commentator was a boy crying wolf.

Not that clichés are altogether intolerable. They can produce pleasure. Mixed and mangled, the cliché has a way of enriching dialogue. Watching "Corner Gas," the prairie sitcom, I was delighted to hear Hank (a character with limited powers of expression) describe some task as easy because "It's not rocket surgery."

Observant readers can take innocent pleasure in the appearance of attachment-clichés, in which one word serves as the inevitable accessory of another. In newspapers we write about only one kind of hoax, the elaborate hoax. In book reviews (as Tom Payne noted in the London *Telegraph*) epics are all sprawling, quibbles minor, insights penetrating and roller coasters emotional. Scholarship, if worn, is worn lightly.

I know people whose faces register delight when some fool says we have to think outside the box. There's fascination, too, in watching the growth of clichés that pointlessly lengthen sentences. People love saying "on a daily basis," for instance, using four words where one will do fine, giving their speech an official, memo-like sound. Those who care about language may not like it, but in some ears it sounds appropriate. The late Alistair Cooke's doctor asked him, "Do you have a bowel movement on a daily basis?" Cooke said no, but he had one daily.

Clichés

There are thousands of clichés and slang phrases that reporters must learn to recognize and avoid. Some of the most common are listed here.

a keen mind	few and far between	pitched battle
ambulance rushed	foreseeable future	police dragnet
around the clock	gained ground	pose a challenge

arrived at the scene	gave it their blessing	proud parents
at long last	get a good look	proves conclusively
at this point in time	go to the polls	pushed for legislation
baptism by fire	got off to a good start	quick thinking
bare minimum	grief-stricken	real challenge
beginning a new life	ground to a halt	reign of terror
behind the wheel	hail of bullets	see-saw battle
benefit of the doubt	heated argument	set to work
bigger and better	heed the warning	smell a rat
blanket of snow	high-speed chase	sped to the scene
blessing in disguise	hits the spot	spread like wildfire
called to the scene	in his new position	start their mission
calm before the storm	in the wake of	still at large
came to their rescue	landed the job	stranger than fiction
came to rest	last but not least	strike a nerve
came under attack	last-ditch stand	sudden death
came under fire	left their mark	sweep under the rug
cast aside	levelled an attack	take it easy
caught red-handed	limped into port	talk is cheap
clear-cut issue	line of fire	tempers flared
colourful scene	lingering illness	time will tell
complete stranger	lodge a complaint	tip of the iceberg
complete success	lucky to be alive	tipped the scales
coveted title	made off with	took its toll
crystal clear	made their escape	too late to turn back
dead and buried	made their way home	tower of strength
decide the fate	miraculous escape	tracked down
devoured by flames	Mother Nature	travelled the globe
dime a dozen	necessary evil	tried their luck
doomed to failure	never a dull moment	under siege
dread disease	no relief in sight	under their noses
dream come true	notified next of kin	undertaking a study
drop in the bucket	once in a lifetime	up in the air
dying breed	one step closer	view with alarm
erupted in violence	in the mix	went to great lengths
escaped death	opened fire	won a reputation
exchanged gunfire	paved the way	word of caution
faced an uphill battle	pillar of strength	words of wisdom
fell on deaf ears	pinpointed the cause	word to the wise

Slang

Journalists avoid slang, which tends to be more faddish than clichés. Some words that started out as slang have won acceptance as standard English. "Blizzard" and "flabbergast" are among such terms. Most slang never makes this transition, however.

Feature stories and personality profiles sometimes employ slang effectively, but it is inappropriate in straight news stories because it is too informal and distracting. Moreover, slang may baffle readers who are not of the right age or ethnic group to understand it.

Slang is often specific to a single generation and rapidly becomes dated so that a term used in a story may already be obsolete. During the 1970s and 1980s, young people overused such terms as "cool" and "freaked out," and over the years those terms underwent subtle changes in meaning; other colloquial expressions have simply become outdated and fallen out of use. By the 1990s, young people found a whole new set of "slammin'" slang terms and "dissed" anyone still using the slang of the 1980s as a "Melvin." A young woman of the early 2000s might show "props" to friends who know the "off the hinges" films showing at the "grindhouse" and get "stoked" about "poppin' tags" and looking for "lollipops" at the mall.

Slang also conveys meanings journalists may want to avoid. It often expresses a person's attitude toward something. Thus, slang terms such as "flaky," "ego trip" and "flatfoot" convey evaluations—often negative and stereotypical—of the things described. Reporters, however, should leave to editorial writers or readers and viewers the job of making evaluations.

Technical Language and Jargon

Nearly every trade or profession develops its own technical language or jargon. When professionals use jargon to impress or mislead the public, critics call it gobbledygook, bafflegab, doublespeak or bureaucratese. Most jargon is abstract, wordy, repetitious and confusing. For example, a government agency warned, "There exists at the intersection a traffic condition which constitutes an intolerable, dangerous hazard to the health and safety of property and persons utilizing such intersection for pedestrian and vehicular movement." That sentence contains 31 words. A good journalist could summarize it in four: "The intersection is dangerous."

Many sources reporters routinely use—doctors, lawyers, business people, press releases, technical reports, and police and court records—speak in jargon. Journalists must translate that jargon into plain English. Here are two examples:

JARGON: Identification of the victim is being withheld pending notification of his next of kin.
REVISED: Police are withholding the victim's name until his family has been notified.

JARGON: Dr. Stewart McKay said, "Ethnic groups that subsist on a vegetarian diet and practically no meat products seem to have a much lower level of serum cholesterol and a very low incidence of ischemic diseases arising from atherosclerotic disease."
REVISED: Dr. Stewart McKay said ethnic groups that eat little meat have low rates of coronary heart disease and related illnesses.

Canadians expect teachers to set a good example for their students by writing clearly and accurately, but even teachers succumb to jargon. Some call themselves "educators" or "instructional units." Desks have become "pupil work stations," libraries "instructional resource centres," hallways "behaviour-transition corridors," and schools "attendance centres."

Readers usually can decipher the jargon's meaning, but not easily. Sometimes jargon is almost impossible to understand:

The semiotic perspective promotes a reflective mode of thinking that requires attention to specific contextual clues and relates them to one's understanding of the world with a kind of "informed skepticism" that the authors believe is fundamental to critical thinking.

This kind of technical language may be appropriate in some specialized publications written for experts in a particular field. It is not appropriate in newspapers written for a mass audience.

Euphemisms

Euphemisms are vague expressions used in place of harsher, more offensive terms. Some etiquette experts say that good manners require the use of euphemisms. Prudishly, some people may say that a woman is "expecting" rather than "pregnant" and that they have to "go to the washroom" rather than "go to the toilet."

Whatever value euphemisms have for etiquette, they detract from good newswriting in which clarity and precision are the most important goals.

Because newspapers are written for a general audience, words or phrases that could offend members of the audience are rarely, if ever, used. But sometimes news events force reporters to use descriptive words in place of confusing and awkward euphemisms. An example is the 1993 case of Lorena Bobbitt, the Virginia woman who used a kitchen knife to cut off her husband's penis after he allegedly raped her. The word "penis" had rarely appeared in news stories, and some news organizations were squeamish about using it, especially in headlines. Euphemisms like "member," "organ" or "offending organ" appeared instead. The widespread coverage the Bobbitt case received apparently diminished journalistic sensitivity to the word. A computer search found more than 1,000 news stories that used the word "penis" in the six months after the Bobbitt story broke, compared to only 20 mentions in the previous six months.

A similar phenomenon occurred with the Monica Lewinsky scandal during U.S. president Bill Clinton's time in office as many reporters and news anchors found themselves writing and talking about oral sex and semen stains.

As with sex, death is frequently referenced by euphemism. People may say that a friend or relative "passed on" or is "no longer with us," not that he or she has died and been buried. Hospitals report a "negative patient outcome," not that a patient died. Funeral directors object to being called "morticians"—a word that itself was originally a euphemism for "undertakers."

During a recession, major companies lay off thousands of employees. Few admit it, however. Instead, corporate executives say they are "restructuring," "downsizing" or "rightsizing" to get rid of "excess workers." Some executives insist such "reductions in force" offer their employees "career enhancement opportunities."

Some people use euphemisms to make their jobs sound prestigious. Garbage collectors call themselves "sanitation workers," prison guards have become "corrections officers," and dogcatchers are "animal welfare officers."

War spawns grotesque euphemisms, perhaps, as some critics say, to hide the human pain and suffering every war causes. Killing the enemy has become "servicing the target." Airplanes no longer bomb enemy soldiers; instead, they "visit a site." And if during the bombing of enemy troops, some civilians are killed, that is "collateral damage." The United States calls the largest of its land-based nuclear missiles "Peacekeepers." Finally, modern armies no longer retreat. Instead, they "move to the rear," "engage in a strategic withdrawal," or "occupy new territory in accordance with plan."

Other Problems to Avoid

Avoid Stating the Obvious: Platitudes

Dull, trite, obvious remarks are called "platitudes," and journalists must learn to avoid them. Platitudes that have appeared in news stories include:

> As it has in most areas of modern life, science has entered the profession of firefighting in recent years.
> Superhighways, high-speed automobiles, and jet planes are common objects of the modern era.

The second example appeared in a story about technological changes that had occurred during the life of a 100-year-old woman. The sentence would have been more interesting if it had described the changes in more detail and clearly related them to the woman's life, such as:

> Lila Hansen once spent three days on a train to visit relatives in California. Now, she flies there in three hours every Christmas.

Students have included these platitudes in their stories:

> Counsellors help students with their problems.
> The mayor said she was pleased by the warm reception.
> The sponsors hope the art show will attract a large crowd.

The writers of these stories were quoting sources who were stating the obvious. Platitudes make for dull quotations, and dull quotations should be deleted:

> The newly elected mayor said, "I hope to do a good job."
> The committee chair said, "Homecoming weekend is going to be big and exciting."

When people stop reading a story, they rarely think about why it bored them. If they re-examine the story, they might realize it is just a series of platitudes. Platitudes say nothing that hasn't been heard before. Thus, people might quit reading the story because it is no longer interesting or newsworthy.

To avoid repeating platitudes, reporters must recognize them when they conduct interviews. Sources often give obvious, commonplace answers to questions. If a bartender is robbed at gunpoint, there is no reason to quote him saying he was scared. Most people confronted by guns are scared, and they often say so. If journalists want to quote the bartender—or any other source—they should ask more penetrating questions until they receive more specific, interesting or unusual details.

Avoid First-Person References

Except in extraordinary circumstances, journalists should remain neutral bystanders. They should not mention themselves in news stories. Journalists should not use the words "I," "me," "we," "our" or "us" except when they are directly quoting some other person.

Beginning reporters sometimes use "we," "us" or "our" when referring to the community in which they work or to Canada. Most newswriters refrain from using the first person. When first-person pronouns appear outside quotation marks, readers usually conclude that the writer is editorializing about the subject:

> He said we must work harder to improve the city's schools.
> REVISED: He said parents must work harder to improve the city's schools.

> The prime minister said we are being hurt by inflation.
> REVISED: The prime minister said Canadians are being hurt by inflation.

Avoid the Negative

For clarity, avoid negative constructions. Sentences should be cast in positive rather than negative form, as in the following examples:

> The student did not often come to class.
> REVISED: The student rarely came to class.

> The defence attorney tried to disprove her client's sanity.
> REVISED: The defence attorney tried to prove her client was insane.

Sentences containing two or three negatives are wordy and even more difficult to decipher. As you read the following examples, you may have to pause to determine their meaning:

> The women said they are not against the change.
> REVISED: The women said they favour the change.

> The MP said she would not accept any campaign contributions from people who do not live in her riding.
> REVISED: The MP said she would accept campaign contributions only from people living in her riding.

In most cases, you can correct the problem by changing just a word or two:

> Most people are not careful readers.
> REVISED: Few people are careful readers.

> The financial planner said he could help people not go into debt.
> REVISED: The financial planner said he could help people avoid debt.

Avoid an Echo

An echo is a redundancy or the unnecessary repetition of a word. Good writing avoids an echo by eliminating redundant words or phrases:

> Her annual salary was $29,000 a year.
> REVISED: Her annual salary was $29,000.

> In Japan, cancer patients are rarely told they have cancer.
> REVISED: In Japan, patients are rarely told they have cancer.

Writers sometimes repeat a key word or phrase for emphasis or to demonstrate an important similarity. If the repetition is needless, however, the result is likely to be awkward, distracting or confusing.

Avoid Gush

Reporters also avoid "gush"—writing with exaggerated enthusiasm. They write news stories to inform members of a community, not to please their sources. News stories should report useful information. They should not praise or advocate.

Two ways to avoid gush are to always use more than one source for a story and to demand that sources provide specific details to support their generalizations. Using multiple sources who are independent of one another prevents reporters from being misled or manipulated by sources seeking favourable publicity. By insisting that sources provide details and specific examples to support their claims, reporters can minimize the tendency of sources to engage in the kind of self-praise found in these examples:

> "We feel we are providing quality recreational programs for both adults and children," Holden said.
> Police Chief Barry Kopperud said the city's mounted horse patrol, which began one year ago, has become a great success.

When a journalist finishes an article, it should sound like a news story, not a press release. Yet one travel story gushed that Mexico is "a land of lush valleys and marvellous people." Other examples of gush include:

> The fair will offer bigger and better attractions than ever before.
> The event will provide fun and surprises for everyone who attends.

This gush cannot be rewritten, because there is nothing of substance to rewrite. It simply should be deleted.

There is a second type of gush—an escalation in modifiers. Columnist Donna Neely explains that what used to be called "funny" is now called "hilarious" and what used to be "great" is now "fantastic" or "incredible."

Exaggerations appear everywhere: in news stories, press releases, advertisements and everyday speech. Sportswriters call athletes not just "stars" but "superstars." Advertisers call their inventories "fabulous" and their sales "gigantic." Delete all such modifiers or replace them with facts and details, and let readers and viewers decide for themselves what adjectives are appropriate.

Avoid Vague Time References

Unless your instructor tells you otherwise, do not use "yesterday" or "tomorrow" in print (hard-copy) news stories to refer to a specific day, and use "today" and "tonight" to refer only to the day of publication. Instead, use the day of the week—Monday, Tuesday, and so forth—to date events that occur within seven days before or after the day of publication. For events that are more than seven days in the past or future, use a specific date, such as July 23 or March 4. Using date or day of the week eliminates the confusion that might arise with the use of "today," "tomorrow" or "yesterday" in news stories that are written a day or more in advance of their publication.

For example, if a fire destroyed a home at 5 p.m. Tuesday, a reporter would write the story later that evening for publication in the Wednesday newspaper. If the reporter wrote that the fire happened "today," readers would think "today" means the day they are reading the story—Wednesday. If the reporter is writing about an event that will happen on the day of publication, the use of "today" is appropriate, as in this sentence in a morning newspaper: "The concert will begin at 3 p.m. today." "Yesterday," "today" and "tomorrow" may be used in direct quotations, and they may be used to refer to the past, present or future in general and not to specific days. Journalists also avoid the word "recently" because it is too vague.

All of this might seem antiquated, given the availability of online communication and with it, the ability to update news stories continuously. But even online newspapers will annoy readers who have to search to discover the time element of a given article.

Use of the Present Tense

Reporters avoid the present tense and terms such as "at the present time" in stories for the printed newspaper, because many of the events they report end before readers receive the paper. A reporter working on deadline should not say, "A fire at the Grand Hotel threatens to destroy the entire block." Firefighters almost certainly would have extinguished the blaze before readers receive the paper hours later. For the same reason, a reporter covering a fatal accident should not say, "The victim's identity is not known." Police might learn the victim's identity in a few hours, and local radio and television stations might broadcast the person's name before subscribers receive their papers. Consequently, print journalists must use the past tense:

> A fire at the Grand Hotel threatens to destroy the entire block.
> REVISED: A fire at the Grand Hotel was threatening to destroy the entire block at 11:30 p.m.

> The victim's identity is not known.
> REVISED: Police were unable to learn the victim's identity immediately.

Stories written for immediate publication on a website or for broadcast are more likely to use the present tense. When the story is likely to reach readers or viewers as the events are unfolding, the present tense may be more accurate and more compelling than the past tense.

Avoid Excessive Punctuation

Journalists avoid excessive punctuation, particularly exclamation points, dashes and parentheses. Exclamation points are rarely necessary and should never be used after every sentence in a story, regardless of that story's importance. Parentheses interrupt the flow of ideas and force people to pause and assimilate some additional, often jarring bit of information:

> He (the premier) said the elderly population (people 65 and older) had grown twice as fast as any other segment of the province's population during the last 20 years.
> REVISED: The premier said the percentage of people 65 and older had grown twice as fast as any other segment of the province's population during the last 20 years.

Sources use a lot of pronouns and vague references. Students often quote these sources, adding explanations within parentheses. If an explanation is necessary, then a direct quote is not a good idea. Instead, reporters use partial quotes or paraphrase what a source has said:

> "I wish they (school administrators) would quit fooling around," she said. "They say they don't have enough money (to hire more teachers), but I don't believe that. I know they have it (the money); it's just a matter of priorities—of using their money more wisely."
> REVISED: She said the school administrators should "quit fooling around." They say they do not have enough money to hire more teachers, but she does not believe that. "It's just a matter of priorities—of using their money more wisely," she said.

 ## CHECKLIST FOR THE LANGUAGE OF NEWS

Choose words that convey your meaning as precisely as possible. Write your story with detail and explanation so it answers all the questions one logically might ask about the topic.

1. Use active verbs and vivid nouns.
2. Prune adjectives and adverbs from your sentences.
3. Avoid clichés, journalese, slang and euphemisms.
4. Avoid loaded words and opinionated or artificial labels.
5. Avoid mentioning yourself in the story and using the words "I," "me," "we," "us" and "our" except in direct quotations from a source.
6. Avoid misleading statements about the time of the story. Use the specific day of the week or the date—not "yesterday," "today" or "tomorrow."
7. Avoid gush, exaggeration, contrived labels, and excessive punctuation.
8. Avoid an echo: Do not unnecessarily repeat the same word in a sentence.
9. Avoid platitudes: Do not state the obvious, such as the fact that a government official was happy to be elected.
10. Avoid the present tense when writing for print media; the events you write about will already have occurred by the time people are reading the newspaper. But for Web or broadcast news stories as well as for some features, the present tense may be appropriate.
11. Cast your sentences in positive rather than negative form.

The Writing Coach

The section on common writing faults in *The Canadian Press Stylebook* pays a lot of attention to the fundamentals of newswriting style, and so should you. Here are some excerpts:

The most common faults in writing are lack of imagination, muted curiosity, and a deaf ear and closed eye for the reader's interests. These faults lead to stories that are predictable, unfocused and boring. By turn or together, they may confuse readers with conflicting information, leave them gasping for missing facts or infuriated at what they know is misinformation. Such stories can puzzle readers with fog and bafflegab and have them wondering what the news means to them and their everyday lives. Bluntly put, they turn readers off.

Active vs. passive: Think of active verbs as power words—words that drive your sentences, keep the reader's attention, and move her briskly along.

Not: The economy experienced a quick revival.

But: The economy revived quickly.

Not: At first light there was no sign of the ship.

But: The ship vanished in the night.

Use the passive when a switch in emphasis is helpful, for instance, to put the news ahead of the source:

Not: A grievance board has ordered the reinstatement of a counsellor fired for kicking a patient.

But: A counsellor fired for kicking a patient has been ordered reinstated by a grievance board.

And the passive may lighten a sentence by removing secondary information that can wait: A banker wanted for questioning in the disappearance of $1 million is believed to have flown to Mexico, police said today. (But be sure a later paragraph gives reasons for the belief.)

More than words: Tell the reader what has happened, certainly. But also help the reader understand why and how it has happened in terms that strike home.

Not: The hurricane caused widespread damage to buildings, farm equipment, trees and hydro lines.

But: The hurricane's winds lifted roofs off houses and barns and flipped over cars, tractors, and even lumbering dump trucks used to carry grain. Almost every fruit and shade tree in the region was knocked over, and linemen said about 3,000 hydro poles had been snapped off.

EXERCISE 1   Vocabulary

Words with different meanings often look or sound similar. As a journalist, you should be familiar with these words and use them correctly. Cross out the wrong words in the following sentences, leaving only the correct ones. Consult *The Canadian Press Stylebook* for preferred usage. Also correct errors in style and possessives.

1. The mayor (accepted/excepted) the offer from the university board of directors to (aide/aid) the city in its (clean up/cleanup) efforts after the storm.

2. The professor (alluded/eluded) to the chapter in the book that mentions that people will (altar/alter) their behaviour if they are (assured/ensured/insured) their efforts will be rewarded.

3. The (cite/site/sight) of the new World War II memorial (peaked/peeked/piqued) the interest of many (people/persons) in the neighbourhood.

4. (Personal/Personnel) were asked to evaluate their (peers/piers) in regard to (their/there) job performance.

5. She was afraid the club members would (waiver/waver) in defence of their actions when it was determined the (principle/principal) planned to (censure/censor) them for demonstrating in front of the school.

6. The restaurant (complemented/complimented) the meal with a delicious (desert/dessert).

7. The team's (moral/morale) was higher (than/then) ever after (their/there/its) undefeated season became a reality.

8. Police said the car was (stationary/stationery) when the truck (collided with/struck) it, causing a quite a (cite/sight/site) for passersby.

9. The beautiful (weather/whether) was one of the reasons that thousands of Canadians turned out to demonstrate at the (Parliament Buildings/Parliament buildings/parliament buildings).

10. The snowstorm during the (assent/ascent) of the mountain peak hampered the rescue workers from reaching the climber who (received/sustained/suffered) a broken leg (due to/because of) a fall from a ledge.

11. The county commissioner felt that passage of the (ordinance/ordnance) was (to/too/two) (elusive/illusive) at this time (due to/because of) opposition to it.

12. She wanted to know with (who/whom) they intended to (pedal/peddle) their bicycles across the province.

13. The provincial fire (marshall/marshal) began investigating the fire at the mall that caused (about/around) $1 million damage and (raised/razed) seven of the mall's 30 stores.

14. Police are looking for a (blond/blonde) male in his (30s/30's) (who/whom) is wanted for questioning in connection with the (bazaar/bizarre) incident at City Hall on Tuesday.

15. The author (implied/inferred) that the government's plan was (impracticable/impractical) because there was not enough money available to make it work.

16. Barbara and her (fiancé/fiancée), (who/whom) is serving in the military, plan on having (their/there/they're) wedding in June.

17. He said it would not have been difficult to be (misled/mislead) by the evidence presented by the defendant's (council/counsel) during the trial.

18. The (envelop/envelope) has been (laying/lying) on the table (that/which) she bought just last month.

19. (Fewer/Less) than 30 (people/persons) attended the meeting at which officials announced employees would have to (forgo/forego) a (raise/raze) this year.

20. The minister (prayed/preyed) that the members of his congregation would not (loath/loathe) the young people (who/whom) had (flaunted/flouted) the law when they vandalized the church.

EXERCISE 2   Verbs

SECTION I: AVOIDING USE OF NOUNS AS VERBS
Rewrite the following sentences, eliminating the use of nouns as verbs.

1. She scripted a movie about life in China.

2. The students partnered with a professional writer.

3. The class interfaced with the teacher by email.

4. The family always summered in the Rockies.

5. He inked a new contract with the team.

SECTION II: USING STRONGER VERBS
List three stronger, more active and descriptive verbs that could replace the verbs in the following sentences.

1. The mayor plans to distribute information over the Internet.

2. The company conducted a study of customers in the area.

3. He got a new job.

4. Kelly is well thought of by her peers.

5. More than 300 people are employed at the plant.

SECTION III: USING STRONGER VERBS
Rewrite the following sentences, using stronger verbs. Also use normal word order (subject, verb, direct object).

1. The car is in need of a new paint job.

2. He was planning to open a restaurant in Moncton.

3. The professor was able to interest many students in his classes.

4. The preschool nutrition program is set up so that the cost is paid by the province.

5. A short circuit in the electrical wiring at the church was the cause of the fire.

6. The cost of a ticket for admission to the amusement park is $25.

7. A trip to the beach is what Karen and David are planning for this summer.

8. To obtain extra money to pay for college, John has picked up a second job.

9. It was suggested by the moderator that the panel participants may want to take a break.

10. The reservations she made at the hotel were for three rooms.

EXERCISE 3   Avoiding Common Errors

SECTION I: AVOIDING GRAMMATICAL AND VOCABULARY ERRORS
Rewrite the following sentences, correcting their wording.

1. The mayor said the city would not agree not to expand the program.

2. The hospital said they would be releasing the man that received a broken leg in the accident sometime Wednesday.

3. Waiting for the right moment, the suspects house was surrounded by police shortly after the robbery.

4. The men and women that are members of the committee hope to settle the dispute soon.

5. The councils concern is the ambiguity they feel exists with regard to providing funding for the program.

SECTION II: KEEPING RELATED WORDS AND IDEAS TOGETHER
Rewrite these sentences, improving the word placement.

1. The referendum was approved by voters to merge the two towns by a 2–1 margin.

2. David Smith pleaded guilty to violating his probation in front of County Judge John Robinson in a burglary case on Wednesday.

3. The parking situation has been a problem for the past few months which will be dealt with by the police chief.

4. The driver was taken to the hospital for observation by the city ambulance after the accident.

5. County commissioners voted to raise taxes by 2 per cent to balance next year's budget last week.

SECTION III: AVOIDING IMPRECISION
Rewrite the following sentences, making them as precise as possible.

1. The mayor ordered the city park benches be replaced at the monthly city council meeting.

2. The pedestrian was killed instantly after she was struck by the car.

3. The delay in construction of the recreation centre caused a reaction in the student population announced by the university president.

4. The judge sentenced the man to five years in prison after pleading guilty to three counts of embezzlement.

5. When the car collided with the fence, the driver and his passenger were hurt.

SECTION IV: DEFINING AND EXPLAINING
Define or explain each of the large numbers or unfamiliar terms in the following sentences.

1. Their son has meningitis.

2. A single B-2 Stealth bomber costs $800 million.

3. The most powerful supercomputer can perform more than 150 billion calculations per second.

SECTION V: AVOIDING CLICHÉS
Rewrite the following sentences, eliminating clichés.

1. Today's sunny weather may be the calm before the storm, as the area could be enveloped in a blanket of snow by the weekend.

2. Police arrived at the scene of the crime five minutes after receiving the 911 call.

3. City council's discussion about raising taxes turned into a heated argument between two council members.

4. The university does not expect to raise tuition in the foreseeable future.

5. Time will tell how John will fare in his new position as manager of the department.

SECTION VI: AVOIDING UNNECESSARY PARENTHESES
Rewrite the following sentences to eliminate the parentheses and other errors.

1. She (the mayor) said (in response to a question about property taxes) that she opposes any such proposal (to increase them).

2. Despite the loss (now estimated at $4.2 million) he said the company should be able to pay all their debts before the deadline (Dec. 30).

3. The premier predicted, "They (members of the legislature) will approve the proposal (to increase the sales tax) within 60 days."

SECTION VII: AVOIDING THE NEGATIVE
Rewrite the following sentences in positive form.

1. Not until last year were they able to buy their new home.

2. The test was not that easy to finish in the allotted time.

3. The students do not have any limitations on which songs they can choose.

4. The car was parked not far away.

5. The mayor said she would not be disinclined to vote against the motion.

SECTION VIII: IMPROVING SENTENCES
Rewrite the following sentences, correcting all their errors.

1. She went by way of train to travel through Europe.

2. The owner of the software company, an alumni of the university, gave $1 million to be used for scholarships by the college of business.

3. The couples twin sons ended up moving to British Columbia after they graduated, a fact that made it difficult for them to visit the boys.

4. The purpose that the after-school program was created for is to give youngsters a place to get help with their homework.

5. Between the two candidates, voters chose the older one who they believed had more experience.

CHAPTER 3

EXERCISE 4   Review

Answer key provided: See Appendix D.

SECTION I: AVOIDING SLANG AND CLICHÉS
Rewrite the following sentences, eliminating their slang and clichés.

1. The president of the company asked employees to give the benefit of the doubt to his restructuring plan, but his plea fell on deaf ears.

2. The crowd erupted in violence when the doors to the club were closed, leaving them outside.

3. The premier said the election had tipped the scales in favour of his party.

4. The students believed the program was doomed to failure because few supported it.

5. Soldiers fought a pitched battle with a group of guerrilla fighters.

SECTION II: IMPROVING VERBS AND SENTENCE STRUCTURE
Rewrite the following sentences, using stronger verbs and normal word order (subject, verb, direct object).

1. The best that can be hoped for is that the decision to postpone construction of the building by university officials will come soon.

2. Sitting across from me at the café dressed in a green hoodie and black hat, he ordered an espresso from the waitress.

3. More than 10 student residences have been broken into and have had things taken in the last two weeks.

4. Patients in dire need of treatment for serious injuries or illnesses are required to be taken to the nearest hospital by paramedics.

5. The three-vehicle accident that closed Main Street for two hours so authorities could investigate was witnessed by a bystander who called police to the scene.

SECTION III: KEEPING RELATED WORDS AND IDEAS TOGETHER

Rewrite the following sentences, moving the related words and ideas as close together as possible. Correct any style or grammatical errors.

1. Over $5 million was needed in order to begin construction of the new arts centre by the city.

2. The letter Mary wrote to her husband was filled with news from their neighbourhood stationed in Afghanistan with the Canadian Forces.

3. The proposal is expected to be vetoed by the premier to raise $1 billion to improve the province's roads by increasing the gas tax.

4. Detectives questioned the suspect in the burglary Thursday night for two hours at the Main Street Restaurant.

5. The accident victim was found with lacerations on his arms and legs trapped under the motorcycle.

SECTION IV: TESTING ALL YOUR SKILLS

Rewrite the following sentences, correcting all their errors.

1. The committee said they feel the program is a beneficial one because a student can get class credit for all he does at the internship.

2. She laid on the beach from 8 AM in the morning until 3 PM in the afternoon realizing what a beautiful day it was.

3. The policeman told the jury that they needed to understand police procedures on investigations to understand how the robbery occurred during the trial.

4. The consensus of opinion among participants in the workshop is that a pay raise of 15 to 20% should be received by the nurses.

5. The woman said her son, who she considered to be a budding genius, was champing at the bit to get to college next year.

6. It was inferred by the author of the book entitled *It's a Great Day in MY Neighbourhood* that everyone can have a good life if they want too.

7. The city council burnt the midnight oil before voting six to one to spend 50 thousand dollars a year annually to the qualified expert whom would serve as consultant on the construction job for the next 3 years.

8. The clothing on display came from the archives collection of the 1930's and the director commented to the effect that they feature adult and childrens clothing in the collection.

SECTION V: AVOIDING JOURNALESE
Rewrite the following sentences, eliminating slang and journalese.

1. She racked up $30,000 in medical expenses.

2. He gave an OK to spending the $26,000 figure for a car.

3. The program is geared toward helping high school students.

4. The new building will carry a price tag of about $6 million.

5. The proposal met with opposition from three council members.

SECTION VI: AVOIDING JARGON
Rewrite the following sentences, eliminating jargon.

1. Police said the perpetrators of the burglary would be arraigned later in the week.

2. Teresa Phillips, a/k/a Marie Phillips, testified that she entered the store and helped the defendant steal an unknown quantity of jewellery from the premises on or about the 9th day of last month.

3. The company said it would maximize efforts and utilize every department it had available to overcome the budget crisis.

4. The mayor said if the sanitation engineers went on strike, he would be forced to have other city workers drive the trucks.

5. Brown's lawsuit charges that, as a result of the auto accident, he suffered from bodily injury, disability, disfigurement, and mental anguish. Browns lawsuit also charges that he has lost his ability to earn a living and that the accident aggravated a previous condition.

4 | Selecting and Reporting the News

I do not hold with the myth of the impartial observer; you cannot watch government as closely as I have over the past eight years and remain a detached outsider unless you are a political eunuch, and no eunuch is a trustworthy guide to the ultimate mysteries.

—Walter Stewart, Canadian journalist, 1971

On the evening of Wednesday, March 19, 2003, then–U.S. president George W. Bush sat at his desk in the Oval Office, ready to announce to the American public that for the second time in 12 years, the United States was at war in Iraq. U.S. forces had just an hour earlier launched the attack, the stated objective twofold: oust Saddam Hussein and eliminate the threat of weapons of mass destruction. The announcement of war came after months of campaigning by the president and his administration to warn of Hussein's threat to American and world interests.

Coverage of the invasion blanketed news media, large and small, in the United States and in Canada. Both countries' media provided extensive coverage of the build-up to the war and of the war itself. People read accounts providing factual details of the bloodshed as well as passionate commentary on both sides of the issue.

Here in Canada, where controversy roiled over then–prime minister Jean Chrétien's refusal to join the American war effort, different perspectives on the attack were apparent almost immediately. On March 19, the *Globe and Mail* ran a front-page story featuring an Iraqi family in Kirkuk scrambling to get out of the city. The family had listened on shortwave radio (illegal activity in Saddam Hussein's Iraq) to the U.S. president's 48-hour ultimatum to Saddam and his sons. Another story on page A5 focused on filmmaker Sacha Trudeau, son of former prime minister Pierre Trudeau, who was among a handful of Canadians refusing to leave Baghdad despite warnings to flee the country from the Canadian Department of Foreign Affairs. Among the Canadians refusing to leave were six peace activists who vowed to remain in Baghdad, declaring that they would attempt to thwart the U.S. military action by acting as "human shields."

The *National Post* reported from Washington that thousands of troops had taken up positions for the imminent invasion after Saddam had refused a U.S. demand that he leave Iraq within 48 hours. The paper reported that the U.S. war effort was backed by a coalition of 45 nations, not including Canada, a fact that "disappointed" the U.S. CanWest Global's TV station, Global National, promised to break from regular programming to bring viewers hourly reports of the invasion.

The *Toronto Star*'s headline story the next morning covered the dawn raids on the Iraqi capital and said that Iraqi officials remained defiant in the face of 300,000 U.S. and British troops, backed by a fleet of warships and 1,000 warplanes. They quoted Iraq's deputy prime minister, who appeared at a Baghdad news conference vowing to rally behind Saddam, and reported that the Persian Gulf state of Bahrain, allied with the U.S., had offered Saddam sanctuary.

The Iraq War posed challenges for Canadian and American news media alike and frayed nerves between the two countries. How to get the story without endangering the war effort, the troops who were fighting, or the journalists who were covering the conflict? After the Vietnam War, in which the news media provided extensive coverage of military operations, the U.S. government imposed tight controls on journalists. Reporters claimed they had little access to information and no freedom in the operational battleground to gather news and write stories. U.S. military operations in Grenada, Panama, and especially in the first war with Iraq in 1991 had seen the news media hampered in getting stories out. During the build-up to the second Iraq War, the military and the news media reached an agreement on how to cover the war. Journalists would be "embedded" with combat and other units to cover the war.

As the conflict unfolded and quick initial success led to a guerrilla-style war with insurgents planting roadside bombs, reporters would begin to unravel the story of how the war began and how it was progressing. By 2006, Canada's military involvement in Afghanistan (as part of a NATO-led International Security Force) had reached a peak, with more Canadian troops deployed and more Canadian soldiers dying. Canada's military involvement had in fact been increasing since the fall of the Taliban in late 2001. By late 2009, Canadian soldiers were still dying in Afghanistan, and Canadian officials were embroiled in a scandal involving allegations from a high-ranking diplomat that the Canadian military in the poverty-stricken and war-torn country was implicated in the torture and abuse of Afghan detainees.

But on March 19, 2003, editors in Canada as well as in the United States had no difficulty deciding what to put on the front pages of their newspapers: war is undoubtedly front-page material. Even when the news day lacks one clearly compelling story, editors tend to emphasize the same stories on the same day because they all apply the same sets of news values—values they have developed through years of experience. Their takes on the story will vary according to their political sympathies, but there will be little disagreement over what "makes" the front page or the top of the newscast hour.

Selecting news stories to publish in a newspaper or air on a news broadcast is a subjective process—an art. No scientific test helps journalists measure a story's newsworthiness. Journalists have tried to define news, but no single definition has won widespread acceptance. Also, no definition acknowledges all the factors affecting the selection process. For newspaper editor and publisher Neil Reynolds, news is "what someone wants suppressed." Famed Canadian culture critic and academic Marshall McLuhan saw news media as social forms with the power to impose assumptions. And a former B.C. premier, W.A.C. Bennett, insisted, "I make the news, I don't read the news."

THE CHARACTERISTICS OF NEWS

Even if journalists cannot agree on a definition of news, they do agree that news stories possess certain characteristics or news values. They agree that a good news story highlights the dramatic by presenting characters who face challenges. Sometimes the characters overcome the challenges, sometimes they are beaten by them. Either way, the structure and method of telling their stories is the fabric of journalism. More traditionally, journalists have said that newsworthy events are those that possess at least some of the following characteristics: timeliness, impact, prominence, proximity, singularity, and conflict or controversy. After all, if news stories contain none of these qualities, the audience is justified in asking, "So what?"

Timeliness

Journalists stress current information—stories occurring today or yesterday, not several days or weeks ago—and try to report it ahead of their competitors. In the past, print journalism used to trail television and radio in reporting the basic facts of a breaking news story and still does with its paper publication, but the Internet and newspaper websites have changed the nature of print journalism in the twenty-first century. Many newspaper reporters provide Web updates for their Web news products before stories are prepared for the print edition. This allows print journalists to get stories to the public sooner than they can with print publication. But in terms of the traditional newspaper, when reporting a story that occurred even hours earlier and that may have already been reported on television, radio, or the Internet, journalists look for fresh angles and new details around which to build their stories. If some background is necessary, they usually keep it to a minimum and weave it throughout a story.

Impact

Reporters stress important information that has an impact on their audience: stories that affect, involve or interest thousands of readers or viewers. A plane crash that kills 180 people is more newsworthy than an automobile accident that kills two. Similarly, an increase in city property taxes is more newsworthy than an increase in dog licence fees because the former affects many more people.

As reporters evaluate events, they must consider the impact or importance of those events for readers and viewers. News stories tend to focus on the most severe storms, the most damaging fires, the most deadly accidents, the most important speeches, and the most interesting organizations because these events are likely to affect the most readers and viewers and have the most serious consequences. They also tend to be relatively easy stories to report because often sources such as emergency response officials make themselves available to the media. Reporters should stay alert to the harder-to-report stories that also affect large segments of their audiences.

Prominence

If an insurance salesperson or a plumber catches a cold, no one cares except that person's friends and family. If the prime minister of Canada catches a cold, the Toronto stock market may lose 500 points. Even routine events become newsworthy when they involve prominent individuals, such as politicians, business leaders, or celebrities. Almost everything the prime minister does is news because he or she is the nation's leader.

Reporters should not cover celebrities to the exclusion of stories about ordinary people, but the public seems to have an insatiable appetite for information about those who are famous. *People* magazine, for example, is successful because it fills its pages with facts and photographs about the lives of glamorous people.

Ordinary people become prominent for the news media when they are involved in a news event. When a crime is committed or an accident occurs, the news media (barring publication bans) will name the suspects or the victims, and they will be considered newsworthy only as long as the event itself is newsworthy. Once the story runs through a news cycle and is no longer considered newsworthy, the prominence of the story's subjects diminishes, unlike the prominence of celebrities who are always in the news.

Sometimes ordinary people become even more prominent in the news, with coverage of their stories lasting weeks, months, or even years. The inquiry into the death of Polish immigrant Robert Dziekanski after he was Tasered during a confrontation with RCMP officers in Vancouver's airport in 2007 is an example of a story that transfixed Canadians as it unfolded in the media.

Proximity

The closer an event is to home, the more newsworthy it becomes. Murders are important news stories locally. Sometimes murder cases attract national attention. British Columbia pig farmer Robert William Pickton was convicted in 2007 for the murders of six women abducted from Vancouver's Lower Eastside. After the verdict, Crown prosecutors decided not to go ahead with a further trial on an additional 27 counts of murder although a substantial amount of evidence was in hand. After his arrest, Pickton allegedly commented that he had planned to murder 50 prostitutes. The story also focused attention on social matters relating to drug addiction, prostitution, and missing women. Most murders, however, lack such shocking or unusual circumstances, so they draw little national attention. Journalists explain that readers and viewers are most interested in and affected by stories about their own communities.

CP PHOTO/Chuck Stoody

Vancouver Police Sgt. Sheila Sullivan (left) and RCMP Cpl. Catherine Gallifor (right) hold up a new poster released by the Missing Women Task Force in Vancouver, Wednesday Oct. 6, 2004. Eight women were added to the list which now stands at 69 missing women.

Proximity may also be more psychological than geographical. Two individuals separated by thousands of miles but sharing a characteristic or an interest may want to know more about each other. A Canadian mother may sympathize with the problems of a mother in a distant country. Canadian college students are likely to be interested in the concerns of college students elsewhere.

Singularity

Deviations from the normal—unexpected or unusual events, conflicts or controversies, drama or change—are more newsworthy than the commonplace. The 1989 shooting of female students at École Polytechnique in Montreal by a man who then committed suicide is more newsworthy than the routine school day experienced by hundreds of thousands of other students on that same day. Similarly, the fact that a city's mayor is squabbling with another city official is more newsworthy than the fact that two other officials are good friends.

Journalists must be alert for the unusual twists in otherwise mundane stories. A story about a house fire in a rural community captured the attention of editors not because it was a house fire but because of the circumstances surrounding it. Fires occur all the time, but if there is no significant damage or people are unharmed, the story may be moved to an inside page or given just a brief mention. The story in this case, however, revolved around a conservative and devout religious sect, a member of which set the fire to punish three people from his church because he thought they were sinners. That, in an editor's mind, is a fire story that does not occur every day, and the story was front-page news.

Critics charge that the media's emphasis on the unusual gives their audiences a distorted view of the world. They say that the media fail to portray the lives of normal people on a typical day in a typical community. Editors respond by saying that because there is too much news to allow them to report everything, they report problems requiring the public's attention. Still, reporters should remember that there is also news when things work as they should in a community: organizations or individuals who help a community improve its education or health care, programs that defeat youth or domestic violence, efforts to reduce teen drinking or pregnancy.

Conflict or Controversy

Two people arguing about their divergent philosophies on a social issue is more newsworthy than two people who agree on everything. The tension between the subjects creates the conflict that often makes a story dramatic and interesting to read. Although conflict between government officials or agencies, private organizations, or private individuals can be viewed as negative news, it often provides readers and viewers with different opinions about policies and problems. Conflict can exist in any story. The single mother working her way through college faces the conflict of time to care for her child and time needed to prepare herself for a better future. A young man fighting AIDS faces the conflict of trying to live his life. An athlete fighting to gain the edge against her competitors in a championship game faces the conflicts of the limits of her body's endurance and the talent and strength of her competition. In each of these stories, the conflict can be positive and no less newsworthy for that.

Other Characteristics

Dozens of other factors affect journalists' selection of news; however, most definitions of news acknowledge only a few of them. Reporters look for humorous stories—anything that will make the audience laugh. They also report straightforward events—fires, storms, earthquakes and assassinations—partly because such dramatic events are easy to recognize and report. Journalists are less adept at reporting complex phenomena, such as the causes and consequences of crime, poverty, inflation, unemployment and racial discrimination. Journalists also have difficulty reporting stories that never culminate in obvious events.

That is changing. The increased use of computers—known as computer-assisted reporting—is allowing journalists to analyze information that in the past was difficult to gather and compare. Stories that report, analyze and explain are becoming more common at larger news organizations. Even small organizations attempt such projects. Although technology has helped, editors still must publish a newspaper or air a broadcast every day, and they may need all their staff members just to accomplish that. Smaller budgets prevent smaller news organizations from hiring the staff necessary to spend time on big projects.

Another characteristic of news is that it varies somewhat from medium to medium, depending on what is called the "news cycle." The news cycle is the time between two publications of the news or between updates. Daily newspapers emphasize events occurring in their communities during the previous 24 hours and so have a 24-hour news cycle. Although most dailies concentrate on local or regional news, a few major dailies also strive to provide extensive national and international coverage. Weekly papers and newsmagazines report events of national interest, often in more depth, and try to explain the events' significance. Television reports headline news—a few details about the day's major stories, often with frequent updates as the stories develop. Also, television news broadcasters favour visual stories—ones with strong, dramatic pictures—over stories that are complicated and difficult to illustrate.

A news organization's size and the size of the community it serves affect the selection of news. A news organization in a small town may report every local traffic accident; one in a medium-sized city may report only the accidents that cause serious injury; and big-city newspapers and television stations may report only the accidents that result in death. Similarly, newspapers in small cities often publish all wedding and engagement announcements and obituaries, whereas newspapers in larger cities publish only those of prominent citizens. Most death announcements in such papers appear not as news stories but as advertisements paid for by families.

The day of the week on which news occurs is important. Newspapers publish more advertisements on Wednesdays, Thursdays and Sundays, the days when readers plan their weekend shopping or have more time to spend reading. Most newspapers attempt to maintain a specific ratio of advertisements to news, often about 60 per cent to 65 per cent advertisements to 35 per cent to 40 per cent news. So on the days they publish more advertisements, newspapers also publish more news.

News organizations also develop tendencies and traditions to emphasize some types of news stories over others. Tabloid newspapers traditionally tend to emphasize crime, sex, sports and photographs. Broadsheet newspapers take a more serious approach, placing greater emphasis on political, business and foreign news. Similarly, some local newspapers diligently investigate the problems in their communities, whereas others hesitate to publish stories that might offend their readers or advertisers.

Few publishers or station managers admit they favour any individuals or organizations. Yet most develop certain "dos and don'ts" that reporters call "policies" or "sacred cows." Sacred cows reflect the interests of an organization's executives. In a few cases, news organization executives have used their power to distort the news, ordering their staff to report only positive stories about their favourite candidates, political parties, causes or organizations.

TYPES OF NEWS

Journalists recognize two major types of news: hard and soft. "Hard news" usually refers to serious and timely stories about important topics. The stories may describe a major crime, fire, accident, speech, labour dispute, or political campaign. Journalists call hard news "spot news" or "straight news." "Breaking news," a similar label, refers to events just occurring, or "breaking," now.

"Soft news" usually refers to feature or human-interest stories. Soft news entertains as well as informs. It may make readers laugh or cry, love or hate, envy or pity. Although still newsworthy, soft news is often less timely than breaking news. Consequently, editors can delay soft stories to make room for more timely stories. Soft stories also may use a less formal style of writing, with more anecdotes, quotations and descriptions.

Non-journalists are more likely to classify news as "good" or "bad." Many critics of the media claim news organizations today focus too much on bad or negative news. Systematic studies have found, however, that most people exaggerate the amount of crime and violence reported by the media. Dozens of studies have examined the issue and found individual newspapers devote anywhere from 2 per cent to 35 per cent of their space to violence. On average, one-tenth of newspaper content concerns violence.

Other critics claim that the news media are becoming detached from the audiences they are supposed to serve and have come to define news in narrow and sometimes destructive ways. In stories about public issues, the news media tend to polarize the discourse, covering the issues as feuds between political opponents rather than informing audiences about the issues. Such reporting tends to turn audiences off, the critics charge, leaving them uninformed and cynical toward their government and bureaucratic officials, as well as toward the news media themselves. A newly minted criticism of the press has evolved in the context of online communication, which also allows for nearly immediate feedback from audiences. To be successful in their role as the eyes and ears of the public, the news media need to make audiences feel less like spectators and more like participants in public life and the news—an objective in which online publications have excelled and, by excelling, have influenced more traditional papers as well as broadcast to follow suit with their invitations to audiences to become part of the endeavour.

PUBLIC/CIVIC JOURNALISM

Nearly 20 years ago, a movement began finding its way into many newsrooms. That movement is influencing how journalists define and gather news. Proponents call it public or civic or citizen journalism. David Beers, founding editor of the award-winning, Vancouver-based online publication "The Tyee," is a leading Canadian advocate of public journalism. In a 2006 article in the *Canadian Journal of Education*, Beers argued that the movement is bolstered when educators and citizens use independent media (such as ezines and blogs) to critique corporate media and to "sharpen competing definitions of democratic discourse." The article also suggested that citizens critique independent media, focusing on potential problems such as lack of credibility and flaming (online defamation). Finally, Beers urged educators to help their students create their own independent online media and do their own original research, "allowing them a taste of the invigorating opportunities and challenges this era presents the engaged citizen journalist."

It has sometimes been observed that if public life is in trouble in Canada, then journalism is in trouble. Therefore, journalists should do what they can to support public life. The press should help citizens participate in public life and take them seriously when they do, rather than treat citizens as spectators to a drama performed by professionals and technicians. The press should nourish or create the sort of public talk some might call a deliberative dialogue. Most important, perhaps, journalists must see hope as an essential resource that they cannot deplete indefinitely without costs to the community.

Supporters of public journalism link it with fundamental concepts of democracy: by participating in self-government, people preserve democracy. The role of the press in a democracy is to keep the public informed, to provide a forum for public debate, and to help citizens make informed choices.

Many Canadians say they are tired of the press because they believe the news is boring and biased. To combat the growing public disenchantment with the press and public life, public journalism offers an alternative set of approaches for reporters. In political coverage, news organizations should turn away from the horse-race aspect of coverage—who's ahead, who's behind. Instead, journalists should conduct extensive interviews, polls, and public forums with voters to find out what issues concern them. This process allows the public to decide what issues are important.

Proponents of public journalism say journalists cannot live in a vacuum as neutral observers. Reporters should listen to all voices, not just the loudest, and listen particularly to people whose views on issues fall near the centre, not just those at the extremes. Proponents of public journalism suggest that the routine five Ws and H questions (who, what, where, when, why, and how) work well but should be expanded. In public journalism, reporters should ask:

- Who—cares, is affected, needs to be included, has a stake, is missing from this discussion?

- What—are the consequences, does it mean to citizens, would this accomplish, values are at work?

- When—were things different, can things be different, should talk lead to action?

- Where—are we headed, is the common ground, should debate take place, is the best entry point for citizens?

- Why—is this happening, do we need discussion, are things not happening, should we care?

- How—does it affect civic life, did the community do, does my story encourage action or help the public decide?

Civic journalism done well pays off in a more informed community and in a stronger readership. Surveys have found that people with a real sense of connection to their communities are almost twice as likely to be regular readers of newspapers. Although the results are not surprising, many newspapers and journalists still need to hear the message.

APPLYING THE PRINCIPLES OF NEWS SELECTION

How do reporters find good news stories? Some reporters can get story ideas from thinking about their own experiences. Things they see or hear about around town or around campus, events they attend, likes and dislikes, and people who interest them all may become subjects for news stories.

Another approach is to ask other people for ideas. Reporters often ask people what they want to know, what puzzles them, or what concerns them. Joseph Alsop, a Washington columnist for many years, said he asked 10 people a day for ideas for columns. By the end of the week, he would have 50 ideas. If only one in 10 proved usable, he still would have enough ideas to write his column for the next week. That type of digging is part of a reporter's job—perhaps the most important part.

THE CONCEPT OF OBJECTIVITY

A previous chapter noted that news stories must be objective, or free of bias. Journalists gather information and report it as factually as possible. They should not comment, interpret or evaluate. If an issue is controversial, journalists interview representatives of all the sides involved, then include as many opinions as possible. Some sources may make mistakes, and some may lie. Journalists may point out inconsistencies or inaccuracies in sources' statements, but they should not call them liars.

Journalists traditionally assumed, perhaps mistakenly, that if they reported all the information, their readers would think about the conflicting opinions and then decide which were most important and truthful. That has not always worked, so newspapers now publish separate stories analyzing major issues in the news. The stories, labelled "commentary" or "analysis," critically evaluate the news to help readers better understand it.

No human can be totally objective. Family, education, personal interests, and religious and political beliefs all influence how reporters cover stories and what stories they see as newsworthy. Nevertheless, they strive to be as impartial and objective (i.e., fair and balanced) as possible. Routine newsroom practices encourage impartiality. News stories are rarely the work of a single individual. Normally, an editor assigns a story, and a reporter writes it. Sometimes several reporters may contribute information to a story another reporter writes. Several editors may then evaluate and change the story. Reporters and editors serve as checks on one another. If one expresses an opinion in a story, another has a chance to detect and eliminate that bias.

Biases, whether intentional or not, often appear in a story when a reporter covers only one side of an issue or gives one side disproportionately more space or time than others. Reporters may talk to more sources supporting an issue than those opposed. Although it may be impossible for reporters to write about every conceivable side of an issue in their stories, they can provide readers with many sides rather than just one or two. By treating various sides of an issue equally and allowing partisans for each to state their case, reporters provide their audiences with facts they need to understand a story more fully. Total objectivity may be difficult to achieve, but balance and fairness in a story can be achieved through thorough reporting and clear writing.

DETAILS NEWSPAPERS ARE RELUCTANT TO PUBLISH

Reporters must learn to recognize what information is not newsworthy. News organizations rarely mention routine procedures, such as the fact that a city council met in a city. Reporters delete the obvious and the irrelevant: the fact that police officers rushed to the scene of a traffic accident or that an ambulance carried the injured to a hospital.

News organizations often must decide whether to use information about a crisis or threat. The so-called Unabomber, whose decades-long series of terror bombings in the United States baffled law enforcement authorities, sent a lengthy manifesto to the *New York Times* and the *Washington Post*. He promised that his killings would stop if the papers published his writings. The newspapers' executives decided to publish, knowing that the bomber might make good on his threat to continue bombing. Not all journalists agreed with that decision, but the publication of the manifesto led to the arrest of Theodore J. Kaczynski. One of his relatives, who noted similarities between the Unabomber manifesto and other anarchist writings by Kaczynski, alerted law enforcement agencies.

Offensive Details

Generally, editors omit material that is obscene, gruesome or in poor taste, usually on the grounds their newspapers or broadcasts reach children as well as adults. What would be the point, for example, of using grisly photographs or video, unless the material was highly newsworthy? Normally, news organizations avoid specifics about sexual assaults and omit most bloody details about accidents.

Different news organizations adopt different policies about what kinds of information they will use. Journalists must understand their employers' policies. When the national wire service Canadian Press runs stories that might offend readers, it generally prefaces the story with some kind of warning to the effect that some readers may find the content disturbing or distasteful.

Sensationalism

Most news organizations avoid sensationalism but not sensational stories. Historically, the word "sensationalism" has described an emphasis on or exaggeration of stories dealing with crime, sex and oddities. Some events, however, are inherently sensational—assassinations, wars and other disasters. News stories do not make such events sensational, but the news media report on them because of their importance.

Journalists evaluating a potentially scandalous or sensational story must weigh several conflicting considerations and may ask themselves:

- Is the story newsworthy?
- Does the public need and have a right to this information?
- How seriously will this story harm the people it mentions?
- How will readers react to the information?

Some journalists might balance these interests by avoiding anything tasteless or sensational, but that approach can make reporting the news more difficult. Now news organizations find themselves reporting stories about obscene words and images used on the Internet. Again, editors must decide what language to use to accurately report messages coming through cyberspace without offending readers and viewers.

There are no set right or wrong answers to these problems; each is a matter of individual judgment. The examples, however, reflect the journalistic dilemma. Journalists are reluctant to report graphic details likely to offend the public. Yet readers denied those details may consider them important.

Rumours

News organizations are reluctant to report rumours, especially harmful ones. Yet the failure to report some rumours may confuse, frighten or alienate the public. As a rumour spreads through a community, more people are likely to become interested in it and believe it. People who hear a rumour but see no coverage of it also are likely to believe journalists are deliberately suppressing the story.

Some rumours involve important issues, such as racial conflicts, and may cause widespread anxiety. Normally, responsible editors investigate the rumours and, if they find no evidence the rumours are true, conclude there is no story. Editors will consider a rumour's effects on the community and especially on innocent people. They may decide a story exposing a rumour as untrue will be more helpful to the people involved—for example, by clearing a person's reputation—than remaining silent on the issue.

Sexual Assault, Youth Crimes and Child Protection Laws

Canadian news organizations are generally prohibited by publication ban from naming the victims of sexual assault. Even if a ban is not imposed, it is unethical to name a sexual assault victim without that person's active consent. In such cases, it is also forbidden to disclose information that could lead members of the community to make an identification, such as an address, a place of business, or a personal relationship.

Canadian journalists are also prohibited by the Youth Criminal Justice Act from naming young persons (from the age of 12 up to the age of 18) involved in crimes, whether as the accused, a victim or a witness. The restriction extends to any information that would tend to identify the young people involved, including deceased victims. Child protection laws apply to all cases involving the custody or care of children (those under the age of 12). While the rules vary from province to province, it is generally a violation of child protection laws to provide any information that identifies or would tend to identify the child or the child's parents or guardians.

In some limited instances, publication bans have been lifted after the name of a person involved in a sex crime or other offence became a matter of wide public knowledge. Some bans have been broken by media from other countries reporting banned-in-Canada details in Internet news coverage. Legal experts and the courts continue to wrestle with the implications of instantaneous worldwide publication by international news organizations that are not subject to control by publication bans set down in Canada.

Other Details Reporters Avoid

Some editors hesitate to mention trade names, because they think publication of trade names is unnecessary and provides free advertising for the products. Detail is important to a story, and the use of specific names can add to that detail, but unless a trade name helps readers understand a story, reporters should use generic names. "Soft drink" is an acceptable generic term for Coke or Pepsi. Similarly, a journalist should report that someone used a "tissue" rather than a Kleenex or made a "photocopy" rather than a Xerox.

Manufacturers encourage journalists to use trade names properly. They place advertisements in magazines read by journalists to remind them to capitalize all trade names. Manufacturers want journalists to use their trade names to describe the products made by their companies, not similar products made by competitors.

If the public begins to use a trade name to describe every product within a certain category, the manufacturer may lose its exclusive right to use that trade name. Some trade names have become generic terms. Manufacturers lost the right to the words' exclusive use when the public repeatedly used the words to describe similar products. "Aspirin" is protected by trademark in Canada, for instance, but some other common examples include:

cellophane
cola
corn flakes
cube steak
dry ice
escalator
kerosene
lanolin
linoleum
mimeograph
nylon
raisin bran
shredded wheat
tollhouse cookies
trampoline
yo-yo
zipper

If carried to an extreme, the media's policy of avoiding trade names can have unfortunate results. When a small airplane crashed during a snowstorm in a mountainous area, a family aboard the plane survived for three days by drinking melted snow and eating boxes of Cracker Jack. In reporting the family's ordeal and rescue, some newspapers pointlessly substituted the term "candied popcorn" for Cracker Jack. Similarly, a copy editor became disgusted because his paper refused to allow him to use the trade name Jeep in a story about several hundred people who had formed a caravan of Jeeps for a weekend camping trip (called a "Jeep Jamboree"). He substituted the phrase "small truck-type four-wheel-drive vehicles of various manufacture." He did not expect his newspaper to print this circumlocution, but it did.

Common sense should dictate when a reporter should use a trade name. Include the trade name in the story if it seems pertinent.

THE IMPORTANCE OF ACCURACY

When Mark Twain began his career as a reporter, an editor told him never to state as fact anything he could not personally verify. Here is his account of a gala social event: "A woman giving the name of Mrs. James Jones, who is reported to be one of the society leaders of the city, is said to have given what purported to be a party yesterday to a number of alleged ladies. The hostess claims to be the wife of a reputed attorney."

Reporters should avoid taking the advice given to Twain as literally as he did, but accuracy is important. Errors affect the public's perception of the media and ultimately the media's credibility with the public.

Accuracy in Facts

The information appearing in newspapers and on television news is more accurate than most Canadians believe. Professionals who manage news organizations do their best to report the news as fairly and accurately as possible. Journalists, however, are not always able to convince the public of that fact. Editors generally require reporters to confirm every important fact with at least two sources. Editors insist on accuracy.

Some factual errors are embarrassing. One daily newspaper was forced to publish a correction after one of its reporters mistakenly quoted a dead sheriff. The reporter had called the sheriff's office to obtain information about an accident and assumed the man who answered the telephone was the sheriff. He was the sheriff, but a new one; his predecessor had died a few weeks earlier. In writing a story about the accident, the reporter—who failed to ask the sheriff his name—attributed all the information to his dead predecessor.

Carelessness and laziness cause most factual errors. After finishing a news story, reporters must recheck their notes to ensure the story is accurate. If reporters lack some information, they should consult their sources again. If the sources are unavailable or unable to provide the information, reporters may have to delete portions of the story or, in extreme cases, kill the story. Reporters should never guess or make any assumptions about the facts; they are too likely to make an error.

Conscientious news organizations check their stories' accuracy. They also check for factual and grammatical errors. Copy editors double-check reporters' math by calculating percentages and statistics in stories. Many errors occur because reporters fail to check their stories' internal consistency; numbers have to add up. For example:

> Of the 10 men and women who were interviewed, five favoured the proposal, three opposed it, and three said they had not reached a decision.

Reporters also must understand a topic before they begin to write about it. Too often, when asked about a fuzzy sentence or paragraph, beginners respond, "I really didn't understand that myself." If the reporter does not understand something he or she has written, neither will the audience. Reporters who do not understand a topic should go back to their source and ask for a better explanation or find a source who can explain it.

Accurate writing requires specifics instead of generalities. Getting specifics requires more effort, but in the end the story will be clearer, more accurate, and more interesting to readers and viewers. The trick is to double-check, even triple-check, all the information, to ask for specifics, to ask for spellings, to ask whether the information you have is correct. Reporters whose stories contain factual errors are admonished to be more careful. Some news organizations identify the reporter or editor who made a mistake. Others believe public humiliation does not solve the problem or help an individual improve. Those who repeatedly submit stories with errors may be suspended or fired.

Sometimes inaccuracies appear in news stories because reporters have engaged in misconduct, such as fabricating quotes, sources or facts, selectively reporting information, or committing plagiarism. News organizations almost always fire reporters caught engaging in these behaviours. A news organization's most important asset is its credibility, and managers believe they must protect that asset.

Accuracy in Names

News organizations are particularly careful in their handling of names. Spelling errors damage a paper's reputation and infuriate its readers, particularly when the misspelled names appear in wedding announcements, obituaries and other stories readers will save. Consequently, many newspapers require reporters to verify the spelling of every name that appears in local news stories. They can do so by consulting a second source, usually a telephone book or city directory.

Other errors arise because of a reporter's carelessness. A source may say his name is Karl, and a reporter may assume his name is spelled with a C rather than with a K. Dozens of other common names have two or more spellings, such as Ann (Anne), Cathy (Cathie, Kathy), Cindy (Cyndi), Fredrick (Fredric, Frederic, Frederick), Gail (Gayle), John (Jon), Linda (Lynda), Steven (Stephen), and Susie (Suzy).

Obstacles to Accuracy

Absolute accuracy may be impossible. Because of the need to meet strict deadlines, reporters work quickly and sometimes lack the time to perfect their stories. Reporters also are vulnerable to misinformation. They get much of their information from sources who may have impressive titles and may sound as if they know what they are talking about. But some sources may be ignorant of the facts, and others may lie. Stephen Colbert, the host of Comedy Central's "The Colbert Report," coined the term "truthiness" to describe statements a person wishes were true but are not supported by facts. The reporter's job is to separate the "truthy" statements from true ones—those supported by facts. Sometimes news organizations unknowingly report a source's misstatements. Other times, journalists report the statements of prominent people and public officials even when they doubt the comments' validity.

Historians can often be more accurate than journalists because they see more of a story before they begin to write. Journalists obtain stories piece by piece and cannot always predict the outcome or significance of the events they cover. Reporters sometimes revisit a story at a key moment to put events into perspective and give them meaning. Such stories allow readers to get a complete picture of events that originally came in piecemeal fashion.

Journalists might eliminate even more errors by giving the people named in news stories an opportunity to read and correct those stories before papers publish them. The idea surfaces most often among science writers and other journalists who deal with complex issues, but editors generally prohibit the practice. They fear that it will consume too much time and that sources may try to change the statements they disagree with, not just correct factual errors.

Researchers who have analyzed sources' corrections have found that sources believe that about half the stories they are shown contain an error, but many perceived errors are judgmental rather than factual. Sources may interpret some facts differently or want to include, emphasize or de-emphasize certain facts. Sources also may complain that a story misquotes them or a headline distorts a story. Only about one-third of the errors that sources point out are typographical or factual errors. Most factual errors involve misspelled names and inaccurate times, dates, numbers, addresses, locations and titles.

Most journalists agree a correction should appear in a paper or on the air as quickly as possible. Some believe it is healthy to go through the catharsis of admitting an error. By correcting errors, journalists show their willingness to respond to public concerns and strengthen their own credibility. Others argue that admitting all errors, including the most trivial, unnecessarily harms a news organization's credibility.

 Guest Columnist

"I Quit: A Feisty Editor of a Small-Town Paper Resigned after She Ran a Front-Page Story Management Considered Offensive."

By Kim Kierans

The tip came into the *Record* in Springhill, Nova Scotia, on Monday morning, June 27— deadline day. Yellow police tape was strung around the taxi stand on Main Street. Editor Susan Belliveau grabbed a camera, her notepad and headed off. Little did she know this story would leave her jobless and homeless.

When she arrived at the scene a crowd had gathered. Word in the town (pop. 4,100) was out. A body had been found in the upstairs apartment. "Despite the 31-degree heat, folks filled the streets, driving back and forth or simply parking and watching," Belliveau wrote. "Everyone's eyes were glued to the building where the body was, waiting for it to be brought out."

Belliveau started talking to people, gathering information and snapping photos. She spoke to people at the cab company, friends of the victim, and police. Belliveau knew this was the most disturbing story she had ever covered in her 17 years at the *Record*.

The body had been in the apartment for days. People working in the cab company spoke of a funny smell wafting down from the apartment.

Maggots had fallen from the ceiling into the taxi stand. The maggots led a worker at the taxi stand upstairs where he found the badly decomposed body of Kenneth Gilroy, who suffered from severe diabetes.

The story, Belliveau said, was "a calm outline of facts." She wanted people to understand that Gilroy was first and foremost a person—a quiet guy, a diabetic, a carpenter who liked camping and fishing. He had told his family he was going away, so nobody missed him. Belliveau also wanted to put rumours to rest. Word was out that it might be a drug hit. (Gilroy died of natural causes.)

As a seasoned reporter, Belliveau knew that the colour photo of police in white suits and wearing masks carrying out the grey body bag would upset some readers. She knew the graphic details of the news story mentioning maggots would also be a problem.

Belliveau emailed her photo to her publisher, Leith Orr of Advocate Media in Pictou. "He said, 'Go ahead, front page,'" Belliveau recalled for journalism students at the University of King's College.

The photo and story of the Gilroy death was the front page of the tabloid (circulation 2,300). After all, it was the talk of the town. The advertising manager at the *Record*, Kevin Cummings, didn't see the story before it went to press. When he did, he was "totally amazed at the graphic nature" of the story. The reference to maggots, he said, went too far.

Cummings is a third generation Springhiller and has spent 22 years in advertising with the *Record*. (Belliveau is from nearby Amherst).

"This was the week of graduation. People were expecting nice photos on page one. The Gilroy story should have been on page three. The photo should have been in black and white to lose impact and the story should have taken out the references to maggots. It had no news value," said Cummings.

Because she knew people would be upset, Belliveau also wrote an editorial to accompany the story and photo to help readers understand what reporters do.

"Like it or not, death is news. Evidence of that is the number of spectators at the death scene," she wrote. "But if you ask any journalist, particularly a small-town reporter, most will say that providing this type of coverage is the worst part of the job, partly because it's so macabre, but mostly because it seems too insensitive and cruel to race around taking photos of such a sad event."

As anticipated, the front page story and photo provoked reaction. Three people wrote letters to the editor criticizing the coverage as too descriptive and sensational. Those were the only three letters the paper received.

Cummings said the phone at the paper "rang off the wall" all week long with people complaining about the photo and story. He said people stopped him on the street to complain and advertising clients said they were "appalled" at the coverage. The newspaper didn't keep a record of the calls. No one cancelled subscriptions because of the story.

Belliveau flew off to Alberta to receive an award for editorial excellence from the International Society of Newspaper Editors. She returned home to find the paper had published a front-page apology on July 13 for "the graphic story pertaining to the death of Mr. Gilroy." The manager of the *Record*, Kevin Cummings, signed it. Belliveau was stunned.

After receiving an angry phone call from the victim's father, Orr and Cummings had reviewed the photo and story and decided to print an apology without consulting Belliveau.

"Knowing Susan, she would have had 15 reasons why we should not publish an apology. I felt a need to act to maintain the integrity of the newspaper," said Cummings.

"I was caught up and never really thought about it, the consequences to the paper. It's a small community and to go into great details was a little bit overboard," Orr said. "There was nothing not true in the article, but why so much detail? Who benefits from it?"

"That apology not only wreaked havoc on my credibility and made me look mean. It made my paper look gutless and that's the worst insult you can say about a newspaper," Belliveau said.

"I don't regret the apology at all," Cummings said. "If Susan feels her integrity as editor was jeopardized with the apology, I say it happened when she wrote the article."

Belliveau felt betrayed. She went back to Orr and asked for editorial control; she offered to go part-time and work from home, a company apartment above the newspaper; she asked for a public apology to her and the newspaper.

"I hoped my publisher would do the right thing to restore my credibility and the paper's credibility. I won't work for a newspaper unwilling to print the news," she said. "If it happened once, it could happen again."

After three weeks of waiting, Belliveau resigned. That move left her jobless and without a home. As soon as she resigned she and her 13-year-old daughter had to leave the company apartment.

In her farewell letter of Aug. 10, Belliveau wrote it was painful to cover such a horrible story, but she made no apologies. "I felt that my duty was to provide the news as it was presented to me by those I interviewed and the things I observed. I reported it in the same manner as I have reported every other news story I've written for this newspaper—with integrity and accuracy." To this day Belliveau maintains she did the right thing.

"The publisher failed me as a journalist, my paper, and my readers who depend on the news," she said. "The publisher should provide journalists with the tools they need to do their job properly. He needs to step back and stay out of editorial decisions unless he has a strong editorial background."

Now that it's all over, Orr says he would have handled this differently. "I probably would not be so quick to do an apology and take more time, wait to get input from the editor."

Orr has nothing but praise for Belliveau. "She's a great reporter and I had hoped she would have reconsidered and stayed."

The new editor, Christopher Gooding, is a Springhiller. He has been a reporter with the *Record* for two years. He said that it's business as usual at the paper. "I'm not into titillation; I'm into all information."

Since Belliveau stepped down, Cummings said, he is "taking greater interest in the editorial content of the newspaper." That means he scans headlines, photos and leads of stories before the paper goes to press. If he's not comfortable with something, he said, he'd approach Gooding.

There are now weekly staff meetings. The six people, two reporters, a designer, the receptionist and sales staff, meet to go over the news agenda for the week. Cummings sees no conflict.

"I feel comfortable with this," Cummings said. "I want to make sure the readers get the best product we can produce. We have a good understanding, and news and advertising can exchange ideas and help each other." Cummings admits that's something Belliveau would not have accepted.

Belliveau moved with her daughter to a nearby rural community in November. Her federal unemployment insurance benefits claim was approved without a penalty for resigning. So while some of the financial pressures are off, she's still dealing with the emotional upheaval.

After 17 years with the paper, Belliveau is suffering from a loss of identity. "I'm finding it difficult to cope with how things could go so desperately wrong in such a short period of time. It's weird to say, but it has some of the very same elements of heartbreak. I feel so incredibly betrayed.

"Perhaps the worst part is the loss of identity. I used to be 'the *Record* lady.' I'm not that anymore and I am left to wonder who I am now." While Belliveau wrestles with that, the *Record* will wrestle with its direction. The paper has lost a feisty and courageous editor. I wish the *Record* and Gooding well.

Kim Kierans is the director of the School of Journalism at University of King's College in Halifax. This article originally appeared in *Media* (January 1, 2006), the publication of the Canadian Association of Journalists.

SUGGESTED READINGS AND USEFUL WEBSITES

Auger, Michel. 2002. *The Biker Who Shot Me: Recollections of a Crime Reporter*. Toronto: McClelland and Stewart.

Beers, David. 2006. "The public sphere and online, independent journalism." *The Canadian Journal of Education* 29 (1): 109–30.

Berton, Pierre. 1982. *Why We Act Like Canadians: A Personal Exploration of Our National Character*. Toronto: McClelland and Stewart.

Bolan, Kim. 2005. *Loss of Faith: How the Air India Bombers Got Away with Murder*. Toronto: McClelland and Stewart.

Cameron, Stevie. 2007. *The Pickton File*. Toronto: Alfred A. Knopf Canada.

———. 1989. *Ottawa Inside Out: Power, Prestige and Scandal in the Nation's Capital*. Toronto: Key Porter Books.

Chodos, Robert, Rae Murphy, and Eric Hamovitch. 1997. *Lost in Cyberspace: Canada and the Information Revolution*. Toronto: James Lorimer.

Gladney, George Albert, Ivor Shapiro, and Joseph Castaldo. 2007. "Online editors rate Web news quality criteria." *Newspaper Research Journal* 28 (1): 55–67.

Hackett, Robert A. 2000. *The Missing News: Filters and Blind Spots in Canada's Media*. Ottawa: Centre for Policy Alternatives.

Journalistic Standards and Practices. 2004. Toronto: Canadian Broadcasting Corporation.

Kostash, Myrna. 2000. *The Next Canada: In Search of Our Future Nation*. Toronto: McClelland and Stewart.

Malarek, Victor. 1985. *Hey Malarek: The True Story of a Street Kid Who Made It*. Halifax: Goodread Biographies.

Canadian Journalism Foundation: www.j-source.ca

The Credibility Gap: Canadians and Their News Media: Five Years Later. Canadian Media Research Consortium, May 2008: http://www.cmrcccrm.ca/en/projects/documents/TheCredibilityGapMay.pdf

The Tyee: www.thetyee.ca

CHAPTER 4

News Judgment

Every day, journalists make difficult decisions involving matters of importance, interest, taste, ethics and myriad other considerations. The following questions ask you to make those types of decisions. After deciding which stories to use and emphasize, compare your decisions with those of your classmates.

1. As editor of your local daily newspaper, you have space for one more photograph on page 1. Circle the photograph in each of the following pairs that you would select.

    A. A photograph showing the Governor General visiting an elementary school in your city.

    B. A photograph of university students protesting an increase in tuition and fees at a university in your city. The increase is the fourth in five years.

    A. A photograph showing two students from one of your city's secondary schools participating in the semi-final round of a national spelling bee.

    B. A photograph of three Grade 12 students being led away in handcuffs after being charged with vandalizing school property over the weekend. The three students caused nearly $80,000 in damage to a computer room and the main office. They sprayed foam from fire extinguishers onto computers and into file cabinets and smashed computer monitors and other equipment.

    A. A photograph of a young child in Afghanistan handing a bunch of flowers to a Canadian soldier.

    B. A photograph of the bodies of an Afghan father and his four children killed in a suicide bombing near a Canadian base in Afghanistan.

2. Rank the following nine stories by their newsworthiness, starting with 1 for the most newsworthy:

    A. _____ Your province's Ministry of Education released a report today saying secondary students in your city have reached an all-time high in scoring on their university placement exams.

    B. _____ The province approved a plan to build a six-lane bypass around your city that will cost $284 million and destroy thousands of acres of prime agricultural and developable land.

    C. _____ A city man was charged in an arson that destroyed an apartment building and killed eight people, including five children.

    D. _____ CSIS investigators visited the public libraries in your city to check on the reading records of several local residents who CSIS believes may be linked to terrorism.

    E. _____ Three Israelis and 10 Palestinians were killed in a suicide bombing at a bus stop in a suburb of Tel Aviv.

    F. _____ The parents of quintuplets in your city saw their five children off to school for the first time, as the three boys and two girls were picked up by a bus that took them to kindergarten.

G. _____ More than 100 people were killed and another 800 injured when a runaway passenger train collided with a freight train in Tanzania.

H. _____ Tennis star Serena Williams today announced that she is retiring from tennis and plans to become a sports announcer.

I. _____ City officials agreed at their Tuesday night council meeting to spend $128 million to build a new trash incinerator that would burn trash from the city as well as from six surrounding counties.

3. Rank the following nine stories by their newsworthiness, starting with 1 for the most newsworthy:

A. _____The driver of a compact car escaped injury early today when her car was struck by a freight train at a railroad crossing.

B. _____ A chest containing manuscripts of music written by Johann Sebastian Bach was discovered today in Russia, more than half a century after it was lost during the Second World War.

C. _____ Police and prison officials in your city were conducting a mock prison escape when three inmates walked out of the prison and disappeared.

D. _____ A new senior citizens' centre opened on the east side of the city offering nearby residents a place to get a hot meal at lunch time, participate in games and educational programs, and pass time with friends.

E. _____ A 14-year-old city girl who had been missing for six months was found safe in Mexico with a man she met on the Internet who turned out to be a convicted murderer.

F. _____An Alberta woman was convicted in the deaths of her four children who were drowned in the family's bathtub. She was found guilty of four counts of second-degree murder.

G. _____ Your provincial Ministry of Labour and Industry announced today that the unemployment rate rose to 7.5 per cent despite a rally that saw significant increases in the stock market.

H. _____ An RCMP officer was arrested and charged with aggravated assault and using undue force after he Tasered a man who was attending a concert. The officer was patrolling the stadium parking lot and mistook the man for a scalper. After an argument with the man, the officer allegedly threw him to the ground before Tasering him.

I. _____ A group of teenagers from a nondenominational church youth organization volunteered to help two elderly sisters maintain their home so that they would not be fined by the city for having a blighted property. The youths mowed grass, trimmed hedges and painted the sisters' house.

4. Patricia Richards, a 52-year-old business woman in your city, today announced that she is running for mayor. You know and can prove all the following facts but have never reported them because she was a private citizen. Mark the facts you would report today.

A. _____ Richards has been divorced three times.

B. _____ At the age of 17, Richards and two friends were charged with stealing a car. The charges were dropped because the car was recovered undamaged and the car's owner, a neighbour, declined to prosecute.

C. _____ Richards has diabetes.

D. _____ Richards has had two abortions.

E. _____ Richards is a recovered alcoholic; she has not had a drink in 20 years.

F. _____ Before going into business for herself, she was fired from two other jobs because of her drinking.

G. _____ Her campaign literature says she attended McGill University, yet she never graduated.

H. _____ She established, owns and manages the city's largest chain of furniture stores.

I. _____ Various tax and other public records reveal that her chain of furniture stores is valued at $20 million and last year earned a profit of $2.3 million.

J. _____ Each year Richards donates more than $1 million to local charities that help troubled young women but always avoids publicity, insisting that the charities never mention her donations.

5. Your provincial MLA Constance Wei was involved in a traffic accident that resulted in the death of another driver and his passenger. Which of the following details would you use and which would you discard?

A. _____ Wei is married and has two children.

B. _____ As an attorney, Wei successfully defended two people who had been accused of vehicular manslaughter.

C. _____ Wei was speeding and ran a red light.

D. _____ A woman, who didn't want to be identified, called your newsroom and said the minivan she and her children were riding in was almost struck at an intersection one time by a car driven by Wei.

E. _____ Friends of Wei said she often joked about having a "lead foot."

F. _____ Police said Wei refused to co-operate with them when they arrived at the scene of the accident.

G. _____ Wei has had five tickets in the past four years for speeding and reckless driving.

H. _____ Wei was first elected to office nine years ago.

I. _____ Wei was driving on an expired driver's licence.

J. _____ Wei once sponsored a bill to eliminate the point system used to penalize drivers stopped for motor vehicle violations. Drivers would lose their licences after accumulating a certain number of points.

5 | Basic News Leads

If you have anything to tell me of importance, for God's sake begin at the end.
— Sara Jeannette Duncan, Canadian journalist and author, 1904

The first paragraph or two in a news story is called the "lead." The lead (some journalists spell it "lede") is the most important part of a story—and the most difficult part to write. Like the opening paragraphs of a short story or novel, the lead of a news story is the part that attracts readers and, if it is well written, arouses their interest. It should tell readers the central point of the story, not hide the subject with unnecessary or misleading words and phrases.

THE SUMMARY NEWS LEAD

Every news story must answer six questions: who? how? where? why? when? and what? The lead, however, is not the place to answer all of them. The lead should answer only the one or two questions that are most interesting, newsworthy and unusual. For example, few readers in large cities know the ordinary citizens involved in news stories, so the names of those people do not have to appear in leads. The exact time and place at which a story occurred may also be unimportant.

To determine which questions are most important for a story, consider the following points:

1. What is the most important information? What is the story's central point?
2. What was said or done about the topic? What happened or what action was taken?
3. What are the most recent developments? What happened today or yesterday?
4. Which facts are most likely to affect or interest readers?
5. Which facts are most unusual?

Each of the following leads emphasizes the answer to only one of the six basic questions— the question that seems most important for that particular story:

Who: ASHEVILLE, N.C.—Evangelist Billy Graham was in fair condition Saturday and resting comfortably in a hospital near his home after he was admitted for evaluation and treatment of an intestinal bleed, hospital officials said.

How: A nearby resident pulled an Antrim Township milk truck driver from his crumpled tanker Tuesday morning after a Norfolk Southern train crashed into the rig at the Milnor Road railroad crossing.

Where: TEHRAN, Iran—Iran has resumed small-scale enrichment of uranium, a senior Iranian nuclear negotiator said today, showing the country is determined to proceed with atomic development despite international moves to restrict it.

Why: Consumers, energized by unusually warm weather and the tame heating bills that went with it, hit the malls with gusto last month, sending retail sales soaring by 2.2 per cent—the biggest jump in six years.

When: Before Friday, Kishan Garib, 12, had never been away from his family.

What: Five school buildings would close and more than 5,300 students would be shifted to different schools this fall under a plan presented to the city's school board last night.

When writers try to answers all these questions in one paragraph, they create complicated and confusing leads. Here's an example of an overloaded lead and a possible revision:

Charles E. Vickers, 47, of 1521 Yarmouth Drive, died, and John Aston Walters, 39, of 1867 Colonial Ave., was severely injured Sunday afternoon when the bicycles they were riding were struck near the intersection of Weston and Falmouth roads by a car driven by a man police said had a blood alcohol count of nearly .23 per cent and was driving without a licence because it had been revoked last year after his fourth conviction for driving under the influence of alcohol.

REVISED: One man is dead and another severely injured after the bicycles they were riding were struck by a drunken driver Sunday afternoon near the intersection of Weston and Falmouth roads.

Because people and what they do are central to many news stories, some journalists recognize two variations on the summary news lead: the immediate-identification lead and the delayed-identification lead. Reporters use the immediate-identification lead when the identities of the major subjects in the story are important or are well known:

Martha Stewart walks out of federal prison in Alderson, W.Va., today to launch an audacious comeback campaign that might be tougher than anything she faced during her five months behind penitentiary walls. (*Washington Post*)

In many stories, the names of the main subjects are not as important as what those people did or what happened to them. For those stories, reporters use leads that withhold complete identification of the people involved until the second or third paragraph. The following leads are examples of delayed-identification leads:

An Ottawa man held his girlfriend's baby at knife point for more than two hours Saturday night before police officers captured him after shooting him with a stun gun.

An 82-year-old Halifax woman is slowly recovering from a gunshot wound to the head, and RCMP say they may be on the verge of charging a suspect with attempted murder.

Leads that hold back details so the reporter can get to the central point of the article more quickly are called "blind leads." Beginners should not misinterpret the terminology. A blind lead does not hide the central point of the story, only information that the reader does not need immediately. Blind leads let the reporter tell readers what the story is about to pique their interest and get them into the story.

A "catchall graf" usually follows the blind lead to identify sources and answer questions created by the lead. Missing details can be placed in subsequent paragraphs. Here's an example of a blind lead:

It was a local company that lost its appeal in court, but it's the provincial ministry charged with overseeing construction matters that's feeling the pain.

In its second paragraph, the article identified the company and what the case involved. In the third paragraph, the article identified the ministry involved and what it had done wrong.

Before reporters can write effective leads, however, they must learn to recognize what is news. After deciding which facts are most newsworthy, a reporter must summarize those facts in sharp, clear sentences, giving a simple, straightforward account of what happened. Examine these leads, which provide clear, concise summaries of important moments in the nation's history:

OKA, Que.—A provincial police officer was shot and killed today as police exchanged hundreds of gunshots with Mohawk Indians at a road barricade. (*The Canadian Press*, John Davidson, 1990)

OTTAWA—Pierre Elliott Trudeau put us on the map. His acid candour, his intellectual acrobatics, his nose-thumbing at the staid traditions of this country's highest political office qualified him as our first existential political hero: The man with the red rose in his buttonhole, who made us so proud that we elected him our prime minister for all but nine months of 16 turbulent years. (*National Post*, Peter C. Newman, 2000)

TORONTO—In spite of the obvious challenges ahead, there are still more reasons for Prime Minister Stephen Harper to celebrate the changing of the guard at the White House than to mourn it. (*Toronto Star*, Chantal Hébert, 2008)

Leads that fail to emphasize the news—the most interesting and important details—are sometimes described as burying the news. Here's an example of a lead that fails to give readers the news:

Wentworth is required to give inmates the same level of medical treatment the general public receives, Corrections Director Maria Sanchez said.

The news in the story, however, was not the level of medical care provided to jail inmates. The news was the financial problems the municipality was facing because of the requirement that it provide medical care to inmates. Here's a rewritten lead that makes the significance of the story clearer:

Wentworth's costs for medical care for jail inmates doubled—from $50,000 to $100,000—last year because of a new provincial regulation.

Friday morning, municipal and provincial officials gathered to find a way to pay the bill.

SENTENCE STRUCTURE IN LEADS

Most leads are a single sentence, and that sentence must follow all the normal rules for punctuation, grammar, word usage, and verb tense. If an event occurred in the past, the lead must use the past tense, not the present. Leads must be complete sentences and should include all the necessary articles—the words "a," "an" and "the."

Some problems with sentence structure arise because beginners confuse a story's lead with its headline. The lead is the first paragraph of a news story. The headline is a brief summary that appears in larger type above the story. To save space, editors use only a few key words in each headline. However, that style of writing is not appropriate for leads:

Headline: Harper denies private accounts in serious trouble

Lead: OTTAWA—Prime Minister Stephen Harper dismissed the notion Thursday that his campaign to create tax-free private accounts was in serious trouble, asserting he was still "at the early stages of the process."

Reporters usually write leads that use normal word order: subject–verb–object. Most leads begin with the subject, which is closely followed by an active verb and then by the object of the verb. Reporters deviate from that style only in the rare case that a different sentence structure better tells the news. Leads that begin with long qualifying clauses and phrases lack the clarity of simpler, more direct sentences. Long introductory clauses also clutter leads, burying the news amid a jumble of less significant details. Writing coaches call this "backing in" to the lead.

> A new pill, approved by Health Canada after 10 years of testing and costing about $100 per pill, could relieve the pain of migraine headaches, medical researchers said today.
> REVISED: A new $100 pill could relieve the pain of migraine headaches, medical researchers said today. The pill has been approved by Health Canada after a decade of testing.

GUIDELINES FOR WRITING EFFECTIVE LEADS

Be Concise

The concise style of writing found in newspapers makes it easy for the public to read and understand leads but difficult for reporters to write them.

Two- or three-sentence leads often become wordy, repetitious and choppy, particularly when all the sentences are very short. Like most multi-sentence leads, the following example can be made more concise by combining the main elements into a single sentence:

> Two women robbed a shopper in a local supermarket Tuesday. One woman distracted the shopper, and the second woman grabbed her purse, which contained about $50.
> REVISED: Two women stole a purse containing $50 from a shopper in a local supermarket Tuesday.

The original lead was redundant. It reported two women robbed a shopper, and then it described the robbery.

Reporters use two-sentence leads only when the need to do so is compelling. Often, the second sentence emphasizes an interesting or unusual fact of secondary importance. Other times, the second sentence is necessary because it is impossible to summarize all the necessary information about a complex topic in a single sentence. The following lead uses a second sentence to illustrate and explain the first:

> A growing number of Canadian soldiers whose body armour helped them survive bomb and rocket attacks are suffering brain damage as a result of the blasts. It's a type of injury some military doctors say has become the signature wound of the conflict in Afghanistan.

Reporters need to be mindful of the length of their leads, as well as the information they contain. Readability surveys show many readers find a 25-word lead "difficult" to read and a 29-word lead "very difficult." A better average would be 18 to 20 words. Reporters should examine their leads critically to determine whether they are wordy or repetitious or contain facts that could be shifted to later paragraphs.

Reporters shorten leads by eliminating unnecessary background information—dates, names, locations—or the description of routine procedures. Leads should not contain too many names, particularly names readers are unlikely to recognize or the names of people who played minor or routine roles in a story. If a lead includes someone's name, it also may have to identify that person, and the identification will require even more words. Descriptive phrases can substitute for names. Similarly, a story's precise time and location could be reported in a later paragraph. A lead should report a story's highlights, not its minor details, as concisely as possible:

A former Saskatoon woman, who has eluded RCMP since she allegedly hijacked a flight from Canada to Cuba using a plastic flare gun in 1983, was arrested Wednesday as she stood alone on a street corner in Montreal, according to the RCMP.
REVISED: The RCMP on Wednesday arrested a former Saskatoon woman who has eluded authorities since 1983, when she was accused of hijacking an airplane.

Although leads can be too long, they cannot be too short. An effective lead may contain only four, five or six words: "The King is dead" or "Americans landed on the moon" or "There's new hope for couch potatoes."

Be Specific

Good leads contain interesting details and are so specific that readers can visualize the events they describe. As you read the following lead, you should be able to imagine the dramatic scene it describes:

At 59, she'd never touched a gun—until someone held one to her head.

The following lead is less interesting because it is abstract and contains vague generalities. Reporters can easily transform such leads into more interesting ones by adding more specific details:

The city council passed an ordinance that will affect all parents and teenagers living within city limits.
REVISED: The city council ignored the objections of the mayor and numerous parents and voted 6–1 Monday to enact a dusk-to-dawn curfew to keep youngsters off city streets.

Some leads use worn-out clichés—a lazy way of summarizing a story. Avoid saying that "a step has been taken" or that someone has moved "one step closer" to a goal. Present specific details:

University officials moved one step closer to increasing tuition and fees for the upcoming school year, leaving students up in the air.
REVISED: University officials voted Tuesday to increase tuition and fees 10 per cent next year to offset cuts in government funding.

Avoid "iffy" leads that say one thing may happen if another happens. In addition to being too vague, "iffy" leads are too abstract, tentative and qualified. Report the story's more immediate and concrete details.

Use Strong, Active Verbs

A single word—a descriptive verb—can transform a routine lead into a dramatic one. As you read the following lead, for example, you may be able to picture what happened:

VICTORIA—After rushing her seven-year-old daughter to safety, Ann Murray raced back to the docks and pounded on her friends' boats while flames and explosions tore through a marina early Friday morning.

Strong, active verbs such as "rushing," "raced," "pounded" and "tore" paint a vivid picture of the scene in readers' minds. Strong verbs capture the drama and emotion of a news event and help readers understand the impact of the story.
The following lead uses several colourful verbs to describe the capture of a wayward Angus steer that escaped his handlers:

The suspect tore through a homeowner's fence, ripped the wires from a satellite dish with his teeth, slammed head-on into a travel trailer, then bolted down the street on his way to a weird encounter with a canoe. (*Orlando [Fla.] Sentinel*)

Avoid passive-voice constructions, which combine the past participle of a verb with some form of the verb "to be"—such as "is," "are," "was" and "were." Strong, active-voice verbs are more colourful, interesting and dramatic:

> One person *was killed* and four others *were injured* Sunday morning when their car, which *was travelling* west on the Trans-Canada Highway, *hit* a concrete bridge pillar and *was engulfed* in flames.
> REVISED: A car *travelling* west on the Trans-Canada Highway *swerved* across two eastbound lanes, *slammed* into a concrete bridge pillar and *burst* into flames, *killing* one person and *injuring* four others Sunday morning.

Writers can easily convert passive voice to the active voice. Simply rearrange the words, so the sentence begins by reporting (1) who...(2) did what...(3) to whom. Instead of reporting: "Rocks and bottles were thrown at firefighters," report: "Rioters threw rocks and bottles at firefighters."

Emphasize the Magnitude of the Story

If a story is important, reporters emphasize its magnitude in the lead. Most good leads emphasize the impact stories have on people. When describing natural disasters or man-made catastrophes, such as airplane crashes, earthquakes or major fires, reporters emphasize the number of people killed, injured and left homeless. They also emphasize the dollar cost of the damage to buildings or other objects. When describing a storm, reporters may emphasize the amount of rain or snow that fell. The following lead does not deal with a disaster or catastrophe, but it shows how magnitude can be emphasized in a story:

> Second-hand cigarette smoke will cause an estimated 4,700 deaths and about 15,000 nonfatal heart attacks in Canadian non-smokers this year, a study says. That's as much as 50 per cent higher than previous estimates.

Stress the Unusual

Leads also emphasize the unusual. By definition, news involves deviations from the norm. Consider this lead from a story about two men who were arrested for stealing a man's clothes:

> OELWEIN, Iowa—Two men have been arrested for stealing a man's clothes and leaving him to wander around naked, officials said. (*Associated Press*)

A lead about a board of education meeting or other governmental agency should not report "the board met at 8 p.m. at a local school and began its meeting with a prayer." Those facts are routine and not newsworthy. Most school boards meet every couple of weeks, usually at the same time and place, and some begin their meetings with a prayer. Leads should emphasize the unique—the action that follows those routine formalities.

Bank robberies are so common in big cities that newspapers normally devote only a few paragraphs to them. Yet a robbery at the Burlington National Bank in Columbus, Ohio, became a front-page story, published by newspapers throughout the United States. A story transmitted by the Associated Press explained:

> A 61-year-old man says he robbed a bank with a toy gun—he even told the FBI ahead of time when and where—because he wants to spend his golden years in federal prison.

After his arrest, the bank robber insisted he did not want a lawyer. Instead, he wanted to immediately "plead guilty to anything." The man explained he recently was divorced, had no family ties, and was disabled with arthritis. He had spent time in at least three federal prisons and wanted to return to one of them. "I knew what I was doing," he insisted. "I wanted to get arrested, and I proceeded about it the best way I knew how."

Reporters must learn to recognize and emphasize a story's unusual details:

> LONDON—A Dutch driver who watched movies and ate dinner while 58 Chinese immigrants slowly suffocated in the back of his sweltering tomato truck was convicted Thursday of manslaughter and sentenced to 14 years in prison. (*Associated Press*)

Localize and Update

Reporters localize and update their leads whenever possible by emphasizing their communities' involvement in stories. Readers are most interested in stories affecting their own lives and the lives of people they know.

Reporters also try to localize stories from other parts of the world. When a bomb exploded in an Air India plane in 1985, newspapers across Canada not only ran the story of the bombing but localized the story on the basis of where the passengers had lived. Similarly, when Statistics Canada reports on the number of violent crimes committed in Canada, reporters stress the statistics for their communities:

> Statistics Canada reported Tuesday that the number of violent crimes in Canada rose 8.3 per cent during the last year.
>
> LOCALIZED: The number of violent crimes committed in the city last year rose 5.4 per cent, compared to a national average of 8.3 per cent, Statistics Canada reported Tuesday.

Reporters update a lead by stressing the latest developments in the story. If a breaking story appears in an early edition of a newspaper, a reporter will gather new information and rewrite the story for later editions. The same thing happens with a television news broadcast. Instead of saying a fire destroyed a store the previous day, reporters may stress that authorities have since learned the fire's cause, identified the victims, arrested an arsonist, or estimated the monetary loss. Stories are updated to offer the public something new—facts not already reported by other newspapers or by local radio or television stations. Major stories about such topics as economic trends, natural disasters, wars, and political upheavals often remain in the news for months and must be updated regularly.

Not every lead can be updated or localized. If a story has no new or local angles, report it in a simple, straightforward manner. Do not distort the story in any way or fabricate any new or local angles.

Be Objective and Attribute Opinions

The lead of a news story, like the rest of the story, must be objective (as opposed to subjective). Reporters are expected to gather facts and convey them to their readers—not to comment, interpret or advocate. Reporters may anger or offend readers when they insert their opinions in stories.

Calling the people involved in news stories "alert," "heroic" or "quick-thinking" or describing facts as "interesting" or "startling" is never justified. These comments, when they are accurate, usually state the obvious. Leads that include opinion or interpretation must be rewritten to provide more factual accounts of the news:

> Speaking to the Downtown Rotary Club last night, Emil Plambeck, superintendent of the City Park Commission, discussed a topic of concern to all of us—the city's park system.
>
> REVISED: Emil Plambeck, superintendent of the City Park Commission, wants developers to set aside five per cent of the land in new subdivisions for parks.

The original lead is weak because it refers to "a topic of concern to all of us." The reporter does not identify "us" and is wrong to assert that any topic concerns everyone.

Here are other examples of leads that state an opinion or conclusion:

Adult entertainment establishments have fallen victim to another attempt at censorship.

Recycling does not pay, at least not economically. However, the environmental benefits make the city's new recycling program worthwhile at any cost.

To demonstrate that both leads are statements of opinion, ask your friends and classmates about them:

- Do all your friends and classmates agree that the regulation of adult entertainment establishments is "censorship"?

- Do all your friends and classmates agree that recycling programs are "worthwhile at any cost"?

Although reporters cannot express their own opinions in stories, they often include the opinions of people involved in the news. A lead containing a statement of opinion must be attributed so readers clearly understand the opinion is not the reporter's.

A lead containing an obvious fact or a fact the reporter has witnessed or verified by other means generally does not require attribution. One editor, instructing reporters to "make the lead of a story as brief and clear as possible," noted: "One thing that obstructs that aim is the inclusion of an unnecessary source of attribution....If the lead is controversial, an attribution is imperative. But if the lead is innocuous, forget it." Thus, if a lead states undisputed facts, the attribution can be placed in a later paragraph:

Cars and motorcycles crash into deer more than 4,000 times a day, and it's taking an increasingly deadly toll—on people.

Strive for Simplicity

Every lead should be clear, simple, and to the point. Here is an example:

Like hundreds of mobile homes throughout the province, the home where Linda McDonald and her family died Monday was built before provincial regulators required fire-retardant walls, accessible windows, and smoke detectors.

Here is an example of a lead that suffers from far too much detail:

Officials of the city and the school district are breathing sighs of relief following a Housing Authority decision to pull out of a plan to build an apartment complex for moderate-income people on 11 acres of land between Southeast Oatfield and Webster roads.

The lead could be rewritten any number of ways. The reporter must decide what the important point is. Here are two versions of a simple blind lead for the same story:

Several city and school district officials applauded the county's decision to scrap plans for a subsidized housing complex.

A new subsidized housing complex will not be built, and city and school district officials are relieved.

AVOIDING SOME COMMON ERRORS

Begin with the News

Avoid beginning a lead with the attribution. Names and titles are dull and seldom important. Moreover, if every lead begins with the attribution, all leads will sound too much alike. Place attribution at the beginning of a lead only when it is unusual or significant or deserves that emphasis:

At a press conference in Ottawa today, Ontario Minister of Labour Peter Fonseca announced that last month the cost of living rose 2.83 per cent, a record high.

REVISED: The cost of living rose 2.83 per cent last month, a record high, the Ontario minister of labour said Friday.

Originally, the lead devoted more space to the attribution than to the news. As revised, it emphasizes the news—the information the Ontario Ministry of Labour released. The attribution has been condensed and can be reported more fully in a later paragraph.

Emphasize the News

Chronological order rarely works in a news story. By definition, news is what just happened. The first events in a sequence rarely are the most newsworthy. Decide which facts are most interesting and important, and then write a lead that emphasizes these facts regardless of whether they occurred first, last, or in the middle of a sequence of events:

The O.J. Simpson trial started with the selection of jurors, which was a long and arduous process. After opening arguments by the prosecution and defence, the prosecutors began calling their witnesses and started building their case against the former football star. After months of legal manoeuvring and bickering, prosecutors rested their case.

Now O.J. Simpson's attorneys plan to call their first witness Monday morning. The next few weeks promise a lineup of Simpson's friends, family and golf chums testifying about his demeanour before and after the murder.

REVISED: Now O.J. Simpson has the ball.

With the prosecution case finished after five months of testimony, Simpson's lawyers are about to begin presenting his side of the story.

City council began its meeting by approving the minutes from its last meeting and then approved paying omnibus budget bills and examined a list of proposed ordinances.

REVISED: City council voted 6–1 Monday night to increase the Parks Department budget by 15 per cent to hire more groundskeepers and buy new equipment.

Look for a story's action or consequences. That's what should be emphasized in a lead. The following lead, as revised, stresses the consequences of the accident:

A 15-year-old boy learning to drive his family's new car struck a gasoline pump in a service station on Hall Road late Tuesday afternoon.

REVISED: A 15-year-old boy learning to drive created a fireball Tuesday. The family car he was driving struck a gasoline pump at a Hall Road service station, blocking traffic for three hours while firefighters extinguished the blaze.

Avoid "Agenda" Leads

An opening paragraph that places too much emphasis on the time and place at which a story occurred is called an "agenda" lead. Although agenda leads are used to announce an upcoming event—public relations news releases use them to promote an organization's product or event—they should never be used in a news story about something that occurred the previous day. A lead should focus on the news, as the following lead, after revision, does:

James Matthews, president of International Biotech Inc., a company that manufactures recycling and composting machinery, was the keynote speaker at Monday night's opening ceremony of the Earth Preservation Society's annual conference.

REVISED: There's gold in the garbage society discards, the president of a company that manufactures recycling and composting machinery said, staking his claim on the future of recycling.

The revised lead focuses on what the speaker said, something the original lead failed to do. Other leads place too much emphasis on the time at which stories occurred:

> Last weekend the women's volleyball team participated in the regional playoffs.
> REVISED: The women's volleyball team won five of its seven games and placed second in the regional playoffs last weekend.

Avoid "Label" Leads

"Label" leads mention a topic but fail to reveal what was said or done about that topic. Leads should report the substance of a story, not just its topic. A good lead does more than report that a group met, held a press conference, or issued a report. The lead reveals what the group did at its meeting, what was said at the press conference, or what was written in the report.

Label leads are easy to recognize and avoid because they use similar words and phrases, such as "was the subject of," "the main topic of discussion," "spoke about," "delivered a speech about," or "interviewed about." Here are two examples:

> The city council Tuesday night discussed ways of regulating a new exotic dance club in the city.
> Faculty and staff members and other experts Thursday proposed strategies to recruit more minority students.

The first lead should summarize the city council's discussion, clearly explaining how the council plans to regulate the club. The second lead should summarize the experts' strategies for recruiting more minority students.

Avoid Lists

Most lists, like names, are dull. If a list must be used in a lead, place an explanation before it, never after it. Readers can more quickly grasp a list's meaning if an explanation precedes it, as the following lead and its revision illustrate:

> The company that made it, the store that sold it, and the friend who lent it to him are being sued by a 24-year-old man whose spine was severed when a motorcycle overturned.
> REVISED: A 24-year-old man whose spine was severed when a motorcycle overturned is suing the company that made the motorcycle, the store that sold it, and the friend who lent it to him.

Avoid Stating the Obvious

Avoid stating the obvious or emphasizing routine procedures in leads. For a story about a crime, do not begin by reporting that police "were called to the scene" or ambulances "rushed" the victims to a hospital "for treatment of their injuries." This problem is particularly common on sports pages, where many leads have become clichés. For example, news stories that say most coaches and players express optimism at the beginning of a season report the obvious: The coaches and players want to win most of their games.

The following lead, before its revision, is ineffective for the same reason:

> The Pearson Park school board has decided to spend the additional funds it will receive from the province.
> REVISED: The Pearson Park school board voted Monday night to rescind the 5 per cent spending cut it approved last month after learning the district will receive more money from the province.

Avoid the Negative

When writing a lead, report what happened—not what failed to happen or what does not exist:

Canadians over the age of 65 say that crime is not their greatest fear, two sociologists reported Friday.

REVISED: Canadians over the age of 65 say their greatest fears are poor health and poverty, two sociologists reported Friday.

Avoid Exaggeration

Never exaggerate in a lead. If a story is weak, exaggeration is likely to make it weaker, not stronger. A simple summary of the facts can be more interesting (and shocking) than anything that might be contrived:

A 78-year-old woman left $3.2 million to the Salvation Army and two cents to her son.

A restaurant did not serve a dead rat in a loaf of bread to an out-of-town couple, a jury decided Tuesday.

Avoid Misleading Readers

Every lead must be accurate and truthful. Never sensationalize, belittle or mislead. A lead must also set a story's tone—accurately revealing, for example, whether the story that follows will be serious or whimsical:

The party went to the dogs early—as it should have.

Parents who host parties for their children can understand the chill going up Susan Ulroy's spine. She was determined guests wouldn't be racing over her clean carpeting with their wet feet. "This could be a real free-for-all," she said.

Even though only seven guests were invited, eight counting the host, that made 32 feet to worry about.

This was a birthday party for Sandi, the Ulroys' dog. (*Ann Arbor [Mich.] News*)

Break the Rules

Reporters who use their imagination and try something different can sometimes report the facts more cleverly than the competition.

Edna Buchanan, who won a Pulitzer Prize for her police reporting at the *Miami Herald*, consistently made routine stories interesting. Here's a lead she wrote with some imagination. Notice the active verbs and description she incorporates into her writing:

Gary Robinson died hungry.

He wanted fried chicken, the three-piece box for $2.19. Drunk, loud and obnoxious, he pushed ahead of seven customers in line at a fast-food chicken outlet. The counter girl told him that his behavior was impolite. She calmed him down with sweet talk, and he agreed to step to the end of the line. His turn came just before closing time, just after the fried chicken ran out.

He punched the counter girl so hard her ears rang, and a security guard shot him—three times.

Remember Your Readers

While writing every lead, remember the people who will read it. Leads must be clear and interesting to attract and keep readers. The following lead, until revised, fails both tests:

Two policy resolutions will come before the Student Committee this week.

REVISED: Two proposals before the Student Committee this week would raise student parking and athletic fees by more than $100 a year.

Is the first lead interesting? Why not? It emphasized the number of resolutions the student senate was scheduled to consider. Yet almost no one would care about the number of resolutions or, from the lead, would understand their significance: the fact that they would affect every student at the school.

Rewrite Leads

Critically examine all leads and rewrite them as often as necessary. First drafts are rarely so well written that they cannot be improved. Even experienced professionals often rewrite their leads three or more times.

APPLY THE GUIDELINES TO OTHER KINDS OF LEADS

The guidelines in this chapter are for effective writing of all kinds of openings, not just leads for news stories. Good writing does not vary from one medium to another. You may want to work in public relations, to write for a radio or television station, to become a columnist, or to write a book. Regardless of your goal, the guidelines will help you achieve it.

Begin to analyze everything you read. You are likely to find some surprising similarities among books, magazines and newspapers. Also watch the opening scenes in movies and on television. Most, like a good lead, begin with a detail (or a story or scene) likely to capture your attention.

These, for example, are the opening sentences of two newspaper columns:

> Ozzie E. Garcia has a shaved head, a crooked grin and three tiny dots tattooed in the shape of a triangle near his right eye.
>
> A 12-year-old girl was jumped in Hull last month. Last week, charges were filed against her alleged assailants—all 21 of them.

Similarly, these are the opening sentences from four books:

> The small boys came early to the hanging. (Ken Follett, *The Pillars of the Earth*)
>
> On the 26th of July, my best friend decided he wanted to kill me. (Wyatt Wyatt, *Deep in the Heart*)
>
> In a hole in the ground there lived a hobbit. (J.R.R. Tolkien, *The Hobbit*)
>
> I did not realize for a long time that I was dead. (Alice Walker, *Possessing the Secret of Joy*)

 ## CHECKLIST FOR WRITING LEADS

1. Be specific rather than vague and abstract.
2. Avoid stating the obvious or the negative.
3. Emphasize the story's most unusual or unexpected developments.
4. Emphasize the story's most interesting and important developments.
5. Emphasize the story's magnitude and its impact on its participants and readers.
6. Use complete sentences, the proper tense, and all the necessary articles—"a," "an" and "the."
7. Be concise. If a lead exceeds three typed lines, examine it for wordiness, repetition or unnecessary details, and rewrite it to eliminate the problems.
8. Avoid writing a label lead that reports the story's topic but not what was said or done about it.
9. Begin leads with the news—the main point of the story—not the attribution or the time and place the events occurred.
10. Use relatively simple sentences, and avoid beginning leads with a long phrase or clause.
11. Use strong, active and descriptive verbs rather than passive ones.
12. Avoid using unfamiliar names. Any names that require lengthy identification should be reported in a later paragraph.
13. Attribute any quotation or statement of opinion appearing in the lead.
14. Localize the lead, and emphasize the latest developments, preferably what happened today or yesterday.

15. Eliminate statements of opinion, including one-word labels such as "interesting" and "alert."
16. Remember the readers. Write a lead that is clear, concise and interesting and that emphasizes the details most likely to affect and interest readers.
17. Read the lead aloud to be certain that it is clear, concise and easy to understand.

 ## The Writing Coach

OH WHERE, OH WHERE DOES THE TIME ELEMENT GO?

If you have problems—and most of us do—deciding where the time element should go, here are some tips from the *CP Stylebook*:

Put the time element where it falls naturally in speech, usually right after the verb or at the end of the sentence.

Not: Veterans Affairs Minister Greg Thompson Thursday said the new policy…
But: Veterans Affairs Minister Greg Thompson said Thursday the new policy…

Try to put the time element at the end if putting it directly between the verb and its object is awkward:

Not: Finance Minister Jim Flaherty announced Wednesday a $2-billion job program.
But: Finance Minister Jim Flaherty announced a $2-billion job program Wednesday.

There are situations where the time element is at home either in the middle or at the end of the sentence:

Dawn Coe-Jones came out of the pack Saturday to score a five-shot victory in the Canadian women's golf championship (Saturday).

Here are six more tips on where to place the time element, from editor Joe Hight:

1. The most natural place to put the day is immediately after the verb or the main clause. Follow the basic formula for writing a lead, especially in a hard news story: who, what, time, day or date, and place.

   The robber was killed Friday at the convenience store.

2. Avoid placing the time element so it appears to be the object of a transitive verb. In such situations, use "on" before the time element.
   Awkward: The city council postponed Thursday a resolution. (This appears to suggest that the council postponed Thursday.)
   Better: The city council postponed on Thursday a resolution.
   Or: The city council on Thursday postponed a resolution.

   Awkward: Deputies arrested Thursday a man wanted for theft.
   Better: Deputies arrested on Thursday a man wanted for theft.

Use "on" if the time element precedes the principal verb.

Awkward: The embassy Friday expelled several diplomats.
Better: The embassy on Friday expelled several diplomats.

And use "on" to avoid an awkward juxtaposition of the day and a proper name.

Awkward: Police told Smith Tuesday. (This could be misread to suggest that the name of the person is Smith Tuesday.)
Better: Police told Smith on Tuesday.)

Remember, however, that you do not use "on" unnecessarily (if the time element is clear without the word "on": The council meeting will be held Wednesday.)

3. Try placing the time element in a different sentence. It doesn't have to be in the lead, especially when you're writing a profile or issue, trend, or feature story. In many cases, the time element can be effectively delayed for later paragraphs.

4. Always read your sentence out loud to ensure that the time element doesn't sound or seem awkward.

SUGGESTED READINGS AND USEFUL WEBSITES

"Common faults." 2008. In *The Canadian Press Stylebook*, 15th edn., 285–94. Toronto: The Canadian Press.

Gibb, Don. *How to Write the Perfect Lead*. A 36-page booklet self-published in 1995, reprinted in 1999 and again in 2007. (Available from the author)

Hart, Jack. 2006. *A Writer's Coach: An Editor's Guide to Words That Work*. New York: Pantheon.

Kilpatrick, James J. 1984. *The Writer's Art*. New York: Andrews, McMeel and Parker.

Robertson, Heather. 1998. *Writing from Life: A Guide for Writing True Stories*. Toronto: McClelland and Stewart.

Stepp, Carl Sessions. 2000. *The Magic and Craft of Media Writing*. Chicago: NTC Publishing.

Sweet, Lois, and Klaus Pohle. 2003. *Writing with Spirit: A Journalistic Guide to Effective Writing*. Kitchener, ON: Castle Quay Books Canada.

Canadian Association of Newspaper Editors (CANE): http://www.cane.ca. CANE was created in 1999 when members of the 51-year-old Canadian Managing Editors Conference (CMEC) voted to change the name of their association and broaden its mandate to become a resource for newspapers editors in Canada. Among other things, the website offers the following guidelines for writing leads:

15 Steps to Writing the Perfect Lead (adapted from Don Gibb's booklet *Writing the Perfect Lead*: www.cane.ca (See under "Editorial Tips")

Don Gibb's 18 Quick Tips on Lead Writing: www.cane.ca (See under "Editorial Tips")

10 Leads That Shout 'Ugh'! by Gregg McLachlan, associate managing editor, *Simcoe Reformer*: http://www.cane.ca/english/me_res_ughleads.htm

EXERCISE 1   Leads

Evaluating Good and Bad Leads

Critically evaluate the following leads. Select the best leads, and explain why they are effective. In addition, point out the flaws in the remaining leads. As you evaluate the leads, look for lessons—dos and don'ts—that you can apply to your own work.

1. A 24-year-old Toronto man was charged with multiple counts of first-degree murder and arson in the deaths of his wife and three children who died in an early morning fire in their home.
2. City Council has to return a grant it received last year to fix deteriorating road conditions on Main Street.
3. People are jumping into swimming pools and switching buttons to high on air conditioners as temperatures in the province soared to record numbers over the past three days.
4. University administrators say they are considering imposing the largest tuition and fee increases in a decade because of provincial budget cuts.
5. A petition filed by City Council member William Bellmonte to force the council into a special session to reduce local property taxes was thrown out in court Monday after it was discovered that half the names listed on the petition were dead people.
6. An 85-year-old woman stepped off the curb and into the path of a moving car. She was struck by the car and tossed 16 metres into the air. She died instantly.
7. Ray's Mini-Mart at 2357 S. Alderman St. was the location of a burglary sometime Friday night.
8. RCMP Constable Barry Kopperud is concerned that crime is rising in the city.
9. This weekend will offer the best chance yet to see a brilliant performance of *My Fair Lady* at the Fairwood Community Theatre, so reserve your tickets now.
10. Loans become a popular way to cut college costs.
11. The right of students to freely express themselves may soon be cast aside if the board of governors votes to restrict access to campus public areas.
12. The tree-lined campus is home to many wild and stray animals.
13. Two men suspected of burglarizing five churches, two homes and a pet store all in one night were captured Wednesday during another burglary attempt.
14. The union representing university secretaries and maintenance workers reached a tentative agreement Friday that will give members a 6.5 per cent raise over three years.
15. Distance education classes offer alternative to classroom.
16. Fingerprints on a candle led the RCMP to a man accused of blowing up the building he worked in to hide the shooting deaths of the man's boss and three co-workers.
17. Around 10 a.m. Wednesday a bank at the intersection of McGill and Hillside streets was the scene of a daring daylight robbery by three armed gunmen.
18. A teenage driver lost control of his car Wednesday night killing himself and a female passenger, while a 14-year-old friend who was riding in the back seat walked away with only scratches and bruises.

CHAPTER 5

EXERCISE 2   Leads

Writing Leads

SECTION I: CONDENSING LENGTHY LEADS
Condense each of these leads to no more than two typed lines, or about 20 words.

1. Christina Shattuck, 43, and Dennis Shattuck, 45, and their three children, ages 7, 3, and 9 months, all of 532 3rd St., returned home from a shopping trip Saturday night and found their two-storey frame house on fire and called firefighters, who responded to the scene within five minutes, but were unable to save the house and its contents, which were totally destroyed.
2. The local school board held a special meeting Tuesday night so Schools Superintendent Greg Hubbard could address a group of angry parents who were demanding to know why they were never informed that a student had brought a gun to school and may have been targeting their children during an incident on school grounds last Friday.

SECTION II: USING PROPER SENTENCE STRUCTURE
Rewrite the following leads, using the normal word order: subject, verb, direct object. Avoid starting the leads with a long clause or phrase. You may want to divide some of the leads into several sentences or paragraphs. Correct all errors.

1. In an effort to curb what city officials are calling an epidemic of obesity among young people in the city, which mirrors national data on overall obesity of the population, your local city council voted 7–0 to offer free memberships at its meeting Monday night to local youth centres and health clubs in the city for children ages 8 to 15 whose parents do not have the financial wherewithal to purchase the memberships.
2. Despite the efforts of Karen Dees, 19, a student at your university who lives at 410 University Avenue, Apartment 52, and performed cardiopulmonary resuscitation for more than 20 minutes, she was not able to help Constable William McGowen, 47, of 4224 N. 21st St, who died while directing traffic after being struck by lightning during an electrical storm.

SECTION III: EMPHASIZING THE NEWS
Rewrite the following leads, emphasizing the news, not the attribution. Limit the attributions to a few words, and place them at the end, not the beginning, of the leads.

1. Health Canada released a report today indicating that more than 90 per cent of all heart attack victims have one or more classic risk factors: smoking, diabetes, high cholesterol, and high blood pressure.
2. Police reported Monday that Stephanie Sessions, 16, daughter of Jeffrey D. and Michelle A. Sessions, of 9303 Vale Drive, had just gotten her driver's licence two days before she was involved in an accident in which she rolled the Jeep Wrangler she was driving, injuring herself and two other passengers.

SECTION IV: COMBINING MULTI-SENTENCE LEADS
Rewrite each of the following leads in a single sentence, correcting all errors.

1. Gary Hubard, superintendent of schools, announced a new program for your local school district. It is called the "Tattle-Tale Program." The program involves paying students to tell on classmates who bring guns or drugs to school or violate other school rules. The program is in response to an incident last month in which a high school student was caught carrying a loaded handgun on school property.

2. Statistics Canada released a report Monday on the number of people in Canada who have spent time in prison. Last year, about one in every 120 adult Canadians was imprisoned or had been in prison at one time. The 861,000 people who were either serving or had served time in prison represented 0.82 per cent of the adult population of 32 million people, according to the report. The figures represent people who served time in federal and provincial prisons after being sentenced for a crime, not those temporarily held in jail.

SECTION V: STRESSING THE UNUSUAL

Write only the lead for each of the following stories, correcting errors if necessary.

1. The city is sweltering under a heat wave. Temperatures have hit 40 degrees-plus for the past week and humidity levels have hovered between 75 and 90 per cent each day. Authorities have been cautioning people, especially the very young and the elderly to stay inside in air conditioning and avoid exerting themselves outside in the sun. Interior Health Authority officials held a press conference this morning to announce that three people had died over the past two days because of the heat. All three were elderly people who lived in the downtown area. Two of the three were a married couple. The one victim was identified as Betsy Aaron, 86, of 410 Hillcrest St., Apartment 302. Aaron was a retired teacher who had taught elementary school for more than 30 years. The other two victims were Jeffrey Ahsonn, 84, and his wife, Teresa Ahson, 79, both of 49 Groveland Ave. Ahsonn was a retired mechanical engineer who had worked for the city for many years. Police and health department officials were alerted to the deaths in each case by relatives who discovered the bodies. When they entered the dwellings, police told officials that they found a pair of fans and an air conditioner in each dwelling. The fans and air conditioners had been delivered by city workers to disabled elderly people to help them cope with the heat wave. But authorities found the fans and air conditioners still in their boxes. They had never been installed.

2. Destiny Schfini is a vice president with SunBank. Schifini is divorced and the mother of two children—a 10-year-old girl and an eight-year-old boy. The children visit her once a month. Schifinis son, Ronald, was visiting this weekend. Schfini is 36 years old and lives at 3260 Timber Ter. Ronald was injured in an accident Saturday afternoon around 2 p.m. The boy was struck by a train. Police said Schifini and her son were riding bikes along Fremont Avenue when the mother decided to take a shortcut across the railroad tracks that run along Fremont Avenue. The boy is on life support in Mercy Hospital and listed in critical condition. He was struck by a train. Witnesses said the mother saw the train coming and crossed anyway and encouraged her son to cross. The boys bike got caught on the tracks and as he tried to free it, the train struck him. Ronald was thrown through the air and sustained broken ribs, a broken pelvis and a bruised heart. Police charged Destiny Schifini with aggravated assault, reckless endangerment, endangering the welfare of a child and failure to obey a train signal. Police said they charged Schfini after they learned from witnesses that Schifini did not help the boy, but taunted him as the train approached.

3. Julius Povacz is a paramedic in your community who serves with the rescue squad in the fire department. The 34-year-old Povaz lives at 210 East King Avenue, Apartment 4. Eight years ago he was tested for human immunodeficiency virus, or HIV, the virus that causes AIDS, and told that the test was positive. Povacz never told his superiors that he had tested positive. A routine check of his medical records last month by fire department officials found the notation that the test was positive. Povacz was relieved of his duties. Povacz said at the time he may have been infected with the virus accidentally by coming in contact with an infected patient at the scene of an emergency. When he learned that he lost his job, Povaz said it was worse than learning that he had tested positive for HIV. Being a paramedic was all he ever wanted to do. He said for eight years he has feared that his medical condition would be discovered or that he would develop AIDS and die. The regional Health Authority computer system tracks HIV

patients and periodically reviews cases. An official at the Health Authority informed Povacz and his superiors yesterday that Povacz is not and never was HIV positive. A second test that was performed eight years ago to confirm the first test indicated no presence of HIV, but the information was never placed in Povaczs medical records by his physician, Dr Nadine Caspinwall, and Caspinwall never informed Povacz. Povacz is now fighting to get his job back.

4. The RCMP in your community are investigating a two-vehicle accident. The accident occurred at 5:38 p.m. Thursday during rush hour. The accident occurred at the busy intersection of Huron Avenue and Timber Trail Road. An RCMP spokesperson said a blue Toyota Camry driven by Cheryl Nicholls, 25, of 1287 Belgard Avenue, ran into the rear of a pickup truck driven by Ronald Dawkins, 44, of 1005 Stratmore Drive. Dawkins is a bricklayer. Nichols Toyota suffered severe damage, but she sustained only bruises and a laceration on her leg. RCMP said the car was a total loss. RCMP charged Nicholls with inattentive driving and operating a cellphone while driving. The cellphone law was passed last year by the provincial legislature and banned the operation of a cellphone while driving. Nicholls was talking to her car insurance company about an error on a car insurance bill when she struck the rear of Dawkins pickup truck.

5. A home at 2481 Santana Ave. was burglarized between the hours of 1 p.m. and 4 p.m. yesterday afternoon. The owner of the home is Dorothy R. Elam, a grade six teacher at Laurier Elementary School. She said no one was home at the time. Neighbours said they saw a truck parked in the driveway but thought some repairmen were working at the home. The total loss is estimated at in excess of $8,000. The items stolen from the home include a colour television, a videocassette recorder, stereo, sewing machine, computer, 2 rifles and many small kitchen appliances. Also, a stamp collection valued at about $1,000, some clothes, silverware and lawn tools were taken. Roger A. Elam, Mrs Elams husband, died 2 days ago. The robbery occurred while she was attending his funeral at 2:30 p.m. yesterday at the Powell Funeral Chapel, 620 North Park Avenue. Elam died of cancer after a long illness.

SECTION VI: LOCALIZING YOUR LEAD

Write only the lead for each of the following stories, correcting errors if necessary. Emphasize the information that would have the greatest local interest.

1. Canada's Department of Justice is calling identity theft the crime of the twenty-first century. Identity theft is the illegal appropriation of another persons personal information—Social Insurance card number, driver's licence number, credit card numbers, etc.—and using them to drain bank accounts or go on a buying spree. Department of Justice officials say it is the fastest-growing crime in Canada. Criminals can get access to peoples personal information by going through their trash or stealing their mail. Industry Canada estimated the dollar loss to businesses and individuals last year was in the billions. The number of victims nationally is running as high as 75,000 a year. The rate of identity theft complaints nationally is averaging 22 victims per 100,000 people. Department of Justice officials say that is too high. But the rate of identity theft complaints in your city is 77 victims per 100,000 people. MP Constance P. Wei is sponsoring a bill that would establish a website that would allow credit card holders check to see if their numbers have been stolen. The bill also would increase the penalties for identity theft and raise the crime from a misdemeanour to a felony.

2. Your province's ministry of education announced that it is awarding more than 30 million dollars in grant money to 53 school districts throughout the province. The money is to be used to offset recent cutbacks in provincial funds given to school districts for educational programs and materials. Among the programs eligible for grant money are innovative programs to help identify and support at-risk youth who are not receiving the help they need. At-risk youth are more prone to failing in school and dropping out, becoming involved with drugs, becoming involved in crime or

gang-related activity, and ending up in prison. The province's Commission on Crime and Delinquency identified your local school district as a leader in the effort to help at-risk youth with its Community Helping Hands program. The program identifies at-risk youth at an early age and then engages teachers, community members and other students to help at-risk youth through academic tutoring, social activities and counselling. The provincial Commission on Crime and Delinquency through the provincial Ministry of Education is providing $1.2 million to your school districts at-risk program. The funds will help support the programs operation for at least three years.

SECTION VII: UPDATING YOUR LEAD
Write only the lead for each of the following stories, correcting errors if necessary.

1. Dorothy Heslin is the manager of the Mr. Grocer convenience store at 2015 North 11th Avenue. Heslinn is a 48-year-old single mother with three children. She is seen as a hero by some and a villain by others. Yesterday, two masked men carrying guns barged into the Mr. Grocer and demanded money. As she reached for the cash drawer, Heslinn pulled a .357-caliber Magnum pistol from beneath the counter and fired four shots, killing one robber and seriously wounding the second. Some in the community say it was justified because her life was in danger, but others say she used excessive force. Police today charged Heslinn with aggravated assault with a handgun, attempted murder, second-degree murder and possession of an unregistered handgun.

2. There was a grinding head-on collision on Cheney Road yesterday. Two persons were killed: Rosemary Brennan, 27, and her infant daughter, Kelley, age 2, both of 1775 Nairn Dr. The driver of the second car involved in the accident, Anthony Murray, 17, of 1748 North 3 Street, was seriously injured, with multiple fractures. Police today announced that laboratory tests have confirmed the fact that Brennan was legally drunk at the time of the accident.

3. The Steak & Ale restaurant is a popular restaurant and lounge in your community. It is especially popular with college students. The restaurant is located at 1284 University Boulevard. Last year, a group of students was celebrating at the restaurant after a football game. The five students became rowdy and were asked to leave by Sarah Kindstrom, a waitress at the Steak & Ale. The students left the restaurant, but one of them, James Ball, who was 18 at the time, of 1012 Cortez Avenue, Apartment 870, became separated from the group, wandered into the street and was struck by a car. He died at the scene. His parents sued the Steak & Ale for serving underage students alcohol and causing the death of their son. Monday the restaurants owners settled the suit for one million dollars.

EXERCISE 3   Pro Challenge

Writing Basic News Leads

Write only a lead for each of the following stories. As you write your leads, consult the checklist on page 19. As you write the leads, correct any errors of spelling, diction, possessives and style.

1. Researchers from Statistics Canada conducted a major study of Canadian marriages and announced their results at a press conference today. Of couples that marry, the researchers found that 43% break up within fifteen years, according to their study of 50,000 women. It helps if women are wealthy, religious, college-educated, and at least 20 years old when they marry. They are less likely to divorce. StatsCan found that half of Canadian women had lived with a partner by age 30. And 70% of those couples that lived together for at least five years eventually walked down the aisle. But their marriages were most likely to break up. After 10 years 40% of the couples that had lived together before marriage had broken up, compared with 31% of those couples that did not live together. That's because people who choose to live together tend to be younger and less religious and have other traits that put them at a greater risk for divorce, the researchers concluded.

2. Your citys downtown businessmen want something done immediately about the problem of panhandling and vagrants, especially on downtown city streets. Some vagrants sleep at night in parking lots or on doorsteps. Passersby they approach for money find them scary, and business leaders don't like them in front of their stores, saying they scare away good customers and give the downtown a seedy image. Businessmen say vagrants also eat, urinate, and sleep in parks, in unlocked vehicles, and elsewhere. So mayor Datolli said today she will introduce a new panhandling ordinance to the city council at its regular meeting at 8:00 pm next Tuesday night. The ordinance calls for the establishment of a program to offer homeless people one-way bus tickets to a town where they have family. A critic, Sandra Gandolf, says it is heartless, since many of the homeless have long-lasting problems including mental illness and/or drug or alcohol addiction and need real help. She favours providing programs to feed and house the homeless and to guide them toward mental health treatment, substance abuse counseling, and job assistance. However, the mayor said today the RCMP now charge vagrants with minor crimes such as indecent exposure and shoplifting, that vagrants clog the jails and the court system, and that they end up right back on the streets. Downtown businessmen have promised to raise all the money needed for bus tickets.

3. Erik Barsh is the son of Margaret and Michael Barsh of 2498 Hazel Lane. He was hit by lightning at a municipal swimming pool last summer. A friend was killed and Erik was injured. Now, Erik is suing the city for his injuries: for the cost of his mounting medical bills that total thousands of dollars each and every month. He says the citys lifeguards knew a storm was coming and were gathering their own equipment but failed to warn swimmers of the danger. He is 17 yrs. old, has dropped out of high school where he was to be a senior this school year, and now takes pain medication daily and says he cannot work or even muster the strength to go to church or to a mall or to a movie theater with friends. He says he can't stand for more than ten minutes at a time. He says his body was set in a slow, painful decline of lightning-induced brain and nerve injuries that he and his lawyers contend may eventually leave him in a wheelchair and destroy his sight and memory. He adds that before the unfortunate incident he was his high schools top male tennis player, earned As in all his classes, and planned to begin playing tennis and studying engineering next year at Carleton University. Alan Farci, your City Attorney, said, "Our position on this is that we didn't have any greater knowledge than he did. The problem was obvious. It had started raining, and we've got a dozen witnesses who heard the thunder approaching and said the lifeguards had, in fact, ordered everyone to immediately get out of the pool, but this kid was horse playing with his friend. Its tragic, but they just didn't listen, and lightning hit before the lifeguards could do anything else."

4. Cynthia Lowrie of 118 Hillside Dr., Apt 74, was arrested today by RCMP. She was charged by them with theft and with defrauding an adoption agency. She had said she was pregnant. She received $12,000 from the Hope Agency to pay all her medical and other expenses while pregnant and had signed a contract to give her unborn child up for adoption. Medical tests given her today showed she isn't pregnant and never has been. She admits submitting at one point to the adoption agency test results from a friend who was pregnant. After all the money, the entire amount, was spent, she cut off contact with the agency and the prospective adoptive parents. A private detective hired by the couple tracked her down. She then said at first that her baby was born dead. Based on the results of todays tests, medical doctors concluded she was not recently pregnant, and she was arrested.

5. Construction workers for a new apartment complex were digging a trench for some underground utilities today. They hit by accident a major water main, shattering it, leaving major parts of the city with low or no water pressure. It may not be fully restored for 24 hours, authorities say. Now, water officials warn everyone living North of Hanson Avenue to boil their cooking and drinking water for the next three days. All water used for drinking and food preparation should be boiled vigorously for at least 3 minutes. The boil-water notice affects about 25,000 customers. The break occurred in a 65-centimetre pipe, a major line running from the citys main water plant. The area was flooded as a fountain of water gushed an estimated sixteen metres upward, flooding the entire construction site near the intersection of Colonial Ave. and Chapman Rd., and the intersection also had to be closed due to being under a metre or more of water. During the repair process dirt is likely to get into the lines and will have to be flushed out.

6. An RCMP constable yesterday arrested an 8 yr. old boy. Today RCMP are conducting an internal investigation. The charges have been dropped but the boys mother is upset, saying const. Roger Temple who arrested her son should have simply separated the 2 children who were squabbling on a playground. The boys mother, Audrey W. VanPelt, said the girls mother was out of control and hysterical, insisting that she wanted to press charges. The boys mother said, "That dumb cop that gave my son a ticket reacted to the womans feelings instead of acting as an officer of the law and trying to calm her down." The incident happened at about 4 p.m. at Riverview Park. The boys mother had taken him there to play with several friends. A girl was trying to use a swing when the children began squabbling, and the boy slapped her on the face leaving a red mark. The girls mom immediately called police and insisted that charges be filed, so officer Tempel took the boy to a juvenile detention facility on a battery charge. An internal investigation will be done to examine the decision to take the boy to the juvenile lockup says the RCMP. The name of the boy was not released because he is a juvenile.

7. Elizabeth Anne Daigel was 102 years old and apparently in perfect health. She never used her health benefits. Investigators called at her home yesterday to find out her secret for good health and longevity. They found she had been dead twenty years. She apparently died of natural causes and her body had been wrapped in blankets and hidden in a trunk in a locked room in the basement of her home at 431 Central Boulevard. Her granddaughter, Annette, told police her grandmother died in her sleep and she hid the body in order to keep collecting her monthly social insurance cheque which Annette said she desperately needs as a divorced mother with four children to support. The government routinely compares the names of those receiving social insurance cheques to the rolls of eligible persons. Today police charged Annette with theft. She could not be charged with improper burial or failure to report a death because the crimes are beyond the statute of limitations. If convicted she could be sentenced to five years in prison and ordered to make full restitution for all the money she collected after her grandmothers death, a total well in excess of 200,000.00, plus interest.

8. Your city needs more money to eliminate a 6 million dollar deficit. So mayor Datolli at a press conference today proposed a fire tax. The tax would put the financial bite on all property owners, without exception, including churches, schools, and non-profits as well as residences and businesses. Under the proposal by mayor Datoli, the city would charge homeowners a $134.00 fee each year regardless of a propertys value. Apartment owners

would pay $89.00 per unit. Churches, businesses, and schools would have various rates based on square footage. Datolli noted that for the past seven years there has been no tax rate increase in the city. Council member Nyad called the idea "bizarre." Nyad said, "We already pay for fire protection through our property taxes. This would tax citizens twice for the same thing. It's the dumbest thing I've ever heard of. You don't tax schools. Where would they get the money from?" But the mayor on the other hand stated, "Its painful but ultimately a good thing. We have to be fiscally responsible. We have to solve our financial problems and provide essential services. I don't want to cut back on them."

9. There's a new program to help your citys teachers. They aren't paid much. Many can't afford a down payment for a house. So local school officials today unveiled a new program that will offer mortgages with below-market interest rates to teachers and administrators in public schools. Its designed for first-time buyers and would offer eligible educators up to 10,000 dollars to help cover down payments and closing costs. They will not have to repay any of that amount provided they both continue to teach and remain in the home for a minimum of the next five consecutive years. Helping teachers buy or rent is becoming a popular incentive across the nation as teacher shortages and attrition continue to plague schools. Cash for the down payments will come from funds already used to help low to moderate income residents buy homes. Program rules have been tweaked so teachers qualify, said school supt. Gary Hubard. There are limits on applicants income and on a homes purchase price, mostly depending on exactly where a home is located.

10. Your citys Fire Chief announced today that the fire department is ending a tradition at least a hundred years old. It's the tradition of sliding down a pole to get to a fire engine. The city, he explained, is phasing poles out as it builds new one-story stations to replace older multistory firehouses. Going down the pole too fast and hitting a concrete floor can cause injuries and was therefore never a good tradition, he said. He explained that fire department records show over the past 20 years at least 12 firemen suffered injuries, especially sprained or broken ankles or legs. Still, crews improved their response time to fires by bypassing staircases from their upstairs living quarters, by cutting holes in the floors of firehouses, and by installing and using the brass or steel poles. The last multi-storey firehouse with a pole is slated for demolition sometime early next year.

11. There's a deadly problem at Pearson High School. Two more students tested positive for tuberculosis last week, indicating they likely picked up the germ from a student with an active case of TB, city health officials announced today. The two students are not yet ill and can not pass the infection on to anyone else but will be given antibiotics to make sure they never develop TB. The two were among 170 persons tested at the school last week. The tests were necessary because health officials determined that one student has active TB, which is contagious. The Health Authority last week tested every student and staff member who was in a class or rode a school bus with the ill student. The ill student is no longer in school, having dropped out for the year. The health officials said there is little danger to the schools nearly 3000 other students. TB is spread when an ill person coughs, but only after prolonged exposure and in poorly ventilated areas. A high school campus isn't likely to be a place for TB transmission. Those two who tested positive will be given a chest x-ray and medication to be sure they don't develop active TB.

12. Community leaders wanted to know who are the homeless in your city, so they raised 50,000 dollars to fund a grant for researchers in the sociology dept. at your institution to study them. The researchers who issued their report today found, "Most thought these people in our community were chronically homeless, that they came here from someplace else and that they had mental health or substance abuse histories. When interviewed, less than 30% informed us of mental health or substance abuse histories. Sixty-seven percent claimed this was their first time homeless. Sixty-eight percent had been homeless for less than six months. Almost 55% had been living in the city when they became homeless because of a job loss, eviction, marital breakup, domestic violence, victimization or having been jailed. Just 14% became homeless while living in another province before moving here. Many were married or unmarried couples with children. Thus, we conclude that homelessness is a local problem. Our citys homeless are mostly neighbours who've temporarily fallen on hard times."

EXERCISE 4   Pro Challenge

City, Provincial and National Leads

Write only a lead for each of the following stories. As you write your leads, consult the checklist on page 42. The first set of stories involves events in your city; the second set involves events in your province; and the third set involves events in the nation. As you write the leads, correct any errors of spelling, diction, possessives and style.

City Beat

1. Two researchers at your school today announced the results of an important study they conducted. Both are psychologists. Their study involved 50 children, all boys between the ages of ten to twelve who attend the University Learning Centre. One by one, the boys were sent into a laboratory furnished to look like a playroom. They were told they could open all the drawers and look on all the shelves and play with whatever toys they found. Among the items under clothes in one drawer was a genuine pistol. The 2 researchers watched and filmed each child. One of the researchers, Aneesa Ahmadd, said many boys found the pistol and played with it and even pulled the trigger without knowing whether or not it was loaded. "They did everything from point it at each other to look down the barrel," said Prof. Ahmadd. About seventy-five percent, or 37 found the gun, and 26 handled it. At least 16 clearly pulled the trigger. Many, when questioned later, said they did not know if the gun was real. None knew it was unloaded and that the firing pin had been removed so it could not possibly be fired. All the childrens parents had given the researchers permission for their offspring to participate in the important study, and Ahmadd said many were horrified by the results, especially since all said they had warned their children never to play with guns. Ahmadd said the studys real significance is that it reveals that simple parental warnings are ineffective.
2. For the last 62 years, Olivida Saleeby has lived with her husband, Wesley, in their home at 1961 Elizabeth Lane, a structure originally built by her parents. The couple has been married all 62 of those years, immediately moving in with her parents after their honeymoon and later inheriting the house. Last week Wesley died, and his body remains unburied in a funeral home. Olivida last night asked the citys Zoning Board at its regular weekly meeting for permission to bury her dead husband in their back yard. By a vote of 7–0, board members refused. Olivida explained that she has no other living relatives, deeply loved her 81-yr.-old husband, and wanted her beloved husband to remain near her. He died suddenly and unexpectedly of a heart attack. Board members rejected her plea and explained burial in a residential neighbourhood would set a bad precedent and bring down property values.
3. Susan Carigg of your city was forty-two years old and the mother of 4 kids, 3 girls and 1 boy. She was in a serious and tragic car accident 7 months ago. Since then, she's been in a coma at Mercy Hospital in your city. Her husband, Craig, now wants to remove the feeding tube that has kept his comatose spouse alive. Susans parents oppose the idea. They are Elaine and Vernon Sindelar, and they appealed to a Superior Court judge to issue an injunction to stop their son-in-law from removing the tube. The judge today ruled that Craig can proceed, clearing the way for the tubes removal by doctors. Three doctors who have treated the woman testified unanimously that she is brain dead with no hope of recovering. Mr Carigg said he will wait until he receives final paperwork and consults again with his wifes doctors. Without the tube Mrs Carigg will die of starvation and dehydration, probably in a period of approximately five to seven days.
4. A judge today issued an important decision that involves your citys school board. A gender-discrimination lawsuit was filed against the school board by girl softball players parents. Judge McGregor ruled that the school district violated provincial and federal gender-discrimination laws by providing better baseball fields for boys than for girls. Two girls high school softball teams in your district have to travel up to 7 kilometres to practise while boys teams have fields on their high school campus. Parents complained the girls

fields are unsafe and substandard, with dirty bathrooms and open-air dugouts. The judge ordered the district to bring the girls softball fields up to par with the boys fields. Like the boys fields, the new fields for the girls must have 2 metre high fencing with backstops, bleachers, dugouts with refrigerated water for each team, electronic scoreboards, batting cages and 3-by-4 metre storage sheds. The School Board estimates that all that will cost approximately $600,000 to build new fields adjacent to the boys fields at the two schools involved, and the board said it does not know where the money will come from.

5. Some people in your city don't like billboards, considering them an urban blight. The issue was brought before the citys Planning Board last night. By a unanimous vote of 7–0 its members recommended banning any new billboards within the city limits and also taking down all existing billboards within seven years. Its recommendations will go to the city council for final consideration, and council members have already said they will hold two public workshops to give interested parties an opportunity to provide their input. There are currently about 180 billboards within the city. A spokesman for the citys billboard companies responded that any edict to remove existing signs is akin to stealing from legitimate businesses. She said the city government must legally pay fair market value for existing signs which are worth millions of dollars, and that local billboard companies will sue, if necessary, to protect their property rights.

6. Deer Creek Park is normally a popular city park but thousands of winged mammals have made their home in the rafters of the parks three picnic pavilions. People who had reserved the pavilions for picnics over the next several days have been notified the areas are now off limits. People can picnic elsewhere in the park but not in the pavilions. "In a general sense, bats are good people to have around," said Carlos Alicea, an epidemiologist for the local Health Authority. "They do a wonderful job of insect control, but the flip side of that is that if you have a one-on-one encounter, there could be a risk of rabies, and there's also a problem with their droppings." The city is waiting to hear from experts about relocating the bats elsewhere in the park. One option is to erect bat houses elsewhere to provide shelter during daylight hours when the bats are inactive, but there is no guarantee the bats would use them.

Provincial Beat

1. There was a daring daylight robbery in your provincial capital. It involved an armored car. It was owned and operated by Brinks. Police say it is unclear whether a second person was involved, but about 400,000 dollars were taken. There were no signs of struggle or foul play, and they are looking for the trucks driver, Neil Santana, age 27. He is suspected of taking the cash while his partner went into a supermarket for a routine money pickup. He is still at large. Officials searched in and around his home and checked airports and are looking for his car. The heist occurred shortly after 4:10 p.m. yesterday afternoon when Santana drove his partner to the supermarket. As his partner went inside to pick up a bag of cash, witnesses said the driver drove off. When his partner returned, the truck was gone and remains missing. The incident occurred at the end of their route, which included a total of 22 stops and pickups. The co-worker called the police. Company officials said the driver started working for the company about five weeks ago and had no arrest record.

2. Your provincial legislature acted today. Its members want to end a serious problem. Each year, a dozen or more little helpless newborn babies in the province are found abandoned, and some are dead. Often, their mothers are unwed and young and don't want the babies or know how to care for their babies, so they abandon them, and some die before being found. Some mothers and some fathers kill some unwanted newborn infants. To end the problem, the legislature today adopted a law that will allow anyone to leave an unwanted newborn at any manned hospital or fire station in the province, no questions asked and with no criminal liability whatsoever. Your premier has endorsed and promised to sign the bill.

3. Jennifer Pinccus, a member of the provincial legislature elected from your riding, is troubled. She says there are too many motor vehicle accidents, and too many of those accidents involve the elderly some of whom, according to her, "are no longer fit to drive."

So she today introduced a controversial bill that would require senior motorists to take an extra test, and it is a controversial piece of legislation which will, to be passed, have to be approved by the provincial legislature and then signed by your Premier. Under her plan, drivers age seventy-five and older would have to renew their licences in person every three years, and would have to submit proof of hearing and vision tests by their physician when doing so. Those eighty-one and older would have to take a road test every 3 years as well as pass the screenings. Now, any driver over age seventeen can renew a six-year licence two consecutive times by mail. So it is possible to hold a valid licence for 18 years before having to actually walk into a provincial driver's service centre which Pincus thinks is too long for seniors whose health can change dramatically in a short time. Seniors are expected to actively oppose the proposal, yet four other provinces have additional testing or renewal requirements for seniors. Many require a doctors vision or hearing certification. Only 2 other provinces require regular road tests.

4. Your provincial Supreme Court acted today. It ruled unanimously that Jason Perez of your city can be kept in prison even though Perez has completed his sentence and has not been charged with a new crime. Health officials believe he is a public health risk, and a lower court judge who heard the case brought by the health officials concluded Perez cannot be trusted to participate willingly in a treatment program. So the 46-year-old tuberculosis patient sits in an isolated 2-by-3 metre cell eight days after his prison sentence for assault with a deadly weapon ended and he was supposed to be a free man. His attorney wants Perez freed on his own recognizance. But before his incarceration for assault, Perez fled three times in violation of court orders and failed to get complete treatment for his drug resistant form of TB, a highly communicable and potentially deadly disease. That's why the regional Health Authority considers him a public health risk. His attorney says he belongs in a hospital, but the Supreme Court today concurred with the lower court that he can be detained so long as he remains a clear and present health threat to others.

5. The Humane Society in your province announced today a new policy. All its city affiliates will immediately stop providing homeless cats to paramedic students. In the past the affiliates provided the cats so the students could practice inserting breathing tubes into humans. For as long as anyone can remember, the Society allowed its affiliates to provide cats scheduled to be euthanized for practice by students in emergency-medical-technician, paramedic, emergency-medical-service, and related programs. The society said it has received lots of complaints since PETA last week denounced its policy as unnecessary, gruesome, and potentially painful to the cats. People for the Ethical Treatment of Animals urged its members to withdraw all funding from the Humane Society and to encourage others to do so as well. A spokesman for the society today said no cats suffered but PETA's criticisms led to a reconsideration of the program. "We concluded there was not a need for us to be involved, and so we're out of it," she said. The cats were anesthetized but still alive when students practised sticking breathing tubes down their throats. After the class, the cats were given a final, lethal shot. Students say they are losing an important training opportunity, especially for dealing with babies and infants, and that some young children may die since no alternatives for practising helping them have been developed.

6. There's a new trend in your province. The population is aging, with more people over the age of 65 than ever before. So throughout your province, new hospitals are being built and old hospitals are being expanded. Provincial health officials calculate that, across the province, the aging and inadequacy of mature buildings has fuelled an unprecedented multi-billion dollar rush of construction by hospitals. Of all existing hospitals in the province, 31% are currently in the process of expanding or renovating. Two dozen of those hospitals are spending at least $25 million, and 14 are known to be spending more than $50 million each. Two dozen hospitals are enlarging crowded emergency rooms to ease overcrowding. Growing numbers of people who don't have family doctors go to ERs for any medical problem, sharply increasing patient volumes at ERs. Many other hospitals are expanding operating rooms, adding outpatient centres, and building physician offices to handle increased businesses. Expansions also are bringing new or larger speciality medical services such as heart surgery centres and cancer programs needed primarily by the elderly.

National Beat

1. Each year Public Safety Canada located in Ottawa gathers a variety of statistics about highway safety. It analyzes data gathered throughout the nation. Today it announced the results of a study of young drivers. It found that, of all young drivers, 16-year-old boys remain the most risky drivers on the road. 16 yr. old boys have more accidents than any other age group, and that's been true since the Institute began analyzing highway data 32 years ago. But this year the institute found that 16-year-old girls are gaining. For every 1000 licensed 16-year-olds girls, 175 were in car accidents last year. That's up 9 percent from just 10 years ago when 160 girls crashed per 1000 drivers. Accidents for 16-year-old boys decreased slightly during the same period, from 216 to 210 per 1000 licensed drivers. A spokesman for the group said boys are crashing less because of safer vehicle designs and less drunk driving.

2. Some men kill their wives and girlfriends. They've been the subject of a major national study. Those men typically have a long history of domestic violence. They own firearms and use them "in a final act of rage against a woman perceived to be their property," concludes the first national review of domestic violence deaths conducted by Statistics Canada. StatsCan today announced that, nationally, about 19 percent of all murders are domestic related. Sixty-two percent involve the spouse or live-in girlfriend of the alleged killer. Children were the victims in roughly 11% of the cases of domestic deaths. In all, about 27% of all violent crimes reported to the RCMP including murder, forcible rape, aggravated assault, and stalking involve domestic issues. And in the vast majority of cases, victims have had plenty of advance warning, as the violent behaviour of their partners escalated over time. Many of those killed had received death threats from spouses who felt betrayed and jealous, StatsCan concluded. Guns were frequent weapons of choice.

3. Its another national study, this one of married men and women. It found that many married Canadians admit keeping a major secret from their spouses, but most secrets have nothing to due with an affair or fantasy. Of those married men and women with a secret:

    - 48% said they had not told their spouse the real price of something they bought.
    - About 40% of the wives and 30% of the husbands said they wish they could persuade their spouses to be less messy.
    - About a quarter of each sex said they cannot get their partners to lose weight.
    - About 20% of the nations marrieds have dreams or aspirations they haven't mentioned to a spouse, ranging from living somewhere else (50%) to getting a dog (8%).
    - 16% of both men and women admitted that, at least once during their marriage, they wished they could wake up and not be married any more.
    - About 15% had not told their spouse about a failure at work.
    - About 15% had not told their spouse about a childs misbehaviour.
    - 14% kept quiet about being attracted to another person.
    - Only 9% of the respondents, equally split among men and women, said they had an extramarital affair that remains a secret.

    The poll was conducted last month by Statistics Canada, which interviewed by phone 700 husbands and 700 wives.

4. A startling new study shows how difficult it is to be a parent. When teens start dating new problems arise. The University of Alberta School of Public Health conducted a comprehensive study of 1,977 high school girls and found that 1 in 5 reported being a victim of physical or sexual violence in a dating relationship. Girls reported being hit, slapped, shoved, or forced into sexual activity by dates. Since this was the first study of its kind its not clear whether such abuse is on the rise. The report concluded that high school girls think they can handle situations they're not ready for. The researchers add that the pressures and status of having a boyfriend can propel girls into unhealthy relationships. And many of these girls never tell their moms and dads about dating violence.

5. Ralph Wick is 5 feet, 5 inches tall and weighs 342 pounds and lives in St. John. He blames fast-food restaurants for his excessive weight. He is suing 4, saying they contributed to his obesity, heart disease, and diabetes. He filed the 4 suits this week and explained at a press conference today he wants 1 million dollars from each. He is only twenty-eight years old and worked as a barber but says he's no longer able to work. He said many other Canadians also should sue the companies which sell products loaded with saturated fats, trans fats, salt, cholesterol, and other harmful dietary content. He says he wants to warn everyone of the adverse health effects that could cause obesity, diabetes, heart disease, high blood pressure, and elevated cholesterol levels. A spokesman for McDonalds, one of the companies he's suing, called the suit "frivolous." The other restaurants he's suing include Boston Pizza, Tim Horton's, and Burger King, since he says he ate at them an average of once or more a day.

6. Kimberley Mchalik, one of Ryerson's most prominent Sociologists, focuses on marriage and family life as her primary area of study. Today she spoke to 6000 delegates attending the national convention of the Association of University Women in Toronto and said: "As women age, more and more who never married or lose a spouse complain there are no good men left. But instead of griping, women should increase their pool of prospects. As women become more successful, independent, and confident, they're better able to dump societys old rules and create new ones. No longer are younger men out of the question. Each generation becomes more tolerant and progressive. Plus, men usually are the ones putting the moves on older women. What attracts them are the older womens accomplishments, sophistication, and self-assurance. And the fact that older women are looking much younger. You've got to realize that women now take much better care of themselves. We eat more healthfully, go to the gym, and spend more time taking care of ourselves. Sure, there can be problems. If the age difference is more than 10 or 15 years, it becomes a little edgy. As you approach a decades difference, you have men and women born in different social contexts that affect their attitudes about marriage and relationships. Whether these relationships work out generally depends on the individuals involved. Couples need to share common values and to figure out whether they're at the same stage of life. Differences in incomes, the desire for children, and decisions about when to retire can be problems. But couples who iron out those differences can go the distance."

CHAPTER 5

EXERCISE 5   Pro Challenge

Emphasizing the Unusual

Write only a lead for each of the following stories. As you write your leads, consult the checklist on page 79. A professional has been asked to write a lead for each of the stories, and these leads appear in a manual available to your instructor. You may find, however, that you like some of your own and your classmates' leads better. As you write the leads, emphasize stories' unusual details. Correct stories' spelling, style and vocabulary errors. Also, none of the possessives has been formed for you.

1. Scott Forsythe is 22 years old. He was killed in a car accident today. RCMP in your city say the accident occurred at about 8:45 AM this morning on Kirkmann Rd. Forsythe was driving a ford mustang. Police estimate the vehicle was traveling at least 160 km/hr. and witnesses told police it was passing slower traffic when a large dog walked into his path. As Forsythe veered to avoid the dog he lost control of his car and hit two trees and a fence before coming to a complete stop, police said. The accident occurred about a kilometre from the church where he was to be married to Sara Howard of 812 Bell Av. at 9:00 a.m. today He was alone in the vehicle. No one else was hurt.

2. Your city needs more money. Its in a financial crisis and trying to trim its expenses. So today city officials announced that every time someone is arrested and the police take mug shots and fingerprints, the jail will charge them $25 for the service. Local RCMP commandant Barry Kopperrud said he wants to make criminals pay a price for their actions. "They have to learn there's a cost for their behaviour," Kopperrud said today. "Decent citizens shouldn't have to pay for this. Let the crooks and other bad guys pay the full cost what it costs to arrest and incarcerate them." The fee will go into effect immediately but will be refunded to people who are arrested and later acquitted.

3. Larry Chavez, a constable with your citys RCMP detachment., went to a football game at Riel High School last Saturday to watch his son play at 2:00 PM. He then recognized a player on the opposing team, a sixteen-year-old from Colonial High School. Chevez arrested him several months ago for armed robbery. The youth is currently under house arrest yet allowed to play football. He robbed a pizza delivery woman at gunpoint. He was charged with armed robbery and released from juvenile detention under house arrest. He was ordered not to leave his house except to attend school, and an electronic bracelet was attached to his ankle. Still, Tony Guarino, coach of the Colonial High School football team, allows him to play for the team. "We just taped the bracelet up real good," Guarino said in an exclusive interview with you today. The constable was amazed, saying today, "I was amazed to see someone charged with an armed robbery playing on the field." School Supt. Gary Hubard said juveniles on home detention are allowed to participate in school functions and that students are not always suspended for crimes committed off campus.

4. There's been a national survey involving a random sample of the nations High School students. It contradicts many negative images or stereotypes. The survey of 2400 High School students paints a largely upbeat picture of Canadian teenagers, showing they are very directed, very motivated, very serious. When asked to rank various pressures:

    ■ 26% said the need to get good grades and go to university was a major problem.
    ■ 16% cited that a pressure to look a certain way was their major problem.
    ■ 15% cited financial problems.
    ■ 14% had a major problem getting along with their parents.
    ■ 12% cited pressure to do drugs or drink alcohol.
    ■ 10% spoke of pressure to have sex.
    ■ 9% listed loneliness and a feeling of being left out as their worst pressure.

    So overall, students said the greatest pressure in their lives was a pressure to take tough courses, earn high grades, score well on university-entrance exams and load their resumes with all sorts of athletic and extracurricular activities in an attempt to succeed in university and in life, according to researchers in the College of Education at the University of British Columbia in Vancouver, B.C.

6 Alternative Leads

*And I say to you that if you bring curiosity to your work it will cease to be merely a job and
become a door through which you enter the best that life has to give you.*

— **Robertson Davies, Canadian novelist, playwright, journalist and professor, 1974**

When the *Toronto Star*'s Peter Gorrie set out to cover a conference of Ban Asbestos
International, he didn't expect the resulting story to win a National Newspaper
Award. He wasn't even sure there was a story.

"Asbestos had been around for a long time," he said, "and I thought it was pretty much
a dead issue. So I went just with that level of curiosity … I wanted to see what was up." He
discovered a campaign by the federal and Quebec governments to "rehabilitate" the public
image of asbestos (from decidedly toxic to perfectly safe). He knew he'd need to figure out how
to frame the piece for readability and how to convey the complex and controversial history of
asbestos without drowning readers in information overload. Because of the sheer mass of information and the wealth of technical data to explain, he "wanted to make it simple and dramatic
without losing accuracy or perspective."

Gorrie is a consummate craftsman, but he says the asbestos story gave him trouble. "This
one drove me nuts.… I started it several different ways and I wasn't happy with any of them. It
was either obvious or dull or it got convoluted."

He knew the lead would be key and struggled with variations on a theme. Then came "the
heaven-sent arrival of the press release written on asbestos paper. As soon as I saw it, the lead
was in my head and the structure of the article finally started to emerge." He wrote:

> The jolt of fright came at the bottom of an information sheet sent to reporters.
> "This press release is printed on chrysotile paper."
> Why should that simple statement lead to nervous tremors?
> Because chrysotile is not just any old ingredient in paper. It's a form of asbestos.
> And asbestos is a convicted mass-killer, one of the most feared substances on Earth.
> (*Toronto Star*)

The lead that Gorrie wrote is an example of an alternative or "soft lead." Journalists
employ at least a dozen variations of soft leads, but most begin with a story's most interesting
details—often an anecdote, description, quotation or question. Stories with soft leads, which
may run four or five paragraphs, usually have a nut paragraph immediately after the lead. The
nut graf states the central point of the story and serves some of the same functions as the summary news lead.

Chapter 5 described basic summary news leads. Summary leads are more common than alternative leads—and probably easier to write. Writing an alternative lead requires thought and imagination: the ability to recognize and convey an interesting idea uniquely. It does not require an unusual story. In the following example, the lead first appears as a routine report about the first day of a smoking ban. The alternative lead captures the news better:

> TYPICAL SUMMARY: A new smoking ban that ends the use of parking lots and outdoor shelters by smokers took effect Monday.

> ALTERNATIVE LEAD: Terre King's Monday morning might have been rougher than just about anyone else's.
> Not only was it the first day in her 16 years at work that she couldn't light up, but as well her job required her to remind people at the entrance about the brand new no-smoking policy. (*Maryland Gazette*)

Here is another example in which creativity lends freshness to a story about a young man waiting for a heart transplant:

> Kyle Bennett poured his heart into becoming this year's valedictorian at his high school. Now the 18-year-old honours student is patiently awaiting a new one. (*Houston Chronicle*)

Good reporters can write many kinds of leads, choosing the appropriate one for each story. This versatility allows reporters to avoid the trap of blindly following a particular formula in newswriting. Although summary leads are effective for many stories, alternative leads allow reporters to stretch the boundaries of their creativity.

Even stories that at first appear minor can provide the impetus and opportunity for alternative leads. Gorrie said he "reworked and reworked" the first section of his asbestos story. "I took stuff out and put stuff in and moved it around. Unless I'm on a tight deadline, I spend a lot of time writing and rewriting. That's actually one of my favourite parts of the job."

Having acted as the editor for the *Toronto Star*'s Insight section, Gorrie had worked closely with reporters on their feature stories. "One thing I tried to instil was that it's actually fun to do it: if it's not right the first time, it's not a big deal. In fact, the reshaping and working at it can be as much fun as doing the research."

Appropriateness is important when considering the use of alternative leads, whose range depends on both the nature of the publication and the self-imposed stylistic restraints of the writer.

When reporters finish a story, their editors expect it to be well-written: clear, concise, accurate and interesting. If a story meets these criteria, editors are unlikely to object if its lead uses an alternative form. Nor are they likely to object to a summary lead that creatively and freshly captures the essence of a story.

On Boxing Day 2005, Toronto shoppers and passersby were caught in the crossfire of two rival gangs on a busy stretch of the city's arterial Yonge Street. The gun fight involved about a dozen young men; during their violent confrontation, seven people (four males and three females) were shot. The single fatality was 15-year-old Jane Glenn Creba, who'd been out shopping with her mother and sister. The *Globe and Mail*, *National Post*, and *Toronto Star* all covered the incident. The *Globe and Mail* used a summary lead; the *National Post* and *Toronto Star* used alternative leads that tried to embed the story in the context of growing gang and gun violence in Canada's largest city. Here are the leads from the three stories:

> Jane Creba, the bright and athletic 15-year-old killed in the Boxing Day shootings on Yonge Street, wandered into the midst of the gunfire that suddenly erupted. (*Globe and Mail*)

(CP PHOTO/Toronto Star–David Cooper)

Schoolmates of Jane Creba cry together at a makeshift memorial outside a store on Yonge Street in Toronto on Thursday, December 29, 2005. The 15-year-old Creba was struck by a stray bullet while taking advantage of Boxing Day sales with her family.

Three weeks before she died, 15-year-old Jane Creba was listening to the same song over and over again.

On the Web log she kept, like many 15-year-old girls, to communicate with friends, Jane professed her love for the ballad Goodbye My Lover by the British songwriter James Blunt. "I really cannot stop listening to it," she wrote in a brief missive posted on Dec. 2 before signing off: "That's it for now and maybe forever."

Police confirmed yesterday that the Grade 10 student of Riverdale Collegiate Institute was killed on Boxing Day while shopping with her mother, Virginia Creba, and sister, Alison, along a crowded section of Yonge Street. (*National Post*)

"I love you Jane and I'm going to miss you 'til the cows come home. I hope you know that everyone loves you . . . you of all people do not deserve this, and I hope those guys burn in hell."

OXOX, Best Friend Forever, Adelaide

There was no time to say goodbye.

Instead, Adelaide's parting words to Jane Creba, the 15-year-old sports star gunned down near the Eaton Centre on Boxing Day, were in an emotional letter. (*Toronto Star*)

CRITICISMS

During the 1960s, large Canadian daily newspapers like the *Globe and Mail* and the *Toronto Star* began to push the envelope on newswriting style and experiment with new and emerging forms such as the soft lead. The *Globe and Mail* led the way, earning itself a reputation as a "writer's newspaper." Since then, other Canadian dailies have given their reporters more freedom to experiment with their writing. Proponents of soft leads say what matters is whether the lead works, not whether it is hard or soft. They disparage the traditional summaries as "suitcase leads." In the past, they explain, newspapers tried to jam too many details into leads, like a traveller trying to jam too many clothes into a suitcase. They say summary leads are unnatural and deter reporters from writing good stories. They further explain that summary leads eliminate the possibility of surprise and make all stories sound alike.

The more literary style of soft lead also may help newspapers compete with television. The style's proponents concede that television can report the news more quickly than newspapers, but by using soft leads and other literary techniques, newspapers can also make their stories more interesting.

Critics call the use of alternative leads "Jell-O Journalism." They complain that soft leads are inappropriate for most news stories: too arty, literary, dangerous and unprofessional. Critics add that soft leads are too long and fail to emphasize the news. If a story begins with several paragraphs of description or quotations, for example, its most important details may be buried in a later paragraph.

The following example illustrates how poorly constructed alternative leads can confuse readers and make them impatient. You have to read more than 145 words before getting to the news—the main point—of the story:

> Eleanor Lago considers herself an intelligent, educated woman.
>
> She's read the information provided her by the Grand Rapids Township Board. She's talked to friends and neighbours. And she intends to vote Tuesday in a special election that could determine the township's future.
>
> "I just want to do what's best," says Lago.
>
> Like many residents, though, she's not sure what that is.
>
> An unusual battle is being fought in this smallest of Kent County townships, a raggedy-shaped 16 square miles set cheek to jowl against the cities of Grand Rapids, East Grand Rapids, and Kentwood.
>
> The battle is not about zoning, the more typical flash point of local politics. Nor is it about leaf burning ordinances or other grassroots laws in this suburb of nearly 11,000 people.
>
> This battle is about what the community can do to keep from being nibbled to pieces by annexation.

The writer's intention was good: describing an intelligent voter who is confused about an important issue. The introduction would have been more effective, however, if it had been cut in half. The writer could have eliminated some description, cut the clichés, and avoided saying what the election was *not* about.

The following sections describe different types of alternative leads and offer examples of each.

"DELAYED" LEADS

A "delayed" lead is the most common type of alternative lead. Typically, a delayed lead begins with an interesting example or anecdote that sets a story's theme. Then a nut graf—perhaps the third or fourth paragraph—summarizes the story and provides a transition to the body. The nut graf states the central point of the story and moves it from a single example or anecdote to the general issue or problem. Like a traditional lead, it summarizes the topic. In addition, it may explain why the topic is important.

Here are two examples of delayed leads. The first is by Lindsay Kines, writing one of the earliest stories in the case of women going missing from Vancouver's notorious Downtown Eastside, a case that ended with a conviction in what is now known as the worst case of serial killing in Canadian history. The second is by Lori Culbert, writing a feature about one of the missing women several years later:

> VANCOUVER—Every night, women stop at the WISH drop-in centre on East Hastings before going out to work the streets.
>
> And most nights, Joanna Russell gives them each a hug and, like a police staff sergeant to departing troops, urges them to be careful out there.
>
> "And every night when they leave the centre, we're at a point, or at least I am," Russell says, " ... where we wonder who we're not going to see tomorrow."
>
> With each passing month, the list of the disappeared continues to grow. Vancouver city police have 20 outstanding files on missing "street-involved" women since 1995—11 from last year alone.

VANCOUVER—A girl and her father play together outside their house.

It is the summer of 1962.

The father is Ernest Albert Crey, 57, a former hard-rock miner and hard-drinking logger. He gave up booze to build a better life for his family and moved them, here, to a new home in Hope.

The girl is the fourth of seven children. Dawn Teresa. She is three years old and plump, with brown eyes and raven hair. A beautiful child.

When her father falls to the ground, she screams for her mother to come and help. Then she holds her father's head in her lap as he dies.

The father's health had been failing, his heart weak.

But the little girl will always blame herself, will always think that she should have gone to get help right away, should have run inside and got her mom sooner.

That picture, the one of her father dying in her arms, will haunt her for the rest of her life.

Her father's death will do worse than that, however; it will tear apart her family, chase her mother back to the bottle, and scatter her brothers and sisters to a series of foster homes in the Fraser Valley.

For years, they will pass each other like ghosts on the streets of Chilliwack. They will lose and find one another, and then lose each other again, until, finally, searching for family becomes the shared narrative of their lives.

In the end, some of them will survive, grow to be native leaders and healers. Others will spiral into despair and drugs and, eventually, death.

Dawn will disappear.

Then Culbert proceeds to the nut graf of the story:

She will drift into drugs and prostitution, endure having acid thrown in her face and, finally, in late 2000, at age 43, she will join the ranks of 45 women missing from Vancouver's Downtown Eastside.

The delayed lead can introduce a complex or abstract problem by showing how the problem affects a single individual—someone readers may know or identify with. Or an anecdote can illustrate a problem and arouse readers' interest in the topic.

Some delayed leads surprise their readers with an unusual twist. If a story is only three or four paragraphs long, journalists may save the twist for the last line. If a story is longer, they use the twist to lure readers to the nut graf, which then provides a transition to the following paragraphs.

MULTI-PARAGRAPH LEADS

Other newswriters think of a lead as a unit of thought. Their summary leads consist of two or three paragraphs that flow into each other as if they were one:

CARLISLE—It didn't take Mark Toigo and Jay Shettel long to realize they had bought an aerodynamic pile of junk.

They had paid $75,000 to a West Coast aircraft broker who'd advertised the early 1950s Grumman Albatross amphibious plane on the Internet auction site eBay.

It was a sight-unseen deal.

Toigo, of Shippensburg, and Shettel, of Carlisle, didn't get a good look at the Albatross until they ventured to a Brazilian air force base outside Sao Paolo, where the venerable old bird was roosting.

The Albatross was grimy, beaten-up, partially scavenged and anything but airworthy.

"Right away, we named her 'Dirty Girl,'" Toigo said.

Four years and about $500,000 worth of work later, Dirty Girl still needs a final face-lift, but she flies. (*Patriot-News* [Harrisburg, Pa.])

No one would begrudge Rite Fletcher a comfy retirement.

Though only 52, she has taught chemistry for 31 years in Salisbury, Md. She could have retired without regret last year after 30 years in the classroom.

But when Fletcher saw what it would cost her and her self-employed husband for health insurance—nearly half of her $1,780 monthly pension—she signed on for another year. "People say, 'Oh, you could retire,' and I say, 'Only if I didn't need food, shelter or health care.'"

As more teachers look ahead to retirement, many are finding themselves in Fletcher's shoes. Benefits they took for granted, such as health care, are becoming prohibitively expensive, both for them and their school districts. (*USA Today*)

USING QUOTATIONS

Reporters usually avoid using quotations in leads. Sources generally do not provide quotes that meet three criteria for leads: (1) they summarize the entire story (not just part of it); (2) they are brief; and (3) they are self-explanatory. Some editors prohibit the use of quotation leads because they lack clarity and are often too long and complicated. As with the use of any quotation in a story, the source's statement should be so effective that the reporter cannot improve it. When used in the first line of a story, a quotation also must tell the reader the point of the story:

> "I wanted to slam the plane into a mountain so I could die with my husband," said Betty Smith, whose husband died at its controls. But then she thought of her children on the ground.
>
> "Our children can't read, add or find countries on a map," the award-winning teacher said Wednesday.

If a quotation is only sensational, then it fails to satisfy the criteria for a lead. It may be suitable to use elsewhere in the story, however. Reporters have other ways of writing leads that will startle readers or grab their attention. Remember that the lead provides the organization for the rest of the story. If the quotation does not lead readers into and set the stage for the rest of the story, then it will only confuse and discourage them. Even within the body of a story, a quotation should be brief. In the lead, brevity is a virtue because a complicated, long quotation will raise unnecessary questions.

Avoid quotations that begin with words needing identification or explanation, words like "he," "she," "we," "they," "it," "that" and "this." If such words open a story, readers have no way of knowing to whom or what the words refer. When the subject's identity is revealed later in a story, readers may have to reread the quotation to understand its meaning.

Leads using a quotation often can be rewritten with a brief introduction to enhance clarity:

> "The water was rising so fast and the bank was so muddy and slippery I just didn't think I could get away from that torrent of water." That's how a Winnipeg man described his ordeal just before rescue workers used a utility truck to pluck him out of a tree he had climbed to escape a flash flood during Monday night's thunderstorms.
>
> REVISED: A Winnipeg man who was rescued from a tree he had climbed to escape a flash flood Monday night said, "The water was so fast and the bank was so muddy and slippery I just didn't think I could get away from that torrent of water."

USING QUESTIONS

Questions can make effective leads. Some editors, though, prohibit question leads because they believe news stories should answer questions, not ask them. Question leads often run the risk of being clichés.

To be effective, question leads must be brief, simple, specific and provocative. The question should contain no more than a dozen words. Moreover, readers should feel absolutely compelled to answer it. Avoid questions if the readers' responses may discourage them from continuing with the story:

> Are you interested in nuclear physics?

A few readers might be interested in nuclear physics, but many would think the story too complicated. This question lead also fails because readers can answer "yes" or "no," possibly ending the reader's interest in the story.

A question should concern a controversial issue that readers are familiar with and that interests and affects them. Avoid abstract or complicated questions requiring a great deal of explanation.

The following question is ineffective because it is too abstract, long and complicated. Moreover, it fails to ask about issues that everyone is certain to care about:

> If you were on vacation miles from your house and you thought the mechanics at a service station deliberately damaged your car, then demanded an exorbitant fee to repair it, would you be willing to file criminal charges against the mechanics and return to the area to testify at their trial?

The following questions also fail, but for different reasons. The first question asks about an issue unlikely to concern most readers. The second question is unanswerable and flippant, treating a serious topic as a trivial one:

> Have you thought lately about going to prison?
> Someone was swindled today. Who'll be swindled tomorrow?

The following questions make more effective leads. Notice that immediately after asking a question, the reporter answers it:

> GAINSVILLE—How much is an inch of height worth? Nearly $900 a year in salary, a new study finds. (*Associated Press*)

> Could this be the end of cereal aisle showdowns between parents and sweet-toothed tots?
> New reduced-sugar versions of popular children's breakfast cereals—everything from Fruit Loops to Frosted Flakes—certainly sound promising, but consumers might want to hold off chiming in when Tony the Tiger says, "They're Gr-r-reat!" (*Associated Press*)

SUSPENSEFUL LEADS

Some reporters write leads to create suspense, arouse readers' curiosity, or raise a question in their minds. By hinting at some mysterious development explained in a later paragraph, this type of lead compels readers to finish a story:

> It is the fire bell that signals the beginning of each firefighter's day.
> It is the same bell that summons firefighters to action.
> And it is the same bell that marks their last alarm. (*Desert Sun* [Palm Springs, Calif.])

> It is difficult to run a successful business when you keep losing half of your work force year after year.
> Just ask James Griffe—or any other beekeeper. (*Patriot News* [Harrisburg, Pa.])

The first story focused on the deaths of several firefighters. The second story reported on the economic devastation an insect parasite was causing for beekeepers.

DESCRIPTIVE LEADS

Other leads begin with descriptive details that paint a picture for the reader before moving gradually into the action. The description should be colourful and interesting so that it arouses readers' interest. The description should also help to summarize the story.

The following examples show the effectiveness of descriptive leads. Notice the use of concrete images and active verbs in the first lead: "sirens wail," "lights strobe," and "vehicles speed."

> Sirens wail in the night. Emergency lights strobe red and blue through the windows as a Lincoln Navigator and Ford Crown Victoria rush through a red light in the city's northwest, the cars ahead of them slowing, pulling to the curb. The big black vehicles speed past, straddling the solid yellow center lines. (*Washington Post*)

> Parkinson's disease worked on Goldie Maurer like a slow-moving robber, taking away things one at a time.
> Baling hay. Birthing calves. Working the controls of a John Deere tractor.
> Each lost activity seemed to pull Maurer further from what she was—a Midwestern-born farm girl, raised in the 1920s on a farm near tiny Lena, Ill.
> The tremors and faulty sense of balance started 25 years ago, long after Maurer moved from Illinois to a farm in northern Dauphin County.
> First, she surrendered garden chores, such as tending strawberry and potato plants. Then, she had to give up handling equipment, such as riding a snowmobile to far-flung parts of her farm.
> It was the tremors, she said. (*Patriot News* [Harrisburg, Pa.])

The second lead sets the scene and provides background details for a feature story about a woman and her husband who suffer from Parkinson's disease. The focus of the story is the doctor who treats them and the relationship his father, who was also a physician, had with Maurer's family as their doctor many years before.

SHOCKERS—LEADS WITH A TWIST

Reporters like "shockers"—startling leads that immediately capture the attention of readers. The following examples have an unusual twist that adds to their effectiveness:

> APOKA—Every night, when Twanyetta Jones puts her 1-year-old son, Terry Jr., to bed, she has to stuff cotton balls in his ears.
> It keeps the cockroaches from crawling in them. (*Orlando [Fla.] Sentinel*)

> MANAGUA, Nicaragua—She had been raped. She was pregnant. And she was poor.
> And Rosa was 9. That gave her one more reason to want an abortion. (*Los Angeles Times*)

IRONIC LEADS

Closely related to shockers are leads that present a startling or ironic contrast. The use of striking details is likely to arouse readers' curiosity:

> For months, second-year high school student Sara Corbett had begged her mother for permission to get her tongue pierced. On Aug. 7, 2004, Sara's mother, Robin DeBaise, relented and the two went to a nearby mall.
> The next day, Sara, 16, was in severe pain. At her aunt's house, she found a couple of methadone pills—amounting to twice the recommended dosage—and took them. She passed out and was rushed to a hospital, where she died. (*USA Today*)

When union activist Oliver French goes on trial today on charges of killing two auto plant colleagues and wounding two others, he likely will be portrayed as the victim. (*Detroit News*)

DIRECT-ADDRESS LEADS

Reporters occasionally use a form of direct address, speaking directly to their readers:

PHOENIX—Picture this scenario. You're walking along when you notice a poster for a Springsteen concert. "The Boss is coming here!!!???" So you grab your cell phone, aim it at a bar code on the poster, and are wirelessly connected to an online ticket agent. (*USA Today*)

If you just spent another Valentine's Day alone and lonely, the state of Maryland can hook you up. (*Baltimore Sun*)

WORDS USED IN UNUSUAL WAYS

If you are clever and have a good imagination (or a good grasp of literature), you can use a common word or phrase in an uncommon way:

Sufferin' succotash—Sylvester had better stay home. An impending vote could pave the way for legally shooting stray cats. (*USA Today*)

Perhaps it was God's joke on a newly ordained priest when the Rev. Jim Farnan, former class clown and no stranger to the detention room, was asked to speak with the occasional clone of his former self at Our Lady of Fatima School. (*Pittsburgh Post-Gazette*)

This style is difficult, because what seems funny or clever to one person may seem corny or silly to another. Also, the subjects may be too serious for such a light touch:

Oakland County Prosecutor Richard Thompson wants to be known by the criminals he keeps. (*Detroit Free Press*)

The story was about the high costs a prosecutor was creating by refusing to plea bargain with criminals.

OTHER UNUSUAL LEADS

The following leads are difficult to categorize. All the leads are unusual yet effective. Notice their simplicity, brevity and clarity. Also, notice the leads' emphasis on the interesting and unusual. The first lead introduces a story describing the effects of unusually cold weather on the economy. The second lead reports the death of actor Audrey Hepburn, who played Eliza Doolittle in the movie *My Fair Lady*. The third lead introduces the man in charge of demolishing Three Rivers Stadium in Pittsburgh, Pa.

WASHINGTON—Jack Frost is nipping at our growth. (*Wall Street Journal*)

Audrey Hepburn was the fairest lady of them all. (*Detroit News*)

Circuses have ringmasters. Military boot camps have drill sergeants. The Three Rivers Stadium implosion has Greg Yesko, who's a bit of both. (*Pittsburgh Post-Gazette*)

The Writing Coach

SOME TIPS FOR TIGHTER SENTENCES

1. Re-read your story, focusing on making sentences shorter.
2. Look for clutter. Remove redundant or unnecessary words that add nothing to understanding the sentence or the story. (Examples: end result; completely destroyed; total number; serious threat.)
3. Read your story aloud to see if you stumble over words or phrases. If so, rephrase.
4. On deadline, keep those periods handy as a quick-fix for long sentences.
5. Remember: If you give readers a long sentence, treat them to a short one.
6. Reduce attribution. If you know something to be true, no need to attribute. If it's clear to readers whom you are quoting (because of an earlier reference), no need for attribution.
7. Use active verbs.
8. Choose short, simple words instead of long, difficult words.
9. Avoid little qualifiers (very, extremely, quite, rather). From Strunk and White: "These are the leeches that infest the pond of prose, sucking the blood of words." Wow ... heavy stuff!
10. Rewrite, rewrite, rewrite is to a journalist what location, location, location is to a real estate agent.
11. Beware of dashes and brackets. If they make sentences too long, consider a separate sentence.
12. Read *The Elements of Style* (Strunk and White), *On Writing Well* (Zinsser), or any other favourite book on writing just to remind you of the pitfalls and to encourage you to strive for better writing.

Source: "Keep those periods handy. Give your readers a fighting chance. Keep sentences short, and limit them to one idea," by Don Gibb, Ryerson University.

Don Gibb is Professor Emeritus of the Ryerson University School of Journalism. Retired since 2009, he continues to conduct seminars and one-on-one coaching at newspapers across Canada. He is a visiting writing coach at the *Globe and Mail*. He can be reached at dgibb@ryerson.ca

SUGGESTED READINGS AND USEFUL WEBSITES

Benedetti, Paul. 2009. "Kick Start." In Ivor Shapiro, ed., *The Bigger Picture: Elements of Feature Writing*, 206–7. Toronto: Emond-Montgomery Publications.

Berton, Pierre. 2003. "Storytelling." In *The Joy of Writing: A Guide for Writers Disguised as a Literary Memoir*, 219–68. Toronto: Doubleday Canada.

Bloom, Stephen G. 2002. *Inside the Writer's Mind: Writing Narrative Journalism*. Wiley-Blackwell.

Cumming, Carman, and Catherine McKercher. 1994. "Writing technique." In *The Canadian Reporter: News Writing and Reporting*, 97–120. Toronto: Harcourt Brace Canada.

Farr, Moira, and Ian Pearson. 2009. *Cabin Fever: The Best New Canadian Non-Fiction*. Banff Centre Literary Journalism Program. Markham, ON: Thomas Allen Publishers.

———. 2003. *Word Carving: The Craft of Literary Journalism*. Banff, AB: Banff Centre Press.

Purdue Online Writing Lab: http://owl.english.purdue.edu

Canadian Association of Newspaper Editors (CANE): http://www.cane.ca

15 Steps to Writing the Perfect Lead (adapted from Don Gibb's booklet *Writing the Perfect Lead*: www.cane.ca (See under "Editorial Tips")

Don Gibb's 18 Quick Tips on Lead Writing: http://www.cane.ca/english/me_res_18leadtips.htm

CHAPTER 6

EXERCISE 1   Alternative Leads

Evaluating Alternative Leads

Critically evaluate the following leads, each of which uses one of the alternative forms discussed in this chapter. Select the best leads and explain why they succeed. Point out the flaws in the remaining leads. As you evaluate the leads, look for lessons—dos and don'ts—that you can apply to your own work.

1. Are you ready for a big change?
2. "I saw the train coming at us, and I knew it would never get stopped."
3. No shirt! No shoes! No service!

    Unfortunately, the 350-pound black bear that wandered into the city limits and pried open a window to break into the Oakhill Restaurant couldn't read. The bear was captured by wildlife officers after it had ransacked the restaurant's kitchen and helped itself to a variety of treats.
4. Amy Clauch sat beside the rough-hewn pine fence, her fingers rubbing the worn knuckles of the knots in the rope she held in her hand.

    The sweet scent of clover hay wafted on the light breeze that blew through the barn. She sucked in a deep breath and held it. The scent lingered. She wished it always would.

    The sun hung in the early morning cobalt blue sky like a spotlight in a theatre, illuminating her, the actor on this stage. This is where she wanted to be—free from the confines of the four pale beige walls that surrounded her in clinical sterility for months.

    She tugged at her jeans. Her lips pursed. "You can do this," she whispered in prayer to herself.

    Clauch rocked the wheelchair to the left and reached for the stirrup hanging limply from the saddle. Pulling herself upright, she grimaced as she felt the braces tighten on her legs. The muscles in her arms clenched as she pulled herself into the saddle. The chestnut mare flinched at the load, and Clauch grabbed the worn leather saddle horn to steady herself. Her smile stretched her cheeks to their limit. She was back where she belonged.

    It had been eight months since a riding accident left Clauch temporarily paralyzed from the waist down.
5. Too much work. Too many demands. Too many responsibilities. Not enough time.

    Stress is killing Canadians, the Canadian Medical Association said in a report released Monday.
6. Should high school students have to take a competency test before receiving their diplomas?
7. The province's motorcycle riders won the right today to have the wind in their hair and bugs in their teeth. The provincial legislature passed a bill eliminating the province's helmet requirements for riders 18 and older.
8. How much would you pay for, say, a triple heart bypass? Or gall bladder surgery? As government officials struggle to rein in health care costs without sacrificing the quality of care, they find themselves confronted with the question of who should pay how much.
9. "If we can't solve the budget crisis today, the students of tomorrow will suffer the consequences," school superintendent Gary Hubbard said about the government's failure to pass a budget before the start of the school year.
10. The Freedonia County Fair begins today, and if you want to catch all the action this week, you better get to the fairgrounds.
11. Billy Lee Anderson pushes the blond hair away from his blue eyes, exposing the dusting of freckles on his forehead.

    The 12-year-old sits in a chair that is a bit too adult for his small frame, his feet, clad in gleaming white athletic shoes, dangling several inches above the floor.

    There is an air of innocence surrounding the boy that will make it hard for any jury to believe that he could have set the fire that killed his parents and baby sister. But that is what prosecutors will attempt to do as Anderson's murder trial gets underway today.

12. You're driving down a tree-shaded city street when a child runs out from between two parked cars. Could you stop in time?

13. Thompsontown hit a grand slam over the weekend as all four of its Little League teams won their championship games.

14. When Jim and Suzanne Baker left the mall, they were loaded down with Christmas presents and laughing about the surprises they had in store for their children. Half an hour later, they were dead.

15. It actually was a dark and stormy night when Sharon Murphy sat down in front of her typewriter to start writing her first novel.

16. A 60-year-old Montreal man who was rescued Monday from a burning building said, "I could hear the sirens of the fire trucks, but they just seemed so far away. I decided that I needed to make peace with the fact that I was going to die."

CHAPTER 6

EXERCISE 2   Alternative Leads

Writing Alternative Leads

Using techniques you studied in this chapter, write an alternative lead for each of the following stories. You may want to use complete or partial quotations, questions, descriptions, delayed leads, multi-paragraph leads, suspense, or chronological order. Or you may want to try a shocking lead, ironic lead, direct-address lead, or a word used in an unusual way. Correct any errors you find.

1. A group of ecologists and biologists at your university and other schools have come up with a unique idea. They want to transplant African wildlife to the Great Plains of North America. Julie Allen, 1504 Lincoln Drive, is an associate professor of biology at your university. She had this to say about the idea, "I think it would be wonderful to drive across the Great Plains and see lions and elephants and giraffes roaming the prairie." The idea was developed by more than 30 scientists as a way to perpetuate species that are slowly facing extinction because of declining habitat in Africa. The scientists say there is plenty of room left in the American West for these types of animals. Relocating the animals could help them increase their numbers. The plan is being criticized by ranchers, developers and other scientists, who say that it would be difficult to introduce animals to a place they had never lived. Ranchers, such as Jim Smithson, who lives in North Dakota and is vice president of the Western Stockman's Association, claims such a move would devastate the regions cattle industry. "How many steers or dairy cows can a pride of lions eat in a week?" Smithson said. Supporters of the idea say the animals they want to relocate would be held in large game parks or private reserves. They would not be allowed to roam free. Other critics say the transplanting of alien creatures could have devastating effects on native creatures. The animals being brought to places they have never lived could introduce new diseases or could destroy native wildlife. In addition, taking wildlife from Africa could hurt the tourist trade on that continent.

2. It was an intense situation for police Wednesday afternoon. It was an adventure for the six-month-old daughter of Michael and Ethel Perakiss of 876 Collins Street. Everything ended OK, police said. Megan Perakiss, the daughter of Michael and Ethel, was in the back seat of a 2006 Ford Explorer sport utility vehicle when it was carjacked by a man who had just held up the convenience store where Ethel had stopped to get gas. The robbery of the Quik Shoppe convenience store at 2752 Michigan Avenue occurred shortly after 2 p.m., according to Police Chief Barry Kopperud. Kopperud said the suspect walked into the store and waved a handgun in the face of Edwin C. Jimenez, manager of the store. He ordered Jimenez to empty the cash register into a cloth bag he threw on the counter and threatened to shoot him if he did not. The thief made off with an undetermined amount of money. Megan was unaware of what was going on. Police said Ethel pulled into the convenience store to get fuel and had just finished pumping the gas when the robber ran from the store and pushed her away from the vehicle. Reports of the carjacking sparked a massive, multi-agency search for Megan that at one point included nearly two dozen units from the city's police force. Ethel Perakiss left her keys in the ignition while she was filling the fuel tank. Police described the armed robbery and carjacking suspect as a 6 foot 1 inch tall white male in his early to mid-20s wearing a white T-shirt and long black pants. He had short, neatly cropped hair. "My baby's in the back seat," Perakiss shouted as the carjacker drove away. About 40 minutes after the ordeal began, Kopperuud said, police officers spotted the missing vehicle abandoned in the parking lot of a Chinese restaurant with Megan inside. The carjacker apparently had fled, leaving the vehicle unlocked and running with the air conditioner on. Police said they were shocked but pleased that the incident ended so quickly and without harm to the child.

3. It's a unique idea. School board members and school administrators in your local school district are considering changing the school week to cut costs. The province announced that

it does not have enough money to fund schools because of the slow economy and schools will have to cut their budgets. Superintendent of schools Gary Hubbard told school board members at Monday night's meeting that the district has cut all the fat out of the budget that it can. "We've cut out after-school programs and eliminated all but the essential teacher's aides positions," Hubbard said. "We've even raised the price of school lunches, but we are still coming up short." Hubbard and school board members are proposing to go to a four-day school week to help the district save money. The school day, which now runs from 8 a.m. to 2:30 p.m., would be lengthened by two hours, running from 8 a.m. to 4:30 p.m. to make up for the loss of one day during the week. Hubbard and the board say the district could save more then one million dollars in transportation, food service, and janitorial costs. The board voted 7–0 in favour of the proposal.

4.   Your city officials received a gift on Tuesday. Attorney Richard Cycler handed a check for over $2 million to Mayor Sabrina Datolli. The money will be used to build the Willie Hattaway Centre in an annex of city hall. Plans to develop the annex into a community centre, senior citizens centre, a historical exhibit hall, and meeting and conference rooms had been postponed for several years because of a lack of funds to complete the project. The city had built the annex with money from a federal grant but could not raise enough money to complete the project. The building has been an empty shell for more than seven years. City officials were using the space to store boxes of old water bills and other papers. Willie Hattaway gave the money to the city in his will. Hattaway died last year. He was 98. He was a widower. His wife, Estelle, died 10 years ago. Everyone, including his neighbours, was surprised that Willie had that much money in the bank. Willie lived in a modest two-story, white clapboard house on Virginia Avenue for more than 60 years. Flowers surrounded the house. Hattaway loved to work in his garden and flower beds. He was particularly fond of roses and grew several assorted varieties. He had entered Sunnyview Retirement Home on Wisconsin Avenue last year, shortly after his 97th birthday. Neighbours said he could no longer take care of himself after he fell and broke his hip. Neighbours said Hattaway drove a car that was 40 years old and never travelled very far from home. The car, a green Chevrolet Impala, is still parked in the garage. Hattaway did not want to sell the car even though he had not been driving since he was 90. He enjoyed sitting on his porch and talking to neighbours or giving neighbourhood children treats of candy or fruit. He did not live extravagantly. "It just goes to show that you never really know your neighbours. Willie was such a wonderful, friendly gentleman. He was so generous with his time helping neighbours and playing with the neighbourhood children. It doesn't surprise me that he would be so generous with his money, too," said a former neighbour Marilyn Boudinot, 41, of 4340 Virginia Ave. Hattaway and his wife had no children. He was a retired construction worker who had invested his money in the stock market for many years.

EXERCISE 3   Pro Challenge

Writing Alternative Leads

Write an alternative lead for each of the following stories, correcting any errors.

1. It was just another car theft in your city. Police were startled when the car thief called them and told them where he would be leaving the vehicle. The vehicle in question was a white 2003 Chevrolet cargo van. The van belonged to Hertz Rent A Car car rental agency. Chief of police Barry Kopperud said the man who stole the van was frantic when he called police around 11 p.m. Thursday. "He jumped in that van and roared off. He didn't know he had a passenger," Kopperud said. Police said the van was stolen while it was parked in front of a residence in the 4000 block of New Orleans Ave. It was stolen at 9:35 p.m. The driver of the van said he was in the residence talking to the homeowner when he heard the door of the van slam shut and the engine being gunned. By the time he got to the front door, the van was speeding down the street. The driver said he had left the keys in the van because he only had to get some paperwork he left in the residence. The van had been rented earlier in the day by Parsons Funeral Home. A spokesperson for the funeral home said both hearses they normally used were in the shop being repaired and the funeral home rented the van to pick up bodies during the day until the hearses were repaired. The driver of the van, William Thomas, 38, of 2838 Vermont Ave, an employee of Parsons Funeral Home, said he was at the residence picking up the body of an elderly man who had died that evening. Thomas was talking to the son of the man who died when the van was stolen from in front of the son's house. The man who stole the van called police to tell them he had just stolen the van he was driving, but he didn't know anything about the body in the back of the van. He said he had nothing to do with the man's death. Police recovered the van shortly after midnight in the 3000 block of Eastland Drive. They believe the thief must have gotten curious about what was in the big black bag in the back of the van because the body bag was partially unzipped when police opened the back of the van.

2. Its an idea that many people are praising. Beginning next year, aspiring doctors will have to take a test. The National Board of Medical Examiners created the examination. The exam will be required of all medical students who want to practise medicine in the United States. While clinical skills are already tested, this examination will test the would-be doctors' bedside manner. Medical students will be required to examine 20 people who will have fictional illnesses. The "patients" will be trained to act like they are sick and complain of various symptoms. They will be trained to test the students' patience and communication skills, such as how they listen to the patient and how well or thoroughly they question the patient. Each of the fictional patients will be examined for 15 minutes. After the examination, they will fill out a report on how the would-be doctor handled the examination. The test will cost $1000 and students will have to travel to major cities, where test sites will be set up. Students who fail the test will be able to repeat the test after 90 days. During that time the students who fail will be offered counselling in developing better people skills.

3. Patricia Richard, 23, of 42 Tusca Trail, got married Saturday. It was a lovely ceremony. Her new husband is Grady Smith, 22, of 8213 Peach Street. Richards was arrested Saturday night and charged with disturbing the peace, criminal mischief, simple assault, and resisting arrest. Police handcuffed Richards and put her in jail. She was released Sunday and left for her honeymoon on Monday after posting a $25,000 bond. Richards said it was all a misunderstanding. The reception was held at the Downtown Club at the intersection of Washington and Virginia avenues. More than 200 guests had been invited to the reception. When the reception dinner was served, it was discovered that the wrong meal had been prepared. Instead of having prime rib au jus and salmon almondine as entries, the reception party was served baked ham and stuffed chicken breasts. Richards said she had already paid the bill and wanted a refund. She got into an argument with Walter Morton, the manager of food service at the Downtown Club. Richards picked up a stuffed chicken

breast and threw it at Morton, striking him in the face. She then grabbed a serving plate of ham and threw it at a waiter. The waiter picked up some of the ham and threw it back at Richards. The ham struck Richards in the chest. Grady Smith tried to stop Richards, to calm her down, and Richards struck him on the head with a serving platter. Richards began throwing food and wine glasses at other waiters and waitresses. By the time police arrived, Richards was throwing hunks of her wedding cake at Morton and staff members of the Downtown Club. Several officers were struck by cake when they tried to take Richards into custody. Richards kicked one of the officers during the struggle. Police said alcohol was a factor in the incident.

4.   There was an attempted burglary at the Wendys Old Fashion Hamburgers restaurant, 1853 Huron Ave. The attempted burglary occurred between 2 a.m. and 8 a.m. Tuesday. Police said the burglary was discovered by the store manager, Jenna Adams, 31, of 550 S. Highland Ave. Police said the burglar attempted to enter the fast-food restaurant through the drive-thru window on the north side of the building. Adams is the day manager. She usually arrives at work around 8 a.m. to begin preparations for the restaurants opening at 11 a.m. Police said her normal routine is to go directly to her office located behind the cooking and serving area of the restaurant. Adams told police she did not notice anything unusual when she first entered the restaurant. Nothing seemed to be missing. About 30 minutes after arriving at the restaurant, Adams heard a noise. She said it sounded like a whimpering animal. She began to look around the restaurant to locate the noise. What she found shocked her. A man was stuck in the drive-thru window of the restaurant. His belt and a belt loop of his pants were hooked on a metal peg used to open and close the window. The upper half of his body was inside the restaurant and the lower half was outside the restaurant, his feet dangling a foot off the ground. Adams said the man apparently had been hanging there for hours. Adams called police and officers managed to free the burglar. Police charged the suspect, Thomas C. Ahl, 19, of 2634 6th Street, Apartment 382, with burglary and indecent exposure. Ahl had torn the seat of his trousers while trying to free himself from his predicament. "I surrender. Now please get me out of here," Ahl said when police arrived at the restaurant.

7

The Body of a News Story

Once we figure out how the dice are made, we may be able to figure out who is throwing them.

— Graeme Ross, correspondent in Fredericton, N.B., 1990

The portion of a news story that follows the lead is called the "body." It contains the information a reporter believes readers need to know. The information can be presented in several styles: inverted pyramid, hourglass, focus or narrative. No technique works best with all readers, all stories or all reporters. All require thorough reporting, and all require reporters to organize the facts and present them effectively. Whatever story style a writer chooses, the important thing for the writer is to determine how to best get the information across to the reader.

Think of writing a news story as driving a train along a track. The rails are the story's central point and give the story direction. The railroad ties—who, what, when, where, why and how—provide a foundation. The train's engine is the lead; it must be powerful enough to pull the rest of the story. Like the whistle of the engine, a story's lead must capture the reader's attention. Each car that follows the lead represents a paragraph containing information and providing structure. The cars (paragraphs) can be arranged in whatever sequence—for example, from most important to least important—seems most effective. The train is strengthened when research, verification, multiple sources, quotes, anecdotes and descriptions fill the cars. The amount of information needed to complete the story determines the number of cars in the train. Holding the train cars together are couplings, which represent the transitions between paragraphs of information. Without strong transitions, the paragraphs disconnect from one another.

This chapter discusses the writing styles and the techniques reporters often use to write effective bodies for their news stories.

THE INVERTED-PYRAMID STYLE

Inverted-pyramid stories arrange the information in descending order of importance or newsworthiness. The lead states the most newsworthy, important or striking information and establishes the central point for the rest of the story. The second paragraph—and sometimes the third and fourth paragraphs—provides details that amplify the lead. Subsequent paragraphs add less important details or introduce subordinate topics. Each paragraph presents additional information: names, descriptions, quotations, conflicting viewpoints, explanations and background data. Beginning reporters must learn this style because it helps them decide what is most important and what is least important. It also helps reporters discover "holes" in their information—details that have not been collected and need to be found.

The primary advantage of the inverted pyramid is that it allows someone to stop reading a story after only one or two paragraphs yet still learn the newest, most newsworthy, and most important facts. The inverted pyramid also ensures that all the facts are immediately understandable. Moreover, if a story is longer than the space available, editors can easily shorten it by deleting paragraphs from the end.

The inverted-pyramid style also has several disadvantages:

- Because the lead summarizes facts that later paragraphs discuss in greater detail, some of those facts may be repeated in the body.

- A story that follows the inverted pyramid rarely contains any surprises for readers; the lead immediately reveals the major facts.

- The inverted-pyramid style evolved when newspapers were readers' first source for breaking news; now radio, television and the Internet fill that role.

- Readers with less than a high school education cannot easily understand stories written in this style.

- The inverted pyramid locks reporters into a formula and discourages them from trying new styles.

Many writing coaches discourage the use of the inverted pyramid, saying it is overused, confusing and often irrelevant. The inverted pyramid remains a common form for organizing news stories, however, because of its inherent advantages: daily deadline pressures encourage its use because coming up with new styles requires additional thinking and, perhaps, more rewriting.

Organizing the Information

If two cars collide and several people are injured, an inverted-pyramid story about the accident might contain the following sequence of paragraphs:

Normally, reporters emphasize people: what they do and what happens to them. Consequently, in the preceding example the injuries to the people are described early in the story. Damage to the cars is less important and reported later. If the damage was not unusual, the story might not mention it. Paragraph three describes the accident itself—the recent action and main point of the story. Quotations, such as those used in paragraphs five, six and seven, add detail and colour as well as a pleasing change of pace. Paragraphs eight, nine and 10 add less essential information and might be deleted if space is limited.

The exact organization of a story will vary depending on the story's unique facts and most newsworthy points. The second, third and, perhaps, fourth paragraphs should provide details that develop and support the lead.

Notice how the leads in the following stories summarize their topics and how the second and third paragraphs present their most important details. Neither story ends with a summary or conclusion; instead, the final paragraphs present the least important details. The stories are cohesive because their leads summarize the main topics and because each of the subsequent paragraphs presents additional information about those topics.

LOTHIAN, Maryland—A Glen Burnie man was in serious but stable condition yesterday, a day after he fell asleep at the wheel and collided with a box truck in South County.

David A. Calligan Jr., 19, was driving a 1998 Ford Explorer east on Route 258 near Brookswood Road just before 3 p.m. when he fell asleep and crossed the center line, county police said.

Lead . . . . Summarizes the story
Paragraph Two . . . . . . Identifies the injured
Paragraph Three . . . . . Explains how the accident occurred
Paragraph Four . . . . . Reports charges fited against driver(s)
Paragraph Five, Six, Seven . . . . Quotes driver(s), police officer(s) and witness(es)
Paragraph Eight . . . . . Describes unusal damage to the cars
Paragraph Nine . . . . . Describes traffic problems caused by the accident
Paragraph Ten . . . . . Presents minor details

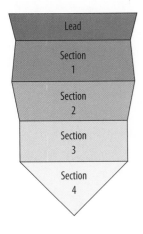

The Ford collided with a westbound GMC box truck, which overturned, trapping Calligan.

A county fire department spokesperson said it took 15 to 20 minutes for firefighters to free Calligan, who was flown by helicopter to the Maryland Shock Trauma Center in Baltimore.

The box truck driver, 29-year-old Ulise Trujillo-Hetteta of Waldorf, and passenger Raphael Ignot, 26, of Fort Washington, were not seriously hurt. (*Maryland Gazette*)

A Carlisle couple is homeless following a house fire Sunday.

The borough's four fire companies were dispatched about 3 p.m. to a one-storey ranch house owned by Suzanne Zeigler at 307 Avon Drive.

"Fire was coming from the roof when we arrived on the scene," Carlisle Fire Chief David Boyles said this morning.

It took firefighters about 45 minutes to contain and extinguish the blaze.

Boyles said the homeowner was out shopping at the time of the fire and no one was home.

The structure sustained heavy fire damage to the roof and severe water damage everywhere else.

He said the fire appears to be electrical in origin and started in the garage.

The Red Cross provided assistance to the homeowner, her fiancé and their three cats and two dogs, said Gene Lucas, executive director.

Boyles said a passerby from the neighbourhood rescued the pets from the home.

One firefighter was treated at the scene for a minor burn. (*Carlisle [Pa.] Sentinel*)

Notice that in both of these inverted-pyramid story examples, an editor could easily remove the last couple of paragraphs if necessary (for space) and still retain the essential information of the story.

Many of the facts reported in longer news stories are of approximately equal importance. These stories are more likely to resemble the diagram shown on this page rather than the perfect triangle shown on page 117.

Immediately after the diagram's summary lead, Section 1 presents several paragraphs that contain information of roughly equal importance. These paragraphs may present some additional information about a single topic or information about several different but related subtopics. Section 2 may describe a somewhat less important aspect of the story. Section 3 presents more facts of about equal importance to one another but of less importance than the facts in Section 2. Section 4 contains the least important details, perhaps routine procedures, background information, or a reminder of related or similar incidents that occurred in the past.

Writing the Second Paragraph

The second paragraph in a news story is almost as important as the lead—and almost as difficult to write. Like the lead, the second paragraph should emphasize the news. In addition, the second paragraph should provide a smooth, logical transition from the lead to the following paragraphs.

Sometimes reporters fail to emphasize the news in a story's second paragraph. Other times they fail to provide smooth transitions. As a result, their stories seem dull or disorganized. The following sections discuss both of these problems and present some solutions.

Avoid Leapfrogging

Reporters often refer to an individual in their lead and begin their second paragraph with a name. However, many reporters fail to say clearly that the individual referred to in their lead is the person named in their second paragraph. Readers are forced to guess. They will usually guess right—but not always.

This problem is so common that it has a name: "leapfrogging." To avoid it, provide a one- or two-word transition from the lead to the name in the second paragraph:

> A man rammed his car into his wife's car, then shot her in the arm and leg before bystanders tackled him, police said.
>
> Police expressed gratitude to the bystanders who helped bring John McDonald, 53, of Allentown into custody Monday.
>
> REVISED: A man rammed his car into his wife's car, then shot her in the arm and leg before bystanders tackled him, police said.
>
> Police expressed gratitude to the bystanders who helped bring the man suspected of the attack, John McDonald, 53, of Allentown, into custody Monday.

Continue with the News

After providing a smooth transition between the lead and the second paragraph, continue with information about the topic summarized in your lead. Mistakenly, some reporters shift to a different topic, a decision certain to confuse their readers:

> The mayor and City Council agreed Monday night to freeze wages and make city workers pay more for benefits in an effort to close a budget deficit that is now larger than officials expected.
>
> Mayor Sabrina Datolli, who has been a lifelong resident of the city, is in her fourth term as mayor. She has seen many ups and downs over her years as mayor but hopes the city can overcome its problems.
>
> REVISED: The mayor and City Council agreed Monday night to freeze wages and make city workers pay more for benefits in an effort to close a budget deficit that is now larger than officials expected.
>
> Mayor Sabrina Datolli said the wage freeze and other measures are needed to prevent layoffs of city employees, cuts in programs, and more drastic fiscal surgery to balance the city's budget.

Before revision, the story seems to discuss two different topics. The lead summarizes a problem that confronts city officials everywhere: balancing budgets. The second paragraph shifts to the mayor's career and hopes. It fails even to mention the problem of balancing the budget.

Names, Names—Dull, Dull

Reporters sometimes place too much emphasis on their sources' identities. As a result, their second paragraphs fail to convey any information of interest to readers. Note how the following example can be revised to emphasize the news—what the source said, saw or did, not who he is:

> A highway engineer was killed Wednesday at a TransCanada Highway construction site when a tractor-trailer owned by Shearson Trucking Inc. plowed through a concrete barrier and struck him.
>
> A materials engineer, Riley Patterson of Independent Testing Laboratory Inc., was killed in the mishap.
>
> Jonathan Martin, a site manager for Baldini Construction Co., saw the accident happen.
>
> REVISED: A tractor-trailer plowed through a concrete barrier at a TransCanada Highway construction site Monday, killing a highway engineer.
>
> The force of the crash pushed the concrete barrier into a piece of road equipment, crushing the engineer, Riley Patterson. Patterson had been using a core-drilling machine to bore a sample hole in the concrete roadbed when the accident occurred. He was pronounced dead at the scene.

Jonathan Martin, a worker at the site, said he saw the truck crash through the barrier but could not warn Patterson because of the noise of the drilling machine.

Background: Too Much, Too Soon

Avoid devoting the entire second paragraph to background information. The second paragraph in the following story is dull because it emphasizes routine, insignificant details:

> Local Red Cross officials expressed alarm Wednesday that blood supplies are dangerously low prior to the beginning of the long holiday weekend.
> Nancy Cross, executive director of the Broward County Chapter of the Red Cross, said the Red Cross strives to maintain an adequate blood supply for emergency situations. "The role of the Red Cross since it was founded is to help people during times of need," she said.

The story shifts from the news—the lack of adequate blood supplies—to the organization's purpose. Yet that purpose has not changed since the Red Cross was established. Thus, the second paragraph says nothing new, nothing likely to retain readers' interest in the story. Fortunately, the problem is easy to correct:

> Local Red Cross officials expressed alarm Wednesday that blood supplies are dangerously low heading into the long holiday weekend.
> Restocking those supplies will require a 50 per cent increase in blood donations over the next three days, said Nancy Cross, executive director of the Broward County Chapter of the Red Cross.
> "Holiday periods are often a problem because people are travelling or have other plans and don't think about the need for blood," Cross said. "But the holiday period is also a busy time for emergency rooms and trauma centres, which increases the demand for blood."

The revised second and third paragraphs describe the solution to the blood supply problem and explain the reasons for the problem—details central to the story, not minor or unnecessary ones.

Complex Stories

Some stories that contain several major sub-themes may be too complex to summarize in a brief lead.

For example, the next story says the Supreme Court of Canada may take an action in a case with a long and controversial history. Such stories require the writer to summarize the relevant history for readers unfamiliar with the issue. The following story begins with the Supreme Court's most newsworthy recent action and then, in subsequent paragraphs, fills in the relevant background:

> TORONTO—Punitive damages in Canada and the United States are under heavy fire, evident by recent decisions of the two countries' supreme courts that drastically slashed such awards and limited the extent to which they should be granted.
> That bodes well for corporations that are found to have breached the law, but not so well for those who suffer harm.
> Punitive damages are granted by courts to address egregious conduct between parties. In Canada, they are relatively rare and seldom exceed six figures. In the United States, however, they can reach into the hundreds of millions of dollars and can form the bulk of the damages awarded to injured parties.
> "Punitive damages may be alive in Canada, but they're not very well," says Alf Kwinter of Singer Kwinter, a member of the plaintiffs' bar. "The Supreme Court keeps raising the standard, saying conduct isn't bad enough to warrant punitives even after trial judges condemn corporate behaviour."

That's not an unfair description of the recent Supreme Court of Canada decision in *Keays v. Honda*, which originated with an employee's poor attendance record over two years, supported only by very summary doctors' notes. When Mr. Keays refused to meet with the company's doctor, Honda terminated him.

The Ontario Superior Court concluded that Honda had engaged in a conspiracy to avoid accommodating Mr. Keays and awarded $500,000 in punitive damages. The Ontario Court of Appeal cut that to $100,000. That didn't satisfy the high court. It ruled that Honda's conduct was not the type of "malicious" or "outrageous" conduct that deserved punishment on its own, and voided the punitives.

The reasoning mirrored that of the court in its 2006 decision in *Fidler v. Sun Life*.

In that case, pain and fatigue left Connie Fidler, a middle-aged receptionist with Royal Bank of Canada in Burnaby, B.C., unable to work. A unanimous Supreme Court found that Sun Life Assurance Co. of Canada was liable for the mental distress Ms. Fidler suffered when the insurer wrongfully withheld disability benefits for five years—but not for the $100,000 in punitive damages that the B.C. Court of Appeal had ordered.

"The Supreme Court has been making the criteria for punitives almost unattainable," Mr. Kwinter says. "It refused to award punitives in *Keays* even though the court called Honda's conduct 'ill-advised' and 'unnecessarily harsh,' and even though it called the conduct in *Fidler* 'outrageous' and 'troubling.'"

Chris Paliare of Paliare Roland Rosenberg Rothstein LLP, who represented NE/FM Action Network, an intervenor in *Keays*, says the case is a big win for employers in particular.

"The ruling is totally antithetical and contradicts everything the Supreme Court has said about employment law for the last decade," he says. "As far as I'm concerned, it demonstrates a lack of understanding and sensitivity on the court's part about the nature of the employment relationship, because it means that employers can get off the hook on punitives for pretty well anything they do, as long as they write nice letters about it to the employee."

In the United States, 10 years of litigation that began with the *Exxon Valdez* oil spill ended with a June decision from the Supreme Court slashing a US$2-billion punitive award to US$500 million. That left native Alaskans and local fishermen and landowners with just 20 per cent of the amount awarded by a federal appeals court.

Mr. Justice David Souter, writing for the majority in a split court, said the punitives should not have exceeded the compensatory damage award of US$507.5 million.

"We're seeing a backlash to what the public and the business community perceived as extreme and disproportionate punitive awards," says Peter Simmons, a litigator at Fried Frank's New York office. "Consequently, federal and state courts and legislators have been trying to eliminate the 'outlier' awards, as opposed to punitive damages in general."

Indeed, Judge Souter's criticism of punitive damages focused on the occasional blockbuster awards, saying they introduced "stark unpredictability" into litigation.

"There's no question that there are cases where punitives are right and reasonable," Mr. Simmons says. "But the chance of an outlier award makes it hard for anyone to predict what their downside risk is. Litigation isn't supposed to be a game of chance or roulette or a lottery."

Meanwhile, in Canada, Mr. Kwinter says the solution for plaintiffs is to elect trial by jury.

"Juries will be the last bastion of punitive damages, because judges don't get so shocked by egregious corporate conduct," he says.

Fortunately for the denizens of Bay Street and their counsel, however, high-profile corporate-commercial litigation almost always ends up before a judge alone. However, other stakeholders in the justice system, like the insurance industry, may find the Supreme Court's distaste for punitives increasingly leaves them subject to the whims of their peers.

Reporters often use lists in news stories that involve several ideas, subtopics or examples. If all the ideas or examples are important, reporters may begin a news story by summarizing one or two main points, adding a brief transition, and presenting the other ideas or examples in a simple, orderly list:

> Assailants attacked three women in the college's parking lots, and Police Chief Alvin Schwab today warned other students that the attacks may continue.
>
> To protect themselves, Schwab recommended that women:

- avoid dark areas;

- park in areas that will be lighted when they return;

- tell friends where they are going and when they will return;

- keep their car doors locked and windows rolled up when driving alone;

- check their car's floor and back seat for intruders before getting into the vehicle;

- report any suspicious activities to the campus police.

Later in a story, reporters can discuss each point in greater detail. The initial summary may contain all the essential information about a topic; in that case, it need not be mentioned again.

Each item in a list must be in parallel form. If one item is an incomplete sentence that begins with a verb, then the rest must have the same structure. For example, each item in the following story is an incomplete sentence that begins with a verb:

> The premier said he wants to raise the province's sales tax and increase spending on education. He told reporters he would use the money to:

- raise teachers' salaries;

- test new teachers to assess their competence;

- place more emphasis on English, science and math;

- reduce the number of students in each class;

- give schools more money to educate gifted students.

Reporters also use lists to summarize less important details placed at the end of news stories. Lists are particularly useful when dealing with chronologies, with minor details that concern several diverse topics, or with material that would be difficult to organize in any other manner:

> OTTAWA—With a federal election now set for Oct. 14, the coming weeks will be dominated by political debate as each party seeks to make its case to voters across the country. The election mode marks an important role reversal—after months of Canadians working to gain the attention of their elected officials, those same politicians will be knocking on doors, making phone calls, and participating in all-candidates meetings in an effort to seek them out.
>
> The 2008 election therefore presents an exceptional opportunity to raise the profile of digital issues. Not only do these policies touch on "core concerns" such as the economy, the environment, education and health care, but they also resonate with younger Canadians, who could help swing the balance of power in many ridings.
>
> In the United States election, both Barack Obama and John McCain have unveiled detailed digital policy positions. Canadian leaders have yet to promote their policies, but there are at least five worth watching and asking about.
>
> 1) Spectrum surplus: The recent wireless spectrum auction generated more than $4 billion for the federal government, nearly triple initial estimates. The Conservatives committed in the 2008 budget to allocate the funds to debt reduction. The Liberals,

meanwhile, focused on the opportunity to use the surplus revenue to kick-start long-delayed plans to provide high-speed Internet access to all Canadians. Where do the parties stand on the use of the spectrum proceeds and on universal broadband access from coast to coast to coast?

2) Wireless competition: The sorry state of the Canadian wireless marketplace has been well documented in recent months with high-profile incidents involving text-message charges and high data pricing. New competitors are slated to debut in late 2009, yet Canadians continue to face high prices and limited choice. Are the political parties content with the status quo? If not, would they consider additional measures such as the removal of foreign ownership restrictions or new openness requirements in the next spectrum auction?

3) Net neutrality: Network neutrality emerged as a major issue this year with a political rally on Parliament Hill, the introduction of a private member's bill, and a heated regulatory battle between Bell and independent Internet service providers at the CRTC. The same is true in the U.S., where the Federal Communications Commission (the CRTC's counterpart) ordered cable giant Comcast to abide by net neutrality principles. Where do Canada's political parties stand on net neutrality? If the CRTC concludes that it does not possess the regulatory power to address the issue, would they be prepared to introduce legislative reforms?

4) Copyright: Few issues generated as much attention this summer as copyright with some members of Parliament acknowledging that the controversial Bill C-61 was one of the most discussed constituent concerns. With the bill now dead, each party should be asked to articulate its plan for the future. Would the Conservatives reintroduce the bill unchanged? Would the Liberals scrap the bill and hold public consultations as several of their MPs have suggested? Would the NDP continue its strong opposition to the C-61 approach?

5) Privacy reform: Over the past year, the Standing Committee on Access to Information, Privacy, and Ethics held hearings on potential reforms to both PIPEDA (the private sector privacy law) and the Privacy Act (the public sector privacy law). These reform initiatives—including a recommendation to implement long-awaited mandatory security breach disclosure legislation—have stalled with the election call. None of the political parties has staked out a clear position on privacy legislation. This election campaign provides an opportunity to put the issue squarely on the policy agenda.

Some newspapers number each item in a list. Others mark each item with a dash, bullet, asterisk, check mark, or some other typographical symbol.

THE HOURGLASS STYLE

Roy Peter Clark, vice-president and senior scholar at the Poynter Institute, notes that the inverted pyramid often forced writers to tell their stories in unnatural ways. It also homogenized the news so stories about bank robberies and parliamentary debates sound the same. At the same time, writers who experimented with narrative structures for their stories often lost sight of the news. The most important and newsworthy information might be buried so far down that frustrated readers never saw it. Clark offered the hourglass style of story writing as one that combines the strengths of the inverted pyramid and the narrative format.

The hourglass story has three parts: an inverted pyramid top that summarizes the most newsworthy information, a turn or pivot paragraph, and a narrative. The inverted pyramid top, which may be only three to five paragraphs, gives readers the most newsworthy information quickly. The narrative allows the writer to develop the story in depth and detail, using the storytelling power of chronology. The key, Clark says, is the turn or pivot, which makes the transition between the two formats. Here's an excerpt from a story illustrating the hourglass style:

TORONTO—On a still but rainy night, the black Nissan Sentra had to thread two needles before plunging into the Rideau Canal just north of Kingston, leaving local detectives baffled.

Organization of the Hourglass Story

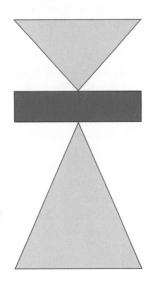

1. An inverted pyramid top

2. The turn

3. A chronological conclusion

The four-door car carrying three Montreal sisters and an aunt to their graves likely turned north off Kingston Mills Road, where it had to skirt a locked green gate barring vehicle access to the canal.

The rocky ground next to the gate would have given the Nissan a bump, but the 1.7-metre-wide compact could probably have squeezed past. It's unlikely the manoeuvre was a simple wrong turn.

The next obstacle was the canal itself, with stone moorings spaced a few metres apart and the ancient black iron control wheel standing about a metre above the canal's edge.

If the car went straight from the road into the water, the driver would have had to make a quick left turn into the canal. Witnesses and police say there are no skid marks in the green grass next to the canal, no telltale signs of sudden braking, turning or acceleration.

It would have been a smooth turn made at a reasonable speed. The stone edge of the canal shows just a few scrapes from the car sliding in.

"The area is fairly level, there are rocky areas, but you'd still have to do some manoeuvring to get out to this spot," said Constable Mike Menor of Kingston police.

The car was discovered at 9 a.m. Tuesday in three metres of water right next to the lock gates. Nearby residents had heard a noise some six hours earlier. The three sisters, aged 13, 17 and 19, and their 50-year-old aunt were found inside.

Investigators say the condition of the bodies suggests they'd gone into the water overnight. Police were withholding their identities yesterday at the request of the family.

Police are left to sort through a myriad of theories, each with glaring problems and unlikely probabilities.

"We're still trying to ascertain the why, the why, the why," said Constable Menor, a 20-year veteran of the force. "It's the unknowns. I can't recall anything like it. It was there for a reason, it didn't drop out of the sky."

Without revealing details, police say the foursome had spent the earlier part of the evening in Kingston.

"We pieced together that they did have a bit of a family vacation west of us on the other side of Toronto and were returning to Quebec," said Staff Sergeant Chris Scott of the Kingston police criminal investigations division.

With picnic tables along the canal shore, the tourists from Montreal may have stopped for a moment before the plunge. But 3 a.m. would be an unusual time for a picnic in the secluded spot.

Perhaps the driver didn't know the canal was there, or perhaps she didn't care. Police have not excluded a suicide pact, murder-suicide or something as simple as the bad luck of a misguided U-turn or mistaking "drive" for "reverse."

Another possibility is that the passengers were already dead and someone else pushed the Nissan into the canal, with the four females inside.

Montreal police said they were asked by Kingston police to locate a second vehicle in Montreal that may have been seen with the Nissan. Late yesterday, Kingston police denied they were looking for another vehicle.

Autopsies were performed yesterday but results could take weeks, investigators said.

Kingston police have refused to reveal if there were signs of violence on the bodies.

The first eight paragraphs tell this story in a modified inverted pyramid fashion, reporting the newsworthy facts about how four women died when their car plunged into the Rideau Canal just north of Kingston and noting that police are at a loss to explain the deaths. The ninth and tenth paragraphs are the turn. They tell the reader that police are withholding the identities of the victims and sorting through a myriad of theories to explain the event. The eleventh paragraph begins the rest of the story, which adopts a more narrative style, using quotations, details and anecdotes to enhance the story.

The hourglass style will not work for all stories. For stories that have no meaningful chronology, such as an account of a city council meeting in which topics are discussed in no particular order, the hourglass style is useless. But for stories about many newsworthy events—sports contests, criminal investigations, natural disasters, and political campaigns—the hourglass can be an effective way of organizing information.

THE FOCUS STYLE

The focus style has been used for years by the *Globe and Mail*. Its news feature stories often employ this format. Many other newspapers and their reporters have been using the focus style as well. The focus style, like the hourglass style, tries to incorporate storytelling techniques in newswriting. But unlike the hourglass, the focus story begins with a lead that focuses on a specific individual, situation or anecdote and uses that to illustrate a larger problem.

The focus story has four parts. The first is the lead, which, unlike the lead for an inverted pyramid story, may run three, four, five paragraphs or more. Also, unlike the hard-news lead, the focus lead describes a person, place, situation or event that may not be newsworthy by itself but exemplifies a larger problem that is newsworthy.

The second part of the focus story is a nut graf—which can actually be two or three paragraphs—stating the central point of the story and how the lead illustrates that point. The third part of the story is the body, which develops the central point in detail. The final part is a one-, two- or three-paragraph close, or kicker, that brings the story to a conclusion. The kicker usually relates to the person, place or situation described in the focus lead. Here's an example of a focus story from the *Globe and Mail*:

TORONTO—The last thing Benjamin ever thought he'd have to do is help his father die.

But after a cancer diagnosis in the prime of life, his father gathered his wife, 20-year-old Benjamin and his older brother around the kitchen table in their Toronto home to discuss exactly that.

"We faced his death together, as a challenge," recalls Benjamin, who asked that his surname not be used to protect the privacy of his grieving mother. "When he knew the end was near, he asked that something good come out of it and that his body be used to help others."

Benjamin struggled to accept the fact that his father, a successful businessman and enthusiastic skier, golfer and runner in his late 50s, had only months to live. Just over a year, as it turned out, from diagnosis to his death last January. When aggressive treatment failed to stop the spread of pancreatic cancer to his internal organs, his father opted for palliative care.

"There was no sugarcoating. We knew he was going to die," says Benjamin, a poised and thoughtful business student. "We were involved in every decision. We normalized it by talking about everything, including all the therapies and procedures my father went through."

With every passing year, as life expectancies increase, there is an illusion we will all last forever. Medical stories often focus on the sexier aspect of medicine—the cure.

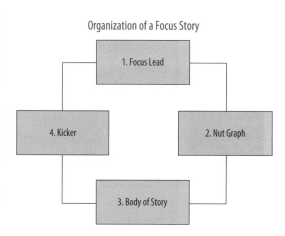

Organization of a Focus Story

1. Focus Lead

2. Nut Graph

3. Body of Story

4. Kicker

But palliative-care experts say the bulk of medicine is about something less cheery: how to manage the care of terminally ill people. Research shows that many doctors, as well as patients, are reluctant to initiate this conversation. A recent study by Queen's University in Kingston found that only 18 per cent of 440 patients with end-stage disease talked to doctors about their prognosis, even though most were likely to die within a few months.

The time has come to put death back on the table for discussion, says Gary Rodin, the head of psychosocial oncology and palliative care at Princess Margaret Hospital in Toronto.

"For years there was a feeling in the medical community that you shouldn't talk about death. This created a conspiracy of silence," says Dr. Rodin, who is also a University of Toronto professor. "But someone who is seriously ill knows it, so if you don't talk about it they feel very alone."

Today, medical students are being taught empathy and communication along with anatomy and physiology.

Doctors understand that terminally ill patients don't want sympathy, or to be deprived of hope. "But hope isn't just about how long you live," says Dr. Rodin, "but about knowing you are loved, and that your life is meaningful."

Researchers have found that the final days of a person's life are often the most expensive, and medically complicated. In many cases, active treatment is maintained, or another round of chemotherapy administered, even if there is no chance it will improve the patient's quality of life.

"There are cases where futile treatment, such as chemotherapy, is given because people are reluctant to have these conversations," Dr. Rodin says, "and patients fear they will be abandoned. Far too often, people are referred to palliative care too late."

If patients plan ahead, there is a greater likelihood that their passing will be more peaceful, and that their death won't in any way diminish the life they have lived. Planning includes a discussion about how and where to die and the writing of a living will and a do not resuscitate order (DNR).

Though Dr. Rodin helped Benjamin and his family cope, a recent U.S. study found that 40 per cent of people with family members in hospice care were provided no information about the loved one's life expectancy, and 20 per cent were never told the illness could not be cured. The study, published last year in the *Journal of Palliative Medicine*, concluded that the most common question was: "How long does my loved one have?" and "What is happening with my loved one?" Many were afraid to ask doctors for a physical description of a dying person's last moments, which can be quite frightening.

In his recent book *The Welcome Visitor*, legendary BBC broadcaster John Humphrys writes about people who are afraid of living too long and having no control over how their lives end.

"Society's approach to death must change as we all live longer," Mr. Humphrys says. He was inspired to write the book by his father's "final sad, lingering and undignified" years. "My father's last years cast a shadow over what had been a good life," he says.

Benjamin knows he is blessed to have well-adjusted parents who helped him face death: "We saw it as our family responsibility."

Dr. Rodin also helped the family decide how to manage their father's care, including whether he should participate in a clinical trial and when to stop aggressive cancer therapies in favour of enjoying the few months he had left. Ultimately, his father decided to work a half-day at the office, and ski and travel as long as he could. The summer after his diagnosis, he even completed a two-day, 200-kilometre bike race to raise money for cancer research.

By the fall of 2008, when his illness became debilitating, he chose to be cared for at home. A palliative-care team installed a hospital bed in his bedroom, and a physician was on call 24 hours a day. His sons and wife helped him with his medication and going to the bathroom.

Two days before he died, his father checked into Princess Margaret's palliative-care unit. A colourful mural decorated the wall of his room, and soothing music from a CD player on his bedside table filled the room. A physician told the family what to expect when his time came, and explained that he wouldn't be in pain.

"He told us it could be a few days or hours. We held my father's hand and told him we loved him, because he could still feel our presence, even though he wasn't responding," Benjamin says. His breathing became laboured toward the end, which was a little scary, but the palliative-care team ensured he had the right balance of drugs.

In his grief, Benjamin felt supported by his close-knit peer group, but also found he had no script for his journey. "I didn't want my friends to pity me or for them to feel hurt. I wanted them to know that I was still the same person," he recalls.

In this, too, his father and Dr. Rodin helped him, advising him how to share news of the illness with friends.

Dr. Rodin notes that things rarely go as smoothly as they did for Benjamin's family. Sometimes, the dying person changes his wishes as he becomes sicker. There is no prescription for a "good death," as it is strongly influenced by a person's religion, culture, age, background and psychology.

But every family can benefit from open communication, early planning and attention to pain relief, Dr. Rodin says. "Birth and death are two major life events. We go to prenatal classes to prepare for birth, and we also need to prepare for death."

The first five paragraphs of the story describe the focus: a single aging father facing a diagnosis of cancer in an era of increased life expectancies. The writer introduces us to Benjamin, the 20-year-old son of the dying man, and it is through Benjamin's eyes that we come to understand how the family dealt with its loss. Those facts are interesting, but paragraphs six and seven—the nut paragraphs—explain in detail the central point of the story: research shows that despite an aging population, palliative care is a subject neglected by most patients with end-stage disease. The last four paragraphs of the story provide the kicker—tying the end of the story back to the beginning and providing a sense of conclusion to the story.

The success of the focus story depends on the selection of the lead. Some beginners start their stories with interesting anecdotes or descriptions that have little or no connection to the central point of the story. If the focus has no connection to the central point, it is likely only to confuse and frustrate readers.

The focus style also has flexibility. The body of the story can be developed in any number of ways. If the story has several subtopics, they can be arranged in descending order of importance. Or if the material lends itself to a narrative structure, the information can be arranged chronologically.

THE NARRATIVE STYLE

A narrative has two components: a story and a storyteller. A storyteller writes as a playwright or novelist would, depicting people interacting with other people and within their surroundings. To write in the narrative style, a reporter must find people who are crucial to the story and record their actions. This technique requires more than just interviewing sources, recording quotes, and reporting numbers. It requires keen observation.

Observation does not mean reporters are free to interject their opinions into a story. It means that reporters observe people, places and events important to a story and describe them in vivid detail. Through those details, readers get a better sense of what is occurring. But to paint a picture with words, reporters must be specific. Notice the difference between the following sentences:

Students are angry about the board of governors' decision.
Students gathered in the administration building lobby waving signs protesting the board of governors' decision.

The first sentence presents an opinion. Without using attribution, it says the students are angry at the board's decision. The reader does not know whether the writer is reporting a fact or her opinion. The second sentence, however, shows the students' negative behaviour in response to the board's decision.

The narrative approach allows reporters to be more creative. Reporters can describe the drama—even if it is not high drama—at a school board meeting, for example. What happened? What did they see? Were people shouting? Were people laughing? Did the participants exchange views? Reporters cannot answer these questions and others unless they take extensive notes.

Longtime writing coach Don Fry describes the style this way:

> Narrative writing requires narrative thinking, narrative reporting and narrative forms.
>
> Narrative thinking means seeing the world in terms of people doing things, not as piles of disparate facts. Actions connect to one another to create meaning, mostly based on human motives. The best journalistic storytellers let their curiosity lead them into stories, because they want to find out why real people do things.

A story written in narrative style can still lead with the news—the most important part of the story—but then quickly switch to using chronology, flashbacks, dialogue and other story-telling techniques. Or the stories can employ a strictly chronological organization, ending with the most recent and perhaps most newsworthy information. Generally, such stories have a beginning, a middle and an end, each of relatively equal importance. It is more difficult to cut the final paragraphs of narrative stories than of stories written in the inverted-pyramid style.

The following story about the St. Lawrence Seaway by *Globe and Mail* writer Erin Anderssen illustrates the narrative style:

> TORONTO—The official opening of the St. Lawrence Seaway was orchestrated to be a breathless moment in history—a "flossy, glossy" ceremony, to quote this newspaper. On the muggy afternoon 50 years ago yesterday, balloons soared, guns saluted, an American president stopped by and a rosy-cheeked Queen, just turned 33, leaned over the railing of her yacht and waved at the cheering crowds.
>
> Cargo freighters had, in fact, been lumbering through the new locks to Toronto and major ports on the Great Lakes for more than a month, smoothing out kinks in advance of the *Royal Yacht Britannia*'s sleek arrival.
>
> As it was, fog interrupted the voyage from Montreal, and the Queen turned up too late to enjoy the dinner carefully prepared for her at the hotel in Long Sault, a town created to house the many families who had lost their homes to the rising waters of the seaway and Ontario Hydro's massive new power dam.
>
> But for most observers that day, a few lost villages was well worth giving ocean vessels access to the Great Lakes; to them, the seaway was an economic bonanza for Canada after decades of bickering with the United States. An engineering marvel finished on time and under budget, it had cost nearly $470-million (US) and taken 22,000 workers four years and nine months to build the vital 306-kilometre stretch from Montreal to Lake Ontario.
>
> The hydroelectric dams—built at the same time and worth an additional $530-million—would fire up the bustling cities and manufacturing plants along both sides of the seaway. And this was the time of the Cold War, when the route promised secure berths for military ships and submarines, with quick passage to the ocean. The canals and locks that had widened and deepened the river path—silencing the famous Long Sault Rapids, which had 400 years earlier frustrated Jacques Cartier's travel plans—now made it possible for a transoceanic freighter the size of two football fields to deliver French perfume and Italian marble (as the first arrivals did) to inland ports such as Toronto before heading to Lake Superior to take home grain from Thunder Bay.
>
> "It has moved the ocean a thousand miles inland," the *Globe and Mail* declared that day in 1959. "The effects of this cannot as yet be estimated, but we can be certain that they will be very great." Or, as the Queen put it: "We can say in truth that this occasion deserves a place in history."

The prediction proved to be true: The seaway, arguably the world's most impressive inland waterway, built at a cost that today would top $7-billion (US), transformed cities along its shores, opening new markets and churning out a reliable stream of electricity. But over time, the story has become less rosy, the seaway's place in history less celebrated, its future uncertain.

Canada paid roughly 70 per cent of the bill, and has divided revenue with the U.S. accordingly. But that revenue has yet to cover the cost of construction, and often has barely covered operating costs.

Even worse, the seaway has wreaked so much havoc on the world's greatest supply of fresh water that some critics now propose that it be abandoned as a route for saltwater ships—the very notion that stirred its creators' imagination.

"It's pretty clear that the seaway has been an economic disappointment and an environmental disaster for the Great Lakes," says environmental writer Jeff Alexander, whose new book, *Pandora's Locks*, chronicles the project's fallout. "I think it would be disingenuous to hold a celebration without recognizing some of the unintended side effects."

MUSSEL POWER

The seaway has always been the tale of two waters—salt and fresh, divided by nature but united by humanity. Even before construction began on the Montreal section, however, it was clear that mixing the ocean with the lakes came with risks. The building of the Welland Canal years ago allowed ships to circumvent Niagara Falls, but it also provided passage to the sea lamprey, a vicious "aquatic assassin," as Mr. Alexander describes it, that broke into the world's largest freshwater fish market with no natural predator to stand against it.

So perhaps it shouldn't have come as such a surprise when, in 1988, two biology students found an unusual shellfish on the bottom of Lake St. Clair, which lies between Lake Erie and Lake Huron. It turned out to be a foreign intruder that had hitched a ride on an ocean freighter and, of course, in the two decades since then, the zebra mussel has become legendary for the many millions of dollars in damage it has caused to its new habitat.

But it didn't come alone: Since the seaway opened, scientists estimate that as many as 57 foreign species (about one-third of the 185 now on record and almost all of those that have been found in the past 50 years) have arrived in the ballast water shed by saltwater ships. They have displaced native plants and animals, decimated fish stocks, even disrupted power plants.

The seaway is hardly the only cause of the Great Lakes' decline—aquaculture and recreational boating have done much damage, along with pollution from industry and agriculture—but many scientists believe that it is responsible for the most harm, and certainly let in the most destructive intruders.

Even worse, environmentalists point out, government agencies that regulate the seaway and shipping have been painfully slow to react. Only in the past two years have seaway authorities on both sides of the border made it mandatory that all ships—including those with just small amounts of ballast from ports overseas—flush their tanks in the ocean before entering the seaway. Even that isn't necessarily foolproof. Flushing may kill 95 per cent of what is in the tanks, but a troublemaker could survive.

So, 20 years after the zebra mussel arrived, "the threat still remains," says Jennifer Nalbone, an analyst with Great Lakes United, a cross-border environmental coalition. "It's a very sober anniversary."

Assessing the economic value of the seaway—and whether the environmental toll and human costs have been justified—is complicated. There is no doubt that having lots of cheap hydro as well as a watery highway has been important to manufacturing cities on the Great Lakes.

Statistics released this week show that more than 2.5 billion tonnes of cargo worth more than $375-billion have passed through the seaway, most of it between Canadian and U.S. ports.

Even so, annual tallies for "salties" have never reached the predictions made on opening day, and the early glow of having ready access to European markets—the romantic focus of those "glossy, flossy" celebrations—soon faded. Demand for grain moved to the west, other markets shifted as well, and long-distance container vessels grew too big to fit in the seaway's locks.

"It was a noble idea—it's been very valuable for domestic bulk cargo," says John Taylor, a transport specialist at Grand Valley State University in Grand Rapids, Mich. "But the seaway has been 'locked' in time. The world has evolved and the seaway has not been able to evolve with it."

Today, as Mr. Alexander points out in *Pandora's Locks*, only about 5 per cent of the world's container fleet can even squeeze into the Great Lakes. By 2007, the volume of cargo carried by ocean-going vessels had dropped to nine million tonnes from a high of 23 million in 1978, and even that figure was well off early expectations.

Prof. Taylor says the salties could be replaced by as few as two 100-car freight trains running each day of the year. A study he co-wrote in 2005 calculated that the cost of closing the locks to transoceanic ships at roughly $55-million, a figure that is widely criticized by the shipping industry but is just a fraction of the $200-million environmental toll he estimates the seaway has taken on the Great Lakes.

But the seaway also has ardent defenders, who make a convincing case that it will play an increasingly important role as transportation costs rise and, ironically, the environment becomes an even greater concern. Because the loads can be so huge, transporting goods by ship uses, on average, far less fuel and doesn't clog up already congested highways.

"One ship can take 800 trucks off the road," says Bruce Bowie, president of the Canadian Shipowners Association.

In addition, the shipping industry is lobbying to have removed the 25-per-cent duty the government charges on vessels built outside Canada, which, he says, has prevented companies from making their fleets even more environmentally efficient. Steps have been taken to modernize the locks, and an incentive program lured nearly two billion tonnes of new cargo to the route last year, according to the seaway corporation. But drawing even more business by staying open through the winter would be costly, and major renovations required down the road will cost more than the seaway currently earns.

As for banishing the salties, Mr. Bowie calls it a "sledgehammer solution" that would only limit future economic growth. The seaway needs to be ready to capture some emerging market abroad, he says, just as lakers have suddenly picked up solid business in the past few years by carrying low-sulphur coal to power plants on the East Coast.

But future prospects aside, it has been a rocky 50 years for Highway H-2O, as the seaway has been branded by the development corporation that now oversees it, and this anniversary is not the exuberant celebration of that June day half a century past. To a large extent, the seaway's prospects depend on the global path of supply and demand. But the next half-century will decide whether it can sell itself as a clean, energy-efficient water route and earn the place in history that the Queen once said it deserved.

Notice how the writer used quotations, dialogue and description to give readers a sense of working on the seaway and of each source's distinctive personality. The details are ones that easily bring images to the mind of the reader. Notice the length of the story. Stories using the narrative style tend to be longer, and yet the rich detail and concrete imagery make the stories easier to read than many shorter straight news stories.

Narrative style can be a refreshing change from the inverted pyramid, but it is not appropriate for all stories. Stories about breaking news events, speeches, or most government meetings, for instance, often make more sense to readers when told in traditional inverted-pyramid fashion. Narrative touches, such as dialogue and colourful descriptions, can make any story more readable, however. Regardless of the occasion, the success of a narrative story depends on the depth of the reporting. A writer who has not attentively gathered details and quotations will have difficulty constructing a narrative story.

USING TRANSITIONS

Transitions help stories move from one fact to the next in a smooth, logical order. Again, think of the story as a train. The engine is the lead, and each car that follows is a paragraph. The couplings that hold the cars together are transitions. Reporters introduce ideas by relating them to ideas reported earlier in a story. Often, the natural progression of thought, or sequence of facts and action, is adequate. Or reporters may repeat a key name or pronoun:

> School board member Diana Maceda voted against the proposed cuts in the school lunch program. Maceda said cuts would hurt low-income families that rely on the program.

> Police Capt. Virginia Detwieler said the accident occurred when a car cut in front of the tractor-trailer, causing the rig to jackknife when the driver slammed on his brakes.
> She added that police investigators had got a description of the car and a partial licence number and were searching for the vehicle to question the driver.

The first example repeats the name of the school board member. In the second example, the pronoun "she" refers to the captain mentioned in the preceding paragraph. Reporters can also repeat other key words, ideas or phrases:

> Richard Nolles, editor of the *Weekly Outlook*, said the newspaper tries to report the truth even when its readers do not want to hear it.
> "A newspaper that reports only what its readers want to hear is dodging its moral obligations," Nolles said.
> In a speech Wednesday, Nolles added that many readers want to avoid unpleasant news and threaten to cancel their subscriptions when he reports it.
> "But if a problem exists, they need to know about it so they can correct it," he said. "Ignorant citizens can't make wise decisions."

Transitional Words

Sometimes a single word can lead readers from one idea to the next. Many transitional words refer to time: words such as "earlier" and "later," "before" and "after," "prompt" and "tardy." Other common transitional words that refer to time include these:

delayed
eventually
finally
formerly
frequently
meanwhile
next
now
occasionally
often
once
seldom
sometimes
soon
then

Using the hour, day of the week, month, season, year, decade or century ("an hour later," "the previous Saturday," and so on) can also provide a transition.

Other types and examples of linkage words include the following:

Addition	Causation
again	accordingly
also	because
another	consequently
besides	hence
beyond	since
extra	so
furthermore	then
moreover	therefore
new	thus
other	
together	
too	

Comparison	Contrast
agreeing	although
conflicting	but
contrary	conversely
different	despite
identical	exactly
inconsistent	however
like	if
objecting	nevertheless
opposite	simply
related	solely
separately	still
similarly	until
	while
	without
	yet

Phrases can also move a story from one idea to another. Examples include these:

along with	in an earlier
as a result of	in another
aside from	in contrast
at last	in other action
at the same time	in other business
due to	on the contrary
for example	on the other hand
for instance	until then
for that reason	years earlier
in addition	with the exception of

Transitional Sentences

Transitional sentences link paragraphs that contain diverse ideas, but the sentences should do more than report that another idea was "introduced" or "discussed." They should present some interesting details about the new topic so that readers want to finish the story. Mistakenly, beginners often use vague generalities. A good transitional sentence often serves the same purposes as a lead, summarizing the topic it introduces and revealing what was said or done about it. The following paragraphs then discuss the topic in more detail:

> She also commented on the legislators' overriding of the premier's veto.
> REVISED: She said the legislators' overriding of the premier's veto would anger supporters of the death penalty.

> He also discussed the budget proposal.
> REVISED: He said the budget had been cut as much as possible.

Questions as Transitions

Transitional sentences occasionally take the form of questions. The questions should be short and, as in the following examples, should be immediately followed by their answers—the new details or topics that reporters want to introduce:

> How does he manage to play the piano so well at such a young age?
> "Practice," he said, the freckles blossoming with the smile that spread across his seven-year-old face. "I practise four hours a day—every day. I practise even when I don't feel like it."

> Forty-seven per cent of the students enrolled in the university will earn a degree within the next six years, according to Robert McMahon, director of the Office of Institutional Research.
> What about the other 53 per cent? They will drop out or transfer to another institution.
> Why? A study just completed by McMahon found that most students who drop out of school accept full-time jobs, get married, have children, or say they lack the money needed to continue their education.

EXPLAIN THE UNFAMILIAR

Reporters should avoid words that are not used in everyday conversation. When an unfamiliar word is necessary, journalists must immediately define it. Stories that fail to define unfamiliar terms may annoy as well as puzzle readers and listeners. A story about a 19-year-old Olympic skater who collapsed and died before a practice session reported she died of clinical terminal cardiac arrhythmia. The journalist placed the term in quotation marks but failed to define it. Yet many people would be interested in the death of an Olympic skater and would wonder why an apparently healthy young athlete had died. Because the story failed to define the term, it failed to satisfy their curiosity about the cause of the young woman's death.

Here are three techniques journalists can use to define or explain unfamiliar terms:

1. Place a brief explanation in parentheses:

    > The law would ban accessory structures (sheds, pool houses, and unattached garages) in new subdivisions.

2. Place the explanation immediately after the unfamiliar name or term, setting it off with a colon, comma or dash:

    > Amy and Ralph Hargis of Carlton Drive filed for bankruptcy under Chapter 13, which allows them to repay their creditors in monthly instalments over a three-year period.

    > About 800 foreign students at the university are on F-1 student visas—which means that they are allowed to stay in the United States only until they complete their degrees.

From the salmonberry thickets and among the thimbleberry canes crowding the fence line of the University of B.C.'s experimental farm here at Oyster River, about midway between Courtenay and Campbell River on the east coast of Vancouver Island, a choir of songbirds raises a boisterous hymn of praise for the morning.

There is a cathedral-like quality to this small corner of forest at the estuary of the river that was doubtless what first attracted the tough First World War chaplain from Vancouver's east-side who sought solace and solitude here with his fly rod and whom the riverside trail commemorates.

Watching a big cutthroat trout as long as my forearm hang motionless in the swift, clear current, I'm reminded of that long-dead angler and his pastoral meditations. He must have been an optimist. He may have fished for souls on East Hastings but for his own sense of peace and salvation he returned to this temple of nature so often that he finally became part of the geography.

If this seems an unusual place to begin a contemplation of the trial by fire through which British Columbia has just passed, perhaps it's not.

For this rich oasis of tranquility, throbbing with life, is the future of all the devastation around Kelowna, Kamloops and Cranbrook that so shocked our urban officials—and those television news directors who bring little historic memory to their coverage but have an insatiable appetite for the dramatic. Those ravaged landscapes might also serve as images from the past of this place of present abundance.

Lieutenant-Governor Iona Campagnolo described the summer's losses as "agony." Premier Gordon Campbell, after flying over the burns in the southern Interior that are expected to cost the province $500 million in fire suppression, said the desolation seemed "endless."

Almost everyone who owned a television could not help but be mesmerized by the images of flaming forests menacing suburban neighbourhoods and the steady mantra intoning British Columbia's worst summer of fire in 50 years. And who could not feel the deepest of pangs for the suddenly homeless?

Reporters who want to describe an object must learn to use concrete, factual details as opposed to trite phrases and generalities. Readers should be able to visualize the scene in their minds:

VAGUE: There were about 50 men and women working in the area.

BETTER: About 50 men and women worked in the area, and most wore hard hats, some yellow, some white, and others red. Four of the workers had tied nail pouches around their waists. Others smoked cigarettes and looked weary in their dirty white T-shirts, jeans and sunglasses.

Vagueness also becomes a problem when reporters attempt to describe other people. Some reporters mistake generalities or their personal impressions for factual detail:

She spoke with authority.

She seemed to enjoy talking about her work.

Neither of those sentences is an actual description. The first sentence concludes the woman spoke "with authority" but fails to explain why the writer reached that conclusion. The second sentence reports she "seemed to enjoy" talking about her work but does not specifically describe either the speaker or what she said.

Generalities are often inconsistent among observers. One student reported a woman "seemed relaxed and very sure of herself." Everything about her "conveyed calmness." Yet another student concluded, "She seemed nervous." The students could have avoided the problem by reporting specific details as opposed to their impressions and opinions.

Reporters train themselves to observe and describe specific details. If they are important to the story, include descriptions of people's voices, mannerisms, facial expressions, posture, gestures and surroundings. Include details about or descriptions of their height, weight, age, clothing, hair, glasses, jewelry and family if they help to bring an image alive. Each factor can be described in detail. For example, a journalist might describe a man's hands by mentioning their size, calluses, nails, smoothness or wrinkles or veins, and jewelry. Avoid generalities and conclusions:

Residents watch the approaching flames in Kelowna, B.C., as police with bullhorns (not shown) order people from their homes in the southern suburbs in this August 22, 2003 file photo.

VAGUE: He is a large man.

BETTER: He is 6 feet tall and weighs 210 pounds.

VAGUE: Butler looked as though he had dressed in a hurry.

BETTER: Butler's shirt was buttoned halfway, his socks were mismatched, his shoelaces were untied, and his hair was not brushed.

Descriptions help the audience see the situation or person through the eyes of the reporter. When describing people, however, reporters should not write anything about a woman that they would not write about a man in the same situation, and vice versa. Don't note, "The woman had long slender legs" if you wouldn't write in the same situation, "The man had long slender legs."

THE USE OF HUMOUR

Editors constantly look for humorous stories and often place them on page 1. But humorous stories are particularly difficult to write. Journalists should not try to inject humour into stories that are not obviously humorous. If a story is funny, the humour should be apparent from the facts. Journalists should not have to point out the humour by labelling it "funny" or "comical." Author and economist John Kenneth Galbraith once explained: "Humour is an intensely personal, largely internal thing. What pleases some, including the source, does not please others."

A story about the peculiar laws in some cities never called the laws "peculiar" or "funny." Instead, it simply listed them so people could judge the humour of the laws for themselves. The laws made it illegal to:

- take a cow on a school bus;
- take a bath without a bathing suit;
- break more than three dishes in a single day;
- ride a horse not equipped with a horn and tail light.

If you were writing about Ann Landers, you might give an example of her famous wit so audience members could judge it for themselves:

While attending an embassy reception, Landers was approached by a rather pompous senator.

"So you're Ann Landers," he said. "Say something funny."

Without hesitation Landers replied: "Well, you're a politician. Tell me a lie."

Humour, when it is appropriate, makes news stories more interesting, but remember that understatement is more effective than exaggeration. Simply report the facts that seem humorous, and hope others will laugh.

THE NEED TO BE FAIR

Regardless of how a story is organized, it must be balanced, fair and accurate. Reporters who write about a controversy should present every significant viewpoint fully and fairly. They must exercise particular care when their stories might harm another person's reputation. A reckless or irresponsible charge may destroy an innocent person's reputation, marriage or career.

If a story contains information critical of an individual, that person must have an opportunity to respond—the right of reply. It is not enough to get the person's response after a story has been published and report it in a later story, because not everyone who read the original criticism will see the second story. Most major newspapers have a policy requiring that a person criticized in a news story have an immediate chance to respond. If the person cannot be reached, editors and reporters should consider holding the story. If the story cannot be held, it must describe the efforts made to reach the person and explain that those efforts will be renewed the next day.

When the subject of a negative story is unavailable or refuses to respond, that fact should be mentioned. A brief sentence might explain:

Repeated attempts to reach a company employee were unsuccessful.

OR: A vice-president at the company declined to comment about the charges.

OR: Company officials did not return phone calls made by reporters.

THE FINAL STEP: EDIT YOUR STORY

After finishing a story, edit it ruthlessly. Novelist Kurt Vonnegut said, "If a sentence, no matter how excellent, does not illuminate your subject in some new and useful way, scratch it out." Vonnegut also urged writers to have mercy on their readers, explaining: "Our audience requires us to be sympathetic and patient teachers, ever willing to simplify and clarify—whereas we would rather soar high above the crowd singing like nightingales."

Good reporters will reread and edit their stories. Lazy reporters immediately submit their stories to an editor, thinking their stories need no editing or expecting the editor to correct any mistakes. That attitude involves some risks. If an editor misses the errors, the reporter will be the one who suffers the embarrassment and bears the responsibility. Or an editor may decide the stories require extensive changes, perhaps even total rewriting. When that happens, reporters often complain about the changes. Reporters who correct their own errors will develop reputations as good writers and earn better assignments, raises and promotions.

 ## CHECKLIST FOR WRITING NEWS STORIES

Use the following checklist to evaluate all your stories:

1. Place the most important details in your lead.
2. Throughout the story, emphasize the details most likely to interest and affect your readers.
3. Include details from your observations to create a picture your readers can visualize.
4. In the story's second paragraph, continue to discuss the topic initiated in your lead.
5. Do not leapfrog. If your lead mentions an individual and your second paragraph begins with a name, provide a transition that makes it clear you mean the same person.

6. Make your sentences clear, concise and to the point. (Avoid passive verbs. Also, use the normal word order of subject, verb, direct object.)
7. Vary your sentence structure.
8. Avoid overloading your sentences.
9. If your story discusses several major subtopics, mention all the major subtopics in your story's opening paragraphs so your readers know what to expect.
10. If you use a list, make sure each item is in parallel form.
11. Provide transitions to lead your readers from one sentence or paragraph to another smoothly and logically.
12. Make your transitional sentences specific; say something intriguing to sustain readers' interest in the topic.
13. If you use a question as a transition, make it clear, short and simple.
14. Avoid generalities that have to be explained in a later sentence or paragraph. Be specific.
15. Resist the temptation to end your story with a summary, conclusion or opinion.
16. After finishing your story, critically edit and rewrite it.

 The Writing Coach

LOSE 10 BAD HABITS IN ONE WEEK

By Gregg McLachlan, associate managing editor, *Simcoe Reformer*

It's totally free and the results are guaranteed. No gimmicks, no monthly fees.

One of the greatest aids to improving your copy is to print out your work and read it as if you were a reader. Reading your work aloud is another routine step that helps produce better copy. So, how often do you include these steps in your daily routine? Sometimes not enough. Make it a habit today.

Breaking habits requires an investment in examining your copy to make the necessary changes.

We can't break habits unless we know our habits. Here's a sampling of steps that can help you improve your work. How many habits can you eliminate in one week—and sustain for the long run?

Give it a shot this week:

1. Avoid patterns
   Reread your work from the past week. Look for habits. Maybe it's that you started multiple leads all in the same way (i.e., with the name of someone) or that you filed multiple run-on sentences. Or that you started multiple paragraphs with a surname. Or that you overused certain words such as the, that, and etc. It's easy to fall into habits. Don't roboticize your work. Evolve it.
2. Eliminate awkward words
   Nobody's asking reporters to dumb down their writing. It's simply a case of being reader-friendly. Write for your readers, not above them. Look for words with fewer syllables to replace long-winded words. Look for places where one word will take the place of two words. Condense. Cut. Tighten.
3. Improve your quotes
   Evaluate your quotes. Are they quotes that add colour to your story, or are you just quoting information that can be paraphrased? Filing quotes such as "If people want more information, they'll have to contact Bob Smith in accounting next week" are a disservice to quote marks. Or, if you repeatedly file quotes that consist of three words

EXERCISE 1   The Body of a News Story

SECTION I: SECOND PARAGRAPHS

Second paragraphs are almost as important as leads. Like leads, second paragraphs must help arouse readers' interest in a topic. Critically evaluate the second paragraphs in the following stories. Judge which of the second paragraphs are most successful in: (1) providing a smooth transition from the lead; (2) continuing to discuss the topic summarized in the lead; and (3) emphasizing the news—details that are new, important and interesting. Give each second paragraph a grade from A to F.

1. A Pinkerton courier was robbed at gunpoint and fatally wounded on Tuesday while leaving Merchants Bank with the day's daily transaction records.

    Edwin James, 59, of 826 Bell Drive, was following standard bank procedures and carrying no money. (Grade: _____)

2. A 41-year-old teacher who fell and broke an ankle while stopping for a cup of coffee on her way to work sued a convenience store Monday.

    The teacher, Tina Alvarez, has worked at Washington Elementary School for 21 years. (Grade: _____)

3. Two young men are presumed dead after falling off a 30-foot rock formation into the Pacific Ocean at a California park Saturday.

    The men remain unidentified, and their bodies have not been recovered. (Grade: _____)

4. Police responding to a 911 call about a shooting at 10 p.m. Sunday discovered Ralph Beasley on Bennett Road with a gunshot wound to his head.

    County sheriff's deputies arrived at about the same time in response to a radio request for assistance. An ambulance was already at the scene, as were Fire Department paramedics. (Grade: _____)

5. A 32-year-old woman who said she smoked marijuana to ease the pain of a rare intestinal disease was charged Tuesday morning with possessing illegal drugs.

    Ruth Howland was stopped at the Municipal Airport after a K-9 dog singled out her suitcase. She and her husband, Terry, were returning from Mexico. (Grade: _____)

6. Three gunmen who entered a restaurant on Wilson Avenue at 10:30 p.m. Tuesday held four employees and 12 customers at gunpoint while taking more than $3,000 from several cash registers.

    Peggy Deacosti, the restaurant's hostess, was on duty when the robbery occurred. (Grade: _____)

7. Eileen Guion, 38, a food and beverage co-ordinator at Walt Disney World for 18 years, died at her home Tuesday of unknown causes.

    Although she was offered many other jobs at restaurants, she never accepted them. She once said, "I've loved working at Disney because I get to work with people from all over the world, and I think that is very neat." (Grade: _____)

8. Police are searching for a man who attacked a woman outside the Bayside Bar & Grill Thursday night.

    Terry Smythe, a bartender at the restaurant, said he heard a woman screaming outside the entrance at 9 p.m. Smythe darted to the foyer, where he saw the woman trapped in the entryway. Smythe said it was "kind of like a tug of war," with the assailant trying to pull the woman outside while waitresses tried to pull her inside. (Grade: _____)

SECTION II: TRANSITIONS

Critically evaluate the following transitions. Which would be most likely to entice you to continue reading the stories? Which provide a smooth, specific, informative and interesting introduction to the next idea? Give each transition a grade from A to F.

1. _____ Other students said they would tell their teachers about cheaters because cheating is not fair to those who take the time to study.

2. _____ But what should happen when a husband and wife disagree about having a baby?

3. _____ A concerned citizen then addressed the commission about the fence.

4. _____ Next, the task force presented its plan for preservation and renovation of the downtown.

5. _____ In a flat, emotionless voice, Howard responded that he and Jackson stole a red Mustang convertible on the night of June 3, picked up the two 14-year-old girls, and took them to the motel.

6. _____ Gary Hubbard, superintendent of schools, then addressed his concerns about security in the city's schools.

7. _____ Police Chief Barry Kopperud said his department is trying to combat juvenile crime by changing the way officers interact with children.

8. _____ He then discussed prejudice as a problem that plagues society.

9. _____ She also spoke about the different religious celebrations and rituals.

10. _____ Parents who love, care for, and respect their children don't raise delinquents, she said.

CHAPTER 7

Writing Complete News Stories

Write complete news stories based on the following information. Be thorough; use most of the information provided. Because much of the material is wordy, awkward and poorly organized, you will have to rewrite it extensively. Correct all errors in your rewrite.

1. A family that owns a farm about 2 kilometres outside your town has decided to sell it. It has been in they're family for four generations. They often bring fresh eggs, produce and other items to the farmers market in town to sell, which is held once a month on the first Saturday. The father of the family told you they are selling because their children are nearly grown and don't want to farm, and that they will be moving to another province to be closer to other family members, but he declined to say any more than that. A real estate developer is buying the property, and he wants to subdivide it for single-family homes and town houses. There would be a total of five hundred new homes as the developer, Eugene McIntry, President of McIntry Realty, has planned it. McIntery has submitted his subdivision plan to the county commissioners. The commissioners and the County Planning Commission are extremely worried about this giant new development. They don't believe their roads and their water and sewer systems can handle all those people. In fact, right now the water system and sewer system don't even run to the farm. The family that lives on the farm have a well and a septic tank for their house and another well for their barn. But, the county doesn't have any zoning, so the supervisors don't think they can keep McIntry from buying the farm and building all those homes. Plus, McIntry has threatened to file a lawsuit if the township tries anything to keep his plans from going through. He said he has a lot of money invested and doesn't want to lose it. Some nearby residents, however, are going to file a lawsuit of their own to keep him from building the houses. They are angry that they're peaceful, quiet stretch of road just outside the city will soon be filled with cars and their view will be ruined by hundred's of new houses. The residents attorney, Hector Salvatore, says he is finishing up the suit and will file it in County Court next week. He said the residents also are afraid they will be forced to hook up to the water and sewer systems if they are expanded out to the farm, which means several hundred dollars out of each of their pockets, which he said is unfair and possibly illegal.

2. A bad accident happened this morning on the interprovincial highway that runs right along the western edge of your city. It is Highway 790. Apparently two tractor trailers collided and started a chain reaction crash. The citys Police Department is not done investigating the accident, which happened at 6:45 a.m. in the morning, but that is what they believe preliminarily. A total of 4 tractor-trailers and fourteen cars were involved, according to Sgt. Albert Wei of the police department. One of the tractor-trailers was a tanker hauling diesel fuel; it was very lucky, Wei said, that it didn't roll over or dump any fuel or catch fire. The truck part of the tanker was damaged when a car hit it, but the truck driver managed to get it stopped along the side of the road. He wasn't hurt, Wei said, but 2 people driving cars were killed and twenty other people were injured and taken to the hospital, four of them seriously hurt. The fire chief, Tony Sullivan, said those seriously hurt people had injuries that were life-threatening. One of the ambulance drivers told him that. Sulluvan said his firefighters had to cut the roofs off three of the cars to free the drivers and passengers that were trapped inside. All five of the fire department's ambulances were on the seen, along with ambulances from four nearby citys' fire departments. Also, the "Life Flight" helicopter from Memorial Hospital in you're city was called to the scene and flew two of the worst injuries to the trauma center in Statesville, 50 miles away. Sullivan said the crash scene looked like something from a war zone when he arrived, with bodies laying along the road, people covered with blood sitting next to their cars, emergency workers running from place to place trying to help the injured, and sirens wailing in the distance as more fire trucks and ambulances were called. He had never seen anything that bad in the 18 and a half years he's been with the fire department. Wie said the police officers on the scene were having trouble

figuring out which people were from which vehicles, and who were the drivers and who were the passengers. According to Wei, the accident, which happened in the northbound lanes, closed the entire highway, north and south. The highway was still closed at 10 a.m., the deadline for your story, and Wei had no idea when it would be open again. It created quite a mess for the rush hour traffic today, since people who normally would have used Highway 790 had to go on Highway 690, on the eastern side of the city, and that backed up traffic on 690 for three hours.

3. It seems to be turning into a controversy in your local school district. The School Board is considering implementing random drug testing of all student athletes at the high school. Students and parents on both sides of the issue plan to attend tomorrow night's board meeting, which was to be in the library at Van Horne Elementary School but has been moved to the cafeteria at Northmount High School to accommodate the expected large audience. The 5 school board members you were able to talk to this morning before your deadline, David DeBecker, Mimi Lieber, Judie Lu, Diana Maceda and Jane Tribitt, were reluctant to say anything before the meeting that might give away their positions on the issue. Gary Hubbard is the Superintendent of schools. He didn't really want to say much either when you called him, but then did admit that he was the one who asked the board to consider the new policy. He believes there are members of the football and boys basketball teams that are using steroids and other performance-enhancing drugs, and said some players on those teams have come to him and complained. The school can't test only certain athletes, Hubberd said, so they have to test players in all sports. DeBecker referred you to the school boards attorney, Karen Bulnes. She said she has drafted a proposed policy for the board to consider, but said she doesn't know how they will vote. She said such a policy is legal based on past Supreme Court of Canada decisions. You were able to talk to some students at the high school this morning before classes started. Hazel Beaumont was dropping off her son, Roger, in front of the school. Roger is a tenth-grader who is playing soccer this fall. He thinks drug testing is a violation of his privacy, but then admitted that he really likes playing soccer and probably would take the test. His mother said she would make him take the test, and said she'll be at the school board meeting. Two girls who play field hockey, Ann Capiello and Amy Deacosti, don't like the idea either, but said they don't have anything to hide and would take the test if required. Both girls are seniors, and when you asked them about the football players taking steroids, Ann said she has heard that. James Carigg and Diana Nyer are seniors who both play basketball, and both are opposed to drug testing. In fact, they plan to go to the meeting and voice they're opinions against the idea. Lu called you back after you had talked with her and said she decided to publicly say that she is in favour of the idea because she thinks it will be a deterrent for students who might be thinking about taking drugs. The meeting will start at 7 p.m.

4. Fire destroyed two businesses downtown last night, and police think it was arson. They also think they know who set the fire, which caused an estimated five hundred thousand dollars' damage. The businesses that were destroyed were Kalani Brothers Bakery and Barton School of Dance. The fire started in the bakery and spread to the dance studio. Fire chief Tony Sullivan said an automatic alarm at the bakery sounded at 11:35 p.m. When the first fire truck arrived on the scene, flames were shooting out the front of the bakery, where a large picture window had burst, and fire was visible on the 2nd floor, where the dance studio was located. The city fire department was assisted by fire companies from two neighbouring towns. A total of 75 firemen and other emergency personnel responded to the call. The first fireman on the scene was Eddy Muldaur, a student at Lake Community College and a volunteer with the city fire department. He told you last night at the scene that there was a lot of smoke and flames coming from the building when he got there. About ten minutes later, the first truck arrived. You were very surprised this morning to find out that Police chief Barry Kopperud issued a news release saying that Muldaur had been arrested and charged with arson for allegedly setting the fire and damaging the sprinkler system so it wouldn't work. He was placed in the city jail on $1 million dollars bail. Eileen Barton, the owner of Barton School of Dance, was inconsolable when you talked to her this morning. She started the dance school 8 years ago. It was the only thing she ever wanted to do. She

CHAPTER 7

EXERCISE 3   The Body of a News Story

Writing Complete News Stories

Write complete news stories based on the following information. Critically examine the information's language and organization, improving it whenever possible. To provide a pleasing change of pace, use quotations in your stories. Go beyond the superficial; unless your instructor tells you otherwise, assume that you have enough space to report every important and interesting detail.

1. The president of your local school board is in trouble. David DeBecker has been a member of the school board for more than twenty years and president for nearly six years. He told school officials and local authorities that he has done nothing wrong. Police have charged Debecker with theft, fraud, extortion, and obstruction of justice. DeBecker, 57, lives on a 15-acre estate at 6540 Meadowdale Road. The property includes an 18-room white brick mansion, a barn and stable, several work sheds, and a large pond stocked with fish. Police said this is what happened. DeBecker is part owner of a janitorial service incorporated as Best Bet Cleaning Services. DeBecker did not disclose the fact that he was part owner of the business when the company bid on the cleaning contract at your local high school. His partner, James V. Stimson, 43, of 2109 Jamestown Drive, is listed as owner and operator of the company. DeBecker runs his own accounting firm, DeBecker Accounting Services Inc. DeBecker became acquainted with Stimson seven years ago when Stimsen came to DeBecker seeking financial advice. Stimson was in trouble with the federal government for owing back taxes and DeBecker was able to fix the problem but demanded to be made a silent partner in the lucrative cleaning business. DeBecker helped Stimson bid on the school cleaning contract and Stimson was awarded the contract as low bidder. DeBecker recruited students from the county vocational school to work with Stimson, but often did not pay the students. DeBecker would pocket the money instead. DeBecker also had the students work on his property to clean and do construction work on various projects. The students were not paid for the work. More than 35 vocational students were involved at one time or another in the scam. Best Bet Cleaning Services was being paid hundreds of thousands of dollars to do the cleaning work at the high school with the stipulation that vocational students be among the workers. The students were never told they were to be paid. They were told by Stimson that they were getting "business experience" as their compensation. Also charged with obstruction of justice is Ruth Gunderson who is accused of destroying email and other records in regard to the work done at the high school. Gunderson is the office secretary for Best Bet Cleaning Services. She is 45 years old and lives at 946 Hillcrest Street with her husband, William Gunderson. Charges are pending against Stimson. A provincial court handed down the indictments after a 14-month investigation. Authorities believe that DeBecker defrauded the school district of more than $850,000 over the six-year term of the cleaning contract. DeBecker is free on $250,000 bond. He faces up to 25 years in prison if convicted of the charges.

2. Fishing is a great sport enjoyed by millions of Canadians. Jeffrey R. Ahsonn loves to fish. He likes to fish for trout and small-mouth bass. The province stocks the fish in two small lakes in your county. The lakes are Lake Raymond and Lake Barton. They are fed by crystal clear underground springs. The water is very clean and clear in the springs that tumble into the lakes that Ahsonn fishes in as often as he can. "My dad got me hooked on fishing. No pun intended. I used to just go along and sit beside him by the stream and watch him bait his hook, cast the line, and reel the fish in. When I got old enough to handle a rod, he showed me how to bait my own hook and cast the line. It was a great time for the both of us. Sometimes we would just sit on the bank of some creek and just talk. There were times he didn't even put a worm on the hook. I think he just wanted to spend time talking to me. I began fishing in Lake Raymond and Lake Barton when I moved to the county more than 30 years ago. I brought my dad here whenever he came for a visit. He always brought his

rod and reel. This was the last place he fished before he died three years ago. He always loved how clear the spring water supplying the lake was. I could drop a quarter into three feet of water and read the date on the back without my reading glasses. You can always come here and catch fish. You can catch trout, bluegill, and bass. I can't remember a day of fishing that I didn't go home with something. I taught my son James to fish in these lakes just like my dad taught me so many years ago." The two lakes are surrounded by oak, willow, and maple trees that turn orange, red, yellow, green, and gold in the fall. They provide shade during the hot summer months. Ahsonn has a favourite spot under a one of the big oak trees on the south side of Lake Raymond. But the favourite spot will soon be gone. The province plans to drain Ahsonns favourite fishing spots because they pose a danger to surrounding communities. Lake Raymond is nearly 175 acres and Lake Barton is just over 90 acres. Both lakes are nearly 16 feet deep at their deepest points. The lakes formed in 1925 when the province dammed up the spring-fed streams. The dams are in need of repair. It would cost the province nine million dollars to repair the dams. Kerwin Dawkins is the county's director of public works. He says the county doesn't have the money and the province doesn't have the money so the only alternative is to drain the lakes. The dams are leaking and provincial and county officials are afraid that a flooding rainfall could collapse the dams. "It's a losing battle. The dams were built in 1925. They may have been safe at one time, but there has been a lot of development in the county since then and if those dams collapsed, it could damage a lot of property and threaten the lives of a lot of people." Dawkins said. The province plans to make small breaches in the dams at each lake and let the water slowly drain out. It will take about two to three months for the lakes to drain completely, Dawkins says. Ahsonn said: "It's a shame that we can't save these two lakes. A lot of people in the county used these lakes to fish and swim in. I'm sure going to miss my favourite fishing hole. I guess I'll just have to find another one." The province and county have no plans for the dried up lake beds at this point. There is some talk that a developer would like to purchase the land and build houses on it. The province has nearly 150 small dams that have been inspected by Canadian Armed Forces officials and declared unsafe. Some of the dams will be repaired for historical reasons, but most will be torn down. Your province is one of only several in the nation that set aside funding for small dam repair on private and public land. Ahsonn is 69 years old. He lives at 49 Groveland Avenue with his wife, Teresa. Ahsonn is a retired construction electrician. He is balding, with only a fringe of gray hair left on his head. His complexion is tanned from being out doors a lot. He has blue eyes, a thin build and stooped shoulders.

3.   It was a potential tragedy that your citys police, rescue, and fire officials say was just barely averted. James Shanahan, his two daughters Alyssa and Adrienne, and his wife, Mary, were travelling from Grand Rapids, Mich. They were flying near your city when the plane they were in had to make an emergency landing. James Shanahan is a licensed pilot. He has been flying for 30 years. He has never had a problem in all that time. No one was seriously injured, but James Shanahan was admitted to Mercy Hospital for observation. Mrs. Shanahan was treated for a broken wrist and a laceration on her forehead and released. Adrienne suffered minor cuts and bruises. Alyssa was not injured. The plane was a four-passenger Mooney Executive 21 propeller-driven, fixed-wing aircraft. The undercarriage of the plane sustained minor damage. There was a small fuel spill, according to the fire department. "They were very fortunate. It could have been much worse than it was. There were a lot of startled people when that plane came at them," said Fire Chief Tony Sullivan. Police Chief Barry Kopperud said the Shanahans left Grand Rapids early in the morning. The flight was proceeding normally until the plane was 100 miles east of the city. The plane began to wander off course and was contacted by the control tower at City Regional Airport. A girls voice responded to the control tower. "The girl I talked to on the radio told me the pilot was having problems. She told me he had slumped in his seat and was unconscious. I could hear the passengers screaming in the background. It was really confusing. I think they were getting a bit panicky up there," said control tower flight manager Peter Jacobs. Police said James Shanahan lost consciousness as he was about to contact the tower to request an emergency landing. His wife, Mary, told police her husband

began complaining about not feeling well. He told her that he felt dizzy and couldn't get his breath. She said he suddenly slumped over in his seat and the plane went into a shallow dive. "There was nothing I could do. I was in the back passenger seat with my daughter Adrienne. I couldn't reach the controls. And even if I could have, I don't think I could have helped because I never learned how to fly. I hate flying," Mrs. Shanahan said. Kopperud said Aylssa Shanahan was seated beside her father. It was she who responded to the towers call about the plane wandering off course. Alyssa pulled her fathers arms away from the controls and his legs off the rudder pedals. She then took over the controls of the aircraft and called the tower for help to land the plane. Jacobs stayed in contact with Alyssa and gave her instructions on what to do. He talked to her the entire time and directed other aircraft away from the airport until the emergency was over. Alyssa was able to locate the airport and brought the plane down. When the plane landed, it overshot the runway and skidded across an open field. The landing gear of the plane collapsed and the plane plowed through a chain-link fence and came to a stop just 10 feet from the northbound lane of Interstate 51. The interstate was crowded with traffic at the time of the accident. The accident occurred at 4:05 p.m., police said. No one on the ground was injured. Alyssa is 12 years old, 4 feet 3 inches tall and weighs 88 pounds. "I've been flying with my Daddy since I was a little girl. He taught me all about flying and even let me handle the controls sometimes. I was a little scared because I couldn't reach the rudder pedals very well. But I couldn't be too scared because I want to be a pilot like my Daddy someday. I was more worried about my Daddy because I didn't know what happened to him. I just wanted to get on the ground and get help for him," Alyssa said. Doctors at Mercy Hospital said Mr. Shanahan was in satisfactory condition after suffering an allergic reaction to a prescription medicine he had begun taking that morning.

EXERCISE 4   The Body of a News Story

Reporting Controversial Stories (Quoting Opposing Viewpoints)

Write complete news stories about the following controversies. As you write the stories, present both sides of each controversy as fully and as fairly as possible. Also, try to integrate those conflicting viewpoints. Instead of reporting all the opinions voiced by the first source, and then all the conflicting opinions voiced by the second source, try—when appropriate—to report both opinions about the story's most important issue and then both opinions about the second, third and fourth issues.

Story 1: School Board Ban

FACTS: The school board in your town made a unanimous decision Tuesday night. It wasn't a popular decision with some students and parents. But school board members said they made the decision for the safety of athletes participating in sports in the school district. The vote was 9 to nothing. The board voted to ban boys from playing on girls' teams. The policy was implemented after four boys tried out for and made the high schools girls field hockey team last year. The boys played on the team last fall and helped the team make the provincial playoffs. The policy banning boys from girls teams says the size, speed, and power of male athletes poses a hazard for female players. Several schools that played your towns high school team last year forfeited their games rather than take a chance of fielding their girls against the boys on the team. The policy takes affect immediately. The policy will ban boys from playing on the girls field hockey, volleyball, and softball teams.

ONE SIDE: High school athletic director Hugh Baker told the board that such a blanket policy could hurt the schools athletics program because the school would have to forfeit games to other teams. "If safety is the issue of concern for the board, then our girls teams would have to forfeit games if there are boys on the opposing teams. If we can't have boys on our teams because the board is afraid girls will get hurt, then our teams can't play against teams that have boys on their teams. Our girls field hockey team would have had to forfeit at least ten of their 18 games last season because we played other schools that had boys on their teams. It would be unfair to force our field hockey team to have a losing record every year because it has to forfeit all those games. Some of the schools we play are smaller schools and they wouldn't be able to field enough players if they didn't allow boys and girls to play on the same team." Jacob Stevens is a senior at the high school. He played on the girls field hockey team last year. He was looking forward to playing on the team his senior year. He spoke to the board during the meeting. "I don't think it is fair. There are countries in the world where men's field hockey is a recognized sport. Not every guy wants to play football, basketball, or baseball. Field hockey is a fast and exciting sport that requires a lot of skill. I enjoy playing the game and I haven't had any of the other female players on the team complain about my being there. If we can't play with the girls, we wouldn't be able to play. There are not enough boys interested to create a mens field hockey team."

THE OTHER SIDE: School board member Jane Tribitt voted for the policy. She proposed the ban after receiving complaints from parents in both the home district and away districts. "I just don't believe the sexes should be mixed in this case. The boys are just too big and physical and it intimidates the girls on the team. It is a matter of safety. And there are other teams that have no boys on their teams that do not want to play our school for whatever reason because there are boys on the team. I think other schools will adopt policies similar to this one and ban boys from their teams as well. The question of forfeiting games will then become a moot point." Sandra Adler is a parent whose daughter was a senior on last years team along with the four boys. Adler also was an all-province consensus pick as player of the year during her senior year

Beverly Cheng, executive director of the Provincial Restaurant Association, said: "This is an example of government taking a good thing too far and then compounding the problem. I see nothing wrong with having separate areas in a restaurant or bar for smokers and non-smokers. That is fair to everyone. But to ban a whole segment of society from doing something they enjoy is unfair. And then to persecute them even more by taking away their right to voice their opinion is adding insult to injury."

8 | Quotations and Attribution

Celebrated American humorist Erma Bombeck, on a trip to promote her book about children surviving cancer, discovered at a Toronto hospital that Canadian kids—even kids battling cancer—not only love to hear funny stories but are also pretty good themselves at the humorous quip.

According to a *Toronto Star* story, one little girl in the hospital had lost a leg to cancer. She was "shrouded in sheets and blankets while being moved onto a wheelchair. The flustered orderly carefully placed one leg on the foot rest, then looked for the other one. 'Good luck,' the girl said sardonically." (Catherine Dunphy, "Kids surviving cancer: How humour triumphed." *Toronto Star* Oct. 2, 1989, p. C1)

The girl's remark is both funny and provocative. It also reveals something of her personality and makes those who read her remark want to know more about her. People reveal themselves through their words. Part of the joy of meeting new people is discovering how they speak and how they view the world. And one way readers meet new people is through news stories.

Quotations add colour and interest to news stories by allowing readers to hear many voices rather than just the voice of the writer. Weaving those many voices into one coherent news story, however, can be difficult. Experienced writers follow certain customs and guidelines to help them handle the difficulties.

QUOTATIONS

Reporters incorporate in their stories information they have obtained from other people in one of three forms: (1) direct, (2) indirect, and (3) partial quotations. Direct quotations present a source's exact words and consequently are placed entirely in quotation marks. Indirect quotations lack quotation marks because reporters use their own words to summarize or paraphrase the source's remarks. Partial quotations directly quote key phrases from a source's statement and paraphrase the rest:

> DIRECT QUOTATION: Ambrose said: "Journalism students should be dealing with ideas of a social, economic and political nature. There's too much of a trade-school atmosphere in journalism schools today. One spends too much time on minor technical and mechanical things, like learning how to write headlines."

INDIRECT QUOTATION: Ambrose said journalism students should deal with ideas, not mechanical techniques.

PARTIAL QUOTATION: Ambrose criticized the "trade-school atmosphere" in journalism schools and said students should study ideas, not mechanical techniques.

When to Use Direct Quotations

Reporters use direct quotations when their sources say something important or controversial and state their ideas in an interesting, unusual or colourful manner. When the *Toronto Star* in 2009 profiled Pura Velasco, an advocate and activist for the rights of foreign caregivers in Canada, the story included a compelling quotation: "I was already a student activist (in the Philippines). It's something I cannot stand if I know that the rights of other people are being disrespected. Your heart will tell you that you can't let it go, and that you have to challenge the oppressor."

Direct quotations are so much a part of news stories that reporters and editors may think a story is incomplete without its quota of quotations. But reporters who merely decorate their stories with quotations are not using them effectively.

Editors have identified the usual instances when direct quotations are appropriate:

- Use quotations to let the sources talk directly to the reader.
- Use quotations when you cannot improve on the speaker's exact words or cannot match the speaker's wit, rhythm, colour or emotion.
- Use quotations to tie a controversial opinion to the source.
- Use quotations as evidence for a statement.
- Use quotations to reveal the speaker's character.

Archbishop Desmond Tutu, recalling the days when he and others worked to end the apartheid regime in South Africa, told of meeting a nun in California who said she prayed every day at 2 a.m. for him and for all opponents of segregation. "We're being prayed for in the woods in California at 2 in the morning. What chance does the apartheid government stand?" Tutu asked. His remark satisfies many of the criteria for direct quotations.

The best direct quotations usually are short and full of emotion. Four words taken from remarks made by Dick Pound, former vice-president of the International Olympic Committee, sparked a complaint from an aboriginal rights group to the IOC's ethics committee. Pound, quoted in a story by *La Presse*, was responding to a question about holding the Olympics in China when he compared China, "a 5,000-year-old civilization," to seventeenth-century Canada, "a land of savages."

Using Direct Quotations Effectively

Direct quotations should illustrate a point, not tell an entire story. Stories composed entirely of quotations seem poorly organized because they lack natural transitions. The following story contains a pleasing combination of quotations and paraphrases:

The most important thing women's basketball coach Vance Coleman carries in his briefcase is not a sketch of a new defensive scheme, a game plan for the upcoming opponent, or even the phone number of a basketball colleague.

It's a crumpled, yellowed piece of paper with a list full of scratches and re-dos. It's his list of five life goals. Coleman lists living a long and healthy life, playing the role of a good father and husband, and earning a million dollars as his top three goals. The other two, he said, constantly change as he ages.

But the point, Coleman said, is to always have them.

"There is an equation I use that works on the basketball court, on the playing field, in business, and in life," Coleman said, "and that is performance equals ability times motivation. You may have all the ability in the world, but with no motivation, you won't accomplish anything. Zero times anything is nothing.

"No matter what you do in life, you have to have goals. And you have to stick to those goals."

Coleman, now in his second year at the university and his seventeenth year of coaching, spoke about goals and motivation to nearly 300 students at the Student Alumni Association Conference Friday.

"The first thing you need is a good attitude," Coleman said. "When you get up at 7 a.m., do you say, 'Good morning, God,' or 'Good God, morning'? Same words, big difference in attitude."

Next, the coach shifted gears to the importance of beliefs.

"When someone asks you what you believe in, tell them with conviction," Coleman said. "Say, 'I believe in myself and what I think with my whole heart and nothing less.'"

Reporters often summarize a major point and then use a direct quotation to explain the idea or provide more specific details about it. But the quotation should provide new information. Here's an example of how a quotation can effectively support a point. It's from a story about a speech given by a 34-year-old African-American corporate executive to a group of college students. He advised students to establish personal advisory boards:

Gather five people in your life who helped to shape your views. Whether it's a mentor, a parent, a preacher or a friend, advisory board people can provide support and confidence, Johnson said.

"My mom is part of my advisory board. As a person of colour, it really wasn't popular to be non-white in my elementary school," he said. "My mom had to come to school every day because I was picked on. She'd say, 'Art, you are the best. Always remember that.' She instilled a sense of self-confidence in me that I still have today."

A quotation should not repeat, or echo, facts reported earlier in a story; this kind of quotation is often called a "stutter quote":

Company officials said they are not worried about the upcoming audit.

"We're not expecting anything to worry about," treasurer Peter VanNeffe said.

Quotations can also help to describe a story's dramatic moments. Because of their importance, these moments should be described in detail and placed near the beginning of a story. As the United States was increasing pressure on Saddam Hussein to disclose the contents of his country's arsenal or face military action, a reporter asked then–U.S. president George W. Bush whether the country was about to go to war with Iraq. Bush replied, "You said we're headed to war in Iraq. I don't know why you say that. I'm the person who gets to decide, not you." Years later, with both U.S. and British troops committed to fighting an insurgency in Iraq, Britain's Prince Harry insisted he would go with his military unit if it were deployed to Iraq. "There's no way I'm going to put myself through Sandhurst, and then sit on my arse back home while my boys are out fighting for their country," he said. Sandhurst is Britain's military academy.

In Canada, a 2009 Canadian Press story revealed that the Conservative government had deleted a section on Vietnam from its federal website "to boost its case for deporting Iraq war deserters." The story quoted an internal document, released under the Access to Information Act, that summarized the government's position: "Unlike American draft dodgers who immigrated to Canada during the Vietnam conflict, the individuals coming to Canada now voluntarily joined the United States military and have subsequently deserted."

Quotations such as these are so interesting and dramatic that they compel readers to finish the story.

When to Use Indirect Quotations

Some sources are more quotable than others, and even colourful sources say things that are not quotable. Reporters may be tempted to use whatever quotations happen to be available. Yet a weak quotation is worse than none. If a quotation bores or confuses people, many will immediately stop reading a story. Compare the preceding interesting quotations with these:

> "It's something that's pretty unique here," she said.
> "We're here for many reasons," he said.
> "The positive response was tremendous," Wesley said.

None of these speakers uses interesting or remarkable phrasing. Each sentence would be better paraphrased or omitted entirely.

Reporters use indirect quotations when their sources fail to state their ideas effectively. Indirect quotations allow reporters to rephrase a source's remarks and state them more clearly and concisely. Reporters also can emphasize the source's most significant remarks and revise or eliminate remarks that are unclear, irrelevant, libellous, pretentious or otherwise unprintable:

> ORIGINAL STATEMENT: Edna Czarski said, "Women do not get the same tax and insurance benefits that men receive, and they do not receive maternity benefits that even start to cover what they should."
> PARAPHRASED: Edna Czarski said women receive neither the same tax and insurance benefits as men nor adequate maternity benefits.

Reporters can never justify a weak quotation by responding, "But that's what my source said." They should use their interviewing skill and judgment to elicit and report quotations that are clear, concise, dramatic and interesting.

Sometimes sources give reporters only routine, boring quotations such as, "I really love to play football." By continuing the interview and asking better questions, reporters can get better responses. Here's the type of quotation reporters want:

> "I really love football," Joe Lozado said. "I've been playing since I was seven years old, and I would feel worthless if I couldn't play. There's no better feeling than just before a game when you run out on the field with all your buddies and see the crowd. You can feel the excitement."

Asking questions that encourage the source to elaborate on her or his ideas or reactions often will produce good quotations.

Avoid quotations—direct or indirect—that state the obvious. The following quotations are likely to sound familiar because they appear dozens of times every year. You may see these quotations in newspapers or hear them on radio and television:

> "We really want to win this game," Coach Riley said. (Readers already know this. Does any coach want to lose?)

> "If we can score some points, we can win this game," Tran Ogbondah said. (A team that does not score points obviously cannot win.)

Equally weak are self-serving quotations in which sources praise themselves and their programs:

> Lyons called her program a success. "We had a terrific crowd and a particularly good turnout," she said.

Reading or listening to someone's self-praise is as interesting as watching a videotape of someone else's vacation.

When to Use Partial Quotations

Sometimes reporters try to get around the problem of weak or confusing quotations by directly quoting only a few words from a sentence. In fact, most partial, or fragmentary, quotations are awkward, wordy or unnecessary. Sentences that contain several partial quotations are particularly distracting. Usually, the quoted phrases can be turned into indirect constructions, with the quotation marks simply eliminated:

> PARTIAL QUOTATION: He said the press barons "such as William Randolph Hearst" created "an amazingly rich variety" of newspapers.
> REVISED: He said the press barons such as William Randolph Hearst created an amazingly rich variety of newspapers.

Reporters also should avoid using "orphan" quotes; that is, they should not place quotation marks around an isolated word or two used in an ordinary way. The addition of quotation marks to emphasize individual words is inappropriate. Similarly, there is no reason to place quotation marks around profanities, slang, clichés, or grammatical errors:

> INCORRECT: He complained that no one "understands" his problem.
> REVISED: He complained that no one understands his problem.

> INCORRECT: She said that having to watch her child die was worse than "hell" could possibly be.
> REVISED: She said that having to watch her child die was worse than hell could possibly be.

At worst, an orphan quotation may be libellous. One newspaper included this sentence in a story about a murder case: "As police delved into his tangled business affairs, several women described as 'associated' with Brenhouse (the victim) were questioned at Hastings Police Headquarters." One of those women, who was named in the story, sued for libel. She argued—and a court agreed—that readers would infer from the quotation marks around "associated" that she had been having a love affair with the victim.

Reporters may use partial quotations to more clearly attribute to a source controversial, important or interesting phrases:

> Phil Donahue accused the television critic of "typing with razor blades."
> The petition urged the City Council to ban the sale of *Penthouse* and *Playboy* magazines "for the sake of our wives and children."

BLENDING QUOTATIONS AND NARRATIVE

Every news story must have a central point, and everything in the story must bear on that point. The sources whom the reporter interviewed, however, may have spoken about a number of topics, some of which may bear only slightly on the story's central point. Reporters must blend the quotations and the narrative they write to create a coherent, well-focused news story. This blending of narrative and quotations presents several problems and dilemmas for reporters.

Explaining Quotations

Sometimes reporters use a quotation and then realize readers need background information to understand it. They might try inserting explanatory material in parentheses. Or they might tack on the explanation after the attribution. Still others might put a large block of background information high in the story, hoping that it will give readers the information they need to understand the quotations and new facts reported elsewhere in the story. None of these approaches works well.

Lazy writers solve the problems of providing explanatory material by inserting it in parentheses in the quotation. When reporters pepper their stories with parenthetical explanations, the stories become difficult to read. Each bit of parenthetical matter forces readers to pause and absorb some additional information before moving on with the rest of the sentence. The occasional use of parentheses to insert brief explanations may be acceptable, but reporters should paraphrase quotations that need several parenthetical explanations. If reporters find themselves using parentheses repeatedly, they should consider reorganizing their stories.

INCORRECT: "When (head coach Tom) Whitman decides on his starter (at quarterback), the rest of them (the players) will quit squabbling," the athletic director said.
REVISED: The football players will quit squabbling when head coach Tom Whitman selects a starting quarterback, the athletic director said.

ACCEPTABLE: Dr. Harold Termid, who performed the operation, said, "The technique dates back before the twentieth century, when it was first used by the French to study ruminants (cud-chewing animals)."

Adding the explanatory information after the quotation or attribution is little better than using parentheses. Such backward constructions force readers to complete the sentence before they can figure out what the topic is. Here's an example:

"We're mobilizing for an economic war with other cities and states," the mayor said of his plan for attracting new businesses to the city.

Instead of using this "said-of" construction, turn the sentence around and use an indirect quotation. For example:

The mayor said his plan for attracting new business amounted to mobilization for an economic war with other cities and states.

Beginning reporters sometimes think they must report their questions so that readers can understand the source's answers. The news is in the answers, however, not in the questions. The use of both questions and answers is repetitive and dull. Reporters usually omit the question. If the question provides important context, reporters incorporate it in the answer:

INCORRECT: The president was asked whether he plans to seek a second term, and he responded that he would not announce his decision until next winter.
REVISED: The president said he would not announce his decision regarding a second term until next winter.
OR: In response to a question, the president said he would not announce his decision regarding a second term until next winter.
OR: During a question-and-answer session after his speech, the president said he would not announce his decision regarding a second term until next winter.

Sometimes, though, the fact a statement has been made in response to a question is an important part of the context. In the midst of a football recruiting scandal at the University of Colorado, Katie Hnida, a woman who had been a place kicker on the team, said she had been verbally abused, groped and raped by a teammate. During a press conference about the allegation, head coach Gary Barnett said: "Katie was a girl. Not only was she a girl, she was terrible. There's no other way to say it. She couldn't kick the ball through the uprights." Some commentators jumped on that quote and accused Barnett of saying it was OK for team members to rape Hnida because she was a poor player. Barnett, however, was responding to a reporter's question about why many Colorado players did not want Hnida on the team and was not condoning rape. He also said her allegation was serious and deserved thorough investigation.

To Change or Not to Change Quotations

Sometimes the exact words a source uses may be inappropriate to use in a news story. To make a quotation usable, reporters may be tempted to alter the words the speaker used. Whether writers should ever change a quotation is a matter of debate among journalists. Some journalists accept making minor changes in quotations to correct grammatical errors or delete profanity. Other journalists say reporters should never change quotations. Extensive changes in quotations are rarely acceptable (if the quotation needs that much altering, paraphrase instead of quoting, and be sure to remain faithful to the speaker's meaning).

Correcting Grammatical Errors

It remains common practice in Canadian newsrooms for reporters to correct grammatical errors in direct quotations. *The Canadian Press Stylebook* has this to say about the proper treatment of quotations:

> Quotes are the lifeblood of any story....They can also bring grief to writers and editors who play loose with them. Some news organizations permit liberties with quotes. CP takes a somewhat stern approach to any tampering with just what was said. In general, we quote people verbatim and in standard English. We correct slips of grammar that are obvious slips and that would be needlessly embarrassing. We remove verbal mannerisms such as *ah's*, routine vulgarities and meaningless repetitions. Otherwise we do not revise quotations.

If a quotation is so ungrammatical that it becomes difficult to understand, the reporter should paraphrase the source.

> GRAMMATICAL ERROR: "The council and the mayor is giving them corporations too much tax breaks so the load's not fair no more," Andrews said.
> REVISED: The council and the mayor have given so many tax breaks to corporations that the tax burden is no longer fairly shared, Andrews said.

Some sources are well known for the way they misuse words or create confusing sentences. Cleaning up their quotations would rob stories about them of their colour. The late Casey Stengel, a baseball manager, was famous for sentences like this one describing an unusually lucky player: "He could fall in a hole and come up with a silver spoon." A more recent example from the United States is former president George W. Bush, whose malapropisms, mispronunciations and fractured syntax often have been made fun of, even by Bush himself. When during his first presidential campaign Bush mispronounced "subliminal" as "subliminable," many news reports noted the slip. Bush later joked about it by intentionally mispronouncing the word. Other linguistic flubs by Bush were widely reported:

> "I am a person who recognizes the fallacy of human beings."
> "I know how hard it is to put food on your family."
> "I think that the vice-president is a person reflecting a half-glass-full mentality."

Using the source's exact words eliminates questions about accuracy. Reporters who are uncertain about the source's exact words (or think a statement needs rewriting) should use indirect rather than direct quotations. Doctoring a quotation could lead to a mistake that would injure the reputation of the source and the career of the reporter.

Even those who oppose altering quotations recognize a few instances where changes are necessary. They usually involve the deletion of unnecessary words, grammatical errors and profanities:

> ORIGINAL STATEMENT: He said, "Look, you know I think nuclear power is safe, absolutely safe."
> REVISION: He said, "Nuclear power is safe, absolutely safe."

Reporters may use an ellipsis (three evenly spaced periods) to show where they deleted a word, phrase or sentence. An ellipsis that appears at the end rather than in the middle of a complete sentence should have four periods. Policies vary from news organization to news organization, and some journalists do not use ellipses in reporting ordinary interviews. Reporters are more likely to use them when quoting formal statements or documents.

Reporters have an obligation to present a source's views as faithfully as possible, so they must be certain that they are not removing important context when they delete words or phrases from a quotation.

In 2009, the Saskatchewan government wanted the Supreme Court of Canada to rule on proposed legislation that would allow marriage commissioners to opt out of performing same-sex marriages if it was contrary to the commissioners' religious beliefs. The government referred the matter to the court of appeal, and the question before the court was whether the proposals meet the requirements of the Charter of Rights. The reporter covering the story, Jennifer Graham of the *Prince George Citizen*, aware of the need to get the legal facts straight, quoted the province's justice minister:

> We've given the Court of Appeal two suggested options: one that we grandfather the existing marriage commissioners that are reluctant or refusing to perform a same-sex marriage, and the other one would be to create a religious exemption for those and for future marriage commissioners. It would require us to have two pools of marriage commissioners—one that would be willing to perform the same-sex marriage and one that would not.

Deleting Profanities

Reporters usually omit profanities from quotations. Editors and news directors say children as well as adults read their newspapers and view their programs. Not only may profanities be inappropriate for children, but some adults also may find four-letter words offensive. News organizations are becoming more candid, however, and some publish mild profanities that are essential to a story. Casual profanities—those used habitually and unnecessarily by many people—remain forbidden in most newsrooms:

> UNNECESSARY PROFANITY: "Shit, I wasn't going to try to stop that damned idiot," the witness testified. "He had a knife."
> REVISED: "I wasn't going to try to stop that idiot," the witness testified. "He had a knife."

For broadcast journalists, deletion of profanities may be required by federal law. The debate over appropriate language in broadcast media heated up in recent decades in the United States, where the Federal Communications Commission has ruled that even a single use of a profanity may subject the broadcaster to fines. The ruling came in a case involving a Golden Globe Awards broadcast. When U2 lead singer Bono accepted one of the awards, he said, "This is really, really fucking brilliant." The FCC decided that the broadcast was legally indecent. Before the Golden Globe case, the FCC had held that fleeting uses of profanities, even of the "F-word," were not indecent. The FCC has said it will consider the context in which profanities appear, so no word is automatically indecent.

In Canada, similar regulations apply to broadcast media, forbidding obscene, profane or indecent language. The Canadian Radio-television and Telecommunications Commission is authorized to levy fines for transgressions, but such matters are normally left to self-regulation by the industry's Canadian Broadcast Standards Council. According to this body, self-regulation within the context of prevailing community standards has functioned well; television and radio stations are familiar with the requirements for content warnings and program ratings; obscene language is permitted only after 9 p.m.

Generally, broadcast journalists, like print and online journalists, should avoid profanities. The laws are still developing, and the price of guessing wrong can be steep.

Editorialization

Avoid unintentional editorials. If worded carelessly, partial quotations, and even the form of attribution used, can express an opinion:

> EDITORIALIZATION: The mayor made it clear that the city cannot afford to give its employees a raise.
> REVISED: The mayor said the city cannot afford to give its employees a raise.

> EDITORIALIZATION: Each month, Sen. William Proxmire presented the Golden Fleece Award "for the biggest, most ironic, or most ridiculous example of wasteful government spending."
> REVISED: Each month, Sen. William Proxmire presented the Golden Fleece Award for what he considered "the biggest, most ironic, or most ridiculous example of wasteful government spending."

Before revision, the first sentence editorializes by saying the mayor "made it clear," which implies that she stated a fact in a convincing manner. Others might regard the statement that the city cannot afford pay raises for employees as an opinion or political posturing. The second sentence reports as fact the claim by Proxmire that all the recipients of his "award" wasted the government's money. Many of the recipients disagreed, and some provided convincing evidence that Proxmire was wrong.

ATTRIBUTION

The Purpose of Attribution

Reporters are experts in finding things out. They rarely possess expertise in the topics they write about, such as city planning, health care, finance or international relations. Instead, reporters must rely on the expertise of their sources. Attribution lets the readers know who the reporter's sources are. Ideally, all direct quotations, opinions, evaluations and second-hand statements of fact should be attributed to specific individuals. This information lets readers draw their own conclusions about the credibility of the story.

Reporters can attribute information to people, documents or publications but not to places or institutions. For example, reporters can quote a hospital official but not a hospital:

> INCORRECT: The hospital said the epidemic had ended.
> REVISED: A hospital spokesperson said the epidemic had ended.

> INCORRECT: Toronto announced that all city offices would be closed Monday.
> REVISED: The mayor of Toronto announced that all city offices would be closed Monday.

Statements That Require Attribution

Reporters do not have to attribute statements that report undisputed facts, such as the fact that the Second World War ended in 1945, that Montreal is in Quebec, or that three people died in an accident. Nor must reporters attribute things they witness. However, reporters must attribute the information they get from other people, especially: (1) statements about controversial issues; (2) statements of opinion; and (3) all direct and indirect quotations. News stories that fail to attribute such statements appear to present the reporter's personal opinions rather than the opinions of the sources. Two or three words of attribution are usually adequate:

> UNATTRIBUTED: The Birthing Centre is an alternative for pregnant women who prefer more personalized care.
> ATTRIBUTED: Director Sally Malone said the Birthing Centre is an alternative for pregnant women who prefer more personalized care.

Reporters must attribute statements that praise or condemn, assign credit or blame to any person or organization. Readers should immediately recognize that a story reports what someone else said, not the reporter's opinions or those of the news organization:

> UNATTRIBUTED: Parliament has wasted time while the problem of unemployment has worsened.
> ATTRIBUTED: The Speaker said that Parliament has wasted time while the problem of unemployment has worsened.

> UNATTRIBUTED: Acting in self-defence, the officer shot the teen three times in the chest.
> ATTRIBUTED: The officer said she was acting in self-defence when she shot the teen three times in the chest.

Statements that imply carelessness or recklessness or culpable conduct can provoke lawsuits. Careful attribution, particularly if the statements can be attributed to official sources, will reduce the risk of being sued.

Guidelines for the Placement and Frequency of Attribution

Attribution may be placed at the beginning or end of a sentence or at a natural break within it. However, it should never interrupt a thought:

> INCORRECT: "I shall," the general said, "return."
> REVISED: The general said, "I shall return."

Readers and listeners should be told who is speaking as soon as conveniently possible; they should never have to guess. If a quotation is long, the writer should place the attribution at the beginning or end of the first sentence or after the first meaningful clause in that sentence. The attribution should not be delayed until the end of the second or third sentence. Similarly, if a quotation contains only one sentence but that sentence is long, the attribution should come at or near the beginning of that sentence, not at the end:

> "However close we sometimes seem to that dark and final abyss, let no man of peace and freedom despair. For he does not stand alone. If we all can persevere, if we can in every land and office look beyond our shores and ambitions, then surely the age will dawn in which the strong are just and the weak secure and the peace preserved," the president said.
> REVISED: "However close we sometimes seem to that dark and final abyss," the president said, "let no man of peace and freedom despair. For he does not stand alone. If we all can persevere, if we can in every land and office look beyond our shores and ambitions, then surely the age will dawn in which the strong are just and the weak secure and the peace preserved."

Attribution should come at the beginning of any quotation in which there is a change of speakers. If reporters fail to provide transitions from one speaker to another, particularly when the statements are contradictory, readers may not understand who is speaking:

> The newspaper's editor said he no longer will accept advertisements for X-rated movies. He explained: "These movies are worthless. They contribute nothing to society and offend our readers. They're depressing and pornographic."
> "Newspapers have no right to pass judgment on matters of taste. If they do, they should also ban the advertisements for other products considered harmful: cigarettes, liquor, and pollutants like automobiles," a theatre owner responded.

These two paragraphs are confusing. Readers beginning the second paragraph might mistakenly assume the editor is contradicting himself. The writer can avoid the confusion by placing a brief transition at the beginning of the second paragraph, such as the following:

However, a local theatre owner responded, "Newspapers have no right…"

Direct Quotations

A direct quotation should be attributed only once, regardless of the number of sentences it contains:

> INCORRECT: "I'm opposed to any laws that prohibit the sale of pornography," the attorney said. "The restriction of pornography infringes on civil rights," he said. "I like to picture myself as a good guy defending a sleazy thing," he concluded.
>
> REVISED: "I'm opposed to any laws that prohibit the sale of pornography," the attorney said. "The restriction of pornography infringes on civil rights. I like to picture myself as a good guy defending a sleazy thing."

Even when a direct quotation continues for several paragraphs, it needs attribution only once:

> Capt. Bonventre eliminated the police department's motorcycle squad.
>
> "The main reason is that there are more injuries to motorcycle officers," he said. "I want to protect my officers. They think there's no danger on a cycle. Well, that's just optimistic thinking; there's a real danger.
>
> "Officers have much more protection in a car. I think that's pretty obvious. If an officer gets in a hot pursuit and crashes, he stands a better chance of escaping injury when he's in a car.
>
> "Also, almost any situation, even traffic, can be handled better in a patrol car than on a motorcycle. There are some places a motorcycle can go more easily, but a car certainly commands more respect."

Reporters also must avoid "floating" quotations: direct quotations that lack clear attribution to a speaker. Direct quotations need attribution only once, but that attribution must be clearly attached to the quotation. Careless writers sometimes name a source in one sentence and then deliver an unattributed quotation in the following sentence or paragraph. The reader must guess whether the quotation comes from the person just named or someone who will be identified later. The uncertainty halts the reader. Several such delays can cause the reader to put down the newspaper. Clear attribution makes the reader's work easier:

> INCORRECT: Wendy Mitchell, a sociologist, said there is a trend toward vocationalism on college campuses.
>
> "Many students now demand from college not a chance to think but a chance to become qualified for some job."
>
> REVISED: Wendy Mitchell, a sociologist, said there is a trend toward vocationalism on college campuses.
>
> "Many students now demand from college not a chance to think," she said, "but a chance to become qualified for some job."

Another confusing practice is reporting a quotation and then attributing it in the following paragraph:

> INCORRECT: "I was scared to death. I knew I was hurt, and I needed help."
> These were the words today of an 18-year-old student trapped in her wrecked car.
> REVISED: "I was scared to death," said an 18-year-old student who had been trapped in her wrecked car. "I knew I was hurt, and I needed help."

Partial Quotations

On the rare occasions when writers quote part of a sentence, they take care to separate it from complete sentences that are also being quoted. Combining partial and complete quotations sometimes causes confusing pronoun shifts, which can be avoided by (1) placing attribution between the partial quotation and the full-sentence quotation or (2) paraphrasing the partial quotation:

> INCORRECT: Ross said he expects to find a job "within a few weeks. And when I do get a job, the first thing I'm going to buy is a new car."
>
> ACCEPTABLE: Ross said he expects to find a job "within a few weeks." He added, "And when I do get a job, the first thing I'm going to buy is a new car."
>
> BETTER: Ross said he expects to find a job within a few weeks. "And when I do get a job, the first thing I'm going to buy is a new car," he added.

The original passage is confusing because of a shift in pronouns. The first sentence uses the third person, referring to Ross as "he." But in the second sentence, which is the full quotation, Ross refers to himself in the first person. Rewriting the partial quotation eliminates the confusion.

Indirect Quotations

Indirect quotations (or paraphrases) need more frequent attribution than direct quotations. Every opinion or unverified fact in an indirect quotation—sometimes every sentence—must be attributed:

> INCORRECT: The police chief insisted that the death penalty must be retained. The death penalty, harsh as it may seem, is designed to protect the lives and rights of law-abiding citizens. Without it, criminals' rights are overly protected. Because of the almost endless mechanisms of the appeal system, it is unlikely that an innocent person would be put to death.
>
> REVISED: The police chief insisted that the death penalty must be retained. The death penalty might seem harsh, he said, but it is designed to protect the lives and rights of law-abiding citizens. Without it, criminals' rights are overly protected, he said. Because of the almost endless mechanisms of the appeal system, he said, it is unlikely that an innocent person would be put to death.

If the police chief's remarks have been paraphrased, the reporter may not attribute them by placing the paragraph within quotation marks because it does not contain the police chief's own words. Similarly, editors should not convert an indirect quotation written by a reporter into a direct quotation. However, reporters and editors may take a statement out of quotation marks and reword it, provided they do not change its meaning.

Every sentence of indirect quotation should have attribution, but writers should avoid inserting phrases that may attribute a quotation twice. For example, the following sentence reports that a fire chief made an announcement, then adds that he "said":

> INCORRECT: In making the announcement, the fire chief said arsonists caused 20 per cent of the blazes reported in the city last year.
>
> REVISED: The fire chief said arsonists caused 20 per cent of the blazes reported in the city last year.

Whether reporting direct or indirect quotations, the writer should strive to vary the location of the attribution. Writing becomes dull if every sentence begins with "she said" or some variation. Moving the attribution to the end or middle of the sentence keeps writing interesting. Often the most effective location for attribution is after the first natural pause in the sentence.

Word Choice in Attributing Statements

The verbs used to attribute statements must be accurate and impartial. For straight news stories they also should be in the past tense. For feature stories, present tense attribution may be acceptable.

Some form of the verb "to say" best describes how sources communicate information. For variety, reporters sometimes use such verbs as "comment," "reply," "declare," "add," "explain," "state," "continue," "point out," "note," "urge," "suggest" and "warn." Each has a more specific meaning than "say" and can be used only when that meaning accurately reflects how the source spoke. "Explain," for instance, means to make something comprehensible or less obscure. Unless the source was discussing a complicated or unclear topic, "explain" would not be an appropriate verb for attribution:

> UNACCEPTABLE: The city council meeting will begin at 8 p.m., he explained.
> ACCEPTABLE: She explained that tort law requires that the injurious consequences of a person's actions be foreseeable before that person can be held liable for damages.

The statement in the first sentence is obvious and needs no explanation; the most appropriate verb of attribution is "said." In the second example, the source talks about a point of law that may be confusing or unclear to the average reader. The source's explanation increases understanding of the issue.

Many editors prohibit the use of verbs such as "hope," "feel," "believe," "want" and "think" to attribute statements. Editors say reporters know only what their sources tell them, not what sources hope, feel, believe, want or think.

Other words are even more inappropriate. People speak words; they do not "grin," "smile," "chuckle," "laugh," "sigh" or "cough" them. Reporters should rephrase such sentences as this:

> "It's a wonderful movie," she smiled.
> REVISED: "It's a wonderful movie," she said.
> OR: "It's a wonderful movie," she said with a smile.
> OR: Smiling, she said, "It's a wonderful movie."

The words "claimed" and "admitted" are especially troublesome. "Claimed" casts doubt on a source's remarks. It suggests that the remarks are controversial and possibly wrong. Similarly, "admitted" implies a source conceded some point or confessed to an error, charge or crime. By comparison, the word "said" is almost always appropriate. Frequent use of "said" may sound awkward at first, but it is a neutral term and can be used any number of times in a story.

Attribution should also be concise. Each of the following phrases (which have appeared in news stories) can be replaced by either "said" or "added":

> made it clear that
> further stated that
> went on to say that
> let it be known that
> also pointed out that
> emphasized the fact that
> stated in the report that
> said that he feels that
> brought out the idea that
> went on to say that in his opinion
> in making the announcement said that
> continued the speech by urging that
> responded to the question by saying that
> concluded the speech with the comment that

Levels of Attribution

Ideally, every source should be fully identified, but sometimes sources want their identities withheld. Experienced reporters and sources have worked out a shorthand for describing how much of the source's identity may be revealed and how much of what the source says may be published. This shorthand system recognizes four levels of attribution: on the record, on background, on deep background, and off the record.

"On-the-record" attribution means that everything the source says may be published and quoted directly and the source may be fully identified by name and title. Reporters should try to keep as much as possible of every interview on the record. This allows readers to see or hear the source's exact words and know who the source is.

"Not for attribution" (also sometimes called "on background") means the reporter cannot quote the source by name and cannot directly attribute the statements to the source. These restrictions may be softened somewhat depending on the understanding developed between the reporter and the source. Although a promise of confidentiality is implied, the reporter may fully use the information but must attribute the information only generally by describing the source as, for example, "a highly placed government insider." In early stories about Maher Arar, a Canadian citizen and Ottawa electronics engineer who was wrongly suspected of terrorism and tortured for a year in a Syrian jail before finally being exonerated by a federal inquiry in 2006, attribution was made routinely to unnamed police sources.

When reporters use such not-for-attribution or on-background information, they should try to describe the source as fully as possible. To say the information came from "a government employee" is meaningless. Saying the source is "a supervisory member of the Canadian Security Intelligence Service" gives readers more information. Sources often will try to keep the identification as vague as possible; reporters try to make it as specific as possible. Because of that tradition, some Canadian journalists were surprised to learn of the possibility that celebrated Canadian journalist Daniel Leblanc could go to jail for honouring his promise to protect the identity of his source in the sponsorship scandal stories. Here's an excerpt from one piece commenting on the possibility:

> MONTREAL—It would be deeply ironic, if not the height of absurdity, should Daniel Leblanc wind up going to jail for his part in the sponsorship scandal.
>
> Unlike others who have gone that route already, or may in the future, Leblanc is not a sponsorship villain. More like a sponsorship hero.
>
> He's the reporter who broke the story of the $100-million boondoggle that ultimately brought down the federal government of the day.
>
> It was a series of articles by Leblanc in the *Globe and Mail* nine years ago that first brought to public light the looting of a fund to promote Canadian allegiance in Quebec by a select group of local ad agencies which, in collusion with a corrupt senior bureaucrat, bilked the government for tens of millions of dollars, some of which was kicked back to the Quebec wing of the governing federal Liberal Party.
>
> The budget for the program, mounted in frantic haste after the 1995 referendum scare when the separatists almost won, was $250 million; it was later established that $100 million of it was simply ripped off by the clubby set of sponsorship culprits who were hired to do the job of promoting the country.
>
> Leblanc was hailed for his sterling journalistic coup by no less than Justice John Gomery who headed the commission of inquiry into the affair. It was Leblanc's reports, the commission report acknowledges, that "made the problems affecting the program a matter of public discussion." Yet despite this signal public service, Leblanc is due to be dragged into court for a hearing that could land him in jail, as was the case with so-far convicted sponsorship felons Jean Lafleur, Jean Brault, Paul Coffin and Charles Guite. Criminal charges are also pending against adman Gilles-Andre Gosselin and Benoit Corbeil, a former director-general of the federal Liberal Party's Quebec wing.
>
> But unlike the rest, who stood before the courts in shame, Leblanc will be standing on principle at his hearing scheduled for this month. He will be asked to name or at least provide vital clues to the identity of the source who put him on the scandal's track, one he promised to keep confidential.
>
> His "Deep Throat" in effect, though Leblanc more demurely nicknamed his leaker "Ma Chouette," which roughly translates as my sweetie. He says he'll stick to the pledge he made Ma Chouette to keep mum come what may.

"On deep background" is a variation of the backgrounder. A source on deep background may not be quoted directly and may not be identified in any way. A reporter must publish the information without any attribution or with a phrase like, "It has been learned that…" Unless reporters have a high degree of confidence in the source and the information and the approval of their supervisors, they should stay away from information given on deep background.

"Off the record" is the final level of attribution. It generally means a source's information cannot be used, but because the term is often misunderstood by non-journalists, it makes sense to clarify with the source. Some people say they are speaking off the record when they really mean they are speaking on background. Also, reporters and sources sometimes disagree as to exactly what "off the record" means. Here's a sports story that takes a light-hearted look at the kinds of misunderstanding that can develop over the meaning of "off the record":

VANCOUVER—The relationship between hockey player and media member is often fraught, no matter how hard both sides work.

The reasons are fairly obvious. The athlete knows he's going to be asked questions he may not want to hear or answer for fear of landing in trouble, even if the original topic seems benign.

The reporter is looking to pry information from the athlete—either a good quote on tape or insight into what's going on inside the room.

Athletes think reporters ask the same questions because they do and that they ask stupid questions because that's often the case, too. Reporters often think players are too guarded, too unaware of their needs to provide a usable answer or that they're unco-operative because they can't be bothered. Tension between the parties is natural.

As soon as the player retires and leaves the game, however, it all changes. Suddenly all those forces at play disappear. The reporter doesn't probe as much because there isn't as much to learn, the player is not nearly so paranoid because what he says can't affect his employment. Relations improve and players become more willing to chat, acknowledging usually for the first time that even reporters have a life, too.

"I think the best analogy of what a player is going through with the media is to compare it with a life of a politician," says Dennis Kearns, who played for 14 NHL seasons and now has a successful career in the insurance business in Vancouver.

"He has to be so careful about what he says, just the way a politician does. I remember that first year we went into those uniforms with the deep 'V' when I got myself in shit. Don Cherry came around and was asking what I thought, and I said to him, 'Last year we played like clowns, and this year we're dressed like clowns.' I thought it was off the record, but he goes on Hockey Night and says Kearns said this. I never heard the end of it.

"But I can honestly say that when I played, I never read the newspaper at all or listened to the radio whenever there was a chance I would see something about hockey. The way I figured it, if it was good, it couldn't help me. If it was bad, I might be the kind of guy who would be bothered by it. I would often hear guys come in the room and say, 'Did you hear what that %4#@& said about you?' I wouldn't know what they were talking about.

"That one year they wanted to kick Al (CKNW sportscaster Davidson) out of the dressing room, Garry Monahan and Cesare Maniago spoke up and said we shouldn't, that the ramifications would be too great. But I was oblivious to the whole controversy at the time. I had to get those guys to explain it to me."

Kearns loosened up after he retired and became quite outspoken. As a salesman for CKNW in December 1981, he found himself in the Canucks office. Kearns was asked by then Vancouver comptroller John Chesman, "How do we stop [Wayne] Gretzky?" After some deliberation the former defenceman quipped, "Let Harry Neale coach him." Needless to say, Kearns was not a big fan of Neale.

"I knew so little about the media. When I retired, I got a call at home from Neil Macrae asking me to go on his show. I said I would and my wife asked me, 'What station is it on, because I want to hear it.' I couldn't tell her. Even though I later sold advertising for them, I had no idea what station he was on."

Ignorance is probably better than rabbit ears for a player, to be sure. But to straddle the line is probably best. Brendan Morrison is a master, being a great quote and yet not getting himself into too much trouble. At least we think he doesn't get into too much trouble.

"I had the least trouble in Japan," says former Canucks forward Monahan, now a successful realtor in West Van. Monahan played three seasons with Tokyo-based Seibu Tetsudo of the Japan Ice Hockey League, retiring after the 1981–82 season.

"The reporters didn't speak English and didn't come to me, and I couldn't read what they wrote. In our day, we had no instruction whatsoever on how to handle our duties with the media. Nobody told you what to say or how to conduct yourself, we were on our own. We had no idea how important it could be to your career or to the team. I mean, what does a 19- or 20-year-old kid with no advice know about handling the media?

"But as a player, you were always on your guard. Even when another guy would bring a friend around, he wasn't privy to what went on in the room, who was getting the crap beat out of them or who the coach was yelling at. So you were reluctant to say much—always suspicious. And later when I was in the media (he did colour on Canuck broadcasts for six years) I found it strange because I was then the outsider. I'd be sitting up front on the bus or plane with the reporters but felt I should be at the back. It was weird."

Fortunately, that weird feeling eventually disappears for everyone.

Many editors and most government offices say reporters may not use off-the-record information in any way. Reporters, however, sometimes use off-the-record information as leads to other sources. Almost every secret is known by several people, sometimes hundreds of people. Once reporters know what they are looking for, they usually can locate public records or sources who can verify the information on the record or on background. Some reporters refuse to listen to off-the-record statements. If one cannot publish or broadcast the information, why listen to it? Others see it as an opportunity to gain insight into official thinking. Or it may help them put the information they can publish in a more accurate context.

Anonymous Sources

If reporters want sources on the record, why do so many stories use anonymous sources? Sometimes sources want to remain anonymous for legitimate reasons. (See the accompanying box for guidelines on when to use anonymous sources.) Corporate or government officials who want to blow the whistle on waste, fraud, or other illegal or unethical conduct at their workplace may fear retaliation. Many have lost jobs or been demoted because they disclosed truths that made their supervisors uncomfortable. Canadian Press policy dictates that all anonymous sources be double-sourced (corroborated by two other sources) and cleared for publication by a senior editor.

Some journalists have deplored the use of anonymous sources as a threat to the independence, accuracy and credibility of the news. In the United States, Benjamin Bradlee, famed former executive editor of the *Washington Post*, said: "Why, then, do we go along so complacently with withholding the identity of public officials? I'm damned if I know. I do know that by doing so, we shamelessly do other people's bidding: We knowingly let ourselves be used....In short, we demean our profession."

In Canada, the Maher Arar affair sparked a wide and passionate debate about the use of anonymous sources. Compare the brief excerpts below, each written by an experienced Canadian journalist and journalism educator. The first excerpt was penned in 2006 before the federal government established a commission of inquiry into the affair; it urges reporters who used anonymous sources in helping to smear Arar to now reveal those sources. The second article, written the following year, says the Arar affair suggests that journalists need to become a lot more discerning in their use of anonymous sources.

The independent inquiry that Arar is demanding may prove to be unnecessary. It is clear from my examination of the media record that there are many reporters and editors in the Ottawa press corps who know the leakers' identities.

They would do well to remember that the first obligation of journalism is to serve the truth and not the interests of state officials who caused grievous damage to an innocent man's life. In particular, the journalists who were complicit—wittingly or unwittingly—in smearing Arar should do the right thing and expose their discredited sources. The truth demands it.

The bottom line is that journalists should not print information by anonymous sources unless they are completely convinced it is true, for it is the reputation of the journalist—not the source—that is on the line.

The lesson of the Maher Arar debacle is not that reporters should expose duplicitous sources. The lesson is that reporters should use anonymous sources far more carefully, and far less often.

There is no immediate sign that lesson has been learned.

The same day that Arar accepted $10.5 million and an apology from Prime Minister Stephen Harper, Canadian Press put out a story saying that Arar would stay on the U.S. no-fly list because of his "personal associations and travel history."

Maher Arar discusses the government's apology and compensation package at a news conference in Ottawa on Friday, January 26, 2007. Arar was wrongfully deported to Syria, where he was detained and tortured.

There were no details about the associations or travel. And the source?

A senior state department official who asked not to be named.

Anonymity allows sources to try to influence the way journalists cover the news. In Ottawa, high-level government sources often demand that their briefings be on background or on deep background. The officials use these briefings to place administration policy in the best possible light. They think they can do that most effectively when their identities and their political motives are hidden from the general public. Reporters abide by the background rules officials set because of the competitive pressures they face to get the story.

The accuracy of information from anonymous sources is always a concern. Even if sources are not intentionally misleading reporters, anonymity protects them from the consequences of their mistakes. The same is not true of the news organizations that publish the information. If several newspapers cover the same prison riot and receive inaccurate information from anonymous sources, the public's right to know is not served.

A final problem with anonymous sources is that under some circumstances a promise to keep a source's identity secret can be enforced in court. Courts have ruled that a source whose identity is revealed after confidentiality was promised may sue for damages.

Guidelines for Using Anonymous Sources

Editors are becoming more reluctant to use anonymous sources. Journalism critics say reporters can get more information on the record by threatening to ignore all information from sources who demand anonymity. If some sources insist on remaining anonymous, reporters might seek the same information from other sources who are willing to be identified. On the rare occasions when justification exists for using anonymous sources, news directors and editors tell their reporters to follow guidelines like these:

1. Do not use anonymous sources without the approval of your supervising editor or news director.
2. Be prepared to disclose the identities of anonymous sources to your editors or news directors and, possibly, to your news organization's lawyer.
3. Use anonymous sources only if they provide facts that are essential to the story, not just interesting quotations or opinions. Be sure the source is appropriate for the story

and that she or he is in a position to give authoritative information. Even then, information from anonymous sources should be verified.

4. Be sure you understand the motives of the anonymous source, such as whether the source is carrying a grudge or trying to puff a program or an agency. The motives help you evaluate the reliability of the information.

5. Identify sources as specifically as possible without revealing their identities so that readers can judge their importance and reliability. For example, instead of attributing information to "an informed source" or "a key official," you might attribute it to "an elected city official." This tells the reader the level of government in which the official works and alerts the reader to the fact that the official may have political interests. Never include any misleading information about the identity of a source, even if your motive is to protect the source.

6. Explain in the story why the source does not want to be identified.

7. Never allow a source to engage in anonymous attacks on other individuals or groups. Anonymous attacks risk involving you and your employer in a libel suit and are inherently unfair to the person attacked.

GUIDELINES FOR CAPITALIZING AND PUNCTUATING QUOTATIONS

The Use of Quotation Marks

Use double quotation marks to set off quotations. Only the quotation, never the attribution, should appear within the quotation marks:

> INCORRECT: "The motorcycle slid sideways and skidded about 100 feet, she said. The driver was killed."
> REVISED: "The motorcycle slid sideways and skidded about 100 feet," she said. "The driver was killed."

If a quotation continues for several sentences, all the sentences should be enclosed within a single set of quotation marks; quotation marks do not have to be placed at the beginning and end of each sentence in the quotation:

> INCORRECT: She said: "I did not see the car when I stepped out onto the street." "But when I saw the headlights coming at me, I knew it was going to hit me."
> REVISED: She said: "I did not see the car when I stepped out onto the street. But when I saw the headlights coming at me, I knew it was going to hit me."

Like any other part of a news story, a long quotation should be divided into short paragraphs to make it easier to read. New paragraphs should begin at natural breaks in the quotation, usually at changes in topic, however slight. Place quotation marks at the beginning of a long quotation and at the start of each new paragraph. Place closing quotation marks only at the end of the entire quotation, not at the end of every paragraph:

> The politician added: "Perhaps the most shocking example of the insensitivity of the Bureau of Indian Affairs' educational system is the manner in which boarding school dormitories have been administered.
> "Psychiatrists familiar with the problems of Indian children have told us that a properly run dormitory system is the most crucial aspect of boarding school life, particularly in elementary schools.

"Yet when a six-year-old Navajo child enters one of the boarding schools and becomes lonely or homesick, he must seek comfort from an instructional aide who has no training in child guidance and who is responsible for as many as 100 other unhappy children.

"The aide spends most of his time performing custodial chores. At night, the situation worsens as the ratio of dorm aides to children decreases."

When a quotation includes another quotation, use double quotation marks to identify the overall quotation and single quotation marks (or an apostrophe on the keyboard) to indicate the quotation within the quotation:

During the U.S. 1960 presidential campaign, Republicans were accusing John F. Kennedy of using his family's wealth to buy the election. Kennedy joked, "I got a wire from my father that said: 'Dear Jack, Don't buy one vote more than necessary. I'll be damned if I'll pay for a landslide.'"

If the passage has a quotation within a quotation within a quotation, use double quotation marks to indicate the third level of quotation, as in this example:

The member of Parliament said: "I had a voter tell me, 'I'm fed up with tax cheats. They get away with "murder."' And I had to agree with her."

Other Punctuation

If the attribution comes before a quotation that contains just one full sentence, a comma should follow the attribution. If the attribution precedes a quotation that contains two or more sentences, it should be followed by a colon. Do not use a period after attribution that comes before the quotation:

CORRECT: James Thurber said, "It is better to know some of the questions than all of the answers."
CORRECT: Mark Twain said: "I apologize for writing a long letter. If I'd had more time, I'd have written a shorter one."
INCORRECT: The council member said. "We need to raise the speed limit."
REVISED: The council member said, "We need to raise the speed limit."

When reporters place the attribution after a quotation, they use a comma, not a period, at the end of the quotation and place a period after the attribution to punctuate the entire sentence:

INCORRECT: "I'm feeling better." she said.
REVISED: "I'm feeling better," she said.

The comma or period at the end of the quotation should always be placed inside the quotation marks. This rule has no exceptions. Colons and semicolons should be outside the quotation marks. Whether a question mark or an exclamation point should appear inside or outside the quotation marks depends on the meaning. If the quotation is a question or exclamation, put the question mark or exclamation point inside the quotation marks. Otherwise, leave it outside the quotation marks:

CORRECT: The politician asked, "How much will the program cost?"
INCORRECT: Why did you say, "It's time to leave?"
REVISED: Why did you say, "It's time to leave"?

Capitalization

The first word in a quotation that is a complete sentence is capitalized, but the first word in a partial quotation is not:

INCORRECT: He said, "life is just one damned thing after another."
REVISED: He said, "Life is just one damned thing after another."

INCORRECT: He called journalism "Literature in a hurry."
REVISED: He called journalism "literature in a hurry."

Word Order for Attribution

Journalists put the name of or pronoun for the speaker and the verb of attribution in their normal order, with the subject appearing before the verb. That is the way people talk, and it is usually the most graceful way to write:

INCORRECT: Said the anti-abortion activist, "I've noticed that everybody who's for abortion has already been born."
REVISED: The anti-abortion activist said, "I've noticed that everybody who's for abortion has already been born."

INCORRECT: "Hard work is good for you," insisted the executive. "Nobody ever drowned in sweat."
REVISED: "Hard work is good for you," the executive insisted. "Nobody ever drowned in sweat."

However, if you place a long identifying or descriptive phrase after the name of the speaker, the normal word order may be awkward. In that case, place the verb first and the subject second:

AWKWARD: "This project will save you many times the $2 million it will cost," Smith, a 29-year-old architect employed by the Manitoba firm, said.
REVISED: "This project will save you many times the $2 million it will cost," said Smith, a 29-year-old architect employed by the Manitoba firm.

CHECKLISTS FOR QUOTATIONS AND ATTRIBUTION

Quotations

1. Use quotations sparingly to emphasize a point or change pace, not to tell the story or state facts.
2. Place only the exact words of the source within quotation marks.
3. Each quotation should serve a purpose, such as reveal the source's character, describe or emphasize a point, or present an opinion.
4. All direct quotations should be clear, concise, relevant and effective.
5. Avoid awkward combinations of partial and complete quotations.
6. Report only the source's answers, not the questions you asked.
7. Eliminate orphan quotations and floating quotations.
8. Make sure the quotations do not repeat facts reported elsewhere in the story.
9. For a one-paragraph quotation that includes two or more sentences, place the quotation marks only at the beginning and end of the entire quotation, not at the beginning and end of each sentence.
10. Capitalize the first letter of all quotations that are full sentences but not of partial quotations.
11. Divide long quotations into shorter paragraphs; place open quotation marks at the beginning of each paragraph, but place close quotation marks at the end of only the final paragraph.
12. Use single quotation marks for quotations that appear within other quotations.

Attribution

1. Attribute all second-hand information, criticisms, statements about controversial issues, opinions, and all direct and indirect quotations. (Do not attribute undisputed facts.)
2. Punctuate the attribution properly. Put a comma after an attribution introducing a one-sentence quotation and a colon after an attribution introducing two or more sentences of quotation.

3. Put the attribution at or near the beginning of a long quotation.
4. Attribution that appears in the middle of a sentence should come at a natural break rather than interrupt a thought.
5. Vary sentences and paragraphs so that all do not begin with attribution.
6. Place the attribution outside the quotation marks.
7. Attribute each direct quotation only once.
8. Attribute each separate statement of opinion in indirect quotations.
9. Attribute statements only to people, documents or publications, never to places or institutions.
10. Provide transitions between statements from different sources, particularly when a quotation from one source immediately follows a quotation from a different source.
11. Select the verb of attribution that most accurately describes the source's actual meaning and behaviour.
12. Do not use such verbs as "hope," "feel," "believe," "think," "laugh," "cough" and "cry" for attribution.
13. Make the attribution as concise as possible.

 ## Tips on Quotations from *The Globe and Mail Stylebook*

By J.A. (Sandy) McFarlane and Warren Clements

Direct quotations add authority to a report, and are our first choice when the speaker is clear and concise, particularly if he or she is also forceful or colourful. But if the speaker is long-winded and confusing, a paraphrase does a better job of conveying information; we can always use partial quotations for important or colourful passages. Here are some points to watch in both direct and indirect quotes:

- If something is enclosed in quotation marks, it should be the speaker's exact words, with the exception of corrected mispronunciations and minor grammatical departures that are common in everyday speech. The spoken "gonna" and "'o" should be changed to "going to" and "of," for example, unless a particular flavour is sought for a feature. However, taking this too far can affect a newspaper's credibility, particularly since the reader may have already heard the statement on TV or radio. An "um" or "ah" may be left out, but we cannot omit such recognizable words as "like" and "you know" and pass off the quote as exact.

- We usually retreat into paraphrase if grammatical and other spoken lapses make a quote rambling or confusing. In particular, do not include such lapses if it will appear that the intention is to hold the speaker up as an uneducated person or user of quaint dialect, except in those very rare stories in which this is the point. Slang may be retained, especially when it is obviously being used for effect, as may regional words and such practices as referring to inanimate things as he or she, but regional pronunciation generally should not be reflected in spelling (pardnuh, de b'y dat builds de boat). This rule applies as well to quotations from people whose first language is not English. Do not retain profanity and vulgarity, even with letters removed, unless there are exceptional circumstances and approval is obtained from the editor-in-chief, deputy editor, Report on Business editor, associate editor or their deputies.

- There is no way of inserting "[sic]" into a quote without implying that the speaker is mis-informed or uneducated, and without bringing readers to an abrupt halt while they fig-ure out the error. If a spoken slip is likely to mislead the reader (as when a person gives a wrong date, or says Second World War instead of First World War), our first choice is to use an indirect quote to report this part of the sentence. If it is vital that the direct quote be used in full regardless of the error (rare indeed is the situation that justifies misleading or confusing the reader even for a moment), we would have to follow the quote immediately with an explanation. We should never call attention to grammatical errors in giving attribution, as in "Mr. Smith said, oblivious to the double negative."

- One common and unacceptable form of straying from the speaker's exact words involves changing tenses and personal pronouns, in effect recasting the quotation into indirect but retaining the quotation marks. For example, if someone says "I will have your jobs," we cannot use quotation marks if we report him saying he would "have their jobs."

- Can a person be misquoted even if we use the exact words? Yes, if we leave out nearby sentences that explain, modify or qualify the remark, or do not report facial expres-sions and gestures that might be important parts of the context. An ironic smile or a rolling of the eyes speaks volumes to the reporter, and these must be conveyed to the reader whenever they affect interpretation.

- Do not place quotation marks around statements people "might" have made—a rhe-torical device that puts words in their mouths for satirical or argumentative purposes. You may have seen such "hypothetical quotes" elsewhere (in some popular biographi-es or histories, for example, and even in these their use is controversial). But they are extremely rare in newspapers, whose readers are typically rushed, reading primarily for information and not expecting this sort of nuance.

- In the spirit of "never say never," there may arise some instance in which it is journal-istically justifiable to use the device of hypothetical quotes, but we should take care to eliminate all confusion by tipping off the reader beforehand, not afterward, that the quote is not real, and we should set it off typographically (introduced by a colon, perhaps, or in italics if necessary), but not with quotation marks.

- Translations of direct quotes from other languages pose a special problem for our for-eign correspondents and for our reporters in Quebec and Ottawa. TV and radio reports can carry the original language at reduced volume as an undertone to the voice of the reporter or translator, a technique that clearly informs the listener that the words are not exactly those of the subject. In print journalism, the lack of a comparable handy device does not reduce our obligation to the reader and the person being quoted. It has become a convention that we may use quotation marks, presenting translations as if they were direct quotes rendered in English, but we should be clear that we have done this.

- If a statement is made on Bulgarian TV, for example, our readers certainly know it was not in English. However, in reporting on interviews, etc. when this is not obvious, *Globe* writers should indicate that the interview was conducted in Spanish, that the news conference was conducted partly or mostly in French, etc. It is then unnecessary to specify the language of each quote, unless this is significant, as when a politician gives conflicting messages to different audiences. (The requirement for indicating that the direct quotes we report are actually translations is relaxed for stories from other sources if it is impossible to determine the original language of the interview or statement.)

- If a colloquial expression makes literal translation of a significant quote difficult, we should inform the reader of the problem and offer the conflicting interpretations. If we have any reason to doubt the accuracy of a translation done by others, we should tell the reader the source (said through an interpreter, etc.).

SUGGESTED READINGS AND USEFUL WEBSITES

Cribb, Robert, Dean Jobb, David McKie, and Fred Vallance-Jones. 2006. *Digging Deeper: A Canadian Reporter's Research Guide.* Don Mills, ON: Oxford University Press.

Jackson, Gordon. *Watchdogs, Blogs, and Wild Hogs.* 2008. Spokane, WA: Eastern Washington University Press.

Manning, Paul. 2001. *News and News Sources: A Critical Introduction.* Thousand Oaks, CA: Sage Publications.

McClelland, Susan. 2009. "He said, she said: Using quotes." In Ivor Shapiro, ed., *The Bigger Picture: Elements of Feature Writing*, 243–45. Toronto: Emond Montgomery Publications.

McFarlane, J.A., and Warren Clements. 2003. *The Globe and Mail Stylebook: A Guide to Language and Usage,* 337–40, 364–70, 382. Toronto: McClelland and Stewart.

"Quotations." 2008. In *The Canadian Press Stylebook*, 15th edn, 15–17, 61. Toronto: The Canadian Press.

Rosner, Cecil. 2008. "Undercover, hidden-camera, and gotcha journalism." In *Behind the Headlines: A History of Investigative Journalism in Canada*, 153–64. Don Mills, ON: Oxford University Press.

Soley, Lawrence. 1992. *The News Shapers: The Sources Who Explain the News.* New York: Praeger.

Using Effective Quotes (Don Gibb): http://www.cane.ca/english/me_res_quotes.htm

Fighting Plagiarism at Journalism Schools, by Ellin Bessner: http://www.j-source.ca/english_new/detail.php?id=2977

CHAPTER 8

EXERCISE 1   Quotations and Attribution

Improving Quotations and Attribution

SECTION I: AVOIDING DOUBLE ATTRIBUTION
Rewrite the following sentences, attributing them only once. Correct any other errors.

1. A report issued Tuesday by the Criminal Justice Branch of the B.C. Attorney General's Ministry said the number of serious crimes committed in British Columbia increased slightly last year.
2. Speaking to more than 3,000 people in the Municipal Auditorium, she continued by stating that only the New Democratic Party favours universal health care.
3. Statistics Canada issued a report today stating that, according to data it gathered in 2001, one in every 10 Canadian households is facing housing affordability issues.

SECTION II: CORRECTING PLACEMENT ERRORS
Correct the placement of the attribution in the following sentences. Correct any other errors.

1. People under 18, she said, should not be allowed to drive.
2. Another important step is to, she said, lower the books prices.
3. "The average shoplifters are teenage girls who steal for the thrill of it, and housewives who steal items they can use. They don't have to steal; most have plenty of money, but they don't think its a crime. They also think they'll get away with it forever," Valderrama said.

SECTION III: CONDENSING WORDY ATTRIBUTION
The attributions in the following sentences are too wordy. They appear in italics and contain a total of 76 words. How many of the words can you eliminate? Rewrite the attribution, if necessary. Correct any other errors.

1. *She concluded her speech by telling the scouts that* the jamboree will be held August 7–13.
2. *He was quick to point out the fact that, in his opinion,* the finance minister has "failed to act effectively to reduce the federal deficit."
3. *She expressed her feelings by explaining that she believes that* all those convicted of drunk driving should lose their licences for life.
4. *She also went on to point out the fact that the results of federal studies show that,* by recycling 1 ton of paper, you can save 17 trees.
5. *In a speech to the students Tuesday, he first began by offering them his opinion that* their professors should emphasize teaching, not research.
6. *He continued by urging his listeners to remember the critical point that* the countrys energy policy has failed: that Canada. is not developing alternative fuels, nor conserving existing fuels.

SECTION IV: IMPROVING ATTRIBUTION
Correct all the problems in the following attributions and quotations and any other errors.

1. He said: "after a certain number of years, our faces become our biographies".
2. Andy Rooney declared "if dogs could talk, it would take a lot of fun out of owning one".
3. "Because that's where the money is" Willie Sutton answered when asked why he robbed banks.
4. He continued by claiming that there are "two" types of people who complain about their taxes: "men" and "women."

5. "Blessed is he" said W.C. Bennett "who expects no gratitude, for he shall not be disappointed." explained Bennett.

6. Mother Teresa then spoke to the youths, telling them that. "The most terrible poverty is loneliness and the feeling of being unwanted."

7. "My views on birth control" said Robert F. Kennedy "Are somewhat distorted by the fact that I was the seventh of nine children".

8. Being a police officer is not always fun and exciting, says Griffith. "Some things you'd just as soon forget." "Some things you do forget."

9. "The art of taxation." claimed a French statesman long ago "Consists in so plucking the goose as to obtain the most feathers with the least hissing".

10. Dr. Hector Rivera said they test for AIDS at the clinic "but do not treat the disease." "People come in to be tested scared to death." "Some leave the clinic relieved, and some don't." he said.

11. Her friendships, home, and family are the most important things in her life. "My husband is my best friend." "Maybe that's why we've lasted so long." "You really need to be friends before you're lovers".

12. "I cheat because professors give too much work." It's crazy, he said. "They don't take into consideration that some people have jobs, families and other outside interests." continued the history major. He then continued by adding that he's never been caught.

13. "My son thinks I'm old." "But I'm actually in good health for my age." "Of course, I have the usual aches and pains of an 80-year-old." "But I can still take care of my own house, and I still enjoy it." "My son thinks I should move into one of those retirement apartments and watch Wheel of Fortune all day." said he.

14. Jo Ann Nyez, a secretary, grew up in Calgary and described a childhood fear: There was this house at the end of my street and none of us would dare go near it on Halloween. It was supposed to be haunted. The story was that the wife had hung herself in the basement and the husband killed and ate rattlesnakes.

EXERCISE 2   Quotations and Attribution

Wording, Placement and Punctuation

Answer key provided: See Appendix D.

Make any changes necessary to improve the attribution in the following sentences and paragraphs. Also correct style, spelling and punctuation errors.

1. "Our goal is peace". claimed the prime minister.
2. Benjamin Franklin said: "death takes no bribes".
3. She said her son refers to her literary endeavours as, "moms writing thing".
4. He is a scuba diver and pilot. He also enjoys skydiving. "I like challenge, something exciting."
5. "The dangers promise to be of indefinite duration." the prime minister said referring to the Mideast crisis.
6. "A free press can of course be good or bad, but, most certainly, without freedom it will never be anything but bad...." "Freedom is nothing else but a chance to be better, whereas enslavement is a certainty of the worse." said the writer Albert Camus in one of his books.
7. Jesse Owens expressed the opinion that "I think that America has become too athletic." "From Little League to the pro leagues, sports are no longer recreation." "They are big business, and they're drudgery." he continued.
8. The man smiled, "It's a great deal for me." "I expect to double my money," he explained.
9. When asked what she likes most about her job as a newspaper reporter, the woman responded by saying—"I'm not paid much, but the work is important. And it's varied and exciting." She grinned: "Also, I like seeing my byline in the paper."
10. The librarian announced to reporters that the new building "will cost somewhere in the neighbourhood of about $4.6 million."
11. "Thousands of the poor in Canada," said the professor, "die every year of diseases we can easily cure." "It's a crime," he said, "but no one ever is punished for their deaths."
12. Thomas said students should never be spanked. "A young boy or girl who gets spanked in front of peers becomes embarrassed and the object of ridicule."
13. The lawyer said, "He ripped the life-sustaining respirator tubes from his throat three times in an effort to die. He is simply a man" the lawyer continued "who rejects medical treatment regardless of the consequences. He wants to die and has a constitutional right to do so."
14. Bobby Knight, the basketball coach at the university, said. "Everyone has the will to win." "Few have the will to prepare." Knight added that. "It is the preparation that counts."
15. She said she firmly believes that the federal government "must do more" to help cities "support and retrain" the chronically unemployed.

EXERCISE 3   Quotations and Attribution

Using Quotes in News Stories

Write complete news stories based on the following information. Use some quotations in each story to emphasize its highlights, but do not use quotations to tell the entire story. Use the most interesting, important and revealing quotations, not just those that happen to appear first. Correct any errors in grammar, spelling or style.

1. Carlos Vacante is a police officer who has worked 3 years for your city's police department. Last night he had an unusual experience. This is his story, as he told it to you in an interview today: "I remember his eyes. They were cold, the eyes of a killer. He was pointing a gun at me, and it fired. I smelled the gunpowder and waited for the pain. I thought I was dead. The whole thing had started at about 11 p.m. This man was suspected of stealing from parked cars, and I'd gotten his description by radio. Then I spotted him in a parking lot. This morning we learned he's wanted in the robbery and murder of a service station attendant in Manitoba. There's no doubt in my mind he wanted to kill me last night just because I stopped him. I was an object in his way. I'd gotten out of my car and called to him. He started turning around and I spotted a handgun in his waistband. As he drew the gun and fired, I leaned to the right and dropped to one knee. It was just a reflex that saved my life. When I heard the shot, I thought he hit me. I couldn't believe it was actually happening to me. I thought I was going to cash everything in. Then I was running—zig-zagging—behind some cars. He fired another shot, but my backup arrived, and he fled. Maybe 60 seconds had passed from the time I spotted him. Five minutes later, we found him at the back door to a house, trying to break in and hide. I ordered him to stop, and he put his hands up and said, 'You got me.' I still smell the gunpowder this morning. I thought I was dead."

2. A rise in insurance rates is being blamed for a rise in hit-and-run motor vehicle accidents within the province. Richard Byrum, provincial insurance commissioner, discussed the problem during a press conference in his office today. He said, "The problem is serious. At first, we thought it was a police problem, but police in the province have asked my office to look into it. There has been a dramatic increase in hit-and-run accidents in the province, particularly in big cities where you find the higher insurance rates. I'm told that last year we had nearly 28,000 motor vehicle accidents in the province, and 4,500 were hit-and-run. People are taking chances driving without proper insurance coverage, or they're afraid of a premium increase if they have insurance and stop and report an accident. They seem to think, 'What the heck, no one saw it, and I won't get caught,' and they just bug out of there. If you look at the insurance rates in the province, its practically impossible for some people to pay them, and as insurance rates go up, the rate of leaving the scene of an accident increases. Drivers with the worst records—those with several accidents and traffic citations—pay as much as $3,600 a year in insurance premiums, and they may pay even more than that if they are young or have a high-powered car. Even good drivers found at fault in an accident may find their rates going up several hundred dollars for the next three to five years. So leaving the scene of an accident is definitely tied to the economic situation, yet the insurance company people I've talked to say they can't do anything about it. Its just not realistic to expect them to lower their rates; they aren't making that much money. Right now, I'm not sure what we'll do about the situation. In the meantime, we can expect more hit-and-run accidents and more drivers going without any insurance coverage because of its high cost."

Interviews

In 1989, [Andrew] McIntosh was recruited to join an investigative reporting team
at the Montreal *Gazette.* It was a chance to broaden his range of stories and spend
time doing more intensive digging. He also learned new techniques from his more
experienced team members, William Marsden and Rod Macdonell. Marsden taught
him the power of chronologies, a technique John Sawatsky and other investigative
reporters of the 1970s had developed. "I think Marsden more than anyone else taught
me how to prepare for an interview, that you don't just wing it. You need to have a
plan; you've got to have your material organized and know what you need." McIntosh
benefited from the trial and error of reporters who had gone before him, gradually
accumulating all the key investigative methods and adopting a systematic approach
to his research. McIntosh, Marsden and Carolyn Adolph worked on an exhaustive,
100-part report into the 1992 shootings of four people at Concordia University.
Over a number of months, the three reporters laboriously compiled their research
and constructed a chronology of the troubled life of Professor Valery Fabrikant. The
result was a dramatic exploration into the psyche of a man and how he came to take
the lives of four of his colleagues. When budget concerns led to the dismantling of
the investigative team, McIntosh returned to business reporting and continued to
accumulate a network of sources that would routinely provide him with exclusive
stories for the newspaper. (Cecil Rosner, *Behind the Headlines,* p. 138)

The interview is a basic tool of all journalists, not just investigative ones. While the journalistic
interview may lack the definitiveness of the physicist's experiment, it can be extremely effective
when used properly. Many other professions rely on interviews for gathering basic information.
Sociologists, anthropologists, police officers, lawyers, psychologists and other professionals
routinely use interviews in the course of their work.

Reporters use interviews in a variety of situations. They may interview legislators about
their plans to introduce a bill or police officers about a recent crime. They may gather the views
of a number of citizens on a matter of public concern. Some reporters specialize in writing
profiles of famous or interesting people. They usually conduct long interviews—sometimes
stretching over several days—with the subjects of their stories.

No matter what kind of story a reporter writes, it usually will require one or more interviews. Successful interviews, however, do not just happen; they are the product of thought and planning by reporters.

PREPARING FOR THE INTERVIEW

Reporters planning to interview a source should ask themselves: Why am I conducting this interview? What kind of story will I write from this information? The answers will determine what kinds of questions they ask, what kinds of sources they seek, and how they conduct themselves during an interview. The reasons for interviewing are as varied as the stories themselves, but most often reporters are seeking information for one of three types of stories: the news story, the feature story, or the investigative story.

Reporters who cover a news story, such as a crime or a city council action, usually need to interview several individuals to gather all relevant information. From each individual, reporters may seek no more than a few specific facts, but from the sum of the interviews, reporters construct a complete narrative. This means reporters must interview sources who will provide the following:

- facts and details, including dates, names, locations and costs;

- a chronology showing the unfolding of events;

- relationships among the people or interests involved;

- context and perspective, including the significance of events or issues and their relationships to other issues;

- anecdotes that illuminate events or issues and make them more dramatic and understandable for readers or viewers.

Reporters interviewing sources to write a feature story, such as a personality profile, need everything they would need to write a news story plus descriptions of the following:

- the environment in which the subject lives or works;

- how the subject appears and dresses;

- the subject's mannerisms;

- smells, sounds and textures associated with the subject's home or work, using every sense to create an image of the interview subject.

Interviews for personality profiles may consume many hours for reporters and subjects, but often they are enjoyable experiences for both. In-depth interviews conducted for investigative stories produce more tension. The purpose of the investigative story often is to expose wrongdoing, and sources may fear losing their jobs and reputations. Reporters working on the investigative story must obtain the same information as those working on more routine news or feature stories, but they also go further to seek some additional data:

- The subject's version of events, which may differ from that of other sources and records.

- Explanations of contradictions. If a subject of a story tells a version of events that differs markedly from that of other sources, reporters must ask for an explanation. A subject's explanation may be reasonable and may resolve the conflict—or it may not.

- Replies to charges and allegations. During an investigation, reporters may gather charges and allegations against a subject of a story. Those charges and allegations should be presented to the subject, who should have the opportunity to reply to them.

Many experienced interviewers think of an interview as a conversation, but it is a conversation with a specific purpose: gathering information for an unseen audience of readers, listeners or viewers. To accomplish that purpose, interviewers must maintain control of the conversation, and they can do that only if they have properly planned for the interview. In the case of in-depth personality interviews or investigative interviews, the planning process may be long and complicated, but even with simpler interviews, it can involve several steps.

- Define the purpose. Is this a news, feature or investigative interview? What information is necessary for the story?

- Decide whom to interview. For some stories, the choice of people to interview may be obvious, but for others, the reporter may have to do some research to determine the best sources.

- Assess the character of the interviewee. This may be crucial for feature and investigative interviews in which the reporter will have to shape the interview strategy to the interviewee's character. For news interviews or interviews of public officials the reporter already knows, this step is less crucial.

- Identify the areas of inquiry. What topics will the interview focus on? What questions will enable the reporter to gather the information necessary to write about these topics?

- Anticipate possible answers to questions. Reporters often can predict an interviewee's answers from their advance research. On the basis of these predictions, the reporter can prepare possible followup questions and plan how the interview will develop.

Selecting the Sources to Interview

Once reporters know the purpose of the interviews, they must decide whom they should interview. If reporters are preparing a personality profile of a prominent person, the subject of that profile and his or her friends, enemies and co-workers should be interviewed. But when the story is about an issue or an event, the reporters may have to figure out which people have the information they need to write the story. Reporters who don't have a deadline looming can try to interview everyone who might have relevant information. They can ask every interview subject for the names of more people who might contribute information, repeat the process until the list of sources has been exhausted, and then go back and re-interview sources to fill in gaps and clear up discrepancies in their stories.

Reporters working on deadline must be more selective in whom they interview. The basic principle reporters follow is to seek the best available source. Such sources possess knowledge, expertise or insight relevant to the story. Sources also should be articulate; they should be able to make complicated matters clear and interesting.

Reporters should remember that sometimes the best available source is a document or record rather than a person. They can save themselves and the people they interview time and trouble if they begin by searching for documents or public records that provide the factual background for a story.

Finding sources who can provide insights and information can challenge a reporter's skill. A number of resources can help reporters locate the people they need to talk to. Many of the most frequently used sources work in local governments: cities, municipalities and school districts. Some of these sources can be found through the telephone book. In some communities, directories of local officials are published by civic groups. Many local governments operate websites that can lead reporters to sources.

Provincial governments annually publish directories of their agencies. Those directories describe each ministry's responsibilities and identify its top personnel. Some directories include the salaries of all or most of the people who work for the province. The directories are available in most community libraries. Provinces also put much of the same information on the World Wide Web.

The federal government maintains the Government of Canada website (http://canada.gc.ca) that contains links to federal ministries and agencies, with contact information and names of employees.

Some excellent news sources work not for government but for private organizations. The *Encyclopedia of Associations*, a reference work found in most college and university libraries, lists thousands of organizations and interest groups; an international directory can be found online (http://library.dialog.com/bluesheets/html/bl0114.html). Each organization is described in a paragraph, accompanied by its address and phone number and the name of its top official. Many of these organizations have helpful information and are eager to share it with reporters.

Reporters can find helpful sources at local colleges and universities. Faculty members often provide background, explain complex issues, and offer insights. College and university public relations offices usually help reporters identify and contact the faculty members who can provide the most useful information.

Finding sources in private businesses may be more challenging than finding government sources. One resource is the directories of members published by local service clubs like Rotary and Kiwanis. Many club members are local business leaders who will be identified by company and title. Some companies publish internal phone books, and reporters may be able to get copies. Most businesses have to file documents and reports with local, provincial and federal governments. Financial statements for all companies incorporated under the Canadian Business Corporations Act (CBCA) must be filed with Industry Canada's Corporations Directorate. Provincial agencies may have the names of principal officers of companies incorporated or doing business in that province. Local governments often issue business licences, which might name key executives.

Reporters should never let any organization, governmental or private, allow its public relations person be the fall guy. The job of the reporter is to hold the real decision-maker accountable. The PR person usually is not the best source.

How Many Sources Are Enough?

Beginning reporters sometimes wonder how many sources they need for a story. The answer depends on at least four factors: deadline pressure, the expertise of the sources, the degree of controversy raised by a topic, and the complexity of a topic.

When stories involve breaking news, which must be published or broadcast as soon as possible, reporters lack the luxury of searching widely for sources and information. They must construct a story from the materials readily available. Still, reporters should get as complete an account of the event and include as many points of view as possible. If a reporter cannot interview a key source before the deadline, the story should say so clearly.

If sources possess broad expertise in a topic, three or four might be enough. If they have more limited experience, reporters may need to speak to dozens. A reporter writing a story about the economic health of a city, for instance, may be able to produce a complete and accurate picture after talking to just a few people with broad expertise, such as academic and government economists, chamber of commerce officials, bank executives, or union leaders. The reporter would have to interview dozens, if not hundreds, of individual business owners for the same story. Individual business owners may know the conditions for their own businesses, but they probably don't know the economic health of the community as a whole.

The degree of controversy also affects the number of sources reporters should interview. If a topic is not controversial—the cause of polio, for example—then one source may be sufficient. However, if the topic is the likelihood of developing cures for diabetes or Alzheimer disease from fetal stem cells—about which experts disagree vigorously—then a reporter must include all reasonable points of view in the story.

As a story becomes more complex, the number of sources needed will grow. A story about a particular crime committed by a particular teenager would be fairly straightforward. Reporters could get a complete picture from only a few sources. A story about the causes of teenage crime in general is much more complicated and would require talking to dozens of sources from such fields as law enforcement, criminology, psychology and social work.

No matter how many sources reporters talk to, they must evaluate those sources. Journalists should do more than simply pass along quotations from other people, even those considered experts. The obligation to evaluate information increases as the complexity of the story increases. Evaluating sources requires reporters to ask how the source knows what he or she purports to know: What is the basis of the source's knowledge? How credible or reliable is the source? The first question calls on reporters to find out and weigh the manner in which the source obtained the information. Water-cooler gossip is not as valuable as information from an eyewitness. When a source makes an assertion, ask, "How do you know that?" The credibility and reliability of the source require asking about the source's credentials and cross-checking information from one source with that from others. The process is not simple or easy, but it is essential if reporters are going to produce sound, accurate news stories.

Researching Sources and Topics

Journalists who have interviewed scores of famous and important people (and who often have authored books about interviewing) agree that the successful interviewer must be well informed. That means spending time in a library or a news organization's clip file reading books and articles by or about the person the reporter will interview, researching a company's annual reports, reviewing public documents, and learning the jargon of an industry or the organization of a company. For example, preparing to interview a well-known writer would entail reading at least a representative sample or portion of that writer's work.

Famed Canadian investigative journalist John Sawatsky typically went after stories that mainstream media either ignored or were oblivious to. In newspaper articles and later in his books, Sawatsky tore the veil of secrecy from important organizations, including Canada's RCMP, to reveal their inner workings. Another great Canadian journalist, Cecil Rosner, in his much-praised book on the history of investigative reporting in Canada, *Behind the Headlines*, noted the significance of Sawatsky's pioneering efforts to bolster the impact of investigative reporting with journalistic technique:

> Sawatsky developed a methodology of investigative work that tried to put research on a more scientific footing. His ideas about organization and classification of material, along with the mindset he brought to approaching sources, were important factors in his success at ferreting out information. Most importantly, he became a student of the mechanics and linguistics of the interview. He demonstrated, in both theory and practice, that the specific sequencing and wording of questions was crucial in providing the highest quality of journalistic information.

Why do reporters attach so much importance to conducting research before they interview people? Reporters who have conducted thorough research have the following advantages:

- They will not waste time by asking about issues that have already been widely publicized.

- They will have more interesting questions. People who are interviewed frequently get bored answering the same questions over and over. Interviewers who have researched their subject will have fresh questions that will elicit fresh answers from their source.

- They are more likely to have documented all relevant facts. Once the reporter and the source agree on what the facts are, they can move on to discussing the meaning of those facts.

- They will not embarrass themselves by appearing ignorant. On the other hand, reporters sometimes want to feign ignorance about a topic to elicit more in-depth, revealing explanations.

- They are more likely to recognize newsworthy statements and ask intelligent followup questions about them.

- They are more likely to spot inconsistencies and evasions in a source's responses.

- They learn about secondary sources, people who are familiar with the main source and who might have insights and information that will help reporters interview the main source.

- They are less likely to have to re-interview the main source. If they interview the main source before doing their research and interviews with secondary sources, their subsequent research may uncover important topics they failed to cover in the initial interview.

- They encourage their sources to speak more freely because sources are more likely to trust reporters who seem knowledgeable.

Reporters who fail to prepare for an interview will not know what to ask or how to report the information they get. Some sources will try to manipulate ignorant reporters or avoid difficult topics. Sometimes, sources will immediately end an interview—and scold unprepared reporters.

Preparing Questions for the Interview

Good questions elicit interesting quotations and details. Reporters begin the process of constructing good questions when they select a unifying central point for their story. With a central point in mind, interviewers can decide whom they should interview and what questions they should ask. Say a reporter is planning a profile of a local bank executive who has won several marathon races. The central point for the story may be that long-distance running enhances the bank executive's personal and professional life. That idea suggests certain questions the reporter may ask the bank executive and his friends and family. If the reporter is investigating the bank's treatment of minorities, however, the reporter may want to interview the same bank executive, but the central point will be different. It may be the way the bank's lending practices affect minorities who want to buy homes or start businesses. The questions reporters would ask to develop a story about treatment of minorities would be much different from the questions they would ask for a feature about running in marathons.

Once reporters have selected a central point and have researched the topic, they write their questions in advance. They need not write out full questions. Often it is enough to jot down a word or phrase to remind the reporter what to ask.

Reporters craft their questions to elicit as much information as possible. This means asking open-ended rather than closed-ended questions. A closed-ended question is one that sources can answer with a yes or no: "Will the province's new tax limitation hurt schools?" If reporters want more information, they have to ask followup questions. An open-ended question would be, "What will be the effect of the province's new tax limitation on schools?" The question requires the source to provide an analysis of the problem with some supporting facts.

Renowned for his interviewing skill, John Sawatsky advises journalists to ask short, neutral questions that begin with "what," "how" and "why" and to a lesser extent "who," "when" and "where." Questions structured as Sawatsky suggests encourage interviewees to tell their stories and reveal their feelings. Questions like "Are you angry?" or "Were you scared?"—besides inviting only yes or no answers—suggest that the interviewer has a preconceived notion about how the subject should have acted or felt. The subject might not want to tell her story to a reporter who appears to have already decided what happened.

When interviewees have a story to tell, such as how they survived a plane crash or what happened during a bank robbery, reporters should simply let that person tell the story. Something like "Tell me what happened to you" might be enough to encourage people to talk. This gives them a chance to tell their story as they remember it. Often the most useful information emerges during this phase of an interview. As interviewees talk, reporters should listen carefully. They might think of the questions as the subject tells the story, but they should not interrupt the interviewee. Rather, they should wait until the interviewee has finished and then ask any specific followup questions.

Reporters ask for clarification when they do not understand things sources say. Sometimes that means asking a question that might appear naive or silly. Reporters should not fear asking those questions, however. Reporters who assume they understand what a source said or who fail to ask a critical question out of fear of appearing ignorant could make serious and embarrassing mistakes when they write their stories.

When reporters seek more specific details, they choose questions that will elicit anecdotes, examples and quotations. Here are examples of such questions:

- What crime was the most difficult for you to solve in your career as a detective?

- What television shows do you consider most harmful for children?

- What do you fear the most when you perform before a live audience?

When news sources generalize or give vague answers, reporters ask for anecdotes and examples that support the generalizations or make the vague responses clearer and more specific. Reporters can use the anecdotes, examples and quotations to make their stories more colourful, interesting and understandable.

For feature interviews or personality profiles, some reporters have questions they often use to try to gain insight into the subject. Here are some examples:

- What do you read?

- Who are your heroes?

- What goals do you have?

- What is a typical day like for you?

- What are your weaknesses or drawbacks?

- How do you compensate for those weaknesses?

- What caused the most significant change in your life?

- How did you cope with that change?

Reporters have an infinite number of approaches they can take to conducting an interview, but they should avoid some traps:

- Ask questions rather than make statements: Questions will elicit the subject's opinions and ideas, but statements might make the subject fearful of expressing ideas that conflict with the reporter's. The interviewee may conclude that the reporter is biased and will not fairly report the interview.

- Don't ask double-barrelled questions, which might have more than one correct answer. For example, one interviewer asked former U.S. president Bill Clinton, when he first ran for president, "Was Gennifer Flowers your lover for 12 years?" Clinton answered, "That allegation is false." But which part was false? The part about Flowers being his lover or the part about the 12 years? By splitting the question into two parts, the reporter might have got better answers.

- Don't use loaded words in questions: "Mayor Datolli, will your budget scheme save the city from bankruptcy?" The word "scheme" seems to be passing judgment on the mayor's proposal. A more neutral term would be "plan."

- Don't ask leading questions that suggest what the reporter thinks the answer should be: A question like "Was the robber carrying a shotgun?" implies that the questioner thinks the robber did so. If the interviewee is uncertain, he or she might be tempted to confirm that suspicion, even if it is incorrect.

CONDUCTING THE INTERVIEW

Selecting a Location for the Interview

The prospect of being interviewed creates anxiety for some sources. Their nervousness will interfere with their ability to answer questions in a natural manner. Reporters can reduce the anxiety of their sources by conducting interviews in places where sources feel comfortable, such as their homes or offices. As well, reporters can learn more about a source by seeing that person's home or office. Take the time to look around for clues and details. The photos sources display on their desks and walls, the lapel pins they wear, or the items they have clipped from newspapers and taped to their refrigerators could give reporters insights about sources or suggest questions to ask them.

Here is an excerpt from the beginning of a feature profile by Chris Koentges of noted Canadian chef Michael Noble. The profile, published in *The Walrus* magazine, is entitled "The Noble Effect: Can a $15-a-plate restaurant chain apportion the genius of one of Canada's greatest chefs?" The piece begins in a test kitchen, and Koentges engages in a lengthy opening that details the environment of the test kitchen before he first quotes his subject. Notice how he uses details he observed to give readers a sense of Noble and his working environment as well as to prefigure the profile's main theme: Haute cuisine is haute cuisine because of the mystique of its chef.

There is nothing remarkable about the Earls Test Kitchen, which is known to insiders as TK1. It is stainless steel and tile, six burners, two long counters, a double fridge, some gadgets. With the door closed it feels like a subway car, its windows revealing the hallway of a much larger kitchen. This larger kitchen opens out to a shiny, boisterous room called Earls Tin Palace, which in turn gives way to the world outside, where fifty-one other Earls are strewn from Fort McMurray almost to the Mexican border. Fifty-three, fifty-four and fifty-five are on the way.

I have spent my life avoiding Earls. Then Michael Noble started working there.

If you live in the east, you may not know Earls, which surfaced in the west, with oversized papier-mâché parrots dangling from its rafters, about the same time as U2 and Tom Cruise. Earls is known for inventing and reinventing much of our casual-dining canon, most notably the dry rib and the hot chicken Caesar salad. It is known for servers who are not exactly hard on the eyes. It is arguably the safest bet for a first date in the history of dining out.

Until recently, a typical Earls was 7,000 square feet and averaged $3 million in annual sales. However, the newest generation of stores have flashier décor and tonier locations like Polo Park in Winnipeg, with sales averaging $5.5 million. One competitor I spoke with equated the Fuller family, which runs Earls and several other high-end chains, to NASA scientists, so systematically have they stayed a teaspoon ahead of the public's tastes. What they've shown in their latest incarnation is that the essential qualities of elite cuisine can be reproduced, packaged, and delivered—without the elitism.

In the autumn of 2004, Michael Noble left Catch, a $5-million fine-dining experiment in downtown Calgary that critics had christened "Canada's best new restaurant," to become Earls' Director of Culinary & Product Development. In the weeks leading up to Christmas, he travelled five times from Calgary to TK1, summoned each time by Earls' Executive Tasting Panel. On this, his sixth trip, things would get interesting. In a span of thirty hours, he would attempt to crank out ten dishes, representing the final crack at his first full-fledged Earls menu. And then, because this is how the stars sometimes align, he would prepare a single course for La Confrérie de la Chaîne de Rôtisseurs, an international gastronomic society dating back to Louis IX's Royal Guild of Goose Roasters that is dedicated to safeguarding fine dining as we know it.

Newsrooms are poor places for interviews. They are noisy and chaotic. Sources unfamiliar with newsrooms might find them intimidating.

Experienced reporters also avoid luncheon appointments. The idea of a leisurely interview over lunch sounds pleasant, but restaurants have several drawbacks as interview locations. Crowd noise and interruptions from waiters interfere with the conversation. Reporters who tape interviews might find that the background noise drowns out the interview. Lunch itself will distract both reporter and news source. Also, reporters or their news organizations should pay for lunch to avoid any appearance that they can be influenced by a generous source. Thus, the practice of interviewing people over lunch can become expensive.

No matter where reporters conduct interviews, they should always arrive early and keep the interview within the agreed-on time. They also should dress appropriately for the interview setting, usually in business clothes.

Organizing the Questions

Reporters should start an interview with a clear statement of its purpose, if that's not already understood. For brief news interviews, reporters usually try to get right to the main questions. For longer interviews, reporters often begin with a few minutes of small talk to put a source at ease.

Once the serious questioning begins, reporters should take charge of the conversation, decide what questions to ask, keep the interview on track, and make sure the source fully answers every question. If a source wanders or tries to evade questions, reporters bring the conversation back to the central topic and politely but firmly ask the source to respond to the questions.

Questions should be grouped by topic. A reporter who is planning to profile a candidate for mayor, for example, may want to cover the person's education, work history, family life, community service, political experience, and proposals for running the city. For each of these topics, the reporter might have four or five questions. Reporters try to organize the topics, making it easy for the interviewee to move from one to the next. Chronological organization would be one way of organizing the topics. Another might be to take them up in reverse chronological order. For a reporter interviewing a scientist about the effects of global warming, chronology is meaningless, so a different organization makes more sense, such as moving from effects on oceans and ocean life to effects on land animals and finally to effects on humans. In still other situations, the reporter might let the conversation follow its own course and let topics arise naturally, simply making sure that the interviewee covers all essential points.

Reporters organize the questions they ask as well as the topics they want to cover. One approach—sometimes called the funnel—starts with a general question and moves to progressively more specific ones. For example, a reporter interviewing a police chief about how an influx of immigrants is affecting law enforcement might ask the questions in this order:

- Has the presence of large numbers of immigrants changed the way the police force operates?

- What kinds of changes has the department made?

- Has the department changed any of its policies to deal with immigrants?

- Is the department requiring or encouraging officers to learn additional languages?

Sometimes reporters might organize their questions in a reverse funnel, starting with specifics and moving to more general matters. The same interview with the police chief using a reverse funnel might go like this:

- How many officers does the department have who can speak a second language?

- Is the department considering encouraging officers to learn a second language?

- What changes might the department make to deal with growing numbers of immigrants?

- How has the presence of large numbers of immigrants affected law enforcement generally?

Many experienced reporters recommend starting an interview with some comments or soft questions that will break the ice and get the conversation going. Once the interviewee becomes comfortable talking, the reporter can ask more difficult questions. As banal as it might seem, even a polite question about the weather can start the conversation. Another way of breaking the ice is to ask the interviewee about some personal effect—a photograph or an award—on display in the person's office or home. Talking about a mutual interest or people both the reporter and the interviewee know is another way to start the conversation.

Reporters save their most embarrassing or difficult questions for the end of interviews. By then, their sources should be more comfortable answering questions. Moreover, if a source refuses to answer embarrassing questions and abruptly ends an interview, the reporter will have already obtained most of the information needed for the story.

Experienced interviewers will have prepared well enough before an interview that they will encounter few surprises, but occasionally an interview yields unexpected information. If the new information is newsworthy, reporters must abandon their original plans and pursue the new angles.

At the end of an interview, reporters should always ask sources if they have anything to add. Sometimes the most surprising and newsworthy information emerges in response to that question. Reporters should also ask sources for the names of other people to interview or for documents that might provide additional information or verification. They also should ask the best time to call sources back if they have followup questions. Finally, reporters should thank sources for granting the interview.

Dealing with Reluctant Sources and Asking Tough Questions

Most sources co-operate with reporters because they welcome the opportunity to tell their side of a story; however, a few dislike talking to reporters or are hostile. They may fear a topic is too difficult for reporters to understand; they may have been embarrassed by reporters in earlier interviews; or they may suspect the resulting story will portray them in a bad light.

Reporters first try to learn why the source is hesitant to speak to them. After learning the reason, they may be able to overcome that specific objection. In some cases, sources fear the interview will turn into an interrogation. Reporters might be able to lessen the interviewee's anxiety by showing empathy and adjusting their personal style to fit the mood of the person being interviewed. Good interviewers convey the feeling they are more interested in sources than in themselves.

When sources fear reporters will distort or misunderstand what is said, reporters can demonstrate their knowledge of the topic and background by asking intelligent questions or pointing to other stories they have written on the topic. The interviewees may then be willing to fill in the gaps in the reporters' knowledge. Explaining the purpose of the interview and the story also can help convince sources that reporters are knowledgeable and trustworthy.

Interviewers have a variety of tactics for getting reluctant sources to talk. If interviewees are unresponsive, reporters may try switching topics, trying to find something that will get the source to talk more. In some instances, reporters can build rapport with sources by expressing admiration (if it is genuine) for something a source did or said. Or reporters might draw on their background to establish a connection with a reluctant source. If the interviewee is a college president, the reporter might mention that her father was a college professor (if that is true).

Some sources fear the story will put them in a bad light and cause them to lose their jobs or money or even to face criminal prosecution. Reporters can soothe these fears by explaining that the interview is an opportunity for sources to put their side of a story before the public and that failure to do so will make them look worse.

Many interviews—whether done for feature stories or investigative stories—require reporters to ask tough questions that the source might find embarrassing or potentially harmful. Failure to ask the questions, however, means an interview will be incomplete and lack news value. Asking tough questions is easier if reporters maintain their neutrality. If interviewees believe reporters are simply asking questions and not expressing opinions, they are more likely to submit to tough questions without ending the interview or criticizing the reporter. Sometimes reporters can enhance this sense of neutrality by asking questions in ways that distance themselves from the opinions the questions may imply. They can, for example:

- Attribute the question or point of view implied in the question to a third party or to public opinion generally. For example: "Chancellor Smith, some faculty members have said you attach more importance to intercollegiate athletics than to academics. What is your response?"

- Sugar-coat questions. Asking a person, "Is there anything about your marriage that you now regret?" is easier than asking, "Did you beat your wife?"

- Ask interviewees to explain their previous statements or actions or give their versions of controversial events.

- Ask interviewees to talk about others. Once they start talking about what other people have said or done, it might be easier to shift the interview to their own conduct.

- Ask interviewees for the names of people who support or criticize them. Then ask the interviewees to guess what their critics are most likely to say about them. This tactic often elicits information as well as tips for additional interviews.

- Be persistent. If sources refuse to talk, hang up the phone, or slam the door in reporters' faces, reporters should go back the next day or the next week and try again.

Sources pressed to talk about sensitive topics may sometimes try to evade the question or may even lie. When sources avoid an issue or give fuzzy answers, reporters can restate the question, forcing sources to be more forthcoming. Reporters can also simply remain silent if answers seem incomplete or evasive. The silence tells sources their answers are insufficient and pushes them to elaborate. In some cases, reporters might want to confront sources directly about evasive answers, saying they will note evasions in the story.

Reporters who have done their homework often will know when a source is lying. American reporter Eric Nalder lets sources he suspects of lying spin out their tales. He interrupts them only to ask for elaboration or more detail. Once he has the source's entire story, he can begin to use the facts he has already gathered to pick the source's story apart and get that person to tell the truth.

Reporters should never try to bully or intimidate hostile sources or try to deceive them about the purpose of an interview. Information obtained from a source who has been intimidated may be unreliable. Sources who have been led to believe an interview will be about one topic when, in fact, the reporters want information about something else will feel unprepared to respond fully and accurately.

Special Situations

Telephone Interviews

Reporters conduct many interviews by telephone. When they do, they always identify themselves and their news organizations clearly at the start of the conversation. They never pose as someone other than a reporter. They always ask permission to tape-record the interview.

Experienced reporters wear telephone headsets, keeping their hands free to type notes directly into a computer as they interview their sources. Some sources become upset when they hear the clicking of the keyboard and realize that reporters are typing everything they say; they begin to speak more cautiously or try to end the interview. If a source cannot be soothed, reporters can take notes more quietly in longhand. Sources used to dealing with reporters become accustomed to the noise.

Telephone calls save enormous amounts of time, since reporters do not have to drive to a source's home or office, wait until a source is free, conduct the interview, and then drive back to their offices. Another advantage is that some sources are more comfortable talking without someone watching them. For others, it might be a welcome break in a boring day.

Telephone interviews have disadvantages too. Some sources might be hesitant to talk. Even if reporters have identified themselves, sources may want to call reporters back to make sure they are who they say they are. More important, telephone interviews need to be brief. Sources usually have other work, and long telephone conversations may bore or annoy them. Particularly frustrating for reporters is playing phone tag or not being able to reach a source while on deadline. Reporters simply have to be persistent and keep calling. They should not wait for sources to return phone calls.

Reporters also have to be alert to the possibility that they may be calling at an inconvenient time for the source. If reporters are calling sources in different time zones, they need to be aware of what the time is where the source lives. A reporter working in Vancouver at 8 p.m. should realize that it is 11 p.m. for a source in Toronto, a time when many people are asleep.

Telephone calls are an unsatisfactory means of conducting in-depth interviews about controversial or complex issues and personalities. It is difficult to cultivate sources known only by telephone and never seen face-to-face. Sources might be reluctant to answer over-the-phone questions about embarrassing or personal matters; thus, telephone interviews tend to be brief and superficial. If reporters want to conduct longer, in-depth interviews, they must visit the source in person.

Email Interviews

Email has opened up another way of interviewing sources. Reporters use email to contact hard-to-reach or reluctant sources. Even people who travel a lot make time to check their email. Sources who dodge phone calls or hesitate to return phone messages may answer a reporter's email. A reporter who is trying to contact several sources for similar information can use email to send the same message to each of them. Email is also a way of keeping in contact with sources, exchanging ideas with colleagues, or communicating with readers or viewers.

Reporters are as polite in their emails as they are in person or on the telephone. They use a salutation (such as "Dear Mrs. Ramirez,") and identify themselves and the news organization they represent. They usually review the background of an event or issue before they ask their questions. Reporters also tell sources their deadline, and they thank the sources for their time and expertise. (After all, the sources are not getting paid to answer the reporter's questions but are donating their time.) Reporters do not write in all capital letters because many email users regard it as shouting. Journalists also avoid using acronyms, such as "BTW" ("by the way"), because not everyone knows what they represent.

Email interviews have some advantages over telephone interviews. Besides being more convenient for some sources, email also affords them an opportunity to develop their thoughts more carefully and in more detail. That means reporters get more thorough answers to their questions. The email also provides a written record of the interviews, lessening the likelihood of misunderstanding or misquotation.

However, interviews by email also have drawbacks. Reporters are deprived of their sources' facial expressions, vocal inflections, and body language, all of which can help reporters understand their sources better. Also, although the email response might be more thorough and thoughtful, it also might be

City of Montreal Mayor Gérald Tremblay smiles during an Internet chat session with reporter Stephane Laporte in this March 15, 2005, photo in Montreal.

CP PHOTO/La Presse–Robert Mailloux

less spontaneous. The offhand responses sources make in personal or telephone interviews give reporters additional information and insights on which they can follow up quickly.

Another drawback to the email interview is the possibility that the person who is responding is not who a reporter thinks he or she is. For example, a business executive might have a public relations person draft an answer to an email from a reporter. In still other cases, email sources might simply be pretending to have credentials or experiences they do not really have. The possibility of such fraud exists even for face-to-face interviews, but posing seems to be easier over the Internet or through email.

Interviewing for Broadcast

Reporters interviewing sources for radio or television have problems print reporters don't face. In an interview with *American Journalism Review*, Terry Gross, host of the National Public Radio program "Fresh Air" and one of the best interviewers in the business, explains the difference this way: "For most print journalists the interview is the raw material for the piece, along with everything else the reporter has seen and heard in researching the story. For me the interview is the piece." Gross tries to arrange her questions so that the answers produce a pleasing narrative, rather than something that sounds like answers to a random questionnaire. Although Gross's program is not broadcast live, giving the program staff time to check and edit responses, the production deadlines are tight enough that extensive editing is impractical.

Television reporters need to plan their interviews in advance with the technicians who will be operating the cameras and sound equipment, especially if the interview needs to be shot quickly for broadcast that day or if the source does not want to appear on camera. They also might want to show the interview subject doing more than talking. Where possible, television reporters might want the subject to demonstrate an activity or respond to a video or another source.

Taking Notes

Reporters conducting interviews balance the tasks of note-taking and questioning. Unless reporters take detailed notes, they probably will forget much of what is said. Many interviewers take copious notes, writing down much more information than they can possibly use. During an interview, reporters may not know which facts they will need or want to emphasize in their stories. If they record as much as possible, they are less likely to forget an important point or make a factual error. They can easily ignore notes that later prove to be unimportant or irrelevant.

Few reporters know shorthand, but most develop their own shortcuts for taking notes. They leave out some words, abbreviate others, and jot down names, numbers, good quotations and key ideas. When sources speak too rapidly, reporters can ask them to slow down or repeat important statements. Note-taking makes some sources nervous. Reporters should explain that the notes will help them write more accurate and thorough stories.

After completing interviews, reporters review their notes immediately while everything is fresh in their minds. They may want to fill in some gaps or be certain that they understand everything a source said. Reporters often write their stories as soon as possible after their interviews. The longer they wait, the more likely they are to forget some facts or distort others.

Tape-Recording Interviews

Tape-recording interviews frees reporters to concentrate on the questions they want to ask and sources' responses to those questions. Tapes also provide verbatim and permanent records, so reporters make fewer factual errors, and sources are less likely to claim that they were misquoted. When reporters replay the tapes, they often find important statements they failed to notice during the interviews.

Tape recording has drawbacks too. After recording a one-hour interview, reporters may have to replay the entire tape at least once, and perhaps two or three times, before writing the story. They also may have difficulty locating important facts or quotations on the tape. By comparison, reporters may need a minute or less to find a fact or a quotation in their handwritten notes from a one-hour interview.

Fortunately, there is a third possibility: reporters may both record their interviews and take written notes. The reporters can consult their notes to write the stories, then use the tape recordings to verify the accuracy of important facts and quotations. If a tape recorder has a counter that indicates how much tape has played, reporters can use that to note the location of important or interesting quotations.

The use of tape recorders for interviews represented an innovation in the journalistic technique of the 1970s. Pre-eminent investigative reporter and interviewing expert John Sawatsky, likely the first print reporter in Vancouver to begin tape-recording his interviews, "believes it allowed him to break stories that other reporters missed. And it also gave him insight into his own skills at approaching and questioning sources, a process that he would refine later in his career." (Cecil Rosner, *Behind the Headlines*, p. 132)

Although tape recorders have become commonplace, some sources still refuse to be taped. Recorders are small enough now that reporters can easily hide them in their pockets or handbags, but taping a conversation without the other party's consent is unethical and sometimes illegal. While it is legal for journalists to tape-record telephone interviews without the consent of the person being interviewed, consent is required if the interview is to be broadcast. Reporters may also listen in on or record private conversations if they have the consent of one of the parties (the originator or intended receiver of the communication), but it is a Criminal Code offence to reveal the content of the communication without the consent of one of the parties. It is also a criminal offence to publish or broadcast a phone conversation that was illegally taped by a third party. In broadcast journalism, under Canadian Radio-television and Telecommunications Commission (CRTC) rules, reporters are prohibited from airing interviews or conversations without the consent of the interviewees. Tape-recording in secret may also present legal problems under various other provisions of the Criminal Code (such as those aimed at trespassing at night). Finally, while the use of hidden microphones and cameras is generally prohibited, the procedure may be defended in cases where it is necessary to expose the truth on a matter of legitimate public interest.

In the usual case of a reporter taping a telephone or face-to-face interview, the consenting party would be the reporter doing the taping. Even where it is legal, though, taping a conversation without the other party's consent raises ethical questions. Undisclosed tape recording seems manipulative and invasive. Readers, viewers and jurors (if a story results in a lawsuit) may consider tainted any information reporters obtain through secret recording.

Final Thoughts

Interviewing is an art form that requires practice. Journalists who are most successful at interviewing have done it for years and have developed insights into the sources they interview and into their own strengths and weaknesses in relating to other people. Terry Gross, a journalist with National Public Radio in the United States, told the *American Journalism Review*: "My theory of interviewing is that whatever you have, use it. If you are confused, use that. If you have raw curiosity, use that. If you have experience, use that. If you have a lot of research, use that. But figure out what it is you have and make it work for you." Student journalists often lack the experience and the maturity to know what they have and how to make it work for them. Their initial attempts at interviewing may yield disappointing results. Young reporters should not become discouraged, however. With time and persistence, they too can become excellent interviewers.

WRITING THE INTERVIEW STORY

Writing a story based on an in-depth interview, such as a personality profile, is little different from writing any other news story. An interview story does raise a couple of unusual problems, however.

One option reporters have when writing an interview story is to use a question-and-answer format. Few do so, however, because it requires too much space and makes it difficult for readers and viewers to grasp a story's highlights quickly. The Q-and-A format works best with celebrity interviews, self-help stories, and sidebars for main stories. Q-and-A stories are never verbatim transcripts of interviews, even though the format may create that impression. The interviews are usually heavily edited to eliminate boring and irrelevant passages.

Most reporters begin interview stories with a summary lead that presents the story's central point. Reporters then present the highlights in the following paragraphs. Reporters also may use an alternative lead, such as an anecdote or description that introduces a nut paragraph containing the central point. Information in the body of the story usually is organized by topic, and facts and quotations are presented in the order of their importance, not the order in which the source provided them. Reporters must be sure, however, that in rearranging information they keep every direct and indirect quotation in its proper context. Reporters usually keep background information to a minimum and incorporate it in the story where it is most necessary and helpful for explaining a source's remarks.

Making sure an interview story adheres to its central point can be difficult. A student interested in Canada's participation in the U.S. space shuttle program interviewed a representative of the National Aeronautics and Space Administration (NASA). The NASA source overwhelmed the student with facts about the technological benefits of the Apollo and Skylab projects. Those were the facts that filled the reporter's story. They were accurate but irrelevant to the student's purpose of writing about the space shuttle program. Had the student kept the interview focused on the shuttle program, the story would have kept its focus too.

Another problem is the overuse of quotations. Some writers think they have done their job simply by stringing together quotations from their sources. Quotations should be used only for emphasis and impact. Reporters should tell most of the story in their own words and use only those quotations that show strong emotion or phrase a point in a particularly effective way.

 ## CHECKLIST FOR INTERVIEWING

1. Determine whether the story will be a news story, a feature, or an investigative story.
2. For all types of stories, interview to get facts, details, chronologies, context and anecdotes.
3. For feature stories, capture the source's environment, appearance and mannerisms.
4. For investigative stories, get the source's version of events, explanations of contradictions, and replies to charges.
5. Identify the best available sources who can provide the necessary information for the story.
6. In deciding how many sources to interview, keep in mind deadlines, the expertise of the sources, the degree of controversy regarding the issue, and the complexity of the issue.
7. Research people and issues as thoroughly as possible before conducting any interviews.
8. Select questions that will address the central point of the planned story.
9. Use questions that will encourage interviewees to talk—and then let them talk with as few interruptions as possible.
10. Interview sources in places where they will be comfortable, not newsrooms or restaurants.
11. Organize questions by topic, and raise topics in an order that will make it easy for sources to move from one to the next.
12. If a source is reluctant to talk or hostile, find out why and try to address the concern.
13. Maintain neutrality when asking tough questions. Sources are more likely to answer tough questions from neutral interviewers than from those who seem to be advocates for a point of view.
14. Telephone interviews save time, but they are unsatisfactory for long, in-depth interviews.
15. Email is an effective way of interviewing some sources, but the interviewer is deprived of information about the source's demeanour and personality.
16. Reporters interviewing for broadcast need to remember that the interview is the story and not just raw material for a story.
17. Take thorough notes during the interview, making sure to write down names, dates, numbers and good quotations.
18. Tape recorders provide a verbatim permanent record, but they are sometimes clumsy to use.

The Writing Coach

INTERVIEWING FOR STORY

By Don Gibb

"What's the weather like?"

Such a simple, conversational question, and yet it led *Globe and Mail* columnist Murray Campbell to a detail that provided a lead for his story on Julia Butterfly Hill, the woman who lived for two years in a 1,000-year-old giant redwood tree in California to prevent it from becoming lumber.

His simple question—along with followup questions—produced rich visual detail for readers. It was a cold, cold rainy day. The protective tarp was flapping in the wind. Butterfly Hill was shivering under layers of clothing. Seven, to be exact. And all of this happening on a platform the size of a double bed—yet another detail to let readers "see" the image in their minds.

He opened the story with this:

It is beginning to hail, and Julia Butterfly Hill is shivering even though she is wearing seven layers of clothing. "It's extremely windy and it's extremely cold," she said, drawing out the syllables of "extremely" to underline the point that she has seen better days.

Ms. Hill was speaking on a cellular phone about halfway up a 60-metre redwood tree in northern California. She was huddled beneath rustling tarps and a platform about the size of a double bed.

Around her were her very few possessions: A single-burner propane stove and a bucket she uses as a toilet, some books and the cardboard on which she writes letters and poems.

What's the weather like? What does your living space look like? What are you doing now? Such simple questions produce the details, anecdotes, quotes, dialogue and scenes writers need to create the images readers need to "see" and to be part of a story. Good writers develop a built-in alarm that goes off every time one of their senses (see, hear, smell, touch or taste) detects a moment worth capturing in more detail.

Like the father, his daughter abducted and murdered a year earlier, who cannot stand to hear the doorbell ring.

Why?

It was a year ago, as he made a pot of tea in the kitchen, that the doorbell rang. He walked past his daughter's high school graduation picture on the piano in the living room, opened the front door, and faced a police constable.

What did the officer say?

"I looked straight into his eyes. He didn't have to say anything. I knew my daughter was dead. Every time I hear the doorbell, the image of the police officer—his eyes—flash back to remind me of my daughter's death." A single, simple detail of the doorbell allows the writer to capture a key moment—a telling anecdote—in the story of a father still grieving as police continue to search for his daughter's killer.

But keep going. *What did the father see in his eyes that told him she was dead? What were the first words the police officer said? Did he come in? Did he have tea with the father? Where was the mother of the girl when the officer arrived?* And then … keep going.

The interview is the key that opens the door to great storytelling. Every interview should be an exploration for interesting, factual, informative and visual detail. It is not simply a question-and-answer exchange or transcribing verbatim what someone says. When done well, it involves getting to the heart of an issue and to the very soul of a person.

Feature writing often offers writers a chance to do more research and more interviews. It gives writers more of an opportunity to see their interview subjects at work, at play, and at home—in other words, to go to the scene or several scenes. And that means the chance to gather more detail. It also offers the luxury of conducting followup interviews with key characters in the middle or at the end of the process or after having talked to others.

To be an effective interviewer, writers need to know simple rules that form the building blocks of creating memorable features. Here are some of them:

- Listen. Perhaps this is *the* most crucial interviewing skill. If you're too busy thinking of your next question or checking your digital recorder, you're not paying enough attention to the words coming from your interviewee.

- Stay in charge. Listen to your sources and listen to their agendas, but don't let them take control of the interview.

- Understand the sequence of events. For readers, nothing adds confusion to a story faster than not knowing where we are in time or place.

- Ask open-ended questions. Asking questions that cannot be answered with a simple yes or no opens the door to essential details.

- Probe for graphic details. Always ask followup questions, and you will quickly discover that the answers generate better and more complete responses as well as added detail to bring more colour to your stories.

- Take one thing at a time. It's a good idea not to leave a topic until you believe you have explored it fully.

- Ask for clarification. Follow this simple rule: do not move into a new line of questioning until you understand what has already been discussed.

- Ask tough questions. First, go in prepared. If you're listening carefully, you're likely to find the right spot to segue to your tough questions.

- Ask dumb questions. Reporters who are reticent to ask dumb questions risk failing to properly understand their story or explain it to readers. Too often, they allow a person's quote to substitute for a proper explanation.

- Don't accept "no" too readily. Before accepting "no" as the final answer to your request for an interview, try to determine and then address what lies behind the potential source's refusal.

- Take careful notes. Use a tape recorder to supplement rather than to replace note-taking. Over-reliance on tape recorders dulls a reporter's listening skills.

- Go somewhere. Getting out of the newsroom and to the scene of an interview allows you to experience the setting where an interview subject works, plays or lives and, based on that experience, to build scenes into your stories.

- Trust your senses. Writers need to record what people say, but they also need to move quickly into observation mode when necessary. Seek the telling detail, and don't be afraid to look for personal objects in an interview setting and ask about them.

- Phone with your eyes open. A telephone interview is second-best to a face-to-face interview, so when doing telephone interviews, be sure to ask the kinds of questions that will allow you to paint pictures for your readers.

- Watch out for hazards. Reporters encounter a variety of hazards in an interview; mostly, these hazards are designed to intimidate the reporter and to wrest control of the interview. (The source who waits till the end of an interview to announce that all the preceding was of course "off the record" is a good example.)

- Snap … Snap … Snap. The best writers collect images detail by detail through questions designed to capture a story piece by piece.

SUGGESTED READINGS AND USEFUL WEBSITES

"Getting people to talk: The art of the interview." 2006. In Robert Cribb, Dean Jobb, David McKie, and Fred Vallance-Jones, *Digging Deeper: A Canadian Reporter's Research Guide*, 118–34. Don Mills, ON: Oxford University Press.

Gibb, Don. 2009. "Interviewing to tell a story." In Ivor Shapiro, ed., *The Bigger Picture: Elements of Feature Writing*, 135–54. Toronto: Emond Montgomery Publications.

"Interviewing." 2008. In Patti Tasko, ed., *The Canadian Press Stylebook: A Guide for Writers and Editors*, 15th edn, 80–5. Toronto: The Canadian Press.

McLaughlin, Paul. 1990. *How to Interview: The Art of the Media Interview.* Vancouver and Toronto: International Self-Counsel Press.

Metzler, Ken. 1996. *Creative Interviewing: The Writer's Guide to Gathering Information by Asking Questions.* 3rd edn. Boston: Allyn and Bacon.

Sawatsky, John. 1989. *Insiders: Power, Money and Secrets.* Toronto: McClelland and Stewart.

Stein, M.L., and Susan F. Paterno. 2001. *Talk Straight, Listen Carefully: The Art of Interviewing.* Hoboken, NJ: Wiley-Blackwell.

The Telephone Interview: How to Do It Well (Don Gibb): http://www.cane.ca/english/me_res_telephone_interview.htm

Interviewing Tips (Paul McLaughlin): http://www.cane.ca/english/me_res_interviewingtipspaul.htm

Teaching Interviewing (j-source.ca): http://www.j-source.ca/english_new/category.php?catid=65

EXERCISE 1   Interviews

Discussion Questions

1. How would you respond to a source who, several days before a scheduled interview, asked for a list of the questions you intended to ask?
2. Do you agree that reporters have an obligation to inform their sources when they plan to record an interview even when it's legal to do so?
3. If a story's publication is likely to embarrass a source, do reporters have a responsibility to warn the source of that possibility? Does it matter whether the source is used to dealing with reporters?
4. Would you be willing to interview a mother whose son just died? Would it matter whether her son drowned in a swimming pool, was slain or was a convicted killer executed in a state prison?
5. Imagine that you wrote a front-page story about students' use of marijuana on your campus. To obtain the story, you promised several sources that you would never reveal their identities. If, during a subsequent legal proceeding, a judge ordered you to identify your sources, would you do so? Or would you be willing to go to jail to protect your sources?

Class Projects

1. List 10 interviewing tips provided by other sources.
2. Interview an expert on body language or nonverbal communication, perhaps someone in your school's psychology or speech department, and report on the information's usefulness to journalists. You might also invite the expert to speak to your class.
3. Interview an expert on interviewing, perhaps a faculty member in your school's psychology department. You might also invite the expert to speak to your class.
4. Interview government officials who frequently deal with reporters. Ask those officials what they like and dislike about the interviews and how they try to handle the interviews and the reporters conducting the interviews.
5. Ask several government officials which local reporters are the best interviewers, then interview those reporters about their interviewing techniques. You might invite one of those reporters to speak to your class.
6. Ask every student in your class to write one paragraph about each of the three most newsworthy experiences in his or her life. Then select the students with the most interesting experiences and have each student in your class interview them, one by one, and write news stories about their experiences.

EXERCISE 2   Interviews

Interview with an Injured Bicyclist

Write a news story based on the following interview with Marsha L. Taylor, conducted this morning, two days after she was released from a hospital after being injured in a bicycling accident. "Q" stands for the questions that Taylor was asked during the interview at her home, and "A" stands for her answers, which can be quoted directly. Taylor manages a McDonald's restaurant and lives at 2012 McKay Blvd. in your city.

Q: How long have you been bicycling?

A: I started when I was in college, but I didn't do any serious cycling until after I had graduated. I spent that first summer looking for work, and cycling was a way of filling in time and keeping fit while I waited for interviews. Eventually I got involved with some groups of cyclists and participating in weekend rides and even some races. Since then it's been a major part of my life. I can't imagine what my life would be like without bicycling.

Q: How active have you been in bicycling recently?

A: I rode a lot this year. Um, I guess I must have ridden at least maybe 5,000 kilometres, because in the spring I rode in the annual Lieutenant-Governor's Bicycle Tour, which goes across the province. And in the fall I rode in a tour across Canada.

Q: How did your accident happen?

A: Well, a lot of it is hazy to me, but it happened shortly after I finished the tour. I had been back in town about two weeks, and I was just out for a short ride of an hour or so. I was riding down 72nd Street almost to Southland Boulevard when a car hit me from behind and sent me flying off my bike. That's all I remember until I was in the hospital.

Q: What were your injuries?

A: Gee, you might as well ask what wasn't injured. I had a mild concussion, a broken neck, six broken ribs, a broken arm, and a broken pelvis.

Q: Were the doctors worried about your condition?

A: Yeah, somewhat. They didn't think there was anything they couldn't control, but there was a lot of stuff broken. They were especially concerned about the broken neck. One doctor said I had what they call a hangman's fracture. She said it was a miracle that I wasn't paralyzed.

Q: Was your recovery pretty smooth?

A: No. In fact I got worse at first. After a couple of weeks, they sent me to a rehabilitation facility, but then I developed complications. The doctors discovered I had some internal injuries. My intestine was perforated, and my liver and gall bladder were injured. All that caused my skin to change colour, start turning bright orange. When my mother saw me she said I looked like a Halloween pumpkin. I had to go back to the hospital because of those complications. But for that, I probably would have been out in two months instead of four. I still have to go back for rehabilitation three times a week.

Q: Have you changed your attitude about cycling since your accident?

A: No. I still want to ride. If I could, I'd be out there right now, but it's hard to ride a bike when you have to use crutches. If you, you know, take precautions and are careful, bicycling's pretty safe.

Q: What kind of precautions?

A: Well, the main thing, you know, is protective clothing, especially the helmet. I never ride unless I have my helmet. It probably saved my life this time.

Q: How long have you lived here?

A: Let's see, ah, 15 years now, ever since I started work for McDonald's.

Q: How long have you been manager there?

A: Four years.

Q: How old are you?

A: Ah, 37. Old enough, yeah.

CHAPTER 9

Interview with a Robbery Victim

Write a news story based on the following interview with Michele Schipper, a second-year student majoring in journalism at your college. The interview provides a verbatim account of a robbery that occurred yesterday. "Q" stands for the questions Ms. Schipper was asked during an interview this morning, and "A" stands for her answers, which can be quoted directly. (This is a true story, told by a college student.)

Q: Could you describe the robbery?

A: I pulled up into the parking lot of a convenience store on Bonneville Drive, but I pulled up on the side and not in front where I should have, and I was getting out of my car, and I was reaching into my car to pull out my purse when this guy, 6 foot tall or whatever, approached me and said, "Give me your purse." I said, "OK." I barely saw him out of the corner of my eye. And then, I, um, so I reached in to get my purse. And I could see him approaching a little closer. Before then, he was 4 or 5 feet away. So I turned around and kicked him in the groin area, and he started going down, but I was afraid he wouldn't stay down, that he would seek some kind of retribution. So when he was down, I gave him a roundhouse to the nose. I just hit him as hard as I could, an undercut as hard as I could. And I could hear some crunching, and some blood spurted, and he went on the ground, and I got in my car, and I went away. I called the cops from a motel down the street. They asked where he was last I seen him, and I said, "On the ground."

Q: Did the police find him?

A: No, he was gone.

Q: Had you taken judo or some type of self-defence course?

A: No, but I used to be a tomboy, and I used to wrestle with the guys, my good friends, when I was young. It was a good punch. I don't know, I was just very mad. My dad, he works out with boxing and weightlifting and everything, and I've played with that, so I've got the power.

Q: Could you describe the man?

A: I didn't see him well enough to identify him, really, but I hope he thinks twice next time.

Q: What time did the robbery occur?

A: This was about 4 in the afternoon, broad daylight, but there were no other cars parked around, though.

Q: Did you see the man when you drove up, or was he hiding?

A: There was a dumpster, and I guess he came from behind the dumpster, like he was waiting there, just like he was waiting there. And I guess he was waiting around the dumpster, because no one was standing around when I pulled up, I remember that.

Q: Were there any witnesses who could describe the man?

A: There was no one around, there were no cars parked. The clerks were inside the store. I didn't see any pedestrians around, and after I did it, I didn't wait to find if there were any witnesses because I wanted to leave right away.

Q: Was the man armed?

A: Out of the corner of my eye I realized I didn't see any weapon. And I guess I thought he was alone. You register some things; you just don't consciously realize it.

Q: What was your first reaction, what did you think when he first approached and demanded your purse?

A: I didn't think of anything, really, you know. I just reacted. I was very, really indignant. Why, you know, just because he wanted my purse, why should he have it? There was really only $10 in there, and I probably wouldn't really do it again in the same situation. And my parents don't know about it because they would be very angry that I fought back.

Q: Had you ever thought about being robbed and about what you would do, about how you would respond?

A: It just came instinctively, and after the incident, you know, I was shaking for about an hour afterwards.

Q: About how long did the robbery last?

A: It really only lasted a second, just as long as it would take for you to kick someone and then to hit them and then drive away in the car. It really only lasted a second.

EXERCISE 4   Interviews

Sleep Shortage

Write a news story based on the following interview with Diana Gant, a member of the psychology faculty at your institution. Gant is recognized as one of the nation's leaders in the study of sleep. The interview provides a verbatim account of an interview you conducted today in her office. "Q" stands for the questions that you asked Gant, and "A" stands for her answers, which can be quoted directly.

Q: You're a professor in the Psychology Department?
A: That's right, for 17 years now. That's how long I've been here, ever since I finished graduate school.
Q: Have you been studying sleep all that time?
A: Even earlier. I started when I was a graduate student and wrote my thesis, then my dissertation, about sleep.
Q: How much sleep have you found most people need a night?
A: Most people need nine to 10 hours a night to perform optimally. Some should be taken in afternoon naps.
Q: I read somewhere that most people need only seven or eight hours of sleep a night and that there are people who need only four or five.
A: Nine hours is better. I know not everyone agrees with me, but that's what I keep finding. Think of sleep like exercise. People exercise because it's healthy. Sleep is healthy.
Q: How much sleep does the average person actually get?
A: About seven hours.
Q: If most people need more sleep, why aren't they getting it?
A: Believe it or not, some people think that going without sleep is the big, sophisticated, macho thing to do. They figure they don't need it, that the rules don't apply to them, that they can get more done. It may work for them for a while, but sooner or later they begin to suffer the consequences. Then you can have some real problems.
Q: How can the average person tell if he's getting enough sleep?
A: It's easy. Ask yourself: Do you usually feel sleepy or doze off when you are sitting quietly after a large lunch?
Q: What else happens if people don't get enough sleep?
A: Going without enough sleep is as much of a public and personal safety hazard as going to work drunk. It can make people clumsy, stupid, unhappy.
Q: Can you give some examples of the problem?
A: I look at a lot of disasters, really major disasters like the space shuttle Challenger, the accident at Russia's Chernobyl nuclear reactor, and a lot of airliner crashes. The element of sleeplessness was involved in all of them, at least contributed to all of them, and maybe—probably—caused all of them. The press focuses on the possibility that somebody was drunk, but working long shifts with no relief can lead to people falling asleep at the wheel.
Q: How did you get interested in sleep?
A: When I started I wanted to write about people who got little sleep and remained productive. The problem was, when my subjects arrived in laboratories and got a chance to sleep in dark, quiet rooms, they all slept for about nine hours. That and other work convinced me that most people suffer from sleep deprivation.
Q: How do you gather your data?
A: Partly laboratory studies and partly statistics, statistics on the connection between sleeplessness and accidents. One thing I've done is study the number of traffic accidents in the province right after the shift to daylight savings time in the spring, when most people lose

an hour's sleep. There's an 8 per cent increase in accidents the day after the time change, and there's a corresponding decrease in accidents in the fall when people gain an extra hour of sleep.

Q: Why's that?

A: What we're looking at when people get up just an hour early is the equivalent of a national jet lag. The effect can last a week. It isn't simply due to loss of sleep but complications from resetting the biological clock.

Q: How else can a lack of sleep hurt people?

A: You feel as if your clothes weigh a few extra pounds. Even more than usual, you tend to be drowsy after lunch. If, say, you cut back from eight to six hours, you'll probably become depressed. Cut back even further, to five hours, and you may find yourself falling asleep at stoplights while driving home.

Q: If people aren't getting enough sleep, or good sleep, how can they solve the problem? What do you recommend?

A: That's easy. Almost everyone in the field agrees on that. First, you need someplace that's dark and quiet. Shut off all the lights and draw the shades. Second, it's good to relax for an hour or so before going to bed. Watch TV, read a good book. Don't drink or eat a lot. That'll disturb your sleep, especially alcohol and caffeine. Plus, it should be cool, about 65 is best for good sleep. Tobacco, coffee and alcohol are all bad. As their effects wear off, your brain actually becomes more alert. Even if you fall asleep, you may find yourself waking up at 2 or 3 a.m., and then you can't get back to sleep. Also avoid chocolate and other foods that contain a lot of sugar. Finally, get a comfortable bed, and keep your bed linens clean and fresh.

CHAPTER 9

EXERCISE 5   Interviews

Interview after a Murder

Write a news story based on the following interview with a bookkeeper at the North Point Inn. "Q" stands for the questions she was asked during an interview at her home this morning, and "A" stands for her answers, which can be quoted directly. (The interview is based on an actual case: a robbery and murder at an elegant restaurant.)

Q: Could you start by spelling your name for me?
A: N-i-n-a C-o-r-t-e-z.
Q: You work as a bookkeeper at the North Point Inn?
A: Yes, I've been there seven years.
Q: Would you describe the robbery there yesterday?
A: It was about 9 in the morning, around 7 or 8 minutes before 9.
Q: Is that the time you usually get there?
A: At 9 o'clock, yes.
Q: How did you get in?
A: I've got a key to the employee entrance in the back.
Q: Was anyone else there?
A: Kevin Blohm, one of the cooks. He usually starts at 8. We open for lunch at 11:30, and he's in charge.
Q: Did you talk to him?
A: He came into my office, and we chatted about what happened in the restaurant the night before, and I asked him to make me some coffee. After he brought me a cup, I walked out to the corridor with him. That was the last I saw him.
Q: What did you do next?
A: I was just beginning to go through the receipts and cash from the previous night. I always start by counting the previous day's revenue. I took everything out of a safe, the cash and receipts, and began to count them on my desk.
Q: About how much did you have?
A: $6,000 counting everything, the cash and receipts from credit cards.
Q: Is that when you were robbed?
A: A minute or two or less, a man came around the corner, carrying a knife.
Q: What did you do?
A: I started screaming and kicking. My chair was on rollers, and when I started kicking, it fell. I fell on the floor, and he reached across my desk and grabbed $130 in $5 bills.
Q: Did he say anything?
A: No, he just took the money and walked out.
Q: Was he alone?
A: I don't think so. I heard someone—a man—say, "Get that money out of there." Then someone tried to open the door to my office, but I'd locked it. Three or four minutes later, the police were there.
Q: Is that when you found Mr. Blohm?
A: I went into the hallway with the police and saw blood on a door in the reception area. It was awful. There was blood on the walls and floor. Kevin was lying on the floor, dead. He had a large knife wound in his chest and another on one hand.
Q: Can you describe the man who robbed you?
A: He was about 5 feet 10, maybe 6 feet tall, in his early 20s, medium build.
Q: What was he wearing?
A: Blue jeans, a blue plaid button-up shirt and blue tennis shoes.

Q: Did you see his face?

A: He had a scarf, a floral scarf, tied around the lower part of his face, cowboy style. It covered the bottom half of his face.

Q: Did the man look at all familiar, like anyone you may have known or seen in the restaurant?

A: No.

Q: Did you notice anything unusual that day?

A: I saw a car in the parking lot when I came in, one I didn't recognize. It didn't belong to anyone who worked there, but that's all I remember.

Q: Do you have any idea why someone stabbed Blohm?

A: No. Kevin might have gotten in his way or tried to stop him or recognized him or something. I don't know. I didn't see it. I don't know anything else.

10 Feature Stories

Look at everybody who crosses this lobby. In every one of them there is a story.

— Jack Scott, journalist, columnist and author

Most news stories describe recent events—meetings, crimes, fires or accidents, for example. Feature stories, by contrast, often are written in narrative form, read more like nonfiction short stories, and have an emotional centre. Many have a beginning, a middle and an end. They inform readers and viewers, but they also amuse, entertain, inspire or stimulate. Because of these emphases, they are also called "human-interest" stories.

Features can describe a person, place, process or idea rather than an event. Their topics might be less timely and less local than those of news stories, but producers and editors find time and space to run them because they are newsworthy and appeal to audiences.

Reporters who write features use no single formula, such as the inverted pyramid. And in general, features explore their topics in greater depth than news stories.

When writing a feature story, journalists can borrow techniques from short stories, often using description, sensory details, quotations, anecdotes and even personification. They might use characterization, scene setting, plot structure, and other novelistic elements to dramatize a story's theme and to add more details.

Feature stories, however, are still a form of journalism; they are not fiction or "creative writing." Nothing is made up. Like news stories, features must be factual and original. They must be fair and balanced, based on verifiable information. They also must be objective—they are not essays or editorials. In short, they are still news, and news, as Canadian journalist Neil Reynolds once said, offering a tongue-in-cheek definition, "is what someone wants suppressed."[1]

SELECTING A TOPIC AND GATHERING INFORMATION

Feature story ideas are everywhere. Almost everything one sees or does has a story behind it—journalists just have to open their eyes and ears. The most crucial step in writing a good feature story is making the topic fresh, dramatic, colourful and exciting. Journalists go to the places they write about and interview people in their customary surroundings. They also do background research to give context to the story. Reporters use all their senses—seeing, hearing, touching, tasting and smelling. They record how people move, speak and dress. They use

---

[1]Neil Reynolds. To a journalism panel conducted by Peter Gzowski, on CBC-TV's "Morningside," May 15, 1995, and cited in *Famous Lasting Words* (Douglas and McIntyre, 2000), p. 363.

descriptive verbs instead of adjectives and adverbs. They give audience members a reason to care about the subject.

Feature writers find story ideas by being curious and observant. News stories may provide spin-off topics for features. Events such as war, school shootings and natural disasters can spark human-interest stories about the reactions of victims, heroism in crises, and other "people" angles that bring the event into sharper focus.

After selecting a topic likely to interest a large audience, reporters must narrow the subject and find a central point that emphasizes, perhaps, a single person, situation or episode. For example, a profile cannot summarize a person's entire life, so a reporter will focus on just one aspect with an emotional edge: a single experience, trait or achievement that sums up the person's character. If reporters fail to identify a central point, their stories become long, disorganized and superficial. This can leave readers and viewers confused, and they will quit the story because the point is lost.

While gathering the information for feature stories, reporters normally consult several sources, perhaps a half-dozen or more, to obtain a well-rounded account. Good reporters gather two or three times as much information as they can use and then discard all but the most telling details.

TYPES OF FEATURE STORIES

Feature stories come in a wide variety. The following are a few of the most common types.

Profiles or Personality Features

Profiles describe interesting people. These people may have overcome a disability, had an interesting hobby, pursued an unusual career, or become famous because of their colourful personalities. To be effective, profiles must do more than list an individual's achievements or important dates in the individual's life. They must reveal the person's character. To gather the necessary information, feature writers often watch their subjects at work, visit them at home, and interview their friends, relatives and business associates. Completed profiles quote and describe their subjects. The best profiles are so revealing that readers and viewers feel as though they have actually talked to the people. Here's a shortened version of a profile about a young autistic man:

> Bullied by other children and bewildered by ordinary life, Daniel Tammet spent his early years burrowed deep inside the world of numbers. They were his companions and his solace, living, breathing beings that enveloped him with their shapes and textures and colours.
>
> He still loves then and needs them; he can still do extraordinary things with them, like perform complicated calculations instantly in his head, far beyond the capacity of an ordinary calculator. But Mr. Tammet, who at the age of 25 received a diagnosis of Asperger's syndrome, a high-functioning form of autism, has made a difficult and self-conscious journey out of his own mind.
>
> "I live in two countries, one of the mind and one of the body, one of numbers and one of people," he said recently. Slight and soft-spoken, dressed in a T-shirt and casual combat-style pants, he sat cross-legged in his living room and sipped a cup of tea, one of several he drinks at set times each day.
>
> Not so long ago, even a conversation like this one would have been prohibitively difficult for Mr. Tammet, now 28. As he describes in his newly published memoir, "Born on a Blue Day: Inside the Extraordinary Mind of an Autistic Savant," he has willed himself to learn what to do. Offer a visitor a drink; look her in the eye; don't stand in someone else's space. These are all conscious decisions.
>
> Mr. Tammet's book is an elegant account of how his condition has informed his life, a rare first-person insight into a mysterious and confounding disorder. He is unusual not just because of his lucid writing style and his ability to analyze his own thoughts and behaviour but also because he is one of fewer than 100 "prodigious

savants"—autistic or otherwise mentally impaired people with spectacular, almost preternatural skills—in the world, according to Dr. Darold Treffert, a researcher of savant syndrome.

He wears his gift lightly, casually. When he gets nervous, he said, he sometimes reverts to a coping strategy he employed as a child: he multiplies two over and over again, each result emitting in his head bright silvery sparks until he is enveloped by fireworks of them. He demonstrated, reciting the numbers to himself, and in a moment had reached 1,048,276—2 to the 20th power. He speaks 10 languages, including Lithuanian, Icelandic, and Esperanto and has invented his own language, Manti. In 2004, he raised money for an epilepsy charity by memorizing and publicly reciting the number pi to 22,514 digits—a new European record. In addition to Asperger's, he has the rare gift of synesthesia, which allows him to see numbers as having shapes, colours, and textures; he also assigns them personalities. His unusual mind has been studied repeatedly by researchers.

Mr. Tammet sees himself as an ambassador and advocate for people with autism.

"Autistic people do fall in love," he said. "They do have joy; they do have sorrow; they do experience ups and downs like everyone else. We may not have the same ability to manage those emotions as others have, but they're there, and sometimes our experience of them is far more intense than the experience of other people."

But he is not an easy person to live with, Mr. Tammet said. He is discomfited by disturbances like a suddenly ringing telephone, a last-minute change of plans, or a friend's unexpected visit. When he gets upset, he paces in circles. He splashes water on his face exactly five times each morning and cannot leave the house without first counting the items of clothing he is wearing.

The full story includes his childhood troubles that stemmed from the syndrome and the love of his large family and partner, which has helped him cope with ordinary daily routines.

Historical Features

Historical features commemorate the dates of important events; news organizations also publicize the anniversaries of the births and deaths of famous people.

Other historical features are tied to current events that generate interest in their topics. If a tornado, flood or earthquake strikes the city, news organizations are likely to present stories about earlier tornadoes, floods or earthquakes.

Historical features might also describe famous landmarks, pioneers and philosophies; improvements in educational, entertainment, medical and transportation facilities; and changes in an area's racial composition, housing patterns, food, industries, growth, religions and wealth.

The following historical feature ties a literary and historical landmark, Anne Frank's diary, to a recent discovery.

On April 30, 1941, just days after a Gestapo courier may have threatened to denounce Anne Frank's father, Otto, to the Nazis, he wrote to his close college friend Nathan Straus Jr. begging for help in getting his family out of Amsterdam and into America.

"I would not ask if conditions here would not force me to do all I can in time to be able to avoid worst," he wrote in a letter that forms part of a 78-page stack of newly uncovered documents released yesterday. "Perhaps you remember that we have two girls. It is for the sake of the children mainly that we have to care for. Our own fate is of less importance."

The writer of this feature educates readers in four ways while weaving the story. Readers learn about the events surrounding the Holocaust, the personalized story of one man's unsuccessful efforts to get his family to safety, the unexpected discovery of Otto Frank's papers in a New Jersey warehouse (the news event to which the story was tied), and the artifacts on display at the YIVO Institute for Jewish Research in Manhattan.

Adventure Features

Adventure features describe unusual and exciting experiences—perhaps the story of someone who fought in a war, survived an airplane crash, climbed a mountain, sailed around the world, or experienced another country. Many writers begin with the action—their stories' most interesting and dramatic moments, and use quotations and descriptions. In the following adventure story, the reporter wrote in first and second person to draw in readers and used description to enable them to imagine standing on the edge of a volcano:

> When the world's most active volcano begins belching molten rock into the ocean, you've got to see it.
>
> Thick, heavy clouds of steam cover the entire shoreline, and each new lava flow adds to the island's land mass—an additional 550 acres at last count. Sounds are whipped away by the wind, but when the wind dies momentarily, you can hear the lava snapping and popping—a reminder that land is being created, right at your feet.
>
> A gaggle of volcano-watchers stood within eyebrow-singeing range of an oozing, sizzling, foot-wide finger of lava flowing from Kilauea to the sea. A wider glob moved at a snail's pace to the edge of a cliff and toppled off. The glowing frost greyed as it cooled. The wind was scorching and relentless.

The journalist tucked into the story the history of Kilauea, Big Island, and the Hawaii Volcanoes National Park. Readers also learn tips on the best way to experience the volcano.

Seasonal Features

Editors and news directors often assign feature stories about seasons and holidays: Christmas, Easter, Hanukkah, St. Patrick's Day, Labour Day and Canada Day. Such stories are difficult to write because reporters must find a new angle to make them interesting. Stories about international holidays, such as the one below, also are informative and entertaining.

> Taiwan's leader marked the first day of the Chinese Lunar New Year on Thursday by giving out 15,000 red envelopes stuffed with cash to people in his hometown.
>
> President Chen Shui-bian handed out a comparable $5.80 in every envelope, totalling about $87,000 in the southern farm village of Kuantien. He ran out of envelopes before he got to the end of a line that stretched about two miles.
>
> People traditionally begin lining up at dawn to get an envelope, which they believe brings them good luck.
>
> People of all ages lined up and patiently shuffled past the sheds, machine shops, and traditional low-slung farm houses with tile roofs in Kuantien. There were mothers clutching babies sucking on milk bottles, elderly men dressed in pinstriped suits, and teenagers in sweat shirts and baseball caps. All were celebrating the new Year of the Ram.

The reporter continued his story by tracing the traditional rituals for celebrating the holiday.

Explanatory Features

Explanatory features are also called "local situation" or "interpretive" features or "sidebars." In these stories, reporters provide more detailed descriptions or explanations of organizations, activities, trends or ideas in the news. These stories might localize national events or personalize an issue or event. After news stories describe an act of terrorism, an explanatory feature might highlight individual victims, discussing their lives, hopes and dreams, or survival through interviews with family and friends. An editor might couple a story about a new science fiction movie with an explanatory feature on the makeup and costumes actors needed to become alien beings. Anniversary stories on natural disasters are often paired with stories on survivors and where they are now. Controversial issues also invite explanatory features. The *Globe and Mail*'s science writer, Anne McIlroy, wrote a story about the commercialization of university research and, specifically, the issue of fraud in science and how instances of fraud are dealt with in the academy. The first three paragraphs of the story and one of two accompanying sidebars are reproduced below.

> TORONTO—When they graduate, medical students at the University of Toronto rise and repeat a version of a moral code that dates to the fourth century BC. The Hippocratic Oath connects them with previous generations of physicians, says Catharine Whiteside, the dean of medicine.
>
> Scientists, unlike doctors, don't have an ancient moral code. Nor do graduates vow to "first do no harm," even though their work—in fields from cloning to climate change—may profoundly affect the human race. And it's not as if science is free of cheats.
>
> Last year, American Eric Poehlman, who had worked at the University of Montreal, was sentenced to a year and a day in jail for fabricating 10 years' worth of data on obesity, aging and menopause. Southern Korean stem-cell researcher Hwang Woo Suk has confessed to faking data, published in largely fictional papers in the respected journal *Science*, showing that he had cloned human embryos.

> **A pledge of allegiance**
> **Scientific Code of Ethics**
> In a bid to boost public trust, Sir David King, Britain's chief scientific adviser, has drafted the equivalent of the Hippocratic Oath for scientists. So far, the code has been backed by the British government and the 44,000 members of the Royal Society of Chemistry. It calls on professionals to:
>
> - Act with skill and care, keep skills up to date.
>
> - Prevent corrupt practice and declare conflicts of interest.
>
> - Respect and acknowledge the work of other scientists.
>
> - Ensure that research is justified and lawful.
>
> - Minimize impacts on people, animals and the environment.
>
> - Discuss issues science raises for society.
>
> - Do not mislead; present evidence honestly.

How-to-Do-It Features

How-to-do-it features tell readers how to accomplish a psychological or physical task, such as keeping emotions in check at the office or how to communicate better with roommates. Stories might focus on strengthening a marriage or overcoming shyness. They can explain how to find a reputable tattooist or how to live on a shoestring budget while in college.

Reporters gather facts from several sources, including books and magazine articles. They also interview experts and get tips from people who have done what their stories describe. In addition, good reporters try to observe or participate in the "how-to-do-it" procedure itself. For instance, they might visit a tattoo parlour or watch a pet masseuse to better understand their topic.

Reporters divide the task into simple, clear, easy-to-follow steps. They tell viewers and readers what materials the procedure requires and what it will cost in money and time. Often they include a chart or end such stories with a list or summary of the process, such as "10 common household products to recycle."

Anakana Schofield of the *Ottawa Citizen* wrote a story about how to help kids become proficient readers by encouraging them to read comics or other publications in "graphic" format. Here is the opening section of the article:

> High school English teacher Guy Demers doesn't hesitate to recommend graphic novels for young readers. "Comics are an art form, much like the novel or poetry," he says. "They offer us new ways to read and to put together meaning.

"The richness in subject matter and approach has given us a body of work that we can see as something truly rich and worth celebrating."

Demers, who teaches English at Sir Charles Tupper secondary school in Vancouver, says his goal with graphic novels is no different than with a novel or short story: He wants to challenge his students to expand and develop their literacy.

"When I suggest students read graphic novels, I don't hand them a stack of Archies or a standard superhero story. I give them a copy of a *Tale of One Bad Rat*, *Palestine* or *American Born Chinese*—all amazing works (by Bryan Talbot, Joe Sacco and Gene Luen Yang, respectively) and all completely different."

Perhaps you recognize this drill: Your child enters the library and races to rummage the Tin Tin, Asterix, Garfield baskets or Bone shelf and returns either satisfied or dejected based on what the rummage produces. Increasingly, the demand exhausts the supply and it's time to look farther afield for graphic novels to satisfy insatiable young appetites.

In my quest to unearth diverse graphic titles, I discovered there are plenty for teenagers but not quite the same plethora for boys below the age of 12.

Fortunately, I got some help from the approachable lads at RX Comics and Lucky's Comics, both in Vancouver, who also reminded me that many vintage comic titles (pre-1985) are suitable for all ages.

Occupation or Hobby Features

Journalists might prepare features stories about occupations that are dangerous (mining) or hobbies that are highly specialized (rock climbing). Or they could report on a job many people think is boring (being a server at a restaurant) and turn it into something exciting (meeting celebrities while working on the job). Reporters can show that workers find even stereotyped jobs rewarding, such as this one:

Twenty-nine-year-old Jordyn James is going through a lot of eggs this morning.

"Eggs are the easiest to do," James said, barely looking up from the yellow batter on the stove top to glance at the seven tickets dangling in front of her. "With eggs, you can do a lot of things at one time. I can work on about six orders simultaneously."

James cracks one after another, and carton after carton is tossed out.

Her hands are working at lightning speed, turning the eggs into scrambled, over easy, Benedict, and poached.

"You know, I've done a lot of other things with my time … " James pauses to place a basket of hash browns on the counter, " … but there wasn't anything that makes me as happy as this." (*Associated Press*)

Collectors and crafts enthusiasts often make good subjects for feature stories because they are passionately involved and often eccentric, quotable and entertaining. Strange or trendy hobbies, such as body art, make good topics too, because they tend to involve colourful characters.

Behind-the-Scenes Features

Behind-the-scenes features convey a sense of immediacy, allowing readers to see, feel, taste, touch, smell and understand the "backstage" work that goes into a public event. Reporters look for people who perform jobs out of the public eye but essential to many citizens. They interview sources, visit them on location, and use the source's own words to tell the story. They also include details they observe, such as atmosphere, working conditions, physical appearance of people and their workspace, specialized terms, and conversations between workers.

Participatory Features

Participatory features give another kind of inside view, this time through the senses of a reporter who is actually experiencing an event or situation. Reporters might immerse themselves in the world of a lifeguard at a beach or a chimney sweep on the job. Or they might spend a day or two shadowing a prime ministerial candidate, a clerk at the office of a minister of state, or a wedding planner. Reporters arrange such experiences with the person they are shadowing or that person's supervisor, making it clear that they are reporters and will write or broadcast a story about the experience.

Whereas news stories are usually written in the third person, with the reporter as a neutral observer or outsider, feature stories can also be written in the second person, addressing audience members directly. Participatory features also can be written in the first person, with the reporter appearing in the story:

> When my husband (then fiancé) suggested we start our married lives together TV-free, I thought he was joking. We hadn't moved in together yet, but weekends with this Big Ten grad, sports lover and Fantasy Football devotee almost always involved at least a glimpse of some game on TV. Had he gone crazy—or was this truly a brilliant idea?
>
> Assured by his promises of more quality time as a married couple—and the chance to stop zoning out in front of the tube together—I agreed. So after our wedding bells rang, my newly betrothed and I moved into a condo together. Our TV had a new home, too: a locked storage unit in the basement. Here's how we endured:

The story reviews one year. Journalist Casey Jones organized it into subheads: The Plan, The Beginning, The Adjusting, The Verdict. She ended with the following sentence: "For now, as peculiar as it may seem, this TV-free experience is giving us a priceless gift: the ability to kick off our marriage with a solid foundation of communication."

To expose bad conduct by businesses or government, journalists sometimes have used undercover, cloak-and-dagger approaches, such as getting arrested to report on jail conditions. These behaviours are ethically questionable and expose reporters and their employers to civil and criminal liability. News organizations that have sent reporters undercover into private businesses to report on allegations of misconduct have been sued for fraud and trespass. And reporters who engage in criminal activities to gather information for a story have been criminally prosecuted. On the other hand, to expose bad conduct by businesses or governments is a standard responsibility of good journalism. On the occasions when undercover work is deemed appropriate, proceed with caution and within the law, using sound research methods and multiple sources.

Other Types of Feature Stories

Successful journalists find the human interest in all kinds of reporting beats and topics—politics, medicine, business, technology, education and science. Reporters find individuals affected by the status quo or by change. They look for emotion. The narratives may portray typical conditions or unique aberrations to common systems, but they all include a human element. Reporters gather facts from documents, experts, and individuals affected by a situation to give a story context and to present it on a personal level. They might talk to family and friends of individuals who are subjects for the story. They use quotes, allowing subjects to tell about their experiences and feelings. Journalists go to the scene of the story—a person's home or a place of business, for example. They observe the details found in the physical surroundings and in people's mannerisms and body language. Other elements such as smell, sounds, taste or texture make the story more interesting and realistic, drawing the reader into the narrative.

PARTS OF FEATURE STORIES

Journalists can be creative in writing human-interest stories. Skilled writers use different techniques for the lead, body and ending, depending on the type of feature.

The Lead of a Feature Story

Some features begin with summary leads. However, features also may start with quotations, anecdotes, questions, action, descriptions, shocking facts, delayed leads, or a combination of these alternative leads, which are described in Chapter 6. The only requirement is that the lead interests people, luring them into the story.

One cannot help but admire the flowing prose in the lead of a story written to commemorate September 11. The five-year anniversary narrative by Robert McFadden and his colleagues appeared in the *New York Times* and was headlined "Nation Marks Lives Lost and Hopeful Signs of Healing":

> Once more the leaden bells tolled in mourning, loved ones recited the names of the dead at ground zero, and a wounded but resilient America paused yesterday to remember the calamitous day when terrorist explosions rumbled like summer thunder and people fell from the sky.

This is a lead that rises to the solemn occasion it represents. It is an emotional, heavy and poetic lead that reflects great sorrow and history.

Not all stories can carry this type of lead. Yet no matter what kind of lead writers choose for a feature story, they should try to make it as distinctive and unique as possible. Dick Thien, an editor-in-residence at the Freedom Forum, notes that some leads, such as questions, figures of speech, and shockers, generally sound trite and should be used sparingly.

The Body of a Feature Story

Like the lead, the body of a feature story can take many forms. The inverted-pyramid style may be appropriate for some features and chronological order for others. Regardless of the form or style chosen, every feature must be coherent. All the facts must fit together smoothly and logically. Transitions must guide the audience from one segment of the story to the next and clearly reveal the relationship between those segments. Transitions should be brief. They might ask a question, announce shifts in time or place, or link ideas by repeating key words or phrases.

Reporters should be concise and never waste their audience's time. Features should emphasize lively details—the action—and they should provide an occasional change of pace. A good reporter never writes a story consisting only of quotations or summaries. Instead, the reporter might use several paragraphs of summary, followed by some quotations to explain an idea, then some description, and finally more quotations or summary. Joe Friesen and Lisa Priest wrote a feature article after the 2009 slaying of eight-year-old Victoria Stafford in the southeastern Ontario town of Woodstock; the feature showed how the tragedy "put the spotlight on a community suffering the scourge of drug abuse":

> WOODSTOCK, Ont.—There is a hollow look to the young addicts who wander Woodstock's main street.
>
> Their cheeks are pulled tight, their limbs gaunt, their eyes dull and vacant. They have followed a high to its logical end, and are now trying to scrape themselves back off the bottom.
>
> They gather daily at the bustling methadone clinic across from the city square for their medicine, a narcotic cocktail called "the drink" made palatable by fruit flavouring. In a city of 35,000, 300 people are on the patient rolls.
>
> "I've lost my whole family pretty much," says Casey, a 25-year-old OxyContin addict. "I'm not your normal street fiend. I've been raised by a good family. My parents both work at Toyota. I was in the interview process to get a job there too, but the drugs were more important so I lost that shot."
>
> This is the unseemly side of Woodstock, a side that has been thrust into public view with the abduction and slaying of eight-year-old Victoria Stafford. The girl's mother, Tara McDonald, confessed to an addiction to OxyContin, and the woman accused in her daughter's homicide, Terri-Lynne McClintic, is also a user, according to neighbours.
>
> Although there's no suggestion that OxyContin contributed to Victoria's killing, the incident has focused public attention on a scourge that is ripping through this

blue-collar town—one of many in North America, usually small and suffering economically, where the drug has cut a swath.

Surrounded by some of the most fertile soil in Canada, Woodstock was the hinterland of Upper Canada when it was settled at the turn of the 19th century by Loyalists fleeing the United States. It has always been at the centre of a farm belt, famous for its statue of a prized cow, but from its origins to the present day the "dairy capital" has wagered its own future on manufacturing.

Throughout the 20th century, that strategy helped Woodstock prosper: This was Ontario's heartland, with ready access to rail and roads linking auto parts and machinery destined for Detroit and textiles and furniture for Southern Ontario. In the city's museum, a 1983 promotional film proclaims "industry chooses Woodstock," over a stream of pictures of molten metal and moving machinery.

But while other Southwestern Ontario cities such as Waterloo, Guelph, and London have gained from the research hubs of their universities, and from the influx of immigration and creativity that those institutions attract, Woodstock has stuck to what it knows.

As the town's mayor, Michael Harding, said this week, "We've always done good with our hands."

That approach has created a remarkably stable population, but one less inclined to education. Two-thirds of the town has lived in Canada three generations or more, according to the 2006 census. But just 10 per cent have a university degree and 29 per cent never graduated from high school. Only 4 per cent of its population belong to a visible minority. Compare that with nearby Waterloo, where 31 per cent have a university degree, only 16 per cent didn't graduate from high school, 29 per cent are first-generation Canadians and 17 per cent visible minorities.

"We are what we are," Mr. Harding said. "We're a slow-growth community, always have been."

Good reporters illustrate character and personality. Instead of telling, they show; instead of saying that a person is generous or humorous, reporters should give specific examples of the subject's generosity and humour. Instead of saying former U.S. president Calvin Coolidge was a taciturn man, it would be better to illustrate his reluctance to speak by quoting Coolidge himself:

A woman meeting then–U.S. president Coolidge for the first time said to him, "My friends bet that I couldn't get you to say three words." The president replied, "You lose."

Successful feature writers also use elements such as characterization, setting, plot and subplot, conflict, time, dialogue and narrative.

Reporters reveal the character of the people they write about with quotations and descriptions of mannerisms, body language, appearance, dress, age, preferences, prejudices, use of personal space, and a host of other traits. The setting reveals the subject's character and provides context for the audience to understand the subject. Geography shapes physical and mental traits, determines lifespan, and influences ways of earning a living. Reporters should tell where a subject grew up, what the person's surroundings are now, and how these factors contribute to who he or she is. Such touches of description sprinkled throughout a story show what the subject is like.

The plot of feature stories is often a description of the obstacles that lie between the subjects of the stories and their goals. The resolution of conflict (frustration induced by the obstacles) presents the theme of every human-interest story. The main variations of the plots are the conflicts between humans and nature, humans and humans, and humans and the inner self. As reporters interview people and ask them about events in their lives, plots naturally emerge. Often a subplot emerges, a secondary line of action that runs in counterpoint to the main action, sometimes helping and sometimes hindering the progress. If reporters listen and identify plot and subplot elements as the subject tells the story, a natural order emerges.

Time can be handled in a variety of ways. To organize some types of features, reporters can use a dramatic episode in the present as an opener, then flash back to the beginning of the story and bring it forward in chronological order. Reporters can foreshadow the future or build in a series of flashbacks, arranged in the order in which they happened.

Feature stories need dialogue. Reporters use dialogue to show temperament, plot, events, time, customs, colour or continuity. They must be careful to choose only the best, most revealing quotes.

Reporters use narrative to weave a story together. Narrative is what summarizes, arranges, creates flow and transitions, and links one idea to the next. Narrative should be unobtrusive and subtle.

The Ending of a Feature Story

A feature should have a satisfying conclusion, perhaps an anecdote, quote, key word or phrase repeated in some surprising or meaningful way. Reporters should avoid ending a feature story with a summary. Summary endings are too likely to state the obvious or to be repetitious, flat or boring.

Some endings come back around to the lead. In an exhaustive series that ran throughout the summer of 2001 in both the *Ottawa Citizen* and the *Vancouver Sun*, veteran investigator Paul McKay examined how the human "love affair with cars is poisoning the planet." Examine the excerpts below, from the first and last stories of the series, to see how McKay echoed the beginning of the series in the closing story.

"The smog monster: Our love affair with cars is poisoning the planet." Series: Reinventing Our Wheels. *Ottawa Citizen*, May 19, 2001, p. A1

After a million years of evolution, the human lung could qualify as nature's most elegantly efficient engine.

For most of us, a few pounds of gently pulsing pink tissue will filter some 600 million litres of air during seven repair-free decades, trading a chemical crucial to our hearts and brains for exhaled chemicals that would otherwise poison them.

Without that ceaseless equilibrium—and the oxygen-rich atmosphere that surrounds our planet—there would be no thought, work, play, laughter, love or art.

You could say lungs work a miracle each time we take a breath.

By contrast, the basic design of the century-old internal combustion engine has evolved little since the days of Henry Ford.

It still runs on a liquid concoction of more than 50 chemicals that is utterly dependent on a global support system of wells, ocean drilling rigs, supertankers, pipelines, refineries, gas trucks and retail pumps.

Think of it as a vastly complex, interconnected I.V. bag for the planet's 700 million vehicles.

Each year, the average Canadian motorist burns 2,200 litres of gas supplied by that network, which itself consumes prodigious amounts of energy to drill, dig, refine and deliver oil.

Yet despite the ingenuity, effort and expense required to get it into your tank, less than 12 per cent of the energy in gasoline is converted to actual traction. The rest is radiated as useless heat, either from engine blocks built to contain the intense compression and combustion cycles, or from the tailpipe.

"Smarter fuels, vehicles, cities." Series: Reinventing Our Wheels. *Ottawa Citizen*, June 8, 2001, p. A14

A century ago, horses were the prevailing public health hazard in Canada's young cities. The bacteria in their wastes, the lack of separated sewer and water systems, and an absence of regulations exposed citizens to fatal pollutants that could only be seen through a microscope.

THE CANADIAN PRESS/Paul Chiasson

Ian Clifford, CEO of Zenn Motor Company, stands next to an electric Zenn car at the company's plant in St-Jerome, Que., Wednesday, December 12, 2007.

The toll of disease and death triggered a movement, led by doctors and engineers, to clean up our cities. Now, every toilet, tub and sink in every major city in Canada is connected to sewer pipes and filtration plants.

For a century, Canadians have collectively accepted that invisible pollutants in water can quietly kill, or sabotage a community's health. When we forget, there is a Walkerton to remind us.

Now, another kind of horsepower is doing the same thing to the air we breathe. Some 18 million tailpipes are emitting invisible but deadly chemicals, gases and particles. They are killing people, and silently stalking lungs where 20 million Canadians live.

Everyone is vulnerable, from the ailing elderly to infants to elite Olympic athletes.

After finishing a feature, a professional is likely to edit and rewrite the narrative many times. A professional will also angle the feature for a particular audience, publication or news program, emphasizing the story's relevance and importance to it.

 ## CHECKLIST FOR FEATURES

1. Select a topic likely to interest a large number of readers. Often a spin-off from a major event can be such a topic.
2. Profiles or personality features should reveal the character of the person about whom they are written.
3. Historical features may be pegged to anniversaries, describe famous leaders or landmarks, or illuminate trends.
4. Adventure features describe what happened to people who had unusual experiences, such as climbing a mountain or surviving a plane crash.
5. Seasonal features are tied to holidays, annual events, or changes in the weather.
6. Explanatory features might illuminate new scientific discoveries or describe how people are coping with the aftermath of a disaster.
7. How-to-do-it features tell readers or viewers how to make something, accomplish some goal, or solve a problem.
8. Hobby or occupation features describe what people in interesting jobs or with unusual hobbies do.

9. Behind-the-scenes features take readers or viewers backstage, describing what is involved in making a public event happen.

10. Participatory features often involve the reporters in the actions they are describing.

11. Feature stories are more likely to use alternative leads—ones that describe a scene or tell an anecdote—than they are to use a summary lead.

12. Features can use an inverted-pyramid form, but often they develop chronologically or use flashbacks or foreshadowing.

13. The ending of a feature story should not summarize the story, but it should use some scene, quotation or anecdote that brings it to a conclusion. Often the ending hearkens back to the lead.

 # The Writing Coach

TELLING PICTURES: REPORTING AND RECONSTRUCTING SCENES

By David Hayes

Early in my career, I was assigned by *Toronto Life* magazine to write a story about pimps and prostitutes in Toronto. In their efforts to charge pimps—who, in addition to being brutal employers, are notoriously elusive—morality squad cops often target their "girls." I tagged along for a couple of nights with two undercover cops and at one point stood inside the tiny rented room belonging to a bespectacled young prostitute, nicknamed "Goggles," who, they knew, was being victimized by a pimp. (As one of the officers pointed out later, she was making several hundred dollars a night, yet neither her surroundings nor her clothing reflected a fraction of that.) Of course, I'd been taught to "show, don't tell" in journalism school, and it was obvious, at this moment, that the details of the young woman's life were telling:

> Goggles is sitting on a narrow cot in a room the size of a walk-in closet. A cracked mirror is propped above an old porcelain sink. A makeshift table is covered in bottles and tins of makeup. There are posters on the walls that might have been taken from the covers of pulp fantasy novels and several photographs of a graceless Goggles modeling department store fashions. A tiny kitten named Minou squeaks querulously under the bed. The room is clean and very neat, as though someone is expecting guests.

When you're in the middle of a scene, the heat of the moment can be distracting. Strangers may stare at you. People may ask why you're there. Resentment, even hostility, may be in the air. It can be hard to stay cool and do your job, and even the most experienced feature writers can miss things that they can never go back and retrieve. Sometimes I repeat a mantra in my head at moments like this: *take a deep breath, focus… think… focus… think…*

When I was standing in Goggles's room, there was another detail that I sensed might be important. Later in the story, this is what I wrote:

> A piece of yellow paper is taped to the wall beside her closet. On it is a handwritten poem that includes the line: *Then love still taunts me with its thorny path.*

The symbolism might have been too neat for fiction, but when you're writing non-fiction the things that really happen, and are really there, nearly always work. Afterward I always feel exhilarated, almost like a runner's high. It's what I call the thrill of the scene.

"Show, don't tell," the fundamental rule in non-fiction writing as well as fiction, refers in large part to letting action and dialogue reveal information to readers through the use of dramatic scenes. This kind of narrative storytelling has long been published in magazines and used by writers of non-fiction books (not to mention documentary filmmakers). But in recent years there has also been a narrative revolution in newspapers in Canada and the United States as publishers and editors have come to realize that old-fashioned storytelling is the unique strength that print journalism has over other media. At the heart of this kind of reporting and writing is an ability to capture the essence of people, environments, and situations as they unfold.

If "show, don't tell" were as simple as it sounds, aspiring writers could transform themselves into working professionals without much effort. Although words can paint pictures that are rich in vivid detail, learning *how* to gather those details, *when* you've gathered enough raw material to tell your story, *which* details are most important, and *where* in your manuscript everything should go is what distinguishes the skilled craftsperson from the amateur.

WHAT DOES IT TAKE TO BE A TOP-NOTCH FEATURES WRITER?

By Bryan Denham, Associate Professor, Clemson University

- Descriptive writing skills. The features writer should be able to "paint a picture" and capture the essence of a subject.

- Good reporting skills. Without the ability to gather information in an efficient manner, the writer will have nothing to discuss.

- Good interviewing skills. It's one thing to conduct a basic interview; it's quite another to draw from a source sensitive or controversial information.

- Good research skills. What, if anything, has been written about the subject you are addressing?

- Respect for sources. Treat people with respect and dignity.

- Ethics. Always use good judgment and attribute quotes carefully.

- Persistence. Good writers don't give up on a story if it gets off to a slow start.

- Confidence. Sources have faith in people who appear confident and professional.

- Experience. The more experiences you have in life, the more perspective you will bring to your writing.

- Curiosity. Great writers are curious about the social world and can distinguish good story ideas from bad ones.

- Eagerness to explore. The best writers crave "small adventures."

- Broad-mindedness. Keep your mind open to new perspectives.

- Appreciation for cultural diversity. Embrace individuals who can offer you insight into different cultural values and traditions.

- Familiarity with trends in popular culture. Always keep "an ear to the ground" and stay attuned to what's going on around you.

- Vision. Great writers can picture how their articles will look in print, and they create the articles to fit in the space allotted for newspaper features.

- Reliability. As with hard news reporting, failure to show up for an interview or return a phone call will undermine your ability to produce good work.

- Appreciation for subtlety. Sometimes the most interesting aspects of an individual do not "leap out" at the writer. Students of the social world and human behaviour can observe things that go straight by others.

- Ability to seek out sources apart from the primary source. If you're profiling someone, for instance, you should talk to a few people who know the person.

SUGGESTED READINGS AND USEFUL WEBSITES

Blundell, William. 1988. *The Art and Craft of Feature Writing: Based on the* Wall Street Journal Guide. New York: New American Library.

Clark, Roy Peter. 2006. *Writing Tools: 50 Essential Strategies for Every Writer.* New York: Little, Brown.

Echlin, Kim, et al., eds. 2000. *To Arrive Where You Are: Literary Journalism from the Banff Centre for the Arts.* Intro. Alberto Ruy-Sánchez. Banff, AB: Banff Centre Press.

Elton, Heather, et al., eds. 1997. *Why Are You Telling Me This? Eleven Acts of Intimate Journalism.* Intro. Alberto Manguel. Banff, AB: Banff Centre Press.

Mitchell, Alanna. 2004. *Dancing at the Dead Sea: Tracking the World's Environmental Hotspots.* Toronto: Key Porter Books.

Moon, Barbara, and Don Obe, eds. 1998. *Taking Risks: Literary Journalism from the Edge.* Intro. Michael Ignatieff. Banff, AB: Banff Centre Press.

Root, Robert L., Jr., and Michael Steinberg, eds. 1999. *The Fourth Genre: Contemporary Writers of/on Creative Nonfiction.* Needham Heights, MA: Allyn and Bacon.

Shapiro, Ivor, ed. 2009. *The Bigger Picture: Elements of Feature Writing.* Toronto: Emond Montgomery Publications.

Stewart, James B. 1998. *Follow the Story: How to Write Successful Nonfiction.* New York: Simon and Schuster.

The American Copy Editors Society (ACES) has on its website a list of cliché leads to avoid:
http://www.copydesk.org/words/clicheleads.htm

Poynter Institute:
http://www.poynter.org

EXERCISE 1   Feature Stories

Generating Ideas and Selecting a Topic

1. Canada's national statistical agency, Statistics Canada, has a helpful website to ignite the imagination on story ideas. The department provides economic, social and census data. Its special-topics areas, studies and media releases offer history and statistics on many subjects. Get to the home page here: www.statcan.gc.ca.

2. The concept of "universal needs" can help reporters choose a topic. Everyone is interested in the needs all human beings have in common and the ways of satisfying these needs. Universal needs are food, clothing, shelter, love, health, approval, belonging, self-esteem, job satisfaction and entertainment. The following exercise demonstrates how students can use universal needs to find a story idea: Write the universal needs (such as food, clothing, shelter, love, health) across the top of a piece of paper. Down the left side, list some current topics in the news or pressing social issues (concerns of the elderly or students or parents, health care, unemployment, and teen suicide). Draw lines to form a grid. Fill in the spaces in the grid with "hybrid" story ideas created by combining the two topics, such as free medical clinics for students (combining the topics of students and health) or suicide rate among the homeless (combining the topics of self-esteem and unemployment).

3. Listen and observe to find a feature topic. Ride a city bus to the end of the line, sit in the student union or in a cafeteria. Watch what people do, and listen to what people are talking about. Make a list of potential feature topics.

4. Survey students to get a story idea. Stand in the lobby of the student union or administration building or other popular places on campus, and ask students about their major concerns. If several students have a similar response, you might find that you have a good feature topic and angle. Qualify or narrow your questions to get informative responses. Do you want students to let you know what they think about the Canadian Forces in Afghanistan, student accommodation on campus, dating practices among teenagers, national politics, or alternative medicine?

5. Read blogs and discussion groups on a news website, citizen journalism website, or other interactive places online. What are the issues people are discussing? What seems to be uppermost on their minds?

6. Go to Google or other Web browsers or search engines that list the top 10 searches for the day or week. These topics list subjects that are interesting to people and can provide the seeds of ideas for feature stories.

7. Pair up with another student. Set a timer and write for 10 minutes, completely free and uncensored, about one or more of the following personal topics: pet peeves, things I avoid writing about, things I am curious about, favourite places in my hometown, a specific holiday such as Christmas or Thanksgiving, my biggest problem as a child (or teenager). Take turns reading your papers aloud to your partner. Discuss how you could conduct research and interviews to make a story from one of the ideas you generated.

8. This time when you pair up with a student, list college experiences, such as advice to first-year students, what you wish you'd known when you first came to college, good experiences, bad experiences, medical facilities, making friends, and living arrangements. Which ones would generate the most interest for a school newspaper? How would you conduct research, and whom would you interview? What type of research is needed for context?

9. Observe your surroundings as you walk to class. Make a list of 10 potential story ideas, such as dangerous traffic circles, bicycle safety, students who talk on cellphones while walking to class, or places to eat on campus.

10. Historical feature ideas: Every region, city and school has experienced interesting events. Some students get ideas for stories by reading newspapers that publish "On This Date in History" columns, by interviewing the historians of clubs, or by visiting the community or provincial historical society. A good feature writer will learn more about those events, perhaps by consulting historical documents or by interviewing people who witnessed or participated in them.

11. Occupation or hobby feature ideas: Scan newspaper notices, chamber of commerce websites, or news websites for community hobby club meetings, senior citizens' activities, church and school events, and speeches on unusual topics.

12. Occupation or hobby feature ideas: Ask other people what they do to relax. Read classified ads and seek out magicians, storytellers, video-game players, basement cleaners, and unicycle instructors.

13. Business ideas: Look for the human interest in stories of promotions, new businesses, the local economy, and even the election of club officers. Try to find a human-interest angle to the economy, new businesses, and promotions by highlighting one person or aspect of local commerce. A wealth of business stories exists in any town. Fad businesses like singing messengers and diaper delivery services come and go. Online dating sites, computer software merchants, and shopping services for elderly citizens respond to new needs in society. Stories on old, established firms, perhaps focusing on the personality of a founder or dynamic leader, are also of perennial interest.

14. Medical feature ideas: You can find good medical features in any community. Mental, emotional and physical health are vitally interesting to the public, and subjects abound: the cost of being sick, new or controversial treatments for illnesses, pregnancy, child rearing, male and female menopause, death and the grief process, support groups, workshops for patients with a chronic disease, volunteer programs, new medical equipment, and ethical issues surrounding medical advances. You can gather facts from medical experts, people with a particular condition, relatives and friends.

15. Al Tompkins of the Poynter Institute offers 50 story ideas at the Poynter Institute website (www.poynter.org/content/content_view.asp?id=3779). Rewrite these ideas for the Canadian situation and a Canadian audience.

CHAPTER 10

EXERCISE 2   Feature Stories

Ideas for Campus Features

Here are 35 ideas for feature stories that you can write on your campus. Interview some students affected by the issues as well as authoritative sources.

1. Tuition is increasing nationally. What is the situation on your campus? How are students paying for their college education?
2. Do more students today than 10 years ago work to support themselves? What are the numbers of students who work full- or part-time? Do they work on campus or elsewhere? How hard is it to find a job on campus?
3. Is the number of international students increasing on your campus? Compare your local statistics to national levels. Why do international students attend undergraduate or graduate programs in Canada instead of elsewhere?
4. What does your campus to do assimilate international students into the student body? Are international students comfortable pursuing a degree on your campus and in your city?
5. Campuses have counselling centres. Who frequents them the most often—undergraduate, master's or doctoral students? What are the most common reasons that students visit counselling centres?
6. Students often experience stress while completing a college or university education. Is there a different type of stress associated with undergraduate, master's or doctoral students?
7. Does your campus have a university ombudsman? What are the most frequent problems he or she hears?
8. Many colleges and universities have study-abroad programs in which faculty members take students to another country to study a topic for credit in a particular class. What are the most popular programs? Why are they so popular? Are there programs in warring countries, and if so, what safety provisions are made? You should get some quotes from students who have participated in these programs.
9. Plagiarism and fabrication seem to be increasing on campuses nationally. What is the situation on your campus? Compare it to national figures. What are the punishments for cheating?
10. Think about a national issue or trend, and make a local comparison, using the people on your campus.
11. What types of fun things do students and their families do as a holiday tradition? What do international students do during the holidays?
12. Interview at least five faculty members who have written textbooks. Describe their work, problems, profits and attitudes.
13. Describe the tenure and promotion system at your university. How easy is it for faculty members to obtain tenure? What must they do? Typically, how many succeed and how many fail? What happens to those who fail?
14. Write about your favourite teacher, a successful coach, or another interesting personality on your campus. Interview other students, friends, relatives and colleagues so you have enough information for a well-rounded portrait of the person.
15. Find a campus club that helps people, such as Alcoholics Anonymous or Gamblers Anonymous. Interview club members about their problem and how it affects their lives.
16. What are the best part-time jobs for students on your campus? Who earns the most money and enjoys the best hours and benefits? (Students who earn tips—bartenders, baggage handlers, servers in restaurants—often earn hundreds of dollars during weekend shifts.)
17. Write about your institution's use of part-time faculty members. Are part-timers well paid? What are the advantages and disadvantages of employing them? Why do they teach, and compared to your full-time faculty members, how qualified are they?
18. What are the excuses your faculty members hear most often from students who miss classes, assignments and tests—or simply do poorly in a class?

19. Do students on your campus ever complain about faculty members they have difficulty understanding, especially faculty members from other countries? How serious is the problem, what's being done to correct it, and how successful is the effort? Also, why does your university or college employ faculty members with language problems?

20. To obtain more practical experience, many students complete internships, and some students must do so. Typically, many interns are not paid, and some companies seem to exploit interns, using them as free labour. Discuss the advantages and disadvantages of internships and any abuses you find on your campus.

21. Write about the problems and perceptions of physically challenged students. You might look specifically at the problems of students who are blind or use wheelchairs.

22. Write a historical feature that describes your institution's establishment and early years.

23. If some buildings on your campus are named after individuals, write about several of these individuals, explaining who they were and why they were honoured.

24. What, if any, are the advantages to being an athlete (or an honours student) at your institution? Do athletes have to meet the same entrance requirements as other students? Do they enjoy special housing, food or financial aid? Do they have special tutors or registration times?

25. Describe the wildlife on your campus, anything from bats to rats, cats, snakes and raccoons.

26. How easy is it for the students on your campus to obtain credit cards, how many overspend, and where do they find help?

27. What percentage of the incoming students at your institution are required to complete remedial courses? Describe the courses, the cause of the problem that prompts remedial courses, and their ramifications.

28. If you have heard horror stories about difficult roommates, write about the problem. What causes the problem, how common is it, and how is it resolved? Cite some of the worst examples.

29. If you have heard horror stories about blind dates, write about the problem. What causes the problem, and how common is it? Cite some of the worst examples.

30. Interview people who come to your campus to interview and hire graduating seniors. What do they look for? What common mistakes should job seekers avoid? What advice would they give students interviewing for jobs?

31. Write about student loans and the ability of students to repay the loans after graduation.

32. Interview the youngest or oldest student on your campus or the youngest or oldest faculty member. What was schooling, fashion, work or etiquette like when the oldest member was growing up? Choose one topic for an in-depth story.

33. Find and write about a campus club that involves an element of danger, such as scuba diving, skydiving, mountain climbing, hang gliding or spelunking (exploring caves).

34. What is your campus doing to recruit more women and minorities for its faculty—and how successful is it? Why? How do other faculty members feel about the issue?

35. About how many students flunk out of your college each year? Why? Is the problem more common in some majors than others? Interview several of the students.

CHAPTER 10

EXERCISE 3   Feature Stories

Information for Features

Write brief feature stories using the following sets of information. Correct all grammatical, spelling and style errors. In the second set of information (Scholarship Searches), assume you are picking this story up from a U.S. source, and write the article for a Canadian audience, revising as necessary. For your feature, find out whether such a situation could occur in Canada.

1. Deer Farms

Kyle White is a farmer, age 41, in your county, married to his wife Rebecca, 42, and parents together of 4 children (3 girls and 1 boy). Their farm is located a distance of approximately 7 miles south of your city.

Their farm originally covered a total of 240 acres of land but eleven years ago they bought a second farm, a retiring cousins, which covered an additional 120 acres of land, so they now farm a total of 360 acres.

Little of the land is good for crops. Its too hilly and swampy, with lots of woods. A low area along the Mequin river often floods in the spring and then remains in a flooded condition for a period of time. Six years ago, Mr. White abandoned his diary herd and hay and vegetables, and pigs, chickens, and other crops and started a new crop: deer. Why? Big bucks.

Some sleek brown bucks weigh as much as 240 pounds or more. Leaner ones (visible in a pasture you visited) weigh only about 160 or so pds. They're kept on the farm by an 8-foot fence topped by barbed wire that now encircles the entire farm area. "The heaviest ones we sell," White said.

Who to? Fine restaurants throughout the entire province. They charge their diners a premium for tender venison which has much less fat than cow or pig. Some day White also hopes to sell his deer which he butchers himself directly to gourmet sections of supermarkets. Its a national trend, he said. Nearly 700 farmers nationwide now belong to the North American Deer Farmers Assn. established in 1978 by German immigrants who established the first venison ranch in the 1960s on a remote patch of rugged hills and woods in upstate New York. All venison ranchers now hope to capitalize on people's current desire to be healthy—to eat well while staying fit. All tout venison as "the meat of the future"—red meat for health-conscious calorie counters. Nutritionists say among red meats only buffalo is healthier. Some animal rights activists raise a ruckus about the human consumption of deer and some consumers shudder at the thought of eating Bambi or any of the other beautiful, graceful members of the species, but deer farmers believe they can gain converts by rattling off the real statistics to further educate consumers. A 7-ounce serving of venison steak gets only 3.2% of its 316 calories from fat. Ground beef is nearly 10% fat and a 7-ounce portion weighs in at far more calories, a whopping total of 432. "Venison has less fat—and fewer calories—than even skinned chicken," White told you. At 6'2" in height, White weighs only a thin 162 pounds and is red headed with a full red beard and red mustache. Others agree about the healthful nature of venison. The Heart and Stroke Foundation of Canada lists wild game as a good choice for your daily serving of meat, poultry, or fish. Weight Watchers also recommends venison as a lean, low-calorie alternative to fatty beef. Still, its a tough sell. Tests show farm-raised venison tastes tender and mild and the meat tends to be smooth without the grains that streak beef steak. Yet many Canadians tend to associate venison with the tough, gamey, shoe-leather meat that many amateur hunters often drag back home after a kill while hunting in the fall and bagging a deer that isn't as well fed and cared for as Mr. Whites.

Plus there's what the farmers call the Bambi Syndrome. Graceful, brown-eyed, white-tailed deer seem to generate more sympathy than almost any other animal but dogs and cats which, by law, many places prohibit people in Canada from eating although both animals are eaten elsewhere in the world along with horse. "Most consumers don't see cows as cute and cuddly like they do a veal calf or lamb or deer," said a spokesman for the Canadian Beef Export

Association. There are doom-and-gloom predictions about the future of beef with all the new competition from deer and other species, even ostrich, but cattle ranchers tend to brush off claims of venisons surging popularity. After all, Canadians gobble up, on national average for every man, woman, and child in this great country, a grand total of 63 pounds of beef each year despite relentless warnings from assorted medical authorities and nutritionists against fat and cholesterol. The average Canadian persons diet also includes 47 lbs. of pork each and every year and almost as much chicken. By comparison, the average Canadian now eats no venison, none whatsoever, which remains at this point in time largely a novelty, sold at a few fine restaurants—never at popular, fast-food restaurants where so many Canadians eat so many of their meals, but those facts also show the markets untapped potential. White says: "Everyone has prejudices, and many involving deer are unfounded: emotional, not intellectual. People see deer on television or movies, then they don't want to eat them. Kids especially, but deer are good for kids, healthy for everyone. Its healthy, tasty, and inexpensive considering the fact its all meat, not fat."

2. Scholarship Searches

Are you thinking about going to college anytime soon? Are you already there? Are you a parent with a kid in college or about to go to college. If so, beware! Don't be swindled like the thousands of other poor innocent victims swindled every year. This story comes in part out of the U.S. capital of Washington, D.C. The Federal Trade Commission issued a warning today. The F.T.C. said there are some legitimate businesses in the field but there are also bogus scholarship search services that fast talk students and their families out of millions of dollars in cash each and every single year. Just last month the same Federal Trade Commission (FTC) in Washington filed charges against eleven companies that it claims stole a total of nearly about $10 million dollars from students located in all of the 50 states who plan to start college next year or who are already in college and from their families. The companies promised to look for money to help the swindled students and their families pay the outrageous cost of college tuition, fees, room and board, and other expenses incurred while attending a college. The numbers are astonishing, truly astonishing. The FTC estimates that each and every year as many as 300,000 students and their families fall for the swindle. They're defrauded. Fooled! Cheated! Swindled! Companies promise to find a scholarship or grant, which are free, never having to be repaid. Some promise to find a scholarship or grant for each and every one of the students using their service and to return peoples money if they don't, but then they don't find financial aid and don't return the money. The FTC said today in its new warning they may never look or they may send you a useless and totally worthless computer printout which lists dozens, even hundreds, of scholarships none of which you may be currently eligible for at all. The FTC warns, simply, that "If you have to pay money to get money it might be a scam. Be wary." Matt Adamopoulos, head of the Office of Financial Aid at your school, points out the fact that high school and college counselors provide free services. So do libraries. He recommends that people use free services exclusively.

None guarantee success. "That's impossible," Adamopoulos told you in an exclusive interview today. "We can almost always help really exceptional students, and sometimes the poor. Its those in the middle we have the toughest time with," he went on to add that. The FTC also warns people not to do stupid things like give these or other companies their credit card numbers or bank account numbers or even social security numbers, since other abuses are also committed, such as emptying a victims bank account or adding other charges to his/her credit cards. But people are desperate, overwhelmed and shocked and frightened by the high and escalating and ridiculous cost of college educations in the United States nowadays which threaten to nearly bankrupt some families, especially those with multiple kids. In desperation, and because they are unfamiliar with the process, they are in many cases easy victims for swindlers. The FTC normally seeks temporary restraining orders prohibiting companies from engaging in activities the FTC has challenged. Or, the FTC freezes the companies assets. But companies can close, move to another city or state and in a matter of a very few days open a new company with a new name that continues the same practices with the same people involved. 17-year-old Susan Carigg is an example of victims of the fraud along with her parents, Susan and Craig Carigg. Young Susan is a senior at Martin Luther King Jr. High School and wants to attend college next year but doesn't have a lot of money or extraordinarily high grades, just a solid 3.34 gpa. She, who wants to be a nurse and her parents paid $799 to the Scholarship Search Institute 3 days after receiving a flier in the mail from its headquarters located in the city of Phoenix. The flier promised that people are "guaranteed many times their investment back" in scholarships, grants, and other financial aid. But the Carigs haven't received anything since sending in their check. Now they can't even find the company anywhere. Postal authorities they called for help are also looking for the company, and say thousands of other gullible people who fell for the scam are doing likewise. An FTC official who asked that she not be identified admitted they almost never recover anyones money. Al Giangelli, another high school senior in the same city, whose parents are divorced and who lives with his mother at 214 Lake Dr., sent $999 to a similar company, Financial Aid Finders, using money he saved working at a Burger King. "I want to go to a private school," Al said in an interview today. "I figure that'd cost maybe $20,000 a year, probably more, and they promised to help, said they help everyone, that there's lots of money for everyone. Now I'm worse off than before. I worked hard for that money and they stole it. Its a ripoff, a damn ripoff. They're crooks is what they are."

11

Advanced Reporting

These days, CAR [computer-assisted reporting] skills are showing up as a requirement on job postings. Canada's journalism schools are making CAR part of the mainstream curriculum, and reporters are having more and more success prying newsworthy databases from the clutches of reluctant governments. It's a good time to have CAR skills, and a good time to learn.

— Fred Vallance-Jones, journalist, journalism educator, and Canadian CAR pioneer

This chapter discusses advanced reporting skills and offers exercises to build those skills. To do well on the exercises, you must apply the skills developed in the earlier chapters, as well as new ones explained in this chapter. Some of the exercises are longer and more complex than those in previous chapters, but all involve the types of stories editors assign to reporters during the first years of their careers. The exercises are divided into five categories:

- In-depth stories (Exercises 1–3). These three exercises are genuine; they involve actual letters, statements and other documents. Only a few names and dates have been changed. Unless the exercises mention another time and location, assume that each story occurred in your community today.

- Statistical material (Exercises 4–6). These exercises range from the simple to the complex. The challenge is to interpret the numbers and make them interesting to the reader.

- Informal polls (Exercise 7). This exercise requires you to pose questions to gauge how people feel about issues and events. The central point of the stories should be about the issue and the results of the poll.

- Computer-assisted reporting (Exercises 8–10). These exercises involve sets of questions to get you thinking like a journalist about where to get information and how to use it to support a story.

- Converging media (Exercise 11). This exercise involves strategies in gathering and presenting news. It involves the newsgathering skills that were discussed in previous chapters along with presentation skills mentioned earlier.

USING STATISTICS

Much of the information reporters gather comes in the form of statistics. Statistics appear almost daily in news stories concerning budgets, taxes, census data, sports, politics, profits, dividends and annual reports. Other news stories based largely on statistics report rates of crime, productivity, energy consumption, unemployment and inflation. Reporters must learn to present statistics to the public in a form that is both interesting and understandable.

Reporters who write news stories based on statistics begin best by translating as many numbers as possible into words, which readers can understand more easily. Reporters also try to analyze the statistics, explaining their significance instead of simply reporting the numbers. Explaining the statistics requires reporters to look for and emphasize major trends, record highs and lows, the unusual and the unexpected.

Numbers by themselves lack context. Reporters need to explain the numbers in terms of comparisons that will help the reader understand. Readers following the war in Iraq read and heard of deaths in Iraq from suicide bombings, death squads, and roadside bombs. At times, 20, 40, 50, or more civilians died daily in attacks. Still others died as a result of military operations by the United States and other members of the coalition that overthrew Saddam Hussein. An organization called Iraq Body Count (www.iraqbodycount.org) tracked civilian casualties from January 2003. According to Iraq Body Count, 12,617 Iraqi civilians died during one 12-month period.

One way to put the Iraq War deaths in perspective is to consider the numbers killed in relation to the total population of Iraq and then compare that to the situation in the United States. The population of the United States is about 11 times greater than that of Iraq. To put the Iraq deaths in a U.S. perspective, multiply the 12,617 by 11. That yields 138,787. If the United States were experiencing the same level of violence as Iraq with the same lethality, it would mean 138,787 additional deaths a year. That's 3.5 times the annual number of traffic fatalities and about 8.5 times the number of Americans murdered every year.

Emphasizing the story's human interest is another technique for explaining statistical stories. Until it was revised, the following example gave numbers only in a routine and dull series. The revision includes a human element. The reporter found someone who received first aid from the fire department. Another version could have examined the false alarms in greater detail. Did they come from a certain area of the city? Was anyone caught and prosecuted for setting off those false alarms? Where were the bomb threats? Was anyone injured?

> The fire department's annual report states that last year it responded to the following numbers and types of calls: bomb threats, 60; electrical fires, 201; false alarms, 459; first aid, 1,783; mattress fires, 59; burned pots left on stove, 78; rescues, 18; washdowns, usually of leaking gasoline at the scene of automobile accidents, 227; and water salvage, 46.

> REVISED: When Sarah Kindstrom needed help, the fire department responded. Kindstrom's heart attack last week was one of 5,024 calls the department answered last year. First aid requests were the most common, according to the department's annual report, which was released today.
>
> The five leading types of calls included, in order of frequency, the following: first aid, 1,783; false alarms, 459; washdowns, usually of leaking gasoline at the scene of automobile accidents, 227; electrical fires, 201; and burned pots left on stoves, 78.
>
> Other types included these: bomb threats, 60; mattress fires, 59; water salvage, 46; and rescues, 18.

Stories that rely too heavily on numbers can be deadly for readers, who might perceive them as boring and hard to understand. The reporter's job is to make the numbers interesting so that readers will stay with the story from beginning to end. The unusual nature of statistical information and its impact on people are what make the story interesting.

Reporters describing election results tell readers more than who won and the number of votes that each candidate received. They search for additional highlights: Did incumbents win or lose? Was any bloc of voters (such as ethnic groups, women or conservatives) decisively for one candidate or another? Were there significant differences in ridings or voting districts from previous elections? Did any candidates win by unusually large or small margins? Answering those kinds of questions can make election stories more interesting than merely reporting who won what races.

Reporters who must include statistics in their stories try to present them as simply as possible. They avoid a series of paragraphs that contain nothing but statistics. Instead, they use transitions, explanations and narrative to break up long strings of numbers and make the information clearer. Reporters also avoid the temptation to editorialize about statistical information. Readers or viewers might not agree with a reporter's characterization of a budget increase as "big" or "huge." Although one person might think a 2 per cent increase in a $1-billion budget is small, another person might think that adding $20 million to the budget is a great deal.

Reporters who do not present statistical information carefully can mislead the reader. To write that the traffic accident death rate in a small town increased by 100 per cent or doubled this year might be accurate. It also might be misleading, however, if one person was killed in a traffic accident last year and two people were killed this year. Placing the statistics in a context that makes their significance clear will prevent distortion.

CONDUCTING INFORMAL POLLS

Reporters often want to know what people think of issues in the news. Traditionally, reporters have gathered opinions by interviewing local experts or people they encounter on the street. Informal polls of this type are fast and cheap, but they cannot accurately describe public opinion because they do not use truly random samples that represent a cross-section of the general population. If reporters go to an area where banks and law offices are concentrated to get public reaction to some issue, they are likely to hear comments different from those that factory workers might express. For this reason, reporters cannot generalize about the results of informal polls. They can report only the opinions of the people interviewed; they cannot suggest that the opinions reflect the sentiment of the community as a whole.

The unreliability of informal polls has encouraged some news organizations to employ more scientific techniques. To conduct a truly accurate poll, reporters must interview a random sample chosen from all the residents in their community. Because that is difficult, some news organizations hire professional pollsters to conduct their polls, especially during election campaigns. A few organizations employ reporters who have the expertise to conduct scientific polls using random samples—usually samples of several hundred people. Because of their more scientific procedures and carefully worded questions, the reporters can accurately determine public opinion about important issues.

Still, informal polls often are interesting and enable reporters to localize issues in the news. Reporters assigned to conduct informal surveys—to ask a dozen people whether they favour a new tax, for example—encourage people to respond with more than a simple "yes" or "no." They ask people why they favour or oppose the tax. If respondents answer with vague generalities, reporters ask them to be more specific. If the responses to the questions are dull, vague or unclear, the story will be equally uninteresting.

Many news organizations conduct informal polls on Web home pages to gauge reader response to issues in the news. Some news organizations offer more extensive surveys, created by the news organization itself or by a research company, in separate locations on the website that readers can access from the home page.

Whether a poll is an informal one or is more scientific, the Internet can be used as a means of gauging the pulse of a community on a variety of issues. And whether a poll is conducted in person, over the phone, or on a website, care must be taken in writing the story. The lead should describe as specifically as possible the major finding, which usually is the opinion expressed by a majority of the people interviewed. The lead must do more than report that a poll was conducted or that the respondents were "divided" about the issue. People are divided about every controversial issue, and conducting a poll is not newsworthy. Only the results are likely to interest readers. For these reasons, three of the following leads need to be revised. Only the fourth is well written:

> NOT NEWS: One hundred college students were polled Tuesday about the war in the Middle East. (This fails to report the news—the results of that poll.)

OBVIOUS: One hundred college students responded with varied answers Tuesday when they were asked, "Should the United States go to war in the Middle East?" (This states the obvious—the fact that people disagree about a controversial issue.)

VAGUE: One hundred college students were interviewed Tuesday, and a majority said the United States should go to war in the Middle East, but only if attacked first. (This lead is too vague; it fails to reveal the size of the majority.)

BETTER: Sixty-eight out of 100 college students interviewed Tuesday said the United States should go to war in the Middle East, but only if attacked first. (Note that this lead does not imply that 68 per cent of all college students hold this opinion.)

The two or three paragraphs following the lead should summarize other highlights or trends. The fourth paragraph might quote the exact question asked of each respondent. If the story shifts directly from the lead to a quotation from one of the people interviewed, the transition might be too abrupt, and the story will seem disorganized. Also, if the quotation placed in the second paragraph reflects the opinion of just one person, it is probably not important enough to merit that position in the story.

Reporters arrange quotations in a logical order, grouping similar responses and placing transitions between those groups. They look for trends—perhaps consistent differences between the responses of men and women, young and old, students and non-students. (When the story is based on an informal poll, reporters are careful not to imply that such trends are present in the entire population.)

After the lead and two to four paragraphs summarizing the results, poll stories usually begin by quoting respondents who expressed the majority viewpoint, then people who expressed opposing viewpoints. Some opinions may be divided into even smaller groups. For example, if the respondents who favour an issue gave four reasons for their beliefs, the story first might quote respondents who mentioned the most popular reason, then quote those who cited the second, third and fourth most popular reasons.

Transitions should be logical and informative, linking ideas from preceding paragraphs. Many summarize the viewpoint of the group of quotations that reporters are about to present. The following transitions appeared in a story about high school students' opinions of the Canadian Forces. The paragraphs following each transition quoted students who expressed the viewpoint summarized in the transition:

> Fourteen students said they consider service in the Forces a patriotic duty....
> Seven students said they plan to join the Forces because they want to travel but cannot afford to go overseas by themselves....
> Four women said the Forces offers higher salaries than civilian employers and is more willing to promote women....

Reporters do not quote simple "yes" or "no" responses when reporting the opinions of respondents. If the fourth paragraph in a story quotes the question that each respondent was asked, and the tenth paragraph reports that one person responded "yes," readers might not realize the person was responding to the question presented six paragraphs earlier:

> Rebecca Pearson of 318 Ashton Drive responded, "Yes."
> REVISED: Rebecca Pearson, of 318 Ashton Drive, agreed that the cost of housing in the city is becoming too expensive for most home buyers.

Reporters also try to be specific and clear in characterizing responses, even if it means briefly restating an idea:

> Sandy Roach, a senior biology major, more or less agreed with Hass.
> REVISED: Sandy Roach, a senior biology major, agreed that government workers are overpaid but said it is the fault of politicians, not of unions representing government workers.

Poll stories should identify fully every person quoted. Reporters identify most sources by name, age and address (or hometown for people from outside the community). Because of concerns about privacy, some news organizations no longer use addresses; instead, they identify sources by occupation, neighbourhood or hometown. Experts or community leaders should be identified by name, title and organization. Identification for students should consist of major and year in school; for faculty, their rank and department; and for non-academic school employees, their departments and job titles.

Some people might refuse to identify themselves. Reporters have three choices for dealing with them: (1) ask them why they do not want to be identified and try to overcome their objections; (2) offer to identify them by age or occupation instead of name; or (3) thank them and find others who are willing to be identified. Editors and news directors tell their reporters which of these options to follow. But it is important that opinions be attributed to their sources so readers don't think they are the reporter's views.

A poll story needs to quote only those respondents who say something colourful, important or unusual, not every person interviewed. Reporters paraphrase or discard responses that are awkward, wordy, unclear or repetitious. They select the most interesting statements and devote several paragraphs to those remarks. A story that quotes 10 or 20 people and devotes one paragraph to each will seem choppy and superficial.

If two people make similar replies to poll questions, reporters can combine their responses in a single sentence or paragraph. Note, however, that because two people are unlikely to use exactly the same words, the same direct quotation cannot be attributed to both of them. Instead, reporters paraphrase their responses or say several people expressed the same opinion and then quote one of them to illustrate that point of view. For example:

> Lionel Jackson and Eugene Bushnell, both seniors majoring in political science, said that the provincial tax discriminates against the poor.
>
> Three students said they dropped out of college for a year or more. Marsha Dilte, a senior, explained: "I was running out of money, and I really wasn't certain what I wanted to do. After two years of working as a secretary, I had enough money to finish college, and I knew I wanted to be a nurse."

Reporters should never criticize or attach labels to respondents' answers. They do not refer to any answers as "interesting," "thoughtful" or "uninformed." They simply report whatever respondents said and let readers judge the remarks for themselves. (Readers' conclusions may be quite different from the reporter's.) Reporters also avoid making comments about the manner in which people responded to questions and are especially careful to avoid trite generalities. For example, they do not report that one person seemed "sincere" or that another seemed "apathetic." However, they might report specific details, for instance describing how one person paused for nearly a minute before answering a question, then addressed the issue for nearly 30 minutes.

Some people reporters attempt to interview might be undecided about or unfamiliar with the topic. People who are undecided or uninformed usually constitute a small minority and can be mentioned in the story's final paragraphs. The final paragraphs also might describe the methods reporters used to conduct the poll: the exact number of people interviewed and the way they were selected. The closing paragraphs, however, should never summarize the findings; a news story contains only one summary, and it belongs in the lead.

USING COMPUTERS TO GET ANSWERS

Newspapers have been using computers for many decades. They make writing, editing, and page layout and design (pagination) much faster and more flexible. In addition, most papers are using computers for handling photographs, eliminating the need for a darkroom. However, news organizations have found an even more powerful use for computers—as a means of gathering and disseminating statistical information. Over the past 20 years, as much information went online or was stored in databases, journalists began viewing numbers in a different way. At many news organizations today, computers rather than pocket calculators

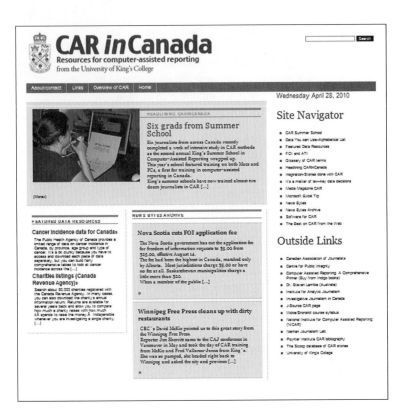

help reporters analyze budgets, reports, surveys and polls.

Twenty years ago, only national or large regional newspapers were using computers to help spot trends and patterns in the information that crossed their desks. Today in Canada, mid-market and even small news outlets have jumped on the technology bandwagon. Surveys of newspaper editors have found that a majority use computers as reporting tools in some manner.

One Statistics Canada study on the growth of Internet use for various functions between 1999 and 2003 found that by far the most common use of the Internet in 2003 was sending and receiving email (52.1 per cent), followed by general browsing (48.5 per cent) and seeking medical and health information (35.6 per cent).

Journalists apply the term "computer-assisted reporting" (CAR) to a wide range of practices. Computers provide access to the Internet, letting reporters use email to communicate with sources and other reporters. Journalists also use the World Wide Web to gather information from search engines such as Google and Yahoo. Perhaps the most sophisticated use of computers in news reporting, however, is to analyze information in electronic databases that reporters have compiled on their own or have obtained from government agencies. These databases contain vast amounts of information, and analyzing them without computers would consume months of time. With computers, however, reporters can analyze data quickly and thoroughly.

Databases are nothing new. A common example is a city directory—an alphabetical listing of people and businesses. But because the data are in a paper format, analysis is difficult. For example, it would be difficult to calculate what percentage of the people listed in the city directory owned their homes instead of renting. Once the data are in electronic form, that calculation can be performed quickly using a database management program. Computer-assisted reporting projects often compare two or more databases to see what they have in common.

Peter Cheney of the *Toronto Star* compiled his own database to tell a series of stories that exposed abuses in the taxi industry in Toronto.

> Once I [built] the database, I saw who owned the plates. I saw there was also this thing called an agent, who handled the plates for people who didn't want to have anything to do with them day-to-day. You wouldn't see any of that without CAR.

Other news organizations have used computer-assisted reporting to obtain stories about agriculture, business, child welfare, crime, discrimination, education, the environment, health care, highway safety and the justice system, to name some general areas. The opportunities are endless. And the stories often attract readers and viewers.

Computer-assisted reporting is an extensive topic, and this section offers only a glimpse of this powerful and increasingly important type of reporting. With continuing advances in computer technology and its use by news organizations, even small papers are using computer-assisted reporting to give their readers more in-depth information on issues. News editors and station managers are requiring more computer-assisted reporting skills on the part of the new reporters they hire. Students who graduate with some basic computer skills in using spreadsheet software (such as QuattroPro, Excel and Lotus 1-2-3) and relational databases (such as FoxPro, Paradox, dBase and Access) will move to the front of the line in the job market. It also will be important for students to prove they can apply that knowledge to real stories. Reporters must learn to see the possibilities, develop story ideas, and write stories that use these skills.

Computer-assisted reporting does not replace good, old-fashioned reporting skills. Computers do not interview sources, and they are only as good as the information that goes into them. They are merely another tool used by reporters to provide information to the public.

CONVERGING MEDIA

Journalists in the future will have to be flexible. Because of technological advances as well as changes in the business of news and mass communication, newswriters will need more skills to navigate the profession of journalism. Students will need not only to become good writers and editors but also to develop good oral communication skills to present news in real time. The growth of media conglomerates owning newspapers, radio stations and television stations or networks, cable news channels, and websites means that news and information may be processed and disseminated in a variety of ways by the same reporter. Print journalists working on a story for their newspaper might find themselves presenting the same story in a segment for the news organization's television station or posting the story to the newspaper's website. Photojournalists might go to a news event armed with a digital still camera and a digital video camera to capture photos for the newspaper and video for the website. The terms being used for these phenomena are media convergence and multimedia journalism.

A "converged" newsroom would bring together a newspaper, television news station, and website in presenting news to a changing audience. Television, newspaper and Web reporters would share the same building, allowing the station manager and production people for the television station to stay in close contact with the news editors on the print side and the webpage editors on the Internet side. Ideas for stories would be shared among the three entities, and teams of reporters from each entity would often work on stories together.

Media convergence is a phenomenon that affects not only future journalists who gather and disseminate information but also audiences who seek and assimilate information. In the past, people read a newspaper and talked to other people to find out what was going on in their communities and around the world. Today, people seek information from many different sources. A radio news report emanating from a clock radio might start their day. As they are eating breakfast or getting ready for work, they might be watching one of the 24-hour cable news channels. As they drive to work, they can listen to an all-news/talk station on their car radio. When they get to work, they turn on their computer and might connect to a newspaper website for the latest business news. When they get home at night, they might sit down with a newspaper or magazine. People get their information from many different sources today, and that trend is expected to continue in the future.

Converging media have changed the nature of the news business in terms of interaction between the news organizations and their audiences. In the past, readers could write a letter to the editor to express their opinion on issues. Or they could submit ideas for stories. Today, with the emergence of Web logs, or blogs, readers can interact with news organizations in a variety of other ways. Some news organizations allow their reporters to create blogs, and some have experimented with allowing readers to create their own blogs on specialty topics in sports, law, medicine or social issues. Blogging can create a dialogue—an interactivity—with the community, something that didn't exist previously. Not everyone is willing to take the time to sit down and write a letter, but many people spend a lot of time on their computers and have easy access to a news organization's website.

To prepare for the future, students will need to learn to adapt the information they gather for presentation on a number of different platforms. Beginning journalists will need to learn how to write well, because no matter what platform the information is presented on, the content needs to be well written. Once they learn the mechanics of good grammar and spelling, CP style, and news story structure, students will need to learn to prepare the information for dissemination in print, on the Web, and through video. In addition to learning how to write news stories, students also should learn how to shoot and edit video, create digital radio spots, and make Web animations. The key to learning about convergence is flexibility.

CHECKLISTS FOR ADVANCED REPORTING

Using Statistics

1. Verify the accuracy of statistical information.
2. Make the central point of your story reflect the most important or unusual aspects of the statistical information.
3. Present statistical information in a concise and understandable way.
4. Look for links between statistics that might make the story more interesting for the reader.
5. Don't editorialize about statistical information. Let the numbers speak for themselves, and let readers make their own judgments.

Conducting Informal Polls

1. Ask questions that encourage respondents to say more than "yes" or "no." Try to get beyond vague generalities to more specific issues and details.
2. Make the lead as specific as possible in describing the results of the poll.
3. Don't shift abruptly from the lead to quotations from respondents. Use three or four paragraphs after the lead to describe the findings and report the exact wording of the question asked.
4. Look for trends or groups of similar responses.
5. Write strong transitions between sections of the story.
6. Don't criticize or editorialize about the responses; simply report them.
7. Never imply that the results of an informal poll can predict what the community in general thinks about an issue.

The Writing Coach

COMPUTER-ASSISTED REPORTING ON THE RISE IN CANADA
By Fred Vallance-Jones (*Media* magazine, Spring 2003)

This corner of *Media* magazine isn't feeling quite as lonely as it once did. In fact, it's getting downright crowded.

The last year has been something of a blur in the world of computer-assisted reporting in Canada.

Natalie Clancy of CBC-TV in Vancouver built a database to probe a string of gangland murders. A team at the *Toronto Star* analyzed police data to reveal a persistent pattern of racial profiling and sweep up the 2002 Michener award and a National Newspaper Award. David McKie of CBC Radio used Health Canada data to investigate faulty medical devices. My own newspaper, the *Hamilton Spectator*, makes CAR a regular part of the daily file.

CAR is coming of age in Canada, and is shedding its image as a reclusive, numbers-driven obsession of a few lonely die-hards.

There was proof of that once again at the recent CAJ annual convention in Toronto as the lineup for the fifth annual CAR award was like an awards show in its own right.

For those of us who have been around since nearly the beginning, since the days when the CAR room at the annual convention was a good place for a bowling tournament, it's more than a little satisfying. These days, it's hard to find a chair in the CAR room, and the training sessions fill up quickly with people eager to learn the mysteries of rows, columns and queries. I marvel at it all.

I remember well the Vancouver convention in 1999, when McKie spent long hours in the CAR demo room, learning how to use Excel. This year, he was one of the teachers, and shows other journalists, and journalism students at Carleton University, how to avoid being overwhelmed by data when writing and broadcasting CAR stories.

These days, CAR skills are showing up as a requirement on job postings. Canada's journalism schools are making CAR part of the mainstream curriculum, and reporters are having more and more success prying newsworthy databases from the clutches of reluctant governments.

It's a good time to have CAR skills, and a good time to learn.

TWELVE KEYS TO SUCCESSFUL INVESTIGATIONS

Adapted from *Digging Deeper: A Canadian Reporter's Research Guide*,
by Robert Cribb, Dean Jobb, David McKie, and Fred Vallance-Jones
(Oxford University Press, 2006).

1. Curiosity
   Curiosity may have killed the cat, but it has given many an investigative story life. It gives rise to the most important questions: I wonder what happened? I wonder why? Who was responsible? How much money was involved? What happens next? How is it supposed to work? How does it really work? The investigative journalist must viscerally want the answers to questions such as these. Curiosity is the engine that powers many other crucial parts of the investigation. It also keeps you going when obstacles and frustrations impede you along the way.

2. Preparation
   This one can't be overemphasized. Being prepared will always, *always* pay off for the investigative reporter. Consider interviews: in daily journalism, they are often conducted on the fly with little time to get to know much about the interviewee, or sometimes even the subject. Investigative interviews, however, are conducted only after careful preparation. You will want to research people, find out not only what they do and what they should know, but also what they are like and how they may react in an interview. You will also examine documents, notes from previous interviews, and electronic data, drawing up a list of questions or talking points before you come close to doing an interview. Preparation is key to other parts of the investigative process as well, especially writing. As much time will be spent on organizing material as on writing itself.

3. Organization
   There are probably as many systems for staying organized as there are investigative reporters. The trick is to find one that works for you. On any project, more and more information accumulates as the researcher digs deeper into the subject. There will be interview notes and transcripts, electronic files, links to websites and printouts, notations, databases and spreadsheet files, and any number of other paper documents. You'll know what each one is for when you obtain it, but weeks or months later, you can become overwhelmed by it all. Some reporters use manila file folders to stay organized; others keep spreadsheets, and some use small file cards. Some make "to do" and "to interview" lists; others keep all of the phone numbers they come across on a single sheet or in a single file. The key is to be able to quickly find any document or interview you need and understand its significance, as well as to

come to understand the bigger picture and develop a list of key points. If you stay organized throughout, you will save hours, or days, of work when you reach the writing stage of your project.

4. Patience

It takes patience to research an investigative story. You are always waiting for something, whether a reluctant source to return your calls, public officials to respond to freedom-of-information requests, or inspiration to hit. For those accustomed to the faster pace of daily reporting, all of this waiting can be frustrating. But it is often the difference between getting most of the story and getting all of it. Some projects can take months to go from idea to publication or broadcast, and you will face many pressures along the way to speed that process up. Of course, you need to know when you have done enough research, when that last document isn't worth waiting for. But rushing can lead to incomplete stories that will fade away as quickly as yesterday's headline.

5. Tenacity

This is one of the most important qualities for the investigative journalist. Many, many times you will face obstacles that will tempt you to give up or give in. Bureaucrats will fight to stop you from obtaining public documents. Key sources will be difficult to find or reluctant to speak to you. Databases will seem impenetrable and unintelligible. Sometimes, you just won't have a clue how to nail a crucial piece of information. The key is sticking with it. Persistence—sometimes even over a period of years—can overcome monumental hurdles, including community indifference—and tell important stories that would otherwise remain untold.

6. Resourcefulness

Not everything will be obvious or easy when you are pursuing an investigative story; you will need to use your initiative in deciding where to look. Information about people can be harvested from unlikely places on the Internet. Online records of a person's political contributions or property tax assessments can reveal his or her home address. Documents obtained through freedom-of-information requests yield leads that take you to new and unexpected facts. While daily reporters generally use their sources directly—describing, for example, what a new report says or what a politician said—investigative reporters often use sources as means to an end. A report might offer you a name that leads to an interview with someone who can put you in touch with the person you really want to talk to, and so on. The creative use of the available resources can help you to assemble your information successfully.

7. Thoroughness and completeness

Investigative reporting differs from the daily variety in that you have the time (and the obligation) to be thorough and complete. While a daily story remains tightly focused, an investigation follows up numerous leads and goes down many roads, not all of them productive. You want to know that you have exhausted, or very nearly exhausted, the possibilities before you state something to be true. The need to be thorough applies to every aspect of an investigation. When you are engaged in the early prospecting stage, you want to *thoroughly* canvass existing information on a subject. This will help you to *thoroughly* plan your research. Once into the research stage, you must *thoroughly* investigate leads. You should *thoroughly* prepare to write, and the writing itself needs to be *thorough* and complete. The result is authority and the potential to make a real difference.

8. **Attention and observation**

   Investigators need to be assiduous observers, always on the lookout for the unexpected and, just as importantly, for any facts that contradict their hypothesis. Investigators read documents with extra attention, listen just a little more carefully during interviews, and constantly assess the progress of their project. While interviewing in the field, the investigative journalist pays special attention to the surroundings. Are there family pictures or other objects that will provide an easy entrance into a discussion of the subject's personal life? Are there objects in the office that provide other insights into the character of the person? The same principle applies when visiting the scene of a crime or an accident. What can you learn about the events simply by observing?

9. **Open-mindedness**

   You want to be accurate and right. You don't want to dissect a government program only to have the media relations department successfully discredit your story. You certainly don't want to accuse someone of wrongdoing and then find out that mistakes have left you open to a million-dollar libel suit or publish an exposé only to discover that you missed the more important aspect of the story somewhere along the way. All of this argues for keeping an open mind. No matter what your hypothesis is, and no matter what pressure you may be under to deliver the story you originally conceived, you have to be ready to change course. Reporters working on investigative stories often become deeply involved in the work and find themselves contained in a narrow silo of facts and evidence that can blind them to what else may be going on. Constantly challenge your assumptions. Try just as hard to disprove your hypothesis as to prove it.

10. **Care, caution, and discretion**

    Those doing investigations often have the reputations of others in their hands. With this power comes great responsibility. Perhaps even more so than in daily reporting, discretion is king. If you promise a source confidentiality, for example, you must adhere to that promise, not only for ethical reason, but also because your own reputation is your most valuable asset. It will not remain intact for long if you are untrustworthy.

11. **Skepticism**

    Paired with the need to keep an open mind is the need to maintain a healthy skepticism. This shouldn't be confused with cynicism, which the *Canadian Oxford Dictionary* defines as "doubting or despising sincerity and merit." A skeptic doesn't dismiss merit but instead tests every fact or statement that comes his or her way. Facts stated in press releases, for example, are checked with original sources rather than just repeated. The same goes for statements made by sources. They need to be verified by other sources or in documents. The better the information seems for your story, the more you need to be skeptical until you are certain. This is at the heart of evolving an investigative frame of mind.

12. **Time**

    Buttressing the eleven key elements mentioned above is the one that makes them all possible. Whether an investigation takes two weeks, two months, or two years, it is the luxury of time that allows the extensive research, backgrounding, and thinking to unfold. Time is the elixir that allows ideas to percolate and evolve and allows the reporter to build the patchwork and connect the dots to bring the investigative story alive. Of course, this doesn't mean that you can't do investigative journalism if you are also doing daily assignments. You will simply have to fit the work in between other responsibilities. This is not impossible, but requires organization and discipline. If you squeeze in a phone call here and read a document there, you'll be amazed how much work you can get done in the time you didn't know you had.

SUGGESTED READINGS AND USEFUL WEBSITES

Cribb, Robert, Dean Jobb, David McKie, and Fred Vallance-Jones. 2006. *Digging Deeper: A Canadian Reporter's Research Guide.* Don Mills, ON: Oxford University Press.

Ettema, James S., and Theodore L. Glasser. 1998. *Custodians of Conscience: Investigative Journalism and Public Virtue.* New York: Columbia University Press.

Meyer, Philip. 1991. *The New Precision Journalism.* Bloomington, IN: Indianapolis: Indiana University Press.

Paulos, John Allen. 1995. *A Mathematician Reads the Newspaper.* New York: Random House.

Protess, David L. 1991. *The Journalism of Outrage: Investigative Reporting and Agenda Building in America.* New York: Guilford Press.

Ruvinsky, Maxine. 2007. *Investigative Reporting in Canada.* Don Mills, ON: Oxford University Press.

Vallance-Jones, Fred, and David McKie. 2009. *Computer-Assisted Reporting: A Comprehensive Primer.* Don Mills, ON: Oxford University Press.

Human Resources and Skills Development Canada: www.hrsdc.gc.ca

"Canada at a Glance," Statistics Canada: www.statcan.gc.ca

Statistics: Power from Data: http://www.statcan.gc.ca/edu/power-pouvoir/toc-tdm/5214718-eng.htm

EXERCISE 1   Advanced Reporting

In-depth Story

This is a report by Statistics Canada on police resources across Canada in 2008. Write a brief story summarizing its content. At the end of the story, list the sources you would interview to write a more thorough story, along with questions you would ask each source.

Police Resources in Canada, 2008

Following a period of decline throughout the 1990s, police strength in Canada has increased over the past decade.

At 196 officers per 100,000 population, the 2008 rate was 8 per cent higher than in 1998, although 5 per cent lower than its peak in 1975.

While police officer strength has been increasing, Canada's police-reported crime rate has been decreasing.

The 2007 crime rate was at its lowest point in over 30 years. At the same time, the proportion of crime solved by police reached a 30-year high.

There were over 65,000 "active" police officers on May 15, 2008, two-thirds of which were employed by municipal police services. However, there were an additional 13,234 "authorized" positions that were not staffed for a number of reasons, including difficulty in replacing officers who had retired or otherwise left the police service, were on maternity/paternity leave, or were on long-term medical leave.

Civilian personnel, such as clerks, dispatch officers, and by-law enforcement officers, has increased over the past 10 years at a rate more than twice that of police officers. In 2008, there were over 25,000 civilian personnel accounting for 28 per cent of all policing personnel or 1 civilian per 2.5 police officers.

As is historically the case, police per capita in 2008 was highest in the territories, where crime rates are well above the rest of the country.

Among the provinces, Saskatchewan reported the highest rate of police officers for the eighth year in a row, while Alberta and Prince Edward Island reported the lowest.

Over the past decade, all 27 census metropolitan areas recorded increases in police officer strength, with the exception of Victoria. The largest gains since 1998 occurred in Sherbrooke, St. Catharines–Niagara and London, all up by more than 20 per cent.

In 2008, Thunder Bay had the highest rate of police officers, followed by Saint John and Regina.

Among Canada's nine largest metropolitan areas, the rate of police officers was highest in Montreal and Winnipeg.

The rate of police strength in Toronto, where crime rates were among the lowest, was also above average compared to the other large cities. Quebec reported the lowest rate of officers as well as one of the lowest rates of crime.

Female officers grew at a faster pace than male officers in 2008, continuing the rise in female recruitment that began in the mid-1970s.

In 2008, females accounted for almost one in five officers in Canada compared to approximately one in eight a decade ago. In 2008, Quebec and British Columbia reported the highest proportion of female officers among the provinces. The lowest proportion was found in Prince Edward Island.

After adjusting for inflation, police expenditures rose for the 11th consecutive year, reaching $10.5 billion in 2007 or $320 per Canadian. Total spending was 4 per cent higher than in 2006 and 43 per cent higher than in 1997.

Generally, about one in every three police-reported crimes is cleared, either by a charge being laid or by other means. In 2007, the proportion of crimes solved by police went up for the third consecutive year, reaching a 30-year high of 37 per cent. Police strength, the volume and type of crimes and the complexity of police investigations are among the many factors which affect clearance rates.

EXERCISE 2   Advanced Reporting

In-depth Story

This is a news release from Health Canada about a federal anti-drug campaign aimed at youth. Write a story summarizing its content. At the end of the story, list the sources you would interview to write a more thorough story, along with questions you would ask each source. Notice that there is a single number in this story, and seek out other numbers to help put the initiative in context: for example: How many young people in Canada use illicit drugs, and what proportion of the total do they represent?

WINNIPEG—Joy Smith, Member of Parliament for Kildonan-St. Paul, announced today, on behalf of the Honourable Leona Aglukkaq, Minister of Health, the Government of Canada's support for a national project that will help prevent youth across the country from taking illicit drugs.

"The Government of Canada is proud to be working with provinces and communities across the country to help prevent illicit drug use among youth," said Minister Aglukkaq. "This project will provide communities across Canada with the tools they need to understand the links between youth at risk of psychosis and illicit drug use."

The Schizophrenia Society of Canada and its partners will develop, implement and promote activities aimed at preventing drug use among youth through its project *Understanding the Link between Cannabis Use and Early Psychosis: an Awareness Strategy for Youth at Risk.* The project will delve into the reasons why youth at risk of psychosis are drawn to using cannabis. It will also increase awareness among youth about the negative impacts of cannabis and the links to psychosis. Training, interviews and focus group testing will take place in several sites across Canada to gain a better understanding of the impacts of illicit drug use and its links to psychosis.

"Raising awareness about substance abuse will help better equip youth to make informed decisions about their futures and their health," said Ms. Smith. "I look forward to seeing the benefits of this project in the months and years ahead."

Initiatives such as this one are another step in implementing the Government of Canada's National Anti-Drug Strategy, which was announced by Prime Minister Stephen Harper in October 2007.

"Through this project, the Schizophrenia Society of Canada will be able to conduct research, promote mental illness prevention, and develop mental health promotional material geared towards youth, by working with youth who have lived the experience of psychosis and cannabis use," said Chris Summerville, CEO of the Schizophrenia Society of Canada.

The federal Drug Strategy Community Initiatives Fund provides financial support for health promotion and prevention projects at the national, provincial and local levels. It addresses a wide range of illicit drug use issues, especially among vulnerable populations such as youth. The Schizophrenia Society of Canada project will receive $559,370 in financial support for this important project.

Please visit the National Anti-Drug Strategy website for more information.

-30-

EXERCISE 3   Advanced Reporting

In-depth Story

The following report about juvenile shoplifters in the United States was written for American readers. Write a brief news story that summarizes this report, but write it for a Canadian audience, making whatever changes are necessary and using CP spelling and style. At the end of your story, list the sources you would interview to write a similar story about juvenile shoplifters in this country, along with the questions you would ask each source. Think about what numbers would help to tell the story.

The Juvenile Shoplifter

Shoplifting is the largest monetary crime in the nation. Annual retail losses have been recently estimated at $16 billion nationally and as high as 7.5% of dollar sales. Shoplifting-related costs have been cited as a prime cause in one-third of all bankruptcies in small businesses. Shoplifting losses are on the rise with a 300 percent increase in the incidence of this crime during the 1990s alone.

Juveniles make up the largest percentage of shoplifters. Several studies have revealed that juvenile shoplifters account for approximately fifty percent of all shoplifting.

To gain further insight into the shoplifting problem, George P. Moschis, Professor of Marketing at Georgia State University, and Professor Judith Powell of the University of Richmond surveyed 7,379 students ages 7 to 19 in urban, suburban and rural areas using methods that insured anonymity of responses.

Some key findings:

- Approximately one out of three juveniles said they had shoplifted.
- Among teenagers 15 to 19, about 43% had shoplifted.
- Male youths shoplift more than females; approximately 41% of the males and 26% of the females reported having shoplifted at some time.
- A large amount of shoplifting is done by relatively few juveniles. Approximately 14 percent of those who admitted to shoplifting indicated repeat shoplifting behaviour.
- In comparison with non-shoplifters, youths who shoplift are more likely to believe that shoplifting is not a crime.
- Motives for shoplifting are primarily social rather than economic, especially among girls.
- A great deal of shoplifting is done because of peer pressure, especially among girls.
- About half of the time shoplifting takes place in the presence of peers.
- Shoplifting with peers is more common among girls than boys (61% vs. 47%).
- Females show greater tendency to shoplift with others than males.
- Boys tend to shoplift more frequently alone (less frequently with others).
- Shoplifting done by juveniles is primarily impulsive; four times out of five it is done on impulse.
- Female juveniles who shoplift are more likely to shoplift on impulse. Approximately 87% of females and 76% of males who admitted they had shoplifted decided to shoplift after they entered the store.
- Older teenage girls are more likely to shoplift on impulse than older teenage boys.
- Older boys tend to plan out shoplifting more than girls.
- There is a decline in impulse shoplifting with age and an increase in planned shoplifting among boys. No decline in impulsive shoplifting behaviour is shown for girls.
- Impulsive (unplanned) shoplifting in the presence of others is not only more common among girls, but it also becomes more frequent with age. Impulsive shoplifting among boys in the presence of others does not increase with age.

The findings regarding differences in shoplifting behaviour due to age and sex characteristics are expected to apply to other parts of the country, and they are consistent with the results of previous studies.

The authors recommend two broad strategies for reducing shoplifting losses: shoplifting prevention and shoplifting detection. Among shoplifting prevention methods, the authors suggest promotional campaigns that would increase awareness of the seriousness of the crime, and methods that would increase the difficulty of shoplifting. Proposed shoplifting detection strategies focus on educating security-detection personnel to be alert to the shoplifter's early warning signals, including knowledge of characteristics of youths most likely to shoplift.

EXERCISE 4   Statistical Material

Study the two tables below, and come up with an idea based on the table(s) for a feature story. List the sources you would need to consult to write the feature and the questions you would ask each source.

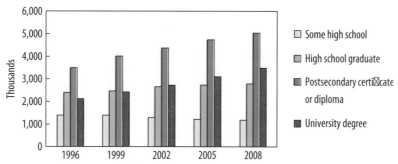

Source: Statistics Canada, CANSIM, table 282-0003. Canada at a Glance, 12-581-XWE 2008001 2009. Released July 3, 2009.

Table 11.1   Tuition fees by province

	1988	1993	1998	2003	2008
			(2002 = 100)		
Newfoundland and Labrador	36.3	57.7	101.3	95.3	97.1
Prince Edward Island	39.5	58.3	82.1	105.8	122.6
Nova Scotia	34.1	51.9	78.5	106.9	120.8
New Brunswick	38.3	56.0	77.2	107.1	136.1
Quebec	30.0	84.5	98.1	100.3	107.4
Ontario	30.0	43.6	76.4	104.1	123.3
Manitoba	38.3	66.6	90.9	100.9	108.9
Saskatchewan	30.0	51.0	73.7	109.3	122.4
Alberta	26.2	46.8	81.5	105.1	122.0
British Columbia	50.7	69.7	90.0	123.0	174.7

Source: Statistics Canada, CANSIM, table 326-0021. Canada at a Glance, 12-581-XWE 2008001 2009. Released July 3, 2009.

EXERCISE 5   Statistical Material

Consult Human Resources and Skills Development Canada (www.hrsdc.gc.ca) for the statistics you will need to complete this exercise.

Write a news brief about the services provided for victims of domestic and sexual violence last year by your province's ministry of human resources. Then develop a list of sources you would need to interview to write a more complete story, along with questions that you would ask each source. In your source list, include (in addition to human sources) sources of statistical information to answer questions such as the following:

- How many agencies did the province fund in the year just past?
- How many agencies did the province fund in the year before last?
- Of the agencies funded, how many were crisis lines, and how many were shelters (or other)?
- What proportion of funding was for sexual assault crisis centres or crisis lines?
- What proportion of funding was for services to victims of domestic violence?
- How many shelter facilities operated in the province?
- How many adults and children did the shelter facilities serve (how many shelter beds)?
- How many had to be turned away from shelter for lack of beds?

EXERCISE 6   Statistical Material

Study the table below, and come up with an idea for a feature story based on the table. List the sources you would need to consult to write the feature and the questions you would ask each source.

Table 11.2   Household participation rates for selected environmental behaviours, by province, 2006

	Low-flow shower-head	Reduced volume toilet	Compact fluorescent light bulbs	Composting	Recycling	Lowering temper-atures
	percent[1]					
Canada	**56**	**37**	**59**	**30**	**97**	**54**
Newfoundland and Labrador	58	27	53	23	94	62
Prince Edward Island	55	27	59	92	99	59
Nova Scotia	54	30	60	71	99	58
New Brunswick	55	31	61	37	96	48
Quebec	59	29	48	14	95	55
Ontario	60	43	65	38	98	51
Manitoba	46	35	50	23	88	50
Saskatchewan	37	34	53	29	96	63
Alberta	49	41	59	24	96	59
British Columbia	53	35	65	31	99	56

1. As a percentage of all households that have a thermostat and that have access to at least one recycling program.

Source: Statistics Canada, Households and the Environment Survey, 2006, Special tabulation. Canada at a Glance 12-581-XWE 2008001 2009. Released July 3, 2009.

CHAPTER 11

EXERCISE 7   Informal Polls

Conducting an Informal Poll

Interview a minimum of 10 people, about half men and half women. Ask them a single question concerning a controversial issue, then write a news story about their opinions. The respondents may be students, professors, non-academic employees, visitors, or anyone else you encounter on campus. Conduct your interviews separately, not simultaneously with other members of your class—if only because it is disconcerting for a respondent to be approached by two or three people, all asking the same controversial question. Identify yourself, explain why you are conducting the poll, and then ask the single question selected by your instructor or class. You may want to use one of the following questions:

1. Do you believe that newspapers and radio and television stations in Canada report the news fairly and accurately?
2. Should faculty members be allowed to date their students, or should your college or university adopt some rules prohibiting the practice?
3. Should your college or university adopt rules prohibiting faculty and students from saying things that are racist or sexist?
4. Would you want your provincial legislature to adopt a law making it legal—or illegal—for women to serve as surrogate mothers for childless couples?
5. If you saw another student cheating on a test, would you try to stop the student or report the student to your teacher?
6. If the administrators at your school learned that several students had AIDS, would you want them to allow the students to continue to attend classes with you?
7. Should the death penalty be reinstated in Canada?
8. Should the government prohibit the sale of pornographic magazines or the showing of pornographic movies?
9. Should churches and other religious organizations be required to pay property taxes for the municipal services, such as police and fire protection, that they receive?
10. Should the federal government allow media companies to own a newspaper and a television station or two or more TV stations in the same town?
11. Do you think the number of terms any one person may serve as a Member of Parliament should be limited by law?
12. Do you think an unwed mother should be required to identify the father of her child before she can receive welfare benefits so the father can be ordered to help support the child?

After you have conducted your poll, write a story about the results. You will have to do additional research to get background information about your poll issue to write a complete story. You might want to do followup interviews with experts on the issue to get their interpretation of the poll results.

EXERCISE 8   Computer-Assisted Reporting

1. If you don't have one already, get an email address for yourself through the proper agency on your campus, and subscribe to a journalism discussion list (a number of websites have such discussion groups). Prepare a weekly report about the mail on the list, summarizing what journalists talk about. Discuss the mail in class. What does it tell you about journalists and the journalism profession?

2. Read this chapter's Exercise 3 about juvenile shoplifting. What databases could be checked or developed that would help you find out whether the recommendations for dealing with shoplifting might be effective? Discuss your ideas with the other members of your class and your instructor.

3. Develop a computer-assisted reporting project from the information given below. What databases could be generated? What kind of information would be important for your story? What comparisons need to be made? Who needs to be interviewed? What questions need to be asked?

    County commissioners for the past 10 years issued licences for duck hunting on three small, unoccupied islands in Ford Lake. Each year there are nearly 100 applications for the five licences the commissioners award. Over the past several years, developers have built a number of homes along the waterfront around the lake. Visitors and residents use the lake for recreational activities—boating, swimming, fishing and picnicking. This year, homeowners want duck hunting to stop. They claim development around the lake has made hunting dangerous. They say pellets from the hunters' guns could hit houses and people along the shoreline. Hunters say the pellets never reach shore.

4. How could computer-assisted reporting help you with a story based on the information given below? What other databases would be helpful? Can the health report listed below be divided into sub-databases? What kind of information would be important for your story? What comparisons need to be made? Who needs to be interviewed for the story? What questions need to be asked?

    Every year, the local health department releases a report that lists the leading causes of death. This report provides the address, age, gender and race of each decedent, as well as the cause of death and the date of death. There were 3,245 deaths in the region last year, including 1,201 from all types of cancer. Other leading causes of death were: automobile accidents (525), heart attacks/strokes (432), and gunshot wounds (57).

5. Your editor hands you a computer printout of a database containing information about the 4,000 parking tickets your local police department wrote over the past year. For each ticket, the printout contains this information: licence plate number, province where licence was issued, year licence was issued, the ticket number, where the ticket was issued (including street and block), time of day the ticket was issued, day of the week the ticket was issued, date the ticket was issued, type of parking violation (expired meter, no parking zone, double parked, etc.), make of the vehicle, amount of the fine, date the fine was paid, and name of the officer issuing the ticket.

    Before your editor will allow you to use the computer to manipulate the data, she wants you to develop three ideas for stories that could result from this single database. She also wants you to list the sources you will need to talk to about each story once the data have been analyzed. Prepare a report for your editor addressing these requirements.

EXERCISE 9   Computer-Assisted Reporting

Market Basket Study

This assignment will give you experience in gathering information from a basic source and compiling a database of statistical information. In addition, it will give you experience in turning the statistics into a meaningful story that interprets the information for your audience. In teams of two to four students, visit two or more grocery stores in your community, and create a computer database comparing prices of 100 food and household items. Design your database so that items are categorized by product type and brand for comparison between stores and the results can be easily turned into charts or graphs for the story you will do. Then conduct interviews with shoppers and other sources, including secondary sources, to give a perspective to the information gathered for the database. Write a consumer-oriented story about your findings.

1. Before you start, ask yourself some questions that consumers, who are your readers, would want to know. Is it cheaper to shop at one store or another? Where do you get the best food bargains? Overall, where will your dollar go further? What are the best buys? These are questions that will help you focus your story.
2. Gather background information on such things as consumer spending patterns, percentage of income spent on food and household goods, or differences in food-buying habits of single people and families. These and other topics can be used in your story.
3. As you select the 100 items for your study, be aware that not all stores carry the same brands of products. You might want to gather information only on national brands that each store carries. Or you might have to compare similar products of different company brands. In that case, make certain that you compare similar-size containers.
4. After gathering the prices of the products, create a database for the statistical material either in a spreadsheet program, such as Excel or Lotus 1-2-3, or a relational database program, such as Access or FoxPro.
5. Divide your database of costs into categories for food items (subdivided into grocery items such as canned goods, meats, dairy products and produce) and nonfood items (such as household cleaning products and detergents) for each store.
6. Make cost comparisons based on individual products, groups of products, and the entire selection of products.

EXERCISE 10   Computer-Assisted Reporting

1. Some of the questions you might want to ask yourself for this assignment include: Are violent crimes on the increase or decreasing in the country? Who are the victims—urban, suburban or rural citizens? What are the levels of violent crime by age group? Are younger people committing more crimes than older people? How many violent criminals are there in prison today? These are just some possible directions the story could take.

2. The first step will be to create a search strategy for locating information on the Internet or in library databases by determining which websites and databases will serve your needs. Before you begin searching, decide on the central point and angle of your story. Put your objectives in writing, and then begin searching for databases and websites. Make a list of keywords to use in your search.

3. When you begin to search online, make a list of the various government or criminal justice websites that provide information for your story. You should document where you are getting your information, both for your story and for future reference. You will need to attribute where you are getting the information in your story.

4. The CD-ROM databases in your library can provide a wealth of information for your story. Many government documents are now available on CD-ROM and require much the same search strategy that you used for your online search of the Internet. You may use the same list of keywords for the CD-ROM databases, or you may add to the list to find the information you need.

5. The list of databases and sources that you use may change as your search progresses—you might find additional information as you conduct your searches, and some databases will provide interesting information that will be irrelevant to the central point of your story. Not all sources will be electronic. Some computer searches may refer you to printed material that you can use in your story but that is not available online.

CHAPTER 11

EXERCISE 11   Converging Media

Working in Print and Electronic Media

This exercise requires you to use material discussed in several chapters in your text.

1. Develop an idea for a story. It could be a hard news story about your local government or your college or university. It could be a feature story from your community or your college or university, such as a personality profile of an individual.

2. As you are thinking about the story, consider the visual possibilities, such as video or still digital images that could be used to illustrate the story. List the types of shots that you would like to use with the story.

3. Check with your department, university library, or campus media services department to see about borrowing a digital still camera and a digital video camera. If you do not have access to a digital still camera, use a traditional film camera and get the film developed. You will have to scan the prints or negatives depending on what scanner technology you have available. Take both the still camera and the video camera with you when you cover the story and conduct interviews.

4. Collect images (both still and video) during your interview, being sure to identify the people and scenes you are photographing. Make sure your interview is thorough. Make sure you obtain the full names and titles of those you interview for the story.

5. Write the story and download the still and video images onto a computer. Edit the story, and select the still photographs and about a minute of digital video to use in a film clip. You will have more visual images than you will need, so edit the images carefully to find the most dramatic and meaningful for the story.

6. Now, turn the camera on yourself. If you don't have a tripod or a steady flat surface on which to set the video camera, ask a classmate to operate the camera for you. Do a one-minute stand-up promotion about the story. You will want to put together a script to have notes to follow for the promo. Tell potential viewers and readers about the story, highlighting important details and telling them what to expect in the story. Or you and a classmate can take turns questioning each other about your stories. Then edit the interviews into 30- or 60-second video stories for the Web.

7. If you have access to a web page, you can upload the images and the story to the Internet for viewing electronically.

12 | Specialized Types of Stories

He told the story of the Maritime fisherman carrying a pail of lobsters up from the wharf. Another fisherman warns him that the lobsters might escape because there's no lid on the pail. "Oh no," says the first fisherman. "These are Canadian lobsters, boys. As soon as one makes it to the top, the others will drag him down."

— Derek Burney, Canadian ambassador to the United States, 1989

Tell a new reporter to write a speech or a meeting story, and he will immediately understand what is asked of him. Someone who has never worked in a newsroom might scratch his head when asked to write a bright, a followup, a roundup, or a sidebar. Yet all are common assignments for beginning reporters.

BRIGHTS

Brights are short, humorous stories that often have surprise endings. Some brights are written in the inverted-pyramid style: After a summary lead, the story reports the remaining details in descending order of importance. Other brights have unexpected or bizarre twists, and reporters might try to surprise readers by withholding those twists until the stories' final paragraphs. Brights that have surprise endings are called "suspended-interest stories." To keep their endings a surprise, these stories often begin with intriguing or suspenseful facts likely to interest readers but withhold until the end facts that are the most newsworthy or put the rest of the story in a new and surprising light. A suspended-interest story cannot begin with a summary lead because it would reveal the surprise ending.

Editors and news directors search for humorous stories and display the best ones prominently in their newspapers and news broadcasts. Brights entertain viewers and readers, arouse their emotions, and provide relief from the seriousness of the world's problems. Here is an example of a bright with a summary lead:

> GREENCASTLE, Ind. (AP)—A consonant-loving thief has police and business owners baffled after dozens of Rs were stolen from signs around the community.
>
> "We've lost our Rs. And we want them back," said Randall Jones, president of Headley Hardware.
>
> The weekend caper targeted gas stations, restaurants, repair shops and medical offices in the city of 10,000 people about 40 miles west of Indianapolis.
>
> The thief also nabbed half a dozen letters from a lighted marquee in front of a National Guard post.

"I don't know if they think it's a joke, but to me it's just theft," said National Guard Sgt. Robert Lamb. "I just think it's disturbing."

Putnam Inn manager Jane Hansen isn't sure how the thief climbed more than 6 feet off the ground to take Rs from a sign in front of her motel.

"Whoever's doing it needs to put their talents to something more constructive," she said.

Greencastle Police said they've been notified about the stolen letters, but many business owners are choosing not to file reports.

The suspended-interest story that follows begins so routinely that at first it might mislead the audience; its bizarre twist is not revealed until the final paragraphs:

Police killed an intruder after he set off a burglar alarm in a clothing store on Main Street shortly after 1 a.m. today.

Police entered the store after customers in a nearby tavern heard the alarm and surrounded the building until the officers arrived.

Police found the intruder perched on a counter and killed it with a fly swatter.

"It was my third bat this year," declared a police officer triumphantly.

Here are two more brights. The first one begins with a summary lead. The second one does not, and its ending might surprise you:

College students often complain about sloppy roommates, and Oscar—the first pig to be evicted from an apartment in the city—may be the sloppiest of all.

Oscar is a 6-week-old, 20-pound Hampshire pig. His owners claim that Oscar is only slightly different from other pets that live in the Colonial Apartments on University Boulevard. But the complex's owners say Oscar has to go.

"He's dug up the entire back yard," co-owner Sean Fairbairn said. "Besides that, he's noisy, and he stinks. We've gotten all sorts of complaints."

Oscar has lived in an old hay-filled refrigerator in Todd Gill's patio for a week. The patio is fenced in, but neighbours complained to the owners. The owners then told Gill and his roommate, Wayne Brayton, that Oscar has to go by noon Saturday.

"I don't think it's fair," Gill said. "People love Oscar. He runs around and grunts and squeals, but nothing too obnoxious. We've only let him out a couple times, and he's dug a hole under the fence once or twice, but no one's complained to me."

Gill and Brayton bought Oscar last week at a livestock auction.

The briefcase was on the floor near the police department's information desk for about 45 minutes. A clerk got suspicious. Maybe it contained explosives, she thought.

She called the department's bomb squad, and it evacuated the building. Members of the bomb squad then carried the briefcase outside and blew it up in a vacant lot.

That's when they learned that the briefcase belonged to their boss, Police Chief Barry Kopperud. He left it at the information desk while visiting the mayor.

"It's my fault," Kopperud said. "I should have mentioned it to someone. My officers did a good job, and I'm proud of them. They did what they were trained to do: to be alert and cautious."

Kopperud added that his son is likely to be upset, however. Today is the boy's seventh birthday, and Kopperud had his present in the briefcase.

Animals are a favourite topic for brights. One big-city newspaper tracked down rumours that a cat had made its home in a busy subway station. The rumours were true, and the cat had been surviving on mice and tins of cat food left by subway passengers. Other brights draw their humour from the stupid things even smart people might do, as in the newspaper story that told of a rookie police officer who left his patrol car running with a suspect handcuffed in the back seat while he investigated a domestic disturbance. The suspect managed to free himself of his cuffs, climbed into the front seat of the car, and drove away.

Writers of brights need to walk a fine line, however. A story that seems to make fun of a tragedy is tasteless, not funny.

FOLLOWUPS

Followups, which are also called "second-day" and "developing" stories, report new developments in stories that were "broken" (or reported) earlier. Followup stories differ from the follow stories we describe in Chapter 14. Follow stories on speeches and meetings are simply the stories written after those events.

Major stories rarely begin and end in a single day, and news organizations prepare a fresh article or package each time a new development arises. Stories about trials, legislative sessions, political campaigns, or flights to the moon might appear in the media every day for weeks. The September 11 terrorist attacks on the World Trade Center in New York City and the Pentagon in Washington remained top news stories for weeks after the events in Canada as well as in the United States. Followup stories described such things as eyewitness accounts, rescue efforts, identification of the terrorists who carried out the attacks, the disruption of air transportation, and plans to increase airport security. Although the followup story is tied to a past event, its lead always emphasizes the latest developments. Followups might summarize previous developments, but that information is presented as concisely as possible and placed later in the story.

Followup stories about disasters are especially common. In the summer of 2009, a massive storm deluged the communities of southeastern Manitoba. The following excerpts, all from the *Winnipeg Free Press*, traced the trajectory of the storm and the story during its first week:

> June 30—Provincial officials have described the weekend's rain storm as one of the worst summer storms to hit the province in 20 years.
>
> The storm deluged communities throughout southeastern Manitoba. The accompanying high winds played havoc with power lines in cottage country and sent waves crashing on Lake Winnipeg, destroying an earthen dike at Winnipeg Beach.
>
> "This was a massive storm that stretched from just north of Fargo to Berens River," Alf Warkentin, the province's river flood forecaster, said. "We've had localized events in the past but nothing on this scale in the summer.
>
> "It's a one-in-20-year kind of event for the summer."
>
> The storm damaged 20 homes and the local community centre at Sagkeeng, where leaders there declared a state of emergency.
>
> At Winnipeg Beach, 20-foot waves destroyed a five-block stretch of an earthen dike and then swallowed up giant chunks of lakefront cottage lots.
>
> Manitoba Hydro crews were still busy Monday, trying to restore power to cottages at Victoria Beach.
>
> At Emerson, the Red River rose three feet in a 24-hour period over the weekend, where the river is now 20 feet above normal summer levels and is expected to rise another six feet.
>
> The storm dumped 125 millimetres of rain onto Garson and 102 millimetres on St. Pierre-Jolys.
>
> At Winnipeg Beach, Mayor Don Pepe credits the clay dike built in 2005 with saving several lakefront cottages in the community but added the storm was so bad that a five-block stretch of dike was destroyed.
>
> With the protection gone, Lake Winnipeg gobbled up large chunks of backyards.
>
> "I've been here 27 years and I've never seen a summer storm like this," Pepe said.
>
> July 3—It will be another two weeks before Winnipeggers can walk instead of swim down the city's river walk.
>
> Alf Warkentin, the province's chief flood forecaster, predicted Thursday the Red River downtown will crest today at 14.8 feet and then begin receding.

"The river is 14.7 feet (on Thursday). It will be the middle of July before the river gets back to 8.5 feet again, the level for the river walkway," Warkentin said.

"The river's normal level is 6.4 feet so we're 8.3 feet above normal."

Warkentin said it was last weekend's major rainstorm that's to blame for water levels rising so quickly on the streams, rivers and lakes in the province.

He said the Red River in Emerson is 23 feet above normal, while the Winnipeg River is six feet above normal.

Warkentin said Lake Winnipeg is currently sitting at 715.35 feet, meaning Manitoba Hydro is mandated to let out as much water as it can through its dam at the north end of the lake.

"There is 145,000 cubic feet per second going out of the lake, but the inflow is about 25,000 greater than the outflow," he said.

"A level of 715.45 is likely and maybe even 715.5. It will be a long while until we get down to 715."

But Warkentin said the lake's level is still a foot less than during the high water conditions on the lake in 2005.

And Warkentin said in 1974—before the lake was regulated by Manitoba Hydro's dam—the lake reached 720 feet.

July 7—Damage from spring flooding in Manitoba is expected to hit at least $40 million, but that doesn't include compensation for the loss of more than five dozen homes in the Red River Valley and the cost of building new dikes to protect against future flooding, a provincial spokesman said Monday.

Intergovernmental Affairs Minister Steve Ashton, provincial minister responsible for emergency measures, said the damage estimate is based on the more than 1,000 claims already submitted to the province under its Disaster Financial Assistance program.

"It certainly indicates the degree of damage this year," Ashton said. "We all know this was the second worst flood of the century in the south of Red River Valley. North of Winnipeg it was the flood of the century, particularly with the damage of ice jams."

The lion's share of damage is to roads and drainage ditches throughout the province, including many outside the Red River Valley that were also hit by high spring run-off. Six First Nations are included on the list of 77 municipalities applying for assistance.

One of the hardest hit areas was the RM of Morris, which was surrounded by flood water for a month.

Reeve Herm Martens said the flood-damage bill for the municipality will be about $7 million, with most going to repair roads and other infrastructure.

Ashton also said the province is changing the cost-sharing agreement with municipalities so that those hit by flooding year after year, like Morris, do not pay beyond what they can afford for after-flood repairs.

The province, at the request of the Association of Manitoba Municipalities, is capping the current cost-sharing sliding scale to five dollars per capita of municipal expenditures. Once municipal spending reaches five dollars per capita, the province assumes 100 per cent of the costs. Up until now municipalities paid the first 10 per cent of their total claim.

Ashton said the new formula will reduce what could have been as much as a $500,000 cost to Morris to about $50,000. "This is important," Ashton said. "This is going to make a real difference for some of the hardest hit municipalities."

AMM president Doug Dobrowolski said the new formula is fairer and helps municipalities in disaster planning. "It doesn't matter what size of municipality you are now, you now know what it will cost you to deal with a disaster," Dobrowolski said.

The DFA is separate from the ongoing process of buying homes destroyed by flooding. Most are north of the city. Earlier this year, the province announced buyouts for cottage owners in the Breezy Point area, and allowed two municipalities north of Winnipeg to expropriate homeowners in flood-prone areas. That process will add several million more dollars to the flood bill.

Ashton said 17 damaged homes in St. Clements and at least two homes in St. Andrews are to be removed. Discussions are still ongoing with 44 Breezy Point residents who lease Crown land.

Each of these stories emphasized the newest and most important developments. Even in stories of lesser disasters, each new event prompts

THE CANADIAN PRESS/Winnipeg Free Press–Joe Bryksa

Two unidentified boaters fight the currents of the flood waters on Red River Drive just south of Winnipeg on Saturday, April 18, 2009.

a followup, and each followup recapitulates earlier stories. Sometimes viewers and readers grow weary of the repetition and believe the news media do it only to sensationalize stories. People who are unhappy with the amount of coverage given to a particular murder trial often express such views. (In the United States, Americans were so enthralled with the trial of O.J. Simpson that the audiences for the nightly network news broadcasts were down as much as 10 per cent because people were watching live coverage of the trial on cable channels CNN and Court TV.)

Yet news organizations cover trials, wars and disasters intensely because large numbers of readers and viewers are interested. Sometimes a followup story does not report new events but adds information unavailable earlier.

Followup stories are becoming more common as news organizations devote more resources to making sure important stories are followed to their conclusions. Media critics have complained that journalists, like firefighters, race from one major story to the next, devoting most of their attention to momentary crises. As one crisis subsides, the critics say, reporters move on to a newer one. The older crisis often disappears from the news before all the questions have been answered. To address this complaint, news organizations regularly return to important topics and tell readers what has happened since the topics dropped out of the headlines. Followups might report that an area devastated by a hurricane has been rebuilt or that victims of an accident are still suffering from its consequences.

ROUNDUPS

To save space or time, news organizations summarize several different but related events in roundup stories. Traffic roundups are most common; instead of publishing separate stories about each traffic death that occurs in a single weekend, newspapers and broadcast stations might summarize several fatal accidents in a single story. News organizations might report all the weekend crimes, fires, drownings, graduation ceremonies, or football games in roundup stories.

Another type of roundup story deals with a single event but incorporates facts from several sources. Reporters might interview half a dozen people to obtain more information about a single topic, to verify the accuracy of facts they have obtained elsewhere, or to obtain new perspectives. For example, if a city's mayor resigns unexpectedly, reporters might ask her why she resigned, what she plans to do after she leaves office, what she considers her major accomplishments, and what problems will confront her successor. They might then (1) ask other city officials to comment on the mayor's performance and resignation, (2) ask the city clerk how the next mayor will be selected, and (3) interview leading contenders for the job. All this information could be included in a single roundup story.

The lead for a roundup story emphasizes the most important or unique developments and ties all the facts together by stressing their common denominator, as in the following example from the Associated Press reporting on Christmas Day happenings around the world:

> LONDON (AP)—Bloodshed marred some of the world's Christmas celebrations and social tensions shadowed others. A grenade killed a girl and two other worshipers at a church in Pakistan, bombs exploded at a church in India, protesters blocked church doors in Yugoslavia.

The story included not only the details of the violence but also reported on the Christmas message from the Vatican urging countries to avoid war, celebrations by U.S. troops at Bagram Air Base in Afghanistan, and year-end remarks by Britain's Queen Elizabeth II.

After the lead, roundup stories usually organize facts and quotations by topic, starting with the most newsworthy accident, crime, fire or drowning and moving on to the second, third and fourth most important.

Some beginning reporters make the mistake of organizing their material by source. For example, they might write a crime roundup by reporting first all the information they got from the police and then all the information they got from the Crown prosecutor. Stories organized by source are disjointed and repetitious. Each source is likely to mention the same events, and comments about a particular event will be scattered throughout the story.

The following roundup story manages to relay a lot of information while maintaining reader interest. It was occasioned by one of the largest military and civilian disaster efforts in Canadian history: In January of 1998, the eastern part of the country was hit with an ice storm that left hundreds of thousands of people struggling without light and heat. Canadian Forces troops were called upon to perform a variety of tasks, including purifying water and taking generators door-to-door to heat houses and provide power. The following roundup story ran on the front page of the *New Brunswick Telegraph Journal* on January 12, 1998.

> SAINT JOHN, N.B.—After a bitterly cold night in Eastern Ontario and Quebec, the largest military and civilian disaster effort in Canadian history continues today in an effort to bring relief to hundreds of thousands of people struggling without light and heat.
>
> Quebec Premier Lucien Bouchard appealed to Montrealers to stay home from work today, leaving roads clear for hydro crews and their military helpers.
>
> He also urged people suffering without electricity to leave their homes and move in with friends and relatives—or join the estimated 100,000 Quebeckers already living in emergency shelters.
>
> "I'm appealing to all Quebecers who have electricity to get in touch with relatives and friends in difficulty to invite them, even persuade them, to come to their house," said Mr. Bouchard. "People must realize they can't stay at home without heat if, as we expect, temperatures start dropping."
>
> Mr. Bouchard said the conditions at emergency shelters are barely adequate.
>
> "There are 1,200 to 1,500 people in the same room sleeping side by side," he said. "They are often depending on generators which supply the minimum power. The best solution is to go to live with friends or family."
>
> Shelters in both provinces were getting mixed reviews.
>
> "I feel like I can cry," said 78-year-old Eleanor Mott, who has been in an emergency shelter in Vankleek Hill, Ont., midway between Ottawa and Montreal, for three days. "It's like World War Two. But it's good here. They have done very well and deserve credit. The army too. They couldn't have been better."
>
> Elsewhere, overcrowding and lack of supplies were fraying tempers. A woman clutching her baby at a shelter in St-Jean-sur-Richelieu, Que., described the emergency accommodation as "hell."

"I'd rather go to be with the devil than stay here any longer," she said. "I just can't take it anymore."

Hundreds of people at another shelter in Ste-Julie, Que., were happier after dining yesterday on donated filet mignon, lobster tails and shrimp.

Robberies and break-ins have been rare in the affected areas. About 600 police cars are patrolling darkened Montreal streets and a total 1,300 officers—three times the usual number—are on duty. City police arrested 17 people for robbery and car theft Saturday night—fewer than usual—and detained others for attempting to smuggle beer into shelters.

About 15 people have died in ice-storm-related incidents. A woman was killed when she was hit by ice falling from her house in Quebec's Beauce region and three people died in Venise-en-Quebec near the U.S. border when fire destroyed their home.

Nearly one million hydro subscribers in Quebec are still without power—down from 1.4 million at the height of the ice-storm last week. The freak weather collapsed about 40 per cent of the province's electricity system.

Ontario crews made significant progress reconnecting customers in the Ottawa area during the weekend—about 8,000 are still without power, down from 60,000 late Friday.

But most of the city of Kingston, Ont., is still in the dark, as are several other smaller cities in the eastern part of the province.

About 80,000 people in rural Ontario have no electricity and may have to wait weeks before they get it.

In more remote towns and villages, the hydro system has been completely destroyed and drinking water, fuel and other essential supplies have run out.

In New Brunswick, utility crews were still busy repairing damage left by the storm. By nightfall yesterday, about 7,000 people in the southwestern corner of the province were facing their fourth night without power—down from 26,000 at the start of the weekend.

In Nova Scotia's Annapolis Valley, the other area of the Maritimes badly hit, only 1,000 customers were still without power.

VIA Rail restored partial passenger service yesterday, reopening routes between Toronto and Kingston and Halifax and Montreal. But the busier routes—Montreal–Toronto, Ottawa–Montreal, and Ottawa–Toronto—remain closed.

As Operation Recuperation grows, the army is sending more troops from every base in Canada to the troubled regions today. By tonight, there will be more than 8,000 troops in and around Montreal and about 3,400 in Eastern Ontario.

Troops are performing a variety of tasks including purifying water and taking generators door-to-door warming houses and providing dairy farmers with the power they need to milk cows.

Responding to a request from the Department of National Defence, the United States Air Force airlifted generators and other heavy equipment by a giant C-17 transport plane into Montreal late yesterday.

The Department of National Defence has also rented two Soviet-built Antonov transport planes at a total cost of about $600,000.

"This is by far the biggest deployment in our history to deal with a disaster in Canada," Defence Minister Art Eggleton said yesterday.

"It is a massive operation and cold weather coming into the region will further complicate matters."

General Maurice Baril, chief of defence staff, said the hardest-hit areas were "like Sarajevo minus the bullets."

SIDEBARS

Sidebars are separate stories that describe developments related to a major event. They are used to break long, complicated stories into shorter, more easily understood ones or to report information of secondary importance. Sidebars can give readers additional information about the main topic, usually from a different source or perspective. They can provide background information, explain a topic's importance, or describe the scene, emphasizing its colour and mood. If fire destroys a nightclub, news organizations might publish or broadcast a sidebar in which survivors describe how they escaped. When a new pope is selected, sidebars could describe his personality, past assignments, philosophy, and trips to Canada. Other sidebars might describe problems confronting churches throughout the world or review the history of a controversial issue. The following example includes one main story (on the rise of public interest in alternative treatments for cancer) and one sidebar, a set of "quick facts" on alternative therapies generally, highlighting some of the most publicized.

MONTREAL (CP)—For years, critics of orthodox cancer treatments have charged that a multibillion-dollar cancer industry suppresses alternative therapies.

Many believe the controversy owes its persistence to the "failure" of orthodox treatments.

"What's fuelling the whole debate is that orthodox methods have failed miserably...in terms of treatment, it's a stalemate situation at best," said Ralph Moss, author of *The Cancer Industry* and former assistant director of public affairs for the Memorial Sloan-Kettering cancer centre in New York.

"After all, you don't see too many unorthodox treatments for polio."

Many alternative therapies are based on strengthening the body's immune system rather than destroying malignant tissue. They are sometimes used in Mexico, the Bahamas and alternative clinics in the United States.

However, radiation, chemotherapy and surgery remain the only "proven" treatments and the only ones covered under government and private health-care insurance plans.

"With chemotherapies, which are given to the vast majority of people with cancer, we clearly have no evidence of survival benefit for 80 per cent of people taking them," said Frank Wiewel, executive director of People Against Cancer.

"Chemotherapy is the snake oil of the '90s," said Wiewel, whose Iowa-based patient advocate group distributes information about alternative treatments to thousands of members around the world. "It is for all practical purposes an unproven therapy used for profit—the U.S. Senate's own definition of quackery."

DOCTOR SHOCKED

"That's incredible," said Dr. Jack Laidlaw, medical director of the Canadian Cancer Society, referring to Wiewel's assessment of chemotherapy as quackery.

"I don't have in my head the information which would tell me if the 80-per-cent figure is correct, but I'd be very surprised if the situation were that bad."

Laidlaw said chemotherapy has proved highly effective against some cancers, including testicular, Hodgkin's (cancer of the lymph glands) and acute childhood leukemia, which today has a five-year survival rate of 73 per cent compared with five per cent in the 1960s.

Yet even some mainstream medical practitioners concede traditional treatments have not been as successful as hoped in treating all patients diagnosed with the more common cancers, among them lung, colon, breast and prostate.

Overall cancer statistics paint a grim picture: 50 per cent of patients won't survive beyond five years, said Laidlaw, noting that cancer is "increasing faster than any other disease," with 110,000 new cases a year in Canada.

But Laidlaw doesn't believe alternative therapies are suppressed: "I have no evidence that that's so in Canada...and I can't believe the same isn't true in the States.

"It's very rare that people touting these new kinds of therapies are studying them in ways recognized by authorities."

But obtaining government approval for a new drug is a lengthy and costly process, taking up to 10 years and costing $200 million to $500 million.

"It's all based on an evaluation procedure that can only be undertaken by (the largest) five or six pharmaceutical companies (in the United States)," Wiewel said.

Meanwhile, numerous alternatives languish untested on the American Cancer Society's Unproven Methods of Cancer Management list.

Case study evidence citing the effectiveness of alternative therapies is often rejected as "anecdotal."

"When you hear about an unproven treatment, all that could mean—and usually does mean—is that no one has attempted to prove it," said Harris Coulter, an expert and author on alternative medicine. "So it's a self-fulfilling prophecy: no one will ever get the money to test them."

Some critics say the public is misled by selectively cited statistics that underplay the failures of orthodox treatments.

Epidemiologist John Bailar, formerly with the National Cancer Institute in Washington and now at McGill University, says the statistics "from NCI and other official agencies are accurate.

"The problem is they're used selectively by people who have a stake in coming to one or another conclusion."

Bailar, former editor of the NCI's professional journal, still advocates "the earliest possible conventional treatment. There is no doubt that there has been major progress against certain kinds of cancer.

"At the same time, there have been some real losses—the death rates and incidence rates are going up."

He believes that despite billions of dollars spent over decades seeking a cure, the war on cancer has been lost.

"For a long time we believed treatment was the way to solve this problem; it hasn't worked," he said.

"It's time to take a whole new approach—and start getting serious about prevention."

QUICK FACTS

The following briefly describes six of the best-known practitioners of unorthodox cancer therapies in the last several decades. The therapies, among the 70 included in the American Cancer Society's list of unproven methods, remain controversial and the subject of ongoing legal battles to provide or prevent access to them.

Lawrence Burton, PhD—Immuno-Augmentative Therapy (IAT), an immune enhancing serum developed from Burton's original discovery in the 1950s of a tumour-inhibiting factor extracted from the larvae of fruit flies. Burton left the U.S. in 1977 and operates a clinic in Freeport, Grand Bahamas.

Stanislaw Burzynski, MD, PhD—Antineoplaston therapy, a cancer-inhibiting chemical derived from urinary peptides. (Peptides are small chains of amino acids, the building blocks of proteins.) Operates a clinic in Houston, Texas.

Max B. Gerson, MD—Elaborate dietary regimen (including liver juice) and detoxification program (involving coffee enemas). Gerson treated Albert Schweitzer, who called him "an eminent medical genius." Gerson clinic continues operation in Tijuana, Mexico, since his death in 1959.

Harry M. Hoxsey—The Hoxsey herbal method, employing herbal remedies for external and internal use. Clinics banned in the U.S. in 1960. Hoxsey died in 1974. Tijuana clinic run by his longtime chief nurse Mildred Cates (Nelson), RN.

Virginia Livingston Wheeler, MD—Immunological therapy based on her theories about the possible microbial origin of cancer, coupled with dietary regimen and vaccine. Livingston Wheeler operates a medical clinic in San Diego, California.

Gaston Naessens—Inventor of somatoscope, a microscope using ultraviolet and laser beam technology, which can examine living blood for evidence of degenerative disease up to two years before the onset of symptoms. At his laboratory near Sherbrooke, Que., produces 714X, an injectable non-toxic liquid that strengthens the immune system.

News organizations also use sidebars to report local angles to national and world stories. In the days following the September 11, 2001, terrorist attacks in the United States, news organizations across this country were finding local angles. Here are excerpts from a sampling of such sidebar stories taken from Canadian daily newspapers in the days after the attacks:

"Canadians working in New York City react with shock to the carnage at the World Trade Center." *Vancouver Sun*, September 11, 2001

Catastrophe in America

Mike Warner, a recent University of B.C. commerce graduate who moved to New York City last month to take a dream job on Wall Street, began his morning watching the World Trade Center towers explode across the street.

Warner, 24, said everything was normal when he arrived for work at 8 a.m. at the Merrill Lynch investment bank in the World Financial Center, located across the street from the World Trade Center towers.

"People on Wall Street were going to work as if it were any other business day. I sat at my desk on the sixth floor, where I have a view of the World Trade Center twin towers immediately next door. Sometime before 9 a.m., there was a sudden shudder, as though something had just broken the sound barrier. My co-workers and I rushed to the window, and heard a rumour that a plane had hit the South Tower. We were all a little shaken, but—if you can believe it—we went back to work, assuming that this was an isolated and accidental incident.

"Eighteen minutes later, a second shudder rocked through the air. A second plane had hit the North Tower. Some of my female workers began to scream, and my co-workers and I realized that this was no accident.

"There was a rush for the doors.

"Everybody at Merrill Lynch evacuated the World Financial Center by way of the stairs. As I stepped outside, I couldn't believe what I saw. The North Tower had a huge gash in its side, literally in the shape of the plane that had hit it. It was something out of a movie. A huge hole in what was probably the most important building on this planet.

"Surprisingly, New Yorkers were incredibly calm. People with strollers walked within blocks of the flaming towers. We assumed this was the end of it. All subways and public transport were shut down, so I walked home towards my apartment on West 21st Street.

"As I walked, I heard radio reports of other events unfolding—the plane crashes at the Capitol and the Pentagon. I wondered what could possibly be next. I heard crazy people wandering through the streets, yelling and warning of World War Three. I am not a pessimistic individual…but then I wondered if they might be right.

"I tried to reach my family on my cell phone to let them know I was alive, but every New Yorker was trying to do the same. Every pay phone in lower Manhattan had a lineup.

"Fire trucks, ambulances, and general traffic chaos everywhere. I finally arrived home, turned on my TV and sent out an email to tell my family and friends that I was alive. And that's when the most shocking news story hit the TV at 10:30 a.m.: the World Trade Center twin towers—collapsed—GONE!!! Hundreds of casualties who hadn't escaped in time, possibly thousands. Bodies flying out of windows and debris surrounding Lower Manhattan.

"I can see a thick brown cloud from my window [at his home]. I still feel sick to my stomach.

"At this moment, all I can feel is total shock. I cannot believe this has happened. I came to New York to pursue a new and exciting career, in the most stable economic climate in the world, or so I thought.

"I wanted to be at the centre of the world's action. If only I had known."

"It started with a scream: A special report on the effect of the terrorist attacks on ordinary people around the globe." *National Post*, September 12, 2001

It was the sound of screaming jet engines that caught David McKenzie's attention. It was 8:48 a.m., and the streets around the World Trade Center were crowded with men and women arriving for work. "Everyone turned and looked up," the 34-year-old research director at a New York options trading firm would later recall. "We could see a huge explosion. There was debris raining down everywhere, shooting out of the 80th floor, all over the place. White office papers, ticker tape, building insulation. I had to squint to see in front of me because there was so much dust. Everyone in the street, including me, turned and ran."

Meanwhile, on the 103rd floor of the World Trade Center's south tower, Clyde Ebanks, an insurance executive, started to the sound of his boss's voice. "Look at that!" his supervisor exclaimed.

Mr. Ebanks had his back to the window, so he caught only the last terrible moment before a full-sized United Airlines jet struck the tower adjacent to him. Flame and smoke poured out the windows around the 80th floor.

It was an unthinkable, unprecedented event, and emergency crews and media immediately sped to the southern tip of the island. The streets filled with the sound of sirens and honking traffic, as the radio and television stations opened up live coverage with reports from the scene. Witnesses who suggested the plane appeared to have been flown intentionally into the tower were cautioned by radio hosts not to leap to conclusions.

Within 18 minutes, it became clear those suspicions were valid. A second airliner, a twin-engine Boeing 767, made for the centre's south tower as television viewers around the world watched in disbelief. At 9:03, the plane plowed into the building near the 67th floor, crashing through the south face with such force it blew out windows and sent a ball of flame out the north side.

Within, there was confusion or horror, depending on where you were. Thirty-three floors below the first crash, Peter Dicerbo of the First Union National Bank teetered as the building rocked beneath his feet. "It knocked me on the floor," he later recalled. "It sounded like a big roar, then the building started swaying. That's what really scared me."

Anne Prosser, 29, rode the elevator high in the north tower, where her global banking office was. As the doors opened, she heard what seemed like an explosion. She didn't know it, but the first plane had just collided with the building, just a few floors above her.

"I got thrown to the ground before I got to our suite," she said. "I crawled inside. Not everybody was at work." She said she tried to leave, but there was so much debris in the air she could not breathe. Rescue workers finally steered her to a stairway.

Jessica Escalera, 22, who worked in a mail room on the 39th floor, had just finished breakfast at her desk when "the floor went up." As she put it: "It swelled up and then swayed back and forth. I thought it was an earthquake or a bomb. We were all panicking. We didn't know what to do."

"Former P.G. man watched as plane hit World Trade Center." *Prince George Citizen*, September 13, 2001

The day after terrorist attacks toppled the World Trade Center on Tuesday, people in Prince George, especially those with family in New York, were still recovering from the shock.

A city woman is trying to figure out how, and if, she'll be able to join her daughter, who is scheduled to deliver a baby within days in New York.

One thing Bev Ramage knows for sure: She couldn't be more thankful she knew right away her son, Steven Brooks, who works in a building that's part of the World Trade Center complex, was alive and well.

Steven's brother Michael had died tragically at age 14 in a car accident in front of College Heights Secondary School in September 1986. Ramage said she doesn't even want to imagine what she'd have done if she'd lost her other son. "I think I said to myself a thousand times, 'Thank God,'" said Ramage. "It's pretty traumatic for everybody, even now."

Brooks, who watched the first jet crash into the World Trade Center towers, called his mom at 6 a.m. on his cell phone to say he was OK.

Brooks, 30, is an accountant for Deloitte Touche in the World Financial Center next to the World Trade Center, but for the first time in months he was out of the office on his way to visit a client in New Jersey. The former College Heights Secondary School student watched with confusion and then horror from his car when he saw a second fireball erupt in the twin 110-storey towers of the Trade Center.

"I was lucky," Brooks said Wednesday from his home in Hoboken, N.J., just across the Hudson River from Manhattan. "The train I usually take to work goes to the World Trade Center. I'd be walking through that building at that time."

Brooks, who had recently been promoted, had been set to attend a reception on the 102nd floor of the Trade Center on Tuesday night.

Sidebars are usually briefer than the main news stories and are placed next to them in a newspaper or just after them in a newscast. If, for some reason, the sidebars must run on a different page of a newspaper or later in a newscast, editors or producers will tell the audience where or when the related stories will appear. Because some people read or view only the sidebars, most briefly summarize the main stories even when the two stories are close together.

CHECKLISTS FOR WRITING SPECIALIZED STORIES

Brights

1. Choose either an inverted-pyramid style or a suspended-interest style for the story.
2. If you use a suspended-interest approach, write a lead that will intrigue readers without revealing the bizarre or amusing twist the story takes at the end.

Followups

1. Write a followup each time something newsworthy develops in a continuing story.
2. Stress the new developments in the lead and body of the story.
3. Summarize the important background and earlier developments.

Roundups

1. Emphasize the most important or unique incident or development in the lead.
2. Explain in the lead what is common to all the incidents reported in the roundup.
3. Organize facts and quotations by topic, not by source.

Sidebars

1. Focus the lead on background, colour, mood, or some other aspect of the story different from the one emphasized in the lead to the main story.
2. Summarize the news event described in the main story.

The Writing Coach

SIDEBAR, YOUR HONOUR

By Paul Benedetti

Q: When should text be broken out?

A: That's not an easy question, because every story is unique, but there are some general guidelines.

A sidebar is generally, though not always, used to manage content that might interrupt the flow of your story, that adds another element to the story, or that more effectively stands alone. Let's look at each possibility.

If you have information that is important but does not fit easily into the story you are telling—for example, historical background, legal explanations, or the terms of an agreement or treaty—it could go into a sidebar. Say you are writing a feature about the battle to preserve a famous local tavern. You may want to break out a list of the building's past owners so the names don't clutter up your story.

Content that adds another element can be as simple as a profile of a great character or an anecdote that you don't want to lose but that doesn't quite fit your story. If you are writing about treating prostate cancer, you might have a short sidebar on one man's battle with the disease or a brisk profile of the doctor who perfected a specific treatment.

What kind of content is more effective standing alone, outside the frame of your story? A glossary of terms might be a great sidebar, particularly in a science or medical story. The actual text of a court ruling or a proposed government bill might be a helpful sidebar to readers. A list of the "players" in the story or a "who's who" is often a good sidebar. A timeline of events may free you up from cluttering your story with dates. Lists, such as dos and don'ts, are often great sidebars because they distil the key messages of your story in a handy way for readers.

Finally, write a sidebar if your editor asks you to! Many feature assignments come with a request for a sidebar or two.

CHARACTER SKETCH

By Paul Benedetti

Q: What do I need to ask a profile subject?

A: The personal profile is one of the most common feature stories assigned and written. Whether you are writing a quick 600-word snapshot of a local businessman or a comprehensive 6,000-word portrait of the prime minister, you need to cover the basics. Too many young reporters come away from a two-hour interview with a subject without some very basic facts. Here's a list of must-haves for a good profile:

1. First, last, and middle name. (Spelled correctly!)
2. Age: If your source refuses, get an approximate age, or use other sources to confirm the date of birth. (Date of birth is important especially if your story may not be published for several weeks or months.)
3. Birthplace: the city or town where the source grew up; where the source now lives.
4. Schools attended; degrees gained. (You may not need all this, but it's important to have it.)
5. Some information about family: mother's and father's occupations; number of brothers and sisters, etc.
6. Marital status: single, married or divorced. Children? This may be crucial or tangential, depending on the kind of profile you are writing, but not knowing these facts is unacceptable.

7. Current job and job title—exactly. Check whether there is more than one. Some people hold multiple jobs and have several titles (for example, Doctor Moira Jones, associate professor of Plastic Surgery at Smithfield University and head of the Reconstructive and Plastic Surgery Department at Mount Vernon Hospital.)

8. Interests, sports, hobbies, etc. Again, this may not make it into the story depending on the length and focus, but if your subject just climbed Mount Everest in her spare time, you'll be happy you asked.

Sometimes, profile interviews are difficult. People are often guarded with their answers, fearful of how they will be represented in your story. Sometimes their answers are short, clipped and colourless. Here are a few questions designed to kick-start a profile interview. Try them—you may be surprised at the answers you get.

- What's the most important thing your father/mother taught you?

- What will you be doing 10 years from now?

- If you weren't a doctor/CEO/teacher, what would you be doing?

- What's the worst thing that ever happened to you?

- What book(s) are you reading right now? What's the best book you read this year?

- What's the most important thing you've learned in life?

- Do you believe in God?

- What was your first job? What was your worst job?

- Who is the person who most influenced you? Why?

- What was the best day of your life?

- If you were reading your own obituary, what would you like it to say?

SUGGESTED READINGS AND USEFUL WEBSITES

Berton, Pierre. 2003. *The Joy of Writing: A Guide for Writers Disguised as a Literary Memoir.* Toronto: Doubleday Canada.

Boynton, Robert, ed. 2005. *The New New Journalism: Conversations with America's Best Nonfiction Writers on Their Craft.* New York: Vintage Books.

Cappon, René. 1989. *The Word: An Associated Press Guide to Good News Writing.* The Associated Press.

Ellis, Sherry. 2009. *Now Write! Nonfiction: Memoir, Journalism, and Creative Nonfiction Exercises from Today's Best Writers and Teachers.* New York: Tarcher.

Emerson, Connie. 1993. *The 30-Minute Writer: How to Write and Sell Short Pieces.* Cincinnati: Writers Digest Books.

Fensch, Thomas. 1988. *Writing Solutions: Beginnings, Middles, and Endings.* Mahwah, NJ: Lawrence Erlbaum.

Fetherling, George, ed. 2001. *The Vintage Book of Canadian Memoirs.* Toronto: Random House of Canada.

Franklin, Jon. 1994. *Writing for Story: Craft Secrets of Dramatic Nonfiction by a Two-Time Pulitzer Prize Winner.* New York: Penguin/Plume.

Shapiro, Ivor, ed. 2009. *The Bigger Picture: Elements of Feature Writing.* Toronto: Emond Montgomery Publications.

"The Working Journalist." 2008. *The Canadian Press Stylebook: A Guide for Writers and Editors*, 15th edn. Patti Tasko, ed. Toronto: The Canadian Press.

Anthologies of Literary Journalism from the Banff Centre:
www.banffcentre.ca/literaryjournalism

How to Write Brights:
http://www.custom-essay.net/
PROFESSIONAL-FEATURE-WRITING/
essay-writing-BRIGHTS-QUIPS.htm

How to Write Sidebars:
http://www.longridgewritersgroup.com
/rx/wc02/phyllis_ring_sidebars.shtml

CHAPTER 12

EXERCISE 1   Specialized Types of Stories

Brights

Use the following information to write "brights," a series of short stories, taking care not to reproduce any errors (e.g., spelling, style) that might appear in the information. Write some brights with a summary lead and others with a surprise ending. Brights are often humorous, but they don't have to be. Stories about people who love unusual occupations or who have overcome difficulties, for example, also make great brights. One newspaper writer told the story of a woman, Lucy Hinkle, who had both qualities. Hinkle owns a business that cleans animal waste from the lawns of her customers, a business she began after she contracted a rare muscle disease that ended her first career as a dental assistant.

1. Squirrels

University officials are blaming squirrels for a rash of problems students, teachers, and staff members have been experiencing with their cars. One person whose car has been damaged by squirrels is Oliver Brooks, an associate professor of English. One of the headlights in his van went out a few weeks ago. He replaced it, but it still didn't work. When he opened the hood, however, he was surprised to find a squirrels nest. "There was a big squirrels nest in the corner where the light wires were," he said. Brookes spent $184 to get the wiring replaced. Linda Kasparov, university dietitian, had a similar experience. She was driving home one night when the headlights, speedometer, and oil-pressure gauge on her new sedan all quit working. She pulled into a service station and asked the attendant what was wrong. She said, "The attendant put up the hood and then jumped back exclaiming, 'My God, what have you got in there!'" She said there was a nest made of sticks, string, and plastic bags. One of the bags started moving, and when the attendant pulled it out, he discovered three baby squirrels. The squirrels had chewed through every wire in the engine compartment except two. The repair bill for Kasparov was $425. Laura Ruffenboch, a wildlife professor at the university, said the insulation on many electrical wires is made from a soybean derivative, and the squirrels may find that attractive. She also said it was unusual for squirrels to make nests in cars that are used regularly.

2. Misdirected Love

Joseph R. DeLoy told the judge today that he's in love. DeLoy, 26, said he loves a 29-year-old woman, Patty McFerren. DeLoy met McFerren while they were both shopping at a supermarket in the city. DeLoy asked McFerren for a date. McFerren refused. "But she was wonderful, and I could tell she really liked me, so I called her," DeLoy said. In fact, DeLoy tried to call McFerren more than 200 times, sometimes in the middle of the night. However, it wasn't really her number that he called. By mistake, he got the wrong number and called Patrick McFerren instead. The two McFerrens are unrelated and do not know each other. Their listings in the phone book are very similar. Patty is listed as "P. McFerren." Patrick is listed as "P.J. McFerren." Patrick informed DeLoy that he was dialling the wrong number. DeLoy said he didn't believe him and continued to call. "I was hoping that she'd answer," DeLoy said in court today. Patrick installed an answering machine so he could screen the calls, and the machine got a heavy workout. Finally, Patrick called the police, and they told DeLoy to stop making the calls, but no charges were filed against him. The calls continued, so Patrick sued, accusing DeLoy of intentional infliction of emotional distress and invasion of privacy. The calls were a costly mistake for DeLoy. In court today, DeLoys lawyer explained that his client was acting "on his heart and hormones, not his head." A jury of 5 men and 7 women decided that his calls were worth $25 each—for a total of $5,000. The jury ordered DeLoy to pay that sum—$5,000—to Patrick. "I'm satisfied," Patrick said.

3. Underage Driver

Charles Todd Snyder was charged with drunk driving following a traffic accident in your city one week ago. He was also charged with driving without a drivers licence in his possession. He was scheduled to appear in court at 9 a.m. this morning. He failed to appear in court. As a consequence, Judge Edward Kocembra ordered police to go to Snyders home and to haul Snyder into court. Police went to the address Snyder had given officers at the time of the accident: 711 Broadway Avenue. The police returned to the court at approximately 10:15 a.m. and appeared before Judge Kosembra with Snyder. Snyder was in his mothers arms. He is a 13-month-old child, and his mother insisted that he drinks only milk and that the only vehicle he ever drives is a stroller. So the judge apologized for the inconvenience and told the officers to give Snyder and his mother a ride back to their home. Snyder, apparently frightened by the unfamiliar surroundings and people, cried. Police said that whoever was stopped had falsely given the arresting officers Snyders name and address when he signed the drunken driving ticket and the ticket for driving without a drivers licence in his possession. They told the judge that they have no idea who that person might be.

4. Truck Theft

There was a motor vehicle theft which occurred in the city at some time in the middle of last night. The vehicle was taken from a building located at 7720 Avonwood Dr. The building was unlocked at the time, and 12 occupants sleeping in an upstairs room said they heard nothing unusual. They were all in bed by midnight and the first got up at 6 a.m., discovering the theft at that time. Police describe the missing vehicle as a bright canary-yellow fire truck, marked with the name of the city fire department. The custom-made truck cost a total of $192,000 and was delivered to the city just three months ago. Firemen said it had a full tank of gas, about 50 gallons. However, it gets only 1.5 miles to the gallon. It contained enough clothing and equipment for six firefighters, a dozen oxygen tanks, 1,000 feet of hose, four ladders (each up to 60 feet tall), plus miscellaneous other equipment. The people sleeping upstairs were all firefighters and the building was a fire station. The firefighters suspect that someone opened the stations main door, then either pushed or towed the truck silently outside and started its engine some distance away from the building. It is the first time in its history that the city fire department has reported that one of its trucks has been stolen. It was not insured. The keys are always left in the truck to reduce the response time when firefighters receive a call for help.

5. Burglar's Escape

Marilyn and Ralph Kubick returned to their home at 1456 North Third Street last night and found a surprise. There was a woman in their house, a stranger they did not recognize, and she was going through the desk in Marylin's home office. The stranger was wearing dark blue jeans and a black hooded sweatshirt with the hood over her head. Mrs. Kubick uses the desk mostly for her writing, but she told you later when you interviewed her, "I keep some extra cash in the top left drawer for emergencies. This woman found it and was stuffing it in a bag when we found her. The bag—it was one of the pillow cases from our bed—already had some stuff in it. Later, we found she had already grabbed all of my jewelry and Ralph's coin collection." Marilyn said as soon as they saw the burglar, Ralph shouted, "Call the cops!" and Marilyn ran to the kitchen phone to call. Ralph said he moved around the left side of the desk hoping to trap the burglar in the office and keep her there until police arrived. "She was sure nimble, though. She juked like an NFL running back and got past me. I grabbed the back of her sweatshirt as she slipped by me. She dropped the bag of loot, but I had a fistful of her clothes and I didn't intend to let go. She was strong, though, and she spun around and twisted and wiggled until she had worked her way out of her sweatshirt, blouse and brassiere. Then she ran out through the front door. I was so astonished I just stood there for a half minute or so. By the time I went to the door to see where she went, she was gone." Officer George Ruis, the police officer who responded to the Kubicks' call, said a neighbour reported seeing a person wearing no shirt get into a Toyota that was about

10 years old and drive away rapidly. The neighbour was not sure whether the topless person was a male or female. Ruiz said the Kubicks described the burglar as Caucasian, about five and a half feet tall, weighing about 120 lbs. She had light brown hair that was pulled into a bun at the back of her head. She also had a small tattoo on her right shoulder blade of a spider or a crab.

6. Bank Regulations

Abraham Burmeister is president of the First National Bank, the largest bank in your community. Each year, in accordance with new federal laws, the bank is required to send all its customers copies of some complex new federal rules concerning the regulation of banks and the procedures followed for money transfers by means of electronic banking. Consequently, the First National Bank prepared a 4,500-word pamphlet describing and summarizing those new federal rules and then sent copies of the rules to all its 40,000 regular depositors and customers. Like many other bankers, Burmeister objected to the federal law, saying it imposed a needless burden and needless expense on bankers since the federal laws that banks are being forced to explain are too complicated for the average person to understand and too dull and uninteresting for people to spend time trying to read. To prove his point, on the last page of 100 of the 40,000 copies of the rules he took a gamble and inserted a special extra sentence. The sentence said, "If you return this pamphlet to any of the banks tellers within the next 30 days, they will give you $50." The 30 days passed yesterday and not one person turned in a single copy of the 100 special pamphlets and requested the $50 due on demand, apparently because no one read the pamphlets. Bank officials calculated that it cost somewhere in the neighbourhood of $25,000 to prepare, print, address, and mail the pamphlets to the 40,000 bank customers, and they said that is a waste of money, yet they must do it every year, even though obviously no one reads the things, as they have just proven with their interesting little experiment.

7. Drunken Rider

Lynita L. Sharp admits she was intoxicated last night but says she should not be charged with drunk driving. Sharp was riding her 2-year-old filly horse along a provincial highway when Scott Forsyth, a local police officer in the sheriff's department, came along. Forsyth said he saw Sharp sitting on her horse in the middle of the road. He said the rider looked to be sick or asleep. He turned on the blue lights on his cruiser, and the horse bolted off. Sharp said she was spending the weekend with her friends who own the farm where her horse is stabled. She had spent part of the evening at the local bar and was riding home. Sharp said the cruisers light spooked the horse and caused her to lose control of it. Forsythe issued Sharp a ticket for operating a vehicle while under the influence of an intoxicating substance. Sharp said her horse, Frosty, is not a vehicle. "Vehicles can't think, but Frosty can think for herself," Sharp said. "I've fallen asleep in the saddle before, but it doesn't matter because Frosty knows the way home." Donald Hendricks, the assistant county attorney, said that the law does not require that a person be operating a motorized vehicle in order to be cited for drunk driving. The law was changed in 1991, he said, and since then 23 people who were not operating motorized vehicles, including a bicyclist and a man in a wheelchair, have been arrested for driving while intoxicated.

EXERCISE 2   Specialized Types of Stories

Followup Stories

Write a story summarizing the initial set of facts and then just the lead for a followup story about the later developments. Or your instructor might ask you to write a complete news story about each day's developments. Be sure to correct any errors of grammar, spelling and style in the notes.

Yesterday

Two boys were playing in Nichols Lake in Lakeside Park in your town. They were wading along the shore of the lake at about 12 noon at a point where the bottom drops off steeply. The two boys were Randy Stockdale, age 9, son of George and Lillian Stockdale, and Edward McGorwan, age 10, son of Karen McGorwan. Edward waded too far from shore, lost his footing, and was unable to get back to shore. He and Randy started to yell for help. A man whose name has not been released by police heard their screams and ran to the lake to help. James Kirkman, a cab driver who was taking his lunch break in the park, heard the screams, too. He radioed his dispatcher who called 911. Kirkman said later that the unidentified man waded out as far as he could and tried to reach out to Edward, but the boy had drifted too far from shore. "When the boy went under and didn't come back up for air, this guy dove under to find him. But he didn't come back up, either," Kirkman said. Police Officers Kevin Barlow and Eddie Linn arrived on the scene at 12:18. Barlow immediately stripped to his shorts and started diving into the lake to find the victims. After several dives, he came back up with Edward McGorwan, who was unconscious. Linn tried to resuscitate the boy, but he was still unconscious when he was taken by ambulance to the Regional Medical Centre. Barlow continued to search for the unidentified man for another 20 minutes until Dorothy Heslin, a scuba diver who assists the police on a volunteer basis, arrived. She pulled him from the water about 1:15 p.m. Wayne Svendson, a paramedic, tried to resuscitate the man. Svendson said the water was unusually cold and hypothermia had set in, which was indicated by the fact the mans skin had started to turn blue. The man was taken to the Regional Medical Centre. Dr. Catrina Lowrie, a physician at the Medical Centre, said the man was pronounced dead when he arrived. She also said that Edward McGorwan was in critical condition. Officer Barlow also was treated at Regional Medical Centre for minor shock caused by the long period of time he spent in the water looking for the victims. He was released that afternoon.

Today

This morning, the police department released the name of the man who died trying to save Edward McGorwan from Nichols Lake. His name is William McDowell and he is an unemployed housepainter. He was 30 years old. Police Chief Barry Kopperud said, "McDowell risked his life without hesitation to try to save someone in trouble. He was a real hero." Also this morning, Dr. Lowrie at the Regional Medical Centre announced that Edward McGorwan had died. "He spent the night on a respirator, but his condition did not improve. This morning, at his mothers request, we took Edward off the respirator. He died less than half an hour later." McDowells sister lives in your town. Her name is Janice Carson. She said her brother had dropped out of Colonial High School one year before graduating and joined the navy. He spent six years in the navy and after he left he held a succession of jobs, including electronics technician, cook, construction worker, and painter. She said he always enjoyed his jobs but was too restless to stay at one for more than a couple of years. "I guess some people would call him a drifter, but to me he was a free spirit. He loved people but he didn't want to be tied down with a house and a mortgage and all of that. There were only two things he never learned how to do. He couldn't hold a job for more than two years and he could never say no to anyone who needed help," she said with tears in her eyes.

CHAPTER 12

EXERCISE 3   Specialized Types of Stories

Followup Stories

Write a story summarizing the initial set of facts and then just the lead for a followup story about each of the later developments. Or your instructor might ask you to write a complete news story about each day's developments. Be sure to correct any errors of grammar, spelling and style in the notes.

Background

Years ago, tuberculosis ranked among the worlds most lethal diseases, and it remains a serious health problem in developing countries. The number of Canadians with tuberculosis has declined dramatically over the last half century. Basically, TB is a bacterial infection. It usually affects the respiratory system. It is spread through coughing, sneezing, singing, or talking. Because of advances in the field of medicine, it is rare for a death to occur because of TB. Modern treatment succeeds virtually 100 per cent of the time. Doctors can prescribe medications to stop the disease if the infection is detected early enough. However, TB can be fatal if undetected. Symptoms include a prolonged and unexplained cough, night sweats, and sudden weight loss. To test for TB, a small amount of dead bacteria is injected into the skin of the upper arm of a person. Health workers know there is an infection when natural anti-bodies, formed to fight the illness, respond to the dead bacteria, and harden the skin around the test area.

Original Story

Maureen Verdugo, principal of Van Horne High School, called a special assembly at the beginning of classes at the school today and made a startling announcement. Verdugo revealed to the students that a 16 year old student enrolled at the school, whose exact identity she in no way revealed, other than as a tenth grader, has been diagnosed as suffering from the disease tuberculosis. Verdugo continued on by announcing that city health officials were notified by the students doctor and will be available at the school all five days of classes next week to give free TB tests to every student enrolled in one of the 16 yr. olds classes, as well as to students known to be the victims friends. "Anyone else—students, faculty members, and school personnel—who fears they may have been infected will also be tested free of charge. The tests will be administered in the school clinic, and students will be excused from their study halls and other free periods to take the tests," Verdugo said. The clinic will be open from 7 am to 5 pm and people can also visit it before or after their classes. "I've been working in high schools for 30 years," Verdugo went on to say, "and this is the first time I've had a problem like this. But I want to reassure you that there's no reason for panic. We're taking all the necessary precautions and have the situation well under control."

Wednesday of the Next Week

On Monday and Tuesday of this week the citys Public Health Dept. had its personnel at the school, busily testing for tuberculosis students that may have come in contact with the infected 16 yr. old student enrolled in Van Horne High School. Initial tests were given free of charge at the school clinic. About 250 of the schools students were singled out by school authorities as having regular contact with the infected teen, either by being enrolled in the kids classes or by having some other close contact with the guy. Other students and teachers went in on their own. The testing is continuing and the final results will be announced sometime during the course of next week.

Of approximately three hundred students tested Monday and Tuesday, six showed signs of infection and were advised to have more testing done on them. "Infected students are being advised to undergo chest X rays and possibly sputum tests to determine whether they have developed TB," said Cathleen Graham, head of the citys Public Health Dept. "Those who are merely infected with the bacteria will be prescribed an antibiotic to prevent the onset of the disease. If the disease has progressed further, students will have to undergo more extensive drug therapy."

Some parents were frightened and dissatisfied. Tanaka Holland, mother of Sophomore Andrea Holland, said during an interview today: "When I called the school with some questions they were totally uncaring, and their procedures stink. Every student in the whole school should be tested. Just because a child wasn't in a class with the carrier doesn't mean he didn't come in contact with the disease," Mrs. Holland said. A second parent, James R. Waundry, agreed, adding, "This isn't anything to mess with. I've heard that people can die of tuberculosis, and how do we know that, uh, it's not going to come back? We've told our son, Paul, to stay home this week, and we're thinking of putting him in a private school."

Friday of the Following Week

In all, 581 Van Horne High School students were tested after learning that a 10th grade schoolmate had TB, Van Horne High School Principal Maureen Verdugo announced today. A total of 23 of the 581 students have tested positive for exposure to tuberculosis but none of the 23 has developed the disease. "The students are not contagious but must take antibiotics for six months to prevent the disease," said Joseph Perez, a health official employed by the city.

Greg Hubbard is the citys superintendent of schools. Hubbard said during a press conference today that he believes that this TB outbreak was the worst in the citys entire history. Hubbard said there is nothing the district can do to prevent occasional health problems like this one. "You're always subject to this kind of thing with the number of kids we have," he said. Health officials added that no one will ever know exactly how the outbreak started.

CHAPTER 12

| EXERCISE 4 | Specialized Types of Stories |

Roundups—Multiple Sources

Write a single news story that summarizes the following information. Organize the information in a clear, logical, cohesive manner. As you write the story, correct the spelling, style, grammatical and vocabulary errors. Also be thorough; report every issue in depth. Notice that the sources' comments appear in quotation marks, so you can quote them directly.

Background

The Sunnyview Retirement Home is an 8-storey brick building located at 410 Hillcrest Street in your community. The building is a former hotel. Ten years ago it was renovated and turned into apartments for retirees. It is privately operated, for profit, with 110 apartments, including 30 for a single resident and 80 for two residents, often couples, sharing an apartment. About 175 people were living there when a fire broke out at approximately 7:10 a.m. this morning. As many as 150 firefighters from throughout your region, including nearby communities, were called in for assistance in battling the blaze and assisting in rescuing all the victims from their peril.

Fire Chief Tony Sullivan

"Its the worst damn fire I've ever seen. We've got seven dead we know of and maybe 20 more that've been taken to hospitals with various injuries, some pretty serious. We just can't tell for sure. There could be lots more in the building, people who couldn't get out. I can't send my men in yet to look for them, not at this point, because its not safe. We've got the fire out, but it was a fierce one, and some floors and walls were weakened and are liable to collapse at any time. We may have to pull them down or they could fall on my men. It may be another day before we're able to make a thorough search and recover all the bodies."

Rescue Worker John Charlton

"People I've talked to say the fire started on the first or second floor. The fire itself wasn't so bad, except on the first couple of floors. Everything on those floors is gone. The fire didn't spread to the upper floors, but most of the deaths occurred up there. It was the smoke that did it. People said they couldn't breathe, and then a lot of them were old and in bad shape to begin with. We've taken the survivors that weren't hurt none to a church just across the street, and they're mostly resting there now. I don't know where they'll go tonight, where they'll sleep. The Red Cross is setting up an information centre for relatives at the church. We've, uh, got all sorts of relatives that've been in and out all morning, looking for their people and apparently bringing them home with them, so we don't know who's missing or dead or home safe with their families."

Retirement Home Director Mildred Anchall

"We don't know how the fire started, just that it started somewhere on the second floor, and our alarms sounded at 7. It happened so fast, it spread so fast, that all we could do was try and get everyone out. No one had time to stop and get a list of all our residents, and now they've been taken a half-dozen different places. We don't have any way of knowing who's safe and who's missing. Besides our residents, I've got my staff to worry about, and some visitors who were in the building. It's a tragedy, a real tragedy, something like this. You hear about things like this happening but never think it could happen at your home."

Building Inspector Ralph Schweitzer

"We inspected the building just a couple weeks ago, and it satisfies all our codes. When it was remodelled 10 years ago we didn't require sprinklers, and they would have saved everyone, would have put the fire out in a minute or two, so they would have really prevented a tragedy like this. Anyone building a nursing home today is required to put in sprinklers, and this is what we have in mind to prevent, a real serious tragedy like this one."

Survivor Steven Minh

"I'm 82, and I've been living here since it opened 10 years ago. Nothing like this ever happened here before. Its like I was back in World War II or something. I lived on the eighth floor, and people up there were screaming for help. The smoke was real bad, and some of us don't move so quick anymore. The firemen got up there real fast and led us down the stairs. There were some real heroes up there. I saw firemen carrying a half-dozen people down 6 or 8 flights of stairs when they could hardly breath themselves, and a lot of us would be dead without them. We couldn't have lasted much longer with the smoke and all. I'd just like to know what started the fire because it spread so fast. One minute everything was OK, then we were all choking on the smoke."

Survivor Betsy Aaron

"It was terrible in there. We began hearing fire alarms, but they weren't loud enough. By the time we realized what it was and went out into the hall it was full of smoke. I had a third-floor apartment, so I was able to get right out. I just took an elevator downstairs. Other people said they weren't working, but that must have been later, after I was out, that the elevators stopped working. When I got out on the street and looked up I saw people I knew leaning out their windows and shouting, 'Help me! Help me!' I couldn't do anything for them, not anything at all."

Fire Chief Marshal R.J. Hilton

"We haven't pinpointed the cause of the fire yet. It's too early, but my personal feelings are, strictly on a preliminary basis, it seems to have been an accidental fire that started in one of the apartments. It'll be at least a day or two before we have anything official on that."

EXERCISE 5   Specialized Types of Stories

Roundups—Multiple Events

Write a single roundup story that summarizes all three of the fires described next. Correct any errors of grammar, spelling, punctuation and style in the notes.

Fire 1

Two police officers patrolling Main St. reported a fire at Frishe's Bowling Alley, 4113 Main St., at 3:32 a.m. today. They smelled smoke, got out of their squad car, and traced the smoke to the bowling alley. Firefighters said the fire was confined to an office, where it caused an estimated $10,000 in damage. Firefighters found evidence of arson and notified police that the office apparently had been set on fire after it was burglarized. Two cigarette machines, a soft-drink machine, and a door leading to the office had been pried open. Police said the thieves probably set the fire to hide the robbery. Art Mahew, manager of the bowling alley, estimated that $20 was missing from the three machines and $50 was taken from a cash box in the office. He added: "That's all the money we keep in the building at night. Except for some change for the next day's business, we just don't keep any money in the building at night. It's too risky. This is the third robbery we've had since I started working here four years ago."

Fire 2

Firefighters were called to 1314 Griese Drive at 8:23 a.m. today. They found a fire in progress on the second floor of the two-storey home. The home is owned by Mr. and Mrs. Timothy Keele. Mr. and Mrs. Keele and their four children escaped from the home before firemen arrived. Firefighters extinguished the blaze within 20 minutes. The fire was confined to two upstairs bedrooms and the attic. Smoke and water damage were reported throughout the house. No one was injured. Damage was estimated at $20,000. Mrs. Keele told firemen she had punished one of her children for playing with matches in an upstairs closet earlier in the morning. Fire chiefs said the blaze started in that closet and attributed the fire to the child playing with matches. Mrs. Keele added that she was not aware of the fire until a telephone repairman working across the street noticed smoke, came over, and rang her doorbell. When she answered, he asked, "Do you know your house is on fire?"

Fire 3

Firefighters responded to a call at the Quality Trailer Court at 10:31 a.m. today after neighbours were alerted by screams from a trailer occupied by Mrs. Susan Kopp, age 71. Flames had spread throughout the trailer by the time firefighters arrived at the scene. The firefighters had to extinguish the blaze, then wait for the embers to cool before they were able to enter the trailer. They found Mrs. Kopp's body in her bedroom in the trailer. A spokesman for the Fire Department said she had apparently been smoking in bed, then awoke when her bedding caught fire. She died of suffocation before she could get out. Neighbours who heard her screams were unable to enter the trailer because of the flames, smoke, and heat.

EXERCISE 6   Specialized Types of Stories

Sidebars

Use the following information to write two separate stories: first a news story reporting the fire, then a sidebar based on the interviews with Mrs. Noffsinger.

Main Story

The Grande Hotel is located downtown at the corner of Manitoba and Barber Avenues. It is a seven-storey structure with a total of 114 rooms. It was constructed and opened for business in the year 1924. In recent years the hotel has been in an obvious state of decline, unable to compete with new facilities in the city and with the convenience of motels located along highways which now bypass the city. Many of the hotel rooms have been rented on long-term leases, often to elderly persons who like its downtown location, which is more convenient for them, since many facilities they use are in walking distance and buses are easily available for other trips they want to make. Three persons died in a fire at the hotel last night. The cause of the fire is undetermined. It started in a third-floor room. It spread and also destroyed the fourth, fifth, sixth, and seventh floors before it was brought under control at 4:30 a.m. today. At about 11 p.m. a guest called the lobby to report the odour of smoke. A hotel employee used a passkey to enter the third-floor room where the fire originated and found it totally engulfed in flames. The room is believed to have been vacant at the time. The employee sounded a fire alarm in the hotel and called firefighters. It was the first five-alarm blaze in the city in more than 10 years. Every piece of fire equipment in the city was rushed to the scene, and off-duty firefighters were called in to assist. Fortunately, said Fire Chief Tony Sullivan, no other fires were reported in the city at the same time or he would have had to send a truck and men from the scene of the hotel blaze. Hotel records indicate that 62 persons were registered in the hotel at the time the blaze initiated; 49 had long-term leases and 13 were transients. All the transients were located on the second floor and escaped safely. The dead, all of whom had long-term leases, have been identified as Mildred Haserot, age 58; Willie Hattaway, age 67; and Pearl Petchsky, age 47. The bodies of all three victims were found on the fourth floor, where they lived. Fire Chief Tony Sullivan said this morning the hotel is a total loss and that some walls are in danger of collapse. He said: "The fire was already out of hand when our first units reached the scene. I was called from home, and by then the flames were breaking out through the third- and fourth-floor windows. We were really lucky there weren't more people killed, but the hotel people knocked on the door of every room that was occupied to get everybody out. Most guests used a back stairway, and we were lucky the elevators kept working for awhile even after my men got into the building, otherwise the loss would have been worse. I'm also told that the top two floors were empty, and that helped keep down the loss of lives."

The Red Cross is caring for survivors, finding them new rooms and providing clothes and emergency allocations of cash, a total of $250 per person. Five people were injured, including one fireman who suffered from smoke inhalation. The others suffered from burns, some serious, and also from smoke inhalation. Three are being treated at Mercy Hospital. Two have been released, including the fireman. Their names and conditions are unknown at this time.

Sidebar

Nora Noffsinger, 74, has been a resident of the Grande Hotel for the past nine years. She paid $880 a month rent for one room on the fifth floor. A retired bookkeeper, she said afterward: "It was dreadfully expensive, but it was a charming old building and I had lots of good friends living there. I was asleep last night when I heard someone pounding on my door. I don't know who it was, but he told me to get out fast, and I did. All I had on were my pyjamas and a robe, but I could see the smoke, even up there on the fifth floor, and I was scared; I knew right away that it was bad. Everyone else was scared too, but we all knew what to do. We'd talked lots about what we'd do if there was ever a fire because you hear so often about fires in old hotels, and we wanted to be prepared. We all kept flashlights in our rooms and planned to go down the back stairway unless the fire was there, and it wasn't. The lights were still on, so we didn't even need our flashlights. Now the Red Cross put me in a motel room a few blocks away, and I guess I should be happy I'm safe, but I lost everything—my clothes, a little money I'd kept hidden in a secret place, all my photographs. My husband's dead, you know, and I lost all my pictures of him. I don't know what I'll do now; I don't have any children. I'm all by myself, except for my friends, and they all lived at the hotel with me."

13 | Libel, Privacy and Newsgathering Issues

Everyone has the following fundamental freedoms: a) freedom of conscience and religion; b) freedom of thought, belief, opinion and expression, including freedom of the press and other media of communication; c) freedom of peaceful assembly; and d) freedom of association.

— **Section 2b of the Canadian Charter of Rights and Freedoms**

The Charter's guarantee of "freedom of the press" has never afforded complete freedom to publish anything at any time. From the very beginning of the federation, courts have held that they may punish obscene or libellous expression. Although Section 2(b) of the Charter guarantees "freedom of the press," this freedom was never meant to be absolute. The first section of the Charter spells this out clearly: "The *Canadian Charter of Rights and Freedoms* guarantees the rights and freedoms set out in it subject only to such reasonable limits prescribed by law as can be demonstrably justified in a free and democratic society." Freedom is not synonymous with licence, and with freedom comes responsibility. Still, the Charter is a step in the right direction for substantive protection of a free press. Before the advent of the Charter (in 1982), there was no substantive protection: cases involving free-expression rights were decided on the basis of the Constitution's division of powers.

Communications law is a broad area involving many aspects of the mass media and a variety of legal principles. Journalism students usually investigate this subject in detail in specialized media law courses. This chapter introduces three areas of communications law that affect reporters almost daily: libel, privacy, and access to news. Libel and privacy are covered extensively because the danger of a lawsuit is high and the cost of defending or losing one can be great. Legal rights of access to news are also covered, although in less detail.

LIBEL

"Libel" is defamation by written words or by communication in some other tangible form, whereas "slander" is defamation by spoken words or gestures. A defamatory statement is an untrue and damaging statement about someone (i.e., an untrue statement to that someone's discredit).

Traditionally, the law has treated libel more harshly than slander because the written word is more permanent and can reach more people than the spoken word. Courts said that the greater power of written words to injure reputation justified harsher penalties and legal rules more favourable to libel plaintiffs than to slander plaintiffs.

One might think that broadcast defamation should be treated as slander because it is spoken, and some provinces do make that distinction, either by statute or by judicial interpretation. More commonly, however, courts treat broadcast defamation as libel because it can reach millions of listeners and be as durable as written defamation. Technological advances generally have allowed spoken words to be recorded and preserved in formats as durable as print, and in practice most jurisdictions refer to a single tort (or non-criminal injury) of defamation that covers both libel and slander. The rise of online communications has complicated the situation by facilitating dissemination of all kinds of messages (including libellous ones) to a potentially global audience.

Libel is a major concern for the mass media. People who feel injured by something in a broadcast, a newspaper story or an advertisement might be quick to sue. The costs of a lawsuit can be great. Damage awards in Canada tended to be modest until the late 1980s, when the Reichmann family brought a $102-million libel suit against *Toronto Life* magazine. More media organizations have been sued for libel since then, and the damages awarded to plaintiffs have been increasingly large.[1]

In the United States, juries have awarded millions of dollars to successful libel plaintiffs. The U.S. Media Law Resource Center surveyed 557 libel trial verdicts over a 26-year period and found that the average damage award by a jury to a plaintiff was $2.85 million, though often the figure was reduced by the trial judge or an appeals court. The average final award was a little more than $560,000. The largest jury award ever was $223 million—$200 million in punitive damages—against Dow Jones for a story published in the *Wall Street Journal*. That award was reduced by the judge and later set aside entirely because of misconduct by the plaintiffs.

Even when media organizations win libel suits, they still might spend hundreds of thousands of dollars on court costs and attorneys' fees. And libel suits place at risk not only the news organization's pocketbook but also its reputation. News organizations build their reputations on fairness and accuracy. A libel judgment blemishes that reputation, sometimes irreparably. Individual reporters, producers and editors also depend on their reputations for accuracy, thoroughness and responsibility. If they lose a libel suit, they could lose that reputation. They might even lose their jobs. For these reasons and others, journalists must know what constitutes libel and what defences can protect them in a libel suit.

The Elements of a Libel Suit

A plaintiff in a libel suit must establish a *prima facie* case by proving three things: (1) defamation, (2) identification or reference, and (3) publication.

Defamation

The essence of a libel suit is vindication of one's reputation. The plaintiff seeks to repair the damage done to his or her reputation by the publication of defamatory remarks. A defamatory statement is an untrue statement about someone that would, if taken to be true, injure the person's reputation, lowering him or her in the estimation of the community, deterring third persons from associating with that person, or exposing the person to hatred, contempt or ridicule. Some statements obviously have the power to injure reputations—for example, statements that a person has committed a crime, has a loathsome disease, is incompetent in her or his business, trade or profession, or has engaged in corruption, conflict of interest, or other serious misconduct. Once the *prima facie* case is established (i.e., the words have been published, identify the plaintiff, and would, if believed, injure the plaintiff's reputation), it is up to the jury (or judge sitting alone) in each case to determine whether defamation has actually occurred (that is, whether the complained of statements are in fact true). Defamation is an *untrue* statement about someone to that someone's discredit (a nasty lie); if the statement, no matter how nasty, is true, then no defamation has occurred (if what's published about a would-be plaintiff is demonstrably true, there would be no basis for a libel suit).

In Canada, the law of libel does not require the plaintiff to prove the allegedly defamatory statements false; instead, it requires the defendant to prove the truth of what was published. Thus, once a *prima facie* case is established, the burden of proof shifts to the defendant. Some critics have argued that this constitutes a "reverse onus" (since it reverses the presumption of innocence that is a cornerstone of the Canadian criminal justice system) and leads to "libel chill"—the idea that journalists will shy away from hard-hitting stories for fear of attracting a libel suit.

In 1997, a TV broadcaster lost his bid to argue that having the burden of proof rest with the defendant contravenes the Charter of Rights; the onus to disprove the truth of the allegedly libellous material, the broadcaster believed, should be on the plaintiff. In *Pressler v. Lethbridge*, the court disagreed. The judge ruled that "while freedom of public debate was very important, so also was reputation, and statements of fact did not contribute usefully to public debate unless they were true."[2]

Innuendo is culpable in libel law. In the case of *Thomas v. Canadian Broadcasting Corporation*, the CBC aired an investigative report on Dome Petroleum, which had acquired a government licence to drill for oil under the Beaufort Sea. The CBC report did not directly accuse the plaintiff of incompetence, conflict of interest or corruption in the matter; it did, however, imply by innuendo that the plaintiff had helped Dome Petroleum acquire its licence and that he was ultimately responsible for an explosion at the site that caused one death and for then moving to cover up the entire affair. The plaintiff sued and won. The court awarded aggravated damages "because of the CBC's failure to include in its broadcast information which it had in its possession and which tended both to be favourable to the plaintiff and to cast doubt on the CBC's interpretation of what had happened."[3]

In the more recent case of *Leenen v. Canadian Broadcasting Corp*, a doctor sued the national broadcaster after it ran a segment about nifedipine, a heart medication that was also being prescribed for hypertension. The judge in the case ruled that the doctor had been portrayed unfairly and that the CBC by innuendo had implied that the doctor ignored the possible dangers of the drug in prescribing it, received kickbacks from the drug company that produced the medication, and, as the chair of an advisory committee assessing the drug, acted dishonestly and with negligence. The doctor was awarded nearly a million dollars in damages, including aggravated and punitive damages, and leave to appeal to the Supreme Court of Canada was dismissed.[4]

Defamatory assertions can refer to corporations (and other legal entities, excluding governments), but in such cases, the allegedly defamatory statements must refer to the entity rather than to its individual owners, officers or employees, and the entity must be capable of performing the action complained of. In the case of the *Church of Scientology of Toronto v. Globe & Mail* (1978), the non-profit group tried to sue for statements published in the *Globe and Mail* that accused some church members of practising medicine without a licence. The court ruled that while the law allows a non-profit corporation to sue for defamation, the statements made in this case logically referred to individual members only, since a corporation per se cannot practise medicine.[5]

Just because a statement angers a person, however, does not make it defamatory, even if the statement is false. For a statement to be defamatory, it must be phrased in such a way that the ordinary reader would understand it as stating facts about the plaintiff. If the statement is so wildly improbable that no one would understand it as factual, it cannot be the basis for a libel suit. Sometimes a statement conveys no obviously defamatory meaning. Rather, a reader or listener must put a statement together with previously known facts to come up with a defamatory conclusion.

Determining whether a statement is capable of having a defamatory meaning requires judges to take into consideration a number of factors affecting how people might interpret the statement. For example, to decide whether statements are defamatory, it's essential to regard those statements in the context in which they were published. In the case of *Brannigan v. S.I.U.*,[6] the plaintiff, a trade unionist, won his case in which he sued a magazine after it published an article that called him a communist. The court held that whether or not it is defamatory to call someone a communist depends largely on the context. The larger context in this 1961 case was that of the Cold War, and the specific context was a raging battle between two hostile trade unions.

Because libel is a tort of strict liability (that is, the intention of the defendant is irrelevant in determining the outcome of the case), allegedly defamatory statements will be judged by how the ordinary person, without special or inside knowledge, would understand their meaning. In *Murphy v. LaMarsh*,[7] a journalist named Ed Murphy sued over ostensibly derogatory statements about him in a book of memoirs published by Judy LaMarsh, a former federal minister (the allegedly defamatory statements included that Murphy was hated by both his colleagues and the politicians he covered). At trial, the former minister and two other journalists called as expert witnesses tried to argue that the complained of statements did not defame Murphy and might even be complimentary to him. But the court differed, emphasizing the strict liability of the tort of libel: what the defendant intended and how "insiders" might interpret the assertions were both irrelevant. The "standard by which to measure whether these assertions were defamatory was that of the ordinary reader." The ordinary reader would assume that there must be something wrong with a reporter who was hated by both his colleagues and his subjects.

For a statement to be defamatory, it must be understood as such by society generally and not only by a select group (of professionals or other "insiders"). In *Burnett v. C.B.C.*, "the court said it could not find a statement defamatory if a person's reputation is only lowered within a particular class or section of the community which has a 'standard of opinion' the courts cannot identify or approve."[8]

While libel plaintiffs usually sue over statements made in the body of a news story, they may also sue over pictures, cartoons, headlines, or some combination of words and pictures that create a defamatory meaning. In *Vander Zalm v. Times Publishers*, a B.C. politician sued after a newspaper published a political cartoon that depicted him gleefully pulling the wings off a fly.[9]

Reference (Identification)

The libel plaintiff must also prove that the defamatory statements refer to him or her, that the audience would associate the plaintiff with the defamatory statement. This requires proving that reasonable readers, listeners or viewers would have understood that the statement was about the plaintiff. Again, because libel is a tort of strict liability, whether the publisher of the statement intended to refer to the plaintiff does not matter. The publication can identify a plaintiff, however, without using a name, and so the question becomes what degree of detail is required to identify the plaintiff.

Usually, libel plaintiffs have no trouble establishing identification in cases involving the news media. News stories normally identify sources or subjects clearly by name. In fact, detailed identification protects reporters against libel suits. Many suits arise from situations in which similar names create confusion. If a Sam Johnson is arrested for selling cocaine, the commonness of the name creates the possibility of confusion. By identifying the person arrested as Samuel H. Johnson, Jr., of 3517 N. Forest St., Apt. 303, the reporter eliminates the possibility of inadvertently defaming other Sam Johnsons in town.

The publication can identify a plaintiff without using a name, however. A publication can identify a plaintiff if the assertion identifies an individual as part of a group. In *Booth v. BCTV Broadcasting System*, a news report quoted a prostitute, and the quotation allowed two police officers to be identified. Eleven officers had sued over the quotation (which alleged that officers in a special squad took payoffs), but the court ruled that only two senior officers in the squad were identified and thus only those two officers could sue; it dismissed the lawsuits brought by the other nine squad members.[10]

Invented names can also lead to libel suits if the presumably invented name turns out to belong to a flesh-and-blood individual. This is what happened in an old English case, *E. Hulton & Co. v. Jones*. A provincial newspaper named the *Sunday Chronicle* published an article about the "scandalous" behaviour of English tourists in Dieppe. The writer of the article used a supposedly made-up name—Artemus Jones—to represent a supposedly fictitious character, a "churchwarden at Peckham," as a typically badly behaved English tourist. It turned out, however, that a real Artemus Jones existed, and he sued for libel. "The court took the view that, since there were not many people called Artemus Jones, people who did know the real Artemus Jones could reasonably conclude that he was the one referred to."[11]

In a work of purported fiction, the standard disclaimer used to deny reference or resemblance to real-life characters living or deceased provides no protection against a plaintiff's charge of libel. In *Youssoupoff v. Metro-Goldwyn-Mayer Pictures Ltd.*, a European grand duchess sued MGM and won over a movie about a supposedly fictional royal family in eastern Europe at the time of the First World War. The son in this royal family suffered from hemophilia, and "at one point, a fictional mad monk appeared and moved into the royal family's palace, claiming he could cure the son." Although MGM tried to argue that the character was invented and that there was no intention to refer to the plaintiff, the court ruled that the plaintiff (the real-life grand duchess) "was the one being depicted. Thus, she had been sufficiently identified and could maintain a libel action."[12]

Publication

Obviously, when a statement has appeared in a newspaper or broadcast it has been published. However, a statement does not have to be so widely disseminated for a person to sue for libel, because the legal definition of publishing is transmission to a third party. All the law requires is that the defendant made the defamatory statement to someone other than the person defamed. Thus, one person slandering another is not actionable, but if a third person overheard the insulting remarks, that would, technically, amount to publishing. The point is that the basic issue of liability doesn't depend on how many third parties were exposed to the libel; one third party is enough. Any repetition of a libellous statement is considered a new instance of publication, for which the publisher can be held liable (i.e., there's no protection in not being the first to publish libellous statements).

What about online content? While the law is still catching up to the wild frontier of online publication, it's safe to assume that what constitutes libel in a broadcast or newspaper (or magazine or other "hard-copy" publication) will also constitute libel online. Posting defamatory comments online carries the same legal risk as publishing them in a newspaper, magazine or book or broadcasting them. Anonymity does not protect from liability; the owners and operators of online sites have been ordered by the courts to reveal the identities of those who post defamatory comments online. Even bloggers who provide hyperlinks to defamatory comments on other sites could be held liable. Mere Internet Service Providers (ISPs) are less likely to be held accountable for distributing defamatory comments (since they could not realistically be expected to monitor all of the thousands of messages purveyed by virtue of their having provided access to the Internet). On the other hand, "the courts may expect them to monitor postings from users with a history of making abusive statements or newsgroups that tend to attract defamatory statements. Once notified of the existence of defamatory statements, an ISP must take prompt action to remove them."[13]

In one recent case, the court ruled that website owners could be held liable for defamation if they intentionally provide on their sites hyperlinks to defamatory material. In *Crookes v. Newton* (2009), the B.C. Court of Appeal said that while in themselves hyperlinks are not dangerous, they could implicate the website owner if he "endorses or adopts the defamatory content, or explicitly encourages the reader to link to the offending material."[14] Merely providing a hyperlink or website address to the libellous material or referring to it in a neutral way does not constitute publication, the court held. Refusing to remove defamatory statements from an online site once the owner or host of the site has been notified of their potentially libellous nature is another matter. A court ruling in the 2001 B.C. case of *Godfrey v. Demon Internet Ltd.* suggests that the website host could be held liable for republication of the offending matter.[15]

Major Defences to Libel Suits

The main defences available to media organizations against a charge of libel are these: truth, also called justification (for matters of fact); fair comment (for matters of opinion); absolute privilege (for government and judicial proceedings); qualified privilege (for matters of the public interest, where there is a duty to report); and consent (for cases in which the would-be plaintiff had agreed to the publication).

Truth or Justification

For a media defendant to succeed with the defence of truth, it must prove at trial the truth of the statements it published, and this can prove difficult. The standard of proof is the same as required in any other civil case (that is, on a balance of probabilities based on the evidence presented) unless criminal or corrupt conduct is alleged, in which case the standard of proof required is higher. In all provinces except Quebec, truth is considered a complete defence (one that cannot be scuttled by proven malice on the part of the defendant). Because media defendants who raise the defence of truth are required to prove the alleged facts of the case, reporters should keep all their notes and any other documentary evidence (including tape recordings) used to write the story and ensure that the sources relied upon are credible and trustworthy.

To prove the truth of a statement or assertion, the defendant may present only direct (not second-hand) evidence, which means journalists should corroborate information with at least two and preferably several sources. Brief references to the following cases underline the importance of sources.

> The point of raising the defence of truth is not to argue that, in some abstract philosophical or moral sense, a story is true. The concrete point is to prove to the satisfaction of a court that it is true. A crucial element in doing this, of course, is to persuade the court to believe the defendant's witnesses—that is, the sources. The issue here is not whether the source is telling the truth, but whether the court believes that the source is telling the truth.[16]

In *Drost v. Sunday Herald Ltd.*, a man told a newspaper reporter that he was driving his car when two police officers pulled him over, ordered him from his car, and beat him at the side of the road. Despite the fact that there were no witnesses to the alleged wrongdoing, the reporter wrote a story about the alleged incident, and the paper ran it. When one of the officers sued for libel, the paper raised the defence of truth. In the absence of provable fact, the court had to rely on the relative credibility of sources (something the paper's reporter and editors ought to have considered before running the story), and the paper lost at trial. "It turned out that this man had an impressive criminal record and was a well-known ne'er-do-well. Two sterling members of the RCMP said none of this ever happened and one man who had a criminal record said it did."[17]

Another case where the defence of truth failed involved a CBC report alleging corruption in the dealings of a former New Brunswick minister of justice. The CBC used the word "kickbacks" to describe monies that were rumoured to have been deposited in a secret Conservative Party fund. *The Fifth Estate* broadcast also claimed that the minister halted an RCMP investigation into the matter. Because the CBC raised the truth defence, it was required then to prove the precise truth of its allegations, but it lost the case, ostensibly because of its use of the word "kickbacks" rather than "political contributions" to describe the goings-on. The result in *Baxter v. Canadian Broadcasting Corp.*[18] (1980) thus turned on language: having raised the truth defence, the CBC was required to prove precisely what its broadcast alleged (that the donations amounted to kickbacks rather than political contributions), and it was unable to do so at trial. The court's ruling does serve to underline the importance of precision in newswriting, but it has been cogently criticized:

> A moment's reflection reveals the flaw in the court's reasoning. Political parties do not keep separate accounts for kickbacks; special receipts marked "kickback" are not given. A kickback is, on its face, a lawful political contribution. It is only after investigation that an ostensibly lawful contribution may be revealed to be a kickback.... But because the matter was not stated with absolute precision, the defence of justification failed. One further sentence added to the script would probably have allowed the CBC to avoid liability.[19]

The defence of truth can also fail when insufficient scrutiny is applied to the motive or agenda of the source relied on, most especially if the source seeks to remain anonymous. There are of course appropriate times for journalists to grant anonymity, but the default position in good journalism is no anonymous sources. (If this were not the case, newspapers and other public media of communication would have no reason, legal or ethical, to bother ascertaining the facts. Rumour and innuendo would serve as well as provable facts, and the former are a lot easier to come by.)

Unless there is good reason to grant a source anonymity (for example, when the source is a bona fide whistleblower whose well-being would be threatened by identifying him or her and there is other corroborating evidence to prove the truth of what the whistleblower contends), reporters should refrain from granting anonymity to sources. They should also look critically at a source's request to remain anonymous. The reporter in the case of *Vogel v. Canadian Broadcasting Corp.*[20] failed to do so; on the basis of an anonymous phone call, he wrote a story alleging that the plaintiff, then deputy attorney general of British Columbia, "had interfered with cases actually before the courts, interfered with the administration of justice, in order to benefit his friends."[21] Vogel sued for libel, and the CBC lost, paying heavy damages.

In the case of *Munro v. Toronto Sun Publishing Co.*,[22] a cub reporter for the *Toronto Sun* wrote a story accusing the plaintiff, then a member of Parliament, of corruption and conflict of interest in the matter of a lucrative government contract for PetroCanada service stations. The reporter, in a meeting with superiors and legal counsel shortly before the story ran on the front page, claimed to have documentary evidence of the allegations on a microfiche. Incredibly, none of the reporter's superiors at the meeting asked to view the evidence; they simply took the reporter's word for it. Further, the reporter never confronted the plaintiff with the allegations before the story ran; in other words, he never offered the right of reply to the target of his "investigation." The plaintiff won his case, and the truth emerged: the reporter had simply made up the story. As the presiding judge in the case observed, the processing of this story broke the basic rules of good reporting and editing:

> [T]here *must* be a separation of functions between the reporter and the editor, it being the responsibility of the editor to confirm the accuracy of the contents of a story before publication.... [T]here must be constant supervision maintained by the editor over the reporter, with a regular reporting requirement.... [I]t is the editor's responsibility to know in detail before publication, the documentation to support the story and the reliability of the sources and so ensure its accuracy.[23]

Finally, the defence of truth does not protect the accurate republication of defamatory charges made by other people. For example, a news organization that reports a defamatory statement that a bank president makes about a competitor cannot escape liability by proving that it accurately quoted the bank president. The news organization is responsible for proving that the underlying statement is true, not merely that it has quoted the source accurately. There are some exceptions to this rule, the main one being the defence of absolute privilege that news organizations have to report on official government and legal proceedings. The principle holds to spoken statements, normally regarded as slander. In *Stopforth v. Goyer*,[24] the court reiterated that when someone speaks defamatory words to the press, knowing or intending that they be published, the speaker, in the event of a libel suit, would be held responsible for libel, not slander.

The requirements of a successful truth defence against a libel action may seem onerous to the media defendant, but they are none other than the requirements of good journalism (backed by evidence and rigorous journalistic technique), and truth remains the touchstone. While it may be difficult to prove the truth of a story in court, truth is also a "pre-emptive" defence, because if the story is true, the target is unlikely to sue. "If anyone is going to know for certain that the story is accurate, it must be the person about whom it was written.... [T]he truth of a story ensures that there will not be a libel action."[25]

Fair Comment

The law of defamation distinguishes between assertions of fact and those of opinion. Everyone has the right to an opinion and to the Charter-protected right to express that opinion, but the law distinguishes opinion based on fact and relevant to the public interest from opinion based on rumour or speculation and motivated by malice (defined in law as "intent to injure"). For the fair comment defence to succeed at trial, the comment must be on a matter of public interest, based on fact, and recognizable as comment, though the commentary must still be based on fact to be considered fair. As well, it must satisfy the "objective" test: Could anyone honestly express that opinion on the proved facts? Finally, there must be no actual or express malice underlying the comment.

The defence of fair comment exists to protect the right to free expression so critical to a democratic society and to encourage the kind of full public discourse necessary to preserve free-speech rights. But the defence does not protect all editorials, columns and reviews or even news stories that offer opinion along with reportage. In fact, any published opinion based on or implying false facts can be the basis of a libel suit. The defence of fair comment does not exist to protect anyone's right to say anything, however harmful and ill-based, at any time; as with other constitutionally guaranteed rights, the right to express an opinion is not absolute. There are limits to the use of the defence:

> It will not protect assertions of fact; to be considered fair comment, a statement must express an opinion and the defence cannot be put forward to avoid the more difficult task of proving the truth of an allegation. If a columnist expressed the opinion that a lawyer is a crook, the columnist would have to produce the evidence needed to prove that the lawyer is a crook. Presenting allegations in the guise of opinion is not fair, let alone fair comment.[26]

On the other hand, the fair-comment defence is reliable when the opinion involves a matter of genuine public interest and does not amount simply to idle gossip or rumour-mongering. The following decided cases serve to illustrate the strength of the defence when it is properly employed.

In the case of *Vander Zalm v. Times Publishers* earlier referred to, a political cartoonist criticized a politician (by depicting him tearing the wings from a fly); the court deemed the cartoon fair comment. As long as the author honestly believes what he says and isn't motivated solely by malice, the opinion does not have to be reasonable; it can "even be exaggerated or prejudiced, as long as it is an honest view that could be held by someone."[27]

The principles of fair comment as they apply to political cartoons were more recently reaffirmed by the New Brunswick Court of Appeal in *Beutel v. Ross* in which the appeal court overturned the decision of a trial court that had awarded damages to an anti-Semitic teacher named Malcolm Ross "after a cartoon compared him to Joseph Goebbels, Hitler's propaganda minister."

> The appeal judges said "cartoons are not to be literally construed but are to be considered as rhetorically making a point by symbolism, allegory, satire and exaggeration." Since the opinion expressed was an honest belief of the cartoonist based on provable facts, he could rely on the defence of fair comment and did not have to prove Ross was a Nazi or actually advocated [the murder] of Jews.[28]

The case of *Pearlman v. Canadian Broadcasting Corp.* arose after the CBC produced a hard-hitting report about a landlord in Winnipeg. In the piece, the plaintiff was called a slum landlord and a person with "no morals, principles or conscience." The plaintiff objected to being so characterized and sued for libel. The CBC report was assiduously researched and reported, leaving no doubt as to the dirty and substandard conditions that the plaintiff's tenants were forced to endure. The court ruled in favour of the broadcaster, judging the opinion expressed as fair comment made without malice.[29]

In a more recent case, the Supreme Court of Canada bolstered the defence of fair comment with a landmark decision—the first consideration of the limits of fair comment—that overturned a court ruling against Vancouver radio broadcaster Rafe Mair. In the case of *Simpson v. Mair and WIC Radio Ltd.*,[30] the high court clarified the boundaries of free speech when it struck down a B.C. Court of Appeal ruling that found against the defendant, the controversial host of a radio talk show. In the original suit, Mair was accused of defaming Kari Simpson, a family values advocate who objected to the province's practice of allowing its schools to use books that portrayed homosexual parents. In the 1999 on-air editorial that became the subject of the suit, Mair criticized Simpson's position as bigotry and compared her views to the kind espoused by infamous racists like Hitler.

By overturning the appellate court's ruling, the Supreme Court suggested that freedom of expression rights demand a wide berth for commentary on matters of public interest and must be balanced against the right to protect personal reputation. Commenting on the case, Supreme Court of Canada Justice Ian Binnie said:

> Public controversy can be a rough trade and the law needs to accommodate its requirements.... An individual's reputation is not to be treated as regrettable but unavoidable road kill on the highway of public controversy, but nor should an overly solicitous regard for personal reputation be permitted to "chill" freewheeling debate on matters of public interest.[31]

The president of Ad Idem, an association of Canadian media lawyers in defence of free-expression rights, also commented:

> It is a long overdue first step by the Supreme Court to modernize libel law, to properly protect free speech.... The Supreme Court has heard very few libel cases in the last few decades and this is the first one where they've really weighed in with an analysis that's [anchored in] the importance of free speech.[32]

Absolute Privilege

The law recognizes certain occasions when people need absolute protection from libel suits. People called to testify in court, for example, cannot be sued for defamation because of what they say on the witness stand, even if what they say turns out to be untrue or motivated by malice. Members of legislative bodies, such as Parliament and provincial legislatures, cannot be sued over remarks they make in the course of their official duties (though the privilege ends outside those forums—for example, after the trial on the courthouse steps or outside the House of Commons in a hallway media scrum). This same privilege, in limited form, is extended to journalists so that they can cover government and open court proceedings without fear of attracting libel suits, but the following conditions generally apply: the report must be a fair and accurate account, must be published contemporaneously, must contain no comment, and must be free of seditious, blasphemous or obscene content. This is in keeping with the overriding principle of openness that is supposed to safeguard the Canadian justice system by ensuring that such proceedings do not occur behind closed doors and that news media are able to cover them, acting as the eyes and ears of the public (or, as the American expression has it, protecting the "public's right to know").

News organizations are covered by absolute privilege when they report on official legislative and judicial proceedings. For example, a news reporter covering a trial cannot be sued for reporting defamatory statements made by a witness in open court as long as the reporter's story meets the standard (i.e., is contemporaneous, contains no comment, and accurately and fairly summarizes the testimony). The following cases illustrate when the defence of absolute privilege as it applies to media coverage will succeed.

In *Geary v. Alger*, the journalist lost his case because he had added to his report the name of a person whose identity had not been revealed in open court. In *Mitchell v. Times Printing and Publishing Co.*, the court said that the defence of absolute privilege would be destroyed by any extra comment or statement imputing guilt. (The report had described the suspect, who was ultimately found not guilty, as a "long-sought killer" who had "finally been caught.") But the decision in *Wesolowski v. Armadale Publishers Ltd.* underlines the potential strength of the defence when it is used to protect a fair and accurate report. "In this case, a person was named in the indictment with the accused, but was not charged. The court said the newspaper's reference to the person as 'an unindicted co-conspirator' was fair and accurate because it adequately described that part of the judicial proceedings."[33]

Qualified Privilege

While the defence of absolute privilege allows for free speech and debate by public representatives in certain public forums, the broader defence of qualified privilege "can be used to defend statements published in the public interest while carrying out a recognized duty, protecting an important interest or reporting on public proceedings."[34] There has to be a moral obligation on the part of the sender to publish and on the part of the receiver, a corresponding right to know. To succeed at trial with the common law defence of qualified privilege, the report must be a fair and accurate account, free of malice, on a compelling matter of legitimate public interest. It would seem that qualified privilege is the right defence for at least some major investigative projects, yet until recently, Canadian courts defined the intended receiver or audience narrowly (expressly excluding the public at large), and Canadian media had little success trying to use the defence in defamation cases. But in a landmark ruling late in December of 2009, the Supreme Court of Canada affirmed a form of qualified privilege, the so-called "public interest responsible journalism" defence, which had been used in two Ontario newspaper cases.[35]

The defence was adopted by the Ontario Court of Appeal in 2007 and had earlier been accepted by leading British and American courts as necessary protection for free-expression rights. The new defence gives the media greater insulation against libel chill as long as the story was properly researched, fact-checked, written and edited, and the matter is one the public has a legitimate interest in hearing about. In other words, if the story meets the public-interest criteria and standards of responsible journalism, it should be protected by qualified privilege.[36]

In the groundbreaking case of *Cusson v. Quan*,[37] an Ottawa police constable with the Ontario Provincial Police decided on his own initiative to go to New York to help in the rescue operation after the September 11, 2001, attacks on the World Trade Center. He was recalled by superiors to his duties at home, but many articles portrayed him as a hero, and the stories provoked controversy. The *Ottawa Citizen* questioned the storyline of the officer as hero and suggested he might have misrepresented himself as an RCMP officer and been a hindrance rather than a help to the rescue effort. The newspaper argued at trial that because the articles in question were matters of the public interest published without malice, they should be protected by qualified privilege. The judge disagreed, finding that there was no compelling moral duty to publish the articles, and awarded the plaintiff $120,000 in damages. In 2007, however, the Ontario Court of Appeal accepted the new defence after considering the classic dilemma presented by the case and the defence of qualified privilege: how to weigh the right to protect reputation against the media's right to free expression.

Now that the Supreme Court of Canada has affirmed the new defence, courts in all provinces, not just Ontario, are required to follow the ruling, which is widely regarded as a progressive modernization of the defence of qualified privilege and an encouragement of public-interest reporting. According to one expert, it will require the courts to "shift their focus away from deciding whether there is truth or some other defence available, to whether the conduct of the media defendant met the standards for responsible journalism. In the view of Ontario's appeal court, 'this is an acceptable price to pay for free and open discussion.'"[38]

Note that the defence of qualified privilege should not be confused with the defence of fair comment. Fair comment defends not the validity of a given opinion expressed but rather the individual's right to hold an honest opinion and to express it. The essence of qualified privilege, by contrast, is the obligation to report, the idea that the person who makes the statement has an ethical duty to do so and those who receive the information, a legitimate interest in hearing it. Until recently, it was difficult for media defendants to succeed with the claim of qualified privilege against a charge of libel because the courts did not regard the defence as applicable to publishing to the general public. The advent of the responsible journalism defence at the dawn of 2010 may also encourage more journalists to produce more stories involving matters of the public interest.

Consent

This defence is rarely raised because normally, no one would consent to be defamed. This was the defence raised, however, in the 1976 case of *Syms v. Warren*. The plaintiff, chair of the Manitoba Liquor Commission, had agreed to appear on a radio call-in show to address rumours about him that were circulating in the community. During the show, a caller accused him of being an alcoholic, and the man sued the radio station. The station raised the defence of consent, arguing at trial that because the plaintiff had agreed to appear on the program, he in effect gave his consent to the broadcast comments. "The court agreed that a defence of consent existed, but said it did not arise in this case. The mere fact that this individual consented to appear on the open-line radio show could not be taken to mean that he consented to the publication of anything that anyone might say about him. It should be added that it is foolhardy for a radio station to air an open-line show without employing a delay mechanism."[39]

Remedies in Libel Actions

The remedies in a libel action are basically twofold: damages, which are awards of money meant to compensate the injured party, and injunctions, which are court orders that either compel a party to the suit to do something (called mandatory injunctions) or forbid a party to do something (called restrictive injunctions).

Of damages, there are two main sorts. General damages are awarded for losses that cannot be easily quantified (so-called non-monetary losses such as pain and suffering) to compensate the plaintiff for the injury to his or her reputation. Special damages are awarded for specific monetary losses. Theoretically, special damages (like general damages) have no limit, but to collect special damages, the plaintiff must provide proof that publication of the libel resulted in monetary loss (for example, lost wages if the libel caused him or her to lose a job).

In *Hill v. Church of Scientology*, a plaintiff successfully sued the church and was awarded $1.6 million in damages. During a news conference, a lawyer acting for the church defamed the plaintiff. At trial, the defendants tried to argue that the law should apply more stringently to public officials, requiring them to "prove knowledge of falsehood or a reckless disregard for the truth." The court stressed the importance of protecting the reputation of public officials and said the defendants "failed to raise enough evidence to establish a constitutional challenge of defamation law."[40] The church, in raising the issue of defamation as it applies to public figures, was referring, albeit inappropriately, to a famous ruling of the U.S. Supreme Court.

The critical 1964 case of *New York Times v. Sullivan* set a higher threshold in the United States for defamation of public officials, allowing for unlimited criticism of them as long as there was no malice or reckless disregard for truth on the part of the media defendant.[41] The case arose in Alabama, and the decision of the U.S. Supreme Court supported unrestrained reporting of the massive civil rights campaigns then being waged in the South. Before this case, regarded as a milestone for freedom of the press, news organizations in the South had succeeded in exercising a "chill" on journalists trying to cover the civil rights movement, with millions of dollars in libel actions outstanding. The plaintiff in the original case was L.B. Sullivan, then a public official in Montgomery, Alabama, whose duties included oversight of the police department. The *New York Times* argued on appeal that the original suit had been brought against the paper precisely to intimidate it and other news media and discourage them from reporting on the often illegal actions of public figures in the South who opposed integration.

The next group, nominal damages, falls within the same compensatory category as general damages, but the amount of nominal damages is minimal. Such damages are awarded to plaintiffs who succeed but whose reputations were poor to begin with. A good example is the 1956 case of *Leonhard v. Sun Publishing Co.*, in which a *Vancouver Sun* article described the plaintiff as a "drug king." At trial, the newspaper brought evidence that the plaintiff was well-known in the community as a gangster with no good name to protect. The plaintiff won his case but was awarded a single dollar in damages. "The risk in this tactic is that if the defendant's evidence as to the plaintiff's generally bad reputation fails to persuade the court, the defendant, as a result, may pay even more in damages."[42]

A final category of compensatory damages is aggravated damages, for cases in which the injury to reputation is particularly serious and the defendant has behaved particularly badly. Part of the award ($500,000) in *Hill v. Church of Scientology* was composed of aggravated damages. The courts have ruled that aggravated damages take into account "the additional harm caused to the plaintiff's feelings" by the defendant's bad conduct.[43]

The final category of damages to be considered is punitive damages. They are in a different class because unlike other kinds of damages, which seek to compensate the victim, punitive damages exist to punish the defendant for outrageously bad behaviour and to deter others from following suit. When a media defendant loses a libel case and is ordered to pay aggravated or, especially, punitive damages, something has gone badly wrong in the newsroom. Consider the three cases already noted in which aggravated or punitive damages were awarded against media organizations: *Thomas v. Canadian Broadcasting Corp.* (in which the CBC failed to include in its broadcast information favourable to the plaintiff); *Vogel v. Canadian Broadcasting Corp.* (in which the broadcast proceeded on the scant evidence of an anonymous source with no right of reply offered to the target of the investigation); and *Munro v. Toronto Sun Publishing Co.* (in which punitive damages were awarded after a cub reporter fabricated a story and, by crowing around the newsroom about having "got" the target, handed the court ample evidence of malice).

A plaintiff must serve notice of his intention to sue a media defendant (within the time period set out in provincial statutes), and the defendant must then decide whether to raise one of the recognized defences or issue an apology. An early and sincere apology may serve to avoid a libel suit altogether or to lower the amount of damages awarded if the case goes forward and the media defendant loses. Notices of intention to sue, however, are more numerous than libel actions that go forward to trial.

One last remedy—injunctions—may occur in response to charges of defamation. Injunctions are sought by plaintiffs to prevent the publication, or republication, of defamatory material. But again, there are serious problems inherent in the issuing of injunctions by courts in civil cases, especially in libel actions:

> The first is that a plaintiff can apply for an interim, or temporary, injunction without having to give notice of such application to the other party. Concretely this means that an injunction could be made against a newspaper or a broadcaster without that newspaper or broadcaster having been given an opportunity to argue against it. The second problem is that an injunction issued during a libel action is as clear an example as one could ask of a prior restraint on publication—censorship in its most basic form.[44]

A Note on Criminal Libel

Civil libel affords a legal mechanism for people to protect their reputations and is the kind that normally concerns journalists, but there also exists a criminal form of libel; its stated purpose is the preservation of public order. Critics have argued that the three categories of criminal libel (seditious libel, defamatory libel, and blasphemous libel) should be removed from the Criminal Code, but as of this writing, they remain.[45]

Seditious libel, traditionally used to prosecute unacceptable political speech, also targets advocating the use of force as seditious. The last prosecution for seditious libel occurred in the 1940s in Quebec after the Jehovah's Witnesses circulated a pamphlet criticizing the provincial government (then led by Maurice Duplessis); the pamphlet was entitled, in the translation from the original French to English, *Quebec's Burning Hate for God and Christ and Freedom Is the Shame of All Canada.* Although the accused were acquitted and there hasn't been another prosecution for the offence since then, seditious libel technically remains a criminal offence.[46]

In defamatory libel (also called criminal libel), a major distinguishing feature is the lack of a publication requirement. In civil libel, the element of publication is one of three that make up a *prima facie* case: for libel to have occurred, there must have been publication to a third party. But in criminal libel, two people exchanging seriously insulting remarks is enough to have them charged with the criminal offence. Further, while civil libel pits individuals against each other in a civil dispute between a plaintiff and a defendant, in defamatory libel (as in all criminal law), it is the state that brings charges against the individual. The ostensible justification for defamatory libel is to punish speech deemed so extreme that it could conceivably undermine public order. In the 1938 case of *R. v. Unwin*, the accused was convicted after having distributed a pamphlet criticizing a group of prominent Edmontonians (calling them "bankers' toadies" and comparing them to "snakes, slugs, snails and other creepy-crawly, treacherous and poisonous things").[47]

In the 1969 case of *R. v. Georgia Straight Publishing Ltd.*, the country's best known "underground" paper of the sixties generation was prosecuted for lampooning criticism of a Vancouver magistrate. In one issue, the paper awarded the magistrate the Pontius Pilate Certificate of Justice, further explaining thus: "To Lawrence Eckhardt, who, by closing his mind to justice, his eyes to fairness and his ears to equality, has encouraged the belief that the law is not only blind, but also deaf, dumb and stupid. Let history judge your actions—then appeal."[48] The court imposed on the defendants a fine of $1,500, but the charge was later thrown out. Since then, legal authorities have recommended that the offence, which carries a maximum penalty of five years' imprisonment, be removed from the Criminal Code, but the crime of defamatory libel has survived constitutional challenges to its legitimacy and remains in the code.[49]

The third kind of criminal libel is blasphemous libel, meant to deter people from making extreme remarks about religious beliefs (which, it is assumed, could lead to public violence). Although prosecutions are rare, the law remains in the Criminal Code and has been criticized for two main reasons: To convict someone of blasphemous libel, the Crown does not have to prove intent, and according to an English court, the offence applies only to Christianity (no decision has been reached on that count in Canada).[50]

The Role of Malice in Civil Libel

Truth is a complete defence (in all provinces and territories except Quebec, which has a Civil Code that governs civil defamation, as opposed to the situation in the rest of the country, where defamation is governed by statutes that have incorporated the main principles of the common law).

To say that truth is a complete defence to a charge of libel means that malice is irrelevant when this defence is raised. But remember that the media organization or individual journalist who raises this defence in a lawsuit is required to prove the truth of the published allegations at trial and that if the defendant is unable to do so (i.e., loses the case), any evidence of malice will tend to increase the damages awarded. But what constitutes malice?

> The case law is clear. Malice will be found when the desire to injure is determined to be the dominant motive in publishing the defamatory material. It is important to note that knowledge that publication may have the effect of injuring the plaintiff is not the same thing as the desire to injure. Go back to the Pearlman case. One would have to be naive not to know that when you say someone has no morals, principles or conscience, the statement is going to cause some injury. But that is not the issue. The issue is whether the defendant was motivated by the desire to cause injury. If the court is satisfied that the defendant was motivated by such a desire or was reckless whether injury resulted, that is malice, and the defences of fair comment and qualified privilege will be lost.[51]

As noted, Canadian libel law differs from U.S. libel law where public figures are concerned. In the United States, public officials must prove malice on the defendant's part before they can collect damages. But Canadian courts have rejected the notion that current libel laws violate the constitutional free-press rights guaranteed by Section 2(b) of the Charter and apply the same standards to public officials as to ordinary citizens in defamation lawsuits. The latter principle was affirmed by the Supreme Court of Canada in the 1995 case of *Hill v. Church of Scientology* already referred to.[52]

Actual malice can be difficult to prove; it refers to more than the commission of simple errors, even though such errors may well indicate sloppy reporting. Evidence that the journalist disliked the plaintiff are also in themselves insufficient. But generally, the courts have ruled that malice can be found when the defendant:

- knew facts that would call the story into question but did not include them in the story;
- refused to examine evidence that would prove or disprove an allegation;
- relied on an inherently unbelievable source;

- relied on an anonymous source without seeking corroborating evidence;

- published a story without adequate investigation;

- exhibited reckless disregard for the truth;

- failed to give the target of an investigation a chance to respond to allegations; or

- conveyed defamatory innuendos about the plaintiff in the published article.

Steps for Avoiding Libel Suits

No checklist or set of steps can guarantee that a news organization will never face a libel suit. Some news organizations have checked stories and found evidence for every potentially defamatory statement but still have been sued. Although the potential cost of defending against a libel suit can be daunting, the conscientious news organization will usually win. As well, virtually all reputable commentators (such as the ones cited repeatedly in this chapter) agree that the best defence against a charge of defamation is first-rate journalism: good reporting and good editing. Here are some of the things journalists can do to protect themselves and their employers:

1. Make sure everything in the story, especially any potentially defamatory statement, is newsworthy. Nothing is gained by risking a lawsuit over a statement that has no news value.
2. Identify everyone mentioned in the story as fully as possible.
3. Ask people who are attacked or criticized in news stories to respond, and include the response in the story, even if it is just a flat denial. If a person refuses to respond, say so in the story.
4. If a person who has been attacked or criticized presents credible evidence to support his or her denials, check out that evidence.
5. Interview every relevant source, and read every relevant document; do not ignore sources or information that might contradict the central point of a story.
6. Find out what basis a source has for making a defamatory charge and what the source's motives might be.
7. If a source for a story has credibility problems, explain in the story what those problems are.
8. Avoid confidential or anonymous sources. Reporters might be asked to reveal their sources at a libel trial. If the reporters refuse to do so, they may be charged with contempt of court, or the judges and jurors may assume the reporters made up the information.
9. Never use confidential or anonymous sources for making attacks on a subject. Use them only for factual information that can be verified by other sources or documents.
10. If a story uses documentary sources, make sure the documents are understood and quoted accurately. Double-check the information in any documents; even official records may have errors.
11. If a story is not breaking news, take additional time to make sure the investigation is thorough and the story is accurate.
12. Adhere to organizational policies regarding keeping notes, tapes and other materials. If the policy is to keep all such materials, be sure everything is kept. If the policy is to destroy materials, make sure all are destroyed. Do not destroy some and keep others.

PRIVACY

Before the turn of the twenty-first century, references to privacy rights were scant in all Canadian jurisdictions. In recent years, that situation has changed, and while there is still no common law tort for invasion of privacy, most jurisdictions now have various regulations and statutes that address the issue. At the time of writing, five Canadian provinces (British Columbia, Manitoba, Quebec, Saskatchewan, and Newfoundland and Labrador) had enacted laws allowing people to seek civil remedies for invasion of privacy. Various federal and provincial laws also protect access to confidential personal and commercial information held by governments.

Journalists need to be aware of their rights to gather and publish information, especially when these rights may conflict with the legitimate rights of others to protect their own privacy and confidential information. Even though the tort of invasion of privacy is still developing and there is little jurisdictional uniformity, various existing laws protect against related forms of interference such as trespassing and harassment. Provincial privacy laws also cover activities such as stalking, wiretapping phones, intercepting messages, eavesdropping, using without authorization personal papers like journals, and using without permission or consent someone's name or image for commercial purposes. Some of these issues are considered in greater detail below.

As the rules continue to evolve and as the ubiquity of online communications continues to complicate privacy concerns, journalists are likely to face new restrictions on what is acceptable practice. "The line appears to be drawn if a journalist uses illegal or covert methods to collect personal information, subjects a person to unwarranted harassment, or discloses information about an individual when there is no wider public interest in the person's private life."[53]

A U.S. judge in 1960 proposed four kinds of invasion of privacy: intruding into a plaintiff's solitude or private affairs, disclosing private facts about the plaintiff, putting the plaintiff in the public eye in a false light, and appropriating the plaintiff's name or image.

In Canada, privacy matters intersect with other legal concerns such as defamation. The Supreme Court of Canada has ruled that damages for defamation and breach of privacy cannot be awarded in the same lawsuit. In the case of a B.C. newspaper that erroneously published a photo of a lawyer in a story about a terrorist group (see *St. Pierre v. Pacific Newspaper Group Inc. and Skulsky*), the newspaper was deemed to have committed defamation, but it was not held responsible for a claimed breach of the plaintiff's privacy rights. (Part of the purpose of Canadian defamation law is the protection of personal privacy; damages for breach of privacy would be awarded only if defamation had not been found.)

Where the privacy rights of innocent parties is at issue, the courts have provided mixed rulings. In one high-profile case, a provincial court judge in B.C. refused to allow CTV to air video of a two-year-old being unearthed from a month-old grave; the judge acknowledged the right to privacy of the child's parents and community as innocent third parties. But in another case involving the alleged privacy rights of an innocent party, a judge ruled that a detective who had been served with a search warrant executed at the police station could not keep that information private because the public interest in having access to information about the warrant outweighed the detective's privacy rights. In general, privacy rights are increasingly seen as relevant when a third party is required to disclose information related to health history, financial status, education, or employment status, or that indicates a person's race or ethnic origin, gender or age.

An English court ruled that the privacy rights of Canadian singer Loreena McKennitt were breached in a book written by a former friend that disclosed details of the singer's intimate sexual and emotional life.[54]

In federal law, the Privacy Act gives Canadians the right to access personal information held by governments, but until recently this right did not extend to personal information held by others. In 2000, the federal government enacted the Personal Information Protection and Electronic Documents Act (PIPEDA) to control the use of personal and confidential information by private enterprises. The Act exempts anyone who collects, uses or discloses personal information for journalistic, artistic or literary purposes. For journalists, one of the disadvantages of privacy laws, including PIPEDA, is the ability of government agencies and business enterprises to use the laws to avoid answering questions from the media. (In one case, Corrections Canada authorities in New Brunswick initially refused to release a photograph of an escaped murderer, saying that privacy laws required them to get the permission of the prisoner.)[55]

Journalists are not prohibited from listening in on private conversations or recording them as long as they have the consent of the originator or the intended receiver of the communication. (There are three other occasions when intercepting private conversations can be legal, but they don't generally apply to journalists: legally authorized wiretaps; during necessary repairs to telephone, telegraph or other communication systems; and during random monitoring by an officer or servant of the Crown.) Under the Criminal Code, it is a separate offence to disclose the content of an intercepted private communication without the consent of one of the parties (or unless the information is disclosed in open court). Surreptitious electronic recordings may present legal problems under other provisions of the Criminal Code, including those aimed at trespassing at night, intimidation, harassing phone calls, and disrupting a religious service.

It is legal for journalists to tape-record telephone interviews, and they do not require the consent of the person being taped unless the interview is to be broadcast. It is a criminal offence, however, to publish or broadcast a phone conversation that was illegally taped by a third party. For broadcast reporters, CRTC rules forbid airing interviews or conversations without the consent of the interviewees, but journalists are generally free to repeat or refer to what was said during the interview. The use of hidden microphones and cameras is generally prohibited but can be defended in the case of journalists working on investigative stories that expose matters involving the public interest.

At the provincial level, as at the federal level, privacy legislation is spotty, but five provinces do have privacy acts (British Columbia, Saskatchewan, Manitoba, and Newfoundland and Labrador, as well as Quebec under its Civil Code). These provisions to protect privacy generally involve matters such as visual invasions (publishing someone's photograph and filming in public places), harassment, and publishing or broadcasting private information or conversations without consent.

In a Quebec case, a teenaged woman launched a civil suit against an arts magazine. A photographer for the magazine had taken a photo of the young woman enjoying the sunshine on a beautiful day in a public place, and the magazine had published the photo, all without gaining the woman's permission. The woman sued for invasion of privacy, and the Quebec trial judge ruled in her favour, awarding $2,000 in damages. A provincial appeal court in the case of *Aubry v. Éditions Vice-Versa* upheld the ruling, and so did the Supreme Court of Canada. A dissenting Supreme Court judge noted, however, that there is no general right to absolute privacy or protection from searches guaranteed in Canada under the Charter or Rights and Freedoms (although Section 8 of the Charter does protect against unreasonable search and seizure).[56]

In terms of photographs and video, standard journalistic practice requires seeking the consent of a person before publishing or broadcasting his or her image. When filming or photographing groups of people, individuals are generally not identifiable, but if a person is singled out in a crowd, seek that person's permission before publishing. On the other hand, journalists are not prohibited from covering a matter of public interest occurring in a public space (where there is generally no expectation of privacy), such as a protest march down city streets.

In a 1985 case in British Columbia, a businessman tried to stop a TV crew from filming employees picketing the man's building. Even though the plaintiff owned the parking lot where the TV crew had set up, a judge ruled that the station was entitled to film the dispute and air the footage and that the businessman's right to privacy had not been infringed, both because the matter was one the public had a right to hear about and because there is little expectation of privacy in a parking lot, regardless of who owns it.[57]

The case of *Robbins v. Canadian Broadcasting Corp.* was one of the first invasion of privacy claims related to the mass media. In the late 1950s, the plaintiff, a doctor, won his case and was awarded damages in his suit against the CBC. He had written a letter of complaint to a CBC television show. The host of the show subsequently read the letter on air and, displaying the plaintiff's mailing address on screen, invited the show's viewers to write to him in order to cheer him up. The plaintiff received letters, phone calls, and even visits to his home, and the court, in finding for the plaintiff, used words like "humiliation," "malicious mischief" and "nuisance" in addition to "invasion of privacy."[58]

In a 1976 Alberta case, the court held that a woman, by subjecting several of her relatives to a continuous series of abusive telephone calls and letters over a period of two years, had committed a tort it called "nuisance by invasion of privacy." The court issued an injunction against the woman.[59] Courts in New Brunswick and British Columbia have gone further, supporting invasion of privacy as a common law tort.

In a 1991 Quebec case, where privacy matters are governed by that province's Civil Code, a teacher with AIDS sued for invasion of privacy and won after a Quebec newspaper published an article about him revealing his disease. The teacher was on sick leave and was offered a full salary to not return to work. Even though he was not named in the article, there were enough details in the story to identify him as the person referred to in the article.[60]

In 1982, an Ontario County Court ruling awarded damages against a defendant who tape-recorded a telephone conversation between himself and the plaintiff and then played the tape at a public meeting without the plaintiff's permission or knowledge.[61]

A related tort, generally called "appropriation of personality," protects people against the unauthorized use of their name or likeness for commercial purposes (for example, to falsely suggest that a celebrity or other well-known person has endorsed a given product).[62]

NEWSGATHERING ISSUES

Section 2(b) of the Charter of Rights and Freedoms expressly protects the right to speak and to publish, but it says nothing about the right to gather information. The Supreme Court of Canada has recognized that freedom of the press means very little if there is no right to gather information, but what rights news reporters have to information are largely defined by a hodgepodge of provincial and federal statutes. This section covers three newsgathering issues: access to non-judicial events and records, access to judicial proceedings, and confidentiality for sources and information.

Reporters should always remember that the Charter's free press guarantee does not protect them from prosecution if they engage in illegal conduct to gather news. Posing as a police officer, stalking the subject of an investigation, buying drugs, stealing documents, and communicating with a prostitute are all illegal activities, and reporters who are prosecuted for engaging in illegal activities will not be allowed to plead that they were doing so to gather information for a news story.

Access to Non-judicial Events and Records

News Scenes

When a river floods a city, a murder is discovered, or a fire destroys a building, police, rescue workers and firefighters try to control the area to save lives and protect property. Some officials, however, worry as much about their images and how they will be portrayed in news accounts as they do about citizens and their property. Such officials often try to control what news reporters and photographers see and how they report what they see.

Reporters and photographers covering the protests accompanying meetings of the World Bank and International Monetary Fund and the Iraq War sometimes were arrested along with the demonstrators. Journalists covering protests, demonstrations and riots face many risks, but they can do some things to minimize the chances of being harassed by police:

- Always carry press credentials.

- Don't trespass on private property or cross clearly marked police lines.

- Don't take anything from a crime scene.

- Obey all orders from police officers, even if doing so interferes with getting the story or the photo. (The alternative might be going to jail.)

- Don't argue with arresting officers.

The normal desire of the authorities to manage crisis scenes intensified after the September 11, 2001, terrorist attacks in the United States. The federal and some provincial and municipal governments have tried to use the terrorist attacks as a rationale for restricting access by reporters to government buildings and government information. Privacy concerns also have been cited as the rationale behind some decisions to curtail access to news scenes in recent years.

Legal restrictions on newsgathering include the tort of trespassing (entering private property without permission), and trespassers can be sued for damages. The Criminal Code gives property-owners or their representatives the right to forcibly remove trespassers. When reporters are charged with trespassing, police are within their rights to seize notes and tape as evidence. Trespassing applies to all private property (including shopping malls, parking lots, and publicly funded sites such as government offices, airports, train stations and bus depots). Trespassing at night is a criminal offence that carries a fine of up to $2,000 or a six-month jail sentence.

Stealing documents and being in possession of stolen documents are crimes, but confidential information per se cannot be stolen (although it is illegal to obtain information by hacking into a computer system). The principle that information itself cannot be stolen is illustrated by the 1989 case of a reporter who got an advance look at a federal budget and was sued by the government. In the case, a reporter for Global Television in British Columbia was leaked a copy of a summary of the federal budget. The reporter was prosecuted by the government for theft but was acquitted because the document he was leaked was a photocopy of the budget document. Legally, information as such cannot be stolen, only information in a particular form; there is no property in the information itself.[63]

Other restrictions on newsgathering stem from police powers. Excessive use of force (force likely to cause bodily harm or death) in administering the law is not considered justified unless the person enforcing the law believes, on reasonable and probable grounds, that it is required for self-protection or the protection of others. The Criminal Code specifies that a person being placed under arrest must be so informed and told the reason for the arrest. Searches of people or places and seizures are not legal without a duly authorized warrant (unless there is consent). A journalist's conflict with police could result in a Criminal Code charge of obstructing justice (but the obstruction has to be actual and wilful). Aside from Charter protections (for example, against unreasonable search and seizure), a reporter's most important right in dealing with police, as for any citizen, is the right to remain silent.[64]

Records and Meetings

The federal government and all the provinces and territories of Canada have laws setting out the public's right to access records by government at all levels. The federal Access to Information Law and the provincial freedom of information laws are meant to provide access to the wealth of information held in government records and by doing so, to protect both the public's right to know and the need to keep governments and their representatives accountable to the public.

These laws have been used in gathering material for investigative stories revealing information about matters of grave public interest that would otherwise have remained hidden from public view, including stories about the use of Tasers and the surveillance of such groups as Greenpeace and the Council of Canadians in the name of fighting terrorism. But access to information laws have also proven a double-edged sword, and it is often only the most persistent reporters who succeed in using the laws to dislodge sensitive information.

A nationwide project to test the openness of governments, co-ordinated by the Canadian Newspaper Association, found that federal departments, school boards, public health agencies, municipal governments and police forces complied with less than two-thirds of requests for basic information about their operations. The requests covered such routine subjects as classroom sizes, reports of schoolyard bullying, the annual cost of sick leave for civil servants, plans for street repairs, the results of restaurant inspections, and the number of public complaints filed against police officers.[65]

The federal Access to Information Act provides public access to its holdings in many government departments and agencies, but exemptions from the Act cover some government organizations, including the CBC and Atomic Energy of Canada, and certain kinds of information, such as cabinet records (for 20 years from the date of creation), classified information, government confidences, business and third-party transactions, and trade secrets and commercial information. Provincial and municipal freedom of information laws also provide access to the records of some public bodies, such as Crown corporations and government-appointed agencies, commissions and boards, and restrict access to others. These provisions largely mirror the federal Act in the kinds of information exempt from the legislation.

Reporters for national newspapers have used access laws to investigate important stories; examples include the series of stories that came to be known as Shawinigate, investigating the role played by former prime minister Jean Chrétien in securing federal grants for a business in which he had an interest, and the scandal of the federal government's advertising sponsorship program, which provoked an audit and sparked a commission of inquiry into kickbacks to the Liberal party in Quebec.[66]

Access to Judicial Proceedings

Freedom of the press is just one of the rights guaranteed by the Canadian Constitution; the Constitution also guarantees the rights of people accused of crimes to a fair trial. These two rights appear to conflict when news organizations publish information that might sway potential jurors. Some authorities have labelled this problem "free press versus fair trial," suggesting one right must be sacrificed to the other. Traditionally, courts have given more weight to the right to due process (fair trial). But in a landmark ruling arising from the 1994 case of *Dagenais v. Canadian Broadcasting Corp.*,[67] the Supreme Court of Canada said that in the matter of publication bans issued to try to protect an accused person's right to a fair trial, the presiding judge should no longer assume that the right to a fair trial automatically trumps that of the press to free expression. Instead, the judge should try to balance the two rights, issuing a ban only if certain conditions are met. The high court ruled that publication bans should be issued only when they are necessary to prevent a real and substantial risk to a fair trial, when reasonable alternatives are not available, and when the effects of the ban in terms of protecting the right to fair trial outweigh the deleterious effects on freedom-of-expression rights. The ruling came to be known as the Dagenais test.

In 2001, the high court updated its test for issuing court orders that restrict access and publication. In the case of *R. v. Mentuck*,[68] the high court said that judges are required to consider two factors before issuing publication bans or other orders restricting access:

> 1) such an order is necessary to prevent a *serious risk to the proper administration of justice* because reasonable alternative measures will not prevent the risk; and
> 2) the salutary effects of the publication ban outweigh the deleterious effects on the rights and interests of the parties and the public, including the effects on the right to free expression, the right of the accused to a fair and public trial, and the efficacy of the administration of justice.[69]

Courts still have a variety of common law and statutory powers to issue discretionary publication bans on information arising from hearings, such as names of victims or witnesses, despite the Supreme Court of Canada rulings in *Dagenais* and *Mentuck* that judges must consider the Charter's guarantee of freedom of the press in deciding whether to issue bans. Only in rare cases will the courts ban publication of the name of a person accused of a criminal offence.

Various sections of the Criminal Code may be used by judges in criminal proceedings to issue publication bans, including bans in sexual offence proceedings on details of applications to introduce evidence of a complainant's sexual history; bans on information revealed at bail hearings and preliminary hearings, including an absolute ban on reporting confessions; bans on disclosing the identities of youth involved in crimes as accused persons, victims or witnesses; bans on publishing evidence given during *voir dires* at jury trials; and an absolute ban on disclosing jury deliberations. The code allows for further bans at the discretion of the presiding judge on information related to search warrants and production orders, the identities of jurors or informants, and disposition information on the mental capacity of an accused person deemed not criminally responsible because of mental disorder. Bans may also be ordered by provincial statutes to prevent the publication of certain information or the names of people involved in proceedings dealing with matters such as coroners' inquests, family law cases, and sexually transmitted diseases.

Although the default position of the Canadian justice system is openness—courts and the hearings or meetings of official bodies that deal with matters of the public interest must be open to public scrutiny, and exceptions to openness must be justified—the Criminal Code may be used, as noted, to exclude the public on specified occasions (meaning that the presiding judge may exclude everyone but the accused, counsel for the accused, and the prosecutor).

Most judicial and quasi-judicial tribunals at the federal and provincial levels also have the authority to exclude the public from certain hearings. The public has limited rights of access to administrative tribunals. As a general rule, public meetings are open to all members of the public, although individuals can be asked to leave by convenors of the meeting. All provinces have municipal law provisions that stipulate that regular city council meetings be open to the public. At the time of writing, electronic news media had no right of access to many court hearings.

In terms of access to court documents, Supreme Court of Canada rulings in recent years have presumed a right of access for the news media to view, copy and publish court documents and exhibits, subject to provisions for preventing serious risk to fair trial rights. Usually, journalists have access to court records setting out the names and addresses of parties involved in lawsuits, the remedy sought, the stage of proceedings of a trial, and the result of a trial. While courts keep pleadings and other pre-trial documents, not all of these records are available to the public. Courts may bar access to personal or financial information, to solicitor–client fee agreements, and to family information in child-custody or child-abuse cases. Under the common law, courts may also restrict access to protect the rights of innocent third parties or the administration of justice. Public access to evidence presented in open court is decided by the presiding judge in a case, but the Supreme Court has instructed judges to weigh the news media's right to freedom of expression before issuing bans or restricting access. Finally, journalists generally have the right of access to search warrants that have been executed in cases where evidence was found and to criminal informations laid before a judge.[70]

Protecting Confidential Sources and Information

For almost as long as reporters have written news, they have used confidential sources. And reporters routinely promise to protect the identities of those sources. Reporters depend on confidential sources for some of their best stories, and in most cases the sources will provide key information only if they know their identities are safe. Yet there is no substantive protection for journalistic privilege in Canada. Courts and legislative bodies can demand the names of a reporter's confidential sources or other information the reporter wants to protect. Law enforcement officials want this information because they think it is relevant to the adjudication of some criminal or civil court case. In such cases, reporters might receive subpoenas ordering them to appear and testify before some official body. The subpoena may also direct them to bring notes, photographs, tapes and other materials they might have collected in the process of gathering news. A person who fails to comply with a subpoena can be cited for contempt of court and sent to jail or fined or both.

When reporters obtain confidential documents and use them as evidence to back up hard-hitting investigative stories, the courts may be able to order the documents returned. As well, people hurt by the release of private or confidential information may be able to sue the journalists and media organizations responsible. For these reasons, the use of both anonymous sources and "secret" documents leaked to the press, though part and parcel of the investigative reporter's toolkit, requires assiduous attention to detail and special care. In all such situations, legal counsel should be consulted before publishing.

Bar–Press Guidelines

Generally, guidelines for the reporting of criminal matters say the media should be free to report the following:

- basic information about a suspect, such as name, age and address;
- the charges against the suspect;
- the circumstances under which the suspect was arrested, including whether any weapons were used;
- if the crime involved a death, who died and how;
- the identities of the investigating agencies and officers.

Under most bar–press guidelines, the following information should not be published:

- the existence and nature of any statement or confession the suspect made to authorities;
- the results of any tests;
- opinions on the credibility of the suspect or any witnesses or any evidence;
- opinions about the outcome of the trial;
- any other statements made outside the presence of the jury that might be prejudicial.

The guidelines usually include special warnings about the publication of the past criminal record of an accused person. Such information is considered highly prejudicial, but it is also a matter of open record in many places. Besides, much of the information might already be in a newspaper's clip file. So it would be impossible to prevent its disclosure. Nevertheless, the guidelines strongly discourage reporting a suspect's record.

Cases in recent years have underscored the dilemma reporters sometimes face when they try to write in-depth stories that involve confidential sources and information. The issue of confidentiality of news sources acquired special prominence with two high-profile cases that were still before the Supreme Court of Canada in December 2009 as this book was being readied for publication.

In 1999, an award-winning reporter named Andrew McIntosh, then working for the *National Post*, began to investigate government and business dealings in which former prime minister Jean Chrétien had an interest. McIntosh had launched his research by

Journalists frantically go through documents regarding the sale of shares by the prime minister in the Grand-Mère Golf Club handed to them minutes before a news conference with ethics counsellor Howard Wilson in Ottawa on Tuesday, March 27, 2001.

scouring documents available in the public realm, such as property and lobby registration records. Methodically piecing together the facts, he was able to reveal "that a Chrétien aide who lobbied local federal officials on behalf of a Shawinigan hotelier … wasn't registered as required by law. That revelation triggered the federal ethics counsellor to call for an RCMP investigation."[71]

In subsequent stories, McIntosh nailed down the facts in the affair that came to be known as "Shawinigate," a controversy that sparked wide public debate, more investigations and, eventually, changes in public policy. A classic work of investigative reporting, the series tried to hold the powerful to account and won for McIntosh the admiration of his peers. The legal troubles began when a confidential source sent McIntosh a document in a plain brown envelope. That document "appeared to be a copy of a Business Development Bank of Canada (BDBC) loan authorization for a hotel in then–prime minister Jean Chrétien's home riding. If genuine, the document could show that Mr. Chrétien had a conflict of interest in relation to the loan. However, BDBC officials claimed that the document was a forgery and complained to the police."[72]

Police wanted to conduct forensic tests to find out who sent the document, and in July of 2002 an Ontario judge issued a search warrant and assistance order (under a section of the Criminal Code) against McIntosh and the *National Post*, ordering that the document and the envelope in which it was sent be handed over to police. The *Post* gave the document in a sealed envelope to the RCMP and then challenged the legality of the seizure. In 2004, Ontario Superior Court Justice Mary Lou Benotto quashed the warrant in a decision that recognized for the first time in Canada that journalists may be entitled to protect confidential sources. Benotto said she based her decision to overturn the order on three main principles: (1) the issuing judge erred in issuing a search warrant without notifying the newspaper; (2) both the search warrant and the assistance order violated the Charter; and (3) both the document and the envelope were protected by journalist–confidential source privilege.[73]

Countering the federal government's position that it was ill-advised to encourage people with evidence of wrongdoing to take their stories to the press, Benotto said, "If employee confidentiality were to trump conscience, there would be licence for corporations, governments and other employers to operate without accountability." Justice Benotto maintained: "It is through confidential sources that matters of great public importance are made known. As corporate and public power increase, the ability of the average citizen to affect his or her world depends upon the information disseminated by the press. To deprive the media of an important tool in the gathering of news would affect society as a whole."[74]

The ruling was hailed as a landmark victory for the media, and the optimistic hoped it was a sign of things to come, that the Charter would work to loosen legal restrictions on freedom of the press. But on February 29, 2008, the government won an Ontario Court of Appeal ruling that reversed the Benotto decision and restored the search warrant. The *National Post* was required to turn over the leaked documents to the Crown. The president of the Canadian Association of Journalists, in a news release issued the same day, called the appeal court ruling "regressive" and "a major setback for press freedom and the public's right to know." She said it was "the latest in a series of attacks on the use of confidential sources in Canada" that would "effectively require journalists to become agents of the state [and] … put a chill on whistleblowers and other people of conscience who would bring matters of profound public importance to light."[75]

For the court, the critical issue "was whether the reporter and his source had a privileged relationship such that the actual documents and the source's name were confidential and beyond the reach of law enforcement.... [T]he appeal court refused the Crown's argument that law enforcement's interest in requiring disclosure 'will always trump the media's claim to a journalist–confidential source privilege.' The Court of Appeal stated that issues of privilege and confidentiality must always be decided on a case-by-case basis."[76] Early in May 2010, just as this book was going into production, the Supreme Court ruled on the *National Post* case, ordering that the documents leaked to Andrew McIntosh during his investigation of "Shawinigate" be turned over to police for forensic tests. For an excellent analysis of the ruling, see Dean Jobb's column on J-source ("The Upside of the Confidential Sources Ruling"), posted May 11, 2010. The post drew interesting comments, including one from the CBC's Cecil Rosner, who noted that for potential whistleblowers, the ruling offered little encouragement.

To decide in individual cases on the rights of journalists to protect their sources, Canadian courts have relied on the Wigmore test, a legal analysis developed in the United

Kingdom that consists of four criteria. (Justice Benotto found that all four criteria were met in *R. v. National Post et al.*) The case meets the standard if the following criteria are met: 1) the reporter has promised anonymity to the source; 2) the promise was crucial to the source's agreement to provide the information; 3) it is in the public interest to foster the confidential relationship; and 4) the importance of protecting the confidentiality of the relationship outweighs the potential benefit of forcing the journalist to reveal a confidential source.

The second major case before the Supreme Court of Canada on the matter of journalistic privilege to protect confidential sources and information arose from the investigation by *Globe and Mail* reporter Daniel Leblanc into a political scandal over federal sponsorship funding. The reporter had begun with an access-to-information request for documents that were never provided.

> But the report's absence, rather than its contents, became the real story that launched a political scandal. Two years later, bureaucrats finally admitted there was no such report.... The story Leblanc had been casually pursuing into federal government sponsorships of community events across the country suddenly took on a dramatic new dimension [indicating] ... 'a probable fraud case instead of just wacky spending.' ... The story (published in March 2002) was among the first in a Pandora's box of revelations about the waste of millions of taxpayer dollars, soon generating headlines and dominating news broadcasts across the country. The stories would trigger deep public outrage, a high profile inquiry, and prompt criminal charges against a federal bureaucrat and the heads of three advertising firms."[77]

Journalism professor and author Dean Jobb has commented on the two cases, noting that they confront the Supreme Court of Canada with a question at the core of free-press rights and force it to draw a line between the journalistic duty to protect a confidential source and the need of the justice system to resolve legal disputes.[78]

Protecting Confidential Sources and Information

In the United States, reporters' rights to protect sources are covered by shield laws in dozens of states. Canada has no shield laws, but journalist and media lawyer Michael Crawford has developed the following advice for protecting confidential sources and information in Canadian newsrooms.[79]

1. The general rule is that courts are unlikely to offer protection to a journalist who does not want to disclose the identity of a source if it is considered relevant or necessary to the proper adjudication of a matter.

2. In a criminal proceeding, courts may use the Criminal Code to compel a journalist to reveal a source. Section 545 allows a justice conducting a preliminary hearing to jail (for up to eight days) a witness who refuses to testify. At trial, a judge can cite a journalist for contempt and order a jail term and/or a fine.

3. In many provinces, civil courts recognize the special role of the news media and follow what is called the "newspaper rule." Under this common law rule, a court will try to avoid ordering a journalist to disclose a source until the matter reaches trial. However, courts in a few provinces don't follow the rule and may order disclosure in the early stages of a court action. (When a news story based on unnamed sources results in a libel suit, reporters may be forced to reveal the unnamed source, who will be called to testify.)

4. Some courts have found that there is no special privilege for journalists in the common law or under the Charter against disclosing a confidential source's name; however, other courts have been willing to give special consideration to the Charter's promise of freedom of the press during pre-trial stages.

5. A journalist should not make promises to sources that he or she doesn't intend to keep (for example, to let the source see the story before it's published). A court may hold the journalist to his or her word and issue an injunction for breach of contract.

6. Some relationships impose an obligation of confidence on the parties (for example, employer–employee, solicitor–client or doctor–patient). If that confidence is breached by one of the parties passing on confidential information to a third party (such as a journalist), the other party may be able to seek an injunction restraining publication.

 ## CHECKLISTS FOR LIBEL, PRIVACY AND NEWSGATHERING ISSUES

Elements of a Libel Suit

1. **Defamation.** Chances are that the story is defamatory if it contains any statements or suggestions about any of the following, whether stated expressly or only implied: criminal, immoral or improper behaviour; information about someone's financial status or health; insults, slurs or critical comments related to a person's business, trade or profession; assertions that would lower the person in the eyes of ordinary people (as opposed to insiders or specialists) or deter them from associating with the person.

2. **Reference (Identification).** The defamatory matter refers to an individual, either directly or indirectly. The element of reference is fulfilled even if the potential plaintiff is not named—for example, if enough details are provided that the person could be identified or if the ordinary reader could assume from the details provided that the plaintiff is the person being referred to. A member of a group may also be identified for the purposes of a libel suit if even one person might think the defamatory matter refers to a specific individual.

3. **Publication.** The element of publication is obviously met if the statements are published in a newspaper or magazine or broadcast. But the element is also satisfied—the comments are regarded as published—once those comments are relayed to a third party. Posting defamatory matter to the Internet is considered publishing.

Libel Defences

1. **Truth.** To rely on the defence of truth, you need proof of the defamatory statements, such as the following: documents; credible witnesses with first-hand knowledge able and willing to testify in court; corroboration from at least two other sources; detailed notes and tape recordings from key interviews.

2. **Fair comment.** The defamatory matter is an expression of someone's honest opinion on a matter of public interest; it is based on provable facts and is free of malice.

3. **Absolute privilege.** The defence of absolute privilege applies to the occasion of a statement rather than to its content; absolute privilege applies to a fair and accurate account of the proceedings of an open court or legislature.

4. **Qualified privilege.** The defence of qualified privilege involves a kind of reciprocity; it applies when the sender has a social and moral duty to publish on a matter of the public interest and the intended audience has a corresponding right and responsibility to know or hear about it.

5. **Responsible journalism in the public interest.** A form of qualified privilege, this defence was affirmed in 2009 by the Supreme Court of Canada. It applies in matters of serious public interest in which the journalists have taken every step to ensure the accuracy and quality of the final story or series, from initial research to final editing.

Privacy [80]

1. In Canada, there is no general right to be protected against invasion of privacy, but various laws protect privacy in select areas.
2. The Criminal Code prohibits the unlawful interception of private communications but allows a reporter (or other individual) to listen to and/or secretly record a private communication as long as he or she has the consent of the sender or intended receiver of the communication.
3. The Criminal Code indirectly protects privacy rights with sections concerning trespassing at night, intimidation, harassing telephone calls, and disrupting a religious service.
4. Other federal laws affecting broadcasters guard against the unauthorized use of radio communications and recordings of telephone conversations.
5. British Columbia, Saskatchewan, Manitoba, and Newfoundland and Labrador have enacted privacy acts that create a civil remedy for invasions of privacy. Quebec's Civil Code can also be used to assert privacy rights.
6. Generally, photographs of people in public places or at public events can be used freely in news reports, particularly when there is a legitimate public interest in the subject matter. However, when using crowd or "generic" shots, journalists should guard against associating pictures of identifiable individuals with potentially defamatory remarks.
7. Trespassing is a form of invasion of privacy and can be pursued in civil or criminal courts. A fence, boundary or sign can serve as sufficient warning to potential trespassers. Even without a warning sign, once a person is told to leave private property, he or she must go. Even in public places, such as government offices or shopping malls, someone in authority can order individuals to leave the property.

Newsgathering

1. The Constitution affords some protection to newsgathering, but generally, reporters have the same right of access to places and information as ordinary citizens.
2. Some federal laws, mainly the Access to Information Act, require the government to disclose information, with certain exceptions and exemptions.
3. Provincial laws regarding open meetings and open records stipulate access to information about government at the provincial and local levels, again with certain exceptions and exemptions.
4. Judges presiding at trials must seek to balance the freedom of the press against the right of accused persons to a fair trial.
5. Judges should impose publication bans and other restrictions on access only if there is a real and substantial risk of prejudicing the outcome of the trial and no reasonable alternative exists to protect the due administration of justice.
6. The guiding principle of openness in the justice system says that the public and the press have a general right to attend court proceedings.
7. Despite this constitutional right to an open court system, judges can use their discretion to close the courtroom under certain conditions.
8. There is no general right of journalistic privilege; journalists may be asked to reveal confidential sources and information.
9. In many cases, federal and provincial courts have recognized a qualified privilege for reporters to withhold confidential information and sources. The rules vary, however, according to jurisdiction and the circumstances of the case.
10. The question of journalistic privilege continues to evolve on a case-by-case basis and pits the rights and responsibilities of a free press against those of a democratic court system and the need to resolve legal disputes.

SUGGESTED READINGS AND USEFUL WEBSITES

Bakan, Joel. 2004. *The Corporation: The Pathological Pursuit of Profit and Power.* Toronto: Viking Canada.

Brown, Raymond E. 2003. *Defamation Law: A Primer.* Toronto: Thomson Carswell.

Crawford, Michael. 2008. *The Journalist's Legal Guide.* 5th edn. Toronto: Thomson Carswell.

Cribb, Robert, Dean Jobb, David McKie, and Fred Vallance-Jones. 2006. *Digging Deeper: A Canadian Reporter's Research Guide.* Don Mills, ON: Oxford University Press.

Demarkos, Antree, Ian D. Levine, Michael G. Crawford, and James Middlemiss. 2006. *Your Guide to Canadian Law.* Toronto: Fitzhenry and Whiteside.

Dranoff, Linda S. 2005. *Every Canadian's Guide to the Law.* Toronto: HarperCollins Canada.

Geist, Michael. 2006. "Our own and creative land: Cultural monopoly and the trouble with copyright." Toronto: The Hart House Lecture Committee (University of Toronto).

Jobb, Dean. 2006. *Media Law for Canadian Journalists.* Toronto: Emond Montgomery Publications.

Martin, Robert. 2003. *Media Law.* 2nd edn. Toronto: Irwin Law.

———. 2003. *Sourcebook of Canadian Media Law.* 2nd edn, revised. Montreal: McGill-Queen's University Press.

McConchie, Roger, and David Potts, eds. 2003. *Canadian Libel and Slander Action.* Toronto: Irwin Law.

Roberts, Alasdair. 2006. *Blacked Out: Government Secrecy in the Age of Information.* New York: Cambridge University Press.

Ad IDEM (Advocates in Defence of Expression in the Media): http://www.adidem.org

Canadian Journalism Project (Canadian Journalism Foundation): j-source.ca/ projetj.ca

CanLII (Canadian Legal Information Institute—for rulings): http://www.canlii.org

Dean Jobb's media law site: http://www.deanjobb.com/media_law.htm

Federal statutes and regulations: http://laws.justice.gc.ca/en/index.html; Criminal Code of Canada: http://laws.justice.gc.ca/en/C-46/index.html

Juristat (Statistics on crime and justice): http://www.statcan.ca/english/indepth/85-002/juhome.htm

Legislation (provinces and territories): http://www.collectionscanada.ca/8/4/r4-201-e.html

NOTES

Note on legal citations: After the name of a case, the year of the judgment is given in parentheses; however, some reporting series also use the year of publication in square brackets to identify the case. If the judgment year and publication year are the same, only the latter is included, in square brackets; if they are different, the judgment year is given first in parentheses, followed by the publication year.

1. Michael Crawford, *The Journalist's Legal Guide*, 5th edn, Toronto: Carswell, 2008, p. 27. The suit was settled out of court in 1991. "In the end, bloody and bowed, *Toronto Life* publicly apologized and admitted it made 'serious mistakes in the writing, editing and presentation' of an article about the family's history." See also Michael Skene and Evan Cooke, "Canadian defamation verdicts, October 23, 2007, to September 30, 2008," accessible on the Ad Idem website, www.adidem.org.
2. *Pressler v. Lethbridge* (1997), 153 D.L.R. (4th) 537 (B.C. S.C.).
3. *Thomas v. Canadian Broadcasting Corp.* [1981] 4 W.W.R. 289 at 302 (N.W.T. S.C.). For a more extensive discussion of this case and the culpability of innuendo in libel suits, see Robert Martin, *Media Law*, 2nd edn, Toronto: Irwin Law, 2003, pp. 151 and 202.
4. *Leenen v. Canadian Broadcasting Corp.*, [2001] O.J. No. 2229, Docket No. C34272 (Ont. C.A.), leave to appeal dismissed [2001] S.C.C.A. No. 432 (S.C.C.).
5. *Church of Scientology of Toronto v. Globe & Mail* (1978), 84 D.L.R. (3d) 239 at 242 (Ont. H.C.).
6. *Brannigan v. S.I.U.* (1963), 42 D.L.R. (2d) 249 (B.C. S.C).
7. *Murphy v. LaMarsh* (1970), 13 D.L.R. (3d) 484 (B.C. S.C.), aff'd (1971) 18 D.L.R. (3d) 208 (B.C. C.A.).
8. Crawford, p. 29. See *Burnett v. C.B.C. (No. 1)*, (1981), 48 N.S.R. (2d) 1 (T.D.).
9. *Vander Zalm v. Times Publishers* [1980] 4 W.W.R. 259 (B.C.C.A.).
10. Crawford, footnote 8, p. 31. See *Booth v. BCTV Broadcasting System* (1982), 139 D.L.R. (3d) 88 (B.C. C.A.).
11. Martin, pp. 152–3. See *E. Hulton & Co. v. Jones* (1910) A.C. 22 (H.L.).
12. Martin, pp. 153–4. See *Youssoupoff v. Metro-Goldwyn-Mayer Pictures Ltd.* (1934), 50 T.L.R. 581 (C.A.).
13. Dean Jobb, "Internet media law 101," j-source.ca. Posted December 30, 2006; updated January 2007.
14. David Crerar and Michael Skene, http://adidem.org/Crookes_v._Newton. See *Crookes v. Newton,* 2009 B.C.C.A. 392.
15. *Godfrey v. Demon Internet Ltd.* [2001] Q.B. 201 and *Carter v. B.C. Federation of Foster Parents Assn.,* 2005 B.C.C.A. 398.
16. Martin, p. 162. See *Drost v. Sunday Herald Ltd.* (1976) 11 Nfld. & P.E.I.R. 342 (Nfld. T.D.).
17. *Drost v. Sunday Herald Ltd.*, as cited above.
18. *Baxter v. Canadian Broadcasting Corp.* (1980), 30 N.B.R. (2d) 102 (C.A.).
19. Martin, p. 168.
20. *Vogel v. Canadian Broadcasting Corp.* [1982] 3 W.W.R. 97 (B.C. S.C.).
21. Martin, p. 164.
22. *Munro v. Toronto Sun Publishing Co.* (1982) 39 O.R (2d) 100 (H.C.).
23. Cited in Martin, pp. 165–6.
24. Crawford, footnote 14, p. 33. See *Stopforth v. Goyer* (1978), 87 D.L.R. (3d) 373 at 375 (Ont. C.A.).
25. Martin, p. 169.
26. Dean Jobb, *Media Law for Canadian Journalists*, Toronto: Emond Montgomery, 2006, p. 286.
27. Cited in Crawford, footnote 81, p. 62. See *Vander Zalm v. Times Publishers*, as cited in note 9 above.

28. Ibid. See *Beutel v. Ross* (2001), 201 D.L.R. (4th) 75 (N.B. C.A.).

29. *Pearlman v. Canadian Broadcasting Corp.* (1981), 13 Man. R. (2d) 1 (Q.B.).

30. *Simpson v. Mair and WIC Radio Ltd.* (2006), 55 B.C.L.R. (4th) 30 (C.A.).

31. Quoted by Tracey Tyler, "Top court ditches libel case against B.C. 'shock jock': Decision on boundaries of fair comment will make it easier to engage in freewheeling debate," *Toronto Star,* June 28, 2008, p. A4.

32. Ibid.

33. Crawford, footnote 53, p. 46. See the following cases: *Geary v. Alger* [1925] 4 D.L.R. 1005 (Ont. C.A.); *Mitchell v. Times Printing and Publishing Co. (No. 2),* [1944] 1 W.W.R. 400 (B.C. S.C.); *Wesolowski v. Armadale Publishers Ltd.* (1980), 3 Sask. R. 330 (Q.B.).

34. Crawford, p. 47.

35. Ottawa: Canada News Wire (CNW) December 22, 2009: "The high court affirmed a new 'public interest responsible journalism' defence in two cases involving the *Ottawa Citizen*'s reporting on Ontario Provincial Police officer Danno Cusson and the *Toronto Star*'s reporting on businessman Peter Grant."

36. Crawford, p. 3.

37. See *Cusson v. Quan* (2007), 2007 CarswellOnt 7310, 2007 CarswellOnt 7311, 2007 ONCA 771 (C.A.), leave to appeal to the Supreme Court of Canada allowed (2008), 2008 CarswellOnt 1862 (S.C.C.), and *Douglas Quan et al. v. Danno Cusson.*

38. Crawford, p. 56.

39. Martin, p. 191. See *Syms v. Warren* (1976), 71 D.L.R. (3d) 413 (Sask. Q.B.).

40. Crawford, footnote 78, p. 60. See *Hill v. Church of Scientology* [1995] 2 S.C.R. 1130, affirming (1994), 114 D.L.R. (4th) 1 (Ont. C.A.).

41. *New York Times v. Sullivan,* 376 U.S. 254 (1964).

42. Martin, p. 199. See *Leonhard v. Sun Publishing Co.* (1956), 4 D.L.R. (2d) 514 (B.C. S.C.).

43. Martin, p. 201.

44. Martin, p. 107.

45. See Martin, pp. 69–76, for an eloquent defence of free expression and a measured diatribe against all three forms of criminal libel.

46. Martin, pp. 70–1. See *Boucher v. R.* [1951] S.C.R. 265 (Quebec).

47. *R. v. Unwin* [1938] 1 D.L.R. 529 (Alta. C.A.).

48. *R. v. Georgia Straight Publishing Ltd.* [1969] 4 D.L.R. (3d) 383 (B.C. Co. Ct.).

49. See *Lucas v. Saskatchewan* (1995), 31 C.R.R. (2d) 92 (Sask. Q.B.), and *R. v. Gill* (1996), 29 O.R. (3d) 250 (Gen. Div.).

50. Martin, p. 75.

51. Martin, p. 185.

52. Crawford, pp. 59–60. See *Hill v. Church of Scientology,* (1995) 2 S.C.R. 1130, affirming (1994), 114 D.L.R. (4th) 1 (Ont. C.A.).

53. Jobb, p. 316. "The CBC's reporting handbook advises that intrusions into the private lives of individuals are warranted only when the person's private life spills over into his or her public life or when private matters become relevant to the discussion of a public issue."

54. *McKennitt v. Ash* (2006), [2007] 3 W.L.R. 194 (C.A.).

55. Crawford, p. 144.

56. *Aubry v. Éditions Vice-Versa,* [1998] 1 S.C.R. 591.

57. *Silber v. B.C. Broadcasting System* (1985), 25 D.L.R. (4th) 345 (B.C. S.C.).

58. Martin, p. 211. See *Robbins v. Canadian Broadcasting Corp.* (1957), 12 D.L.R. (2d) 35 (Que. S.C.).

59. Martin, p. 211. See *Motherwell v. Motherwell* (1976), 73 D.L.R. (3d) 62 (Alta. C.A.).

60. *Valiquette v. Gazette (The)* (1991), 8 C.C.L.T. (2d) 302 (Que. S.C.).

61. Martin, p. 212. See *Saccone v. Orr* (1981), 34 O.R. (2d) 317 (Co. Ct.).

62. Martin, p. 211. See *Krouse v. Chrysler Canada Ltd.* (1974), 1 O.R. (2d) 225 (C.A.).

63. Martin, pp. 64–5.

64. Crawford, pp. 330–1.
65. Robert Cribb and Fred Vallance-Jones, "Access denied," *Toronto Star,* May 28, 2005, cited in Jobb, p. 340.
66. See Andrew McIntosh, "Into the rough," *Media,* Summer 2000, p. 6–7, and Edward Greenspon, "Four years of dogged digging unravelled sponsorship scandal," *Globe and Mail,* February 14, 2004.
67. *Dagenais v. Canadian Broadcasting Corp.,* [1994] 3 S.C.R. 835.
68. *R. v. Mentuck,* [2001] 3 S.C.R. 442.
69. Crawford, pp. 214–15.
70. Crawford, pp. 316–17.
71. Robert Cribb, Dean Jobb, David McKie, and Fred Vallance-Jones, *Digging Deeper: A Canadian Reporter's Research Guide*, Don Mills, ON: Oxford University Press, 2006, p. 53. See *R. v. National Post* (2004), 69 O.R. (3d) 427 (S.C.).
72. *R. v. The National Post*, 2008 CarswellOnt 1104, 2008 ONCA 139.
73. Cited in Jobb, p. 308. See *R. v. National Post* (2004), 69 O.R. (3d) 427 (S.C.J).
74. Ibid.
75. CAJ president Mary Agnes Welch, in a CNW release, February 29, 2008.
76. Crawford, pp. 107–8.
77. Cribb, Jobb, McKie, and Vallance-Jones, p. 151.
78. Dean Jobb, "Protecting confidential sources," in *The Lawyer's Weekly*, October 16, 2009. Also posted online at j-source.ca: http://www.lawyersweekly.ca/index.php?section=article &articleid=1021.
79. Crawford, pp. 121–2.
80. Crawford, pp. 171–2.

CHAPTER 13

EXERCISE 1   Libel

Decide which of the following sentences and paragraphs are potentially libellous. Place a D in the space preceding each statement that is dangerous for the media and an S in the space preceding each statement that is safe.

1. _____ The police officers said they shot and wounded Ira Andrews, a 41-year-old auto mechanic, because he was rushing toward them with a knife.

2. _____ Testifying during the second day of his trial, Mrs. Andrea Cross said her husband, Lee, never intended to embezzle the $70,000 but that a secretary, Allison O'Hara, persuaded him that their actions were legal. Her husband thought they were borrowing the money, she said, and that they would double it by investing in real estate.

3. _____ A 72-year-old woman, Kelli Kasandra of 9847 Eastbrook Lane, has been charged with attempting to pass a counterfeit $20 bill. A convenience store clerk called the police shortly after 8 a.m. today and said that she had received "a suspicious-looking bill." The clerk added that she had written down the licence number of a car leaving the store. The police confirmed the fact that the $20 bill was counterfeit and arrested Mrs. Kasandra at her home about an hour later.

4. _____ Margaret Dwyer said a thief, a boy about 14, grabbed her purse as she was walking to her car in a parking lot behind Memorial Hospital. The boy punched her in the face, apparently because she began to scream and refused to let go of her purse. She said he was blond, wore glasses, weighed about 120 pounds, and was about 5 feet 6 inches tall.

5. _____ Police said the victim, Catherine White of 4218 Bell Ave., was too intoxicated to be able to describe her assailant.

6. _____ "I've never lived in a city where the officials are so corrupt," Joyce Andrews, a Cleveland developer, complained. "If you don't contribute to their campaigns, they won't do anything for you or even talk to you. You have to buy their support."

7. _____ The political scientist said that Americans seem unable to elect a competent president. "Look at whom they've elected," she said. "I'm convinced that Carter was incompetent, Reagan was too lazy and senile to be even a mediocre president, the first George Bush cared nothing about the people, Clinton was a scoundrel, and the second George Bush—the worst of the bunch—was a liar and a buffoon."

8. _____ The newspaper's restaurant reviewer complained: "I've had poor service before, but nothing this incompetent. The service at The Heritage Inn wasn't just slow; it was awful. When she finally did get to us, the waitress didn't seem to know what was on the menu. Then she brought us the wrong drinks. When we finally got our food, it was cold and tasteless. I wouldn't even feed it to my dog. In fact, my dog wouldn't eat it. The stuff didn't even smell good."

9. _____ Police Chief Barry Kopperud said: "We've been after Guiterman for years. He's the biggest drug dealer in the city, but it took months to gather the evidence and infiltrate his operations. His arrest last night was the result of good police work, and we've got the evidence to send him away for 20 or 30 years."

10. _____ A police officer in your city, George Ruiz, today filed a $100,000 personal injury suit against Albert Tifton, charging that Tifton punched him in the nose last month while the police were responding to a call about a domestic dispute at Tifton's home. "It's the third time I've been hit this year," Ruiz said. "I'm tired of being used as a punching bag by these criminals, and I'm doing what I can to stop it."

11. _____ There was an emergency meeting of about 100 angry parents at the Wisconsin Avenue branch of the YMCA at 8 p.m. yesterday, with its director, Marty Willging, presiding. Willging said he called the meeting to calm the parents' fears and to respond to rumours. A parent asked whether it was true that the YMCA's janitor had been dismissed for molesting several boys. Willging responded that there had been some unfortunate incidents and the janitor had been discharged, but some of the allegations were exaggerated. When asked whether the police had been called in, Willging answered that they had and that their investigation is continuing. He assured the parents that the YMCA will see that the matter is resolved appropriately.

EXERCISE 2   Libel

Write an essay analyzing whether the news organization in the following situation can be sued successfully for libel. Consider all the elements of a libel case and how likely the plaintiff would be to prove each. Finally, consider what defences the news organization might use.

When Local 1313 of the Municipal Employees Union and the Beacon City Council negotiated a new labour contract for the city's employees last year, the union was represented by Sam Fong, its chief negotiator. The Beacon negotiations were stressful and stormy, with accusations of bad-faith bargaining made by both sides. At one point, the union threatened to strike if its demands were not met.

As the strike deadline approached, Hilda Jackson, reporter for the *Beacon Daily Light*, prepared a story that profiled Fong and described the union's negotiating strategy. Jackson talked to a number of people familiar with Fong and the way he conducted labour negotiations.

Jackson's story included the comments of Paula Williams, a city councillor, who said during a council meeting: "Fong is a first-rate bastard. That S.O.B. is trying to extort a fortune from the city. If we give him what he wants, we'll be broke, and if we don't, he'll shut down the city with a strike."

Another of Jackson's sources is Ben Davis, a union member with a grudge against Fong and a history of alcoholism. Davis said Fong had promised to keep union members informed about negotiations and to get their advice and guidance, but instead he had kept the members in the dark. Davis also said he suspected that union money had been used to hire prostitutes for union officials. He said a union bookkeeper had information that could confirm his story, but Jackson did not talk to him. Nevertheless, she included Davis's allegations in her story.

Jackson also reported that Fong had been convicted of automobile theft when he was 19 and had spent five years in a federal prison. Because Jackson failed to read the entire record of the case, her report was incorrect. Fong had served only 18 months of his five-year sentence and was placed on parole because of his good behaviour.

Immediately after Jackson's story was published, Fong's wife sued him for divorce, alleging adultery and citing the allegation that union officials had engaged prostitutes as an instance of adultery. National union leaders also commenced an investigation of how Fong was spending his expense account money. The national union concluded that the charges of misuse of union money were groundless, but it dismissed Fong anyway for having failed to disclose his conviction for auto theft when he applied for his job.

Fong sued the *Beacon Daily Light* for libel.

EXERCISE 3   Privacy

Write an essay analyzing whether the news organization in this situation can be sued success-fully for invasion of privacy. Consider the various forms of invasion of privacy, and decide whether the plaintiff would be able to prove any of them.

Jasmine Lynd is a model-turned-actress who has appeared on the covers of many fashion magazines and in several major motion pictures. She attended a reception at the premier's mansion and stayed late for a private cocktail with the premier. The next day, Lynd reported to the police that the premier had raped her. The incident drew intense coverage from the press, including the *Weekly Intelligencer*, a tabloid newspaper sold mainly in supermarkets. In the past, Lynd had angered *Intelligencer* editors by refusing requests for interviews and threatening libel suits. One editor told the reporters covering the case, "This is our chance to pay her back."

Lynd would not talk to *Intelligencer* reporters, so they spoke to a number of her friends and acquaintances. One friend described Lynd's high school career, saying that she had been a "party girl" who had barely passed her courses and had frequently been in trouble with school authorities. Another source mentioned that Lynd had overcome, with great effort, a severe stuttering problem as a teenager.

Other *Intelligencer* reporters examined court records and learned that Lynd had three arrests for speeding and one for drunken driving. Other records showed that her husband had divorced her because she had been unfaithful. Her ex-husband said in an interview with reporters that he had discovered Lynd's infidelity when she gave him a venereal disease she had picked up from her lover, a professional wrestler. The wrestler told reporters that Lynd had an irrational fear of food preservatives, chewed her fingernails compulsively, and always slept in the nude. Lynd has denied none of these statements.

The divorce records on file in family court also provided reporters with information about Lynd's finances, including the fact that she had purchased a controlling interest in a television production business and several pieces of commercial real estate, all of which more than tripled in value in only two years. One of Lynd's former friends, a woman who had known her in high school but had not seen her for 15 years, said that Lynd never made a business investment with-out consulting the famous astrologer Wesley Wilson. Wilson denied that Lynd was one of his clients, but the *Intelligencer* published the assertion anyway.

The *Intelligencer*'s editors dispatched two teams of photographers to get photos for the story. One team followed Lynd wherever she went—work, shopping, social events—constantly snapping photos. On one occasion, trying to get a photo of her driving on the freeway, they manoeuvred their car so close to hers that she swerved to avoid them and grazed a safety railing. Another team of photographers stationed themselves at the side of a highway on a hill over-looking Lynd's expensive home. From that location, the photographers used powerful telephoto lenses to get pictures of Lynd sunbathing and swimming in her back yard (which is surrounded by a high privacy fence).

Even though Lynd had not talked to reporters since she charged the premier with rape, the *Intelligencer* promoted its story about her with an advertisement in several newspapers saying, "Meet Jasmine Lynd. Find out what Lynd told the *Intelligencer* that she would tell no one else. You can depend on the *Intelligencer*—just as Lynd does—to deliver the truth!"

Lynd has filed a lawsuit alleging that the *Weekly Intelligencer* has invaded her privacy by photographing her without her knowledge or consent, stalking and harassing her, disclosing private information about her, and appropriating her name and likeness.

14 Speeches and Meetings

Reporter: Why is the invasion of Kuwait by Iraq more problematic
than the invasion of Tibet by China?
Dalai Lama: Because we have no oil.
— Alice Klein, journalist, 1990

Many news stories report what important or interesting people say in speeches or the actions people take at public meetings. Even in small towns, dozens of speeches and meetings happen every week. In large cities, there might be thousands. Some speeches and meetings involve government agencies. Others are sponsored by clubs, schools, religious and business groups, and professional organizations. Journalists cover only the speeches and meetings most likely to affect or involve large numbers of people.

News organizations often publish two stories about major speeches and meetings: an "advance" story before the speech or meeting and a "follow" story, which reports on the speech or meeting itself.

ADVANCE STORIES

Advance stories alert readers, listeners and viewers to coming events they may want to attend, support or oppose. Most advance stories are published the same day a speech or meeting is announced or shortly thereafter. As a reminder to their audiences, news organizations may publish a second advance story a day or two before the speech or meeting.

News organizations publish several advance stories about events of unusual importance. If, for example, the prime minister of Canada announced plans to visit your city, local newspapers and radio and television stations would immediately report those plans. As more information became available, news organizations would publish additional advance stories about the prime minister's schedule, companions and goals—and about opportunities the public would have to see the prime minister. All advance stories emphasize the same basic facts:

- what will happen;
- when and where it will happen;
- who will be involved.

Reporters and camera operators jam a board meeting of the Toronto District School Board during a debate about creating black-centred public schools in Toronto, Tuesday, January 29, 2008.

The advance stories for speeches identify the speakers, report the times and places they will speak, and describe their topics. The advance stories for meetings identify the groups scheduled to meet, report the times and places of the meetings, and summarize the agendas. Advance stories also may mention the event's purpose or sponsor, whether the public is invited, whether those who attend will have an opportunity to participate, and whether there will be a charge for admission. Some news organizations publish advance stories for only those events open to the general public.

The leads for advance stories should emphasize what is important and unusual, not just the fact that someone has scheduled a speech or meeting. Often, leads mention celebrities who will be involved in the events or the topics that will be discussed. For example:

Singer Céline Dion has agreed to perform in Ottawa at a dinner expected to raise more than $5 million for the Canadian Cancer Society.

Members of the British Columbia Civil Liberties Association will meet at 8 p.m. Friday at the YMCA to discuss charges that the RCMP refused to hire an applicant because he is a homosexual.

Advance stories are short and specific. They often contain only three or four paragraphs:

The last time the City Commission discussed Memorial Hospital there was standing room only.
The city planner's advice for Tuesday's meeting? Come early if you want a seat.
The commission will meet at 4:30 p.m. to discuss a 10-year master development plan that would change the hospital from a community to a regional facility.
The commission will also discuss spending $10,810 for signs, installing speed bumps in hospital parking lots and driveways, and the proposed closing of Eddy Drive.

Because of time limitations, broadcasters usually carry advance stories for only the most important speeches and meetings. Newspapers run more advance stories, but to save space, they may publish them in roundups or digests (often called "Community Calendars") that list all the newsworthy events for the coming week.

COVERING THE SPEECH OR MEETING

Speeches and meetings quickly become routine assignments for most reporters, but covering them effectively requires perfecting some basic reporting skills: advance preparation, sound news judgment, accuracy, an ear for interesting quotations, and an eye for compelling details.

Reporters may cover speeches about topics with which they are unfamiliar or meetings about complicated issues. Meetings of some public agencies can be particularly confusing. In larger communities, a city council might vote on issues without discussing them at its regular meeting because all the discussion occurred in committee meetings days or weeks earlier. Unless reporters are familiar with the committee action, they might misunderstand the full council's action or fail to recognize newsworthy developments.

Planning and preparation help reporters cover speeches and meetings. Reporters usually try to learn as much as possible about the participants and issues before a speech or meeting. As a first step, reporters might go to their news organization's library and research the topic for the speech or meeting, the speaker, or the group.

Reporters who cover meetings should learn all the participants' names beforehand to identify the people who are speaking or making decisions. So that they understand everything that is said, reporters should also learn as much as possible about every item on the agenda. Reporters can get agendas before many meetings. The agendas identify what topics the group will consider, and reporters can research these issues.

In some cases, agendas provide more than just lists of topics. The agenda may be a small packet with supporting information on each item coming before the board or council. For instance, if a school board is considering a pay increase for substitute teachers, the agenda packet might include the superintendent's rationale for the increase, projections of its impact on the budget, and comparisons with the pay that substitutes earn in nearby districts. Even if the published agenda lists only the topics to be considered, additional documents and information presented to board and council members are public records under most laws, and reporters can get copies simply by asking and paying for them.

Sometimes, unexpected or confusing issues arise during a meeting. Reporters prepare for these situations by arranging to see the leading participants after a meeting adjourns to ask followup questions.

Reporters who cover speeches often try to talk to a speaker to clarify issues or get additional information. The groups that sponsor speeches will sometimes accommodate reporters by scheduling press conferences with speakers before or after the speech. If no formal press conference is arranged, reporters may ask to see speakers for a few minutes immediately after their appearances. Reporters also like to get advance copies of speeches when speakers make them available. Then, instead of having to take notes, reporters can follow the printed text and simply record any departures from the prepared remarks and note important areas for more in-depth research.

Some steps reporters take are common to covering both speeches and meetings:

- They arrive early and find seats that will allow them to hear and see as much as possible. Some public bodies that news organizations regularly cover set aside seating for reporters.

- They introduce themselves to speakers, if possible, or the participants in the meeting, if they have never covered the group before. They may also ask a few quick questions or arrange to talk with speakers or meeting participants later.

- They take detailed notes. Thorough notes will help them recall and understand what was said or done and reconstruct it for their audience.

- As they listen to a speech or meeting, they try to think of groups or individuals who might have different points of view or who might be affected by any actions taken. Reporters will try to speak to these individuals or groups later so they can provide readers or viewers with as complete a news story as possible.

FOLLOW STORIES

Follow stories are published after speeches or meetings and report on those events in detail. Therefore, they are longer than advance stories and harder to write.

Speech and meeting stories need a central point as much as any other news story, but the fragmented nature of most meetings and some speeches makes identifying that idea difficult. An expert on economic development in rural areas might describe the obstacles such areas face in attracting new businesses and their resources for overcoming the obstacles. Should the central point be the obstacles or the resources? Or should it be broad enough to cover both and therefore risk being vague and difficult to understand? A school board might at one meeting adopt a set of achievement standards for district pupils, announce a major expansion of the district's soccer facilities, and hear a report on why construction of a new high school has been delayed. All are important issues, and none is related to the others. How can a writer work all three issues into a single coherent news story?

Organizing the Story

Usually, reporters select one idea or issue from a speech or meeting as the central point for the story. Which idea or issue they emphasize will depend on their news judgment about what is going to be most important and interesting to their readers or viewers. If a speech or meeting involves several important topics, reporters usually focus on the most newsworthy item in the lead and summarize the others in the next two or three paragraphs. Reporters then develop each topic in detail, starting with the most important. If the opening paragraphs mention only one topic, readers or listeners will think the story discusses only that topic. If that topic fails to interest them, they may stop paying attention.

Here are three solutions to the problem of organizing a story about a speech or meeting:

Solution 1

If a speech or meeting involves several major topics, select the one or two most important topics and summarize them in the lead. Summarize the remaining topics (rarely more than two or three) in the second and third paragraphs. Then discuss the topics in the order of their importance:

> The Board of Education gave final approval Tuesday night to its annual budget—two weeks after the new school year had started.
>
> Members also approved instructions to a subcommittee that will represent the board as it intervenes in a lawsuit over the formula for provincial aid to schools.
>
> And the board set a special meeting to plan for hiring a search firm to find a new superintendent of schools.

Solution 2

If a speech or meeting involves several major topics, select the most important, and summarize it in the lead. Provide a brief transition, and then briefly describe the meeting's other major topics, using numbers, bullets, or some other typographical device to introduce each item. Remember that such lists must be parallel in form: if the first item in a list is a complete sentence, the following items must also be complete sentences and use the same verb tense.

Normally, reporters will return to each topic later in the story, discussing it in more detail:

> Carlos Diaz, a Conservative party candidate for MLA, promised last night "to cut the province's taxes by at least 20 per cent."
>
> Diaz said the province can save millions of dollars a year by:

- eliminating at least 10 per cent of provincial ministry employees;

- hiring private companies to build and operate provincial prisons;

- establishing a "workfare" system that will require every able-bodied adult on the province's welfare rolls to either work or go to school;

- reforming the province's post-secondary education system by abolishing tenure and reducing the number of administrators.

Solution 3

If a speech or meeting involves one major topic and several minor topics, begin with the major topic, and after thoroughly reporting it, use bullets or numbers to introduce summaries of the minor topics in the story's final paragraphs:

In response to questions asked after her speech, LeClarren said:

- Most colleges and universities are still dominated by men. Their presidents, deans, department chairs—and most of their faculty members too—are men.

- A subtle, often unintentional, discrimination steers women away from fields tradition-ally dominated by men such as mathematics, business and engineering.

- When two university students marry, the husband rarely drops out to support his wife. Rather, the wife drops out to support her husband.

- Some parents discriminate against their university-age daughters by giving them less help and encouragement than they give their sons.

Never simply report in a story's final paragraph that a speaker or group "discussed" or "considered" another topic. If a topic is important enough to mention, give readers meaningful information about it. As specifically as possible, summarize the discussion or action:

VAGUE: Finally, Councillor Cycler expressed concern about the Senior Citizens Centre on Westhaven Drive.

REVISED: Finally, Councillor Cycler said several people have called her to com-plain that the staff members at the Senior Citizens Centre on Westhaven Drive are arrogant and unhelpful.

Writing Effective Leads

Inexperienced reporters often err by writing leads for stories about speeches and meetings that are so broad they contain no news. The overly broad lead may say that a speaker "discussed" a topic or "voiced an opinion" or that a group "considered" or "dealt with" an issue. Here are examples of overly broad leads:

FOLLOW STORY LEAD (SPEECH): The president of the Chamber of Commerce discussed the dangers of higher taxes in a speech Tuesday night.

FOLLOW STORY LEAD (MEETING): The city council considered the prob-lems of billboards and panhandlers in an eight-hour meeting Monday.

Neither lead contains any news. The advance stories for these events would already have informed readers and viewers of the topic of the chamber president's speech and of the agenda for the city council meeting. The news is what was said or done about these issues. The leads might be revised as follows to emphasize the news:

REVISED LEAD (SPEECH): If the city continues to raise property taxes, major businesses will leave town, throwing hundreds of people out of work, the president of the Chamber of Commerce warned Tuesday night.

REVISED LEAD (MEETING): The city council voted to ban most billboards and to restrict panhandling to only two zones downtown during a meeting that lasted eight hours Monday.

Usually, leads for follow stories emphasize the most newsworthy information to emerge from a speech or meeting. Often, that is the speaker's main point or the most important action taken or issue discussed at a meeting. Sometimes, other aspects of the story are more newsworthy:

FOLLOW STORY LEAD (EMPHASIS ON MAIN POINT): OTTAWA— The fate of accused war criminal Omar Khadr rests with an American military commission after the Supreme Court of Canada concluded it can't make the federal government try to bring him home, Justice Minister Rob Nicholson said today. The court said bluntly that Canadian officials violated Khadr's constitutional rights when they questioned him at the Guantanamo Bay detention centre in 2003 and 2004. But it disagreed with two lower courts that said the federal government must request his repatriation.

Although justice ministers are newsworthy people, the most newsworthy point here is the decision by the Supreme Court of Canada, not the fact that the announcement came from the justice minister. At other times, who said something is more important than what was said:

FOLLOW STORY LEAD (EMPHASIS ON SPEAKER): OTTAWA—July 16, 2009, marks the 25th anniversary of the Canadian Security Intelligence Service, and the agency's director, Richard B. Fadden, said it has evolved from a fledgling organization into a solid, professional intelligence service that is respected and relied upon both domestically and internationally.

So the newsworthy angle to this story was the statement by the CSIS director that the agency is both reliable and respected (despite having come under heavy criticism almost since its founding a quarter of a century earlier). Sometimes, the most important news is not made in the speech or the meeting but in reaction to it:

FOLLOW STORY LEAD (EMPHASIS ON REACTION): University students at a B.C. school, shouting "Common Grounds Forever," pulled the plug on a spokesman for a major food company who gave a speech dismissing the ill-effects of consuming trans fats, common in processed foods.

Yet another approach to the follow story uses a lead that might be an anecdote from the speech, a description that sets a scene, or a bit of dialogue from a meeting to introduce a nut paragraph that states the central point:

FOLLOW STORY LEAD (ANECDOTAL): Cheetos may be a popular snack food in Canada, but they were a flop in China, Roger Enrico, chief executive officer of PepsiCo, said Friday.
When PepsiCo's Frito-Lay subsidiary tried to introduce Cheetos in China, the company discovered that Chinese consumers don't like cheese and they don't like snack foods that leave yellow dust on their fingers, Enrico told an audience in the university's College of Business Administration. Now Frito-Lay is marketing to Chinese a steak-flavoured cheese puff.
Companies engaged in international business often experience frustration and setbacks, as PepsiCo did with Cheetos, Enrico said, but for those organizations willing to be flexible and realistic, doing business overseas offers excitement and rewards.

Anecdotal or other delayed leads offer an opportunity to hook readers with a bit of narrative or description. But the anecdote or description must clearly lead into and support the nut paragraph. (See the sidebar on pages 316–17 for an example of a speech story that uses a descriptive lead to engage readers.)
Quotations also can hook readers with a colourful phrase, but they rarely make good leads. As a rule, writers should use a quotation in the lead only if it accurately and succinctly states the most newsworthy point of the meeting or speech. In practice, few quotations will satisfy that standard.

Use Dramatic Elements in the Lead

Here's a speech story that illustrates how a description of a dramatic part of the speech can make an effective lead.

INTERNET BRINGS PORNOGRAPHY TO CHILDREN, RESEARCHER SAYS
"I sit down as a 14-year-old and type in a few words and let the mouse roam where the mouse will roam," said Edward Donnerstein, as he started to demonstrate what's available on the Internet.

And roam the mouse did.

Donnerstein, a professor of communication and dean of the division of social science at the University of California at Santa Barbara, typed the words "free porn" into the computer search engine he was using. The program responded with a list of dozens of websites offering pornographic images.

Donnerstein clicked on a few of the links as his audience of university students and faculty watched, and he brought to the screen still and moving pictures of naked women and men, vaginas, erect penises, and couples having intercourse. And then he moved on to the rough stuff.

From sites that specialized in bondage and sadomasochism, Donnerstein opened photographs of women tied up and tortured. One image showed a naked woman with what appeared to be cigarette burns covering her breasts, belly and thighs.

"That's a 14-year-old not being asked age, not paying a cent, and getting some pretty violent things," Donnerstein said.

Sex, violence, hate-group messages, bomb-building instructions, and promotions for tobacco and alcohol are just some of the culturally nonconformist messages children have access to over the Internet, Donnerstein said Monday during a lecture on children and the Internet at the student union. And the most frequently mentioned solutions to the problem—government regulation, blocking software, ratings systems, and safe sites for children—have weaknesses. The lecture was part of a series on media and children sponsored by the university's Family Research and Policy Initiative.

Some parents may decide the best solution is to keep children off the Internet all together, but Donnerstein said that was wrong.

"The solution is not to pull the plug. In fact, it's just the opposite," he said. Children need to be online to access valuable educational information, Donnerstein said, adding that he cannot imagine writing a scholarly paper without using the World Wide Web. And Internet access is likely to become more important, he said, as people conduct online more and more of their daily business, from trading stocks to seeking medical advice.

Children have embraced the Internet, Donnerstein said, but parents have little knowledge or understanding of what their children are doing.

Of children between 9 and 17, Donnerstein said, 79 per cent say they are online daily and prefer using their computers to television or the telephone. And 44 per cent of those children say they have found X-rated material; 25 per cent say they have seen hate-group sites; and 14 per cent have seen bomb-building instructions.

By comparison, parents are ignorant of computers, the Internet, and what their children are doing with them, he said. The Internet is the first mass medium in which children and parents are at opposite ends in terms of their use and knowledge of the medium. Most parents, he said, don't know what sites their children visit, don't have rules for using the Internet, and haven't installed blocking software, even if they own it, because it's too complicated for them.

Every new medium—movies, radio, television—has raised concerns among parents about how it will affect children, but the Internet is different, Donnerstein said. The sex and violence in the movies and on television, even cable, are benign compared to what is on the Internet.

"The Internet is whatever you want. Things that have no other media correlation are available," Donnerstein said. Also, the interactive nature of the Internet may heighten any arousal the user experiences. Theoretically, he said, the effects of the Internet may be much stronger than those of older media.

Parents are justified in worrying about what effects exposure to Internet sex and violence may have on their children, but the most frequently mentioned solutions have shortcomings.

Government regulation won't work, he said, in part because of constitutional protections for freedom of expression rights, which allow government to prohibit only messages that meet the stringent legal definition for obscenity or that are child pornography. Even if a democracy's constitution allowed greater regulation of the Internet, it would not stop access to sex and violence. Many of the most salacious sites, Donnerstein said, are based overseas, beyond the reach of Canadian and American law.

Ratings systems suffer a similar defect. They rely on the content providers to rate content as to its level of sex and violence, Donnerstein said. The systems are voluntary and would not bind content providers from other countries.

Parents can buy computer programs that block access to certain websites. But Donnerstein said studies of these programs show that sometimes they fail to block pornographic sites. Other times, he said, they may block access to valuable information, such as sites that deal with breast cancer or AIDS.

Websites specifically designed for children can provide a safe environment. Donnerstein mentioned Yahooligans, Dig (a Disney site), and Apple Kid Safe as sites that allow children to see educational materials but not pornography, violence and hate. Such sites are not likely to satisfy older children, he said.

The best approach may be for parents to learn more about the Internet and what their children are doing with it. Parents can teach their children "critical viewing," he said, in which the children and parents view websites together and discuss what they see.

Children are aware of computer technologies and will make use of them, Donnerstein said; parents need to teach children how to use those technologies productively and safely.

Solving Problems of Sequence and Attribution

Two common weaknesses in speech and meeting stories are reporting events in chronological order and failing to vary the location of the attribution.

Some beginners report events in the order in which they occurred, as if the sequence were somehow important to readers. The agendas for meetings rarely reflect the importance of the topics discussed. Major issues may be taken up early or late, but news stories should not make readers or viewers endure descriptions of minor actions before learning about important ones. Although speeches usually have a more logical order, speakers rarely put their most important points at the beginning. Rather, they save them for the middle or end of the speech.

Experienced reporters write most follow stories in the inverted-pyramid style, presenting information in the order of its importance—not in the order in which it arose during a speech or meeting. Reporters can move statements around and may begin their stories with a statement made at the end of a one-hour speech or meeting, then shift to a topic discussed midway through the event. If topics brought up early are unimportant, reporters may never mention them at all.

Beginners also tend to start every paragraph with the speaker's name and attribution. As a result, their stories become dull and repetitious.

Reporters should look at the paragraphs of their finished stories. If they see this pattern or something like it, they need to rewrite:

> City Manager Faith An-Pong began by discussing the problems that recycling is creating for the city.
> Next, An-Pong said…
> Turning to a third topic, An-Pong said…
> She then went on to add that…
> Continuing, An-Pong said…
> In conclusion, she added…

Writing Transitions

Transitions shift a story from one idea to another. A good transition will show readers how two ideas connect and will arouse readers' interest in the topic being introduced.

Transitions should be brief. The repetition of a key word, phrase or idea can serve as a transition to a related topic, or it can shift the story to a new time or place. If the new topic is markedly different, a transitional sentence or question might be necessary. The transition should not, however, simply report that a speaker or group "turned to another topic." Instead, the transition should function as a secondary lead, summarizing the new topic by giving its most interesting and important details:

WEAK TRANSITION: The board also considered two other topics.

REVISED: The board also considered—and rejected—proposals to increase students' health and athletic fees.

WEAK TRANSITION: Hunt then discussed the problem of auto insurance.

REVISED: Hunt then warned that the cost of auto insurance rose 9.6 per cent last year and is expected to rise 12 per cent this year.

REMEMBER YOUR READERS

Reporters should write with their readers in mind, clarifying issues so that readers can understand how events will affect them and their neighbourhood, city or province. Sometimes reporters forget this rule and try to please the people they are writing about instead of the people they are writing for. One news report of a city council meeting began by saying three employees received awards for working for the city for 25 years. Placing the presentation of the awards in the lead probably pleased the city officials, but few readers would care about that. Readers were likely to have a greater interest in a topic presented later: plans for the city government to help people with low incomes buy their own homes.

Reporters also need to clarify jargon, especially the bureaucratic language used at government meetings, so that readers and viewers can understand their stories. A story reported that a municipal commission had imposed "stricter signage requirements" for adult bookstores, theatres and clubs. Instead of repeating such jargon, reporters should give specific details. In this case, the commissioners limited the size and location of outdoor signs advertising adult entertainment businesses.

Check Facts

The reporter has an obligation to go beyond what is said or done at the speech or meeting to check facts, find opposing points of view, and get additional information and comments.

People say things in speeches that may not be true or may be largely opinion. And because a speech represents the views of only the speaker, a reporter who does nothing more than report the speaker's words may be presenting a one-sided and inaccurate view of a topic.

News organizations are more likely to expect reporters to check controversial statements of fact or opinion made in speeches or meetings and get reactions from sources with other points of view. When Stephen Harper became prime minister of Canada in January 2006, he gave a speech thanking Canadians for the victory and promised to govern in "a spirit of hope, not fear." In concluding his speech, Harper ended with the phrase "God bless Canada." Angry controversy erupted almost immediately in the Canadian media. Well-known *Toronto Star* columnist Linda McQuaig called Harper's words "ominous," and the *Vancouver Sun*'s Barbara Yaffe declared them "crass." The Montreal *Gazette*'s Sue Montgomery said Harper had raised the "red flag" of religion, and other critics deemed his comments "un-Canadian." Still others charged that Harper was "under the influence of a malign puppet master," then–U.S. president George W. Bush. Canadian news organizations included such criticisms in their initial stories, in sidebars, or in followup stories published a day or two after the speech.

Double-checking personal attacks and getting responses from the targets may help to avoid libel suits. If a defamatory personal attack is made during a speech or meeting that is not an official government proceeding, a person who is attacked may sue for libel both the speaker and any news organizations that report the statement. The fact that news organizations accurately quoted a speaker is not a defence. Even if a personal attack is not defamatory or is made in an official government meeting—and therefore cannot usually be the basis for a libel suit—the journalist still has an ethical obligation to check facts, get opposing points of view, and give people who have been attacked a chance to respond.

ADDING COLOUR

Report What You Hear

Quotations, direct and indirect, help the writer describe debates that take place in a public meeting. The people who read and view the news need to know why certain actions were taken or why their elected representatives voted a certain way. Simply recording votes and actions will not give readers and viewers the information they need to make informed judgments. They also need to know the competing points of view.

Describe What You See

Vivid descriptions of participants, audiences and settings add drama to speech and meeting stories. The descriptions can appear anywhere. The following example shows how vivid description can enliven a meeting story:

> A public hearing on an ordinance that would limit the number of animals allowed in homes drew a standing-room-only crowd to a city council meeting Thursday.
>
> Some of the spectators wore T-shirts inscribed with pictures of their pets, primarily cats and dogs.

A combination of quotations and descriptions can make stories even more interesting:

> Baker loudly objected to each vote in favour of the project.
> "We're citizens," she yelled. "You should consider us."
> After all the votes were cast, she threw her petition to the floor and stormed out of the room, shouting: "This is not a dictatorship! You should listen to us."

CHECKLISTS FOR REPORTING ON SPEECHES AND MEETINGS

Advance Stories

1. Report what speech or meeting will happen, when and where it will happen, and who will be involved.
2. Keep advance stories short—normally three or four paragraphs.

Covering the Speech or Meeting

1. Get background information on the group or speaker, including a copy of the agenda or the speech, if it's available.
2. Learn the names of all participants.
3. Find out if there will be an opportunity to interview the speaker or the participants before or after the event.
4. Arrive early, and find a seat where you can see and hear as much as possible.
5. Introduce yourself to the speaker or the participants in the meeting if they do not know you.
6. Take detailed notes, making sure you record colourful quotations, information about the setting of the event, and the responses of the participants and observers.
7. Identify and seek responses from people who may be affected by what happens or who may have views or interests different from those expressed at the speech or meeting.

Follow stories

1. Identify the issue or decision that is most likely to interest your readers and viewers, and make that your central point. If other important issues or decisions arose in the speech or meeting, be sure to mention them early.
2. Focus the lead on specific actions or statements to keep it from being overly broad.
3. Organize the story in inverted-pyramid fashion, not according to the order in which statements were made or topics considered.
4. Vary the location of the attribution in direct and indirect quotations so that the story does not become monotonous.
5. Provide transitions from one topic to another.
6. Avoid generalities, and eliminate or explain jargon or technical terms.
7. Check controversial facts, and give any person or group who has been attacked in the speech or meeting an opportunity to respond.
8. Include colour in speech and meeting stories by providing direct quotations and descriptions of speakers, participants, settings and audience responses.
9. When covering speeches or meetings, go beyond the "stick people" approach, which includes only basic information such as name, address, age and past job experience.
10. To flesh out real people for your readers, find out and include in your story information about the following:

   - personality/character (each person is different);
   - beliefs (religious, personal, political);
   - environment (surroundings, friends, family, hobbies, etc.);
   - likes/dislikes.

The Writing Coach

Q.U.O.T.E. (QUESTIONS UNMISTAKABLY OFFBEAT THEY'RE EFFECTIVE)

By Gregg McLachlan

Want to know more about me? Go ahead. Ask me anything. Ask me where I went to school. Ask my age. Ask where I live. Ask about my family?

Sure, they're all basic questions that have merit.

Routine questions? Yep. Routine answers? Probably. Sure, they're all basic questions that have merit. But remember the opening question? No, not the one about where I went to school. The first question: Want to know more about me?

Whether you're writing an advance, a followup, or a profile, you're writing about people. It's all about peeling back the surface layers (i.e., beyond those routine questions and answers about age, employment, family, hobbies) and getting to know more about what drives a person's personality.

When we do this, we're investing in a person's character. We're committing ourselves to give readers more by giving them the opportunity to get to know a person. The ultimate compliment is having a reader remark, "I feel as though I've got to know this person" after reading your story.

Readers don't get to know a person when we report only age, occupation, home town, etc. We're not reporting to fill out a bank form to open a new account—a process we all know is boring and time-consuming.

You need more.

Think back to high school. We discovered more about a person's personality by reading a yearbook.

Plenty could be crammed into that 30-word blurb next to your graduation photo.

Next time you do an interview, and the situation is right, throw some Q.U.O.T.E at your subject and you may discover a gem. This approach is especially effective for profiles.

The Q.U.O.T.E approach is effective because it involves questions whose answers can't be rehearsed beforehand. Your subject will have to look to his/her inner self to answer. It may take a minute. There may be silence for an extended period. That's OK. That's exactly what we want. We want the subject to dig deep for an answer.

Obviously, I'm not suggesting you throw Q.U.O.T.E in every interview. Pick the time and the subject.

Develop a whole list of Q.U.O.T.E questions that you can keep handy. The possibilities are endless.

Yes, as journalists, we need to be serious and professional. But we also need to put our subjects at ease… and become candid. Think Q.U.O.T.E. Here are 10 examples of questions that can lead to telling quotes:

1. If you could have dinner with anyone, living or dead, who would it be? Why?
2. If you could be one animal, what would it be? Why?
3. What kind of car do you drive? Some say a car reflects the owner's personality. What do you think your car says about your personality?
4. If you were on a desert island, what three CDs would you take along, and why?
5. Can you describe your ideal vacation?
6. Some people have bumper stickers on their cars that read, "I'd Rather Be Sailing." What would your bumper sticker read…I'd Rather Be…?
7. In high school, you would have been considered the person most likely to….
8. Can you describe what your life six months from now would be like if you won the lottery?
9. If you could be in any other profession, what would it be?
10. If you were prime minister, what's the first thing you'd do to make life better in Canada?

SUGGESTED READINGS AND USEFUL WEBSITES

Auger, Michel. 2002. *The Biker Who Shot Me: Recollections of a Crime Reporter.* Toronto: McClelland and Stewart.

Benedetti, Paul, Tim Currie, and Kim Kierans. 2010. *The New Journalist: Roles, Skills and Critical Thinking.* Toronto: Emond Montgomery Publications.

Elton, Heather, et al., eds. 1997. *Why Are You Telling Me This? Eleven Acts of Intimate Journalism.* Intro. Alberto Manguel. Banff, AB: Banff Centre Press.

"Getting people to talk: The art of the interview." 2006. In Robert Cribb, Dean Jobb, David McKie, and Fred Vallance-Jones, *Digging Deeper: A Canadian Reporter's Research Guide*, 118–34. Don Mills ON: Oxford University Press.

"Interviewing." 2008. In *The Canadian Press Stylebook: A Guide for Writers and Editors*, 15th edn, 80–5. Toronto: The Canadian Press.

Miller, John. 2004. *Yesterday's News: Why Canada's Daily Newspapers Are Failing Us.* Halifax: Key Porter Books.

"Quotations." 2008. In *The Canadian Press Stylebook*, 15th edn, 15–17, 61. Toronto: The Canadian Press.

"The Working Journalist." 2008. In *The Canadian Press Stylebook*, 15th edn, 37–202, 332–52. Toronto: The Canadian Press.

Yagoda, Ben. 2004. *The Sound on the Page: Style and Voice in Writing.* Toronto: HarperCollins Canada.

Using Your Senses:
http://www.newscollege.ca

Twenty Tips on Interviewing:
http://www.newscollege.ca

Don't Forget the Followup:
http://www.newscollege.ca

EXERCISE 1   Speeches and Meetings

Evaluating Speech and Meeting Leads

Critically evaluate the following speech and meeting story leads, giving each a grade from A to F. Then discuss the leads with your teacher and classmates.

1. City council voted unanimously Tuesday against raising the tourism tax by one cent to pay for a new baseball stadium. (Grade: _____)

2. A spokesperson for Citizens Against Crime warned parents Wednesday night about violent crime and its impact on families in the city. (Grade: _____)

3. By a vote of 5–4, the city council rejected on Monday night a proposal to build an apartment complex near Reed Road and Highway 419. (Grade: _____)

4. A heated debate took place at the city council meeting Thursday night over the need for police dogs. (Grade: _____)

5. Fifty per cent of the drug abusers entering treatment centres go back to using drugs within a year, Mimi Sota told an audience here Monday. (Grade: _____)

6. In a speech Monday, reporter Samuel Swaugger talked to journalism students about his past as a journalist and his experiences with the two largest newspapers in the province. (Grade: _____)

7. During a speech to the Canadian Legion last night, former Lt. Gen. Romeo Dallaire discussed his work as a member of the Senate. (Grade: _____)

8. Commissioners heard testimony from more than 20 people Tuesday morning on plans to license and regulate snowmobiles. (Grade: _____)

9. The Lands Commission reviewed a resolution Wednesday to create a committee that will identify conservation and recreation lands within the regional district. (Grade: _____)

10. Blasting opponents of the plan, Mayor Sabrina Datoli last night defended a proposal to establish a police review board. (Grade: _____)

11. Travelling by airplane has never been more dangerous, Ramon Madea charged in a fiery speech Sunday night. (Grade: _____)

12. City council voted unanimously Monday to change the zoning along three streets from residential to commercial. (Grade: _____)

13. The business before the School Board flowed smoothly Tuesday night as the board proceeded through the agenda. (Grade: _____)

14. The county commissioners continued to struggle with the issue of protecting the water quality in Butler Lake at their meeting Monday. They eventually denied a petition to build a new boat ramp on the lake. (Grade: _____)

15. The County Commission unanimously passed an ordinance that makes it illegal for anyone to possess an open container of alcohol in a vehicle. A previous law made it illegal to drive while drunk but legal to drink while driving. (Grade: _____)

EXERCISE 2   Speeches and Meetings

Speeches

Write separate advance and follow stories about each of the following speeches. Because the speeches are reprinted verbatim, you may quote them directly. Correct the stories' grammatical and spelling errors, including all possessives. You may want to discuss with classmates the problem of handling speakers' errors in grammar and syntax and statements that seem sexist.

Canadians' Work

INFORMATION FOR ADVANCE STORY:

Leslee D'Ausilio will speak this forthcoming Saturday night to the Chamber of Commerce at the organizations annual meeting. The affair will start with an open bar at 6:30, dinner at 7:30, and the speech to begin promptly at 8:30 PM, all in the spacious Grand Ballroom of the Downtown Hilton Hotel. Cost for the dinner and speech: $39.00 for members and their guests, $49.00 for non-members.

Tickets are conveniently available at the Chamber of Commerce office until Noon Saturday. The speaker, a famous celebrity and frequent CTV guest commentator, is the author of 3 best-selling books, all about Canadian workers, their jobs, their characteristics, their problems. She received her B.A. and M.A. from the University of Regina where for both degrees she majored in Sociology, and Ph.D. from Harvard where she majored in Management with a speciality in Labour Relations. She currently teaches at Harvard, serves as a consultant, and was Deputy Minister of Labour under Jean Chrétien. Her announced topic will be "Today's Workers, Workweeks, And Productivity."

SPEECH FOR FOLLOW STORY:

Today, Canada ranks Number One in the world in productivity per worker. That has both advantages and disadvantages for workers, their families, and employers.

On the upside, Canadian families are enjoying more prosperity, but not due solely to rising wages. More family members are working, especially among minority families. During the last 10 years, the average middle-class familys income rose 9.2% after inflation, but the typical familys wage-earners had to spend 6.8 percent more time at work to reap it. Without increased earnings from wives, the average middle-class familys income would have risen only 3.6%. The share of married women working full-time rose from 41 to 46%. Plus, the average workers workweek has risen from about 38 hours for full-time workers to slightly more than 41 hours a week. Executives, on average, work 47 hours a week.

On the downside, workers complain they're working harder and that they're having difficulty balancing their jobs and personal lives. Canadian workers seemed to be squeezed during both booms and busts. In expansions, companies keep giving their workers more work, and in recessions companies downsize. Then, with fewer employees, those that remain have to work longer and harder to get everything done. So its not surprising that Canadian workers are sometimes frustrated. Forty-one per cent feel they do not have enough time to accomplish all their tasks each day.

Its a complex issue, and there're also other culprits. One is technology. More than ever before, technological advances keep people tethered to their office by cellphone and computer. Think about it! It doesn't matter where you go: to a movie, a nice restaurant, or even a golf course or your church. People carry telephones everywhere and, while some calls are social, many are business.

There's also the Canadian psyche and culture. Much of the increase in time spent at work is voluntary. Workers want to earn more and to move up economically. They're eager to make a good impression: to impress their boss and co-workers. Also, work is important to them, sometimes the most important thing in their lives. Many are ambitious, even obsessed, with getting ahead. Increasingly, then, some Canadians work even on holidays and are forgoing vacations and time with their families and friends.

During the past decade, Canadians added nearly a full week to their work year, working on average 1,978 hours last year. That's up 36 hours almost a full week from ten years ago. That means Canadians who are employed spent nearly 49 weeks a year on the job. As a result, they worked longer than all other industrial nations last year. Canadians work 100 more hours (2 weeks per year) than Japanese workers. They work 250 hours (about 6 weeks) more per year than British workers, and 500 hours (12 weeks) more per year than German workers.

Why? Among the reasons for the differences are the fact that Europeans typically take 4 to 6 weeks of vacation each year while Canadians take only 2 to 3 weeks. Also, while Canadian employers offer or require lots of overtime, the French government has reduced that countrys official workweek to 35 hours. That's because the unemployment rate in France is high, and the government wants to pressure companies to hire more workers.

Clearly, all these trends, whether good or bad, have contributed to our countrys outstanding economic performance, which translates into more income for employees and more profits for employers. So, no one can deny that Canadians are working harder, and I don't like that, but I don't see the situation as all bad. Our economy is booming. There are good jobs for most workers, and incomes are going up along with our productivity.

EXERCISE 3   Speeches and Meetings

Speeches

THE POLICE AND THE PRESS

Write separate advance and follow stories about the following speech. Because the speech is reprinted verbatim, you can use direct quotations. Correct any spelling or grammatical errors.

INFORMATION FOR ADVANCE STORY:

Barry Kopperud is scheduled to speak to the local chapter of the Society of Professional Journalists Monday of next week. The club meets for dinner the second Monday of every month at the Blackhawk Hotel. Both the dinner and the speech are open to the public.

The dinners are $17.50 per person. Those wishing to hear the speech only may attend free. The evening begins with a social hour and cash bar at 6 p.m. Dinner starts at 6:30 p.m., and Kopperuds speech will begin at 7:30 p.m. Anyone wishing to attend the dinner must make reservations in advance by calling LeeAnn Verkler at the university.

Kopperud is the chief of police, and he will speak about issues regarding press coverage of crime and the police.

SPEECH FOR FOLLOW STORY:

Good evening, ladies and gentlemen. I've met most of you before. A couple of you I've seen just within the last hour. I'm glad we have this opportunity to talk under conditions that are more pleasant than when we usually meet.

The police beat is among the most active beats for any reporter. I've noticed that a good share of the content of the news broadcasts and the newspaper comes from the police.

This heavy reliance by the media on the police probably accounts for a situation police and news people have observed in many towns and cities. There is a symbiotic, co-dependent, love-hate relationship between cops and reporters that develops about everywhere.

Obviously, reporters rely on the police to provide information about some of the most important and dramatic events of the day. But police need reporters to get out information on the things they want to promote. Police understand that people read and watch news stories about crime. One of the first places people turn to when they get their daily paper is the police blotter.

Although the police department has had generally good relations with the press, there are some common problems—points of friction, you might call them—that arise from time to time. One of these points of friction involves the release of information through unofficial channels.

The police department has lots of information, some of it secret that it doesn't want released to the public. A classic example is information relevant to a homicide, such as autopsy information and details about the scene of the crime. Why do we want to keep this information secret? Because doing so helps us investigate the crime. A few years ago we had a homicide in which a man was bludgeoned to death with a tire iron. The killer then doused the body with gasoline and tried to set it afire. The body was in a wooded area and not discovered for several weeks. We got a lot of tips about that murder. We also had a couple of people show up trying to confess. Because we withheld the details about the crime scene and cause of death, we were able to distinguish the real culprit from the cranks and the real sources from the phoney ones. Because the details were never published in the media, we could trace leads back to the one person with firsthand knowledge—a person who is now serving a life sentence. But those details are exactly the kind of thing reporters most want.

One of the banes of my existence is that there are people in the police department who like to release that kind of information. Maybe these leaks are intentional—from disgruntled officers—or maybe the leaks are unintentional, where an officer tells a friend who tells a reporter. Either way, reporters will call us back asking for confirmation of these leaks, but the police department will never confirm or deny anything.

That brings me to some ethical questions. Both police and reporters deal with ethical issues. Sometimes we err and release information that we shouldn't. Sometimes we wonder why you folks in the media publish what you do. I just want to share with you some recent incidents that raise ethical issues and ask you to consider them.

A few weeks ago, a police dog bit its handler's daughter. The dog was retired from service but had been living with its handler. As a result of the incident the girl needed stitches. Somehow a TV reporter got onto the story and wanted to do an on-camera interview with someone from the department. We refused. The reporter suggested it was because the story would embarrass the department or suggest irresponsibility or create problems with the city council. But none of those was correct. We refused because the dog had been put down, and the little girl didn't know that. She was fond of the dog, and the dog had meant a lot to her. Her mom and dad asked that the story not be released, and we agreed.

In another recent case, we had an accidental death of a graduate student in a university dorm. The man had suffocated to death, and the newspaper reported—correctly—that he had died while practising autoerotic asphyxiation. I read that article and thought, "How crass!" Imagine how that must have made that students mother and father feel. I'd like to think that reporters would take that kind of thing into account before they publish a story. Sometimes the feelings of the family outweigh the publics need to know.

The case that for me presented the most searing ethical problem was the Wendy Ray case. You all remember that Wendy was a university student who was abducted from just outside her parents apartment one night, repeatedly raped, tortured, and then murdered.

For weeks she was just missing, and no one knew where she was. We got our first break in the case when we arrested a couple of men for burglarizing an electronics store. After we had charged them, Donald Hendricks, the Crown prosecutor, called and said one of them, Scott Reed, wanted to cut a deal: He'd tell us about Wendys murder if we promised to seek a lighter sentence for him. Reed told us where to find Wendys body.

At this point, I went to Bill and Liz Ray, Wendys parents, and told them we had remains and believed them to be Wendys, pending a dental match. I also told them that we knew a lot more about how she had died and that I would tell them as much as they wanted to know when they wanted to know it. They understood that I meant there were grisly details about Wendys death. A few hours later, we had a positive dental match, but before I could get back to Wendy's parents, one of the radio stations had aired a news story with all the gory details. I can't tell you how devastated the Rays were. I think it was not a good way for the family to learn those details.

I guess the moral of these stories is a simple one: People really are affected by news stories. I hope reporters have enough humanity not to get caught up in the competitive practices of the business and realize how they may hurt others. I understand some people may reach different decisions about how to handle these ethical issues. I have no problem with someone who disagrees with me. I have a real problem, however, with reporters who won't consider other points of view.

EXERCISE 4   Speeches and Meetings

Speeches

HEALTH MINISTER'S SPEECH

Write a news story that summarizes the following speech given by the Canadian Minister of Health, Leona Aglukkaq. Assume that the minister spoke at a provincial education convention in your city at 8 p.m. yesterday. Assume that this is a verbatim copy of a speech given by the minister and can be quoted directly. As you write the story, assume that it is just a few days before Halloween. Correct any spelling or grammatical errors.

I am pleased to be here today with representatives of several organizations who recognize that alcohol is the nations number one drug problem among youth and who share my concern that the alcohol industry has targeted Halloween, a traditional holiday for children, as their latest marketing opportunity.

Just as Saman, the ancient Keltic Lord of the Dead, summoned the evil spirits to walk the earth on October 31, modern day distilleries, breweries and vineyards are working their own brand of sorcery on us this year. On billboards and at supermarket check-out counters we are being bombarded with exhortations to purchase orange and black 12-packs and even "cocktails from the Crypt."

Well, as your Minister of health I'm here today with my own exhortation: Halloween and hops do not mix.

Alcohol is the number one substance abuse problem among Canadas youth. In fact, it is the only drug whose use has not been declining, according to our most recent survey of Grade 12 students. The survey shows that, currently, nearly a million teen-agers have a drinking problem.

Why do so many of our young people drink? There are no easy answers to this question, but clearly the availability of alcohol and its acceptance, even glamorization, in our society are factors. We know that before turning 18, the average Canadian child will see 75,000 drinking scenes on television programs alone.

In just two days many of our young people will be celebrating Halloween. Many children look forward to this day as much as they do Christmas and Hanukkah. Who among us can forget the excitement of dressing up as ghosts and goblins and going from door to door shouting "trick or treat," and coming away with a fistful of candy?

Trick or treat.

This year the alcohol industry has given new meaning to those innocent words of childhood. They are serving up new treats—and new tricks.

They are saying: "It's Halloween, it's time to celebrate, it's time for a drink!" Beer companies offer free Halloween T-shirts, bat sunglasses, and glowing cups. Halloween parties sponsored by a major brewer are being held across Canada.

What I say is scary is the possibility of increased carnage on our highways, the real spectre of more binge drinking by our young people, and the absolute reality of those smaller, less dramatic cases of health and emotional problems caused by alcohol consumption.

Last year alone, we lost 358 young people in alcohol-related crashes, some in every province. Fully 40 per cent of all deaths in young people are due to crashes—698 last year, and, as you can see, about half are related to alcohol.

What is also scary to me is the encouragement of "binge drinking" by our young people.

Some of these Halloween ads encourage the purchase of 12 or 24 packs of beer, and who will drink all that beer? 43 per cent of college students, 35 per cent of our Grade 12 students, and 26 per cent of Grade 8 students have had five or more drinks in a row during the past two weeks. And beer and wine coolers are their favourite alcoholic beverages.

I also find it scary that we continue to think of beer and wine as "soft liquor." There's nothing "soft" about ethyl alcohol. And there's just as much ethyl alcohol in one can of beer or one glass of wine as there is in a mixed drink. That is the hard fact.

Finally, as the nations minister of health and a caring mother, what I find scariest of all is that alcohol affects virtually every organ in the body. Alcohol consumption is associated with

EXERCISE 6   Speeches and Meetings

Meetings

School Board Meeting

Assume that your school board held its monthly meeting at 7:30 p.m. yesterday. Write a news story that summarizes the comments and decisions made at this meeting. Correct all errors.

The school board opened its meeting by honouring seven retiring teachers: Shirley Dawsun, Carmen Foucault, Nina Paynich, Kenneth Satava, Nancy Lee Scott, Lonnie McEwen, and Harley Sawyer. Paynich worked as a teacher 44 years, longer than any of the others. Each teacher was given a framed "Certificate of Appreciation" and a good round of applause.

The school board then turned to the budget for next year. The budget totals $618.7 million, up 5% from this year. It includes $9.3 million for a new elementary school to be built on West Madison Ave. It will be completed and opened in two years. The budget also includes a 4.5% raise for teachers and a 6% raise for administrators. Also, the salary of the superintendent of schools was raised by $10,000, to $137,000 a year. The vote was unanimous: 9–0.

The school board then discussed the topic of remedial summer classes. Board member Umberto Vacante proposed eliminating them to save an estimated $2.1 million. "They're just too expensive, especially when you consider we serve only about 900 students each summer. A lot of them are students who flunked their regular classes. Often, if they attend the summer classes, they don't have to repeat a grade. If we're going to spend that kind of money, I think we should use it to help and reward our most talented students. They're the ones we ignore. We could offer special programs for them." Supt. Greg Hubbard responded, "Some of these summer students have learning disabilities and emotional problems, and they really need the help. This would hurt them terribly. Without it, they might never graduate." The board then voted 7–2 to keep the classes one more year, but to ask its staff for a study of the matter.

During a one-hour hearing that followed, about 100 people, many loud and angry, debated the issue of creationism vs. evolution. "We've seen your biology books," said parent Claire Sawyer. "I don't want my children using them. They never mention the theory of creationism." Another parent, Harley Euon of 410 East Third Street, responded: "Evolution isn't a theory. Its proven fact. Creationism is a religious idea, not even a scientific theory. People here are trying to force schools to teach our children their religion." A third parent, Roy E. Cross of 101 Charow Lane, agreed, adding: "People can teach creationism in their homes and churches. Its not the schools job." After listening to the debate, the board voted 6–3 to continue using the present textbooks, but to encourage parents to discuss the matter with their children and to provide in their individual homes the religious training they deem most appropriate for their families.

Finally, last on its agenda, the board unanimously adopted a resolution praising the school systems ADDITIONS: adult volunteers who contribute their spare time to help and assist their neighbourhood schools. Last year, Supt. Greg Hubbard reported, there was a total of 897 ADDITIONS, and they put in a total of 38,288 hours of volunteer time.

EXERCISE 7   Speeches and Meetings

Meetings

City Council Meeting

Assume that your city council held a meeting at 8 p.m. yesterday. Write a news story that summarizes the comments and decisions made at this meeting. Correct all errors.

BACKGROUND

For 10 years, a downtown church in your city (the United Church at 680 Garland Avenue) has provided a shelter for the homeless, allowing them to sleep in the basement of its fellowship hall every night and feeding them both breakfast and dinner. The church can house 180 people each night and relies on a staff of more than 200 volunteers. In recent years, they've been overwhelmed, and the church, by itself, is unable to continue to afford to shoulder the entire burden. It has asked for help: for donations and for more room, especially in winter, for the homeless to sleep. Civic leaders have formed the Coalition for the Homeless, Inc., a non-profit organization, and hope to build a new shelter. The coalition has asked the city to donate a site, valued at $500,000. Coalition leaders said they will then raise the $1.5 million needed to construct the shelter. The coalition leaders say they will also operate the shelter, relying on volunteers; a small, full-time professional staff; and donations from concerned citizens.

FIRST SPEAKER: IDA LEVINE, PRESIDENT OF THE COALITION FOR THE HOMELESS, INC.

"As you, uh, know, what we're trying to do here is raise $1.5 million to build the shelter. We're approaching everyone that might be able to help and, so far, have collected about $200,000 and have pledges of another $318,000, and thats just the beginning, in two months. So we're certain that if you provide the land, we'll be able to, uh, come up with all the money for this thing. The site we have in mind is the old fire station on Garland Avenue. The building is so old that its worthless, and we'd tear it down, but its an ideal location for our purposes."

SECOND SPEAKER: LT. LUIS RAFELSON

"I'm here officially, representing the police department, to say that we're all for this. It costs the taxpayers about $350,000 a year to arrest homeless people for violating city ordinances like trespassing on private property and sleeping at night in parks and such. During the average month last year we arrested 300 homeless people, sometimes more. It takes about 2 hours to arrest a person and do all the booking and paperwork, while taking five minutes to transport them to a shelter. So you're wasting police time, time we could be spending on more important things. So if the city spends $500,000 on this deal, it'll save that much in a year, maybe more."

THIRD SPEAKER: BANKER IRVIN POREJ

"The people who stay in shelters are just like you and me. The difference is that we have a place to go. They're good people for the most part, just down on their luck. This would provide a temporary shelter for them, help them get back on their feet. Until now, we've had churches doing this, and the Salvation Army has a shelter, too, but we should put an end to the church shelters. Its not fair to them because the churches are burdened by a problem that everyone should be helping with, and the problem is getting too big for them to handle."

FOURTH SPEAKER: COUNCIL MEMBER SANDRA BANDOLF

"We have to address this problem. It's not going to go away. And with this solution, it really won't cost the city anything. No one's asking us for money or anything, only for a piece of land that's been lying unused for years."

FIFTH SPEAKER: COUNCIL MEMBER WILLIAM BELMONTE

"I suppose I'm going to be the only one who votes against this. Why should taxpayers suddenly start paying for this, people who work hard for their money and are struggling these days to support their families? And what happens if the coalition doesn't raise all the money it needs for the shelter, what happens then? What happens if they breach the agreement? Then we'll be left holding the bag, expected to pay for this damn thing and to support it for years. That'll add a whole new bureaucracy to the city, and where'll the money come from then?"

SIXTH SPEAKER: TRINA GUZMAN, PRESIDENT OF THE DOWNTOWN MERCHANTS' ASSN.

"The members of my association are strongly opposed to this. We agree that the city needs a shelter, that we have an obligation to help the people who are really homeless and needy, but not on Garland Avenue. That's just a block from downtown, and we've been having trouble with these people for years. Some of them need help, have all sorts of problems like alcoholism and mental illness that no one here's talking about. Remember too that these people aren't allowed to stay in the shelters during the day. Theoretically, they're supposed to go out and work, or at least look for work. What some of them do is hang around Main Street, panhandling and annoying people and using our parking lots and alleys for toilets. We've got customers who tell us they won't come downtown anymore because they're afraid of being approached and asked for money and being mugged or something. Let's feed these people and help them, but put them out somewhere where they can't hurt anyone."

OUTCOME

The council voted 6–1 to donate the land. Belmonte cast the single vote against the proposal.

15 | Public-Affairs Reporting

I've always figured my job is simple: to tell people what I know—within the laws of good taste and libel. Readers should know what the insiders know, and that's what I have tried to do here.

— Stevie Cameron, parliamentary correspondent, 1990

Crime and taxes. Those two things will pique the interest of every newspaper reader and television viewer. Throw a recession into the mix, with government stimulus money being spent by the trainload, and the possibilities are limitless. Reporter Mike DeSouza focused public attention on the opportunity for faltering construction companies and organized crime to cash in when he wrote a story for the *Ottawa Citizen* warning about stimulus project bid-rigging in June 2009. During an interview, Competition Bureau Canada official Chris Martin warned DeSouza that "[w]henever there's an economic downturn, companies that have otherwise been competing well and earning profits ... sometimes will seek to replace those competitive profits with profits through monkey business such as illegal conduct out of the Competition Act."

While one federal agency was sounding an alarm about bid-rigging, the federal Transport, Infrastructure and Communities Ministry was saying staff had no intention of "micromanaging" the process of handing out cash. Opposition Liberals accused the federal government of failing to put adequate safeguards in place to insure proper use of taxpayers' money. DeSouza's background research told him the Competition Bureau had co-operated with police to raid several Quebec construction companies. In direct questioning, however, bureau spokesman Martin said he could not be sure those raids were a direct result of bid-rigging on stimulus infrastructure contracts.

All levels of government were feeling the pressure to get an economic recovery underway, as evidenced by the extreme frustration of Transport, Infrastructure and Communities Minister John Baird, who commented in front of media a week later that the City of Toronto had failed to properly fill out an application for a piece of the $4-billion stimulus pot. Baird, who did not realize he was walking into a media room, told an aide that the City of Toronto was "bitching at us" and said the city should "**** off." DeSouza's subsequent story on the comment netted a public apology from Baird to the mayor of Toronto.

News organizations should report on public affairs and serve as watchdogs over government. Crime and the efficient use of tax money are relatively straightforward public-interest issues. Reporters need to be detail-oriented to cover them effectively: knowing what's next in a court case or being able to follow a budget spreadsheet on Excel are skills all reporters should develop. In addition, many stories of this type play out over extended time periods. Reporters need to stay abreast of developments, deciding what needs to be published immediately and what is background or secondary information that can be published later. Other public-affairs stories involve more abstract and complicated issues, such as zoning regulation, urban redevelopment, or health-care policy. News organizations devote substantial time and money to reporting on public-affairs issues because journalists know such matters affect their communities. The challenge for reporters is to make the effects of policy decisions clear to their readers and viewers and to keep the audience's attention engaged with a story that has many twists and turns.

The public-affairs reporter, to be successful at any level, must cultivate certain habits, including these:

- Diligence. Public-affairs reporters, whether assigned to local, provincial or national stories, must follow a regular pattern of checking sources. Often, reporters discover important stories simply by regularly inspecting documents filed with the register of deeds or contracts awarded by government agencies. Maintaining an ever-expanding network of human contacts helps reporters stay up-to-date with process developments and also identify new story ideas that may be just coming into bloom.

- Knowledge of sources. The sources for public-affairs stories may be the people who work in government or those who are affected by its decisions. Or the sources may be records kept by governmental agencies. Public-affairs reporters must know how to use both people and documents to find information quickly.

- Accuracy. Government agencies deal with complicated matters. The reporters who cover public affairs must report the details of these issues correctly, whether they involve the name of a person arrested for a crime or a contractor's winning bid on a street-improvement project.

- Ability to write clear explanations. Public officials often speak in jargon and euphemisms. Reporters cannot simply reproduce that linguistic fog; they must explain issues and decisions clearly to readers, listeners or viewers. Unless reporters explain governmental actions clearly, citizens will not understand how their lives and interests may be affected.

Reporters who develop these traits might find public-affairs reporting the most rewarding and satisfying aspect of their work, for nothing else a journalist does has the potential to affect so many people.

CRIME AND ACCIDENTS

The first assignment given to many newspaper reporters is the police beat. Beginning television or radio reporters might have more varied assignments, but covering crimes and accidents will be a major part of their jobs.

Not all police reporters are beginners; some have covered that beat for many years. Nevertheless, the police beat is an excellent training ground, for several reasons:

- It forces young reporters to learn the community, both geographically and sociologically.
- It trains reporters in news value and in the need for accuracy.
- It gives reporters an opportunity to develop sources who will serve them for many years.

The police beat places reporters under a great deal of stress. Police reporters mainly cover breaking news, so deadline pressures are constant. Also, they witness some of the harshest aspects of social life: homicides, fatal accidents and suicides. Being on the streets means that police reporters are in greater danger than most other reporters. Some reporters burn out because of the stress of police reporting, but others thrive on it. Many news organizations rotate police reporters to other beats after a few years, partly to prevent burnout but also to discourage reporters from becoming too friendly with the police officers they cover.

The work of police reporters varies with the size and type of community they are covering. In a small community, almost any crime—even a minor theft—might be newsworthy. In big cities, where two or three homicides a week may be common, only the most bloody, most unusual crimes will receive detailed coverage. Police reporters also cover the activities of the police department, including community service projects, promotions, retirements and internal investigations. They might cover traffic accidents but usually only the most noteworthy ones.

A lot of the information for these stories is available at police headquarters or the precinct stations. Reporters might be able to write their stories without ever leaving headquarters or the newsroom. But experienced reporters know that they must go to the scenes of crimes and accidents to be able to report on them accurately, thoroughly and vividly.

Being There for the Victims

Ethan Baron of the *Vancouver Province* covered nearly every day of the trial of Robert William Pickton for the first-degree murders of six women abducted from the city's Downtown Eastside. Pickton was charged in the murders of 26 women, most of them sex workers. The Crown opted to try Pickton for the murders of six women who disappeared between 1997 and 2001, with a second trial expected in which he would face charges for the other 20 murders. The first trial was expected to last one full year and began in January 2007. Because many of the victims had been homeless or had worked in the sex trade, their families complained, the RCMP had not pursued an investigation of missing persons that could have stopped Pickton's rampage sooner. Despite heavy security, Baron attended as many of Pickton's court dates as he could, even when the matter under consideration was only a procedural point. To a fellow journalist, he remarked that on many days he was the only spectator. Members of many of the victims' families could not afford the time to attend as spectators and only attended when they were appearing as witnesses. Despite the trauma of seeing Pickton and hearing the evidence of his crimes, Baron persisted in the belief that someone needed to be on hand to observe the process and report. The women themselves could not speak, and so Baron took on the task of keeping the trial in the public awareness.

Ultimately, Pickton was convicted of six counts of second-degree murder. B.C. Attorney General Wally Oppal decided not to pursue trial on the remaining 20 murders, saying that justice had been served with Pickton's convictions on the earlier six. The families of the remaining victims protested that their loved ones were being denied a voice for justice, but the trials did not move ahead. In the end, a journalist who was often the only visitor in the courtroom was the only voice these women would ever have in their defence.

Police Sources

Reporters and law enforcement officers are often leery of one another, which sometimes prevents thorough reporting. Police forces are organized along military lines, and many members follow the military ideals of duty, discipline and deference to superior officers. Reporters tend to be more individualistic and less deferential to authority than police officers are. A more important obstacle is that police officers can be wary of news coverage. They fear stories will sensationalize their work, portray them in a bad light, or get them in trouble with their superiors. They see few, if any, benefits from news coverage, except under circumstances they can control.

For their part, reporters tend to see police officers as tight-lipped and secretive, who will use claims of privacy or investigative necessity to keep interesting and important information from the public.

Reporters must work to overcome police officers' suspicion and distrust, because they need information from police sources to write their stories. The first step toward gaining the confidence of police officers is to spend as many hours as possible at police headquarters and precinct stations. Reporters should chat with officers about their work and their professional concerns. They also should try to get permission to ride with officers in patrol cars. Those who do will see how officers spend their time and will learn what officers' lives are like. The best way for reporters to build trust with police officers is to demonstrate their professionalism by reporting on police matters accurately and thoroughly and by treating sources fairly.

How well police officers co-operate with reporters depends on the public-records laws of each province and on the traditions and culture of each community. Even if a police department's public information officer provides information readily, reporters still need to talk to the officers who investigated the crime or accident. Reporters should not stop with the "official voice." Check with witnesses, people living in neighbourhoods, people affected by a crime or accident, or anyone responsible for helping in a recovery effort (such as ambulance attendants, rescue crew members or insurance agents).

Reporters need details to make their stories complete. Public information officers, who rarely visit crime scenes, cannot furnish these details. Only the officers who were present have the information that a reporter needs. Reporters will find it easier to get the information they need for their stories if they develop good work habits. This means following a regular pattern for checking sources, such as police reports, jail records, the medical examiner's office, and the department's public information officer. Other helpful sources reporters should cultivate are police union leaders, prosecutors, defence attorneys and bail bond agents. They also need to learn how to listen to the police scanner.

Reporters should know the most frequently used channels for police and fire communications, including the ones used by special response teams or other emergency units. The chatter on the scanner is preliminary information at best, however, and reporters must check it out thoroughly before publishing it. Advances in computer-encrypted wireless communications and widespread use of cellphones is reducing police agencies' reliance on the traditional radio dispatch. While law enforcement agencies claim the change prevents criminals from listening in for advance warnings, it also means newsrooms rely increasingly on tips from people on the scene calling on their cellphones.

Documentary Sources

Police keep records to plan their investigations, keep track of suspects, prepare to testify in court, and justify their budget requests, among other things. Officers do not prepare their records for the convenience of news reporters, but many police records are open to the public, and journalists should learn how to use them. Here are brief descriptions of some of the records of crimes and accidents available from police departments, courts and other agencies:

- Police blotter. This document goes by different names, but it usually records all calls for assistance received by the police. The log provides such basic facts as the location of an event, the time and a brief description. It might also tell who has been arrested, the charge and the time of the arrest. Blotter information is sketchy and best serves as a lead to other sources.

- Incident reports. The incident report gives a more complete description of a crime. It describes the nature of the crime, the location, the name of the victim, when the crime occurred, what property was stolen or damaged and the name of the investigating officer. Other information might or might not be available, depending on the law of the province.

- Arrest warrants, search warrants and affidavits. Police officers usually have to get a warrant from a magistrate before they can arrest a suspect or legally search private property. Police investigators get warrants by filing affidavits with a court identifying the suspect they want to arrest or the place they want to search and what they are searching for. The warrants also provide more details about the suspects and their alleged crimes than police might be willing to divulge directly to reporters. Nevertheless, the warrants and the affidavits usually become public records once the arrest or search is complete. The affidavits help reporters understand what police are doing and why. After a search has been conducted, police also must file a report of what items were actually taken during the search. Warrants, affidavits and related documents are usually found in court files, not at the police station. Sometimes courts temporarily seal the warrants and the affidavits if the search or arrest is part of a larger investigation and police do not want to alert other possible suspects.

- Jail booking records. These records indicate when a person is taken into custody and when that person is released. The booking records will even name people who are in custody but have not been charged with a crime and who therefore might not show up on other records.

- Autopsy reports. In cases involving violent or unexplained deaths, coroners perform autopsies to determine the cause and manner of death. The cause of death is the medical reason the person died, such as poisoning or a gunshot wound to the heart. The manner of death refers to the circumstances under which the person died: accident, suicide or homicide.

- Medical examiner's report. This report may be separate from the autopsy, and it often includes information about the crime scene, witnesses and next of kin that might not be in the police incident report.

- Arrest reports. The arrest report describes a person who has been arrested and the offence, names the officers involved, lists the witnesses and eventually gives the outcome of the case.

- Criminal history information. Information that a suspect has prior arrests and convictions is likely to turn public opinion against that person and make it harder for him or her to receive a fair trial. To protect the suspect's right to a fair trial, law enforcement authorities hesitate to disclose such information.

- Police misconduct investigation records. Sometimes citizens complain that police officers have broken the law or violated department regulations. The complaints usually lead to an internal investigation. The RCMP has been the focus of several high-profile cases involving alleged officer misconduct. Police often cite laws protecting personnel records or investigative records to withhold information about investigations of police misconduct.

- Accident reports. These records describe motor vehicle accidents and identify the time and place of the accident, drivers involved, passengers, injuries and property damages. The reports usually describe how the accident occurred as reconstructed by the investigating officer.

The names of confidential sources and undercover police officers, along with information about confidential investigative techniques, usually can be withheld indefinitely. Privacy laws also allow police to keep some records confidential, such as the names of rape victims or the identities of juvenile suspects. These secrecy provisions mean the police reporter must combine human and documentary sources to prepare complete news reports.

In addition to knowing the records that track specific crimes and suspects, police reporters should be familiar with a variety of other documents pertaining to the police department. The department's rules and regulations along with training manuals will tell the reporter how the department is supposed to work.

Libel, Sensationalism and Other Problems

A story reporting that a person has been arrested in connection with a serious crime is likely to harm that person's reputation. Therefore, reporters covering the police and courts must be careful to avoid writing anything that could trigger a libel suit. Reporters can say a person has been charged with a crime. However, they cannot say or imply that the person is guilty until he or she has been convicted by a judge or jury. Criminal defendants in Canada are presumed innocent and have a right to be tried in a court of law, not by a mob on a street corner or by their local newspaper or television news broadcast.

Reporters may be tempted to ask experts or law enforcement officers to speculate on or predict the outcome of an investigation. Speculations and predictions, even if carefully considered, are still likely to be wrong and may convict a possibly innocent person in the public's mind. Thoughtless crime reporting can also interfere with police work, as in a reporter citing sensitive information or speculating to "fill time" during a television report. When reporters use expert academic sources who study particular crimes, the reporters may try to have the sources speculate or speak about matters outside their areas of expertise. Unfortunately, some sources will attempt to answer such questions, which could mislead the audience. Perhaps the fault for errors lies not with the reporters' star sources but with the reporters themselves and the questions they ask. Instead of asking experts to guess and predict, reporters should ask for facts and background, such as how profiling works and what information police look for to construct a profile of a criminal in the course of an investigation.

The following story does not libel the defendant because it never reports or implies that the defendant committed the crime. Rather, the story seems to be describing two different people: (1) the suspect and (2) the criminal. The reporter carefully avoids saying that the suspect actually committed the crime:

> A 22-year-old woman is suing a downtown hotel because she was raped in the hotel's indoor parking garage on her wedding night.
>
> On Monday, the woman filed a suit in B.C. Supreme Court, charging that the Superior Hotel failed to adequately protect its guests.
>
> The hotel's general manager, Mark Thomas, responded that the hotel's security is adequate.
>
> According to the woman's attorney, Jeff R. Daniels, the rape took place behind an empty security office—a glassed-in booth with a view of the entire garage.
>
> The attack occurred when the bride returned to her parked car for her suitcase at about 12 a.m. Police arrested a suspect a short time later.
>
> The suspect, Charles Henry, 21, of Kelowna, has been charged with sexual battery and is scheduled to stand trial next month.

Several high-profile criminal investigations illustrate how thoughtless crime reporting can injure the reputations of innocent people or interfere with police work. Richard Jewell was a private security guard working at the Atlanta Olympics in 1996. After a bomb exploded in a park filled with Olympic spectators, killing one person and injuring several others, Jewell became a suspect. He was never charged with a crime, but law enforcement sources leaked their suspicions about him to local and national news organizations. To millions of news readers and viewers, Jewell appeared to be the prime suspect. Eventually, investigators focused on a different suspect, Eric Rudolph, who was arrested years later. Jewell sued several news organizations for libel; some settled out of court, but he never won any judgments in court.

In some cases, suits are brought by the law enforcement personnel themselves. On October 14, 2007, Polish immigrant Robert Dziekanski arrived at Vancouver International Airport to join his mother, who had journeyed 350 kilometres from Kamloops to welcome him. Dziekanski spent several hours wandering the arrivals area, looking for help, but airport staff and Canada Border Services Agency workers said Dziekanski never approached them. His mother inquired whether he had arrived and later testified that she was told he had not been on his scheduled flight and she was sent home to Kamloops. In the meantime, Dziekanski, frustrated, tired and unable to find a Polish speaker to help him, began acting erratically, blocking doorways and moving furniture. Airport staff called the RCMP. As an onlooker recorded the scene on his cell-phone camera, four officers confronted Dziekanski, shocked him multiple times with a Taser, wrestled him to the ground and handcuffed him. Video showed the officers standing apart from Dziekanski, who was lying still on the floor. He had died by the time ambulance crews arrived. The resulting case and news coverage delved into the backgrounds and careers of the four officers and the events leading up to the confrontation—in particular, whether the officers had decided to simply Taser Dziekanski without trying to talk him down or find out why he was upset.

The four Mounties were transferred to other assignments. One, Const. Kwesi Millington, ultimately filed a libel suit against the CBC claiming that coverage of the incident over two years (from November 2007 to November 2009) had brought him "serious embarrassment and distress" and exposed him to "public ridicule." After the incident, Millington was transferred to Toronto. All four RCMP members had testified in the official inquiry that they "feared for their lives" when confronted by a distraught Dziekanski holding a stapler he had picked up from a nearby desk. As of early 2010, results of a formal inquiry into the death had not yet been released, and Millington's case had not been resolved.

Elements of Crime and Accident Stories

Most crime stories have summary leads that identify the central point immediately. Usually, that point is the aspect of the crime that makes it newsworthy—deaths, large amounts of money taken, or some unusual or ironic twist to the story. When writing about unusual crimes, reporters sometimes use delayed leads, which place an anecdote or a description of a scene or person ahead of the nut paragraph containing the central point. Nevertheless, all crime stories contain basically the same information:

- Any deaths or injuries. When they occur, these are often the most important facts and should appear early in the story.

- The nature and value of any property stolen or damaged.

- As complete an identification of the suspect as possible: the suspect's full name, including middle initial, as well as his or her age (if over 18), address and occupation. Complete identification of the suspect guards against the possibility that readers or viewers will confuse the suspect with someone else who has a similar name, because that kind of confusion can lead to libel suits.

- Identification of victims and witnesses. To protect victims and witnesses, some news organizations will not publish their addresses. News organizations are required by law to withhold the names of youth and victims of sex crimes.

- Whether weapons were used in the commission of the crime and, if so, what types.

- The exact charges filed against the suspect.

- A narrative of the crime.

News stories should describe the specific crimes involved, not just the legal charges. The legal charges often fail to reveal exactly what happened. Moreover, because they are expressed in general terms, the same legal charges could be repeated in thousands of stories:

VAGUE: Three people arrested in a church parking lot Sunday morning were charged with petty larceny.
REVISED: Three people arrested in a church parking lot Sunday morning were charged with siphoning gasoline from a car.

Here's an example: Say a city council has decided to set next year's budget at $19 million. The council expects to take in $8 million from sales taxes, provincial and federal grants and various fees. The remaining $11 million will have to come from property taxes. Assume the total assessed valuation of all property in this city is $875 million. Dividing $11 million by $875 million produces a tax rate of .01257. That means a person would pay 1.257 cents in taxes for every $1 in taxable property he or she owns. Sometimes property tax rates are expressed as mills. A mill equals one-tenth of a cent (or one one-thousandth of a dollar), so the tax rate in this example is 12.57 mills. Most readers and viewers will see the tax rate, whether expressed as cents or mills, as just another number. The news reporter must explain it in terms that will have meaning to them. One way is to say how much people will have to pay in taxes for every $100 in the assessed valuation of their property. Multiplying the tax rate of .01257 by $100 yields $1.26. That means people will pay about $1.26 in taxes for every $100 of taxable property they own.

Another way to explain property taxes to readers is to show what the tax bill would be for a typical home. Say the median price of a home in a community is $119,000 and personal homes are assessed at 100 per cent of their market value. Multiply $119,000 by the tax rate, .01257. The result, $1,495.83, is the amount the owner of a $119,000 home would have to pay in real property taxes in the coming year.

The annual budget is a news story in itself, but it can also be the starting point for other important and interesting stories about local government. For instance, how much is the city spending on fire protection? Is the spending concentrated in certain neighbourhoods? Another possible budget story would look at the amounts budgeted for snow removal or storm damage cleanup and whether they are in line with what has actually been spent over the past several years. Dramatic changes in revenue from fees, such as building fees, might be a story too. If revenues from building permits have increased markedly, that could indicate a building boom in the community. A curious reporter who examines a local government budget closely can discover a wealth of story possibilities.

City Sources

Covering city hall requires establishing a routine for visiting the various offices and departments and taking the time to get to know each officeholder or department chief. Reporters also should cultivate contacts among the assistants, staff members and secretaries who work in the various offices. Such workers can steer reporters to information for a story and help them find important documents.

Some local officials fear press coverage or want to control information released to the press. More successful are government efforts to channel the flow of information through public information officers, who present only the information top officials want revealed.

When they do talk, government officials often speak in jargon and technical terms: "ad valorem taxes," "capital outlays," "tax-increment financing," "percolation ponds," "promissory notes," "rapid infiltration basins," "secured and unsecured debts" and "tangible personal property." If a legal or technical term is essential to a story, the reporter should define it. Otherwise, these terms should be replaced by simpler and more familiar words. For example, while writing about plans to fix a sewer system, one reporter explained that the repairs were necessary "because of groundwater infiltration." Another reporter explained more clearly that the sewer pipes were so old and cracked that water was leaking into them.

City hall reporters also need to be familiar with public records. Not every document held by government is a public record; nevertheless, some local government records are usually available to the public, including:

- Purchase orders (paid and not paid). These orders show what products or services were obtained from what vendors at what prices.

- Payroll. This record tells not only how much each employee was paid but also deductions and time records, as well as sick leave, vacations and other absences. Although payroll information is usually obtainable, governments can and do withhold certain privacy information such as social insurance numbers of employees. Other personnel information is often exempt from disclosure.

- Expense records. These records may show which public officials travel, where they go, and how much they spend. Telephone records, including cellphone records, for top officials may show who is trying to influence government decisions.

- Bids and bid specifications. When a governmental unit plans a major construction project or a major equipment purchase, it usually asks for bids. Laws usually require local governments to seek bids for all purchases above a certain amount. The bid specifications are the government agency's description of what it wants to buy or build and are sent to all contractors or vendors that might want to submit bids. The businesses submit sealed bids, which are opened at a public meeting. The specifications are public records as soon as the local government has distributed them. The bids become public records when they are opened.

- Contracts. When a government buys goods or services, it often signs a contract with the vendor or provider. Sometimes it awards contracts without taking competitive bids. The contract shows who is getting paid, how much and for what. If certain companies seem to get the lion's share of government business, a reporter should ask why, particularly if the company's executives are major contributors to the campaigns of government officials.

- Licences. Cities issue licences for various kinds of businesses, pets and many other things. Who gets a licence might be determined by political connections and contributions.

- Inspection reports. Fire department officers inspect certain public buildings regularly for fire hazards. The reports they prepare usually are public records. So are reports prepared by building inspectors who make sure that new buildings adhere to construction codes and by health inspectors who examine restaurants.

- Zoning records. Maps, reports, petitions and case files pertaining to planning and zoning actions are usually public.

- Campaign contributions and financial statements. Public officials must disclose who contributed to their campaigns and how they are spending the money. Officials might also have to disclose the sources of their income and where they have their money invested. If an official makes a decision that benefits a business in which he or she has an investment, that could be a conflict of interest, and it might be illegal.

- Resumés. Resumés tell where public officials were educated, where they have worked in the past, and what they've done. Although it might seem a stupid thing to do, some people have falsified their resumés.

Other Sources

In addition to consulting city government sources, reporters can find useful information for local stories in county and provincial records—for example:

- Tax assessment records. These records reveal the owner, legal description, and assessed value of the land and buildings for each piece of property in a community. The records usually are cross-indexed so they can be accessed in a number of ways.

- Motor vehicle registration records. These records show who owns what vehicles, their value and the taxes paid on them. In Canada, the provinces keep records on motor vehicles. In British Columbia, for instance, the Insurance Corporation of British Columbia—a Crown Corporation—is the issuer of licence plates, driver's licences, basic insurance and vehicle registrations. ICBC also keeps track of claim histories for all registered vehicles in the province. Reporters can use provincial freedom of information legislation to obtain information about automobile accidents, driving violations and the status of driver's licences. For example, reporters have used computer databases of motor vehicle records to find out how many school-bus drivers have been convicted of driving while intoxicated.

■ Deeds. The register of deeds office keeps track of all transfers of real property in a county. The records reveal who owns what property, when it was purchased and from whom. In some jurisdictions, the actual sales price of a piece of real estate is confidential.

For generations, local governments have kept these records and many others on paper. Now, computers are changing the way governments do business. The electronic transformation of public records has created both problems and opportunities for reporters. Most records are considered public whether they are in electronic or paper form. However, jurisdictions differ on whether reporters and citizens are entitled to copies of records in electronic form. The difference is important, because reporters can analyze data that are available in electronic form in ways that would be impossible with paper documents.

For most people, parking tickets are an unpleasant fact of life. But for reporters, a city's computerized records of parking tickets can be fertile ground for news stories, as *Ottawa Citizen* reporter Glen McGregor discovered when he went looking. Parking enforcement officers in Canada's capital city are known as "green hornets" because of their uniforms and the financial sting of their citations. In his series, entitled "The Hornet's Sting," McGregor analyzed 2.3 million citations and found that city employees were issuing more than 1,100 tickets every day, bringing in an estimated $13 million each year to city coffers. His analysis enabled him to pinpoint the enforcer who wrote the most tickets, identify the areas in town that were most heavily targeted by officers, and locate the meter in Ottawa where the most tickets were written. He even spent a day in traffic court to find out what defences would work best to reduce a fine or have a charge dismissed. His series also revealed that the tickets involving the heaviest fines were issued by a private security firm that was being paid by the city for every ticket it wrote.

Geographic Information Systems, or GIS, are large-scale databases that tie physical locations to the events that have occurred in them. Many police agencies use GIS databases to map crimes by neighbourhood, tracking trends and using the information to allocate resources and spot areas where increased vigilance might foil a possible crime. Nina Chiarelli of the Moncton, N.B., *Times-Transcript* discovered that local RCMP officers were not willing to release GIS-related information for her area, but other reporters have found that information for Toronto and Ottawa was freely accessible—mapped to a Google application. Information on GIS databases can be requested under freedom of information laws.

School Districts

Public education absorbs more local tax money than any other area of government. That fact should encourage local news organizations to provide thorough and continuing coverage of schools. Most journalists, however, say education is poorly covered.

The responsibility for the poor news coverage of education rests partly with journalists and partly with educators themselves. Understanding what teachers and administrators are doing requires that reporters learn something about curriculum, educational methodology and child psychology, as well as budgets, taxes and school finance laws. These are difficult subjects to master, so many news organizations simply focus on what school boards decide or top administrators say. Yet such coverage reveals little of what happens to children in the classroom. Educators have compounded the problem with their fondness for opaque jargon, calling libraries "learning resource centres" and schools "attendance centres." Many of them also tend to fear news coverage, sometimes out of a desire to protect students and teachers but other times to protect themselves from criticism.

Many newspapers prepare report cards for local school districts. Reporters have discovered that they must do more than simply report scores on standardized tests and compare the scores of different schools and different districts. Test scores can be dramatically affected by such things as the proportion of pupils who have one or more parents with a college degree, parents' income (often assessed by the proportion of pupils who qualify for free or reduced-price lunches), what percentage of pupils enter or leave school during the year, and the percentage of pupils for whom English or French is their second language. Accumulating all of the data for a school report card and analyzing it correctly can take months, but the work can pay off in a story or series that many people will read or watch.

School Sources and Documents

Education reporters should remember that the sources who are highest placed and most often quoted could have the least knowledge of what is happening in classrooms. Boards of education often concentrate on financial and administrative matters and pay less attention to curriculum issues. The superintendent of schools has day-to-day authority to direct the district and carry out policies set by the board. Superintendents generally deal willingly with reporters, but their knowledge of the classroom might be limited. In large districts, a number of assistant superintendents and program administrators may report to the superintendent. They may have information about specific areas, such as elementary education, art education, nutrition and foreign language instruction. Principals and teachers know the most about what is happening in classrooms, but they might be among the least accessible sources. Some of the best sources could be next door—or at the next desk. Neighbours, friends and colleagues who have school-age children could have a wealth of ideas or anecdotes for fleshing out stories.

Schools are semi-public places. Officials try to control access to school buildings to protect students and prevent disruption of the educational atmosphere, but sometimes officials use the restrictions to harass reporters. Such confrontations are rare, but reporters who want to cover stories about classroom activities should arrange their visits in advance with the teacher and the principal and possibly with the superintendent as well. In many schools, parents must sign forms or otherwise give their permission for their children to appear in the media. Check in with the school office on any visit. This allows administration and teachers to remove any children who do not have parental approval for media exposure before reporters or photographers enter a classroom or playground.

Some school records are closed to the public. Educational records on specific students are closed by provincial and federal laws, although directory information on specific students— name, age, address, major areas of study, and height and weight (for athletes)—is normally available unless a student objects to its release. Personnel records for district employees and supervisors usually are confidential.

Although student and personnel records are closed, access to information laws can give reporters access to other records:

- Laws and policies. Provincial education laws and school board policies should be a starting point for any story about or investigation of a school. Until reporters know how a school or a program is supposed to run, they cannot evaluate how well it is operating.

- Budget and financial records. All records on school district revenues and expenditures are open to the public. The budgets reveal the district's priorities, and a comparison of budgets over several years can indicate how these priorities have shifted. Bills and warrants show how a district actually spent its money. Documents about government grants are worth a look too. Reporters can compare what administrators said grants would be used for with the vouchers showing how the money was actually spent.

- Salary information. Teachers' salaries are often on the public record, as are employment contracts for school superintendents and principals in many areas. These contracts reveal what perks an administrator is receiving in addition to a salary—such as travel expenses, automobile allowances and club memberships.

- Accreditation reports, audits and other assessment records. Many public schools are accredited, a process that requires the school to prepare a self-study report. A visiting team uses the self-study to guide its on-site investigation of the school and then issues a final report. In addition, districts and individual schools usually prepare a variety of reports for education officials. School districts may submit several reports describing curriculum, personnel, students and district finances. These reports, which might include recommendations for upgrading school facilities, curriculum or personnel, can give reporters criteria for evaluating school performance and progress over time.

- Food service records. Reporters generally have access to records about the school lunch program, including analyses of menus and receipts and expenditures.

- Transportation records. If a district operates school buses, it is likely to keep the vehicles' inspection and servicing records. Reports on accidents, even minor ones, often must be kept as well.

COURTS

Some legal proceedings attract national or even international media attention. The trial of Robert William Pickton for the murder of six women in Vancouver grabbed headlines around the world. Pickton was arrested following an investigation into the disappearances of 65 women from Vancouver's Downtown Eastside. Investigators found the personal effects of some of the missing women, as well as DNA evidence, in several areas on Pickton's pig farm.

The Braidwood Inquiry into the Tasering death of Robert Dziekanski and suits filed against the Mounties involved shone a spotlight on police use of a supposedly "safe" means of restraining agitated people. A series of high-profile cases involving Tasers and people who died or were severely injured after police use of the device tarnished the RCMP's reputation.

In the mid-1990s, headlines around the world focused on Karla Homolka and her then-husband Paul Bernardo. Bernardo was convicted of the brutal rape and murder of two teenage girls and given a life sentence, while Homolka, following a plea bargain, was sentenced to 12 years in prison for manslaughter. After her release, Homolka was hounded by the media and ultimately decided to move to the Caribbean to escape media and public attention.

People might think criminal prosecutions depend heavily on scientific evidence, such as DNA tests. In fact, police and prosecutors on tight budgets often skimp on laboratory tests and rely on confessions to build their cases. People also might think court trials are long, requiring weeks or even months. In fact, most trials last less than a week. And while sensational cases might lead people to think that lawyers engage in courtroom theatrics and make inflammatory statements to reporters, attorneys generally behave courteously toward one another and are restrained in what they say to the media. Some have a policy of never talking to reporters.

Most trials lack the profile and drama of Pickton's, but they can make interesting and important news stories. Crimes disrupt the community and challenge its moral order. People want to know that the moral order will be maintained. Citizens also want to know that law enforcement officers, prosecutors, defence attorneys and judges are doing their jobs. In most instances, the law enforcement system works well, but in a number of cases, innocent people have been damaged or have gone to prison. Reporters who cover the courts must remain vigilant and skeptical about the actions and decisions of police, prosecutors and judges. When malfunctions occur in the Canadian justice system, these failures receive wide coverage in the media. Two widely reported miscarriages of justice concerned David Milgaard and Steven Truscott.

David Milgaard was sentenced to life in prison in 1970 for the murder of Gail Miller, a nursing assistant in Saskatoon. His conviction was overturned by the Supreme Court of Canada in 1992. Then in 1997, Milgaard's name was fully cleared after re-examination of DNA evidence. The report of a commission of inquiry released in 2008 found that investigators should have re-opened the case in 1980 when the then-wife of serial rapist Larry Fisher told police she was convinced her husband was connected to Miller's murder. Fisher has since been convicted of the crime.

Although the inquiry's head, Commissioner Edward MacCallum, wrote that police, RCMP, Crown prosecutors and federal justice officials had "acted in good faith" in the Milgaard case, he recommended that the wrongful convictions in Canada be examined and reviewed and that all such reviews be conducted by a non-political independent review board, as is done in other countries.

Steven Truscott's case—much older than Milgaard's—also received judicial review in recent years. Truscott's path through the Canadian justice system started in 1959, when at the age of 14 he was tried, convicted and sentenced to death by hanging for the murder of Lynne Harper near Clinton, Ont., a sentence that was commuted to life by the federal cabinet. Truscott's controversial conviction was one of the factors that led to the abolition of the death penalty in Canada.

Truscott was released from prison in 1969 but consistently maintained his innocence. During his time behind bars, he had been given LSD and sodium pentothal in an effort to have him confess to the crime. Despite decades of media-reported lobbying on Truscott's behalf, his case did not receive a judicial review until 2004. Truscott was formally acquitted of Harper's death in 2007. The following year, he was awarded $6.5-million as compensation for his wrongful conviction.

General Information about the Court System

Knowledge of the court system is important for all reporters, not just those who make the courts their beat. Courts are important sources for all kinds of information. Business reporters, education reporters, even sports reporters may follow paper trails to courts. For example, a business reporter might be seeking information about a corporation that plans to locate a new factory in the community. The corporation's public relations office will provide only the facts the corporation is willing to release. Thus, the reporter needs other sources, and one possibility is court records. If the corporation has sued or been sued, it will have disclosed a lot of information to the other party as part of a pre-trial process called "discovery." Some of that information might become part of the court record available to the public. The records might reveal more detailed information about the corporation's finances, structure and operating style.

In general, there are two kinds of court cases: criminal and civil. Criminal cases represent society's efforts to protect the public good or control and correct wrongdoing. Civil cases arise out of disputes between private individuals or corporate entities. In both cases, reporters must be sensitive to the need for absolute accuracy and compliance with all orders issued by a judge in the matter, as well as with the general requirements of Canadian law. While they have common elements, criminal and civil cases proceed sufficiently differently that we will examine them separately below. Further, since court systems in the various provinces and territories differ significantly, reporters should familiarize themselves with the system in their own province or territory.

Criminal Cases

Criminal offences are either *summary conviction* or *indictable* offences. Summary conviction offences are considered less serious and may be dealt with in a streamlined process in which the accused goes directly to trial without a preliminary hearing. Public drunkenness, causing a disturbance, and indecent exposure in a public place are examples of summary conviction offences. Trial is by a justice of the peace or by the lowest-level provincial court. There is no jury. For some offences that fall close to the dividing line between summary conviction and indictable offences, the Crown has the discretion on how to proceed.

Indictable offences are more serious. For some indictable offences, such as armed robbery and arson, the Crown usually can choose the level of court before which the case will be brought, while the accused can choose whether a jury will hear the case or not. For the most serious indictable offences, such as murder or treason, the case must be tried in a superior court before a jury, unless both the accused and the provincial attorney general agree that it may be heard without a jury.

After a verdict has been handed down, an appeal may be filed. Provincial courts of appeal hear appeals of cases involving indictable offences; appeals on summary conviction verdicts are heard by any of several courts, according to the law in each province. The Supreme Court of Canada will hear an appeal on criminal cases only if some point of law is involved and if "leave to appeal" has been granted by a provincial appeal court or by a panel of three Supreme Court of Canada justices.

The first step in a criminal court case is generally *arraignment.* In arraignment, the accused is brought before a judge, the charges against him or her are read, and the accused is asked to enter a plea of guilty or not guilty. If the accused refuses to enter a plea, the court may record a plea of not guilty in order to move matters along. A guilty plea generally moves the case directly into the sentencing phase, while a not-guilty plea triggers the process of conducting a trial. During arraignment, judges may also hear statements from mental-health professionals as to the accused's fitness to understand the charges and stand trial. The presiding judge will usually issue a ban on publishing such evidence, but if a ban is not issued, the information may be reported, and normally, no other restrictions apply to reporting on arraignments. Decisions about bail can be made at the arraignment or at a separate bail (or interim release) hearing later. If an accused requests a ban on publicity, the judge must grant it. The ban prohibits publishing any information revealed at the hearing, including the judge's reasons for granting or denying bail; only the matter of whether bail was granted and if so, any conditions of release, may be reported. An accused person's criminal record should not be reported, and an absolute (Criminal Code) ban prohibits reporting confessions.

Following arraignment, the court holds a *preliminary inquiry* to determine whether there is enough evidence to proceed to trial. If the accused asks for a publication ban, the judge is required to grant it. The ban prohibits publishing evidence presented during the inquiry; journalists can then report only the exact charge, whether the accused was sent to trial, the number of witnesses heard, and any relevant comments (excepting those that refer to the evidence presented). Publication bans imposed during a preliminary inquiry remain in effect until a verdict is reached, at which point the testimony may be published. If there is insufficient evidence at the inquiry to warrant a trial, the banned testimony becomes publishable once the accused is discharged.

If the judge determines that there is sufficient evidence to proceed to trial, the process of naming counsel and empanelling a jury begins—in much the same way as depicted in film and TV dramas. Most court cases unfold as a vast and stately judicial ballet, with all players carefully rehearsing and performing their parts. With such a wealth of detail that must be presented, reporters who hope to specialize in court matters must be thoroughly familiar with the Canadian Criminal Code and with the laws in their province or territory.

Once a jury and alternates are selected and the trial is underway, the general rule is that all evidence presented in open court can be reported. There are restrictions, however, so consult a court official and your editor to determine whether you can report a development. Publication bans are much more common in Canada than they are in the United States. In Canada, a web of statutory and non-statutory (or "discretionary") bans may apply or be imposed at successive stages of a legal process.

The legal dangers of reporting on criminal trials include revealing an accused's criminal record and revealing information about a *voir dire* (a proceeding within a trial, held without the jury present, to determine whether evidence is admissible in open court).

CP PHOTO/Chuck Stoody

A sheriff posts a notice of ban of publication on the courthouse doors in Port Coquitlam, B.C., on Wednesday, January 15, 2003. The preliminary hearing for accused serial killer Robert Pickton was delayed for a portion of the day by presentations from media lawyers.

On rare occasions, judges may ban the public and the media from the courtroom to preserve order and due process or to protect national security or the public interest.

Publication bans remain in effect until a verdict is handed down, at which point journalists may normally report on all the facts of the case, including previously banned information, as well as on the views and comments of relevant sources, such as the parties involved, legal experts and editorial writers.

Specific rules apply to publication bans regarding young offenders—those between the ages of 12 and 18. The Canadian Youth Criminal Justice Act (which replaced the Young Offenders Act in 2003) bans identifying the accused (unless he or she has been sentenced as an adult, and even then, only if no ban has been imposed). The act also prohibits identifying youths involved in crimes as victims (including deceased victims) or witnesses; exceptions require the permission of the parents and the court and from the young offenders themselves once they have reached the age of 18. However, in such instances reporters must be careful not to fall afoul of the ban by identifying others involved who have not reached 18 (not only by naming them but also by revealing information that would allow identification).

After the conclusion of a trial, the verdict may be appealed. In general, any occurrence or statement in an open appeal court can be reported, but all the general rules of fair and balanced coverage apply equally to appeal courts as to trial courts; for example, suggesting that a judge is biased or prejudiced would qualify as contempt of court. If a new trial is ordered, the assumption is that the previous trial holds no weight and that all procedures and restrictions imposed or agreed to previously no longer apply.

Civil Cases

Remember that civil cases involve disputes between members (or groups of members) of society, unlike criminal law, in which the Crown prosecutes individuals. Thus in civil cases, there is no prosecutor or accused, no acquittal or conviction. The person who launches a civil suit is called the plaintiff (or petitioner), and the party complained of is called the defendant (or respondent). If the suit succeeds, the plaintiff is awarded damages (sums of money) to compensate for the injury, but since the injury is non-criminal, no one is sentenced.

Civil cases may be small claims, intermediate claims or larger claims. They may involve suits brought on behalf of groups of people (class action lawsuits), or they may deal with disputes at a more individual level, such as suits regarding the administration of wills or estates. Small claims cases are usually heard only by a judge, with the parties representing themselves. Two neighbours disagreeing over a fence between their properties might take the matter to small claims court. Intermediate claims may be heard at lower or intermediate courts, generally with lawyers representing the parties and without a jury. The largest civil claims are usually heard in provincial superior courts by a judge alone or with a jury (except in Quebec, which no longer provides for juries in civil trials).

Class action lawsuits are initiated on behalf of a group of people who see themselves as victims of a common action. For example, a group of mill workers who all suffered ill effects as a result of exposure to hazardous chemicals during a mill fire might join a class action lawsuit. The group agrees that their cases are sufficiently similar that the facts will stand for all of the participants, who will share proportionately in any damages awarded.

Before a civil trial, the parties go through a process known as *examination for discovery*. This process is similar to a preliminary inquiry in a criminal trial. In the case of a civil suit, the examination for discovery allows the parties to examine each other's case presentations and agree on the issues to be decided in the course of the trial. Unlike a preliminary inquiry, however, examinations for discovery are not made public.

CHECKLISTS FOR PUBLIC-AFFAIRS REPORTING

Crimes and Accidents

1. Spend time at the police station and talk to officers; learn their concerns.
2. Get as much information as possible from the investigating officers, witnesses, victims and suspects.
3. Learn what records are available at the police station and what information they do and do not contain.
4. When writing crime stories, avoid implying that a suspect is guilty.
5. Avoid referring to a suspect's race or religion unless it is clearly relevant to the story.

Local Government

1. Learn how your local governments are organized, what their powers and limitations are, and how the various governmental units interact.
2. Study the budgets of local government units, and learn how governments raise their money.

3. Develop a routine for visiting the local government offices on your beat, and become familiar with the people who work in those offices.
4. Learn what public records are kept in each office and how to use them.
5. Go beyond covering school board meetings; visit schools and talk to principals, teachers, parents and students.

Courts

1. Remember that the Crown files criminal charges against people suspected of violating criminal laws, whereas civil cases are usually between private parties.
2. Learn how Canadian courts are organized, the names of the various courts and what kinds of cases they hear.
3. Learn how court records are kept and how to find the records on any particular case.
4. Do not imply that a defendant in a criminal case is guilty; only the jury or the judge can decide that.
5. Be skeptical of allegations and damage claims that appear in civil complaints; they present only one side of the story.
6. Be alert to the possibility that a plea bargain or a settlement will end a case before or during a trial.

A NOTE ABOUT THIS CHAPTER'S EXERCISES

Many of the documents available to a public-affairs reporter—lawsuits and police reports, for example—provide all the information needed for minor stories. Examples of such documents are reproduced in the following exercises. Write a news story based on the information in each document. Unless the instructions say otherwise, assume that the police reports have been prepared by officers who investigated incidents in your community and that all other legal documents have been filed in your city hall, provincial courthouse, or federal building.

CHAPTER 15

EXERCISE 1   Public-Affairs Reporting: 911 Emergency

A Child's Heroism

A six-year-old girl placed the following call to a 911 dispatcher. Assume that the girl placed the call in your city today. She is Laura Burke, the daughter of Lynn and Randy Burke of 412 Wilson Avenue.

Police arrested a neighbour, Andrew Caspinwall of 416 Wilson Avenue, and charged him with raping Mrs. Burke. Bail has been set at $250,000, and Caspinwall, 24, is being held in the local jail.

DISPATCHER:	911 emergency. Hello?
GIRL:	My mommy needs help.
DISPATCHER:	What's wrong?
GIRL:	Somebody's hurting my mommy.
DISPATCHER:	Where do you live?
GIRL:	At home with my mommy and daddy.
DISPATCHER:	No, uh, that's not what I mean. Can you tell me where your house is, your address?
GIRL:	Wilson Avenue.
DISPATCHER:	Do you know the address, the number?
GIRL:	Hurry. My mommy's crying.
DISPATCHER:	No, honey, do you know your address?
GIRL, CRYING:	I gotta think. It's, uh, it's, uh, 4 something, I'm not sure. 412. 412.
DISPATCHER:	OK. I'll send help.
GIRL, CRYING:	Hurry.
DISPATCHER:	What's your name?
GIRL:	Laura. Laura Anne Burke.
DISPATCHER:	Can you tell me what's wrong, who's hurting your mother?
GIRL:	A man. He came in the back door and hit my mommy.
DISPATCHER:	Where are you now?
GIRL:	Upstairs.
DISPATCHER:	Does the man know you're there?
GIRL:	No. I'm hiding.
DISPATCHER:	Where are you hiding?
GIRL:	In my mommy and daddy's room. Under the bed.
DISPATCHER:	Can you lock the door?
GIRL:	I don't know. Maybe.
DISPATCHER:	Don't hang up. Just put the phone down and go lock the door. Then come back, talk to me some more.
GIRL:	My mommy. What'll happen to my mommy?
DISPATCHER:	We've got three police cars coming. They'll be there in a minute. Now go lock the door, and don't let anyone in until I tell you. OK?
GIRL:	I guess so.
DISPATCHER:	Hello? Hello? Laura, are you there?
GIRL:	I locked the door.
DISPATCHER:	How old are you, Laura?
GIRL:	Six.
DISPATCHER:	You're doing a good job, Laura. You have to be brave now to help your mommy. Tell me, is the man armed?
GIRL:	What's that mean?
DISPATCHER:	Does he have a gun?
GIRL:	No. A knife.

DISPATCHER: OK, a knife. Is the man still there, Laura?

GIRL, SOBBING: I don't know. I'm afraid. Will he hurt me too?

DISPATCHER: No one will hurt you, Laura. Be brave. The police are outside now. They'll be coming into your house. You may hear some noise, but that's OK. Stay in the bedroom, and don't let anyone in, OK?

GIRL: OK.

DISPATCHER: Your daddy's coming, too. We've found your daddy.

GIRL: Soon?

DISPATCHER: The police say they're in your house. They're helping your mommy now. They've found your mommy, and they're going to take her to a doctor, a hospital.

GIRL: The man?

DISPATCHER: He's been caught, arrested. It's OK. It's safe to go downstairs now. There are people there to help you. They want to talk to you, Laura. Can you unlock your door and go downstairs? Laura? Hello? Are you there? Laura? Hello? Laura?

CHAPTER 15

EXERCISE 2   Public-Affairs Reporting

Assume that the police department for your city released the following report of a traffic accident. Write a story that summarizes the accident. Following the report is an explanation of the codes used in the report and some additional information for followup or sidebar stories. Your instructor might ask that you write only about the accident or write followup or sidebar stories as well.

TRAFFIC ACCIDENT REPORT

DIAGRAM WHAT HAPPENED – (Number each vehicle and show direction of travel by arrow)

← To 44th St.   ← Baltimore →   To 45th St →

INDICATE NORTH WITH ARROW

≡ = gouges
● = utility pole
⊗ = mail box
⊕ = tree

Driveway

4410 Baltimore Av

POINT OF IMPACT

Vehicle	1	2	
	☒	☐	Front
	☐	☐	Right front
	☐	☐	Left front
	☐	☐	Right side
	☐	☐	Left side
	☐	☐	Rear
	☐	☐	Right rear
	☐	☐	Left rear

DESCRIBE WHAT HAPPENED – (Refer to vehicles by number)

V1 was travelling eastbound on Baltimore at high rate of speed. After cresting a hill east of 44th V1 bottomed out. V1 then left the roadway striking the south curb of Baltimore before proceeding eastbound through yard of 4410 Baltimore, striking mailbox and tree. Witness Herwarth observed V1 eastbound on Baltimore accelerating rapidly, squealing its tires and revving its engine before V1 lost control and left roadway.

WHAT VEHICLES WERE DOING BEFORE ACCIDENT

VEHICLE No. 1 was traveling ☐☐☒☐ N S E W On Baltimore Av at 70 Approximately M.P.H.

VEHICLE No. 2 was traveling ☐☐☐☐ On _____ at _____ M.P.H.

Vehicle 1 2	Vehicle 1 2	Vehicle 1 2	Vehicle 1 2	
☒☐ Going straight ahead	☐☐ Making right turn	☐☐ Slowing or Stopping	☐☐ Starting from parked position	
☐☐ Overtaking	☐☐ Making left turn	☐☐ Changing lanes	☐☐ Stopped or parked	
			☐☐ Other (explain above)	

WHAT PEDESTRIAN WAS DOING

☐ Along

PEDESTRIAN was going ☐☐☐☐ N S E W ☐ Across or into _____ from _____ to _____
(Street name, highway no.)   (N.E. corner to S.E. corner, etc.)

Color of Clothing ☐ Dark ☐ Light

☐ Crossing at intersection	☐ Stepped into path of Vehicle	☐ Getting on or off Vehicle	☐ Playing in roadway
☐ Crossing not at intersection	☐ Standing in roadway	☐ Hitching on Vehicle	☐ Other roadway
☐ Walking in roadway – with traffic	☐ Standing in safety zone	☐ Pushing or working on Vehicle	☐ Not in roadway
☐ Walking in roadway – against traffic	☐ Lying or Sitting on roadway	☐ Other working in roadway	☐ Other (explain above)

DRIVERS AND VEHICLES

		VEHICLE 1	VEHICLE 2
PHYSICAL DEFECTS (Driver)		01	
VEHICLE DEFECTS		01	
CONTRIBUTING CIRCUMSTANCES		04	09

ACCIDENT Characteristics

LIGHTING CONDITION	01	ROAD DEFECTS	01	TRAFFICWAY CHARACTER	02	CLASS OF TRAFFICWAYS	01
WEATHER	01	TRAFFIC CONTROL	01	TRAFFICWAY LANES	02	TYPE TRAFFICWAY	01
ROAD SURFACE	02	TYPE LOCATION	03	VISION OBSCURED	01		

WITNESSES other than occupants

NAME Ruth Herwarth   ADDRESS – Number and street 4410 Baltimore Av   City and State / Zip Code

FIRST AID GIVEN BY Bryan Best
☐ Doctor or Nurse   ☒ Cert. First Aider
☐ Cert. First Aider (Police)   ☐ Other (Explain)

CHEMICAL TEST: YES NO
Driver No. 1 ☒ ☐   TEST RESULTS: Neg.
Driver No. 2 ☐ ☐

INJURED TAKEN TO Sacred Heart Hosp   BY: _____
☒ Priv. Ambulance   ☐ Other (Explain)
☐ Gov't. Ambulance

ARREST
NAME Anthony K. Gould   CHARGE manslaughter   Citation No. AO-17355
NAME _____   CHARGE _____   Citation No. _____

PHOTOGRAPHS TAKEN
☒ Yes ☐ No
☐ Invest. Agency
☐ Other (Explain)

TIME NOTIFIED OF ACCIDENT 19 ___ 3:27 p.m.   TIME ARRIVED AT SCENE 3:34 p.m.   WAS INVESTIGATION MADE AT SCENE (If not where) Yes   IS INVESTIGATION COMPLETE (If not why) Yes

Explanation of Codes for Traffic Accident Report

Vehicle Damage Area
 01-Front
 02-Passenger side front
 03-Passenger side
 04-Passenger side rear
 05-Rear
 06-Driver side rear
 07-Driver side
 08-Driver side front

Damage Scale
Rate from 1–5 with 1 being no visible damage and 5 being extensive damage.

Damage Severity
Rate from 1–5 with 1 being little or no damage and 5 being inoperable and unrepairable.

Safety equipment (on vehicle)
01-No lap belts, shoulder belts, or airbags
02-Lap belts only
03-Lap and shoulder belts only
04-Airbags, driver's side only
05-Airbags, driver and passenger
06-Airbags, front and side
07-Other
08-Unknown

Race
C-Caucasian
N-Negro
A-Asian
U-Unknown

Sex
M-Male
F-Female

Safety E. (Safety Equipment Used)
01-None used
02-Lap and shoulder belt used
03-Shoulder belt only used
04-Lap belt only used
05-Airbag deployed
06-Airbag not deployed
07-Airbag not available
08-Child safety seat used
09-Child booster seat used
10-Helmet used
11-Restraint use unknown

Eject (Ejected/Trapped)
01-Not ejected or trapped
02-Partially ejected
03-Totally ejected
04-Trapped; occupant removed without equipment
05-Trapped; equipment used in extrication
06-Unknown

Injury (Injury Severity)
01-Killed
02-Disabled; cannot leave scene without assistance (broken bones, severe cuts, prolonged unconsciousness, etc.)
03-Visible but not disabling (minor cuts, swelling, etc.)
04-Possible but not visible (complaint of pain, etc.)
05-None

Drivers and Vehicles (Indicate All That May Apply)

Physical defects prior to accident
01-Apparently normal
02-Eyesight impaired, wearing corrective lenses
03-Eyesight impaired, not wearing corrective lenses

04-Impairment to hands or arms
05-Impairment to feet or legs
06-Impairment to hands/arms and feet/legs

Vehicle defects prior to accident
01-None
02-Broken or inoperable headlights
03-Broken or inoperable tail lights
04-Broken or inoperable turn signals
05-Cracked or damaged windshield
06-Cracked or damaged side or rear windows
07-Insufficient tread on tires
08-Malfunctioning brakes
09-Malfunctioning steering
10-Other
11-Unknown

Contributing Circumstances
01-No improper driving
02-Failed to yield right of way
03-Disregarded traffic signs, signals, road markings
04-Exceeded authorized speed limit
05-Driving too fast for conditions
06-Made improper turn
07-Wrong side or wrong way
08-Followed too closely
09-Failed to keep in proper lane or ran off road
10-Operating vehicle in erratic, negligent, reckless, careless or aggressive manner
11-Swerved due to wind, slippery surface, other object, or pedestrian
12-Over-correcting/over-steering
13-Visibility obstructed
14-Inattention
15-Mobile phone distraction
16-Distracted—other
17-Fatigued/asleep
18-Operating defective equipment
19-Other improper action
20-Unknown

Lighting Condition
01-Daylight
02-Dawn
03-Dusk
04-Dark; lighted roadway
05-Dark; roadway not lighted
06-Dark; unknown roadway lighting
07-Other
08-Unknown

Weather
01-Fair
02-Cloudy
03-Fog, smog, smoke
04-Rain
05-Sleet, hail, freezing rain/drizzle
06-Snow
07-Severe crosswinds

08-Blowing sand, soil, dirt, snow
09-Other
10-Unknown

Road Surface
01-Concrete
02-Asphalt
03-Brick
04-Gravel
05-Dirt
06-Other

Road Defects
01-None
02-Oil, sand or gravel on surface
03-Ruts, holes, bumps
04-Construction zone
05-Worn, polished surface
06-Obstruction in road
07-Traffic control device inoperative
09-Shoulders (none, low, soft, high)

Traffic Control
01-None
02-Traffic control signal
03-Flashing traffic control signal
04-School zone signal
05-Stop sign
06-Yield sign
07-Warning sign
08-Railroad crossing device
09-Unknown

Type Location
01-Intersection (3-way)
02-Intersection (4-way)
03-Public street or highway
04-Private driveway or parking lot

Trafficway Character
01-Straight and level
02-Straight and on slope
03-Straight and on hilltop
04-Curved and level
05-Curved and on slope
06-Curved and on hilltop

Trafficway Lanes
01-One lane
02-Two lanes
03-Three lanes
04-Four lanes
05-Five lanes
06-Six or more lanes

Vision Obscured
01-No obstruction
02-Obstruction in one or more of the vehicles (passengers, cargo, etc.)
03-Shrubs, trees

04-Walls, buildings
05-Roads intersect at odd angle
06-Other vehicles

Class of Trafficway
    01-Residential street
    02-Arterial street
    03-Highway, uncontrolled access
    04-Highway, controlled access

Type of Trafficway
    01-Undivided two-way traffic
    02-Two-way traffic separated by yellow line
    03-Two-way traffic separated by median
    04-One way traffic
    05-One-way traffic with two or more lanes

Additional Information

Ruth Herwarthe, witness: "The car came over the hill just this side of 44th Street, and for a moment it seemed to be airborne. Then when it hit ground, that's when it seemed to go out of control. In a flash it was over the curb, and then it hit my tree so hard I thought it was going to knock it over. Two of the kids in the car were hurt pretty bad. I think the girl hit the windshield with her head. Her face was all bloody and she wasn't moving. One of the boys was hurt bad enough he couldn't walk. The other boy—I don't know if he was the driver—seemed just fine."

Barry Kopperud, police chief: "Nicole Ping was in the back seat and was not wearing a seat belt. The force of the impact propelled her into the windshield, which she struck head first. She was not responsive at the scene of the accident and was taken to Sacred Heart Hospital at 3:45 p.m. She was pronounced dead about an hour later. The driver, Anthony Gould, was also taken to the hospital. I understand he's been released but did receive serious injuries. Gould wasn't wearing a seat belt or shoulder harness, but his airbag did deploy. The third person in the car, Kevin Shadgott, was the only person wearing a seat belt. Gould had his licence revoked two months ago after two previous incidents of negligent and reckless driving. Neither of those incidents resulted in injuries, but one did involve his losing control of the vehicle, leaving the roadway and striking a mailbox."

Information about Nicole Ping

Nicole Ping was a sophomore at Colonial High School. Hundreds of students and teachers participated in a memorial for her three days after the accident. After playing some of Nicole's favourite songs, her friends, teachers and relatives gave brief remembrances of her. Sara Shepard, the daughter of Frank and Helen Shepard and a close friend of Nicole's said, "I just started screaming when I heard Nicole had died. I can't believe she's gone. We both loved music and science and math. We helped each other and cared for each other. Now she won't be there anymore." Jeanette Weinstein, a teacher at Colonial, said Nicole was a 4.0 student and was especially strong in mathematics. "She was so bright that there was no topic she could not master. She was just one of the best," Weinstein said. Louis Ping, Nicole's father, said, "For Nicole's mother and me, the light of our lives has just gone out. The shock and emptiness are beyond words right now. I don't understand what has happened or why it has happened. I just know that life will never be the same."

Anthony Gould's First Court Appearance

Two weeks after the accident that killed Nicole Ping, Anthony Gould appeared in the courtroom of Judge Marci Hall for first appearance on charges of manslaughter and driving without a licence. Hall set bond at $25,000. Helen Wehr, assistant county attorney, has asked that bond be set at $40,000 because Gould had failed to appear at an earlier hearing and because he had been cited again since the accident that killed Nicole Ping for driving without a licence. Hall said she was concerned about Gould's continuing to drive without a licence, but the failure to appear had been because Gould had fractured his hip in the accident. When he appeared in court, he was in a wheelchair. Hall asked Gould if he had anything to say in his behalf. Gould said, "The other guys in the car were talking about taking the hill on Baltimore. We had gone over it the night before, so we went in that direction. When I got to 44th and Baltimore I built up speed to go over the hill. I guess I was going about 100. I slowed down a little bit before I jumped it. I jumped the hill, and there was this truck in front of me that I would have crashed into—but I swerved out of the way. I must have blacked out because I don't remember what happened next. I woke up in the ambulance. I had no idea. No one wanted it to happen. It wasn't something that someone saw coming. I don't like hurting people or anything like that. Nobody knew it was going to happen. I don't think I should be put away for it, 'cause technically I didn't kill anybody."

EXERCISE 3   Public-Affairs Reporting

Assume that the police department in your city released the following injury reports this morning. Write a story that summarizes both reports. Your instructor might ask that you write about only one of the reports.

						Victim's Name (last - first - middle)		Comp. No.
Submitting Agency **Police Dept.**						Alvarez, Thomas J.		87B-1241-GL

Description of Victim	Sex	Descent	Age	Height
	M	Hispanic	20	6'

Weight	Hair	Eyes	Build	Complexion
160	Brown	Brown	M	Clear

Location of Occurrence	Dist.	Type
Tom's Pizza	4	

Date & Time Occurred	Date & Time Reported to P.D.
11 PM yesterday night	11:07 PM yesterday night

Type of Premises (loc. of victim)	Cause of Injury (instr. or means)
Carry-out pizza restaurant	Pistol

Identifying Marks and Characteristics

None visible at scene

Reason (Acc.-ill health, etc.)	Extent of Injury (Minor or Serious)
Robbery/shooting	Fatal

Remove To (address)	Removed By
County morgue	Coroners office

Investigative Division or Unit Notified & Person(s) Contacted
Homicide

Clothing & Jewelry Worn

Restaurant uniform of tan pants
& shirt & cap

INJURY REPORT   UCR

CODE	R - Person Reporting	D - Person Discovering	W - Witness

	Victim's Occupation	Resident Address City	Res. Phone	x	Bus. Phone	x
	College student/part-time worker	854 Maury Rd., Apt. 11B	823-8892		823-5455	
W/R	Name
Anne Capiello	8210 University Blvd., #311	823-4117		None	
W	Andrew Caspenwall	416 Wilson Avenue	823-4417		823-5455	

(1) Reconstruct the circumstances surrounding the injury. (2) Describe physical evidence, location found, & give disposition.

The deceased, a pizza clerk, was shot fatally at about 11pm in a failed robbery attempt. A lone gunman entered the premises and faked that he wanted a pizza. When asked what he wanted on it suspect #1 said "I really want all your money". The clerk appeared to reach beneath the counter and suspect #1 then shot him although we found no alarm or weapon the clerk might have reached for, but our suspect claims that's what triggered the shooting. The suspect then ran behind the counter and tried to open the register, even throwing it to the floor but didn't know how to open it and then emptied his gun into it, 5 or 6 shots. He proceeded to run outside to a waiting vehicle described by 2 eyewitnesses as an old Ford mustang white in color. It was driven by another white male, and a deliveryman arriving at this time chased the perpetrators vehicle. In the area of Pauley Park the perps fired several shots at deliveryman Caspenwall who was not hit. Said getaway vehicle attempted to make a left turn onto Parkvue Av. but was speeding too fast and flipped on its side. Suspect #1 William McDowell, 1429 Highland Dr., was found dazed inside but otherwise unhurt and was identified as the shooter. We are continuing to look for suspect #2. Witness #1 (Capiello) identified herself as the victims girlfriend. She was present when the shooting occurred, and the gunman may not have seen her as she was studying in a back corner of the kitchen. McDowell said he has no job and admits to having a crack problem and that he went in to rob the place for money. He's charged with murder.

If additional space is required use reverse side.

Supervisor Approving	Emp. No.	Interviewing Officer(s)	Emp. No.	Person Reporting Injury (signature)
Sgt. A. Wei		Detective J. Noonan		*Anne Capiello*

602 - 07 - 23A   INJURY REPORT

Submitting Agency	Police Dept.			

Description of Victim	Sex	Descent	Age	Height
	M	AA	8	4' 1"

Weight	Hair	Eyes	Build	Complexion
70	Black	Black	Medium	Clear

Identifying Marks and Characteristics

Chipped front tooth.

Small scar on lower left leg.

Clothing & Jewelry Worn

T-shirt, bluejeans,

white sneakers.

Victim's Name (last - first - middle)	Comp. No.
Curtis, Derek Andrew	87B-1336K

Location of Occurrence	Dist.	Type
663 Harding Av.	2	

Date & Time Occurred	Date & Time Reported to P.D.
About 4PM yesterday	6:52 PM

Type of Premises (loc. of victim)	Cause of Injury (instr. or means)
Family home	Fall into freezer

Reason (Acc.-ill health, etc.)	Extent of Injury (Minor or Serious)
Accident	Fatal

Remove To (address)	Removed By
Mercy hospital	Paramedics

Investigative Division or Unit Notified & Person(s) Contacted

None. No further action required

INJURY REPORT   UCR

CODE	R - Person Reporting	D - Person Discovering	W - Witness				

	Victim's Occupation	Residence Address	City	Res. Phone	x	Bus. Phone	x
	Child	663 Harding Av.	Yes	823-8019			
R	Name Sara Curtis	663 Harding Av.	Yes	823-8019		823-6400	
D	Danny Jones, grandfather	1152 Arlington	Yes	823-1097		823-4110	

(1) Reconstruct the circumstances surrounding the injury. (2) Describe physical evidence, location found, & give disposition.

The deceased was located in a box-type freezer in the garage area at his home. He apparently fell in while trying to reach some popsicles. There was a small tool chest and some other boxes piled in front of the freezer that he apparently used as steps. It now appears that the deceased crawled high enough to open the lid and tumbled in. The lid closed on him & latched. We were dispatched to the scene in answer to a call of a missing child. The victims mother Sara Curtis said the boy disappeared at about 4pm after returning from school. He'd asked for one of the popsicles and she said she told him to eat some fruit instead. Neighbors aided in the search and at 8:30pm we instituted a full scale search of the neighborhood using dogs, the dept. helicopter, and more than twenty officers. The boy was recovered during a 3rd search of the premises by a grandfather at 11:10pm. Paramedics already on the scene said the boy, who was age 8, had no heartbeat and a body temperature of only 70. Icicles had formed on his body and he apparently spent approximately around 7 hours trapped inside the freezer. Hospital personnel said they managed to get the boys heart beating and returned his body temperature to normal while on life support but he never regained consciousness and died shortly after 1am today. When we opened the lid and let it go it did fall back in place and latch itself each time. A box of popsicles was open and its contents scattered over the bottom of the freezer, which was only about 1/3 full of food.

If additional space is required use reverse side.

Supervisor Approving	Emp. No.	Interviewing Officer(s)	Emp. No.	Person Reporting Injury (signature)
Sgt. T. Dow		M. Hennigen		Sara Curtis

602 - 07 - 23A   INJURY REPORT

EXERCISE 4   Public-Affairs Reporting

Assume that the fire department in your city released the following two reports this morning. Write a story that summarizes both reports. Your instructor might ask that you write about only one of the reports.

FIRE/INCIDENT REPORT

Date of incident: _____Today_____ Time call received: ____01:34____ Time of arrival on scene: ____01:38____

Time of return to station: ____08:12____ Total time at scene: _6 hr., 34 min._ Response time: ____4 min.____

Address of location: _____2048 Main Street_____ Type of premises: ____218 seat restaurant____

Name of owner: _____Mr./Mrs. Michael Deacosti_____ Telephone: ____823-0666____

Nature of call: _____ 911 __X__ Phone _____ Box _____ Police _____ Other _____ Alarms sounded: 1 ② 3 4 5

Units dispatched: __4__ Pumper __2__ Ladder __1__ Rescue _____ Chemical __X__ District Chief _____ Other

Injuries: __X__ Yes _____ No _____ Fatalities: _____ Yes __X__ No

Commanding officer's narrative: First call came by phone from a passing motorist at 01:34 today regarding a fire at Deacosti's Restaurant. The structure was already fully involved when the 1st units arrived on the scene with flames having broken through the roof and shooting some twenty to thirty ft. up into the air. Heavy black smoke was pouring from the structure and flames flaring out the front door. We got 4 men inside via a west side window and a second alarm was immediately sounded. Upon arrival the District Chief ordered everyone outside for safety reasons.

The original building is old, having been opened somewhere around 1940 and was a wooden structure, remodeled and expanded several times. Fire was between and behind the current walls and difficult to reach and extinguish. Two tower trucks and 4 pumpers with deck guns doused all the flames by approx. 02:30. Two pumpers remained at the scene until approx. 08:00 when power company and other crews began coming to the scene in case any flames were re-ignited. Fire apparently started in the back NE corner of the restaurant, in either the kitchen or possibly an adjacent office area, possibly due to electrical problems, after the 11:00 closing hour. Private investigators from the insurance company are helping in the inquiry and an electrical engineer will inspect the damages later today. This may be a slow investigation because of extensive damage to the building which was totally and completely destroyed. There were no sprinklers. If it was constructed or remodeled today current codes would require the restaurant to have a sprinkler system. It would have been a whole different story if there were sprinklers. Sprinklers possibly could have saved the building.

2 firefighters were injured. FF John Charlton was taken to Mercy Hospital for treatment of smoke inhalation and released this a.m. FF Al Moravchek received 2nd and 3rd degree burns to his face, hands, and neck and is reported to be in satisfactory condition at the same hospital where he remains, having suffered said injuries during an explosion within the kitchen area at about 02:08 that sent a ball of flames up into his overhead ladder. No estimate of damage is likely to be available for several days. The premises were insured for $1.2 million.

Alarm system on premises: _____ Yes __X__ No   Alarm system activated: _____ Yes _____ No

Sprinkler system on premises: _____ Yes __X__ No   Sprinkler system activated: _____ Yes _____ No

Premises insured: __X__ Yes _____ No   Insurer notified: __X__ Yes _____ No

Recommended followup:
_____ None _____ Arson Squad __X__ Fire Marshal _____ Inspection Division _____ Prevention Division

Commanding officer's name: _____Lieut. Ron Sheppard_____ Signature ____Ron Sheppard____

FIRE/INCIDENT REPORT

Date of incident: ____Yesterday____   Time call received: ____16:48____   Time of arrival on scene: ____16:52____

Time of return to station: ____17:57____   Total time at scene: __1 hr., 5 min.__   Response time: ____4 min.____

Address of location: ____West end of Liberty Av.____   Type of premises: ____Pond/undeveloped field____

Name of owner: ____Wagnor Development Corporation____   Telephone: ____823-3404____

Nature of call: __X__ 911 __X__ Phone _____ Box _____ Police _____ Other   Alarms sounded: ① 2   3   4   5

Units dispatched: __1__ Pumper __1__ Ladder __2__ Rescue _____ Chemical __X__ District Chief _____ Other

Injuries: _____ Yes __X__ No _____ Fatalities: __X__ Yes _____ No

Commanding officer's narrative: The victim has been positively identified as a boy, age eleven, by the name of James Roger Lo, son of Joan and Roger Lo, home residence at 1993 Collins Av. The deceased was a student at Lincoln Elementary School. Witnesses at the scene said the deceased and 3 other neighborhood boys were digging a tunnel in the side of a hill overlooking a pond at the West end of Liberty Av. and it collapsed. One boy ran for help while the others began trying to dig him out. The one boy's mother dialed 911, then ran directly to the scene with neighbors. When we arrived about twenty adults from the neighborhood and passing motorists were at the scene, digging mostly with their hands and few shovels. We took over the work and got the boys head exposed about ten minutes into the rescue but before medics could begin resuscitation efforts another collapse occurred. Victim was freed at 17:24, taken to the Regional Medical Center, and pronounced dead there by doctors from an extensive lack of oxygen. The collapse occurred about 16:40.

Neighbors and witnesses at the scene were angry, expressing that they had told the property owner on numerous occasions and written him that the area was dangerous and that they needed a good fence around the entire pond area so none of the neighborhood children would drown in it, as it was apparently a popular play area for them. The survivors said they were building a fort and while the deceased was in it the walls caved in. When we arrived the boy had been buried about 12 minutes and completely covered. We found his body six feet from where the opening had been. It was basically a crawl-type cave, and getting the boy out was difficult because dirt (the sides and roof) kept collapsing back on us, and we had to be careful not to hit and further injure the victim without equipment. For that reason we were unable to use any heavy equipment. To expedite the rescue we tore sections from a fence at a residence at 8397 Liberty Av., using it as makeshift shoring in an effort to hold back the sand and dirt continuing to cave in on our men removing the interior dirt. The homeowner should be contacted as they may file a claim or have to be compensated for fence repairs.

Alarm system on premises: __NA__ Yes _____ No   Alarm system activated: _____ Yes _____ No

Sprinkler system on premises: __NA__ Yes _____ No   Sprinkler system activated: _____ Yes _____ No

Premises insured: _____ Yes _____ No   Insurer notified: _____ Yes _____ No
                    Unknown

Recommended followup:
_____ None _____ Arson Squad _____ Fire Marshal _____ Inspection Division _____ Prevention Division
Notify City Attorney of fence and Zoning Board of possible hazard for children

Commanding officer's name: ____Lt. Steven Chenn____   Signature ____Steven Chenn____

EXERCISE 5   Public-Affairs Reporting

School District Budget

Write a news story summarizing the statement from the superintendent of schools and the proposed school district budget that follows. The statement appears verbatim and may be quoted directly. Accompanying the budget are figures showing enrolment by grade and the number of people the district employs. As you write your story, you might want to use a calculator (or a computer spreadsheet program) to find some numbers the budget does not provide, such as the percentage by which spending will increase or the average annual salary for teachers. Because this exercise is retained from the original U.S. edition, some of the terms will sound inappropriate ("state taxes" instead of "provincial taxes") or unfamiliar ("paraeducators" for "educational assistants"). Since school district budgets in both Canada and the United States are largely similar, however, the exercise retains its usefulness. Once you've practised on this budget, ask the same questions about the public school budget for the district where you live.

Statement on the Proposed Budget
By Gary Hubbard
Superintendent of Schools

The development of this budget for the coming year was a challenging process. The district staff had only one overriding premise: What educational programs will provide every student with the opportunity to reach his or her fullest potential and provide the community with contributing citizens? This is an important goal, because if this community is to continue to grow, prosper and maintain its quality of life, we must have educated citizens. This community historically has committed itself to maintaining the quality of the school system, and we are sure it will continue to do so.

This budget proposal shows what the district staff thinks is necessary to maintain the quality of schools and is based on certain assumptions, which should be made public:

1. We expect growth in the district's assessed valuation of 28 per cent next year. The assessor will not certify the final assessed valuation for the district until after the deadline for adopting this budget.
2. The government has changed the formula by which aid is distributed. The impact of that change is not clear, but we expect that aid will increase only slightly for the next year but more substantial increases of $700,000 to $1 million may be coming in the two or three years after next.
3. Student spending will remain at about $3,000 per pupil, and the district's enrolment will grow modestly.
4. The ratio of teachers to students will remain constant.
5. No new programs will be started.
6. No programs will be restarted.
7. Salaries and fringe benefits will not increase, but spending on non-salary items will increase 2.5 per cent in accordance with the consumer price index.

The General Fund Budget shows the staff's proposals for expenditures for most of the district's day-to-day operations, including all instructional programs. All expenses for operating the district's three high schools, nine middle schools, and 33 elementary schools are in the general fund. It also includes all salaries for administrators, certified teachers, and classified non-teaching employees.

The Building and Construction Budget shows spending on the construction of three new elementary schools and the work being done to renovate and remodel two middle schools. The district is nearing completion of the building program voters approved five years ago when they passed a $54-million bond issue. Some of the construction and renovation work that had been budgeted for this year was delayed because of bad weather. Therefore, money the district had expected to spend last year has been included in this year's budget.

The Interscholastic Athletics Fund Budget covers expenditures on interscholastic sports, such as football, girls' volleyball, girls' and boys' basketball, boys' baseball, and girls' softball. Salaries for full-time coaches come from the General Fund. The salaries paid from the Interscholastic Athletics Fund go to referees, parking attendants, concessions workers and security personnel.

The Debt Service Fund shows district payments on the principal and interest for the various bond issues outstanding.

Definitions of Budget Categories:

1. Salaries—Funds paid to employees under regular employment contracts with the district.
2. Benefits—Funds for the district's share of Canada Pension Plan and employees' pension plan contributions, employment insurance premiums, and health insurance premiums.
3. Contracted Services—Funds to pay for services provided by individuals or firms outside the district. Examples are attorneys' fees, consultant fees, and fees pertaining to maintenance agreements for equipment.
4. Supplies—Funds for consumable materials used in providing district services, such as textbooks, pencils, chalk, paper, floor wax and gasoline.
5. Instructional Development—Funds allocated to improve instructional programs and for professional growth activities by employees.
6. In-District Travel—Funds paid to reimburse district employees who are required by their job assignments to travel within the district.
7. Repair Equipment—Funds allocated to repair equipment such as typewriters, film projectors, lighting fixtures, and musical instruments.
8. Replace/New Equipment—Funds for the purchase of equipment to provide new services or enhance current programs. Examples are computers, copying machines, vehicles, tools and furniture.
9. Fixed Charges—Funds allocated to purchase various kinds of insurance for the district.
10. Transfer—Funds transferred from the General Fund to support athletics, debate, journalism and other student activities.
11. Contingency—Funds budgeted for unexpected personnel and non-personnel items and which can be expended only with board approval.

School District Budget			
Description	Last Year Actual	This Year Budget	Next Year Proposed
GENERAL FUND			
Beg. Balance 9/1	14,727,807.00	17,552,056.00	14,174,366.00
Receipts			
Property Taxes	91,798,484.00	91,485,010.00	102,793,572.00
State Aid	29,236,428.00	31,373,050.00	31,427,590.00
Other Local	5,785,741.00	5,847,000.00	5,971,000.00
County	857,522.00	1,000,000.00	841,000.00
State	18,744,139.00	21,566,000.00	21,451,000.00
Federal	2,950,850.00	3,457,000.00	3,625,000.00
Total Receipts	149,373,164.00	154,728,060.00	166,109,162.00
Total Revenue Available	164,101,335.00	172,298,116.00	180,283,528.00
Property Tax Rate	1.5571	1.6453	1.4126
Valuation	5,572,804,000.00	5,702,528,000.00	7,301,758,000.00
Expenditures			
Personnel Expenses			
Salaries			
Administration	7,924,457.00	8,320,440.00	8,447,610.00
Certificated	76,144,423.00	80,556,450.00	87,034,960.00
Classified	19,413,780.00	21,297,550.00	21,982,000.00
Total Salaries	103,482,660.00	110,174,440.00	117,464,570.00

Description	Last Year Actual	This Year Budget	Next Year Proposed
Benefits	26,117,570.00	29,405,560.00	30,723,020.00
Total Personnel Expenses	129,600,230.00	139,580,000.00	148,187,590.00
Non-Personnel Expenses			
Contract Services	1,716,125.00	2,588,010.00	2,570,590.00
Supplies	6,685,297.00	7,586,510.00	7,650,980.00
Utilities	3,081,556.00	3,036,980.00	3,566,700.00
Professional Development	386,739.00	384,430.00	391,930.00
In-District Travel	171,513.00	163,900.00	163,750.00
Repair Equipment	265,977.00	317,430.00	317,930.00
Replace/New Equipment	2,738,604.00	3,093,640.00	3,147,250.00
Fixed Charges	1,507,858.00	1,409,200.00	1,447,400.00
Transfers	395,380.00	363,650.00	348,150.00
Total Non-Personnel Expenses	16,949,049.00	18,943,750.00	19,604,680.00
Total Expenses	146,549,279.00	158,523,750.00	167,792,270.00
Contingency	0.00	100,000.00	0.00
Grand Total Expenses	146,549,279.00	158,623,750.00	167,792,270.00
Ending Fund Balance	17,552,056.00	13,674,366.00	12,491,258.00
BUILDING AND CONSTRUCTION FUND			
Beginning Balance 9/1	3,383,807.00	54,536,777.00	46,633,343.00
Receipts			
Property Taxes	8,206,489.00	7,895,636.00	6,419,926.00
In Lieu of Taxes	241,790.00	260,000.00	260,000.00
Interest on Investments	97,280.00	1,550,000.00	1,730,000.00
Land Leases	5,024.00	10,000.00	5,000.00
City Reimbursements	510,898.00	580,000.00	75,000.00
Miscellaneous	42,394.00	50,000.00	50,000.00
Roof Replacement Fund	0.00	1,000,000.00	900,000.00
Motor Vehicle Taxes	28,578.00	20,000.00	20,000.00
Bond Proceeds	53,705,054.00	0.00	0.00
Tax Anticipation	0.00	5,828,700.00	3,198,344.00
Total Receipts	62,837,507.00	17,194,336.00	12,658,270.00
Total Available	66,221,314.00	71,731,113.00	59,291,613.00
Expenditures			
Construction	8,535,662.00	29,923,852.00	55,390,460.00
Renovation	2,933,242.00	1,150,000.00	1,000,000.00
Connectivity	0.00	0.00	1,225,000.00
Roof Replacement	0.00	1,000,000.00	959,153.00
Purchase of Sites	7,883.00	0.00	0.00
Tax Collection Fee	75,892.00	80,000.00	82,000.00
Rating and Management Fees	131,858.00	0.00	0.00
Contingency	0.00	500,000.00	0.00
Not Completed Projects	0.00	3,545,348.00	1,000,000.00

Description	Last Year Actual	This Year Budget	Next Year Proposed
Principal/Interest Accrual	0.00	0.00	335,000.00
Total Expenditures	11,684,537.00	36,199,200.00	59,991,613.00
Ending Balance	54,536,777.00	35,531,913.00	0.00
DEBT SERVICES FUND BUDGET			
Beginning Balance 9/1	799,305.00	8,689,915.00	1,342,124.00
Receipts			
Property Tax	2,305,785.00	7,075,000.00	7,442,500.00
In Lieu of Tax	61,198.00	100,000.00	100,000.00
Motor Vehicle Taxes	7,578.00	10,000.00	10,000.00
Interest	159,196.00	218,660.00	100,000.00
Refunding	7,945,815.00	0.00	0.00
Total Receipts	10,479,572.00	7,403,660.00	7,652,500.00
Total Available	11,278,877.00	16,093,575.00	8,994,624.00
Expenditures			
Bond Principal			
4,280,000 Issued six years ago	325,000.00	3,225,000.00	0.00
5,000,000 Issued five years ago	345,000.00	4,005,000.00	0.00
3,500,000 Issued four years ago	240,000.00	380,000.00	415,000.00
4,220,000 Issued three years ago	110,000.00	180,000.00	190,000.00
8,020,000 Refunding two years ago	430,000.00	1,255,000.00	1,285,000.00
54,480,000 Issued last year	0.00	475,000.00	1,475,000.00
Total Principal	1,450,000.00	9,520,000.00	3,365,000.00
Bond Interest	1,091,477.00	6,096,168.00	5,529,489.00
Tax Collection Fee	21,455.00	70,000.00	70,000.00
Management Fees	26,030.00	33,241.00	30,135.00
Total Expenditures	2,588,962.00	15,719,409.00	8,994,624.00
Ending Balance	8,689,915.00	374,166.00	0.00
INTERSCHOLASTIC ATHLETICS FUND BUDGET			
Beginning Balance 9/1	71,272.00	72,303.00	72,229.00
Receipts			
Football	125,036.00	75,000.00	75,000.00
Basketball (Boys')	48,922.00	40,000.00	50,000.00
Basketball (Girls')	24,794.00	25,000.00	25,000.00
Other	104,148.00	100,000.00	100,160.00
Transferred from General Fund	294,120.00	238,390.00	228,230.00
Total Receipts	597,020.00	478,390.00	478,390.00
Total Available	668,292.00	550,693.00	550,619.00

CHAPTER 15

Description	Last Year Actual	This Year Budget	Next Year Proposed
Expenditures			
Salaries, supplies, equipment	595,989.00	505,964.00	505,964.00
Total Expenditures	595,989.00	505,964.00	505,964.00
Ending Balance	72,303.00	44,729.00	44,655.00
SUMMARY OF ALL FUNDS			
Total Available Revenues	242,269,818.00	260,673,497.00	249,120,384.00
Total Expenditures	161,418,767.00	211,048,323.00	237,284,471.00
Ending Balance	80,851,051.00	49,625,174.00	11,835,913.00

District Enrolment			
Grade	Last Year	This Year	Next Year
Kindergarten	2,348	2,193	2,349
1st	2,367	2,347	2,225
2nd	2,378	2,377	2,347
3rd	2,415	2,371	2,373
4th	2,421	2,406	2,386
5th	2,326	2,424	2,398
6th	2,322	2,319	2,435
7th	2,292	2,367	2,302
8th	2,071	2,289	2,335
9th	2,118	2,082	2,265
10th	2,078	2,141	2,112
11th	1,969	2,015	2,089
12th	2,070	2,057	2,006
Special Education	296	367	367
Head Start	267	265	265
Total	29,738	30,020	30,254

District Employment (Full-Time Equivalency)			
Category	Last Year	This Year	Next Year
Administration	127.95	131.30	132.30
Certificated	2,225.63	2,313.38	2,369.26
Technician	62.00	65.70	136.14
Office Personnel	270.60	274.55	263.05
Paraeducators	574.74	599.97	549.54
Tradespersons	435.13	467.50	467.55
Total	3,696.05	3,852.40	3,917.84

16

Writing Obituaries

Obituaries—descriptions of people's lives and notices of their deaths—compose one of the most popular sections of the newspaper. Relatives scrutinize obituaries, townspeople inspect them, and others who have moved away but still subscribe to their hometown newspaper peruse them.

Obituaries are popular because of their importance to the people involved. Few other stories are as likely to be laminated, pasted in scrapbooks, fastened to refrigerators, or mailed to friends. Also, obituaries are well read because only newspapers report them. Radio and television stations might mention the deaths of celebrities, but most newspapers publish obituaries for everyone in their communities.

Obituaries report on the lives of people who have died. Well-written obituaries capture people's personalities. They convey the feeling that the people they describe possessed unique personalities and sets of experiences. They make the person who died seem warm or interesting.

In some respects, an obituary resembles a feature profile—it describes a person's life and work. Thus, reporters report and write obituaries as they would news stories about living people. Although journalists might be reluctant to question grieving relatives and friends, they soon discover that most family members are willing to talk about the deceased.

Some critics contend that obituary writing requires the best writer on the staff—the one who has the most life experiences and understands what a death means to the family and to the community. Unfortunately, at some newspapers, the newest reporter is assigned to writing obituaries. Young reporters write obituaries that follow a standard formula, show little regard for the deceased's character, and lack quotes from family and friends. Often, obituaries are poorly written because newspapers devote inadequate resources to them. A single reporter might be assigned to write all the obituaries before deadline and must assemble the facts for the report without leaving his or her desk. As a result, obituaries often seem detached or unfeeling because journalists lack the time to go into depth.

Newspapers try to publish an obituary for everyone who lived in their circulation area and for well-known community members who might have moved away from the area. Newspapers in smaller communities usually publish longer obituaries. Everyone in a small community knows almost everyone else. In large cities, a smaller percentage of readers will know any of the people described on the obituary page. Thus, the amount of space devoted to obituaries varies with the size of the newspaper. Other decisions about space arise because newspapers have limited room for obituaries. The addition of headlines and perhaps photographs leaves even less room for each obituary.

At one time, reporters wrote all obituaries, which were free in all newspapers. That standard has changed because newspapers now have fewer resources (reporters and page space) to devote to the obituaries section. Also, many family members want much longer obituaries than newspapers can afford to publish. And while reporters write objectively, family members want to include words that subjectively describe the deceased.

Many newspapers do not charge for short death or funeral notices but have a variety of fee structures for biographical obituaries appearing in the newspaper and online. Certainly there is no charge when a reporter writes an obituary or if an obituary appears as a news story in a different section of the newspaper. Some charges might seem invisible to the deceased's family because the funeral home writes the obituary and its cost is included in the overall fee for funeral and burial arrangements. Other charges are applied directly to family members who want the obituary to appear exactly as they have written it. Charging for obits gives everyone the opportunity to have an obit in the newspaper. In addition, when family members write obits, the printed record is precisely as they want. A criticism of paid obituaries, however, is that newspapers lose their ability to check the obit for accuracy and completeness.

Obituary databases have become a popular part of online newspapers. Some newspapers, such as the *Globe and Mail*, offer death notices, archives and a search engine.

TYPES OF DEATH REPORTS

Death or funeral notices, biographical obituaries, and feature obituaries are different types of articles that cover someone's death. Death or funeral notices include only basic information—name, age, city of residence, date of death and funeral home. Biographical obituaries include more, such as lists of accomplishments and survivors. Feature obituaries are full stories on the news pages and cover noteworthy individuals whose names are likely familiar to most readers.

Death or Funeral Notices

Usually, funeral directors write and place short death or funeral notices, and the fee for publishing them is added to the cost of funerals. Some newspapers print death notices for free. Funeral notices usually run in alphabetical order, usually near the obituaries or among the classified advertisements. Most are one paragraph long. A paid funeral notice ensures publication of information about someone's death. Thus, everyone with some type of memorial observation usually has a funeral notice, and some will have both an obituary and a funeral notice (and perhaps a feature story as well).

Most death or funeral notices indicate the person's name, age, when he or she died, and the funeral home handling the arrangements, unless the family's wishes dictate otherwise. At a minimum, the notice will usually announce someone's death and the funeral home to contact for more information. Funeral directors might also include the cause of death, the deceased's profession, and the times of the memorial or burial. Here are some examples of short obituaries (called death notices):

> McDonald, Janice MCDONALD, Janice. Passed away peacefully at Sunshine Manor Retirement Home, with her family by her side, on Monday, January 5, 2010, at the age of 59. Predeceased by her husband Edward. Loving mother of Elaine (Dennis) and Megan. Proud grandmother of Lily. Dear sister of Edward. Special friend of Mark. Friends may call at the Johnson & Morgan Chapel, 1222 Ellen St., Toronto, on Monday, January 10, 2010, at 2 p.m. for a Service of Remembrance in the Chapel, with visitation beginning two hours prior. If desired, donations to the Alzheimer Society would be appreciated by the family.

> Dion, Mila (Mia) DION, Mila (Mia). Was called to the house of our Lord on February 5, 2010, Dion, Mila (MIA), beloved wife of the late Gerry Dion, loving mother of Mary (Chuck Depluis) and Kelly (Bob Cooper). Proud grandmother of her four granddaughters, Rose, Janna, Alison, and Mimi and her three great-grandchildren, Justin, Dean, and Melanie. She also leaves to mourn an extended family in France. To

celebrate Mia's life, a memorial service will be held at the Dunder Funeral Home, 111 Dennison Blvd., Wiarton, tel.: 222-555-5555, fax: 222-555-5555, on Tuesday, February 9 at 11 a.m. In lieu of flowers, donations, in her memory, may be made to the Heart and Stroke Foundation.

Rodriguez, Fernando RODRIGUEZ, Fernando 1919–2010. Beloved father, grandfather, great-grandfather, and devoted husband of Jane, Fernando passed away quietly on January 29, 2010, after a long illness. Arriving in Canada with nothing more than the clothes on his back, he raised three devoted children, Emilia, Jennifer (deceased), and Cynthia, and built a better life for his family. Also left behind to mourn him are his four grandsons Keith (Edith), David, Jamie (Samantha), and Joey, along with his great-granddaughters Eliza and Emma. Although he was taken from us suddenly, we are comforted in the knowledge that he is now with his beloved daughter and that they are both watching over us all. Adeus papa. Visitation at Stevenson's Greens, Montreal, Wednesday, February 2 from 1 to 4 p.m. and from 6 to 9 p.m. The funeral service will be held at the chapel of the complex at 10 a.m. on Thursday, thence to Green Valley cemetery.

Biographical Obituaries

The difference between a funeral notice and biographical obituary is that the funeral notice announces who died and the funeral home making the arrangements, while the obituary written by a newspaper reporter focuses on how people lived their lives.

Obituary Characteristics

Information commonly presented, and its approximate order, in an obituary includes:

1. identification (full name, age, address);
2. unique, outstanding or major attribute;
3. time and place of death;
4. cause or circumstance of death;
5. major accomplishments;
6. chronology of early life (place and date of birth, moves, education);
7. place and date of marriage;
8. occupation and employment history;
9. honours, awards and offices held;
10. additional interests and accomplishments;
11. memberships in churches, clubs and other civic groups;
12. military service;
13. surviving relatives (spouse, children, grandchildren, etc.);
14. religious services (location, officiating clergy, pallbearers);
15. other burial and funeral arrangements.

Gathering Facts

Funeral directors give newspapers much of the information they need to write obituaries. Funeral homes, eager to have their names appear in newspapers as often as possible, obtain the information when families arrange services. Some funeral directors have the families fill out forms provided by the newspapers and immediately deliver the completed forms to the papers. Just before their daily deadlines, reporters may call the funeral homes to be certain they have not missed any obituaries.

If the person who died was prominent, reporters might learn more about the person by going to their newspaper's library and reading previous stories published about him or her. Journalists can also call the person's family, friends and business associates to obtain additional information and a recent photograph. Most people co-operate with reporters; they accept the requests for information as part of the routine that occurs at the time of death. Also, people want their friends' and relatives' obituaries to be accurate, thorough and well written.

The Lead

After reporters have gathered the details they need, they begin the obituary by establishing as the central point the unique, most important or most interesting aspect of the person's life or some outstanding fact about that person, such as a major accomplishment. The lead also includes the person's name and identification.

> Arizona D. Markham of North 13th Street died when a car hit her while she was jogging two miles from her home Saturday. She was 42.
> REVISED: Arizona D. Markham, who never missed a trip to Vancouver Island in 23 years, died Saturday at the age of 42.
> Michael J. Jacobs, 68, of Eastwood, died Wednesday at his home surrounded by family and friends.
> REVISED: Michael J. Jacobs, who was an award-winning fisherman and avid sportsman, died Wednesday at the age of 68.

The original leads contained dull, routine facts: the people's ages, addresses and causes of death. Dull, routine facts make dull leads. The revisions contain more specific and interesting facts about the lives of the people who died and their accomplishments. Other good leads might describe a person's interests, goals, hobbies, philosophy or personality.

The Body

An obituary's second and third paragraphs should immediately develop the central point stated in the lead. For example, if the lead reports that the deceased was an electrician who also won ballroom dancing contests, the next two or three paragraphs should describe that person's work and hobby.

Mistakenly, inexperienced journalists quickly shift to chronological order and, in their second paragraph, report the earliest and least interesting details of the person's life: the dates of birth, graduation from high school, or marriage. Instead, if time and space are available, reporters should include anecdotes about the person's life and recollections of friends and relatives, as well as other biographical highlights.

Direct and indirect quotations make obituaries more interesting, as shown here in an obituary for Ron Meyers, a well-known Manitoba judge. The obituary, which appeared in the *Winnipeg Free Press*, also illustrates how facts are generally ordered in obituaries:

> RAISED in a family rife with domestic violence, Ron Meyers rose to become a well-respected judge pushing for family violence courts who, after hanging up his judicial robes for the day, would tread the boards of local musical theatre stages.
> The former provincial court judge—who only retired on Jan. 4—died Friday morning of a massive heart attack. He was 75.
> In a statement, provincial court Chief Judge Ken Champagne said the sudden passing of Meyers "has brought great sadness" to both judges and court staff.
> "He was a great friend and mentor to many and his jovial and approachable style endeared him to all who came to know him. Ron Meyers was a generous, involved and caring human being and his loss will be felt by many in Manitoba's legal system."
> Veteran defence counsel Hymie Weinstein said Meyers's passing from a heart attack was so sudden "everyone is in a state of shock."
> "I don't remember hearing anyone being critical of Ron Meyers on the bench," he said. "Most times it was a joy being before him. He had a sense of humour and he wasn't arrogant. Sometimes he gave lawyers a rough time, but it was done with humour and a smile."
> Tony Kavanaugh, president of the Manitoba Bar Association, said the organization thought so highly of Meyers it honoured him with its Distinguished Service Award last year—the first provincial court judge to be honoured with it.

"He just lived life to the fullest and our lives will be emptier without him," Kavanaugh said.

Meyers was also a fixture on the stage of the Winnipeg Press Club's annual Beer and Skits and the Manitoba Bar Association's annual fundraising theatre show for the Manitoba Theatre Centre. Meyers already had a role in this May's production of *The Producers* and was singing at Monday's rehearsal.

MTC artistic director Steven Schipper called Meyers "an artistic director moonlighting as a judge."

"He researched new musicals, old musicals, all musicals and inspired Rainbow Stage's artistry. He was also an actor in many of our MBA co-productions … he'll be sorely missed on and off stage."

Meyers also assisted behind the scenes, travelling to New York City and other U.S. cities numerous times to help pick Rainbow Stage shows and serving 18 years as a board and executive member of the Winnipeg Jewish Theatre.

Ken Peter, Rainbow Stage's executive producer, said Meyers "was a walking encyclopedia of shows."

"You could talk to him about any theatrical show and most times he would start singing songs from the show. I wondered, 'how does he remember these words?'

"He will be missed by the city's artistic community because he gave so freely of himself."

In the life story Meyers contributed to the Jewish Foundation of Manitoba's Endowment Book of Life, he credited the Young Men's Hebrew Association's third-floor auditorium stage and gymnasium for his lifelong love of theatre and sports.

"I lived for singing, speaking, writing and basketball," Meyers wrote.

"If it were possible, I would have lived there 24 hours a day."

Jane Graham, a former president of the Winnipeg Press Club and a fellow Beer and Skits cast member, said Meyers was very dedicated to the roles he played. "He would practise and practise … and he would laugh at himself."

Meyers was also inducted into the Manitoba Basketball Hall of Fame as a builder and the Manitoba Sports Hall of Fame's media roll of honour.

Meyers was longtime treasurer of the Manitoba Sportswriters and Sportscasters Association, a position he still held at his death.

Bob Picken, the association's secretary, said Meyers put himself through university covering high school and university sports for the *Winnipeg Tribune*.

"He always was interested in sports," Picken said.

Meyers is survived by his wife, Tzivie, sons Jeffrey and Brian and daughter, Adrienne.

A Life Well-lived

- Began practising law just after his mother died in 1962, specializing in family law.

- Took the job of secretary of the law society's Legal Aid Program in 1969, with the understanding the province would begin fully funding it. Became Legal Aid Manitoba's first executive director when the province created it in 1971.

- Appointed a provincial court judge in 1977.

- In 1990, he helped organize Canada's first family violence court.

- In 1994, after being quoted in a *Free Press* story recounting his own abuse-torn childhood, including his father's jabbing of a lit cigarette into his mother's eye and using a razor strap on him and his younger brother, he was abruptly reassigned to rural circuit court. Judicial officials never confirmed what sparked Meyers's transfer.

- One of the last prominent cases Meyers presided over was the teenager who laughed when she heard the truck she was a passenger in had killed a cab driver. "I saw a girl who revelled in her smugness," Meyers said in June 2008, while sentencing the then-16-year-old to two years of supervised probation.

Here are two excerpts from obituaries written about Kate McGarrigle, a well-known Canadian singer-songwriter. The first obituary appeared in the *Vancouver Sun*, the second in the *Ottawa Citizen*. While both pieces contain much of the same information, they take distinctly different approaches. For example, the first article begins with an anecdote and doesn't list musical accomplishments until halfway through the piece, while the second begins with McGarrigle's achievements in the music world and enters into her personal and family life only briefly; the first makes extensive use of quotations from family members, while the second uses quotations sparingly and from sources other than family members. Both articles help illustrate the thought and creativity that go into a well-written obituary.

Juan Rodriguez, "'Accidental' artist set the bar high," *Vancouver Sun* January 20, 2010, p. E4

Kate McGarrigle wore faded white gloves the last time I bumped into her a couple summers ago in Montreal. When I awkwardly asked her how she was, struck with cancer, she managed a "fine" but made no attempt to sound convincing. "You don't want to look at my hands," she said, describing in gruesome detail the painful sores on them.

She never ran away from the important things in life and, now, the great inevitable. With her salt-and-pepper hair done in a bun, posture defiantly erect, a slightly harrowed look on her face, she had an almost Victorian regal bearing.

McGarrigle did not suffer fools gladly, and was quick with a quip, a crack that jolted you back to earth. Spontaneity was part of her soul, a reality-check against the pat and formulaic. False starts were part of the game. Yet she was a charmer but always on her terms. So when she broke out in a smile, it really meant something.

Kate's divorce from singer-songwriter Loudon Wainwright III was acrimonious, something both her son Rufus and Martha alluded to in song. Rufus paid homage to his mother on his 1998 eponymous debut in Beauty Mark, referring to Kate's distinctive facial characteristic. Martha tackled her mom's battle with cancer on In the Middle of the Night, from her 2008 album I Know You're Married but I've Got Feelings Too.

In a remarkably candid 2004 interview with the *Telegraph*, Rufus opined that his mother's "strict French–Irish Catholic background left her pretty mixed up. By the time [he and Martha] came along, she had a kind of love-hate relationship with the church. I've come to realize divorce is shattering for everyone involved, not just the kids. My parents were just struggling to survive the trauma of it all."

In the same interview, Kate said: "[Loudon] was at a point in his career when he was frustrated, while my sister and I had made a record that was being touted as the best thing since sliced bread. It was sad because Loudon and I had wonderful times together and our love was intense."

She said that Rufus "is so like his father. I keep having these deja vu moments—I'll be with Rufus but I'm seeing Loudon all over again. The difference with Rufus is … I can disagree with him and he's not going to turn around and divorce me.

"I sometimes look at people who have children and they have so much trouble reaching out to them or relating to them. When you start realizing how finite everything is, then all your differences and misunderstandings and pain should fall away."

Kate McGarrigle's impact on the Canadian music scene was significant and far-reaching, according to Montreal *Gazette* music critic T'cha Dunlevy.

"In terms of folk music internationally, she was an icon," Dunlevy said. He noted that the sisters were influential with both English and French audiences and regularly covered Quebecois artists' songs.

Mike Regenstreif, 55, a music writer and producer of the McGarrigle sisters' tours in the 1970s, described Kate as "one of Canada's greatest singers. It was the sisters' wonderful harmonies that first attracted me to them."

"Sweet harmony: Kate McGarrigle gave the world some memorable folk-pop music," *Ottawa Citizen* January 20, 2010, p. C7

a bodice of Chantilly lace and a floor-length skirt. White Shasta mums," she added, "formed the backdrop of the wedding."

As an arts writer, Evans-Smith (she changed her name to King when she married in the early 1970s) once reviewed an early stage appearance by a future media star.

Covering a production by the University of Ottawa Drama Guild in November of 1965, she offered a generally positive review but said: "On the debit side, the production is marred by poor articulation, particularly in the opening scenes. One grave offender is Mary Lou Finlay as Millinette, the French lady's maid."

(Finlay went on to host CBC Radio's "As It Happens").

King's newspaper career was just one chapter in a life that included a 22-year marriage to commissionaire Herbert King and the birth of what she called the couple's miracle baby. Although she had been told by doctors that she would not be able to have children, King gave birth to daughter Sarah, her only child, in 1974, when she was 47.

Later in life, she spent more than 10 years as a volunteer for the St. John Ambulance, where she trained in first aid and was working at events into her early 80s, doing first aid or acting as den mother to students involved in the organization's training program for young people.

"She was like a mother to many of us, and was one of the warmest and most caring people I've met," said Lyn Kennedy, a St. John Ambulance volunteer who said King supported her during a difficult illness and treated her like a daughter.

King died Dec. 28 at an Ottawa hospital. At the funeral service Saturday at Woodvale Pentecostal Church, fellow St. John Ambulance members in uniform paid tribute to her dedication and support of the organization.

[…]

The family has requested that donations in her memory be made to the St. John Ambulance Federal District Youth Program.

Grania Litwin, "Talented poet 'left the world a brighter place,'" *Ottawa Citizen* January 16, 2010, p. G8

Note: Obituary of P.K. Page

Award-winning poet, novelist, artist and librettist P.K. (Patricia Kathleen) Page died this week at her Vancouver Island home. She was 93.

The grand dame of Canadian letters—who was born in England but moved to Canada with her family in 1919—received many honours during her long life, including the Governor General's Award for Literature, the Order of Canada and the B.C. Lieutenant Governor's Award.

She was renowned as a poet, but also wrote more than a dozen books (five in the last year)—fiction and non-fiction—as well as librettos for opera, and her paintings were sought after. Several of her works hang in the permanent collections of the National Gallery of Canada and the Art Gallery of Ontario.

"Page was a towering talent in Canadian poetry, and in world poetry," said Molly Peacock, poetry editor for the *Literary Review of Canada* in Toronto and series editor for the *Best Canadian Poetry in English*. "We will miss her imagination, and her affable gratitude for all that came to her in the literary world."

Page's only brother, Michael, 86, said her death was a blessing.

"She'd had a wonderful life and was ready to go. She was afraid her brain would go before her body did, so this was very good news. She was so intelligent, a very literate, accomplished woman with a tremendous sense of humour."

In an interview five years ago, Page said the gods were kind to her and gave her many gifts. She became a scriptwriter at the National Film Board, where she met commissioner Arthur Irwin, former editor of *Maclean's* magazine. They married in 1950 and she enjoyed years of world travel and high society as a diplomat's wife. He was

Canadian high commissioner to Australia, then ambassador to Brazil, then Mexico, and finally, after retiring from External Affairs, became publisher of the *Victoria Daily Times*. He died at 101 a dozen years ago.

"She was a celestial jeweller who polished everything beautifully and left the world a brighter place," said Victoria poet laureate Linda Rogers.

While noting Page could be sharp and adversarial sometimes, Rogers applauded her generous spirit. "P.K. once told me she most wished to be remembered for her poem Planet Earth, which talked about custodianship of the Earth." By a special resolution of the United Nations, in 2001 the poem was read to commemorate the UN Year of Dialogue among Civilizations. [The poem "Planet Earth" appeared with the original obituary]

In 2009, the *Toronto Star* published an innovative story about a San Francisco man who tried to honour the memories of thousands of soldiers who died in Afghanistan and Iraq by creating an Internet memorial that featured photos, hometowns and obituaries of the fallen soldiers:

How would the Internet generation honour fallen soldiers?

With an Internet memorial.

That's what Sean Askay, a 30-year-old Google Earth engineer in San Francisco, has done. He has created a remarkable map that honours the thousands of soldiers—including Canadians—who have died in Afghanistan and Iraq.

"This was the best way I thought I could put information out in a way that touched people and told them who these soldiers were," said Askay in a phone interview. "It's a memorial for my generation of soldiers from my generation."

Using Google Earth 5, the virtual globe, Askay has developed a feature that allows browsers to view each of the 5,700 coalition soldiers represented by a yellow pin connecting their hometown to where they died. Anyone can see photos of the soldiers, read a bit about their lives, how they died and pay their respects in a guest book.

Askay has also linked the soldiers' obituaries and memorial sites to their story. He sourced data from the first death—on Oct. 10, 2001—up to March this year. He has told stories of soldiers from 31 countries, including Canada, England, Germany and France. "Each one of these soldiers has a rich story to tell," said Askay, who doesn't have immediate family in the military but feels a strong connection with those serving overseas. "I felt I had to do this."

He started the project as a graduate student in environmental science at the University of California, Riverside, more than four years ago. Askay, who describes himself as a curious "people person," was learning to navigate Google Earth when he stumbled upon icasualties.org, a website that tells stories of American soldiers who died up to October 2005.

"I saw names and bits of stories but it struck me there was no website which provides information at a broader yet personal level," he said.

Askay decided to map each of their hometowns—the humongous task has consumed his life since.

One of the first things he did was write a program that visited more than 30,000 websites and collected information about the soldiers. A major chunk of the data came from the U.S. Department of Defense's Statistical Information Analysis Division, icasualties.org and similar websites. While he was still working on the map of the fallen, his thesis work on visualizing sensor networks in Google Earth landed him a job with Google in 2007. He plugged away on his pet project whenever he could, spending hundreds of hours. But a few months ago, he decided to complete it by May 25, Memorial Day.

"It was on my mind always," said Askay. "I would work on it all day and wake up in the middle of the night with some ideas."

Askay has chronicled some of his adventures in his blog, www.mapthefallen.org.

A copy of Thailand's *Daily XPRESS* newspaper carrying the obituary of actor David Carradine, is seen at a newsstand in Bangkok on Friday, June 5, 2009. Carradine, star of the 1970s TV series "Kung Fu," who also had a wide-ranging career in the movies, has been found dead in the Thai capital, Bangkok.

Map the Fallen was launched on May 24.

But before that, Askay reached out to dozens of families asking for their feedback. It was positive.

A mother of a dead soldier told Askay that tombstones are set in stone and cold. "The website was full of life and will always be there," she said.

But there were several mistakes—like spellings of names or where the soldiers were from—because the information has been culled from different sources. Askay is now working on a corrections form, which will allow families to tell him what needs to be fixed. There's a link for corrections in every profile.

Since the map has been put up, he has been inundated with questions. Many people want to know why he has included only soldiers who have died in Iraq and Afghanistan. He's explained information about them is easily available.

"I've also told people that I am updating the map with profiles of those who have died after March."

Another question is about civilians, contractors and reporters who have died in combat zones.

That's next on his Google Earth plate, he says.

Reporting the Good and the Bad

Newspapers and magazines devote a lot of space to a celebrity's obituary. Obituary writers may recall anecdotes or tales that will reveal more about the person's life and character. They often describe the hurdles that the celebrity overcame. Many journalists also insist that obituaries should not simply praise individuals but should report their lives: both the good and the bad.

An obituary in *Time* magazine for the Queen Mother Elizabeth recalled an anecdote during the Second World War to describe her conduct:

> During the war, the couple became highly visible symbols of the nation's resolve, climbing over rubble as they visited bombed-out areas of London. The queen defiantly insisted on staying by her husband's side even during the Blitz, prompting Adolf Hitler to call her the most dangerous woman in Europe. Her sense of duty and steadfastness never waned, even when Buckingham Palace itself was bombed. On VE Day, when she stood waving on the balcony, the palace's windows were still obscured by blackout shutters.

Obituaries reported the hurdles Katharine Meyer Graham overcame in her personal life as she transformed a mediocre newspaper, the *Washington Post*, into one of the world's most important media companies. *Newsweek* published that "Katharine Meyer grew up in a kind of chilly grandeur. She was surrounded by governesses and private tutors, but once had to make an appointment to see her mother. Agnes Meyer was a self-dramatist who fed her own ego by trampling on her daughter's." The *Orlando Sentinel* reported that her father invited her husband, Philip, to become publisher at 31 and later gave him the newspaper. "Eugene Meyer also arranged for him to hold more stock in the company than his daughter because, he explained to her, 'no man should be in the position of working for his wife.'" *U.S. News & World Report* reported: "Manic-depressive illness turned Phil into an erratic, abusive husband who played upon his wife's insecurities. Taunting her before friends with the nickname 'Porky,' he briefly abandoned her for another woman."

Another example of reporting the bad happened years ago in Europe—with good results. Alfred Nobel was born in Stockholm in 1833 and became a chemist and engineer. Nobel invented dynamite and other explosives, became an armaments manufacturer, and accumulated an immense fortune. In 1888, Nobel's brother died, and a newspaper in Paris published an obituary for Alfred by mistake. The newspaper's obituary called Alfred "a merchant of death." Nobel was so shocked by the obituary's description of him that when he died in 1896, he left the bulk of his estate in trust to establish the Nobel Prizes for peace, literature, physics, chemistry, and physiology or medicine. Thus, Nobel used his wealth to honour people who do the most to advance humanity rather than simply kill them off, as his products had done.

Newspapers are more likely to publish negative information about public figures than about private citizens. Also, large dailies are more likely than smaller daily and weekly newspapers to mention a person's indiscretions. Smaller newspapers tend to be more protective of their communities and of the people living in them. Journalists in smaller cities might know the people who died and find that the critical information will anger friends and relatives and disturb the entire community.

PREPARING OBITUARIES

Many news services prepare some celebrities' obituaries in advance and update them periodically. When a particular person dies, a reporter adds final information to the lead, and the news service disseminates the obituary across the country. The prewritten obituary is stored in a computer system until it is needed. An outline of Bob Hope's canned obituary was miscoded and inadvertently appeared on a wire service's website for 45 minutes. The headline on the obit copy read: "Bob Hope, Tireless Master of the One-Liner, Dead at XX."

Journalists need to be careful when strangers call with obituaries. The callers might provide all the necessary information. They also might explain that a funeral home will not be announcing a service or burial because the deceased's body will be cremated by a private burial society or donated to medical research. Or callers might say the deceased had been a member of the community but moved to another town. Most such calls are genuine, but sometimes they are hoaxes. Later, the people described in these obituaries call the newspaper, insisting that they are not dead. Because of the possibility of a hoax, editors should require their reporters to call a second source and confirm the details in every obituary before it is published.

Even the information provided by funeral directors should be checked for errors. Survivors might be upset and flustered about the death of their friend or relative. Thus, when they make funeral arrangements, they could be mistaken about some of the information they give to funeral directors. They might not know or remember some facts and might guess at others. Furthermore, funeral directors might make some mistakes while recording information and could misspell names, especially names of unfamiliar individuals and cities.

Obituary writers must be especially careful and accurate. Obituaries are usually the last stories written about a person. If a reporter makes an error, it is likely to infuriate the person's friends and relatives. The error could also be difficult to correct.

OBITUARY WRITING CONSIDERATIONS

1. Obituaries become more interesting when reporters go beyond the routine and do more than list the events in a person's life—that is, when they take the time to include additional details and to explain their significance. For example, instead of just saying that a woman owned a flower shop, the obituary might include what inspired her to buy or open the shop and how her shop differed from others. In addition to reporting that a man enjoyed playing chess during his retirement, the obituary might describe his favourite spot to play, how often he played, and whether he was any good at the game. The reporter might describe the person's character and physical appearance. If the person who died was young, his or her goals or hobbies might be reported.
2. The addition of anecdotes and quotations from family and friends gives a personality to the subject of the obituary.

3. Reporters should avoid euphemisms for "died," such as "departed," "expired" or "succumbed." Airplanes depart, driver's licences expire, and defeated athletes succumb to the victors, but people die. Obituary writers must also avoid the sentimental language used by funeral directors and by grieving friends and relatives—terms such as "the loved one." They should also resist the temptation to write eulogies—speeches praising the deceased.

4. Obituary writers encounter problems other reporters rarely face. Many people hesitate to reveal a deceased relative's age, particularly if the relative had falsified it or kept it a secret. Reporters should always double-check ages by subtracting the date of birth from the date of death. Also, obituary writers might prefer to report that someone died in a hospital but not identify the hospital because the information might unfairly harm its reputation.

5. A woman is survived by her husband, not her widower. Similarly, a man is survived by his wife, not by his widow.

6. A Catholic funeral mass is celebrated, said or sung, and in CP style, the word "mass" is never capitalized.

7. Because burglars sometimes break into surviving relatives' homes while they are attending a funeral, most newspapers no longer print survivors' addresses in obituaries.

8. Many editors object to reporting that a death was "sudden," explaining that most deaths are sudden and a more accurate term may be "unexpected."

9. Medical examiners conduct autopsies to determine the cause of death. When that happens, simply report, "an autopsy will be (or has been) conducted." If you report, "an autopsy will be conducted to determine the cause of death," you will be stating the obvious—and thus wasting your readers' time and your newspaper's space.

10. Avoid suggesting that one relationship is inferior to another. Unless the family requests that you do so, do not create separate lists of natural children and adopted children or of sisters and half-sisters, for example.

 ## CHECKLIST FOR REPORTING AND WRITING OBITUARIES

1. Gather basic information about the individual's life: name, age, occupation, area of residence, activities (hobbies and organizational memberships), honours and awards, survivors, and funeral arrangements.

2. Find the unique trait or ability of the individual that makes this person stand out from all other individuals and that can be expanded into another paragraph or two.

3. Paint a picture of this person, using character traits and personality and, perhaps, physical characteristics.

4. Gather quotes from family and friends. Perhaps repeat something the deceased had said, if it reflects his or her personality.

5. Consider the good and not-so-good. No one is perfect, and it is often people's quirks that make them human or give them character.

6. Add some historical context to give readers a better feel for what it was like to grow up or live as this person did.

7. Remember that the obituary is about a life, not a death.

SUGGESTED READINGS AND USEFUL WEBSITES

Baranick, Alana, Jim Sheeler, and Stephen Miller. 2005. *Life on the Death Beat: A Handbook for Obituary Writers.* Portland, OR: Marion Street Press.

Johnson, Marilyn. 2007. *The Dead Beat: Lost Souls, Lucky Stiffs, and the Perverse Pleasures of Obituaries.* New York: HarperCollins.

Sheeler, Jim. 2007. *Obit: Inspiring Stories of Ordinary People Who Lived Extraordinary Lives.* Boulder, CO: Pruett Publishing.

The Craft of Writing an Obituary: http://www.rrj.ca/online/522

Tips on Writing Obituaries: http://www.newscollege.ca/p33.htm

EXERCISE 1   Writing Leads for Obituaries

Write an interesting lead from the following facts. Use your judgment, based on what you have read in this chapter, as to what should be remembered about the person.

1. Carmen L. DeLaurent, 9, of Spencer, died of head injuries Sunday. She fell in gymnastic practice at the Riordan Studio at 5045 Grant Ave.

   - was the daughter of Steven and Marie DeLaurent;
   - fell while practising for the Youth Gymnastic Meet to be held here next month;
   - studied gymnastics since age four at Riordan Studio and hoped to be in the Olympics one day;
   - was a student at Ridgeville Elementary School.

2. William Robert Bailey of Westwood died of heart failure while mowing his lawn at home Thursday. He was 88.

   - graduated from City Industrial College in 1951 with a B.Sc. degree in business management;
   - was a bombardier in the Royal Air Force stationed at Harrington, England, in the Second World War and was shot down by the Germans over Belgium;
   - owner and president of Bailey's Hardware in Westwood;
   - started Bailey's Thanksgiving Table in 1953 to serve 35 hot dinners to people in need. The annual tradition now serves more than 600 dinners at the City Industrial College Auditorium and relies on 75 volunteers.

3. Eva M. Longworth, 37, was a fourth-grade teacher at Central Elementary School in Middlebrook. She died of non-Hodgkin's lymphoma on Monday in Mercy Hospital.

   - was among the first group of patients to receive a bone marrow transplant at Mercy Hospital in Middlebrook 12 years ago;
   - started the cancer survivors' park for teens at Mercy Hospital;
   - accepted a teaching post at Central Elementary School after graduating from Lakeview College in 1991.

4. Ronald (Casey) H. Sikes, 62, of East Landon, a mechanic for T.K. Best Co. gasoline stations, died Saturday.

   - restored 1960s-era Corvette convertibles and owned three—one in red, yellow and blue;
   - graduated from Landon High School in 1963 and worked for Truck & Motor Assembly until it closed in 1987;
   - drove one of his Corvettes in the East Landon Labour Day Parade, beginning in 1966.

5. Elizabeth (Liza) Sasso, 20, of Middlebrook, died at Mercy Hospital on Friday after a brief illness. She was the daughter of Catherine and Thomas Sasso.

   - was a second-year student at the local university;
   - loved hiking and exploring rivers and streams;
   - joined the university's Environmental Group as a first-year student;
   - photographed her outdoor excursions and posted them on her website and advocated against harmful pollutants in regional waterways.

EXERCISE 2   Writing Obituaries

Write obituaries based on the following information. Use your judgment, based on what you have read in this chapter, in deciding whether to use the most controversial details.

Obituary 1: Carol Shadgott

Identification: Carol Shadgott. Born March 20, 1956. Address: 8472 Chestnut Dr.

Circumstances of death: Died yesterday at Sacred Heart Hospital of melanoma at 9:20 p.m. She underwent treatment for six weeks in the outpatient cancer clinic before being admitted to the hospital two days ago.

Funeral services: The memorial service will be at Mt. Zion Apostolic Church at 11 a.m. Friday. The family plans on receiving visitors at the church's Cartwright Library from 9 a.m. to 10:30 a.m., before the service. She will be buried in Serenity Gardens cemetery immediately following the service. Donations may be sent to the Sacred Heart Hospital Community Sports League Fund and to the Metro Art League Scholarship Fund.

Survivors: Second husband Frank D. Shadgott, MD, daughter Amanda Blake, sister Alice Cyclor of the City Council, stepson Bill Shadgott—all from this city. She is the daughter of Nora Hoffsinger and the late Robert Hoffsinger of this city. Her first husband was Mark Evans, a county social worker. They divorced in 1985.

Accomplishments: She obtained a bachelor of fine arts degree from McGill University in 1977 and was employed as director of art education at Mt. Zion Apostolic Church Summer Camp in the 1980s. She also was a member of the choir for many years.

Additional information: She was active in the Volunteer Alliance at Sacred Heart Hospital and has been chairman of the membership committee, secretary, vice-president and president. Her favourite project was the hospital's annual street fair for better health. She also enjoyed watercolour painting and designed a promotional poster for the health fair in 1992. She liked to garden and paint vegetables and flowers on greeting cards. Mainly, she sent her cards to friends, but she also sold some at the Metro Art League to raise money for art scholarships.

Obituary 2: Cathy Vernel

Identification: Cathy S. Vernel. Born July 29, 1963. Address: 1010 Vermont St.

Circumstances of death: Died at 4 p.m. today in Roosevelt Hospital. Vernel was admitted to the hospital almost three weeks ago and very slowly died from the AIDS virus.

Funeral services: A memorial service at All Faiths Church will be held at 4 p.m. Saturday. Burial immediately following at Clover Field Cemetery. There will be no viewing of the body. The family will receive visitors Friday from 5 p.m. to 7 p.m. They request no flowers and that expressions of sympathy be in the form of contributions to All Faiths Church.

Survivors: An ex-husband from years ago, Joe Simmons of Hawaii; an adopted daughter, Raynelle of this city; parents, Barbara and Paul Wyman of this city; lots of cousins.

Accomplishments: Born and attended elementary and high schools in this city. Was graduated with honours from State University with a degree in accounting about 20 years ago. Worked as an accountant in Chicago for about 15 years, the last five as a senior accountant and the last two as head of the department.

Additional information: Quit accounting to become a cab driver in this city. Bought a horse farm. Got into debt and had to sell some of the horses. Was trying to save money to open a horse-riding business for little kids. This was something she had always wanted to do.

Obituary 3: Joel Fouler

Identification: Joel Fritz Fouler. Born March 13, 1984. Address: 2006 Hillcrest St.

Circumstances of death: Taken to the emergency room at Mercy Hospital at 1 a.m. yesterday, where he died shortly thereafter. An autopsy will be conducted because police found some drugs in his residence, which he shared with another student.

Funeral services: The family will see people at Safe Haven Funeral home from 2 to 4 p.m. tomorrow and the funeral follows at 5 p.m. Burial immediately following at Glenn Acres Cemetery. Donations can be made to the school for a scholarship in Fouler's name.

Survivors: His parents, Barbara and Fritz of 88 Eastbrook Avenue. Three sisters, Wendy, Sierra and Regina, all at home. A brother, Frederic, a soldier stationed in Germany. Also, his college roommate of the last two years: Timothy Bolankner, also of 2006 Hillcrest St.

Accomplishments: In the top 10 per cent of his graduating class at Central High School, where he was a member of the baseball, basketball and soccer teams, a member of the student council, a member of the National Honour Society. Now a second-year student studying veterinary medicine in hopes of becoming a veterinarian someday. He maintained a 3.8 GPA in college and was on the Dean's List. He was also on the baseball team.

EXERCISE 3   Writing Obituaries

Some newspapers give blank obituary notice forms to funeral homes and ask the people working there to fill out the forms when friends and relatives come in to arrange a funeral. The system makes it easy for newspapers to obtain all the information needed to write most obituaries. Use the information in these forms to write obituaries for the individuals they describe.

Obituary Notice

Please supply the information asked for below and send it to the newspaper office as quickly as possible after death. Relatives, friends and neighbours of the deceased will appreciate prompt reporting of this news so that they may attend funeral services or send messages of condolence.

Full Name of Deceased <u>Terrence C. Austin</u>   Age <u>81</u>
Address <u>418 Cottage Hill Rd.</u>
Date and Cause of Death <u>Died late last Sunday of cancer of the throat</u>
Place of Death <u>Mercy Hospital</u>
Time and Date of Funeral <u>4 p.m. Friday afternoon so his entire family have time to travel here for the funeral</u>
Place of Funeral <u>St. Mark African Methodist Episcopal church</u>
Place of Burial <u>All Saints Cemetery with a reception afterwards at the family home</u>
Officiating Cleric <u>The Rev. James J. Burnes</u>
Place of Birth <u>Chicago</u>
Places and Length of Residences <u>Mr. Austin moved here as an infant with his family and lived in the city all his entire life except three years' service in the Armed Forces during the Korean War.</u>
Occupation <u>Retired. Former chef at Deacosta's Restaurant</u>
Did Deceased Ever Hold Public Office (When and What)? <u>None</u>
Name, Address of Surviving Spouse <u>Wife Anna Austin, 418 Cottage Hill Rd.</u>
Maiden Name (if Married Woman) <u>   </u>
Marriage, When and to Whom <u>Married to his wife the former Anna L. Davis 56 years</u>
Names, Addresses of Surviving Children <u>Three sons. Walter J. Austin and Terrence L. Austin both of Calgary. Also James K. Austin of Halifax, NS. Two daughters who live locally, Heather Kocembra of 388 31st St. and Betty Sawyer of 2032 Turf Way Apt. 512</u>
Names, Addresses of Surviving Brothers and Sisters <u>Brothers Edward John Austin of Chicago, Illinois, and Robert Wesley Austin of Montreal</u>
Number of Grandchildren (Great, etc.) <u>14 grandchildren, 27 great-grandchildren and 2 great-great-grandchildren.</u>
Names, Addresses of Parents (if Living) <u>Mother Lulu T. Austin died 10 years ago and his father Frank died 27 years ago.</u>
Other Information <u>Mr. Austin was a retired chef for Deacosta's Restaurant for more than 25 years. He was also a member of the New Day Singers male chorus and a member of St. Mark African Methodist Episcopal church. After retiring from the restaurant he and his wife catered for weddings and other social gatherings. He learned to cook as a child from his mother and was further trained as a cook in the military but then was moved to rifleman, winning the Medal of Military Valour during service in Korea. He was wounded twice in combat. After returning home he got a job in a restaurant kitchen and learned more via on-the-job training. In recent years he never tired of playing with his grandchildren and great-grandchildren. He said he missed spending as much time with his own children as he wanted since he often went to work at 11 a.m. or 12 noon and didn't get back home until after midnight.</u>

REPORTER'S ADDITIONAL NOTES—INTERVIEWS WITH FRIENDS, RELATIVES AND CO-WORKERS:

His wife said, "He worked hard cooking all week at work and then relaxed by cooking at home, but he refused to do the dishes which was fine with us. Until he retired, his job didn't often allow him to be with the family for the holidays. Those were the times he worked 12 hours a day preparing other people's feasts. Since he retired he just loved singing at church. But he smoked those damn Camels, 2 or more packs a day, and that's what killed him, caused his cancer. I wanted him to stop but he was hooked, really hooked on 'em ever since Korea."

His son Walter said, "Dad loved to cook, and he loved working with people. During the holidays and family gatherings he'd cook up a storm. As soon as we stepped in the door we'd smell the hams, turkeys, greens and baked pies. He liked Deacosta's because they let him use his imagination to create new dishes and they gave him a big bonus every Christmas. He always went right out and spent every penny of it on toys for us kids and things for the house and Mom, which made Christmas a really happy time for our family."

Peggy Deacosta said, "His specialty was creating dishes filled with edible colours and designs using fresh fruits and vegetables. Plus desserts, he made the best desserts in town."

Obituary Notice

Please supply the information asked for below and send it to the newspaper office as quickly as possible after death. Relatives, friends and neighbours of the deceased will appreciate prompt reporting of this news so that they may attend funeral services or send messages of condolence.

Full Name of Deceased <u>Anne "Kitty" Capiello</u>   Age <u>20</u>
Address <u>8210 University Boulevard, Apartment 311</u>
Date and Cause of Death <u>Police say apparent suicide via overdose of prescription drugs.</u>
Place of Death <u>Corpse found at 7:40 this morning on a bench in Riverside Park</u>
Time and Date of Funeral <u>Not yet scheduled. Body awaiting autopsy. Coroners report on cause of death is due in a few days.</u>
Place of Funeral <u>University Chapel</u>
Place of Burial <u>Body to be cremated/no burial</u>
Officiating Cleric <u>Campus ministry/The Reverend and Professor Mildred Berg</u>
Place of Birth <u>Mercy Hospital in this city</u>
Places and Length of Residences <u>A life-long resident of the city</u>
Occupation <u>College student currently in her 2nd year of study, major in pre-med.</u>
Did Deceased Ever Hold Public Office (When and What)? <u>no</u>
Name, Address of Surviving Spouse <u>Parents said she was committed to her boyfriend, Jorge Alberto Coto. The two shared a college apartment.</u>
Maiden Name (if Married Woman) <u>   </u>
Marriage, When and to Whom <u>Never married</u>
Names, Addresses of Surviving Children <u>Gave up her only child for adoption 3 years ago, a baby girl</u>
Names, Addresses of Surviving Brothers and Sisters <u>A brother, Burt, age 17, and a younger sister, Amy, age 15, both still living with their mother and stepfather</u>
Number of Grandchildren (Great, etc.) <u>None</u>
Names, Addresses of Parents (if Living) <u>Mother Sara Knoechel and stepfather Alvin Knoechel; father and stepmother Otto and Sandra Capiello</u>
Other Information <u>An honours student at Macdonald High School in this city and on the dean's list at your college with a 3.92 GPA (only 1 B and all her other grades As) during her first completed semesters of college. The winner of several scholarships. Enrolled in your college's Honours Program. Not a member of a sorority or any church. Secretary of the Pre-Med Club. To help pay her college expenses she worked part time, twenty hrs. a week, as a clerk in the Student Health Centre.</u>

CHAPTER 16

**REPORTER'S ADDITIONAL NOTES—INTERVIEWS WITH FRIENDS,
RELATIVES AND CO-WORKERS:**

Friend Thomas Alvarez said, "She was a top student, got As in everything. She was very giving, caring, and I think that's why she wanted a career in medicine. She was a smart, beautiful person, but never very secure. She'd do anything for you and never ask anything in return."

Sue DaRoza, another friend, said, "At first she wanted to major in engineering, then switched to pre-med, but wasn't always certain if she wanted to be a nurse or a doctor. She loved kids and wanted to help them, kids with special needs. I think she really wanted to be a doctor, but her family couldn't afford to send her to med school, and she didn't want to be a burden."

Friend Patricia Richards said, "Anne was very serious, very competitive, always pushing herself, trying to do better, to be Number One. We've been friends since elementary school. She was 14 when her parents got divorced, and that really hurt her. I'd gone through the same thing, and we were always talking about it, trying to understand it. She wanted to marry Jorge, but he said he wanted to wait until they finished college, and then they started having problems a couple months ago, and she caught him with someone else. They'd been going together since high school, and it was hard, so hard for her."

EXERCISE 4   Writing Obituaries

1. Write an obituary for another student in your class. Assume the student died of unknown causes early today and the student's funeral arrangements have not yet been made. Do not write a news story about the person's death but an obituary about his or her life. Include the student's philosophy and goals and interesting experiences or major accomplishments. You might also describe the student's physical traits. Avoid generalities and clichés.

2. During a two-hour class period, go out onto your campus, and look for two people together, both strangers to you. With their consent, interview one of those persons to write an obituary about the other person. Continue the interview until you obtain some good quotations and specific details about the "deceased." Then return to your classroom and write an obituary before the end of the period. Assume the person died of unknown causes early today and the funeral arrangements have not yet been made.

3. Write an in-depth obituary for a celebrity. Briefly report that the person died of unknown causes at home last night and the funeral has not been scheduled. Do not make up any other facts or report only what you remember about the person. Instead, use your campus library to thoroughly research the person's character and accomplishments. (Consult and, on a separate page, list a minimum of 10 sources you used while writing the obituary.)

4. After your lead, immediately report additional highlights—interesting and important details—that help describe the person's life, character and accomplishments. Avoid dull lists, and avoid reporting the information in chronological order. More routine details (such as the person's place of birth, education, and survivors) should be placed near the end of the obituary, not near the lead.

5. Celebrities and other well-known people about whom you might write an obituary include musicians, athletes, political figures, journalists, entertainers and authors. You might write an obituary on your mayor, premier, lieutenant governor, MP or MLA.

17 | Writing for Broadcast

Broadcasting is fleeting—once you utter it, it's gone. In ten minutes it's winging its way around Mars.
— **Rex Loring,** CBC **Radio announcer,** *Globe and Mail,* **Aug. 17, 1990**

Broadcast stories inform their audiences, but they do so in different ways from text-based media. For example, online news is written for users scanning a screen with their eyes, whereas print news publications provide detailed, tangible information structured to be reread. Broadcast news is written for listeners and viewers tuning in with their ears, and sometimes eyes, which requires journalists to learn how to balance important information with aural and visual elements.

Although the writing styles vary among media, the types of stories chosen do not. The best broadcast stories typically resemble the best stories for print or online. They involve the audience. Compelling themes and writing draw audience members into a story, encouraging them to connect to the issue.

In addition to identifying a newsworthy angle for a story, journalists for all media must thoroughly research and report the issues and events to accurately tell a story that reflects reality. They identify a central point to find the best angle, conduct background research on their sources to ask important questions, and employ good interviewing skills to obtain interesting quotes. Furthermore, they must be good writers and spellers so their copy flows easily for both the announcer reading the story and the listener hearing it.

Broadcasters are facing new challenges, including how the transition to online affects their work. Good writing has become more important. In the past, listeners did not see a broadcast journalist's written work, whereas today, many broadcast journalists' words are published online. Also in the past, broadcast stories were ephemeral, but on the Web, broadcasters' stories linger for months or years, encouraging audiences to analyze more closely the reporting of a story.

This chapter presents the basics of broadcast newswriting, which begins with radio, and later explains how radio and television newswriting differ from one another and from other media—such as with the addition of natural sound. Natural sound is a recording of the sounds at a news scene to complement the text written by the reporter. Natural sound and video affect how a news story is structured for broadcast.

Throughout this chapter, the term "broadcast" is used generally to include all types of radio and television signal transmissions, including cable, satellite and broadcast. With the growth of social media and the prevalence of online video portals, an increasing number of people are viewing television programs and listening to audio materials over the Internet. While this practice blurs the definition of what constitutes "broadcast," most alternative phrases are cumbersome and more complicated to use. In any event, what sets this style of newswriting apart is the way that additional channels of communication (audio and video) are brought into the storytelling process.

WRITING FOR YOUR LISTENER

Broadcast journalists adhere to a combination of general rules from Broadcast News (the broadcast arm of the Canadian Press) and a broadcast presentation style. Many networks and stations have their own style guides. The broadcast guidelines presented in this chapter point out the major differences between print and broadcast writing styles.

A broadcast journalist thinks in terms of time, whereas print reporters think in terms of newspaper page space. Broadcasters also structure stories with impatient, multitasking consumers in mind. Thus they focus their story on one or a few angles. Broadcast newswriters appeal to the ear to attract and hold the attention of listeners and viewers who might be doing other things while the news broadcast airs. The following guidelines help journalists meet the challenge of keeping the audience interested:

- Adopt a conversational, informal and relaxed style. Broadcast news is written in the way that one friend would talk to another. Often, writing coaches emphasize, "Tell the story the way you'd tell it to your friend." Sometimes this style includes using contractions, incomplete sentences, and first- and second-person pronouns (e.g., I, me, us, we, you) to establish a rapport with listeners. Still, keep the conversation more formal than casual.

- Write short, declarative sentences that are to the point and limited to one idea. People cannot listen to a long sentence and always associate the end with the beginning. The sentences often have fewer than 15 words, and none should have more than 25 words. They should be simple sentences in the active voice, keeping the subject, verb and object together—and in that order. It is best to cut unnecessary words and break up long sentences into two or more shorter ones, because the announcer will likely run out of breath reading the script:

  WRONG: A man who escaped from prison has been charged with murder in the killings of a couple from Alberta who were attempting to retrieve money from an automated teller machine in southern Alberta on Friday.
  RIGHT: A prison escapee has been charged with the murder of an Alberta couple last night. The man killed the couple as they were trying to retrieve money from an ATM machine.

- Use present-tense verbs to emphasize recentness. Examples include "says," not "said"; "is searching," not "searched." If the present tense does not work, try the present perfect tense:

  A wildlife biologist has traced two eaglets to a large nest on Jamison Island.

- If past tense is used, include the time element immediately after the main verb to tell listeners how recent the information is:

  MLA Dave Thornton [THORN-ton] announced this morning that he will not run for MP on his party's ticket.

- Round off numbers. It is difficult for someone to remember the exact figure of 2,898. It is easier to remember "almost three thousand."

■ Give numbers meaning. What does it mean to the listener that the premier's proposed budget will cut more than 100-thousand dollars from the school district? Sound overwhelming? Saying the cut is "about 55 dollars per student" gives listeners a personal context and clearer understanding. All sentences should be clearly communicated so the journalist does not lose the listener as the story progresses.

■ Shorten long titles. Titles sometimes fail to describe a person's job. Also, long titles make people forget what else the story has to say. For example, "Andrea Dove is a lottery advocate with the North American Association of State and Provincial Lotteries." This long title would use most of the time allotted to the story. Shorten the title to a word or two, such as "lottery advocate Andrea Dove." In television, journalists also can use visual space on screen when Andrea Dove appears on camera. The announcer can say "lottery advocate Andrea Dove," while the words "North American Association of State and Provincial Lotteries" appear on the screen when the interview subject is talking.

■ Never put an unfamiliar name first in a story. Listeners might miss it. Also, sometimes the individual's name is less important than the actual focus of the story. Delay the name until the story has captured the audience's attention or at least until the second sentence of the script:

The uncle of the two missing boys says he is praying for their safe return. Charles Hastings says the police plan to look for the two boys near the family's lake cabin this morning.

■ Omit a person's middle initial, unless it is commonly recognized as part of that person's name. Remember that broadcast writing uses a conversational style and speakers rarely refer to others by their initials in conversation.

■ Place the description, age or identification before a person's name. Newspaper style, with description often placed after the name, is not conversational. Instead, put the description before the name to keep the subject, verb and object together:

WRONG: Jorge Morales, 13, a Riversmeet Secondary student, has won the national championship spelling bee.
REVISED: A Riversmeet boy is being celebrated this afternoon in Ottawa. Thirteen-year-old Jorge Morales [HOR-hay mo-RAH-lays] spelled remblai [ron-BLE] to win the national championship spelling bee.

■ Leave out ages and addresses if they are unimportant to the story. Time is short in broadcast, and ages and addresses are usually not central to the news story. However, writers might need to use information that will differentiate people with similar names, especially in stories reporting arrests or allegations of criminal conduct.

■ Place the attribution before what is said. The broadcast formula "Who Said What" is the reverse of newspaper style ("What, Who Said"). In broadcast news, reporters need to prepare listeners for the quotation or paraphrase coming next to allow them to concentrate on what is being said:

B.C. Supreme Court Justice Horacio Diddi said that his colleague engaged in disruptive behaviour while presiding over cases last week.

■ Avoid writing direct quotes into a broadcast story. Most quotes on broadcast stories are recorded as spoken by the source. If you must write a quote to be read by the announcer, remember that listeners cannot hear quotation marks. Broadcast journalists paraphrase what someone said. If a direct quote is necessary, use special language to make it clear:

And quoting directly here, "…

In a prepared statement issued to the media by his publicist, Jackson said, "…
As she put it, "…
In his own words, "…

- Avoid homonyms. Words that sound alike but have different meanings and spellings can confuse listeners. ("The gambler cashed/cached his chips and went to his room.") Audience members might miss the rest of the story if they spend time wrestling with a confusing sentence.

- Try to avoid pronouns. With several women in a story, it is often difficult for a listener to figure out to whom the announcer is referring: "Heddy Markum and Sung-Mi Lee reported that their purses were stolen. An hour later, police officer Serena Jorges found her purse in her bedroom."

- Use descriptive language, but sparingly. Some descriptive words help a listener to better visualize an event (e.g., "hurled" instead of "threw"). But too much description can take away from the rest of the story by confusing the listener or using precious seconds needed elsewhere. The audio or video that often accompanies broadcast news stories can provide the description. In broadcast copy, simple words work best because they are layered with audio and sometimes video. Journalists must delicately balance words with these elements. Flowery words can either confuse listeners or distract them from other supporting elements of the story.

WRITING FOR YOUR ANNOUNCER

Broadcast copy must be "announcer-friendly." At some stations, the writer is the announcer, but at many stations, writers and announcers are different people. The copy is often finished minutes before a newscast airs, allowing an announcer only a single quick practice read before going on-air. Therefore, a broadcast journalist needs to write stories so they can be delivered aloud by someone else.

Here are common writing tips that broadcast writers use to make announcing easier:

- Add phonetic spelling. To mispronounce a name on the air is a journalistic sin, but not everyone knows how to pronounce everything correctly. Announcers often need the name of a place or person spelled out phonetically, either directly after or in the space above the word.

    Juanita Diaz [Wha-NEE-ta DEE-ahz] has placed first in the Rifle Association's annual sharpshooters' contest.

- *The Canadian Press Stylebook* has a pronunciation guide for various Canadian place names, although some common mispronunciations are not included (the correct pronunciation of Calgary as "CAL-gary" for instance).

- Sometimes, the same word can have different spellings: al Qaeda or Al Qaida [al-K-EYE-(eh)-duh].

- Hyphenate words that go together in a group. Announcers will then avoid taking a breath between these words, saying them as a group:

    A 16-year-old boy has graduated with honours from college.

    The 18-52 book of Uncle Tom's Cabin is a first edition.

- Spell out numbers one through eleven. Spell out eleven because it might look like ll (two letter ls) instead of 11 (two numeral ones). For example, an announcer might pause when reading "11 llamas" instead of "eleven llamas."

- Use numerals for 12 to 999, unless they begin a sentence or indicate an age, address or date.

- Use a combination of numerals and words for large numbers (e.g., "40-thousand"). Announcers might pause at the numeral "$10,110,011" but can glide along more easily when reading (and rounding) "about ten (m) million dollars." Insert an m, b or t in parentheses before the words "million," "billion" or "trillion" to confirm the amount. The numeral 6,500 should be written as six-thousand-500 or as 65-hundred.

- Use words instead of abbreviations. Spell out rather than abbreviate titles, places, months of the year, measurements, and other words so an announcer can easily recognize and pronounce them without guessing their meaning.

Saint or Street, not St.

Association, not Assn.

kilometres-per-hour, not km/hr.

- Spell out figures, signs and symbols. And never use a period for a decimal. Try to round numbers or use fractions instead of decimals.

80-per cent, not 80%

300-dollars, not $300

two-and-a-half-(m) million, not 2.5 million or two-point-five-million

- Hyphenate some numbers and some abbreviations on second reference. Hyphens let an announcer know that the letters are to be read not as a word but individually:

C-B-C News

N-D-P

Acronyms, such as NATO and NASA, are written without hyphens because they are pronounced the way they are spelled. Some acronyms may require an additional "pronouncer." NASA, for example, is often mispronounced "nass-AW" by Canadian announcers. The correct pronunciation is "NASS-uh."

- Use hyphens for numbers to be read individually. Numbers in phone numbers and addresses are usually read individually.

That telephone number is 5-2-7-0-0-6-6.

His apartment number is 21-85.

- Avoid alliterations or tongue twisters that might trip up an announcer. The late Laurie MacMillan, a BBC radio announcer, refused to read on air a story with the phrase, "dismissed this as a myth," fearing she might stumble over the words. Also avoid words in a series that have several snaking "S" sounds or popping "Ps." They don't translate well into a microphone.

- Limit punctuation, because it functions as a brake. Use only periods, commas and ellipses. While reading the script, a period denotes a slight pause, a comma represents a little longer pause and an ellipsis (…) means that the announcer should take a much longer pause. However, in print an ellipsis means that there is an omission of words, not that the reader should pause. All other punctuation is unnecessary in broadcast because the listener cannot see it.

LEADS FOR BROADCAST STORIES

The summary lead used for print news often is too long for broadcast news and too difficult to follow when read aloud. Too much information (who, what, where, when, why, and how) frustrates listeners. They cannot digest it all at once. The audience will understand the story better if the information is delivered in separate sentences.

Broadcast news stories follow two types of formulas depending on the type of story being reported. Hard or straight stories follow the "pyramid" formula: The most important element of a story comes first, followed by the rest of the information. The lead does not have to tell the whole story. And because newscasts are timed before they are aired, journalists can write a complete story without fearing that the ending sentence or paragraph will be edited out at the last moment.

Soft or feature stories follow more of a wineglass structure. The most important or emotional information is placed toward the top of the story to catch the listener's attention, followed by details important to understanding the issue or event, usually in the form of expert sources. The story should then close with a memorable ending, sometimes a lesson learned from the main subject of the story.

Leads for both kinds of stories must capture the attention of listeners immediately. The lead should tell listeners one or two important facts and ease them into the rest of the story.

The best leads capture attention by engaging listeners in some way. Many people might disregard a story about corn prices because they think it does not involve them. A good lead convinces them otherwise. Even if they are not farmers, almost everyone will encounter the domino effect of market prices when they shop at the grocery store for fresh, frozen or canned sweet corn and also meat from animals that eat feed corn. Consumers also will feel the effect of corn market prices because of other competitive uses, such as fuelling furnaces with corn pellets and vehicles with corn ethanol, not to mention the widespread use of corn sugar in many processed foods.

Yet the lead must not give away too much important information. Listeners usually don't hear the first two or three words of a lead, but they "tune in" when they hear something that interests them.

Broadcast journalists rewrite leads throughout the day for ongoing or developing stories (just as wire service reporters do). For broadcast or online, it has become important to quickly rewrite information for the same story topic. Thus, broadcast news needs to be rewritten each time to refocus on a new angle, to update, or to localize the story. Where a newspaper journalist might write a single longer story to cover a number of angles, a broadcast reporter will tell several shorter stories to focus attention on different angles or new information throughout the day.

Four common types of leads are the hard lead, the soft lead, the throwaway lead, and the umbrella lead. Each is written to intrigue and interest the listener and provide a transition to the rest of the story.

The Hard Lead

Hard leads give important information immediately. Some broadcasters believe that as a result, the important facts that listeners need to know are gone before listeners realize they needed to "tune in" to what is being said, but some listeners want to hear the most meaningful information first.

> LEAD: A Grande Prairie man charged this morning with two counts of sexual assault also may be responsible for similar attacks in neighbouring cities.
> REST OF THE STORY: Police say Marcus Sodderby [SOD-er-bee] would look for the glow of computer screens and TV sets in windows late at night when hunting for his victims....

Here is another example of a hard lead:

> LEAD: Police will be giving 9-1-1 domestic violence the same priority as homicide, assault and rape calls.

REST OF THE STORY: Police Chief Hugh Joplin says that the policy changes were incorporated after a woman was killed while on the phone to a 9-1-1 dispatcher. The call terminated abruptly, and police arrived about an hour-and-a-half later to find the woman and her husband dead....

The Soft Lead

The soft lead tells a broadcast audience that something important is coming up and invites them to continue listening to hear the story. Soft leads, like soft-news stories, "featurize" information before getting to the hard news. A soft lead usually tells listeners why the information is important or how it affects them:

LEAD: After last month's deadly porch collapse, one lawmaker wants to put warning signs on porches.
REST OF THE STORY: MLA Josie Williams of Peachland wants the signs to state the exact number of people that can be on the porch at the same time....

Here is another example of a soft lead:

LEAD: An official with the Transport Ministry says the agency spent a record amount this year to maintain roads and bridges.
REST OF THE STORY: Ministry spokesman Jason Taylor says the province spent about one- (b) billion-dollars on 513 road projects this year, making this year the costliest in history. Some of that money was spent on overtime for workers, enabling about 80-per cent of the year's road construction projects to finish before winter....

The Throwaway Lead

The throwaway lead intrigues listeners. After they have "tuned in" to the story, the next sentence begins the real lead. A story would make sense without the throwaway lead—but without it, the story might not have attracted listeners:

LEAD: What was anticipated to be a zoo of a sale turned out to be just that.
REST OF THE STORY: Hundreds of brides-to-be mashed into Bobbi's Bridal Boutique in the Galleria to save on gowns, all of which were on sale for 225-dollars. Some of the dresses were originally priced at ten-thousand-dollars....

Here is another example of a throwaway lead:

LEAD: Finally, it's beginning to feel a lot like Christmas.
REST OF THE STORY: After more than a week of unseasonably warm weather across the province, cold temperatures are back. Light snow is possible today from northern B.C. all the way down to the American border. Today's highs are expected to reach about two-degrees in the south, while northern temperatures will not get above minus-ten....

The Umbrella Lead

The umbrella lead summarizes or ties together two or more related news stories before delving into each separately. The lead tells listeners the relationship between the stories:

LEAD: Fires at two area churches last night have police asking whether they're both arson cases.
REST OF THE STORY: Flames destroyed the education building of the Faith, Hope and Love Church on Clinton Avenue at about one o-clock this morning.

About three hours later, firefighters were called to the scene of a fire at Divinity Chapel on Cooper Street that caused about 50-thousand dollars in damages....

THE BODY OF A BROADCAST NEWS STORY

In broadcast news, every sentence of a story is important because when listeners choose to leave the story, they are usually leaving the newscast. In addition, listeners generally cannot digest a lot of information all at once, so broadcast stories are short. Every sentence needs to be heard. Stories need to be tight, with no extraneous information or loose ends. Although the most important information is given first, what follows is important too. Sometimes facts are presented in descending order of importance and sometimes in chronological order with a narrative format. Overall, sentences are shorter and contain fewer facts than those used in print stories because additional details appear in the form of audio and video.

Descending Order of Importance

The broadcast journalist must first figure out the most significant piece of information to tell listeners. It usually goes in a story's lead. Then the journalist must anticipate what else listeners want to know. This information makes up the body of the story.

Although a story may contain several pieces of information, their order is usually dictated by the facts given in the lead. If the lead indicates that a minister was killed late last night, listeners will want to know the victim's name. They will also want to know where, how or why the victim was killed. And they will want to know what police are doing about the case:

> Police are looking for a man who posed this afternoon as an evangelist and used a hammer to attack a Roseville couple.
>
> Janna and Dylan Banner are in stable condition at Community Hospital after Marten Keller repeatedly hit the couple and forced his way into their home.
>
> By the time police responded to a neighbour's 9-1-1 call, Keller had already fled in his car, a 2007 white Taurus. Janna Banner had a restraining order on Keller, who is her ex-husband.
>
> He is six-feet-tall and was last seen wearing a light blue suit.

Chronological Order

In the chronological type of broadcast news story, the climax—the most significant part—makes up the lead. Then, as in chronological print stories, the details are related to listeners in the order of their occurrence. Journalists relate the story in the order of when events happened, not the order in which they found out about each fact:

> A Roseville couple was hospitalized this afternoon after being repeatedly attacked with a hammer by the woman's ex-husband.
>
> Authorities say Marten Keller knocked on the Banners' door at noon, posing as an evangelist. When Dylan Banner tried to shut his door, Keller became violent, repeatedly hitting Banner with a hammer while forcing his way into the house. Keller then attacked Janna Banner when she came to the aid of her husband.
>
> Keller had already disappeared in a 2007 white Taurus by the time neighbours called police, who arrived about 15 minutes later.
>
> An ambulance took the Banners to Community Hospital where they are in stable condition.
>
> Police are looking for Keller, who is six-feet-tall and was wearing a light blue suit at the time of the attack.

UPDATING BROADCAST NEWS STORIES

Many radio and television stations have several newscasts throughout the day. Although new stories might replace old ones, stations must keep listeners up-to-date on important, ongoing events. Thus, the same story may be repeated throughout the day but freshened with new angles, additional interviews, or more recent information. The lead sentence and body of the story should never stay exactly the same in successive newscasts. Here are three updated leads:

1. A Roseville man accused of a hammer attack on his ex-wife and her new husband has been arrested in Brandon. (Or, Police have arrested a Roseville man…)
2. Police say the man who attacked his ex-wife and her new husband was trying to regain custody of his son.
3. A woman and her husband are out of the hospital this afternoon after her ex-husband attacked them with a hammer Thursday.

WRITING TO PICTURES AND AUDIO

Journalists should not write their script until they have reviewed their audio and video clips captured in the field. It is important that journalists use natural sound and visuals gathered at the scene so listeners can experience the story. The strength of broadcast stories is that they can trigger senses that cannot be experienced through other media because the audience can see or hear those affected. To write to video and audio effectively, journalists should write text that matches the pictures or sound, and they should be careful not to write words that repeat what the audience member already is hearing or seeing on the screen.

Even simple sounds—a tire spinning on ice, a crowd cheering, wind blowing, or sirens going past—can bring the listener into the centre of the story. With video, showing the scene from various angles, showing people moving around, or capturing action as it happens provide the same immediacy and "you are there" feeling to the viewer. Journalists should always be alert to the sounds, sights and words that will encapsulate the story. Once compelling audio and video have been chosen, the broadcast journalist's job is to be the "tour guide" for the listener or viewer.

GUIDELINES FOR COPY PREPARATION

The format and aesthetics of broadcast news copy are important because too many extraneous marks can distract an announcer and consequently detract from the news story. If an announcer gets confused, then listeners surely will be, and they may switch radio or television stations or go to another online site for their multimedia news.

Most of the information in this chapter applies to both radio and television broadcasts. However, these copy guidelines and some of the following sections are written mostly with the radio journalist in mind because many students learn about radio before advancing to television. Copy preparation differs from station to station, but the basics are outlined here:

- If your station uses paper or printout for announcers, use standard 8½- by 11-inch paper so all stories fit neatly together and smaller ones don't slip out.

- Type on only one side of the paper so an announcer knows immediately where the next story is. This also prevents on-air paper shuffling.

- When you are loading stories and writing scripts in a computer-based system, follow system guidelines to indicate when a new story is beginning. Some systems allow a separate page for each story, while others use some divider, such as "xxxxxxxxxxxxxxxxxxxx," to indicate the break between stories.

- Double-space to visually separate lines for announcing and to give more room for editing.

- Standardize copy with either all uppercase letters or a combination of uppercase and lowercase letters.

- Place only one story on each page. If more stories are written than can be used during a newscast, the announcer might become confused about which of two stories on a page should be omitted.

- Most computer scripting systems allow for a "read-rate" calculator. On-air staff will read a set script and note the time it takes. This value is then used to calculate how long it will take that staff member to read a particular script. Anchors and on-air reporters can use the read-rate calculator to program newscasts that will closely fit the time available.

- Put a slug in the top left corner of the page. The slug contains the story identification in one or two words, the reporter's name, the date, and the time of the newscast. If the story runs longer than one page, the slug on subsequent pages should include the page number, repeated several times for clarity (e.g., "2-2-2"). Rarely is a story more than one page long.

- Begin each story about six lines below the slug. The space between the slug and the story can be used for editing or adding transitions between stories.

- Omit datelines, because most broadcasts reach only local listeners. (National wires use datelines because they are syndicated across the country.)

- Indent the first line of each paragraph of a story five spaces to indicate a new paragraph.

- Never split a sentence or paragraph across pages of copy. The announcer needs to read smoothly and should not have to look for extended endings on other pages. Furthermore, the story will sound less confusing if a thought (paragraph) is completed, even though the rest of the story happens to be on another page that is missing.

- Use an end mark at the end of the story to indicate there is no more. Some journalists prefer a traditional end mark ("###" or "30").

- Add "MORE" or a long arrow pointing to the bottom of the page to indicate that the story continues onto the next page.

- Television scripts require additional graphical information that appears on air, such as the names and titles of the people being interviewed. This information must be spelled correctly on the script.

- Most television stations require that all words and names be spelled correctly because many people will see the script. Directors use the cues and timings to direct studio camera shots and tell operators when to insert pre-recorded story elements. The station's computer system will use commands to insert names and other information over video (such as "Joe Smith, Narrow Heights resident"). Anchors read the script from the teleprompter screen, and the script is usually available as "closed captioning" text on the screen for hearing-impaired viewers.

BROADCAST COPY EXAMPLE

```
Escaped Convict
Davenport
1/12/00
6 p.m.
```

:32
8 lines

```
       Police are looking for a Lansing woman who fled the Jackson

County Courthouse moments after being convicted today.


       Assistant prosecutor Reggie Maxim says the trial had just
```

ended when Lucretia Morris hit a guard and ran to freedom, at

about three o'clock.

The 28-year-old Morris had just been convicted of assault and

robbery charges from last May.

Sheriff Bobbi McNeil says the woman was wearing jeans, and a

white short-sleeved shirt and tennis shoes.

Police say Morris is dangerous.

EDITING COPY

- Never use newspaper copy-editing symbols. They are too difficult for an announcer to interpret while reading on air. To edit a word in print copy, black it out completely and rewrite it in the space above it.

- Limit the number of handwritten words inserted into print copy.

- If print copy requires a lot of editing, type a clean copy. The fewer editing marks, the fewer times an announcer will hesitate or stumble while reading.

- Ensure that electronic copy is free of partial words or misspellings.

- Write the timing of the story (for example, ":20") and number of lines in the top right corner of the copy page. Remember that for most announcers, 15 lines of copy equals one minute of reading time. Some journalists prefer to denote only the number of lines. (Count two half-lines as one full line.)

- Copy that contains sound inserts (known as "actuality") should include the "outcue," or ending of the actuality, with a timing. This lets the announcer know what to listen for so he or she can return to reading the script smoothly.

  JONES:…AND THEN IT JUST FELL DOWN. :14

- If you are preparing a script for a self-contained report (known as a "package"), include the introduction ("intro") as well as, at minimum, the outcue and the timing of the piece, as well as the "outro" that the announcer will read to transition out of the package and into the next news item. "SOQ" stands for "standard out cue" and means any kind of standardized ending used in a station, such as "… for 97 News, Terry Pilchuk reporting."

  INTRO: A Fairview man says he's lucky to be alive this afternoon after his car stalled on railroad tracks south of town. Bob Anderson was cut out of his car by rescue crews after a CN freight rammed into it. Terry Pilchuk files this report:

SOQ 1:10

OUTRO: CN spokeswoman Sarah Freely says the Broad Street crossing will be closed until about noon tomorrow to let crews fix damage to the crossing gates and roadway.

- Circle all information in print copy that is not to be read on air, such as the slug, end mark, and timing.

Reviewing Copy

A journalist or announcer should read all copy aloud to become familiar with what has been prepared for the newscast. If the reader stumbles, the story must be rewritten. While reading each story, the announcer should confirm that his or her reading time matches the average number of lines per minute. The announcer should also mark—or personalize—the copy for word emphasis or difficult pronunciations.

Story Length

Story value can be denoted by the time allotted for the story. Broadcast stories can run from 10 seconds to five minutes in length. If the story is not visually or aurally interesting, it should run less than a minute. If the story warrants special attention, it should run from one to three minutes in length. The journalist should let someone else listen to the story to determine whether it is complete or too long. If the story feels too long, determine whether additional details are taking away from the focus of your story, and cut them out.

SOURCES FOR BROADCAST NEWS

Broadcast journalists get their news from the same sources as other types of journalists. However, instead of writing down what a source has said, broadcast reporters tape their sources' comments to be played on the air. This change in voice—the use of sound bites— gives variety to newscasts and lends authority to the news. In addition, broadcasters some- times use the telephone rather than personal interviews. Because newscasts are so frequent, little time is available to work on stories. Common sources for broadcast news include news services and wire feeds, people, newspapers, news releases from public relations agencies, and Internet sources.

News Services

In days gone by, wire machines would continuously print out all news, weather and sports stories that correspondents wrote from different parts of the country and beyond. Typically, a subscribing station's morning reporter would open the office door to find on the floor yards of paper filled with stories from a wire machine, which typed throughout the night. (Or, if the Teletype malfunctioned or jammed, a silent machine and a lack of news to start the day!) This Teletype machine would continue to print news and information throughout the day, occasion- ally ringing a bell for a particularly important story, and stopping only for someone to change its ribbon or paper.

The old term "rip and read" came from reporters ripping stories off the Teletype and immediately reading them over the air. Often nothing was changed because wire copy com- ing into broadcast stations was already written in the accepted broadcast style by wire service reporters and editors working for the broadcast arm of the Canadian Press (Broadcast News).

Today, the wire services are termed "news services," and Teletype machines have been replaced by computers. The steady clacking of Teletype keys and ringing of the bell are gone. News service stories continue to stream into stations, but they are no longer printed. Instead, the stories are recorded in a computer system. Reporters look at national or regional headings and read every story on a computer screen. They then print only the stories they want to use or send them to the system's script cache for later reading at a terminal in the broadcast booth.

News feeds are another news source. They also come from news services, but instead of being written, they are audio or video stories that journalists can tape and integrate into their newscasts. At designated times of the day, forthcoming story topics and lengths are listed on a computer, and the news feeds are transmitted to subscribing stations. Journalists can record any stories they want. Once the story is recorded, journalists simply add the opening and closing to the story.

Newspapers, Online News, and Broadcast News Sources

Other news outlets are an important source of information. Frequently, commercial broadcast stations have only one or two news reporters, who lack the time to cover all stories in person. Thus, they learn about many important events from local newspapers, broadcast competitors, or online news sites. If journalists use information from their competition, it is important to rewrite the story in broadcast style for newscasts, giving credit to the source.

Public Relations News Releases

The government and businesses hire public relations practitioners to promote their image or product. News organizations receive a flood of print and video news releases announcing events or happenings, such as the promotion of an executive officer or the introduction of a new product line. Rarely are news releases objective; never are they negative.

However, news releases can be quite helpful on slow news days. Journalists can look to them for additional information about changes within the community or updates on local companies. Ideally, the release should be regarded as a news tip, to be followed up with background research and interviews with competing organizations or people with opposing viewpoints. Unfortunately, too many journalists simply take a news release, shorten it for broadcast, and read it on the air.

People

Many good news tips come from people who call stations to give information about an event that has just happened or is about to happen. Some stations encourage these tips by advertising a telephone number people can call with news. Following up on these tips with in-depth questions and research can uncover more sources and interesting stories. In addition, interviewing people about one subject can lead to tips and ideas on additional subjects.

Blogs, Wikis, Databases, and Government and Organization Websites

The Internet presents an opportunity for journalists to access background or alternative information from numerous sources. It is important to use many of these sites to begin your query when reporting your story rather than as a main source for information, unless you can verify the accuracy of information published on the site.

A clue to the veracity of online content is to note whether the site has a date adjacent to the information telling when it was published. The site should also provide contact information for the authors and their credentials. Another indicator of a website's credibility is whether it allows users to publicly question the material and to have access to material the author used to construct the article. If outside users edit or add to the information, as in wikis, for example, the information should never be cited or trusted as a reputable source. It is important to email or call an online source to verify the information published on the site.

BROADCAST INTERVIEWING

Interviewing for broadcast requires reporters to behave differently from the way they would while interviewing for print because the audio or video footage is recording all sounds. Broadcast journalists need to minimize their movements for sound quality—so that the microphone does not pick up unnecessary and distracting noise. They also respond nonverbally to their subjects during the interview so that their voices will not be recorded.

Radio journalists frequently do telephone interviews or "phoners." Most telephones used for interviews are modified to allow the microphone to be cut off to prevent noises or words in the studio from being recorded. Many radio journalists also interview and record through a studio mixing board, which allows them to control sound levels for the interviewee and the studio microphone.

Journalists should select sound bites—short portions of a longer recording—that convey the heart of the story. To encourage interviewees to provide these sound bites, journalists should ask open-ended questions.

Journalists write a script around the selected sound bites that most represent the issue or event. Sound bites should tell the story better than the journalist could in his or her own words. The typical length of one sound bite is from six to 21 seconds. The script should set up the upcoming sound bite but not repeat what the subject will say on tape.

THE NEWSROOM ENVIRONMENT

Commercial television and public radio stations typically schedule longer and more frequent news and information programs than do commercial radio stations. Thus, they need more journalists, more space for newsrooms, and a larger news budget. Commercial radio stations often regard news as a brief update for their listeners. They have small news budgets and sometimes only one journalist. That one journalist, who has the title "news director," is the entire news staff.

At smaller television news organizations, reporters must take on multiple roles if they want to advance to higher markets. To start out in the business, a new employee is sometimes the reporter, writer, videographer and editor. This means that students must learn multiple skills while in school.

Not only must the journalist balance multiple duties, but sometimes in a smaller market, journalists report on several stories a day. Many young journalists regard television reporting as glamorous, but it requires hard work. Television reporters are responsible for obtaining the news from news releases or local news sources, calling sources to verify information or to ask for interviews, writing the news, reading it aloud, and editing it for broadcast. Reporters often lack time to research stories in depth, and they must learn how to connect to sources quickly while covering the issue accurately and efficiently. Television requires reporters to be physically at the location to cover the story, rather than gathering information via phone. Those who can become proficient at conveying the heart of a story in a few words should do well in broadcast news.

The Canadian Press Images/Maclean's Magazine/Andrew Tolson

News anchor Suhana Meharchand on the set of CBC Newsworld, Toronto, December 15, 2009.

ONLINE NEWS OPPORTUNITIES AND CHALLENGES

The traditional structure of broadcast news stories is changing. In the past, a news package consisted of a story featuring video or solely audio, usually with multiple sources and reporter narration. In the online environment, news can be a traditional news story, or it can be an element of a text news story. These elements consist of edited interview segments, audio, photo slideshows with audio, or just B-roll of shots (supplemental or alternate footage intercut with the main shot) edited together with natural sound. This new approach to storytelling means video and audio are featured online only when their inclusion aids understanding of the issue.

As news organizations move online, the shift is changing a journalist's workload. Reporters must rewrite their story for the various newscasts throughout the day, but they must also rewrite their story for their online publication. This requires journalism students to understand both online and broadcast writing techniques to communicate their story to a potentially new audience.

Broadcast journalists now have more career opportunities beyond simply working for a commercial broadcast news organization. Their skills are needed at newspapers and alternative news organizations, many of which are experiencing convergence of media. In many of these organizations, multimedia capabilities also are in demand.

 ## CHECKLISTS FOR BROADCAST NEWSWRITING

Writing Style

1. Write in a conversational style for the listener.
2. Make your copy announcer-friendly for quick, easy reading.
3. Use the present tense.
4. Construct simple sentences in subject–verb–object order.
5. Find the one important news element to focus on when framing your story.
6. Do not start a story with a person's name or important information; save it for later when the listener has "tuned in."
7. Use few numbers, round them, and give them meaning.
8. Write out titles, numbers and symbols.
9. Keep sentences short, about 15 words or fewer. Details are added through the use of audio and visuals.
10. Place a person's title before his or her name.

Copy Format

1. Use only one side of the paper.
2. Double-space.
3. Put the slug in the top left corner, and then skip about six lines to begin the story.
4. Do not split a sentence or paragraph across pages.
5. Write reading time for the story in the top right corner.
6. Black out words to be edited out. Write the corrected word above the line.

The Writing Coach

WRITING FOR BROADCAST

Although good writing transcends medium, there are important differences between writing for print and writing for broadcast. The following tips have been adapted from *The Canadian Press Stylebook*:

Paint a picture: Good broadcast writing puts listeners and/or viewers at the scene by painting pictures with words. Don't be a slave to rules or formulas, but do use concise everyday language.

Leads: Broadcast leads should be short and "punchy." Remain true to the facts, but don't try to cram them all into the lead. Avoid long sentences, mixed metaphors and tired clichés. Incomplete sentences are acceptable, especially in leads, as long as they are not used excessively. The same goes for question leads (generally not acceptable in print reporting). Make each word count: Extra words in broadcast writing mean wasted time. Summarize the essential elements of the story in a single sentence, and then add the detail, context and colour to keep the audience tuned in. Boil the story down to its main elements, and tell it in plain, conversational English.

Bring life to your copy: Your job is to make the story interesting to people, showing them how events and issues addressed in a story affect them. Don't embroider the facts, but do dramatize them with colourful, descriptive language, short sentences and present tense. Always ensure that the story includes the latest information available.

Avoid direct quotes: Unless a direct quote adds something to the story, paraphrase instead. Direct quotes don't usually work because they sound as if the newscaster is talking about himself. When a direct quote would add something to a story that could not be captured as well by paraphrasing, include an introductory phrase (such as "in her own words") that makes clear a source, not the reporter, is speaking.

Watch your choice of words: Correctness counts in broadcast writing: check the accuracy of spelling and follow the rules of grammar. For example, use singular verbs with singular subjects, and plural verbs with plural subjects. Avoid unnecessary and ambiguous words, excessive alliteration, and phrases that are hard on the announcer's voice and the listener's ear.

Don't editorialize: Just as in writing for print, the journalist's touchstone is truth, not opinion. The only place for the reporter's opinion is in a broadcast editorial, identified as such. Also, don't report the opinions of others as if they were fact. Avoid loaded words and phrases (ones that include personal bias or judgment of the facts). Instead of saying that someone snuck out the side door, say he left the room without taking questions from reporters.

SUGGESTED READINGS AND USEFUL WEBSITES

"Audio." 2008. In *The Canadian Press Stylebook*, 15th edn, 37–40. Toronto: The Canadian Press.

"Broadcast Formats." 2008. In *The Canadian Press Stylebook*, 15th edn, 454–60. Toronto: The Canadian Press.

"Canadian Press Policies." 2008. In *The Canadian Press Stylebook*, 15th edn, 11–34. Toronto: The Canadian Press.

Hale, Constance, and Jessie Scanlon. 1999. *Wired Style: Principles of English Usage in the Digital Age*. New York: Broadway Books.

"Online News." 2008. In *The Canadian Press Stylebook*, 15th edn, 90–4. Toronto: The Canadian Press.

"Pronunciation Guide." 2008. In *The Canadian Press Stylebook*, 15th edn, 355. Toronto: The Canadian Press.

"Reading the News." 2008. In *The Canadian Press Stylebook*, 15th edn, 130–3. Toronto: The Canadian Press.

"Video." 2008. In *The Canadian Press Stylebook*, 15th edn, 169–70. Toronto: The Canadian Press.

"Writing for Broadcast." 2008. In *The Canadian Press Stylebook*, 15th edn, 183–93. Toronto: The Canadian Press.

McGuire, Mary. "Ethical Guidelines for Editing Audio": http://jsource.ca/english_new/detail.php?id=1638

Poynter Institute for Media Studies. Sound in the Story: Balancing the Tools in New Media Journalism: http://www.visualedge.org/lessons/SoundStory.pdf

Shapiro, Ben. The Transom Review (vol. 7, issue 2): http://transom.org/?p=1897

Teaching Broadcasting: http://jsource.ca/english_new/category.php?catid=66

EXERCISE 1   Writing for Broadcast

Identifying Broadcast Style

The following are correctly written broadcast leads. Explain how they differ stylistically from leads written for newspapers. Think about time, verb tense, titles, personal identification, amount of information, and a conversational mode.

1. A Halifax woman was killed about 8:30 a-m yesterday when her pickup hit a curb on Seagull Street and struck a utility pole.
2. A seven-year-old girl is credited with saving a man's life near Airdrie, Alberta.
3. Ryan Jennings, a council member, wants to put an end to motorists' text-messaging while driving in city limits.
4. Minimum wage is expected to be raised by eight per cent in five months. Minimum wage workers currently earn eight dollars an hour.
5. Canada has begun extradition procedures against the political leader of an Islamic militant group.
6. Prosecutors want more time to build a case against a city official accused of illegal trading.
7. After encountering barriers to raising enough money to pay for the new stadium, officials said construction is expected to begin next year.
8. Medicare officials said that the audits showed that insurers would be held accountable.
9. About 41 members of the Canadian Forces returned to CFB Wainwright today after serving a year in Afghanistan.

EXERCISE 2   Writing for Broadcast

Identifying Different Broadcast Leads

The following broadcast leads and the second paragraphs are written correctly. Identify the style of each lead: hard news, soft news, throwaway or umbrella.

1. LEAD: The man who raped three men, killing one of them, was sent to prison for life today.
    REST OF THE STORY: Ervine McMitchelle drew a life term for the first-degree murder of Henry LaForge last year. Justice Ashley Monahan also gave McMitchelle 50-to-75-years for each of three counts of rape. The rapes occurred over the last three years.

2. LEAD: If you think your pampered pooch or cuddly kitty deserves the national spotlight, here's your chance.
    REST OF THE STORY: The International Pet Cemeteries Foundation in Austin, Texas, plans to build a Canadian Pet Hall of Fame within two years. The president of the foundation, Heidi Hills, says members hope to provide education about pets and also memorialize famous and not-so-famous Canadian pets.

3. LEAD: A Friendswood teen-ager is the centre of attention today at the B.C. legislature.
    REST OF THE STORY: Sixteen-year-old Gordon Elliott has received a Heroism Award for saving two children from drowning in Grand River last fall.

4. LEAD: Smoke still fills the air over western Alberta.
    REST OF THE STORY: A wildfire that injured 30 firefighters and threatened homes has already burned almost five-thousand hectares. High temperatures and strong winds make the job harder for the 15-hundred firefighters who continue working around the clock.

5. LEAD: A Presbyterian minister has been found dead in her church office.
    REST OF THE STORY: First Presbyterian Church secretary Robert Abrahm found the door unlocked and the Reverend Sarah Chen dead when he came to work this morning.

6. LEAD: Police are looking into the possibility of a connection among 20 recent dognappings in the area.
    REST OF THE STORY: Parson's Animal Shelter Director John Ertos says he has received 12 inquiries about lost dogs since yesterday. Most of these dogs were in fenced-in backyards or on leashes.
    In nearby Colleyville, police officer Annie Bearclaw says the station has logged eight calls reporting missing dogs within two days.

7. LEAD: Police are looking for a South Bend man who fled the courthouse moments after being convicted today.
    REST OF THE STORY: Prosecutor Lonnie Howard says the trial had just ended when Lee Chang hit a guard and ran to freedom, at about three o'clock.

8. LEAD: You can be 25-thousand-dollars richer if you tip police with information that helps solve a homicide case.
    REST OF THE STORY: Metropolitan Police Chief Stone Willows says that people who provide information that leads to a conviction stand to receive ten-thousand-dollars more than they did last year.

9. LEAD: More than 165 passengers are safe, after a seven-47 jetliner made an emergency landing at Pearson International Airport today.
    REST OF THE STORY: Airport director Jean Richards says shortly after takeoff, a door blew open in the luggage compartment. The plane then dumped its fuel and returned to the airport.

EXERCISE 3   Writing for Broadcast

Identifying Different Broadcast Leads

The following broadcast leads and the second paragraphs are written correctly. Identify the style of each lead: hard news, soft news, throwaway or umbrella.

1. LEAD: You hear a ring, and reach for your cellphone to find out that it actually is not ringing.
    REST OF THE STORY: McGill University researchers are calling this state of panic… "ringxiety." Researcher David Hill says people feel as though the phone is another limb of their body. The cellphone has become people's connection to their friends, family, and colleagues. The ring of the phone acts as a reassuring mechanism to let them know that they are not isolated from other people.

2. LEAD: Prosecutors charged two women today with the murder of a fisherman on Lake Alvin.
    REST OF THE STORY: Forensic evidence and inconsistencies in their statements led police to arrest suspects Felicia Delgado and Erin Lewis for the stabbing of Alessandro Cortez. A young boy found Cortez's body last month near their lake home. Authorities claim that Delgado and Lewis lied about their alibi on the day of the murder, and they found a knife with blood matching that of Cortez in Lewis's apartment. Police believe the two women murdered Cortez on his boat, and threw his body overboard to cover up the crime.

3. LEAD: A hungry seven-year-old who stole his grandmother's car to get food is safe at home tonight.
    REST OF THE STORY: Police say the boy's grandmother, Ellen Reynolds, was mowing her lawn when her grandson stole her car to look for a hamburger. Police say someone called in a slow-moving car with no apparent driver travelling down Vine street. The boy was using both of his feet to run the gas pedal. He made it only three blocks before police picked him up. The grandmother won't face any charges related to the incident.

4. LEAD: The Canadian Auto Workers announced that it is calling off the strike after reaching a tentative agreement with Chrysler.
    REST OF THE STORY: Union President James Vanderbee says the workers can report to their shifts starting tomorrow. The auto company has agreed to restructure the worker's retirement package in exchange for lowering hourly labour costs.

5. LEAD: A Montreal journalist is at home with his wife after being imprisoned for seven months according to consular officials.
    REST OF THE STORY: Ali Kaabi was arrested for "crimes against national security" at the Tehran International Airport in Iran. Kaabi was in the country visiting his sick mother.

6. LEAD: When faced with the choice of paper or plastic, environmentally conscious grocery shoppers should choose neither.
    REST OF THE STORY: It is more environmentally beneficial to instead purchase reusable quality bags or carts to take with you to the grocery store according to the Globe and Mail. Plastic bags are not biodegradable, and paper cannot degrade because of a lack of water and light available at most landfills.

7. LEAD: Even the South is no escape from cold weather this week.
    REST OF THE STORY: According to Environment Canada, temperatures in southern British Columbia will reach an icy minus-20 degrees over the next two days.

8. LEAD: An Edmonton mother convicted of locking her son in a cage has been sentenced to five years in prison.
    REST OF THE STORY: Lacy Warren apologized to the judge for her behaviour. She told the judge that she was not evil. Warren begged the judge to understand that as a single mother she had difficulty coping when she had lost her mother earlier that year to cancer.

18 | The News Media and PR Practitioners

Every man for himself, as the elephant said while dancing among the chickens.
— **Tommy Douglas, former NDP leader, 1968**

News reporting and public relations are two different professions, but they share some of the same goals; for example, both attempt to communicate with and inform an audience. As well, the target audience for news media is the public at large, a target audience often shared by public relations practitioners. Moreover, reporters and PR practitioners often work in a symbiotic relationship. PR practitioners want to reach journalists' large audience of daily viewers and readers. Journalists often turn to PR practitioners to get sources and information for stories because newsrooms do not have enough resources to discover and cover every newsworthy event. For the relationship between the news media and public relations practitioners to work, each must understand how the other thinks and operates.

Public relations practitioners provide a valuable service for both their clients and the public. To succeed, they must understand how the media operate and provide information that is clear, concise, accurate and objective.

Public relations practitioners need good writing skills; the ability to translate complicated information into clear, readable stories; and an understanding of journalists' definitions of news. They need to be available and respond quickly to questions from reporters. The best practitioners know their client or organization well, locate information quickly, and arrange interviews with experts and top executives when needed. PR practitioners use these skills to build trust and a working relationship with reporters.

WHAT IS PUBLIC RELATIONS?

Public relations involves planned and continuous communication designed to provide information about an organization, an issue or a product to the public. Unlike advertising, which is paid promotion, public relations agencies and practitioners use the news media as a means to promote an organization or a product.

Public relations practitioners and reporters cross paths almost daily. Most PR practitioners want to get their client's name in the news without having to pay for the publicity, so the practitioner's allegiance is to the client. The reporter's objective, on the other hand, is to inform readers or viewers, so the reporter judges a news release on its value to the public. In addition, space in a newspaper or time on radio and television is limited.

It is important, then, that PR practitioners think and write like reporters. This will help them write news releases that are newsworthy and conform to news style. News releases should sound and look as though they were written by reporters.

Public Relations Agencies

Some practitioners work in a public relations agency, representing companies or other organizations either throughout the year or for special events, such as a festival or sporting event, the launch of a new product or service, a fundraising campaign, or a political election campaign. Public relations practitioners in agencies handle several "accounts" simultaneously. Agencies may be as small as a one-person consultant contracted to write and edit a company's communications, develop brochures, news releases, and web pages for target audiences (external communications) or shoot training videos for employees (internal communications). Or an agency can be a large, international network of offices. International conglomerates usually hire worldwide agencies to handle their public relations needs in different countries and cultures.

Corporate, Non-profit and Government Public Relations

Public relations practitioners may work within a company (such as the Ford Motor Company), a non-profit organization (such as Médecins sans frontières/Doctors without Borders), or a government agency (such as Fisheries and Oceans Canada). Practitioners in corporate, non-profit or governmental settings have two audiences they must communicate with—an internal audience of officers and employees and an external audience of consumers, investors and the general public. Practitioners may handle either internal or external communications, or both, depending on the size of the organization.

Internal Communications

Practitioners handling internal communications work to keep company employees informed about the organization. They ensure that all employees, whether in the same building or in a branch office in another province or even another country, think of themselves as part of the company.

For example, employees in a Ford Motor Co. plant in Ontario might believe company officials in the U.S. headquarters do not understand production problems that affect their work. The public relations practitioner creates lines of communication between administrators and employees to make the employees aware of their roles in and contributions to the company's operations. Through the company newsletter or annual report, the practitioner informs employees of activities at the headquarters as well as other plants or offices. The practitioner helps employees understand changes in policies or business practices that will affect them, such as the closing of a plant or the launching of a new retirement plan.

Some practitioners write feature stories about employees and their contributions to the company. Others publish photographs and brief biographies of new employees in a newsletter or news video. Some may manage a company's social networking site or Facebook presence for employees. Still others may stage companywide competitions or host awards banquets for all personnel. Usually, the public relations practitioner stays in the background, allowing company executives to benefit from the increased goodwill.

THE CANADIAN PRESS/Darren Calabrese

Magna International Inc. chairman Frank Stronach speaks to the media as a member of his public relations team stands by following the company's annual general meeting of shareholders in Markham, Ontario, on Wednesday, May 6, 2009.

A department head is interviewed and quoted in the feature story, praising the employee. The CEO shakes the hands of the winners of the companywide contests, and a president reads the speech prepared by the practitioner at the awards banquet. In many ways, the practitioner resembles the theatre director who never appears onstage but co-ordinates the performances of others.

External Communications

Public relations professionals in corporations or non-profit organizations also have to deal with the public—the people outside the organization who are its investors, customers, clients or contributors. PR practitioners promote a positive image of the organization by identifying different publics and researching the best way to reach them. To influence opinions or project a positive image, most practitioners write news releases and features and send them to the media. Other PR tools and skills include developing press kits that contain information about the company; setting up speakers' bureaus; staging events; filming news clips; writing public service announcements; holding meetings; designing posters, brochures and pamphlets; and creating websites and online content. All these activities help disseminate information about the company or its products and services to the public. Many companies have public relations departments that manage all external communications, while other companies hire public relations agencies to handle special needs.

Whether corporations or organizations have an internal public relations department or hire a public relations agency to represent them, they might sometimes face a crisis that requires working with the news media to keep the public informed. Hiding information from the media and the public can create a crisis in public confidence toward the corporation or organization. The Wall Street accounting scandals at AIG, Bear Stearns, and other large corporations shook public confidence in the financial markets and the corporate world. The announcement by the Canadian Food Inspection Agency that Maple Leaf Foods packing plants had produced tainted food sent consumers into a panic. To protect the organization's reputation, PR practitioners need to be able to deal with such crisis situations and get truthful information out to the external publics the organization serves.

BECOMING A PUBLIC RELATIONS PRACTITIONER

Most Canadian universities and colleges offer majors or concentrations in public relations, usually through journalism programs. Schools require students preparing for careers in PR to enrol in a newswriting and reporting class. The class covers such things as how journalists define "news," newswriting style, and the importance of deadlines. Public relations professionals agree on the importance of such classes. (One U.S. survey of 200 PR agencies found that professionals consider news reporting courses more important for PR majors than any course in public relations.)

Many journalists who decide to leave the traditional news business accept jobs in public relations. Companies hire reporters and editors as public relations practitioners because they have writing skills that are essential to the job. It is less common, and more difficult in Canada, to go from a career in public relations to one in journalism.

WORKING WITH NEWS MEDIA

Public relations practitioners use the media to get information about their client to the public. Therefore practitioners must determine which media outlets—newspapers, trade publications, radio, television, or online venues—will best serve their purposes. In addition, practitioners know the writing styles, deadlines and other procedures of each target medium. News releases sent to newspapers are written in Canadian Press style. Releases sent to radio stations are written in the style and format of Broadcast News so radio announcers do not have to rewrite them; they can read them verbatim over the air.

To make their promotional efforts effective, PR practitioners also must learn whom to contact. They should identify the proper news departments and the people in charge of the departments before sending out a release. "Shotgunning" a release, or sending it to multiple departments and department heads in a news organization, is a waste of time and money. For example, most editors will discard a news release about a company employee's promotion, but a business editor might report the promotion in a weekly column or section devoted to local promotions. Similarly, most editors would discard a news release about a Christmas program at a church, but a religion editor might mention it in a roundup about Christmas activities. By sending news releases to the right editor, practitioners increase the likelihood the releases will be used and decrease the chance of harming their reputations by wasting an editor's time.

Many news stories have public relations origins. PR practitioners bring information about a company or organization to journalists' attention, often through a news release. If the release is well-written and a journalist believes it contains something newsworthy, it has a better chance of being used by the media to develop a full-fledged journalistic story. If the news release is poorly written or contains nothing newsworthy, it usually receives only a quick glance before landing in a trash basket.

Reporters generally follow up on an idea presented in a news release but interview their own sources, write their own stories and present their own angles. Thus, although it appears PR practitioners are using journalists to achieve their goals, news releases may help journalists stay informed about their community. Journalists choose whether or not to use the releases.

ELEMENTS OF A NEWS RELEASE

Journalists reject news releases for many reasons:

- They are not newsworthy.
- They are poorly written.
- They fail to include important information.
- They read like advertisements.
- They have not been localized or are too long.
- They are not timely.
- They are sent to the wrong person.
- They are written more for clients than for the public.

The following sections describe how to write a successful news release for print media, but they also apply to writing releases for broadcast news.

List a Contact Person and a Followup

Reporters might want to follow up a news release to verify information or get answers to questions. They need to know whom they can call to get more information. Thus, an effective news release lists the name and phone number of a contact person, someone familiar with the subject of the release who can answer questions.

Reporters often complain that no one is available to answer questions about a release. If a contact person is not available, then another person in the organization should be briefed about the release and given authority to respond to questions.

Some news releases, such as those for a new organization or product, might include a cover letter to the editor with more information about the sponsoring company. Some practitioners use cover letters to suggest ideas for using the attached release. Such suggestions can help the editor decide whether to use the release and how to develop story ideas involving the organization or product.

Send the Release on Time

Timely information is as important to PR practitioners as it is to news reporters. Timeliness is one of the several characteristics of news and is used by reporters to judge the importance of a story. A news release received too close to deadline is less likely to be published or broadcast because editors have little or no time to verify information or get answers to questions.

News releases can be sent to news organizations by conventional mail, fax or email. If releases are sent by conventional mail, PR practitioners must allow adequate time for mail to be handled and delivered. If they are sent by fax or email, PR practitioners must know the correct fax number or email address so the release gets to the proper department or person. If the release is sent as an email attachment, PR practitioners must make certain that the news organization can open and read the release. It is good practice to save and send the release in several versions (e.g., a Microsoft Word document and one in Rich Text Format [RTF]) so the news organization can open the file. Whether releases are sent through conventional mail, faxed or emailed, practitioners need to know news organization procedures and deadlines and deliver the release in time for processing for publication.

Use Journalism's Five Ws

The opening paragraph, or lead, of a news release should provide the who, what, when, where and why of the subject of the release. Journalists respect public relations practitioners who understand their definitions of news. Journalists want to be informed about major stories. They do not want to be bothered with stories that obviously are not newsworthy. Unfortunately, most news releases either lack any news or are written so poorly the news is buried near the end of the release.

The best news releases are so good that news reporters and editors don't need to wonder why they were sent at all; they include the point of the news release in the first paragraph. Here are the leads from three news releases that get to the main point:

The Willow Grove Town Band will present a Canada Day public concert of marches at 7 p.m. Monday, July 5, at the Memorial Park band shell.

The Central Okanagan Legal Services Committee is seeking book donations from the public for its upcoming book sale April 5–8 to benefit the Emergency Legal Services Fund, a program that provides legal aid to low-income residents.

Sacred Heart Medical Centre's Healthy Living Services will present "Beating Stress in Everyday Life," a program Thursday to introduce the public to the benefits of yoga and other stress-reducing techniques.

Analyze those leads. Notice that like good news story leads, all three emphasize the news—and are clear, concise and factual. They also follow Canadian Press style in regard to addresses, time elements and sentence structure.

Write Well

Editors complain that many news releases are poorly written or written for the wrong audience. Newspapers have a diverse audience whose reading abilities range from elementary to college level. For a news release to be used in a newspaper, it must be written so all readers can understand it. News organizations usually write for an eleventh-grade reading level. Journalists will throw away difficult-to-understand releases. News organizations would reject this news release:

DATALINE Systems has earned the "Excellence in Customer Satisfaction" Award from ADI, a manufacturer of VOIP and digital telecommunications systems. 2006 marks the third consecutive year that DATALINE Systems has won this immensely prestigious award. ADI stated that DATALINE Systems consistently exhibits ADI's ultimate ideals for customer satisfaction. ADI further stated that DATALINE Systems is an asset and business partner not only to ADI but also to every customer who does business with DATALINE Systems. DATALINE Systems sells, installs, and services Avaya, ADI, Executone, Bogen, and other major voice, data, and sound systems for industrial, retail, and residential applications. DATALINE Systems' line of secure voice and data networks are hallmarks of the voice and data distribution industry and are compliant with all major digital operating systems. DATALINE Systems serves 40 cities across Canada.

Editors would reject it because it is written more for the client than the public and contains jargon that few people would understand. When writing a news release, practitioners should write as journalists. Words should be simple. Sentences should average about 20 words. Paragraphs should be short and get to the point immediately. Practitioners should write in the active voice, using the passive voice only when necessary.

Proofreading is essential. Editors reject news releases with grammar and spelling errors or missing, buried or erroneous information. Practitioners must care about the quality of the work they produce to see it used in newspapers and news broadcasts.

Practitioners should think of their news releases as a community service providing information the public needs. Their writing should be lively and to the point, not boring and rambling.

Localize Information

News releases often present generalized information, failing to indicate how that information affects people in a community. Too often, practitioners confuse "localization" and "proximity." In fact, localizing can mean reflecting a psychological as well as a geographical closeness. A university's health science centre submitted news releases with the following leads, which illustrate that principle:

> While many Canadians may be eating less red meat to lower their cholesterol and fat levels, researchers at the University of Western Ontario are investigating the possibility that older Canadians should, in fact, be eating more.

> Doctors have some unseasonable advice for pregnant women heading outdoors to enjoy this summer's warm weather: Bundle up. Although the risk is small, they could get bitten by ticks carrying Lyme disease, a rare but disabling illness that University of Western Ontario physicians say can be transmitted by infected mothers-to-be to their unborn babies.

The first news release discusses a topic that concerns many adults—their cholesterol level—but it also points out an unusual or unexpected twist: that older Canadians might need more red meat. The second news release concerns another unusual topic: the fact that pregnant women need to bundle up, even in summer, to protect their unborn babies from Lyme disease (a disease often in the news). Identifying the source, in this case the University of Western Ontario, localizes the releases geographically. However, because the releases discuss topics that affect the everyday lives of hundreds of thousands of readers and viewers, they are also psychologically close to the audience.

Provide Visuals

Visuals, such as photographs, graphs or charts, catch the eye of readers, draw them into the story, and illustrate major points. Many newspapers use visual elements on their pages so their audience can get information easily and quickly.

Public relations practitioners should think about what visuals might be relevant to a release. Can a photograph help illustrate the information in the release? Can an infographic, chart or other visual help the audience grasp the information? Thinking visually can help practitioners get their releases accepted by editors. But don't overwhelm editors with visuals. Keep them simple and to the point. Usually, one or two will do.

Provide a Link to a Website

The Internet is a major source of information, and some research can be conducted quickly and efficiently from a newsroom when reporters have a link to a website.

Most organizations or corporations have websites, which can provide additional information on the topic addressed in the release. Statistical information to support the release or links providing additional information can be included with the release to help reporters answer questions they might have. In addition, many corporations or organizations belong to trade or professional associations that can supply expert sources for a story if reporters want to follow up the release. Links to those associations also can be provided. It is important that the release provide not only adequate information but also the means for reporters to get additional information, especially since reporters will want to corroborate with independent sources the information they publish or broadcast.

Format the News Release Properly

A news release—whether it is sent by regular mail ("snail mail"), fax or electronic mail—should follow a standard format so an editor can quickly determine who sent it and what it is about.

At the top or bottom of the release, include the complete address of the organization sending the release and the names, titles and phone numbers of people who can be contacted for more information. It is a good idea to include both a daytime and a night-time telephone or cellphone number, as well as an email address, because many reporters and editors work at night. It is also important to ensure that the people listed as contacts are actually available to reporters and editors at the times stated in the release.

At the top of the news release, put a "release" date, which indicates whether the item can be used immediately or is to be released at another specified time. The release date tells the editor when the information may be published. The release date might say, "For Immediate Release" or "For Release at Will" (whenever the newspaper has space available), or it might specify a date and time (for example: "For release at 10 a.m. EST Wednesday, Feb. 10"). Finally, the news release may request an "embargo": that the information not be released before a certain date and time. News organizations have no legal obligation to adhere to release dates, but they usually do so as a matter of professional courtesy. Failing to honour a release date, including an embargo, can cost a news organization its credibility with sources and, perhaps, deprive it of information in the future. Another problem with not honouring a release date is that the information could turn out to be inaccurate. The information in a release may change between the time it was written and the release date. The source of the release might have been prepared to update it in light of changing circumstances. However, if a news organization, has already published the release, both the source and the news organization look foolish.

On the other hand, embargoes may constitute attempts to control the flow of news or interfere with publication. The Canadian Press has this advice for its editorial staff about embargoed news releases:

> Entertainment newsmakers are increasingly demanding embargoes or other restrictions before they will provide information or interviews.
>
> Sometimes the request is reasonable; an embargo on an announcement of a major book prize winner, for instance, seems reasonable in return for getting the information early so a full story can be constructed. . . .
>
> In other cases, the newsmaker's motivation seems more self-serving: a TV network asks for an embargo on news about one of its shows until after the network can announce the information on one of its own shows. Or an over-zealous PR agent might block an interview unless a reporter promises not to ask certain questions.
>
> The news report should not be held hostage by such requests, which need to be considered on a case-by-case basis. Consult a supervisor before agreeing to any conditions.

The body of the news release should begin one-third of the way down the page to allow space for the editor to make comments to the rewrite person who will prepare it for publication. A headline or title for the release should appear in all-capital letters and underlined above the text of the release; the release itself should be double-spaced. If the release runs more than one page, the word "more" should be placed within brackets (like this: [more]) or dashes (like this:—more—) at the bottom centre of the page. The following pages of the release are identified by a slug line (a word or short phrase indicating the topic of the release) followed by dashes and the page number at the top of the page, either on the left or the right side.

At the end of the release, type the word "end" or the number "30" within quotes or dashes to indicate to the editor that there is no more text. Some editors use three number signs (###) to indicate the end of the text.

Here's a sample format for a news release:

Canadian Builders' Association – Eastern Newfoundland
222 Dark Forest Road
St. John's, NL P1F 1T1
Release Date and Time: Saturday, Mar. 27, 2010, 10 a.m. EST
CONTACT: John Smith
Office phone 012-555-5555
Cellphone 012-555-1224
Email john@nfb.com
(Body text of the release begins one-third down the page)
THE TITLE GOES HERE IN UPPERCASE AND UNDERLINED

Body of the release begins under the title and is double spaced, making it easier for editors to edit the copy.

At the end of the release, type an end mark to indicate the text is finished.

TYPES OF NEWS RELEASES

News releases serve a variety of objectives, such as publicizing a new company, explaining a new company policy, or pointing out the effects a company has on a community. The most common types of news releases are advance stories, event stories, features and discoveries.

Advance Stories

Practitioners write announcements whenever their company or client plans to sponsor an activity such as a speech or seminar. Advance stories often use an "agenda" lead like the following to provide information on the activity or event to the public:

Sacred Heart Hospital's Prevention Health Group will be offering free non-invasive and painless health tests to screen for the risk of a stroke during the hospital's "It's a Healthy Day" activities April 25.

The five free tests will be available to residents from 9 a.m. to 4 p.m. on a first-come, first-served basis. The screenings will be held in the hospital's Prevention Health Group Annex, 1863 W. Milford St.

The screenings detect the risk of a stroke by determining the amount of plaque build-up in arteries in the neck and legs. In addition, the tests check for possible abdominal aneurysms.

Each year more than 50,000 Canadians suffer a stroke, and last year more than 14,000 of those stroke victims died. Stroke is the third leading cause of death in Canada.

For registration and more information about the free stroke screening, call 555-2121 or 1-800-000-0000.

Event Stories

When practitioners write a story before an event, they write it as though the event already has happened and the news organization is reporting on it. A release written in this manner serves two main purposes: first, it lets reporters know what will occur at the event in case they want to cover it; second, it frees reporters from writing the story.

Reporters rarely publish such a release verbatim, however. They might attend the event, perhaps simply to verify the release's accuracy. Reporters often rewrite releases so identical accounts do not appear in other publications.

Practitioners also give reporters copies of speeches before they are delivered. This practice enables reporters to quote the speakers accurately. However, reporters generally attend the speeches because speakers may change some of their comments at the last moment.

"With the constant stream of data arriving daily from the surface of Mars, the fundamental question of humanity has never been so significant," says CATP Principal Investigator Lyle Whyte, Canada Research Chair in Environmental Microbiology and an associate professor of Natural Resource Sciences at McGill.

"What makes it so compelling is the recent realization that microbial life is extremely hardy and can survive and even thrive in very harsh environments previously thought uninhabitable on Earth like acidic streams, alkaline ponds, salt lakes, and hot springs," says CATP Co-Investigator Neil Banerjee, an assistant professor of Earth Sciences at Western.

For program information or to apply, please visit http://create-astrobiology. mcgill.ca/index.html

MEDIA CONTACT: Jeff Renaud, Senior Media Relations Officer, The University of Western Ontario, 519-661-2111, ext. 85165

THE JOURNALIST'S PERSPECTIVE: WORKING WITH PRESS RELEASES

Newspapers are besieged by individuals and organizations seeking publicity. Large newspapers receive thousands of news releases and other requests for publicity each week. Even small-town newspapers receive hundreds of releases in a week.

For most news organizations, news releases are an important and convenient source of information and story ideas. No news organization can afford to employ enough reporters to cover every story occurring in a community. Instead, news media depend on readers and viewers to notify them about church and school activities; charitable events and fundraisers; business and medical news; art, music and theatre events and schedules; speakers; and festivals.

Reporters handle news releases as they would any other type of story. Their first task is to identify a central point. If the release lacks a central point, the reporter discards it. If a central point is there, then the reporter identifies the relevant information and discards the rest. Reporters also use the central point to identify what information is missing.

Reporters then critically examine whatever information the news release provides and summarize that information as clearly, concisely and objectively as possible. The task is often difficult, because some news releases fail to emphasize any news. Others contain clichés, jargon and puffery. Moreover, most fail to use the proper style for capitalization, punctuation and abbreviations.

Typically, editors will discard 100 news releases for every three or four they accept. Even those they accept will be rewritten. Some editors do not even open all the news releases they receive in the mail. Rather, they glance at the return address to see who sent the release, then immediately throw it away if they recognize that it came from a source that regularly submits trivial information. For example, journalists are unlikely to use a news release from a company that has no presence in a community or surrounding area, such as manufacturing plants or franchise outlets. Yet some companies send out announcements about the promotion of executives at corporate headquarters hundreds of miles away. Few news organizations will use such releases, because they are of little interest to people in their community.

The worst news releases, usually those submitted by local groups unfamiliar with the media, lack information that reporters need to write complete stories. They also omit the names and telephone numbers of people whom the reporters might call to obtain more information or explanations of unclear facts. Some news releases provide telephone numbers that journalists can call only during the day, not during the evening, when the reporters employed by morning dailies and the broadcast media often work.

Editors rarely use news releases as submitted. Instead, they have reporters rewrite them, confirming the information and adding to it with quotes and additional facts. These editors might explain that they want their stories to be distinctive. Also, wary about the accuracy and truth of information submitted by publicists, they will want to corroborate the information independently.

Other editors use news releases primarily as a source of ideas. If editors like an idea provided by a news release, they will assign reporters to gather more information and write a story. Sometimes the published story is much different from the picture presented in the news release.

THE NO. 1 PROBLEM: LACK OF NEWSWORTHINESS

Journalists obviously prefer news releases about topics that satisfy their definitions of news. They look for topics that are new, local, interesting, unusual, relevant and important to their audience. Journalists also look for information likely to affect hundreds or even thousands of people. Action is more newsworthy than opinions, and a genuine or spontaneous event is more newsworthy than a contrived one. Unless they serve very small communities, news organizations increasingly refuse to publish news releases about ribbon-cutting and groundbreaking ceremonies. Newspapers also generally refuse to publish photographs showing people passing a cheque or gavel.

Limited Interest

News organizations might not use releases like the following because their topics would not interest many people—except, of course, members of the organizations they mention. Those organizations can use other means, such as newsletters or website announcements, to communicate with their members. That is not the job of a news organization:

> Cromwell Manufacturing Co. announces the selection of Alan Smith as the employee of the month for June. Smith, who has worked for Cromwell for 18 years, is a line supervisor in the Quality Assurance Department.

> Marilyn Watkins, president and CEO of Protec Home Security Services, has been selected to attend the Eastern Canada Business Leadership Conference to be held in Halifax the first week in April.

Contrived Events

Reporters are likely to discard the following news releases, because they announce contrived events:

> The premier has joined with the blood bank community in proclaiming January as National Volunteer Blood Donor Month and is urging everyone who is healthy to donate blood to help others.

> Mayor Peter Willowman has proclaimed April 20–26 as Literacy Week in the city, to coincide with the declaration of National Literacy Week during the same period.

Every week and every month of the year is dedicated to some cause or commemoration, ranging from Canada Day to Remembrance Day. Furthermore, the two news releases above state the obvious. Most responsible adults would urge "everyone who is healthy to donate blood to help others." In the second release, because a National Literacy Week already exists, a provincial declaration is an unnecessary duplication. Stories about such proclamations are often trite, dull, repetitive and devoid of news value.

Rewriting for Newsworthiness

Many of the people writing news releases seem to be more interested in pleasing their bosses than in satisfying the media and informing the public. To please their bosses, they begin news releases with their bosses' names. Or they might begin with the organization's name and information about the organization before focusing on the news aspect of the release.

Other news releases are editorials that philosophize or praise rather than report information beneficial to the public. A news release submitted by the Alberta Beef Producers declared:

> Alberta beef helps fuel Beijing Olympians and other world class athletes through the Fuel for Gold initiative.
>
> For the second year, Fuel for Gold, sponsored by ABP, in conjunction with turkey, pork and egg producers will help some world-class athletes to worry less about eating, and more about training. The program helps bring nutritious protein to an athlete that is healthy, affordable and quick.
>
> "I eat lots of high quality beef cuts because of the program," said Louis Poirier, a PhD student and bobsledder attending the University of Calgary. "I need to put on lean muscle, and beef helps me do that."
>
> The Canadian Sport Centre Calgary (CSCC) provides the lunch program for its registered athletes. It was designed to provide Canada's best athletes training in Calgary with the nutrition they need to be successful in their sport; the weekly menu has been created by the CSCC dietitians, strength trainers and a Fuel for Gold chef.
>
> The primary purpose of this program is to provide high performance athletes with convenient, affordable and nutritious lunch options.
>
> Fuel for Gold offers nutritious meals for optimal exercise recovery at a time of day when athletes' bodies are most receptive to restoring energy and repairing muscle tissue after a hard morning of training.
>
> "The nutritional aspect of being an elite athlete is critical," said Beijing Olympic gymnastics contender, Nathan Gafuik. "This helps me get the food I need at a reasonable cost."

Newspapers and newscasts should not praise or editorialize in a news story. That is not their job, nor is it ethical for them to do so.

THE NO. 2 PROBLEM: LACK OF OBJECTIVITY

Too many news releases promote rather than report. They contain laudatory adverbs and adjectives, not facts.

Advertisements

The worst news releases are blatant advertisements, obviously written to help sell commercial products. Most journalists would reject the following news releases for that reason.

> Dogs may be considered man's best friend, but for many walkers, joggers and cyclists, dogs can be their worst enemy. According to the Canadian Veterinary Medical Association (CVMA) more than a million people are treated each year for dog attacks, and on average, 12 people a year die as the result of dog attacks.
>
> Some of these victims are walkers, joggers and cyclists who are attacked by dogs while enjoying the sport they love. Meeting the needs of today's sports-minded and exercise-dedicated active Canadians, Pace Consumer Products (PCP) is introducing DOG GONE! Canine Repellant Spray. Based on proven technology developed for law enforcement agencies, DOG GONE! is a non-life-threatening, momentarily debilitating chemical spray that causes temporary irritation of an animal's nose and eyes, rendering it incapable of attack.

> The Hair Affair Styling Salon will now carry the latest line of hair care products from Nature Born Salon Specific.
>
> Marie Benson, owner and operator of The Hair Affair, said she is proud to carry the full line of Nature Born hair care products for her customers. The product line will

include shampoos, conditioners, scalp treatments, hair colouring products and styling products for all types and styles of hair.

Nature Born is the only company producing totally organic hair care products sold exclusively at hair salons throughout the country.

Although most newspapers would not use such releases, they might be valuable to the trade press or news media in affected communities as leads for stories in the business section of the newspaper.

Laudatory Adjectives and Puffery

Journalists eliminate laudatory adjectives in rewriting news releases. Terms such as "world famous," the "best" or the "greatest" are subjective at best and difficult to verify. Every speaker does not have to be called a "guest speaker," and none should be labelled "famous," "prominent," "well-known" or "distinguished." If a speaker truly is famous, the public already will know the person—and will not have to be told of his or her fame.

No news story—or news release—should call a program "wonderful," "successful," "timely" or "informative." Similarly, nothing should be called "interesting" or "important." Reporters also avoid phrases such as "bigger and better," "the best ever" and "back by popular demand."

Puffery often appears in leads of news releases:

Anyone wanting to learn how to deal with conflict needs to talk to a professional—and that professional is Mark Richards. Richards is a well-known expert and extremely talented speaker on the subject of handling conflict. His five-step program on conflict resolution has been touted as the best program ever to help ordinary people deal with the huge conflicts that can arise in their lives and rob them of the quality of life they so richly deserve. Richards will be presenting a two-hour seminar about his program beginning at 7 p.m. Thursday, Sept. 9, in the Fellowship Hall of St. Luke Chapel, 1457 Downing Ave. The title of the program is "Managing Conflict in Your Life."

REVISED: Mark Richards, who is an expert in conflict resolution, will present a seminar on his five-step program for resolving conflict beginning at 7 p.m., Sept. 9, in the Fellowship Hall of St. Luke Chapel, 1457 Downing Ave.

The Creative Art Gallery, devoted exclusively to fine art photography, proudly announces an event of international significance in the photographic community: an exhibition of the works of Jerry N. Uelsmann and Diane Farris.

REVISED: The Creative Art Gallery, 324 N. Park Ave., will exhibit the photographs of Jerry N. Uelsmann and Diane Farris from Jan. 4 to Jan. 29.

Telling the Public What to Do

Instead of reporting news, some releases urge readers and viewers to donate their time and money, to buy new products, to attend events or to join organizations. For example:

You have to see this display to believe it!

Every dollar you give—whether $10, $100 or $1,000—stays in your community. So give—you'll be glad you did.

Tickets are available for $60 per person, or reserve a table of eight for $400. That's a savings of $80. Seating is limited, so get your tickets right away!

Journalists delete such editorial comments or rewrite them in a more factual manner. Reporters might summarize a story and then, in the final paragraph, tell readers how they can respond but not say that they should respond:

Tickets for the program are available to the public at the Performing Arts Centre and by calling 422-4896 for $5 each. Seating will not be reserved, so the public is urged to arrive early to hear this most important message on the subject of health care.

REVISED: Tickets cost $5 and can be obtained at the Performing Arts Centre or by calling 422-4896.

OTHER PROBLEMS WITH NEWS RELEASES

Stating the Obvious

Public relations writers who lack journalism training and do not know what makes a successful news story often write releases that state the obvious:

The office of the Provincial Fire Marshal today emphasized the importance of having working smoke detectors in homes and businesses as a way to save lives.

Parents are worried more than ever about the amount of violence in our society.

A fire marshal is expected to encourage the use of smoke detectors to save lives. That is a routine part of the official's job and not news. Similarly, violence has always been a problem; generations of parents have worried about it.

In many releases, the real news is buried in the second—or even twenty-second—paragraph.

Helping people is a rewarding experience, especially for those who volunteer their time or donate money for their local communities. The reward is seeing friends and neighbours, as well as strangers, benefit from the time and money donated for community projects. Dr. Ronald Bishop, a social psychologist specializing in the subject of private giving, claims that the act of giving is part of the social fabric of a community and helps people become more connected to their community.

Bishop is one of several experts who will present a program on volunteerism and how to get involved with your community that will be presented at 7 p.m. Tuesday, March 5, in the Town Hall auditorium. This interesting and challenging program is designed to raise awareness of volunteering as a way for communities to help themselves develop and achieve common goals.

REVISED: Ronald Bishop, a specialist in private giving, will be one of several people presenting a program on volunteerism and community involvement at 7 p.m. March 5 in the Town Hall auditorium.

Absence of Solid Facts

Other sentences contain generalities, platitudes, self-praise and gush but not facts. By rewriting news releases, journalists eliminate every one of those sentences. Here are three examples:

It will be an exciting theatrical presentation that will heartily reward audiences.

An impressive array of speakers will share their wonderful experiences.

The library has a reputation as a friendly, pleasant place to visit.

Such gush often appears in direct quotations, but that never justifies its use. If a quotation lacks substance, reporters will discard it too:

Councillor Jaitt stated, "The fair is the best ever, with a dazzling lineup of new entertainment."

"We're very excited about the opening of the new store," said Mark Hughey, president. "The store represents a new direction for us and extends our commitment to provide customers with the highest-quality products at the lowest possible prices."

The platitudes and generalities sound familiar because they are used so often. For example, the following platitudes are similar but appeared in news releases that two different companies used to describe new employees:

> We are fortunate to have a woman with Russell's reputation and background as a member of the team. Her knowledge and experience will be invaluable as we broaden our sales and marketing base.

> We were impressed with Belmonte's accomplishments and his professionalism. We're extremely pleased with our good fortune in having him join us.

One-sided Stories

People and organizations submit news releases to the media because they hope to benefit from the stories' publication. Almost all news releases are one-sided. They present only the source's opinions and often present those opinions as fact. The news releases that do mention an opposing view usually try to show that the other side is wrong.

Reporters might be tempted to accept the information provided by a news release because doing so is fast and easy. Reporters who fail to check the facts, however, are likely to make serious errors. For example, a college newspaper missed a major story because it received and immediately published a news release announcing that eight faculty members had received tenure and promotions. The news release failed to reveal the real story: the fact that the college had denied tenure to a dozen other faculty members, including some of the college's most popular teachers, because they were not considered good researchers. Moreover, the faculty members who did not get tenure were, in essence, fired. A single telephone call to a faculty representative would have uncovered the real story.

Using the Media

Other news releases encourage controversy. Here too, media that publish such news releases allow themselves to be used. In dealing with these and all the other problems that they encounter while handling news releases, reporters regularly condense four- and five-page handouts into three- and four-paragraph stories.

SOME FINAL GUIDELINES

Whenever possible, reporters localize the news releases they handle. From a release distributed by Thompson Rivers University in Kamloops, B.C.:

> Thompson Rivers University awarded $409,000 to 470 students at its 27th annual Foundation Awards Ceremony on Thursday evening.
> It was standing room only on the floor of the TRU Gymnasium as student recipients met with donors to receive financial support from the 254 donor-sponsored awards.
> Thursday's awards are a part of the expected $1,420,000 that students will receive throughout the year in the form of scholarships, bursaries and awards from the TRU Foundation and internal university funding. In addition to this, many students take advantage of thousands of dollars available in government grant programs.

Perceptive reporters would contact the university for a list of students and their hometowns so they could localize their stories' leads, focusing on the winning students from their area.

Second, avoid unnecessary background information, especially statements about a group's philosophy, goals or organization. The information is rarely necessary. Moreover, it would become repetitious and waste too much space if reporters included it in every story about a group:

MDCA is a private, non-profit arts organization dedicated to the presentation and advancement of the fine arts in our area.

Throughout the year volunteers give unselfishly of their time as Big Brothers and Big Sisters. "The lives of boys and girls in this community are enriched by their caring," said Joe Midura, executive director, in announcing the Volunteer Appreciation Week event.

 ## CHECKLISTS FOR PR PRACTITIONERS

When writing a news release, ask yourself the following questions:

Does the news release provide the proper information?
1. Does it list a contact person and a telephone number?
2. Does it list the address of the public relations agency or department?
3. Does it clearly identify the client?
4. Does the news release have a release date, indicating an appropriate publication date? Normally, news releases are written in advance of an event.
5. Does the release include a cover letter to the editor indicating more about the sponsoring company or ideas for using the attached news release?

Is the news release written in journalistic style?
1. Does the opening paragraph, or lead, of the release focus on the who, what, when, where and why of the story?
2. Is there a short headline summarizing the contents of the release?
3. Does the text begin one-third of the way down the page and use "more" or "#" or "end" on the appropriate pages?
4. Does the text conform to Canadian Press style, especially in the handling of addresses, employee titles, dates, and time elements?
5. Are creative visuals, such as graphs or charts or photographs, included with the story? Visuals catch the eye of readers, drawing them into the story, and help to illustrate a point.

 ## CHECKLISTS FOR HANDLING NEWS RELEASES

When evaluating a news release, ask yourself the following questions:

Does the news release have news value?
1. What is the central point of the release?
2. Is it newsworthy?
3. Does it involve an issue likely to interest or affect many members of your community—or only a few, such as the members of the organization distributing the news release?
4. Does it involve a genuine rather than a contrived event, such as a proclamation, ground-breaking or ribbon-cutting?

Does the news release need rewriting?
1. Does the lead emphasize the news, or is it buried in a later paragraph?
2. Does the lead begin by stating the obvious?
3. Does the lead begin with an unnecessary name?
4. Does the lead need to be localized?
5. Is the release clear and concise?
6. Does the release contain only information necessary to fully develop its central point?
7. Does the release contain all the information necessary to develop the central point?
8. Does the release contain any clichés, jargon or generalities? Even if they appear in direct quotations, eliminate them.
9. Whom does the news release benefit, the public or its source?
10. Is the release objective?
    - Does it contain any puffery: words such as "best," "exciting," "famous," "interesting," "important," "successful" or "thrilling"?

- Does it promote a private company or commercial product?
- Does it make unsubstantiated claims about a product or service being the "cheapest," "biggest" or "best"?
- Does it urge the public to act?

11. Does the news release present every side of a controversial issue? If it does, are its presentations adequate—that is, fair and thorough?

 ## Guest Columnist

ANYTHING CAN HAPPEN

By Megan Walde Manlove

When I was a daily newspaper reporter, I cherished the notion that anything could happen.

One day I'm sent to interview suburban residents who claimed their drinking water had been contaminated by sloppy practices at a neighbouring business that emptied and cleaned portable toilets. The next day, my feeble number skills have to make sense of a controversial school district budget proposal. The next week, I apply for a press pool badge to cover a VIP's stop in our community.

Different stories to be told, and how to tell them was largely up to me.

Usually, I began with a phone call to the experts—an environmental engineer, the finance director, a local political analyst. Many times, that meant dealing with PR staff, many of whom had a reputation of not returning phone calls in a reasonable time or setting up interviews with utter disregard for deadlines.

As a rule, we reporters commonly referred to them as "flacks."

Imagine the crisis of self-esteem, then, when I considered joining the PR and marketing office for a large medical centre and research institution.

I would get to write about medical science, a passion that preceded even my interest in journalism, all the time rather than for the exceptional assignment. The pay and hours were a significant improvement on what the newsroom offered.

But I feared I was trading in a noble profession to become one of them.

Soon I came to understand my reaction was normal. And I found my skills as a reporter a solid foundation for my new role in PR.

A major part of my job now is to grow awareness of the work done by our biomedical researchers. I spend time in their labs and offices—reporter's notebook in hand—trying to absorb as much as possible about the cellular mechanisms of this protein or the DNA target of that molecular compound. Then, it's back to the office to make sense of the discovery for public consumption.

Our primary tool? The humble news release. Yet I remember the stack of releases that sat unclaimed by the newsroom fax machine every day and the many more banished to my email junk bin—two-thirds unread thanks to a bland or unclear lead paragraph—later in my career.

Two weeks into my new job, a cancer geneticist from the college called to tell me about a recent bit of his work that was to be published three weeks hence as the cover article of *Science* magazine, a leading scientific journal. This was a first in the history of our institution. And his findings didn't have to do with cancer but with skin colour.

It took me a week to read and process the paper, to decide what it meant to peer researchers and the lay public, then to write the first draft. The researcher and I spent the next week making sure my English translation of the science was sound and rewriting for clarity. My final task was this: He was prepared to answer questions about the science, and I had to prep him for questions about what the science meant to social notions of race and ethnicity, the kind of questions I knew reporters would ask and to which I knew the public would want answers.

The story was picked up around the world in print and on the radio, TV, and Internet: At one point, it had well over 1 million references online. This was an awesome success for the institution.

Almost two years later, I still find it difficult to navigate the labyrinth of our Biomedical Research Building, its confusingly simple layout offering few unique landmarks from floor to floor, wing to wing. During on-location interviews, I try to accommodate reporters and their story needs. I try to ensure our presence there doesn't significantly affect the work environment.

I am no longer the storyteller. Neither am I an obstacle to the story's telling. I am a facilitator, helping identify important stories or finding that one telling anecdote from the lab or clinic that will make the story click for readers or viewers.

Reporters get the story. The story is told. I've done my job. The "us vs. them" mindset looks much different from this perspective.

There are still deadlines, though more erratic and usually less demanding. My editors here are scientists more concerned with content than with style or structure. Unlike the newspaper, my audience changes day by day. Yet I still work for a noble cause—that medical research is the key to a better health care future. I still have a part in witnessing dramatic stories unfold every day.

And still, anything can happen.

SUGGESTED READINGS AND USEFUL WEBSITES

"News releases and PR representatives." 2008. *The Canadian Press Stylebook*, 15th edn, 136–7. Toronto: The Canadian Press.

"Public relations and the news media." 2008. *The Canadian Press Stylebook*, 15th edn, 481–8. Toronto: The Canadian Press.

Evans, Harold. 1973. *Editing and Design: Newsman's English.* London: Heinemann.

Fee, Margery, and Janice McAlpine. 2007. *Guide to Canadian English Usage.* Toronto: Oxford University Press.

Heath, Robert L. 2005. *Encyclopedia of Public Relations.* Thousand Oaks, CA: Sage Publications.

Nelson, Joyce. 1989. *Sultans of Sleaze: Public Relations and the Media.* Toronto: Between the Lines.

Robertson, Stuart M. 1991. *Robertson's Newsroom Legal Crisis Management.* Dunedin, ON: Hallion Press.

Canadian Public Relations Society: http://www.cprs.ca

International Association of Business Communicators: http://www.iabc.com

Public Relations Career Tips: http://www.topstory.ca/careers.html

PR Direct: http://www.prdirect.ca/en/home.asp

EXERCISE 1   The News Media and PR Practitioners: Writing News Releases

The following information is from actual news releases. Write a news release from each set of details. Remember to use Canadian Press style. Use as much information as you think is necessary to create an effective release. Add phrases and transitions to make the news releases acceptable to editors. List yourself as the contact person for each sponsor, decide on the release date and write a headline.

1. The following program is being sponsored by Parks Canada.

    - National Park Day Program.
    - National Park Day annual historic preservation event.
    - Nationwide effort to help clean and restore Canada's historic battlefields, cemeteries, shrines and parks.
    - More than 80 sites across Canada have been targeted for work on April 18.
    - The National Park Day Program is in its 11th year of providing volunteer assistance from members of the public to help maintain Canada's public spaces.
    - Participants gather at designated sites to help with activities that range from trash pick-up to trail building.
    - Volunteers receive a free T-shirt and have an opportunity to learn about the significance of the site in exchange for their time and effort.
    - Volunteers are needed to clean up trails and stream banks, clear vegetation, and assist with ongoing restoration and historic preservation projects.
    - Information on the program and how to register to participate is available from Parks Canada at 1-800-555-1212 or at its website www.pc.gc.ca.
    - Necessary equipment for the work will be provided at each site where volunteers will be participating, but participants are asked to dress appropriately for weather conditions, wear sturdy shoes or boots, and bring a pair of leather gloves.
    - A picnic-style lunch will be provided on site as well as bottles of water.

2. The following program is being offered by the Student Government Association at your university.

    - Adopt-A-Street program.
    - More than 600 students from 18 on-campus organizations are involved in the program.
    - Students will be working with members of the community to help clean up and beautify the community and the campus.
    - Members of the program meet at 8 p.m. Tuesdays in Room 210 of the university's student union building to plan projects and co-ordinate cleanup schedules.
    - The program is the latest volunteer service project by members of the university community, including students, staff and faculty.
    - Students annually contribute more than 10,000 hours of volunteer service to the community, while staff and faculty contribute several thousand more hours with various community groups.
    - Community members or students interested in participating in the Adopt-A-Street program can call the Student Government Association through the university's student affairs office at 555-1111.
    - The first cleanup project is planned for sometime in the fall semester and will involve basic cleanup and leaf raking in selected areas.
    - Cleanup projects also will be assigned to groups for the spring semester to remove trash and debris left from the winter months.

- Participating groups include the Greek Affairs Council (representing 12 fraternities and sororities), the Resident Halls Association, Student Senate, Criminal Justice Club, and student members of the Canadian Public Relations Society.
- The university still is looking for volunteers from the community, as well as the university.
- Streets selected for cleanup this fall include Richard Avenue, High Street, Fort Street, Britton Road, Queen Street, Burd Street, Earl Street, Prince Street, King Street, Martin Avenue, Middle Spring Avenue, Orange Street, Macdonald Street, Morris Street and Elm Street.

EXERCISE 2   The News Media and PR Practitioners: Writing News Releases

The following information is from actual news releases. Write a news release from each set of details. Remember to use Canadian Press style. Use as much information as you think is necessary to create an effective release. Add phrases and transitions to make the news releases acceptable to editors. List yourself as the contact person for each sponsor, decide on the release date and write a headline.

1. The following information is being released by Elections Canada in your region.
    ■ Anyone who wishes to vote in the upcoming federal election must be registered to vote.
    ■ The deadline to register to vote in the election is April 16.
    ■ Voter registration information can be obtained by calling Elections Canada at 1-800-463-6868 or online at www.elections.ca.
    ■ The registration form must indicate any change in name or address.
    ■ Electors who will not be able to go to the polls on election day can vote during three days of advance polls, by special ballot through the mail, or at the office of their returning officer.
    ■ Applications to vote at advance polls or by special ballot are available by calling Elections Canada.
    ■ Applications to vote at advance polls or by special ballot must be received by May 8.
    ■ Except for voters who have a disability, all special ballots must be delivered in person or through Canada Post. Special ballots delivered by any other means for voters who do not have a disability will not be accepted or counted by the Chief Electoral Officer.

2. The following program is sponsored by your regional Women In Need (WIN) Victim Services.
    ■ Women In Need (WIN) is in need of help from members of communities across the region.
    ■ The prevention of any crime begins with awareness and the commitment and resolve to get involved.
    ■ The work of preventing sexual violence is a work that must become the commitment of everyone in every community in the county.
    ■ One in four girls and one in six boys will become the victim of sexual violence before their eighteenth birthday. This kind of violence has a devastating effect on both its victims and on those who love them.
    ■ This month is Sexual Assault Awareness Month, and WIN Victim Services is encouraging the community to take action against this silent crime.
    ■ There are many ways to take action against sexual violence, but sexual violence is a crime not often talked about openly. Campaigns against bullying and for respecting others can influence the amount of sexual violence occurring in communities throughout the county. Ways that can work to make a difference include:
    ■ Families should talk openly in regard to age-appropriate discussions about healthy sexuality and the importance of loving and respectful relationships.
    ■ Educators should be encouraged to teach non-violent conflict resolution skills and promote anti-bullying values.
    ■ Employers should be encouraged to contribute resources to programs that work to make a difference and promote violence-free workplaces by enforcing policies against sexual harassment.
    ■ Young people can learn to value everyone's uniqueness and begin to recognize positive relationships and reach out to at-risk peers. They can learn leadership skills and show respect, modelling these behaviours as positive ones to their peers.

CHAPTER 18

- Community groups can invite WIN into their meetings to learn how they can identify and support a victim of violence.
- Creating change starts with each individual family. Parents can teach their children well when they teach them to respect others.

3. The following program is sponsored by your province's Arts Board.

- Your city is one of eight in the province receiving 11 grants to support arts and cultural affairs education.
- A total of $495,500 has been awarded to 11 recipients out of 21 grant applicants.
- The grant program, "ArtsSmarts," is funded by the Arts Board to teach students about art and culture.
- "Our province's tremendous cultural resources add beauty and richness to the lives of our citizens," said Wallace Chandler, director of your province's Department of History, Arts and Libraries, which is administering the program. "This program will help to build connections between schools, students, arts and cultural institutions, and artists."
- Projects funded by the program are intended to aid development of student interest in the arts, support partnerships between schools and cultural institutions, improve arts education curriculum in schools, and introduce students and teachers to the rich variety of art and culture in the province.
- "ArtsSmarts" also will target teacher education in the arts, striving to improve the quality and depth of arts education.
- Information on the "ArtsSmarts" program is available at 111-555-4444.

EXERCISE 3   The News Media and PR Practitioners: Evaluating News Releases

Critically evaluate the newsworthiness of the following leads. Determine whether each release is usable as written and why. Then discuss your decision with your classmates.

1. Pregnant women throughout the province are finding it more difficult to locate an obstetrician willing to deliver their baby because of the number of obstetricians—80 last year alone—who are discontinuing the practice because of the high cost of malpractice insurance, according to a survey by the Saskatchewan Obstetric and Gynecologic Society.

   EVALUATION:_____

2. During October, millions of high school seniors and their families will attend recruitment fairs and tour campuses nationwide as they select a college or university for next fall. Planning experts at Morris College say that families should not automatically eliminate a college because of its sticker price.

   EVALUATION:_____

3. High interest rates, coupled with low prices for most agricultural commodities, are causing serious "cash flow" problems for farmers, pushing some toward bankruptcy, according to a study by the Canadian Institute of Food and Agricultural Sciences (IFAS) at a university in your province.

   EVALUATION:_____

4. Nail polish remover is still being dropped into the eyes of conscious rabbits to meet insurance regulations, infant primates are punished by electric shocks in pain endurance tests, and dogs are reduced to a condition called "learned helplessness" to earn someone a PhD.

   With the theme "Alternatives Now," People for the Ethical Treatment of Animals (PETA) is sponsoring a community rally on Friday—World Day for Laboratory Animals—at 1 p.m.

   EVALUATION:_____

5. Until recently, a missing lockbox key could be a major security problem for homeowners selling a house. But today, a missing electronic key can be turned off, protecting clients and their homes. More and more home sellers are using an electronic lockbox, the Superior KeyBox from Williams, on their properties to provide added safety, security and convenience for their homes.

   EVALUATION:_____

6. *Natural Gardening*, the world's largest-circulation gardening magazine, has announced that it has retained Balenti Associates to represent its advertising sales in the Prairie provinces and western Canada. The 27-year-old company is one of the largest advertising sales firms in Canada, with sales offices in the top five Canadian markets as well as major European cities.

   EVALUATION:_____

7. "The Changing Face of Men's Fashion" will be illustrated in a fashion presentation in Robinson's Men's Shop at 5:30 on Thursday. A special feature of the event will be commentary on the distinctive directions in men's designs by fashion designer Anna Zella.

   EVALUATION:_____

8. In cooperation with Health Canada's Consumer Product Safety office, the Moro division of the Petrillo Group of Italy is announcing the recall of 31,000 London branch LP gas Monitor Gauges. Some of these gauges may leak highly flammable propane gas that could ignite or explode. Health Canada is aware of five incidents of gas leaks catching fire. Two of these fires resulted in burn injuries.

   EVALUATION:_____

CHAPTER 18

9. Dr. Zena Treemont, who recently retired after 35 years with Agriculture and Agri-Food Canada, has assumed her new duties as Chief Investigator for Brucellosis and Tuberculosis with the Alberta Ministry of Agriculture and Rural Development, Minister George Groeneveld announced today.

    EVALUATION:_____

10. Women have made much progress against discrimination through social and legal reforms, but they are still the victims of a very disabling form of discrimination that largely goes unnoticed: arthritis. Two-thirds of the Canadians who suffer from arthritis are women, according to a study by the Arthritis Society of Canada.

    EVALUATION:_____

EXERCISE 4   The News Media and PR Practitioners: Rewriting News Releases

This is an actual news release mailed to a news organization. Only the locations and the names of some individuals have been changed. Use the name of your university as the source of the release. Your instructor might ask you to write only the lead or to write the entire story. The exercise contains numerous errors in style, spelling and punctuation. Correct all errors.

University Student Volunteers Help Meet Community Needs

Press Release

The universitys Volunteer Services Office serves as a centre for five service-oriented groups on campus and provides opportunities for students and others who want to volunteer there time to help others. The V.S.O. also acts as a clearinghouse for community agencies seeking university student volunteers. This service is completely free of charge to the community.

Almost 400 students, including many repeat volunteers, worked on projects as diverse as cleaning up Duncan Provincial Forest, helping the elderly in local retirement homes, and assisting the Red Cross with a blood drive.

Tara Osborn started volunteering as a first-year student to meet the requirements of her social work classes at the university but, like a lot of other students, she discovered she enjoyed volunteering and continued her service without further classroom credit.

"I really liked it," said Osborn, now a third-year student who heads T.O.U.C.H., a campus group that promotes volunteerism. "I like making a difference and helping people."

Osborn and other students volunteered 1,714 hours during the fall semester, donating time and energy to about thirty projects on campus and the surrounding communities.

They volunteered through TOUCH (Today's Organization Utilizing Concerned Humans) and other student-run organizations including Alpha Phi Omega, Big Brothers/Big Sisters, Circle K, Student Environmental Action Coalition and Women's Rights Council. Circle K members, for example, volunteered 564 hours, including forty-seven at Valley View Retirement Community, where they helped push residents in wheelchairs to and from therapy sessions.

"That is a high-energy job," said Linda Ellerman, director of volunteer services at Valley View. "That is definitely a great help for us. A lot of our other volunteers are retirement-age people and they are not able to take on that kind of responsibility."

The residents benefit from interacting with young people, she said. "Just seeing the young faces in the building and having the compassion of a young adult is a very positive thing."

The students, in turn, gain an understanding of the aging process and an appreciation for the work at a retirement home. "They could choose that as a career," Ellerman said. "We've seen that a couple of times."

Other T.O.U.C.H. projects included volunteering at a local homeless shelter, visiting the elderly at Manor Rest Nursing home and working with Head Start children at the university's daycare centre. The Student Environmental Action Coalition helped with recycling drives in Gibson City and cleanups in Duncan Provincial Forest. Alpha Phi Omega members visited the old folks at Episcopal Village Retirement Centre. Circle Ks other projects included helping with the Red Cross blood drive, cleaning a local highway and rails-to-trails path, and volunteering at the King's Kettle Food Pantry. Big Brothers/Big Sisters members spent a total of 464 hours with area children, including activities such as bowling and camping.

For the number of groups that we have, I think they've done an excellent job," said Ann Hoffman, director of volunteer services at the university. "It gives students some life experiences as far as feeling they have accomplished something for themselves. They certainly grow and learn from their experiences."

Student volunteers are planning a number of projects to be held over the next few months including the eighteenth annual Childrens Fair to be held in the universities athletic center. It will feature games, prizes, food, a petting zoo, educational displays and entertainment.

- Should still images, video or graphics go with the story?
- Should the visual be a close-up or a medium or long shot?
- Where to place the story in a newspaper, broadcast or Internet format?

This chapter should help students understand ethical issues, develop personal and professional ethical guidelines and practices, and articulate the reasons behind their decisions and actions.

MEDIA CREDIBILITY

The Canadian public is becoming increasingly skeptical about the information it receives from the mass media. According to a study by the Canadian Media Research Consortium, nearly half of Canadians (48 per cent) think that news stories are often inaccurate, and nearly two-thirds believe that the news media cover up their mistakes.

The Media Research Consortium findings are troubling, because media must maintain credibility for two main reasons. First, people depend on the media for their information. Mass media research shows people use local and national television news programs to find out about breaking events and they monitor radio news for updates. People who want more detail about issues or events turn to newspapers, the Internet and magazines.

Second, media must be credible to succeed as businesses. The media need readers, viewers and listeners to attract advertisers, who provide financial support. If audiences doubt the credibility of a particular news organization, they will stop buying the newspaper, change the channel, or go to a different website. When audiences turn away, advertising revenues decline. Then the media organization's budget shrinks, which often means even poorer news coverage. The downward spiral usually continues until that news organization is no longer in business.

ETHICAL DECISION-MAKING

When a story is wrong or unethical, people usually berate the organization that published it. The organization might then reprimand or dismiss the reporter or editor responsible for it. This alone gives journalists a powerful reason to think through ethical issues. Furthermore, the media are quick to report on journalists who act unethically, whereas the thousands of moral journalists who make good decisions do not make the news.

Guiding Questions

A journalist can ask several questions when facing an ethical decision. Two of the most important are:

- Who will be hurt, and how many?
- Who will be helped, and how many?

Many news stories do hurt someone or some group. Weighing the hurt against the benefits, and justifying that hurt, can help journalists make the right choice. If the story hurts several people and helps several hundred, then publishing the story is most likely justified. Perhaps a veterinarian has been accused of misdiagnosing symptoms, which has led to incorrect surgeries or the deaths of many pets. The story will embarrass the veterinarian's family and affect business, but it would help many people when choosing a doctor for their sick animals. Sometimes, journalists get too involved with the details of writing and publishing a story and forget to ask these all-encompassing questions:

- What is the objective of the story?
- Will my decision contribute to the reason for writing the story?

A retired journalist and professor, H. Eugene Goodwin, used to tell his reporters and students to ask themselves six additional questions while making an ethical decision:

1. What do we usually do in cases like this? (What is the news organization's policy on this type of situation, and is it a good policy?)
2. Is there a better alternative? (Harmful results often can be avoided or eased by trying something different.)
3. Can I look myself in the mirror tomorrow? (You must think about how you feel and whether you can live with your decision.)
4. Can I justify this to family, friends and the public? (If we know we have to explain our decisions to the public—in an editor's column, for example—then we might be more careful about our decisions.)
5. What principles or values can I apply? (Some overarching principles, such as truth, justice or fairness, will take priority over others.)
6. Does this decision fit the kind of journalism I believe in and the way people should treat one another? (Our judgments should correspond with the way we believe the media ought to be and the way people in a civilized society ought to behave.)

Macro and Micro Issues

Journalists wrestling with ethical decisions should identify a story's macro and micro issues. Macro issues are the main reasons for publishing the story—the objectives. Micro issues—such as the wording of a story or its headline, what visuals accompany it, and where it is placed—tend to be less consequential but still important.

Too often, journalists get caught up in micro issues and forget a story's macro issues. Journalists in doubt about a story need to review the objective for the story. They also need to ask their standard questions: Whom does it hurt, and how many? Whom does it help, and how many?

For example, in some cities, coalitions of merchants, homeowners, and government officials have organized to combat the problem of prostitution because it is often associated with drugs and violence. They encourage the police to make more arrests, and they ask newspapers to publish the names of both prostitutes and their "johns," or customers. Editors realize that publicity could ruin reputations, marriages and careers. Customers and prostitutes often have spouses, children and colleagues who know nothing of their outside activities or of their criminal actions. In a big bust of 20 accused, one customer was a scout leader, and another was in a seminary. One of the prostitutes was in law school, and another was trying to make ends meet financially for her family. Customers and prostitutes were both male and female. An editor might decide that identifying prostitutes and their clients could hurt the offenders and their families but benefit an entire community.

As the editors discussed the story, they initially focused on several micro issues: (1) placement—a story placed on an inside page is less damaging to the accused than a story on the front page; (2) space—a short story is not as noticeable as a longer one; and (3) graphics and visuals—the type and number of illustrations, if any, can set a tone.

Then the editors revisited the macro issue (the reason for the story)—ridding the community of an unsavoury business associated with drugs, violence and disease that affects businesses, neighbourhoods and children. Once focused on the macro issue, they were able to resolve the micro issues more easily. The newspaper printed the story on page 1 with a list of the names of both the accused customers and prostitutes.

ETHICS ISSUES

The public questions the techniques some journalists use to obtain the news. Rude, aggressive reporters seem willing to do anything to get a story: invade people's privacy, invent details, and interview the victims of crimes and accidents while they are still in shock. Reporters have slanted some stories and invented others. Some reporters have stolen pictures from the homes of people involved in the news, and others have impersonated police officers or accepted expensive gifts from people they wrote about.

The media are quick to report on journalists who act unethically, whereas the thousands of moral journalists who make good decisions do not make the news. Despite the public's criticisms and the sometimes all-too-real misconduct of reporters, today's journalists act more ethically and professionally than their predecessors. They are better educated and better paid. They are also doing more to raise their ethical standards.

On some issues, Canadian journalists have reached almost universal agreement. They agree, for instance, that it is unethical to fabricate information or to accept valuable gifts from a source. On other issues, ethical journalists might differ because competing values are involved. A journalist might want to report an important story but fear that it would intrude on an individual's privacy. Or a journalist might want to publish an important document but hesitate because a source stole the document or because a federal official insists that it is secret. Furthermore, reporters must be concerned with audience perception of their behaviour, even when they are acting ethically.

Journalists must consider each ethical situation individually, balancing the competing values or deciding which value is most important. While covering one story, journalists might decide to protect an individual's privacy. While covering another story, journalists might decide that the community's need to know is more important than protecting privacy. Although a journalist's decision should satisfy most people, some criticisms may be inevitable. The rest of this section discusses some of the major areas of ethical concern for journalists.

Stealing and Fabricating Information: Never Acceptable

"Plagiarism," according to the *Canadian Oxford Dictionary*, is using or taking someone else's work (writing, thoughts, inventions, etc.) and trying to pass it off as one's own. Universities have experienced an increase in plagiarism offences, a rise that some critics attribute to the ease of copying and pasting information from the Internet. Failing the assignment, failing the course, or being kicked out of school are punishments for plagiarism. Some universities use a special symbol on transcripts that indicates a course was failed because of plagiarism. Furthermore, graduate students have had their master's or doctoral degree revoked because of plagiarism.

It is illegal for a journalist to use another's work, but it also is unethical and says something about the journalist's moral character. Journalists who plagiarize or fabricate (make up) information are fired.

Journalists who plagiarize or fabricate often complain that deadlines and competition forced them to act unethically. Legions of other journalists, however, work under the same deadlines and uphold high principles. They understand that no matter the explanation, if they plagiarize or make up information, they are lying to the public. One newspaper editorial argued that journalists who make up stories or plagiarize are stealing something more valuable than money. They are stealing the public's trust and the newspaper's credibility.

Using Sources

Journalists search for and interview people who can be sources for their stories. A source may be someone who witnessed an accident or who is an authority on a particular issue. Journalists seek sources with different opinions so all sides of an issue are presented. They should also seek varied sources, not people who consistently hold the same background as the reporter.

Using Friends and Relatives

Students in journalism classes and professionals should guard against using their friends and relatives as sources in their stories. It compromises a journalist's integrity. Also, relatives and friends often offer complete freedom for the journalist to make up or change a quote so it better fits into the story. Furthermore, when a journalist uses a friend as a source, the friend expects to be presented in a positive manner, or the journalist tries to make that friend look good in exchange for having agreed to be in the story. A small circle of acquaintances will associate the sources with the reporter, which lessens the credibility of the story and the reporter.

Scratching Backs

Journalists need to know where to draw the line between being friendly and being friends with sources. Once the line is crossed, it becomes harder for journalists to remain objective. Also, sources who become friends expect to be treated with favouritism. They may assume that journalists will clean up their bad language or omit quotes that would reflect badly on them.

Certainly, it is important to get to know sources on beats. Sources give credibility to stories, offer ideas, add a different perspective, and help with leads for information. The line between business and friendship becomes blurred when meetings happen frequently and occur at dinner or over drinks.

The old adage "scratch my back and I'll scratch yours" is applicable here. Sources do not consistently give information and their time freely or out of the goodness of their heart. They usually expect something in return. They might hope the journalist will investigate an issue they think needs examining. They might want their point of view published. They might expect publicity to further their own interests. And many do not want to be named, further lessening the credibility of the reporter and the story.

A journalist's job is to be honest. When journalists' integrity is compromised, they lose the respect of their viewers and readers, and that reflects on the industry.

Journalists should cultivate a variety of sources representing different opinions. When reporters write stories that might cast a reliable government source in a negative light, that source might freeze them out for a while, but not forever. Reporters gain respect for writing balanced, fair stories. And new sources usually are forthcoming once they realize the reporter is not in cahoots with particular politicians.

When a particularly negative story surfaces about an important source, the reporter might request the story be assigned to another reporter. Finally, when journalists find that they are becoming too chummy with a source, it is time to ask the editor for a change in beats.

Quoting

Journalists use sources' words in their stories in the form of direct quotes, partial quotes, indirect quotes, or paraphrases. All require attribution. Direct quotes and partial quotes necessitate quote marks to signify the source's original, exact wording. Indirect quotes do not use quotation marks because they paraphrase or restate in different words what the source said.

To increase the public's confidence in media accuracy, some news organizations have begun to check accuracy with people who are a part of stories. These random checks are a version of the followup that many journalism instructors perform when grading student stories. The practice educates reporters, corrects the record, and promotes goodwill with the community.

Profanity

Reporters have a difficult decision to make about repeating profanity. Profanity often is regarded as a negative reflection on the individual. Also, it can offend readers and viewers. Journalists guard against repeating profane words unless they show something about the character or passion of the speaker that is relevant to the story.

How to Get Information out of Sources Without Cozying Up

By Dave Cuillier

Here are 10 tips on how to keep and maintain relationships with sources without getting buddy-buddy:

1. Be up front with sources from the start. Tell them, "I am not on your side." Set the standard that you are going to seek the truth and that you are going to dig deeply for it. People will take you seriously, sources will open up, and you will get better stories.
2. Be respectful, friendly, accurate and honest. Sources will respect you and talk to you even if they don't like what you report.
3. Avoid surprises. If you are going to publish or air something negative about someone, let the person know in advance and get his or her side. The person won't like it but will understand.

4. If you go to lunch with a source or to a social gathering, be there as a journalist, not a participant. Do not accept gifts, and pay for your own meals to delineate the boundaries.

5. One of the best ways to get to know something is through feature writing. Write positive stories as you try to get to know an agency, but make sure they are newsworthy features. Make sure the stories are legitimate and helpful for the public.

6. Even more important, don't be afraid to write negative, legitimate newsworthy stories about your sources early on. This will make clear the role you play in society. As long as you are accurate and upfront, most sources will understand. Also, it will loosen up other tips about wrongdoing and problems.

7. Remind yourself: Public officials need me more than I need them. They will come back, and even if they are less forthcoming, I can get the information through other means.

8. Be transparent. If my boss or, more important, readers and viewers knew what I was doing with my source, would they approve? Always think of your reporting as transparent.

9. If you feel that you can't pursue a negative story for fear of alienating important sources, discuss it with your boss, and ask that another reporter be assigned to that story. Also, it might be time to shift to another beat.

10. If you're a supervisor, make sure your reporters know they can talk to you about these issues. The alternative is that they might hide good stories from you.

Source: *Quill* April 2007.

Attributing to Anonymous Sources

Journalists make clear at the beginning of an interview that everything is on the record and attributable. It is suspicious when a source does not want to be held accountable for what he or she says, and credibility of the story might diminish with no one to back up assertions. In the few exceptions when a source may supply initial information but doesn't want the information to be attributed to him or her, the reporter must work harder to corroborate the story and find someone else willing to talk on the record, if the story is important.

Recording Interviews: Tape Recorders and Video Cameras

Journalists strive to act and appear ethical; thus, they should not secretly record their interviews with sources, because the tactic is devious and unfair.

Reporters let sources know they would like to record the interview. They use tape recorders to protect themselves in case they are accused of lying. Reporters fear that sources might claim the reporters had misquoted them or even fabricated the entire interview. Some sources honestly forget what they said. Others are shocked by how awful their statements appear when publicly disseminated. To defend themselves, the sources claim the statements attributed to them are inaccurate. If reporters record their interviews, however, they can prove their stories are accurate. They can also protect themselves more easily in libel suits. In cases when reporters record a conversation, they should do so openly, with their source's permission.

The use of hidden cameras raises some issues audio recordings don't raise. Audiotapes record only a person's voice, and reporters use them to make sure they have complete, accurate information. Reporters rarely publish the tape itself or even a transcript of it. Video cameras, however, also record people's faces, clothing and actions. These tapes often end up on television or the Internet. Many people would consider hidden cameras a greater violation of privacy than hidden tape recorders.

Lawsuits for invasion of privacy can arise when reporters use video cameras or tape recorders in places where the people being recorded reasonably can expect their words and actions to be private. Lawsuits and public disapproval—time, money, bad publicity, and the appearance of irresponsible behaviour—should discourage journalists from using hidden cameras or tape recorders unless the story is extraordinarily important and they have exhausted all other means of getting the information they need.

Conflicts of Interest

A conflict of interest exists when journalists, their friends or relatives, or news organizations are in a position to benefit directly from the stories they cover. In other cases, the public might perceive the appearance of a conflict, which results in lessening the journalist's and the media industry's credibility. These conflicts can take various forms, but many news organizations have adopted policies to cover the most common ones.

Accepting Gifts: "Freebies"
Most journalists refuse to accept money or anything else of value from the people about whom they write. Gifts could bias a reporter's story. Most newspapers spell out this policy against accepting gifts (even if the reporter is not biased, the appearance of bias exists), and at most newspapers, the flouting of this policy is a firing offence.

Businesses usually do not give gifts without expecting something in return. Although journalists might believe their stories are not biased by gift-giving, they cannot control the public's perception of their reporting once it is known the journalist accepted a gift. Gift-givers may assume they are influencing positive relationships, unless told diplomatically that their gift cannot be accepted, perhaps because of policy guidelines. Most news organizations sharply limit the gifts reporters and editors may accept. Some news organizations allow their journalists to accept items worth only a few dollars: a cup of coffee or a souvenir T-shirt, for example. Other newsroom guidelines require journalists to politely return the gift, share the gift with everyone else in the newsroom, or send the gift to a charity.

Accepting Trips: "Junkets"
Free trips, called "junkets," once were common. Fashion writers were invited to New York, and television critics to Hollywood, with all their expenses paid. Sportswriters might accompany their local teams to games in distant cities, with the teams paying all the writers' expenses.

Many travel writers insist they could not afford to travel if hotels, airlines or other sponsors did not pay for them. Their stories are often compromised and unrealistic, however, because people on holiday do not get complimentary trips with first-class travelling and managers' red-carpet treatment. Thus, the reporter's experience neither resembles that of most travellers nor helps them decide how to spend their vacations.

General Motors offered student journalists in the United States free round-trip airfare to Las Vegas, a night's stay at a hotel on the strip, and the opportunity to drive new sports cars and SUVs in its First College Journalists Event during a weekend in September. The event was part of GM's campaign to target the 25-and-under set. The car manufacturer knew it might encounter an ethics backlash, so its PR representative extended the invitation to students by phone and followed up by email, refraining from announcing the event beforehand or its success afterward in press releases. Student journalists from many universities took the bait. One reporter for a student newspaper said that she was "inspired" by the junket and was going to suggest they run a full page on cars.

Conversely, professors and advisers noted that the trip contradicted the tenets taught in ethics classes and that it was wrong for GM to lure student journalists, who were still learning about their profession. Many students overlooked the fundamental issue: Was the trip newsworthy? Was the staged event important enough to justify coverage by student newspapers across the country? Or did recipients use the invitation as an excuse to accept a free trip to Las Vegas?

Participating in the News
Journalists want to avoid conflicts of interest that compromise their objectivity. Journalists must also avoid even the appearance of a conflict and therefore the appearance of bias.

Reporters have lives outside the newsroom, and sometimes those outside activities turn reporters into newsmakers. When that happens, editors worry that their reporters' involvement in events might undermine public confidence in the news organization's objectivity. Editors insist reporters' first obligation should be to their primary employer, and they say journalists continue to represent their employers as objective news gatherers and reporters even after they leave work for the day. Journalists should refrain from participating in associations and activities that could compromise their integrity or damage their credibility.

Editors generally agree reporters should not hold public office, either elected or appointed. Most editors also agree reporters should not serve as party officials or help with anyone's election campaign. A business writer's running for city council might not pose a direct conflict; a business writer might never cover the city council. However, the public might suspect that other writers would slant the news in favour of their colleague's campaign. When in doubt about a possible conflict, journalists talk with their supervisors.

Freelancing

Journalists at most news organizations are free to accept outside jobs, provided they do not conflict with the journalists' regular work. Typically, journalists can work as freelancers, but they cannot sell their work to their employers' competitors, such as other media in the same market.

Maintaining Objectivity

Objectivity has two components: absence of bias and accuracy. Everyone has biases and opinions. Journalists' biases can greatly affect a story. Biases may subtly influence selection of story topics, sources, questions asked, story angle, organization and presentation. For instance, journalists who are passionate about banning executions might have difficulty writing about capital punishment. They might unintentionally interview only sources who share their opinions. Reporters should interview people who have other ideas. They also interview people from diverse cultures who might have something to say about the issue or event.

Journalists who are aware of their prejudices might overcompensate in the opposite direction in their effort to present an objective story. To alleviate the problem of bias, reporters avoid topics about which they have strong opinions. In addition, reporters let their editors know when they cannot cover a subject objectively. The editor will assign the story to another reporter.

Sometimes, reporters do not realize that they have formed strong opinions that affect their reporting. Sports reporters agree that their enthusiasm for baseball was the reason that they overlooked the problem of steroid use in Major League Baseball for too long. Steve Wilstein, an Associated Press sports writer and columnist, told *Editor & Publisher* that his inclusion of testosterone-boosting androstenedione in a story about Mark McGwire was not picked up by sportswriters because they "didn't want to believe it." They did not want to recognize the signs that other baseball heroes were using steroids. "It probably put a little pressure on other baseball writers," Wilstein said, "because it threatened the sport they loved and required them to write about something that they probably did not want to write about."

Objectivity also means integrating balance, fairness and accuracy within stories. Objective facts without context can create inaccurate impressions. In *Quill*, Sally Lehrman, who teaches and practises science reporting and writing, criticized journalists who simply repeated a scientist's claim that Maori, the native people of New Zealand, carried a "warrior" gene that promoted aggressiveness and violence and was linked to their high rates of alcoholism and smoking. Other reporters examined crime rates among Maori, which seemed to support the findings. If reporters had been critical thinkers

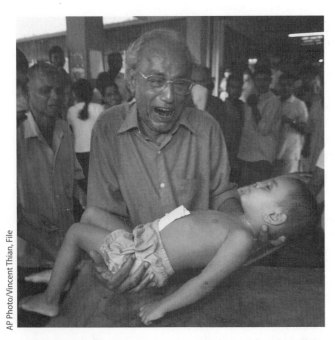

AP Photo/Vincent Thian, File

A Sri Lankan man carries body of his son killed by the tsunami out from hospital in the town of Galle, 117 kilometres (70 miles) south of Colombo, Sri Lanka, in this December 27, 2004, file photo.

instead of merely transcribers, they would have looked at the Maori in a social context to interpret the scientist's findings. The Maori, descendants of the Polynesians, generally experience discrimination compared to white people in New Zealand. A well-established link exists between violence and poverty and lack of opportunity (high unemployment, low education levels, low incomes, health disparities). First, instead of automatically reinforcing a stereotype, Lehrman said, reporters needed to dig deeper to explain context. Second, by explaining context, reporters would have exposed and possibly helped the Maoris' situation by encouraging greater understanding.

AP PHOTO/Ramon Espinosa

A man pulls the body of an earthquake victim from a coffin in order to steal the coffin at the cemetery in Port-au-Prince, Friday, January 15, 2010. A 7.0-magnitude earthquake hit Haiti on Tuesday, January 12, 2010, leaving thousands dead and many displaced.

Reporting or Exploiting Grief

One survey found that more than half of U.S. adults believe the media do not care about the people they report on and have no regard for their privacy. Only one in three Canadians thinks that the news is usually fair and balanced, according to a study by the Canadian Media Research Consortium. About half think fairness and balance is a problem or is becoming more of a problem. The public is especially critical of the way media cover death and tragedy by photographing and interviewing victims and grieving relatives. Journalists need to be sensitive to victims and the public's sense of decency.

Interviewing Victims

Few journalists are psychologists. They might not realize that many disaster victims and their family members are in shock for several days or months after an event. The shock can last for a few days or a long time and can affect people in different ways.

Reporters often harm a news organization's reputation when they scramble to get an early interview. Sometimes victims in shock inadvertently twist facts. Or they might want to please reporters by answering questions, even if they are not certain of the accuracy of the details they supply. Victims often complain later that they were in shock at the time of the interview and are unable to recall even talking to a reporter. They sometimes recant their stories or accuse reporters of making up the interview.

Many journalists have found they obtain more accurate and complete stories if they wait several days to interview victims. Hard news stories can be written immediately after an event, with accurate, informative followup stories later.

Victims or their family members sometimes choose to speak to one reporter during their time of grief. Usually families select reporters who are respectful and considerate. These reporters ask to talk to the family's representative, who might be another family member or close friend. In addition, reporters give their names and telephone numbers to the victim or the victim's representative, not asking for an immediate interview but asking the victim to call if and when the victim feels ready to talk. Compassionate journalists who do not pressure victims and their families receive more in-depth information about the victim and the event.

Hurting Victims Again: The News Story Is a Second Wound

A news story could inflict a second injury on victims and family members who lived through a disaster and experience it again when seeing it described on television or in a newspaper. For example, the details surrounding a tragic killing of toddler twins included much gore. Had

A police officer guides students from Dawson College after reports of a gunman in the building in Montreal, on Wednesday, September 13, 2006. A trenchcoat-clad gunman turned a college cafeteria into a combat zone with a commando-style assault that left the suspect and a young woman dead.

reporters described the killings in detail and used tasteless, sensational photographs, the story could have been more painful for the victims' family. Instead, editors reviewed the objective of the story, omitted sensational details, and published only what the public needed to know.

Compassionate photojournalists, reporters and editors often ask themselves how they would want the press to treat them or their own family members if they were in the victim's situation. Journalists discuss the purpose of the story, what the public needs to know, and alternative ways to portray the emotion. They also weigh these crucial questions: Who will be hurt, and how many? Who will be helped, and how many?

News organizations often run stories on the anniversary of a tragic event. Again, the fundamental questions as to the objective of the story must be considered.

Covering Victims

In their zeal for presenting facts, journalists can give the wrong impression. When reporters do not know why things happen, they sometimes speculate. Their speculations, however, often err and mislead the public. Journalists should refrain from guessing the "why" or "how" until the information is known for a followup story. For instance, a few cars had gone over the edge of a bridge, sometimes because of high winds. In one case, reporters investigated the bad driving record and drinking habits of a victim, leading readers to believe he might have been intoxicated. In reality, the victim had been depressed and ended his life. In another example, reporters said a victim of a shooting was a single man who kept pornography. In reality, the victim was divorced and supported two children who lived with him. This former public official, who was a victim of a gunman's shooting spree, had one 1950s *Playboy* magazine in a stack of other old magazines in his garage.

Reporters can transform heroes and victims into bad guys by presenting allusions and incomplete facts. When two teenage boys were sitting outside one of the boys' homes, they saw and tried to stop a burglar from getting into a neighbour's home. One of the boys was killed in the scuffle. One newspaper stated that the victim was out at 4 a.m., smoking, had a gun, and was a high school dropout. An anonymous source said the boy "liked to party." Very little information was presented about the burglar. A different newspaper called the boy a hero and quoted the positive things his family and friends had to say. This newspaper story noted that the boys were sitting on the porch because they were minding the rules that smoking was not allowed in the house. The victim was enrolled at an alternative school for dropouts because he was determined to graduate, and he had a job. The gun belonged to the other boy, whom the victim was defending when the burglar stabbed him. The burglar had been arrested several times prior for burglary and aggravated assault with a deadly weapon.

Journalists steer clear of sensationalism, are respectful of an individual's privacy, and are mindful of the objective of the story.

Covering Killers

People remember events based on how the media covered them. When news stories, photos and video focus on killers and not the victims, some critics say the media has glorified the killer and sent the message that killers are important and victims are not. Even when the media are handed video clips and still photos by the killer, is it important to run the material? Is it sensationalism or is it news? What are the answers to the fundamental questions of journalism ethics?

Critics charge that because of media's preoccupation with violence, many killers use their acts of cruelty and brutality to achieve fame. Media coverage can encourage copycat killings with repeated coverage, glorifying a killer and speculating on motive.

Media experts debate whether news coverage of a gunmen's attacks at Canada's Dawson College (one student killed, 19 wounded) and Pennsylvania's Amish school (five girls killed) influenced an additional four school attacks, all within six weeks.

Using Visuals: Newsworthy or Sensational?

The visual coverage of disasters has challenged many editors. They seek the proper balance between providing the public what it needs to see without presenting unnecessarily gory images or descending into sensationalism. Too much repetition of the same graphic—the jetliners flying into the World Trade Center towers, for example—can numb viewers' reaction to the horrific events. Pictures of death from hurricane winds and water can anger audience members, which might distract them from the purpose of the story. Yet visuals of young people and children dying show the reality of war.

Editors and producers run photographs or videotapes because they help tell a story. People upset by the images they see accuse the media of acting sensationally. Critics denounce a news organization's decision if a photo or video is used for shock. Many consumers questioned the news value of seeing all of Saddam Hussein's execution and hearing his final discussions, recorded by a cellphone, aired by TV networks and online. Media critics complain that a numbing, saturation effect takes place in which viewers become less sensitive to such acts of violence. They are concerned about a visual's effects: about whether the footage is gratuitous and tasteless.

Editors and producers often feel cornered. Should they shield the public from unpleasantness or educate them? All media make ongoing decisions, sometimes on a case-by-case basis. As with all wars, battles in Iraq were bloody and gruesome. Images of torture victims and the burned bodies hanging from a bridge scaffolding after an ambush in Fallujah shocked viewers. Editors said words alone did not convey the situation as well as photographs did.

News organizations must keep in touch with the public's attitudes. Also, journalists who cover a lot of murders and accidental deaths might no longer be able to objectively judge what the public will find acceptable.

Invading Privacy

The media sometimes intrude on the privacy of individuals. Although they are often within their legal rights, do they have the moral or ethical right?

Respecting Private Individuals
Some events are more obviously newsworthy than others. People who become involved in major lawsuits, crimes and accidents may expect to be mentioned in news stories about them. Other citizens might be surprised to find themselves standing in the media spotlight.

Sometimes journalists must make difficult decisions about whom to subject to public scrutiny. News organizations are prohibited by law from identifying

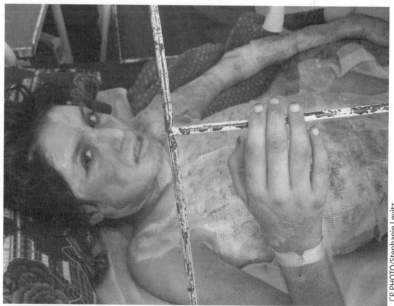

CP PHOTO/Stephanie Levitz

Bora Gull Heha lies in a hospital bed in Kandahar, Afghanistan, on Sunday, July 8, 2007. Gull Heha, 16, doused herself in lamp oil and lit her body aflame, desperate to escape a violent family. Self-immolation has become a horrid last resort for more and more Afghan women each month who see death as the only option for escaping abuse.

young offenders. But if several teenagers are arrested and charged with committing rapes and burglaries that terrorized a neighbourhood, they will likely be sentenced as adults, and editors might feel a need to identify the youths and perhaps their parents as well. Editors might decide their obligation to calm people's fears by informing the neighbourhood about the arrests outweighs their normal obligation to protect the teenagers and their families; the number of people who will be helped is larger than the number who will be hurt.

Reporting on Public Figures and Celebrities

Journalists are often criticized for their treatment of government officials and other public figures. Journalists argue that the public's right to know outweighs the right to privacy of a government official or public figure. Most Canadians seem to agree that journalists should expose government officials who abuse their power by steering lucrative contracts to cronies or coercing a government worker into having an affair or those who have personal problems, such as alcoholism, that affect their work.

But does the public have a right to know about a public official's private affairs, such as adultery? Some people say adultery does not affect a politician's public decision-making. Other critics argue that if a politician breaks a solemn promise, such as a marriage vow, then promises to his or her constituency might also be meaningless. These critics say the public has a right to know about the character of the person who represents them. Another variable is whether the affair is with a member of the government, because it shows potential abuse of power and favouritism.

Many critics think the news media have gone too far in the direction of entertainment and away from traditional reporting. They believe that the public would be better served if the same space and time were filled with stories that help people make informed decisions to lead productive lives. Much of the entertainment includes delving into private lives. Are all stories newsworthy? How important was it to follow family members and photograph the saga of Anna Nicole Smith's funeral, the frolics of Britney Spears, and the spat between Paris Hilton and Nicole Richie?

Deciding When to Name Names

Normally, journalists want to identify fully everyone mentioned in their stories. Most news organizations have adopted policies requiring reporters and editors to do so. However, the participants in some stories might make forceful claims for anonymity: for example, young offenders, sexual assault victims, homosexuals, and prostitutes and their clients. Because each situation is different, reporters and editors examine them individually.

Naming Juveniles

Canadian law prohibits identifying minors (youths between the ages of 12 and 18) who are connected in any way to a crime. Minors are not capable of dealing with the infamy associated with the news account, which might affect them for the rest of their lives. Traditionally, the criminal justice system also has shielded children under 18 who are accused or convicted of a crime. This protection has been explained on the grounds that juveniles understand neither what they did nor the consequences of their actions. In most cases, journalists co-operate by not publicizing young offenders' names. The main exception occurs when juveniles are being sentenced as adults because the crimes of which they are accused are more serious than the ones juveniles usually commit or the suspects have already been punished for earlier serious offences.

Writing about Victims of Sexual Assault

Canadian law also allows for a prohibition on naming or otherwise identifying the victim of a sexual assault, and news organizations normally do withhold the names. (Remember that Canadian law gives the judge presiding in a sexual assault case the power to ban identifying the victim; the judge must impose the ban if the Crown or complainant requests one and may impose a ban even if the Crown or complainant does not request one.) Editors explain that the nature of the crime traumatizes and stigmatizes victims in unique ways. They also realize that sexual assault is an underreported crime and that news coverage discourages some victims from going to police. That is one reason why reforms were made in 1983 and again in 1992 to the Criminal Code provisions for dealing with sexual offences: to address the problem of under-reporting of the crime by protecting the identities of victims, thus encouraging them to come forward and press charges. Studies have shown that before the legal reforms, most rape victims were angry about being identified and a few said they would not have reported the crime if they had known news media would name them. As a result of being named, most victims reported emotional trauma as well as embarrassment, shame, and difficulties in their relationships with others. One victim, who subsequently left college, realized reporters had discovered her school schedule when she found them waiting for her at the door of her classrooms and interviewing classmates.

Some critics say the practice of not naming rape victims constitutes a dual standard: media identify people charged with rape but not their accusers. One study conducted with readers and viewers suggested that most people oppose the news media's identifying victims. The respondents were divided about naming the rape suspect, but most indicated the accused's name should be included. Rape suspects, like those in all other crimes, are always identified so that the public will have full knowledge about how the law enforcement and judicial systems are performing their duties. Bystanders might come forward with information about the accused. Neighbours of the accused would like to be aware of a potential problem and take steps to protect themselves. The same study concluded that identifying victims had little effect on how people viewed either a rape story or the crime but had potentially negative effects on the victim. The study indicated that naming the victim helps no one and hurts the victim again.

Until the 1983 reforms, counsel for the alleged offender was able, as in most other criminal prosecutions, to cross-examine the Crown's witnesses, including the complainant herself, especially about her sexual history. According to one media law expert, the desire to cross-examine the alleged victim was rooted in the sexist and "illogical assumption" that a person's sexual history could constitute a guide to her credibility, that "the more sexual experience a woman had had...the less likely it was that she would tell the truth."

Practicing Deceit: Is It Justified?

Journalists want everyone to believe and trust them. Most reporters believe that deceit is a form of lying and that lying is unethical. Some journalists, however, think deceit is the only way to get some stories. A story might be important and help thousands of people. It might, for example, expose crime or a government official's abuse of power. However, some journalists say the press should not criticize deceitfulness by public officials or businesses if reporters themselves are lying while pursuing a story. But a true investigative story—with many in-depth interviews and extensive background research—provides a better story than one in which journalists misrepresent themselves.

Posing and Misrepresentation

Few reporters misrepresent themselves to sources. On some common occasions, however, reporters may simply fail to reveal themselves. Restaurant reviewers would be ineffective if everyone knew their identities. Restaurant owners, eager to obtain favourable publicity, would cater to the reviewers, offering them special meals and special service. Reviewers would be unable to describe the meals served to the average customer.

Other journalists might want to shop anonymously at a store where employees have been accused of misleading customers. Or reporters might want to visit a tattoo parlour or attend a protest rally. If protesters realized several reporters were present, they might either act more cautiously or perform for the reporters, behaving more angrily or violently to ensure that they got into the news. Protesters might also harass or attack reporters who identified themselves.

Usually, such instances of passive posing, in which the reporter might appear to the business owner or government official as simply another member of the public, present few ethical problems. The reporter is gathering only that information available to any person. More serious ethical—and legal—problems arise when reporters go "undercover" and actively misrepresent themselves to gain access to places and information closed to the general public.

Journalists might lie about their identities by posing as patients to gather information about a mental hospital. Or they might pretend to be labourers while writing about migrant workers' exposure to the chemicals sprayed on farm crops. Although journalists could be exposing a social ill, they could also discover that the public disapproves of their conduct. They might even face legal penalties because of their dubious methods of gathering information.

Reporters must talk to their editors before they use any form of deceit. Typically, editors allow their reporters to pose only when a story is important and no other safe way exists to obtain it. A good example is the investigation by two *Toronto Star* reporters of fraudulent telemarketing scams in the city's downtown core, a probe that revealed Canada's dubious distinction as an international haven for the multibillion-dollar industry. The reporters went undercover for the assignment, getting jobs at one of the downtown "boiler rooms," as the establishments were called. They collected scripts and other documents and at one point even wore concealed mini-cameras; their "eyewitness" and insider status allowed them to document the fraud. Still, going undercover remains a difficult and risky venture, and the technique is used only when there is no other way to nail down the story. One of the *Toronto Star* reporters described the process of arriving at the editorial decision to go undercover on the telemarketing scam story:

It took us a while to get to that point. It's a sort of last-ditch strategy—you always try to figure out other ways to do a story. It's complicated, it's time consuming, it's dangerous. So we had long debates about how to do the story. And at the end of the day, you have to justify this ten ways to Sunday, to editors, before you can do undercover—it's very controversial. It has to be ethically justifiable.... You have to sit before the senior editors and make a pretty compelling case that this is ethically defensible... because, of course, the standard operating procedure in journalism is to present yourself as who you are and identify yourself and be up front and open and clear.

So when we take this step, at least at the *Star*, it's not taken lightly. You have to answer two basic questions: Is there a strong enough public interest in the story? In other words, is it important? And is there any other way to get the information?

Reporters should admit their use of deception in the stories they publish or broadcast and explain to readers why it was necessary. They also should afford the right of reply to sources by calling all people criticized in their stories and giving them an opportunity to respond.

Reporting Rumours and Speculation

Journalists are supposed to publish facts but are often tempted to publish rumours. When a gay blogger claimed U.S. Senator Larry Craig had had sex with men, the *Idaho Statesman* started to investigate. But reporters were unable to find information that would confirm the rumours, which Craig had vigorously denied. Months later, Craig was arrested in a Minneapolis airport and charged with disorderly conduct for having tried to solicit sex from an undercover male police officer in an airport restroom. Craig pleaded guilty to the charge, and at that point the *Idaho Statesman* decided it could publish its story. Although the *Statesman* might have had a more dramatic scoop if it had published the story earlier, it adhered to journalistic standards by publishing only what its reporters and editors knew to be true. Even when a rumour seems credible, journalists risk publishing false information if they have not checked it out.

Sometimes, reports of unsubstantiated information can have serious impact, as in the case of reporters covering a mine disaster that trapped 12 miners. When one tired reporter pulled away to return to his motel for the night, he heard shouts of "They're alive!" People were crying with joy, and he thought he heard an official say that miracles could happen. Like most of the reporters at the scene, he immediately called his editor, and the happy news ran on the front page. Unfortunately, it was incorrect news. Only one of the miners was rescued. The reporter ran with second-hand information and did not substantiate it.

When an event occurs, some of the news elements, such as the "who," "what," "where" and "when," are readily available. It might take several days, weeks or months to find out the "why." Yet journalists sometimes try to provide their readers and viewers with the "why" immediately through speculation and interpretation, which could mislead readers and viewers. Theories and conjectures are not news and waste readers' time.

Witnessing Crimes and Disasters

Reporters and photographers might witness terrible tragedies, such as people drowning, falling to their deaths, or fleeing from fire. Journalists help other people who are in danger, particularly if they are the only ones on the scene. Journalists say they would react the same way that they would if they saw a member of their family in physical danger. Furthermore, they hope other journalists would help—not simply record—human beings in trouble. But when a victim is already receiving help from rescue workers, police officers, firefighters or medical technicians, journalists will stay out of the rescuers' way and concentrate on reporting the event.

Reporters occasionally learn about a crime before it is committed or while it is in progress. They might either go to the police or watch the crime and interview the criminal. A newspaper and a radio station in Tampa, Fla., were soundly criticized when they telephoned a killer holding a hostage. The man had killed a four-year-old boy and three police officers and was holding a hostage in a gas station. A radio reporter called the gas station and aired live the conversation with the gunman. The newspaper also interviewed him. Ethics experts said the potential risk to the hostage outweighed the value of the information gleaned. The hostage situation was in progress. Listeners and readers would have been as well-served if the news organizations had learned the information later from police as opposed to learning it at that moment from the killer. Furthermore, the news organizations interrupted police officers trying to do their jobs, which could have resulted in an obviously unstable man killing another victim. Journalists are not hostage negotiators.

Reporting on Terrorism

Terrorists usually want publicity and have learned to create news so compelling that news organizations cannot ignore it. The terrorists provide genuine drama: hijackings, demands, deadlines, and the threat of mass murder—such as the bombings of the World Trade Center in New York and the Pentagon in Washington on September 11, 2001. Terrorists can add to the drama by moving from one place to another and by releasing or murdering hostages.

To attract even more publicity, terrorists conduct press conferences. Some allow journalists to photograph and interview their captives. Others make videotapes of their captives, sometimes showing the hostages pleading for their lives, reading the terrorists' demands, and warning that they will be killed if the demands are not met.

Some critics insist that media coverage encourages terrorists. They believe that if the media ignored terrorists, they would become discouraged and abandon their acts of violence. Former British prime minister Margaret Thatcher urged journalists to stop covering terrorists, to starve them of "the oxygen of publicity." Other critics note that people have a right to know what is happening in the world and that a news blackout might result in rumours about the terrorists' activities that are more frightening than the truth. They also fear that if reporters ignore the terrorists, they will escalate their violence.

This video grab from Al-Arabiya TV footage aired February 13, 2006, shows Thomas Nitschke and Rene Braeunlich, left, two German hostages surrounded by their kidnappers who threatened to kill them unless the German government meets their demands.

Altering Images

The digital revolution has caused great debate about altering photos. Using Adobe Photoshop or similar image-editing software, photojournalists can remove a distracting object in the background of a photo without changing the essence and meaning of the picture. Initially, many argued that it was no different from the earlier practices of cropping photos or burning images to provide more contrast. Today, the pendulum has swung back, and photojournalists are loath to change the content of their photos in newspapers or online. Why? Because it is dishonest and unethical. Just as writers do not lie about the content of their stories, photographers do not lie about the content of the captured image. Yet clearly, the advent of digital and online communications will continue to raise ethical questions in photojournalism.

Censoring Advertisements and Advertiser Pressure

Many Canadians oppose censorship of any type, and journalists are especially vigilant in their efforts to combat it. Yet news organizations regularly refuse to publish some advertisements submitted to them. They clearly have the legal right to do so. Canadian courts have consistently ruled that editors have the right to reject any advertisement they dislike, regardless of the reason.

In their early history, newspapers published virtually every advertisement that was submitted to them. Editors rarely felt responsible for the content of advertisements. Rather, the editors' philosophy was one of "let the buyer beware." In the early nineteenth century, newspapers published advertisements for slaves, prostitutes and quack medicines. Some medicines contained enough alcohol to inebriate the people using them. Others contained so much heroin, opium and morphine that the people using them became addicts.

During the late 1800s, a few periodicals began to protect their readers from fraudulent advertising, and during the early twentieth century, some newspapers launched campaigns to clean up their advertising columns, even though it might mean lost ad revenues. Now, media managers are expected to act ethically, rejecting advertisements that are tasteless or promote illegal, obscene, immoral or harmful products.

Many managers reject advertisements that might be harmful for members of their community: tobacco products, alcoholic beverages, X-rated movies, sexual aids, mail order goods, abortion services, handguns, massage parlours and escort services. Some newspapers, concerned about their readers' health and safety, no longer accept restaurant and bar advertisements for "happy hours" during which drinks are cheap or free, fearing that the ads will contribute to drunken driving. Another common concern among journalists is advertisers who want to dictate news content and placement of their ads.

CODES OF ETHICS

Major professional organizations in journalism have adopted codes of ethics. The codes encourage organization members to adhere voluntarily to the guidelines. They also serve as models that individual media companies follow when setting their own policies. Broadcast stations and newspapers adapt the ethics codes to reflect local standards. What is acceptable in a metropolitan area might not be permissible for news media in a rural community. See the excerpts from the Canadian Association of Journalists Code of Ethics in the box that follows.

 Canadian Association of Journalists Code of Ethics

STATEMENT OF PRINCIPLES

Preamble
It is our privilege and duty to seek and report the truth as we understand it, defend free speech and the right to equal treatment under law, capture the diversity of human experience, speak for the voiceless and encourage civic debate to build our communities and serve the public interest.

Freedom of Speech

The Canadian Charter of Rights and Freedoms guarantees freedom of expression and freedom of the press. A free flow of information sustains and vitalizes democracy because understanding emerges from vigorous discussion, openly reported. Our legal traditions give media privilege and protection. We must return this trust through the ethical practice of our craft.

Fairness

Our reporting must be fair, accurate and comprehensive. When we make mistakes we must correct them. We must not ignore or temper the facts in order to curry favour or avoid retribution. We must hold ourselves to the same standards that we set for others.

Diversity

Our stories will capture the rich and diverse values, viewpoints and lives of the people in our communities. We need to understand how our own beliefs and biases can interfere with our ability to see and report fairly and courageously.

The Right to Privacy

The public has a right to know about its institutions and the people who are elected or hired to serve its interests. People also have a right to privacy, and those accused of crimes have a right to a fair trial. There are inevitable conflicts between the right to privacy, the public good and the public's right to be informed. Each situation should be judged in the light of common sense, humanity and the public's rights to know.

The Public Interest

The right to freedom of expression and of the press must be defended against encroachment from any quarter, public or private, because we serve democracy and the public interest. Journalists must be alert to ensure that the public's business continues to be conducted in public. Journalists who abuse their power betray the public trust.

* * *

Members of the Canadian Association of Journalists, in holding to these principles, promote excellence in the practice of their craft.

Fairness

- We respect the rights of people involved in the news and will be accountable to the public for the fairness and reliability of our reporting.

- We will not allow our own biases to influence fair and accurate reporting.

- We respect each person's right to a fair trial.

- We will identify sources of information, except when there is a clear and pressing reason to protect anonymity. When this happens, we will explain the need for anonymity.

- We will independently corroborate facts if we get them from a source we do not name.

- We will not allow anonymous sources to take cheap shots at individuals or organizations.

- We will avoid pseudonyms and not use composites. If either is essential, we will tell our readers, listeners or viewers.

- Reporters will not conceal their identities, except in rare cases.

- When, on rare occasions, a reporter needs to go "undercover" in the public interest, we will clearly explain the extent of the deception to the reader or listener or viewer.

- We will not commit illegal or improper acts.

- We will give people, companies or organizations that are publicly accused or criticized prompt opportunity to respond. We will make a genuine and exhaustive effort to contact them. If they decline to comment, we will say so.

- We will report all relevant facts in coverage of controversies or disputes.

- We will clearly identify news and opinion so that readers, viewers and listeners know which is which.

- We will be wary of informants who want to be paid for information. The quality of their information and their motives should be questioned.

Accuracy

- Reporters are responsible for the accuracy of their work. Editors must confirm the accuracy of stories before publication or broadcast. Editors must know in detail the documentation to support stories and the reliability of the sources. Editors are responsible for the accuracy of any facts they add or changes they make.

- We will correct mistakes of fact or context promptly and ungrudgingly. We will publish or broadcast corrections, clarifications or apologies in a consistent way.

- We will not mislead the public by suggesting a reporter is some place that he or she isn't.

- Photojournalists are responsible for the integrity of their images. We will not alter images so that they mislead the public.

- We will explain in the photo caption if a photograph has been staged.

- We will label altered images as photo illustrations.

Privacy

- The public has a right to know about its institutions and the people who are elected or hired to serve its interests. Their role is public, and in matters concerning these roles they are accountable to the public.

- Individuals have a right to privacy except when that right is superseded by the public good.

- We will not harass or manipulate people who are thrust into the spotlight because they are victims of crime or are associated with a tragedy.

- Relatives of people in the news sometimes become newsworthy, but we will guard against voyeuristic stories.

Access
Newspapers, radio, television and the Web are forums for the free interchange of information and opinion. We will encourage our organizations to make room for the interests of all: minorities and majorities; those with power and those without it; disparate and conflicting views.

Off the Record
There are no shield laws protecting journalists in Canada. We may be ordered by a court or judicial inquiry to divulge confidential sources upon threat of jail, so we must understand what we are promising:

- Not for attribution: We may quote statements directly, but the source may not be named, although a general description of his or her position may be given ("a government official"' or "a party insider"').

- On background: We may use the thrust of statements and generally describe the source, but we may not use direct quotes.

- Off the record: We may not report the information, which can be used solely to help our own understanding or perspective. There is not much point in knowing something if it can't be reported, so this undertaking should be used sparingly, if at all.

Discrimination

- We will not refer to a person's race, colour or religion unless it is pertinent to the story. We will exercise particular care in crime stories.

- We will avoid thoughtless stereotypes of race, gender, age, religion, ethnicity, geography, sexual orientation, disability, physical appearance or social status.

Polls

- We should use polls prominently only when we know the full context of the results: the names of the sponsor and the polling agency; the population from which the sample was drawn; the sample size, margin of error, type of interview; the dates when the poll was taken and the exact wording and order of the questions. When possible, we should broadcast or publish this information.

- Polls commissioned by special interest groups and politically sponsored think tanks and institutes are especially suspect. It is easy to frame questions or choose a sample designed to produce an answer favourable to a particular point of view.

Copyright and Plagiarism

- There is no copyright on news or ideas once a story is in the public domain, but if we can't match the story, we will credit the originating source.

- While news and ideas are there for the taking, the words used to convey them are not. If we borrow a story or even a paragraph from another source, we will rewrite it before it is published or broadcast. It we do not rewrite it, we will credit the source because failure to do so is plagiarism.

- Using another's analysis or interpretation may constitute plagiarism, even if the words are rewritten, unless it is attributed. This is especially true for columnists.

Act Independently

- We serve democracy and the public interest by reporting the truth. This sometimes conflicts with the wishes of various public and private interests, including advertisers, governments, news sources and, on occasion, with our duty and obligation to an employer.

- Defending the public's interest includes promoting the free flow of information, exposing crime or wrongdoing, protecting public health and safety and preventing the public from being misled.

- We will not give favoured treatment to advertisers and special interests. We must resist their efforts to influence the news.

- Columnists should be free to express their views, even when those views are contrary to the editorial views of their organization, as long as the content meets the generally accepted journalistic standards for fairness and accuracy and does not breach the law.

- We should not accept or solicit gifts, passes or favours for personal use.

- We must pay our own way to ensure independence. If another organization pays our expenses to an event that we are writing about, we should say so, so that the reader, viewer or listener can take this into account. (We will make sure exceptions are understood. For example, it is common practice to accept reviewers' tickets for film previews and theatrical performances.)

- We will promptly return unsolicited gifts of more than nominal value. If it is impractical to return the gift, we will give it to an appropriate charity or institution.

- Use of merchandise for review: We will not accept the free use or reduced-rate use of valuable goods or services when the offer is extended because of our position. Within narrow limits, it is appropriate to use a product for a short time to test or evaluate it. (A common exception is unsolicited books, music or new food products sent for review.)

Conflict of Interest

- Note: There is a tradition in Canada of media organizations that support and advocate particular ideologies and causes. These ideologies and causes should be transparent to the readers, listeners or viewers. Journalists for these organizations sometimes choose to be advocates or are hired to be advocates and this, too, should be transparent.

- In our role as fair and impartial journalists, we must be free to comment on the activities of any publicly elected body or special interest organization. It is not possible to do this without an apparent conflict of interest if we are active members of a group we are covering.

- We lose our credibility as fair observers if we write opinion pieces about subjects that we also cover as reporters.

- We will not hold elected political office, work as officials on political campaigns, or write speeches for any political party or official.

- Editorial boards and columnists or commentators endorse political candidates or political causes. Reporters do not.

- We will not make financial contributions to a political campaign if there is a chance we will be covering the campaign.

- We will not hold office in community organizations about which we may report or make editorial judgments. This includes fundraising or public relations work and active participation in community organizations and pressure groups that take positions on public issues.

- We will avoid participation in judicial and other official inquiries into wrongdoing. Such inquiries are often prompted by our stories.

- We will not accept payment for speaking or making presentations to groups we report on or comment on. If access to a journalist depends on fees, there will be the same appearance of advantage we perceive when businesses buy access to a cabinet minister or the prime minister. If everyone else on a panel is being paid an honorarium, that honorarium can be directed to a charity or worthy cause.

- We will not participate in demonstrations or sign petitions if there could be an appearance of conflict with our role as fair and impartial journalists.

- We will not report stories about people or organizations if we have asked or applied to work for them.

- We will not report about subjects in which we have a financial interest.

- We will not use our positions to obtain any benefit or advantage in commercial transactions not available to the general public.

- Note: Life does not always conform to guidelines. For example, the only way to subscribe to some publications is to be a member of the group that is publishing. Having a non-journalist in your organization subscribe on your behalf would be one solution. Discussing the exception and subscribing yourself might be the most sensible path.

Police

- Police and lawyers try to involve us in the judicial process by asking for tapes, notes and photographs and by calling reporters or photographers as witnesses in criminal and civil cases. In effect, we become a shortcut for outside persons trying to prove a case.

- This poses difficulties for two reasons. If we are seen to be a part of the judicial process, it damages our credibility as critics of the system and may limit our access to sources. If we promise confidentiality to a source and we are then summonsed as a witness, we may be asked to break that promise upon the penalty of a fine or jail sentence. Accordingly, we will be wary of approaches from the police or lawyers for assistance on a case.

- If we know a confidential document was obtained illegally, there may be legal implications for our organization if its contents are published.

- We will avoid reporting confidential conversations overheard through eavesdropping or monitoring cellular phone calls, although it is legal to report these. Any exception will be explained publicly.

Criminal Charges against Journalists

If we are charged with a criminal offence for activities unrelated to work, it may be wise to report the charges. The charge may be one that would go unreported if it happened to somebody else, but because we have a public profile, a different standard applies, just as it does for elected officials who are charged.

Ethical codes for newspapers differ in details but concur on the basics. Newspapers should act responsibly by being truthful, sincere, impartial, decent and fair. News organizations adopt codes of ethics to discourage the most obvious abuses, especially freebies, junkets and conflicts of interest. Although codes serve as guidelines for journalists' actions, some exceptional cases arise. The codes cannot solve every problem. Thus, decisions will always vary from one news organization to another—and that might be one of the system's great strengths. After considering their news organization's code of ethics, journalists decide which course of action is right or wrong, ethical or unethical. Inevitably, some journalists will be mistaken. But any effort to change the system—to force every journalist to conform to an identical predetermined standard—would limit the media's diversity and freedom. It would also limit Canadians' access to information.

The professional standards in journalism are improving. Journalists are becoming better educated, more responsible and more ethical.

CHECKLIST FOR IMPROVING MEDIA CREDIBILITY

Here are six areas in which journalists should concentrate to improve news media credibility:

1. Inaccuracies. Factual, grammatical and spelling errors undermine a story and its reporter's credibility.
2. Sensationalism. Sensational stories are often chased and over-covered because they are exciting, but they might be less important than other stories.
3. Objectivity. Journalists should avoid the appearance of bias in their reporting—what stories are covered and how they are covered. A bias is a predisposition or a prejudice; a biased report or reporter is one that fails to approach a story with an open mind and a neutral attitude toward the facts. To be biased is to have an agenda and try to shape the news to report it or to show favouritism to a particular social or political group.
4. Freedom from manipulation of the press. The public believes the press can be manipulated by powerful people, organizations and advertisers who want to shape news stories. A big criticism is that newspapers are trying to make a profit instead of serving the public interest.
5. Name sources. Using anonymous sources reduces the credibility of a news story. Many people would not run the story at all if a source declined to go "on the record." Journalists should tell the public why an anonymous source is used.
6. Corrections. Admitting errors and running corrections help credibility; they don't hurt it.

A Memo from the Editor

SOME THOUGHTS ON PLAGIARISM

By Tommy Miller

Plagiarism is like speeding on the highways. It likely will never go away, but that doesn't mean a promising career can't crash and burn after one stupid lapse in judgment. Even lifting part of a story or using quotes from other newspapers without proper attribution counts as plagiarism.

In recent decades, plagiarism has embarrassed the journalism profession a number of times. One of the most infamous cases occurred at the venerated *New York Times* when reporter Jayson Blair stole quotes and descriptions from other stories and lied to readers by filing stories with false datelines. Blair was fired, and the controversy over the newspaper's management style, or lack thereof, led to the resignation of editor Howell Raines.

If plagiarism, intentional or unwitting, can occur at the *New York Times*, it can occur anywhere. This means that plagiarism needs constant vigilance and discussion.

Making up entire stories leaves the most damaging wounds on the reputations of newspapers and other news media, but typical plagiarism incidents focus on these questions:

- How should information be handled when it is obtained from other newspapers, wire services or the electronic media?

- What information can be used from other stories and what can't?

- What is background information, and how should it be handled?

- When should quotes be attributed to other media?
- When are quotes in the public domain?
- When is a fact a generally known fact?

Quotations Are Sacred
There is no room here for embellishing, fudging or guessing.

Readership trust hinges on the belief that words inside quotation marks are true and that the person or entity the quote is attributed to can be held accountable.

Background Facts
Here's one rule you can count on: Generally known facts can't be plagiarized.

For example, for some paragraphs of this article, I gathered information from several stories in other newspapers and trade publications. The information is background for this story, and the facts are that the *New York Times* editor resigned over a plagiarism controversy. Some of the information for this story was written in much the same way that it was written in several other accounts. Because the information now falls into the category of generally known facts, there is no need for me to tell readers specifically where I got that information.

Attribution
But consider this situation:

Let's say that the *Globe and Mail* moves a story on its news service reporting that former Calgary police chief Elizabeth Watson will become the new police chief in Toronto.

Of course, *Calgary Herald* reporters would immediately try to confirm that report, and if they did, no attribution to the *Globe and Mail* would be needed. But if the *Calgary Herald* was unable to confirm the *Globe and Mail* report, the *Calgary Herald* story would need attribution, such as: Former Calgary police chief Elizabeth Watson will become the new police chief in Toronto, the *Globe and Mail* reported.

The previous example seems elementary. But the debate about attributing information usually centres on information of much less impact, primarily because many newspapers lift what is often described as routine information from wire service stories without telling the reader where it was obtained.

For example, I once asked a newspaper reporter about one of her bylined clips about violence in Montreal theatres where the movie "Boyz N the Hood" was showing. The story carried no dateline, and most of it focused on the violent incidents.

About midway through the story, the reporter had written: "In other incidents, reported across the nation Friday night…" This sentence was followed by a list with specific information about incidents in other Canadian cities.

I asked the reporter where she had got the information for the list. "Oh," she said. "That came from the Canadian Press." In a spot news story such as this, a reporter should tell readers where the information came from. For example, the sentence setting up the list should have said: "The Canadian Press reported these other incidents across the country…" Or at the very least, a Canadian Press contributor line should have been at the bottom of the story.

Public Domain
Background is substantiated information that has stood the test of time, putting it in the public domain.

Let's say that the first sentence in a newspaper editorial about a bank scandal is this: "Asked why he robbed banks, Willy Sutton said, 'Because that's where the money is.'" The editorial doesn't say when Sutton said it, or where he said it, or who first reported that he said it. And the editorial assumes that readers know that Sutton was an infamous bank robber. Why? Because the quote has been used so much throughout the years that it's considered in the public domain and doesn't need attribution.

How do you decide what's in the public domain? Time is one element, such as how long the quote has been around. General usage is another. If the quote has been used often in a variety of media, it has moved into the public domain. The exclusive, initial report of a quote is usually the guideline for deciding when a quote is not in the public domain.

But plagiarism problems usually don't come from pragmatic bank robber quotes. It's the routine quotes that cause problems. Too often, reporters read stories from other papers, or from other media sources, and use quotes without attribution. There's no problem with using good quotes that are relevant and important to a story. They simply must be attributed to the proper source.

Description

Description can be another problem area.

For example, let's say you visit Vancouver and write a piece in which you say that Vancouver is a beautiful, haunting city. No problem there. In fact, your problem isn't plagiarism. Your problem is lifeless, bland description.

But let's say you write it this way: "It's the enchanting symphony of metropolitan noise—the stray foghorn in the night, the panting automobile in second gear, the dreamy ageless silence of Stanley Park, the staccato snap of the traffic signal and the wail of the ferry's siren, telling the world defiantly that the old landmark still has its job to do and is doing it…"

Now you've got a problem, because that's *San Francisco Chronicle* columnist Herb Caen's description of San Francisco in a column on July 2, 1940.

But let's say you write it this way:

"It's the enchanting music of metropolitan sounds—the stray foghorn in the darkness, the struggling car in second gear, the dreamy ageless silence of Stanley Park…"

You've still got a problem. You've done nothing more than steal Caen's structure and cadence while filling in the blanks with other words.

What about press releases? Generally, press releases need more reporting and, therefore, should be rewritten. Additionally, length, style and the proper emphasis in the lead paragraph are frequently reasons for rewriting press releases.

As for quotes in news releases, tell readers that the quotes were in a news release or printed statement. This shows that the source provided the quotation in a printed statement or release and was not available for further questioning.

With some straightforward, routine public service news releases, rewriting simply doesn't make sense. For example, "The University library will display a rare collection of first-edition James Thurber books in its foyer from Aug. 1 to Aug. 20. Call 555-1212 for further information."

The bottom line on plagiarism is to do your own reporting, write your own description and attribute quotes and information whenever it is needed. Common sense usually indicates when material should be attributed. When in doubt, attribute! Or get a second opinion.

Source: Adapted from "Some thoughts on plagiarism," published in August 1992 in *The Write Stuff*, an in-house publication of the *Houston Chronicle*.
Tommy Miller is the Roger Tatarian Endowed Chair of Professional Journalism at California State University, Fresno. He is a former managing editor of the *Houston Chronicle*.

SUGGESTED READINGS AND USEFUL WEBSITES

Adam, G. Stuart, and Roy Peter Clark. 2005. *Journalism: The Democratic Craft.* New York: Oxford University Press.

Bakan, Joel. 2004. *The Corporation: The Pathological Pursuit of Profit and Power.* Toronto: Viking Canada.

Cohen, Elliot D., ed. 1992. *Philosophical Issues in Journalism.* New York: Oxford University Press.

Ettema, James, and Theodore L. Glasser. 1998. *Custodians of Conscience: Investigative Journalism and Public Virtue.* New York: Columbia University Press.

Innis, Harold A. 1951. *The Bias of Communication.* Toronto: University of Toronto Press.

Jobb, Dean. 2005. *The Acadians: A People's Story of Exile and Triumph.* Toronto: Wiley Canada.

Kovach, Bill, and Tom Rosenstiel. 2001. *The Elements of Journalism: What Newspeople Should Know and the Public Should Expect.* New York: Three Rivers Press.

Miller, John. 1998. *Yesterday's News: Why Canada's Daily Newspapers Are Failing Us.* Halifax: Fernwood Publishing.

Rosner, Cecil. 2008. *Behind the Headlines: A History of Investigative Journalism in Canada.* Don Mills, ON: Oxford University Press.

Ruvinsky, Maxine. 2008. *Investigative Reporting in Canada.* Don Mills, ON: Oxford University Press.

Seib, Philip, and Kathy Fitzpatrick. 1997. *Journalism Ethics.* Fort Worth, TX: Harcourt Brace.

Silverman, Craig, and Jeff Jarvis. 2009. *Regret the Error: How Media Mistakes Pollute the Press and Imperil Free Speech.* New York: Union Square Press.

Sotiron, Minko. 1997. *From Politics to Profit: The Commercialization of Canadian Daily Newspapers, 1890–1920.* Montreal: McGill-Queen's University Press.

Ward, Stephen J. 2006. *The Invention of Journalism Ethics: The Path to Objectivity and Beyond.* Montreal: McGill-Queen's University Press.

Canadian Association of Journalists: http://www.caj.ca

Canadian Centre for Investigative Reporting: http://www.canadiancentreinvestigates.org

Canadian Committee for World Press Freedom: http://www.ccwpf-cclpm.ca/links

Canadian Community Newspaper Association: http://www.ccna.ca

Canadian Journalism Project: http://www.j-source.ca; http://www.ProjetJ.ca

Canadian Media Research Consortium: http://www.cmrcccrm.ca

Canadian Newspaper Association: http://www.cna-acj.ca

Centre for Journalism Ethics: http://www.journalismethics.ca

Reporters without Borders: http://www.rsf.org

Pew Center for Civic Journalism: http://www.pewcenter.org/index.php

Poynter Institute for Media Studies: http://www.poynter.org

EXERCISE 1   Ethics

Discussion Questions

Read the following situations, marking those actions you would take. Discuss your decisions with the class.

1. Students are sometimes not sure about what constitutes plagiarism. Put a check in front of those actions that you consider a form of plagiarism.

    _____ To turn in a paper purchased online.

    _____ To use, without attribution, a 20-word sentence from the Internet.

    _____ To use, without attribution, a 20-word paragraph from a magazine.

    _____ While writing about a celebrity, to reuse several quotations you found in several other newspapers.

    _____ To use your own words but another writer's ideas, seen on television.

    _____ To use, but totally rewrite without attribution, a story from another newspaper.

    _____ To use, but totally rewrite with attribution, a story from a webpage.

    _____ To use a press release without changing a word.

    _____ For background while working under deadline pressure, to reprint verbatim several paragraphs from an old story written by another reporter at your newspaper.

    _____ While working for a radio or television station, to read your city's daily newspaper to determine what's happening in your community and what stories you should cover.

    _____ While working for a radio or television station, broadcasting news stories published by your local paper without rewriting or attribution.

    _____ While working for a radio or television station, rewriting stories from your local newspaper and attributing them to the newspaper.

    _____ While working for a radio or television station, rewriting stories from the Internet and attributing them to the Internet.

2. If you edited your student newspaper and received an anonymous letter that accused a faculty member of repeatedly making sexist remarks, would you publish the letter?

    _____ Yes _____ No

    If your answer is "No," mark the point below at which you would change your mind. (You can mark more than one response to this and other questions.)

    A. _____ The student who wrote the letter identifies herself but because she fears retaliation insists that you keep her name a secret.

    B. _____ Two more women come in and corroborate the letter's content but also insist that you keep their names a secret.

    C. _____ All three students agree to let you quote them and publish their names.

    D. _____ The three students play a tape they secretly recorded in class, a tape that clearly documents their complaints.

    E. _____ The students complain that the faculty member also touched them.

3. As editor of your student newspaper, mark any of the following gifts you would allow members of your staff to accept.

    A. _____ Free tickets to local plays, movies and concerts for your entertainment editor.

    B. _____ Free meals at local restaurants for your food critic.

    C. _____ Free trips to out-of-town games with your college team for your sports editor.

    D. _____ Free loan of a sophisticated computer that a computer manufacturer offers to your technology editor for the school year so she can test new games and software.

    E. _____ Free one-week trip to Daytona Beach, Fla., for your entertainment writer and a friend to write about the popular destination for students on spring break.

4. As editor of your online newspaper, mark all the products and services for which you would be willing to publish advertisements.

    A. _____ Pistols

    B. _____ Cigarettes

C. _____ Fortune-tellers

D. _____ Juice bars that feature nude dancers

E. _____ Couples who want to adopt white newborns

F. _____ Abortion clinics

G. _____ Escort services and massage parlours

H. _____ An essay claiming the Holocaust is a hoax

5. As editor of your television evening news, mark all the cases of deception that you would permit.

A. _____ A young reporter to pose as a high school dropout and join a teen gang.

B. _____ A reporter using a fake identity to join a white supremacist group, which often marches and holds rallies in the region.

C. _____ After hearing that some people may be cheating local charities, collecting food and money from several simultaneously, a reporter suggests posing as a destitute mother who visits several local charities to see how much food and money she can collect in one day. The reporter promises to return everything after her story's publication.

D. _____ Two reporters to pose as a gay couple and try to rent an apartment. Friends have told members of your staff about instances of discrimination.

E. _____ A reporter informs you that his brother is opening a bar and that city inspectors seem to be asking for bribes to approve the bar's plumbing, electrical and health systems. The reporter suggests that you notify the district attorney, install hidden cameras in the bar, and begin to pay the bribes.

6. As editor of your local daily, mark the practices you would permit.

A. _____ The sports editor to host a daily program on a local radio station.

B. _____ The sports editor to appear in television advertisements for a chain of sports stores in the city.

C. _____ The business editor to own stock in local companies.

D. _____ The education writer to remain on the same beat after marrying a high school principal.

E. _____ A popular columnist, a local celebrity, to charge $1,000 for each one-hour speech she gives.

F. _____ A local freelance cartoonist, whose cartoons your newspaper has agreed to publish regularly on the editorial page, to donate money to local politicians.

EXERCISE 2   Ethics

Discussion Questions

Read the following situations, marking those actions you would take. Discuss your decisions with the class.

1. Without your knowledge, a talented young reporter on your staff breaks into the computer system at a second daily in your city, a bitter rival. The reporter gives you a list of all the stories the rival's staff is working on. Would you:

   A. _____ Compliment the reporter on her initiative and quickly assign your own staff to cover the stories so you won't be scooped?

   B. _____ Destroy the list and tell the reporter to never again enter the rival's computer system?

   C. _____ Reprimand the reporter, suspending her for a week?

   D. _____ Notify your rival and apologize for the reporter's actions?

   E. _____ Notify the police that the reporter may have unknowingly violated a law?

2. One of your reporters is writing about a local private club that, she learns, excludes Jews, African Canadians and aboriginals. The reporter also learns that your publisher and other influential members of your community are members of the club. Would you:

   A. _____ Abandon the story?

   B. _____ Inform your publisher about the story and suggest that she (the publisher) resign from the club?

   C. _____ Tell your reporter to interview the publisher and give her an opportunity to explain her membership in the club?

   D. _____ Publish the story but never identify any of the club's members?

   E. _____ Publish the story, listing your publisher and other prominent citizens who belong to the club?

   F. _____ List all 1,200 of the club's members?

3. As editor of your local daily, you learn that the next day's instalment of Doonesbury, a popular comic strip, shows a bigot using a word certain to offend many readers. Would you:

   A. _____ Publish the strip without change or comment?

   B. _____ Kill that day's strip?

   C. _____ Stop publishing the strip forever?

   D. _____ Change the word to something less offensive?

   E. _____ Move the strip to your newspaper's editorial page and publish an editorial explaining that although you dislike its content, you believe in freedom of speech?

   F. _____ Kill that day's strip but in its place publish a brief explanation and offer to mail copies of the strip to any readers who request it?

4. Each year, a professional organization in your province sponsors an awards competition. Minutes ago, you learned that a reporter on your staff won second place in feature writing and that your chief photographer won third place in another category. However, another newspaper in the city—a bitter rival—won five awards, and a local television station won four. How would you handle the story?

   A. _____ Ignore the story.

   B. _____ Report all the awards, beginning with the first-place awards.

   C. _____ Report only the two awards won by your staff.

   D. _____ Start by reporting the two awards won by your staff, then briefly mention the awards won by all the other media in your city.

5. You run the evening news, and a sports reporter mistakenly credited the wrong football player with scoring two game-winning touchdowns. Would you:

   A. _____ Broadcast a correction the next evening?

   B. _____ Broadcast a correction and identify the reporter responsible for the error?

   C. _____ Broadcast a correction and punish the reporter, placing him on probation?

D. _____ Broadcast a correction that identifies the reporter and reports his punishment?

E. _____ Order the reporter to write a letter to the school, apologizing for his error?

F. _____ Privately punish the reporter, placing him on probation, but publish nothing, treating the incident as a private personnel matter?

G. _____ Do nothing, hoping nobody noticed?

6. Journalists must make difficult and controversial decisions. Decide how you would respond in each of the following situations.

A. As news director of a local television station, you think an emphasis on crime and violence is bad journalism but don't know whether it affects your newscasts' ratings. Would you continue to emphasize crime and violence? _____ Yes _____ No

B. A reporter on your newspaper's staff has terrible vision, undergoes a new laser procedure to correct her nearsightedness, and wants to write a series about the operation and the doctor who successfully performed it. The story is likely to interest thousands of readers, but you learn that the reporter's operation was performed for free. Would you let her write the series? _____ Yes _____ No

C. After serving three terms, your city's mayor—a popular and successful Conservative—decides to step down. She then applies for a job as a political columnist for your editorial page and is obviously a good writer. Would you hire her? _____ Yes _____ No

D. Thousands of people live in your city's slums, and most have little education. Advertisers prefer reaching people who are wealthy and well-educated. To improve your newspaper's demographics, would you, as publisher, instruct your circulation staff to ignore your city's slums and their residents? _____ Yes _____ No

E. A member of your provincial legislature proposes applying your provincial sales tax to advertisements, a policy that would cost the newspaper of which you are publisher millions of dollars a year. When asked, would you contribute $50,000 to a campaign your Provincial Press Association is waging against the tax? _____ Yes _____ No

Would you report in your newspaper your decision and the size of any contribution? _____ Yes _____ No

F. Because of a decline in advertising revenue, you decide to lay off 42 employees, primarily employees in your newspaper's production department. Would you publish a story reporting the layoffs? _____ Yes _____ No

Would you report your newspaper's annual profits? _____ Yes _____ No

G. An extortionist says he has poisoned groceries in your town's largest chain of supermarkets. Customers continue to shop in the supermarkets. Police say the threat is almost certainly a hoax and that it will be easier for them to catch the extortionist in a day or two if you delay publishing the story. Would you immediately publish the story? _____ Yes _____ No

Nouns

A noun is a name for any animate or inanimate thing: people, animals, places, qualities, acts or ideas.

Common nouns name any member of a class of things: "cow," "town," "soldier," "refrigerator," "computer," "honesty." Proper nouns are names for specific individuals, animals, places or things: "Robert," "Melissa," "House of Commons," "Vancouver." The first letter of a proper noun is always capitalized; the first letter of a common noun is capitalized only when it is the first word in a sentence.

Nouns are also classified as concrete or abstract. Concrete nouns name tangible objects such as "table," "book" or "tree." Abstract nouns name intangible things or ideas: "laziness," "creativity" or "beauty." Nouns may indicate various levels of abstraction, becoming more abstract as they become more general. "Animal" can refer to any of millions of kinds of organisms from bacteria to humans. "Mammal" is more specific, referring to thousands of species that share certain physiological characteristics. "Dog" is still more specific, identifying a particular species of mammal. "Fido," a name for a specific dog, represents the most concrete level.

Newswriters try to use the most concrete and most specific nouns possible. Stories filled with such words are easily understood and more interesting than stories filled with abstract nouns.

Verbs

Verbs are the most important part of speech. Whereas nouns are static, verbs describe action; they tell what things and people do. Examples are "run," "steal," "hesitate" and "reflect." Verbs not only show action but also change form to tell the reader who is doing the acting and when. For example, past tense tells the reader that the action being described has been completed.

All verb tenses use one of four main forms of the verb: the infinitive (to walk), or present-tense form (I walk); the present participle, which is the "-ing" form of the verb (I am walking); the simple past-tense form (I walked); and the past-perfect tense (I have walked). These are called the principal parts of a verb. Regular verbs add "-ed" to form the past and past-perfect tenses, and they add "-ing" to form the present participle. For irregular verbs, consult a dictionary for the verb's principal parts. Here are the principal parts of a few common verbs ("sail" and "talk" are regular verbs; "write" and "run" are irregular verbs):

Infinitive	Present	Present Participle	Past Tense	Past Participle
to sail	sail	sailing	sailed	sailed
to talk	talk	talking	talked	talked
to write	write	writing	wrote	written
to run	run	running	ran	run

English has a dozen possible tense variations to show the time of the action but only three main tenses: present, past and future. The most often-used tenses are the three simple tenses (present: talk; past: talked; future: will talk) and the three "perfect" or compound tenses (present perfect: have talked; past perfect: had talked; future perfect: will have talked). A verb can also be used in a progressive tense, to show that an action is continuing (present progressive: am talking; past progressive: was talking; future progressive: will be talking). Finally, a verb can be in a perfect-progressive tense (present perfect-progressive: have been talking; past perfect-progressive: had been talking; future perfect-progressive: will have been talking). Here's an example of what a verb ("to vote") looks like in all twelve possible tenses:

Simple present: I vote.
Simple past: I voted.
Simple future: I will vote.

Present perfect: I have voted.
Past perfect: I had voted.
Future perfect: I will have voted.

Present progressive: I am voting
Past progressive: I was voting
Future progressive: I will be voting

Present perfect-progressive: I have been voting
Past perfect-progressive: I had been voting
Future perfect-progressive: I will have been voting

Verbs give readers hints about who is doing the action. For most verbs, the third-person singular in the present tense has a distinct form, usually created by adding "-s" to the end of the verb (I vote, you vote, but he *votes*). "Argues," for example, tells the reader that the arguing is going on in the present, and a person other than the speaker of the sentence is doing the arguing.

Because verbs pack so much information, good writers pay close attention to the selection of verbs. The best verbs convey strong actions that readers can easily visualize. Sentences with strong verbs and concrete nouns need little help from adjectives and adverbs.

Adjectives

Adjectives describe nouns and pronouns. In many instances, the adjectives precede the nouns they modify: the *thick* book, the *yellow* flower, the *sleepy* town. Other times, the adjective follows some form of the verb "to be"—the town is *sleepy*.

Adjectives may have "more," "most," "less" or "least" before them or have "-er" or "-est" attached at the end to indicate degrees of comparison. English has three degrees of comparison: positive, comparative and superlative. The positive degree is the basic form of the adjective and merely states that a particular thing possesses a quality. The comparative degree is used when comparing two things in the degree to which they possess a quality. The superlative degree is used when three or more things are being compared. Here are some examples of regular forms:

Positive Degree	Comparative Degree	Superlative Degree
the thick book	the thicker book	the thickest book
the beautiful flower	the more beautiful flower	the most beautiful flower
the popular candidate	the less popular candidate	the least popular candidate

Some adjectives take irregular forms for the comparative or superlative degree. These are a few examples:

Positive Degree	Comparative Degree	Superlative Degree
good	better	best
bad	worse	worst
little	less	least

Almost any word can be used as an adjective to modify nouns. Two or more words can be combined to create adjectival phrases, as in these examples:

Nouns modifying nouns: *car* insurance, *school* assignments, *government* official

Present participles modifying nouns: *soaring* airplane, *ironing* board, *winding* road

Past participles modifying nouns: *hardened* criminal, *trusted* friend, *softened* butter

Adjectival phrases: *sky-blue* shirt, *full-time* employee, *man-eating* shark

Note that the words combined to form adjectival phrases are often hyphenated.

Articles

The indefinite articles are "a" and "an." The definite article is "the." Most grammarians consider the three articles special kinds of adjectives. The use of an indefinite article implies that the writer is referring to any member of a class of people or things. The definite article implies that the writer is referring to a specific member of a class.

Jane checked out a book from the library. (The book could be any in the library.)

Jane checked out the book from the library. (A given book has already been specified.)

"A" is used before nouns that begin with consonant sounds; "an" is used before nouns that begin with vowel sounds. In most cases, the choice is obvious, but some words that start with consonants sound as if they start with vowels. In "honour," for example, the "h" is silent, so it requires "an" instead of "a."

He received an honorary degree.

In other cases, words that start with vowels sound as if they start with consonants. "Europe" sounds as if it starts with a "y"; therefore, it uses the indefinite article "a."

They plan a European vacation.

Reporters who misuse the definite article confuse readers by implying that an object being referred to is the only such object in existence. If a reporter writes that three people were taken to "the hospital," yet the story's earlier paragraphs never mentioned any hospital, then the use of "the" implies the area has only one hospital. Similarly, a story reporting someone had coffee at "the Second Cup in Vancouver, British Columbia," implies, wrongly, that there is only one Second Cup in the city.

Adverbs

Adverbs modify verbs, adjectives and other adverbs. Like adjectives, adverbs describe the words they modify. They may show manner, degree, direction, cause, affirmation, negation, frequency, time or place. Many (but not all) adverbs end in "-ly." The following sentences illustrate some of the uses of adverbs. The adverbs are italicized:

Rose *quickly* paid her bills.

Canadian Forces are *fully* committed to the mission.

He recited the alphabet *backward.*

Gordon travels *weekly* to Toronto.

The couple walked *arm in arm* down the aisle.

Like adjectives, adverbs can show degrees of comparison. Most adverbs form the comparative and superlative degrees by combining with "more," "most," "less" or "least." Here are some examples:

Positive degree: The Queen Mary bus runs *frequently.*

Comparative degree: The Peel bus runs *more frequently* than the Queen Mary bus.

Superlative degree: The 27th Street bus runs *most frequently* of all city buses.

Pronouns

Pronouns can replace proper or common nouns, allowing the writer to avoid needless and confusing repetition of a noun. The noun the pronoun replaces is called its antecedent. "Antecedent" means "that which goes before," and the pronoun usually (but not always) follows its antecedent.

> Bill overcame his fear and took the test.

> In spite of his fear, Bill took the test.

In both of these sentences, "Bill" is the antecedent for the pronoun "his," but in the second sentence, the pronoun precedes the antecedent. Whether the pronoun follows or precedes its antecedent, the writer must be sure the meaning is clear. Sometimes the pronoun "it" is used as the subject of sentences that state the time, describe the temperature or weather, or suggest some other environmental fact: for example, in "It often rains in Vancouver."

Grammarians generally recognize six kinds of pronouns: demonstrative, indefinite, interrogative, reflexive, relative and personal.

Demonstrative

Demonstrative pronouns designate or point out the things referred to. English has two demonstrative pronouns: "this" and "that" and their plural forms, "these" and "those." "This" and "these" refer to things that are close in time and space; "that" and "those" refer to things that are more remote. Demonstrative pronouns are used alone (Give me *that*); when they are used to describe a noun or pronoun, they are called demonstrative adjectives (Give me *that* book).

> You neglected to mention *that*. (demonstrative pronoun)

> This piece of fruit is sweeter than *that* one. (demonstrative adjective)

Demonstrative pronouns may have specific nouns as their antecedents, or they may have entire phrases or clauses as antecedents. In the following sentence, the antecedent for "that" is the entire opening clause:

> The bill may be amended before it is enacted, but *that* will be up to the committee.

Indefinite

Indefinite pronouns refer to objects or people generally or indeterminately. The pronoun may refer to any of a class of people. In the next sentence "each" is an indefinite pronoun:

> Each of the workers received a pay raise.

Some of the common indefinite pronouns include these: "all," "another," "any," "anybody," "anyone," "both," "each," "either," "every," "everybody," "everyone," "few," "little," "many," "much," "neither," "nobody," "none," "one," "other," "several," "some," "somebody," "someone" and "such."

Interrogative

Pronouns used to ask questions—such as "who," "which" and "what"—are called interrogative pronouns; they have no antecedents. Here are some examples:

> *Who* has the key?

> *Which* are yours?

> *What* are her reasons?

Conjunctions

Conjunctions are words, phrases or clauses that connect other words, phrases and clauses in sentences. Conjunctions are generally classified as co-ordinating or subordinating. Co-ordinating conjunctions connect elements of equal grammatical standing—words to words, phrases to phrases, clauses to clauses. Subordinating conjunctions connect dependent clauses to the main or independent clauses in sentences.

The seven most common co-ordinating conjunctions are "and," "or," "but," "nor," for," "yet" and "so." Conjunctions show different relations—for example, addition, contrast, separation and consequence. Writers can make transitions smooth and clear by selecting the conjunction that most accurately reflects their meaning.

Subordinating conjunctions are more numerous than co-ordinating conjunctions, but they too can show a variety of relationships: cause, comparison, concession, condition, manner, place, purpose or time. Here are some of the more common subordinating conjunctions:

after	in order that	until
although	rather than	when
because	since	whenever
before	so that	where
hence	though	whether
if	unless	while

Independent clauses joined by a co-ordinating conjunction should use a comma before the conjunction.

> The message arrived, but he ignored it.

> The afternoon was hot, so I went for a swim.

If the independent clauses have no co-ordinating conjunction linking them, use a semicolon.

> The company issued its report Wednesday; the price of its stock fell 40 per cent the next day.

Use a semicolon, too, if the independent clauses are linked by a conjunctive adverb. Some of the conjunctive adverbs are "however," "moreover," "nevertheless" and "therefore."

> The premier agreed to the tax increase; however, he opposed the plan for a new prison.

> We were out of town last week; therefore, we missed the show.

Some conjunctions come in pairs. They are called correlative conjunctions and include the following:

> *both–and:* Both the president and the vice-president will attend the dinner.

> *either–or:* Either the president or the vice-president will attend the dinner.

> *neither–nor:* Neither the president nor the vice-president will attend the dinner.

> *whether–or:* Whether the president or the vice-president will attend the dinner is unclear.

> *as–as:* Workers hope their pay increase will be as large this year as it was last year.

> *if–then:* If the company refuses to increase pay, then the workers will strike.

Interjections

Interjections are words or short phrases that express strong emotions. Interjections bear no grammatical relation to the rest of the sentence and are considered independent or absolute constructions. Some common interjections are "aw," "bravo," "goodbye," "hey," "hush," "nonsense," "oh," "oh, dear," "ouch," "well," "whew" and "wow."

Interjections usually are punctuated with exclamation points, which can come either after the interjection itself or at the end of the sentence containing the interjection.

> Nonsense! I never said such a thing.

> Nonsense, I never said such a thing!

The placement of the exclamation point depends on whether the strong emotion attaches to the interjection alone or to the entire sentence.

BASIC SENTENCE STRUCTURE

Simple sentences usually include a subject, a verb and an object. The subject is the person or thing doing the action. The verb describes the action. The object is the person or thing acted on. Consider this sentence:

> The batter hit the ball.

"Batter" is the actor (the subject of the sentence). "Hit" is the action (the verb), and "ball" is the thing acted on (the object).

Sometimes sentences include indirect objects, which tell to whom or for whom an action was done. The test for an indirect object is to place "to" or "for" before the word. The following sentences have both direct and indirect objects.

> Juan sent Maria a Valentine card.

> Samantha bought her mother a new CD player.

Subject	Verb	Indirect Object	Direct Object
Juan	sent	Maria	a Valentine card
Samantha	bought	her mother	a new CD player

When a noun alone is used as an indirect object, it usually comes between the verb and the direct object, as in the preceding examples. But when the indirect object takes the form of a prepositional phrase, it usually follows the direct object.

> Juan sent a Valentine card *to Maria.*

> Samantha bought a new CD player *for her mother.*

Verbs that have direct objects are called transitive verbs; verbs without direct objects are called intransitive verbs. Many verbs can be used in both transitive and intransitive ways. Take the normally intransitive verb "to walk," for instance. In the sentence "I walk every evening," the subject ("I") is doing something, but not to or for anyone or anything. Here is the same verb as a transitive verb: "I walk the dog every evening."

In the sentence "She flew the flag," "flew" is used as a transitive verb: the verb has a direct object ("flag"). But in this next sentence: "The flag flew from the pole," "flew" is used as an intransitive verb (the flag did something, but not to or for anyone or anything).

A complete grammatical sentence needs only a subject and a verb, but sentences usually contain other words, including direct and indirect objects. Writers can embellish the simple sentence (which has one main clause) in various ways. For example, they can combine two main clauses to make a compound sentence.

> Ice skating is her favourite sport, but she enjoys roller skating too.

> She is an engineer, and he is a teacher.

Another way is to combine an independent clause with a dependent one to make a complex sentence. Dependent clauses are introduced by subordinating conjunctions and are unable to make sense standing alone (they need to be attached to an independent clause to make sense).

As noted, subordinating conjunctions are words and phrases like "because," "as a result of," "after," "before," "whenever" and "as long as."

> I eat dinner *after my last class is over.*

> I visit my aunt *whenever I go home for the holidays.*

Writers may use one or more dependent clauses together with two or more independent clauses to create compound-complex sentences.

> I visit my aunt whenever I go home for the holidays, but I call her almost every week.

Sentences can also contain phrases, which are related groups of words that lack a subject/verb combination. Prepositional phrases and verbal phrases are common types. They may be incorporated in the body of the sentence, or they may introduce the main (or independent) clause. The first of the following sentences ends with a prepositional phrase, and the second begins with a verbal phrase:

> People spend more time outdoors *in the springtime.*

> *Tired from her bicycle ride*, Suzanna took a nap.

Sentence parts can be combined and arranged in many ways. Writers vary sentence structure to keep their prose from becoming too predictable and simplistic, but as a general rule, simple sentences that stick to subject–verb–object order are the clearest and most easily understood.

ACTIVE AND PASSIVE VOICE

Sentences that use the subject–verb–object order are sentences in active voice. A sentence in passive voice turns that order around. The direct object of the active-voice sentence becomes the subject of the passive-voice sentence; the subject becomes part of a prepositional phrase; and the verb is replaced with its past participle and some form of the verb "to be."

Notice that in the following examples, the passive-voice sentence takes two words more than the active-voice sentence to say the same thing. Those extra words are unnecessary stumbling blocks for readers.

> ACTIVE VOICE: The batter hit the ball.

> PASSIVE VOICE: The ball was hit by the batter.

Notice, too, that the actor or subject can disappear from a passive-voice sentence:

ACTIVE VOICE: The mayor gave Alex an award.

PASSIVE VOICE: An award was given to Alex.

Some writers make the mistake of using the indirect object as the subject of the passive-voice sentence. This mistake is most common with verbs like "give" or "present." In the preceding example, for instance, some writers might try to make "Alex" the subject of the passive-voice sentence. Some grammarians call this a false passive and consider it an error.

FALSE PASSIVE: Alex was given an award.

TRUE PASSIVE: An award was given to Alex.

The false passive is an error because it suggests that "Alex" is what was given. But the award is what was given, and Alex was the recipient of the award.

Writers should avoid the passive voice not only because it is wordier than the active voice but also because it often camouflages responsibility. If a disaster strikes or a defective product harms someone, then government or business officials may admit "mistakes were made," but that passive construction reveals nothing about who made the mistakes or why. The passive voice is the ally of all who seek to evade responsibility; it is the enemy of all who seek clarity.

AGREEMENT

Nouns, pronouns and verbs are either singular or plural. Nouns and pronouns also indicate gender: masculine, feminine or neuter. A basic principle of grammar is that nouns and verbs should agree with each other and so should nouns and pronouns. Singular subjects should have singular verbs, and plural subjects should have plural verbs; plural nouns should have plural pronouns; and so forth. The principle is simple, but the opportunities for error are numerous.

Subjects and Verbs

If the subject of a sentence is singular, use a singular verb, and if the subject is plural, use a plural verb. Getting subjects and verbs to agree is easy when sentences are simple. But when prepositional phrases separate subjects and verbs or when the subject is a collective noun, agreement becomes trickier. In the first example shown next, the singular noun "team" is the subject, and the prepositional phrase "of researchers" describes the subject. The verb must agree with the singular "team," not the plural "researchers." In this example, the subject is in italics, and the verb is underlined:

WRONG: A *team* of researchers <u>have gathered</u> the information.

CORRECT: A *team* of researchers <u>has gathered</u> the information.

WRONG: Three *teams* from the university <u>is gathering</u> the information.

CORRECT: Three *teams* from the university <u>are gathering</u> the information.

Some nouns may appear to be plural because they end in "s," but they are considered singular in some senses. Some examples are "economics," "politics" and "physics."

WRONG: *Economics* <u>are</u> a required course.

CORRECT: *Economics* <u>is</u> a required course.

Singular common nouns that end in "s" need an apostrophe and an "s" ('s) to form the possessive.

Singular common noun ending in "s"	Possessive	Sentence
witness	witness's	The witness's testimony failed to sway the jury.

Grammarians differ on this point, but according to *The Canadian Press Stylebook*, singular proper names that end in "s" (or an "s" sound) normally take an "'s" to form the possessive:

Singular proper name ending in "s"	Possessive	Sentence
Chris	Chris's	Chris's proposal was approved.
Strauss	Strauss's	Strauss's operas are still performed.

Pronouns have distinct possessive forms and do not need an apostrophe or an "s" to show possession: mine, yours, his, hers, its, ours theirs.

Many students confuse "its" with "it's." The first is the possessive pronoun, which does not need an apostrophe. The second is the contraction for "it is," and the apostrophe substitutes for the "i" in "is." Similarly, the possessive pronouns "his" and "hers" do not need apostrophes. Students also confuse the plural possessive pronoun "their" with "there," which refers to a place, or "they're," which is the contraction for "they are."

See Appendix C for more guidelines on forming possessives.

"THAT" AND "WHICH"

"That" and "which" are little words, but they can make a big difference in the meaning of a sentence. The following sentences illustrate how changing "that" to "which" changes the meaning of the sentence:

She told Shannon to take the lawn mower that is in the barn to Jason.

She told Shannon to take the lawn mower, which is in the barn, to Jason.

In the first sentence, the use of "that" suggests there is more than one lawn mower on the property—in the yard, the garage, and the barn, for instance—but Shannon should take the one from the barn. In the second sentence, the clause introduced by "which" suggests there is only one lawn mower on the property, so it is the only one Shannon can take to Jason. In the first sentence, the clause is restrictive and uses "that" and no commas; in the second, the clause is non-restrictive and uses "which" and commas. Note that the second sentence adds information but not information that is essential to the meaning of the sentence.

Here's a rule that can help decide between "that" and "which": If the subordinate clause can be removed and the sentence meaning does not change, use "which" and commas. Otherwise, use "that" and no commas.

"WHO" AND "WHOM"

"That," "which" and "who" (also "whom" and "whose") are relative pronouns. "That" and "which" introduce clauses referring to ideas, inanimate objects, or animals without names; "who" is for clauses that refer to people and animals with names.

WRONG: It was Morgan that came by the house yesterday.

CORRECT: It was Morgan who came by the house yesterday.

WRONG: It was a stray cat who ate the bird.

CORRECT: It was a stray cat that ate the bird.

The distinction between "who" and "whom" torments some writers. "Who" is the subject of a clause; "whom" is the object of a verb or a preposition. Whether the word is a subject (in subjective case) or an object (in objective case) might not always be clear in sentences that depart from normal word order, such as questions. Whether "who" or "whom" is correct depends not on word order but on the word's grammatical relationship to the rest of the sentence. These two sentences illustrate the difference:

Who gave you the scarf?

Whom do you prefer as student council president?

In the first example, "who" is the subject of the clause, the initiator of the action "gave." In the second sentence, "whom" is the direct object of the verb "prefer." Here are two more examples:

WRONG: Who did you speak to?

CORRECT: Whom did you speak to? (To whom did you speak?)

WRONG: The report names the man who the police suspect of the crime.

CORRECT: The report names the man whom the police suspect of the crime.

In the first sentence, the relative pronoun is the object of the preposition "to." In the second, it is the direct object of the verb "suspect"; it refers to the person the police suspect. Both should be "whom."

One way to avoid or reduce confusion over "who" and "whom" is to replace them with a more familiar personal pronoun. Isolate the "who" or "whom" phrase. If "he" or "she" is required, then use "who." If "him" or "her" is needed, use "whom." Do that in the following sentence, and it is easy to see that "whom" is wrong:

The candidates discussed whether whom was responsible for the tax increase.

At first, the pronoun "whom" might sound correct," but when the pronoun is replaced with the more familiar "him" or "her," the error becomes apparent. The pronoun is the subject of the clause "was responsible for the tax increase" and so must be in subjective case. No one would say "her" was responsible or "him" was responsible; it's obvious that "she was responsible" or "he was responsible" are correct. The relative pronoun to use here is "who."

MISPLACED MODIFIERS

Modifiers are words or phrases that limit, restrict or qualify some other word or phrase. Modifiers should appear as close as possible to the word or phrase they modify. Misplaced modifiers can make sentences ambiguous, confusing or nonsensical:

CONFUSING: She retold the ordeal of being held hostage with tears running down her cheeks.
REVISED: With tears running down her cheeks, she retold the ordeal of being held hostage.

CONFUSING: The gunmen tied the victim and left him with his hands and feet taped and lying on the back seat.
REVISED: The gunmen tied the victim, taped his hands and feet, and left him lying on the back seat.

In the first example, the phrase "with tears running down her cheeks" follows "hostage," and readers might think the phrase modifies "hostage"—that she was crying while she was a hostage. But the phrase really tells how the woman behaved as she talked about her ordeal. The second revision shows that the victim, not just his hands and feet, is left lying on the back seat.

Sometimes the meaning of a sentence can change dramatically simply by the positioning of a modifying word or phrase. Look at how the following sentences change in meaning by moving the word "only":

Only Smith's farm produces the best apples in the county.

Smith's only farm produces the best apples in the county.

Smith's farm only produces the best apples in the county.

Smith's farm produces only the best apples in the county.

Smith's farm produces the best apples only in the county.

Careful writers choose the word order that accurately conveys their meaning.

DANGLING AND MISPLACED MODIFIERS

Modifiers dangle when the word or phrase they are supposed to modify does not appear in the sentence. That may happen when a thoughtless or hurried writer starts a sentence intending to state an idea one way and then switches in mid-sentence to express it in another way:

CONFUSING: Pleased with everyone's papers, the class received congratulations.
REVISED: Pleased with everyone's papers, the teacher congratulated the class.

Modifiers should be placed as close as possible to the word or phrase they modify; when they aren't correctly placed, they cause confusion.

CONFUSING: Angered by the unannounced closure of the plant, security guards hurriedly cleared the area.
REVISED: Security guards hurriedly cleared the area of employees angered by the unannounced closure of the plant.

Readers understand introductory words to modify the subject of the sentence, "security guards." The first sentence suggests it was the security guards who were angered by the closure; the revision makes it clear that the employees were the ones angered.

PERSONIFICATION

Avoid treating inanimate objects or abstractions as if they were human. Objects such as buildings, cars, stores and trees cannot hear, think, feel or talk. Yet some writers treat them as people. The writers see—and repeat—the error so often they fail to recognize it and continue to personify such things as corporations, countries and machines.

Memorial Hospital treated her for shock and a broken arm.

She was driving west on Columbia Street when two cars in front of her slammed on their brakes.

Can a hospital treat patients, or is that the job of a hospital's staff? Can a car slam on its own brakes? Of course not. Such personifications are easy to correct:

The store said it will not reopen.
REVISED: The owner of the store said she will not reopen it.

The intention of the road was to help farmers transport their crops to market.
REVISED: Highway planners intended the road to help farmers transport their crops to market.

Personification also contributes to two other problems. First, audiences cannot determine a story's credibility if reporters fail to identify their sources. Readers can assess the credibility of a statement attributed to a mayor or premier but not the credibility of a statement attributed to a city or province.

Second, personification allows people to escape responsibility for their actions. Individual officials cannot be held responsible for their actions if reporters attribute those actions to a business or government.

PARALLEL FORM

When writers link similar ideas, they do so with parallel structures. Grammatically parallel structures create harmony and balance in writing, and they help readers compare and contrast the ideas that are linked within the sentence.

The principle of parallelism requires that every item in a series take the same grammatical form: all nouns, all verbs, or all prepositional phrases. If the first verb in a series uses the past tense, every verb in the series must use the past tense, or if the first verb ends in "-ing," all must end in "-ing." If reporters fail to express like ideas in the same grammatical form, their sentences become convoluted and confusing:

NOT PARALLEL: She enjoys writing, researching and reading her published work is great fun, too.

PARALLEL: She enjoys writing, researching, and reading her published work.

NOT PARALLEL: Police said the plastic handcuffs are less bulky, not as expensive and no key is needed to remove them from a suspect's wrists than metal handcuffs.

PARALLEL: Police said plastic handcuffs are less bulky, less expensive, and less difficult to remove from a suspect's wrists than metal handcuffs.

NOT PARALLEL: The Greenes have three children: 4-year-old Gordon, Andrea, who is 3, and little Fielding is not quite 25 months.

PARALLEL: The Greenes have three children: Gordon, 4; Andrea, 3; and Fielding, 2.

"BECAUSE" AND "DUE TO"

Students often misuse "because" and "due to." "Because" is a subordinating conjunction, used to introduce a subordinate clause, as in the following sentence: "The train arrived late because it encountered bad weather between Saskatoon and Edmonton. "Due to" is a preposition meaning "ascribed to" or "attributed to"; it is used after a noun (the train's late arrival, due to bad weather, forced a change in their itinerary) or after a linking verb (the delay was due to bad weather). "Due to" is always followed by a noun or noun phrase. Using "due to" to mean "because of" (the train was late due to bad weather) is common but considered incorrect in formal usage.

SPELLING

Readers complain about inaccuracies in news stories, and they are often referring to spelling errors. Misspellings reflect laziness on the part of the writer, and they sometimes cause readers to doubt the facts in the story.

Correct spelling is as important for writers in broadcast journalism as it is for those in print journalism. News announcers often lack time to review the reporter's copy for misspelled words, and misspellings may cause them to make mistakes on air.

Commonly misspelled words make up some of the exercises at the end of this chapter. Common phrases such as "a lot" and "all right" are frequently misspelled. Five other words that students often misspell are "medium," "datum," "graffito," "criterion" and "phenomenon." All five are singular forms. Students often use the plural form instead: "media," "data," "graffiti," "criteria" and "phenomena." Thus it would be correct to say, "The four criteria are adequate" or "The datum is lost," but not, "The media is inaccurate" or "The phenomenon are unusual."

Reporters usually follow formal rules for spelling. For example, they normally use "until" rather than "till" and "although" rather than "though." They also avoid slang.

A final point about spelling: Spell-check programs for computers help many writers, but a computer program can look only at the spelling of a word, not at how it is used. If a student were to write, "There cats name is Savannah," the spell-checker would note that every word in the sentence is spelled correctly. It would miss two errors: "There" should be "Their" and "cats" should be "cat's." No one should depend solely on a spell-check program.

Words that look or sound alike but have different meanings, such as "accept/except" and "capital/capitol," can also be confusing. Test your vocabulary skills on confusing words with the exercises at the end of this chapter and at the end of Chapter 3 The Language of News.

 ## GRAMMAR CHECKLIST

1. Use subject–verb–object order for sentences.
2. Use verbs in active voice, not passive voice.
3. Use singular verbs with singular subjects and plural verbs with plural subjects.
4. Make sure that pronouns agree with their antecedents.
5. Spell plurals and possessives correctly.
6. Use "that," "which," "who" and "whom" correctly.
7. Place modifiers immediately before or after the word they describe.
8. Avoid personification; do not suggest inanimate objects can talk, think or feel.
9. List items in a series in parallel form.
10. Use the articles "a," "an" and "the" correctly.
11. Reread copy several times for spelling and other writing errors.
12. Do not depend solely on spell-check programs to find misspelled words.

SUGGESTED READINGS AND USEFUL WEBSITES

Bell, James B., and Edward P.J. Corbett. 1977. *The Little English Handbook for Canadians.* Toronto: Wiley Canada.

Editing Canadian English. 2003. 2nd edn. Catherine Cragg et al., eds. Prepared for the Editors' Association of Canada/Association canadienne des réviseurs. Toronto: McClelland and Stewart.

Fee, Margery, and Janice McAlpine. 2007. *Oxford Guide to Canadian English Usage.*

2nd edn. Don Mills, ON: Oxford University Press.

Hacker, Diana. 2007. *A Canadian Writer's Reference.* 4th edn. Bedford / St. Martin's.

Oxford Canadian A–Z of Grammar, Spelling, & Punctuation. 2006. Katherine Barber and Robert Pontisso, eds. Don Mills, ON: Oxford University Press.

Paperback Oxford Canadian Dictionary. 2006. 2nd edn. Katherine Barber, Heather Fitzgerald, Tom Howell, and Robert Pontisso, eds. Don Mills, ON: Oxford University Press.

Ruvinsky, Maxine. 2009. *Practical Grammar: A Canadian Writer's Resource.* 2nd edn. Don Mills, ON: Oxford University Press.

Red River College, Interactive Grammar Lessons:
http://xnet.rrc.mb.ca/leshanson/Writing_Resources.htm

University of Victoria Language Centre:
http://web2.uvcs.uvic.ca/elc/studyzone

EXERCISE 1   Recognizing and Correcting Newswriting Errors

Answer key provided: See Appendix D.

SECTION I: AGREEMENT
Edit the following sentences, correcting agreement and other errors.

1. The committee submits their data this weekend which they expect will help their church.
2. She said the company failed to earn enough to repay their loans, and she does not expect them to reopen.
3. The jury reached their verdict at 1 a.m., concluding that the media was guilty of libelling the restaurant and their twenty-two employees.
4. The decision allowed the city council to postpone their vote for a week, and they suggested that the sites developer design a plan to save more of it's trees.
5. A representative for the organization said they help anyone that is on welfare obtain some job training and raise their self esteem.

SECTION II: PLURALS AND POSSESSIVES
Edit the following sentences, correcting for plurals, possessives and other errors.

1. The womens car was parked nearby, and sheriffs deputies asked to see the owners drivers licence.
2. The juror said she opposes assisted suicide "because a doctors job is to save peoples lives, not end them."
3. Last years outstanding teacher insisted that peoples complaints about the schools problems are mistaken.
4. Manvel Jones parents said there younger childrens teacher earned her bachelors degree in philosophy and her masters degree in eductaion.
5. Everyones money was stolen, and the neighbourhood associations president warned that the police are no longer able to guarantee peoples safety in the citys poorest neighbourhoods.

SECTION III: PLACEMENT
Rewrite these sentences, keeping related words and ideas together. Correct all errors.

1. The board of trustees voted 8–1 to fire the college president for his sexual misconduct during an emergency meeting Thursday morning.
2. On their arrival, the hotel manager took the guests' bags to their rooms.
3. The union representative urged Canadians to support better working conditions for the country's immigrant workers at the Unitarian church Sunday.
4. Jogging around campus, a thorn bush ripped a hole in Zena's shirt.
5. A suspect in the burglary case was arrested after a high-speed chase involving two lawn mowers stolen from a hardware store.

SECTION IV: PERSONIFICATION
Rewrite the following sentences, eliminating personification and other errors.

1. Slamming on its brakes, the car turned to the left, narrowly missing the dog.
2. The city said it cannot help the three businesses who asked for better lighting.
3. After detecting the outbreak, the hospital admitted that 7 babies born this month were infected, including one that died.
4. The Fire Department treated the child for smoke inhalation, then transported her to Mercy Hospital, which treated her broken legs.
5. The corporation, which denied any responsibility for the deaths, will appear in court next month.

SECTION V: PARALLEL FORM
Rewrite these sentences in parallel form, and correct all errors.

1. He was charged with drunken driving and an expired drivers licence.
2. Karen Kim was a full-time student, Air Force reservist, and she worked part-time for a veterinarian.
3. To join the club, one must be a sophomore, junior or senior; studying journalism; be in good academic standing; and have demonstrated professional journalistic ability.
4. The mayor warned that the neighbourhoods high crime rate causes residents to flee, contributes to more unemployment for workers, and the city loses tax revenue, along with lowering everyones property values.
5. She said the other advantages of owning her own business include being independent, not having a boss, flexible hours, and less stress.

SECTION VI: MULTIPLE ERRORS
Rewrite the following sentences, correcting all errors. Most sentences contain more than one kind of error.

1. A sheriffs deputy saw the teenagers Chevrolet pull out of the alley, driving recklessly without its headlines on, and arrested it's driver.
2. The city also said that they cannot silence Sooyoung Li, the woman that fears pollution is likely to effect the neighbourhoods 300 residents.
3. Seeking more money, publicity, and to help the poor, the churchs members said it wants the city to help it by providing food and offer housing for the homeless.
4. The Public Works Department said they could pave the developments road themselves for less than $1.2 million, the Roess Company submitted a bid of $2.74 million.
5. A jury awarded almost $10.5 million to the operators of an abortion clinic that charged that picketers tormented them and there clients. The clinics operators praised the jury's verdict, saying their courage and understanding set a needed precedent.

CHAPTER 20

EXERCISE 2   Recognizing and Correcting Newswriting Errors

SECTION I: AGREEMENT
Edit the following sentences, correcting agreement, ambiguity and other errors.

1. Every one of the news stories were accurate in their description of the accused.
2. Are seven dollars enough to buy the book?
3. Spagetti and meatballs are my favourite dish.
4. The board voted to raise they're salaries 10 per cent.
5. The cat and dog, whom ate off her plate, was punished severely.

SECTION II: PLURALS AND POSSESSIVES
Edit the following sentences, correcting errors in plurals and possessives as well as any other errors.

1. The women's liberation movement continue to help champion their cause for equality.
2. Experts fear the grey wolfs are a endangered species.
3. The fishes scales glowed in the dark from being exposed to pollution.
4. She acknowledged that the mistake was her's.
5. Their going to take they're trip to Jamaica this year.

SECTION III: PLACEMENT
Rewrite these sentences, keeping related words and ideas together. Correct all errors.

1. While baring it's teeth, the dogcatcher caught the racoon.
2. The teacher said that grading was tiring and exhausting for her students papers.
3. Too cold to move, her coat was inadequate for her outing.
4. The mother knew that going to war would be hard for her baby, who was a sergeant in the military.
5. The firefighter saved the child as she ran into the burning house.

SECTION IV: PERSONIFICATION
Rewrite the following sentences, eliminating personification and other errors.

1. The jets unloaded their bombs in the no-fly zone.
2. The funeral home said the former mayors burial was at 4 p.m.
3. What the newspaper says is all ways right.
4. The governors meeting voted to raise taxes.
5. Her watch said it was noon time.

SECTION V: PARALLEL FORM
Rewrite these sentences in parallel form, and correct all errors.

1. She goes to college majoring in journalism to write news.
2. The mayor promised improvements in employment, education and to fix up roads in the county.
3. Tracy went to the store for eggs and butter and also to buy milk.
4. Sept. 11, 2001, was sad, had offensiveness and many students believe it is upsetting to their classmates.
5. She asked the victim to describe the muggers's height, weight and if he knew what she wore.

SECTION VI: MULTIPLE ERRORS

Rewrite the following sentences, correcting all errors. Most sentences contain more than one error.

1. As it rolled along the floor, her foot was run over by the chair.
2. The electricians's union told their members to go on strike and to also demonstrate their disagreement.
3. Detailed and tricky, the class finished their exams.
4. The hockey team was given their five goals by their principal player, Annie Bearclaw.
5. None of the witnesses were available to the reporter that had a deadline.
6. The beautiful flower, black and blue, was stepped on by the gardeners dog.
7. The teacher that was interviewed by the reporter asked for her email.
8. All the people in the neighbourhood was given a good citizenship award by the mayor.
9. The woman could not be a juror due to she said the judge was an hypocrite with her rulings.
10. He likes to watch movies which make him cry and also gets him to feeling sentimental.

EXERCISE 3   Recognizing and Correcting Newswriting Errors

SECTION I: MODIFIERS

Edit the following sentences, correcting for misplaced or dangling modifiers.

1. Riddled with errors, the teacher graded the assignment.
2. The president met with the committee wearing a blue suit today.
3. Although it had a slightly green peel, the monkey at the zoo ate the banana.
4. The rancher wore a leather belt into the church with a bronze bull-riding buckle.
5. The mayor gave an emotional speech to the spectators outside the new library that had stood there for hours.

SECTION II: WHO AND WHOM

Choose the correct relative pronoun in the following sentences.

1. To (who/whom) did you hand your article?
2. You chose (who/whom) to write a series of stories on Hurricane Katrina?
3. (Who/Whom) is going to receive the award this year?
4. On (who/whom) did she blame the robbery?
5. (Who/Whom) asked for the story on the fighting in Afghanistan?

SECTION III: PLURALS AND POSSESSIVES

Edit the following sentences, correcting errors in plurals and possessives as well as any other errors.

1. The hostess's stool was missplaced during the rearrangement of the restraunt.
2. The poker player's finally agreed to end thier game at 3 a.m.
3. "Its Kris' turn to drive the race car," said the manager of the team.
4. The monkeys's cages was cleaned out Saturday by the small team of zookeepers.
5. Looking really nice in her new dress, the gloves were new ones for Loreli.

SECTION IV: ACTIVE AND PASSIVE VOICE

Edit the following sentences, changing passive to active voice.

1. The pitchfork was thrown into the corner by the farmer.
2. An antique train engine will be sold by the Smith Auctioneers next month.
3. The child was handed a football by his uncle on Thanksgiving.
4. A new movie was watched by several students during the festival.
5. The stolen car was given a new paint job.

SECTION V: AGREEMENT

Read the following sentences, correcting for subject–verb agreement and subject–pronoun agreement.

1. The congregation of the church were playing bingo on Wednesday evenings.
2. The family walking into the store are going to buy their groceries for the week.
3. The bar association says they will enforce stricter rules in the conducting of their examinations.
4. The emails from the office of the dean deals with the new policy on student loans.
5. The group of journalism designers want training in Flash.

EXERCISE 4   Spelling

Cross out the word that is misspelled in each of the following pairs. Always use the spelling recommended by the Canadian Press.

1. a lot/alot
2. acceptable/acceptible
3. accidently/accidentally
4. accommodate/accomodate
5. advertising/advertizing
6. adviser/advisor
7. afterward/afterwards
8. alright/all right
9. baptize/baptise
10. boy friend/boyfriend
11. broccoli/brocolli
12. canceled/cancelled
13. catagorized/categorized
14. cemetery/cemetary
15. comming/coming
16. commited/committed
17. congradulations/congratulations
18. conscious/concious
19. contraversial/controversial
20. credability/credibility
21. critized/criticized
22. cryed/cried
23. defendant/defendent
24. desert/dessert (food)
25. despite/dispite
26. deterrant/deterrent
27. dilema/dilemma
28. disastrous/disasterous
29. dispise/despise
30. elite/elete
31. embarass/embarrass
32. emphasize/emphacize
33. employe/employee
34. endorsed/indorsed
35. exhorbitant/exorbitant
36. existance/existence
37. explaination/explanation
38. fascination/facination
39. favoritism/favouritism
40. Febuary/February
41. fourty/forty
42. fulfil/fulfill
43. glamour/glamor
44. goverment/government
45. guerrilla/guerilla
46. harassment/harrassment
47. humorous/humerous
48. independant/independent
49. indispensable/indispensible
50. infered/inferred
51. innuendo/inuendo
52. irrate/irate
53. irregardless/regardless
54. it's/its (possessive pronoun)
55. janiter/janitor
56. judgement/judgment
57. kindergarten/kindergarden
58. license/licence (noun)
59. lightning/lightening
60. likelyhood/likelihood

21

Format, Copy Editing and CP Style

Writing is no trouble; you just jot down ideas as they occur to you.
The jotting is simplicity itself—it is the occurring which is difficult.
— **Stephen Leacock, Canadian writer, humorist and economist**

Journalism is a rewarding profession, but it requires honest hard work and dedication. News judgment, critical thinking and good writing permeate the craft of journalism, whether the medium is newspaper, radio, television or online/multimedia. Training to become a journalist can be one of the most challenging and rewarding adventures of your life. Learning how to report and write in journalistic style—identifying leads, researching events and issues, organizing thoughts and writing concisely—will be one of your most useful experiences, because the ability to communicate will benefit you throughout life.

Being a journalist is a privilege and a responsibility. You have the unique opportunity to record people's private thoughts and enjoy the advantages of sometimes being one of the first to learn about new issues, ideas and events. Yet you must be accountable for the decisions you make, because journalists tell people the news and information they need to make productive decisions about their lives. After all, to what profession did the world turn to find out news in the wake of the global financial crisis of 2008? On whom do people depend to give updates about hurricanes? Who tells the stories that unfold in the midst of a war? And where do people go to learn about local candidates' platforms or school closings?

Although the purpose of reporting the news has remained the same for decades, the tools for gathering, producing, presenting and disseminating news and information have changed. Only 20 years ago, few editors knew what an online database was, and most thought it unimportant. Today, reporters must know how to gather and present information using the Internet, CD-ROMs, public records, online databases, electronic morgues and newspaper databases in addition to traditional reporting skills.

The essential skills of journalism are astute news judgment, reporting aptitude and writing ability. Traditional journalists, visual communicators and digital journalists all use basic news judgment skills. Once journalists understand the fundamentals of writing clearly and concisely, they can transfer these skills to different media. This chapter focuses on basic print copy-editing skills and Canadian Press style as a starting point.

PRODUCING COPY

More changes than ever are happening in newsrooms. Until about 40 years ago, reporters rolled two sheets of paper divided by a carbon into their manual typewriters. Reporters kept one copy of the story in case the editor lost the other. They used a pencil to correct their errors with copy-editing marks in the story before handing it to an editor. The editor would often make further changes on the paper using copy-editing symbols before giving the reporter's story to a typesetter to compose stories on the news page. Starting in the 1970s, media organizations experienced a period of rapid technological change from manual typewriters to electric typewriters to video display terminals (VDTs) to computers, which are now used in all stages of the news process, ranging from writing stories to producing high-resolution digital images of news pages (large-scale desktop publishing). Journalists now keyboard their stories on computers and correct their errors instantly. When journalists finish their work, their stories are stored in a computer until an editor is ready to view them on another computer. The final, edited stories are transmitted to other computerized machines, which set them in type. Everything is done electronically.

Although journalists use technology to enhance their reporting and writing, they still correct their errors on paper with the traditional format and copy-editing symbols, which are a national standard for reporters, freelance writers, public relations practitioners, and others.

The traditional format and copy-editing symbols are helpful in classes in which students' stories are printed for instructors' comments and editing. Although most assignments are keyboarded, students might notice an error in their work after their story is printed. They are expected to make corrections using the same format, editing and style guidelines professional journalists use. The guidelines presented here are a standard, but some news organizations may have slightly different practices.

NEWS STORY FORMAT

Reporters have developed a unique format for their stories, and each story they write follows the guidelines presented here. Although minor variations exist from one news organization to another, most publications are remarkably consistent in their adherence to these rules. Also, most computer word processing programs in the newsroom are programmed for standard margins and provide a special space for the reporter's name, the date and the slug (a short description of the story).

- Print each news story on one side only of separate 8½-by-11-inch sheets of paper.

- Leave a one-inch margin on each side and at the bottom of every page. Standard margins help editors and production workers gauge the length of each story. Instructors use this space to write comments.

- Keyboard your name as the journalist, the date the story is written, and a slug-line (one or two words describing the story) on the upper left-hand corner of the first page:

    Maxine Ruvinsky

    July 14, 2011

    Girl Hero

Slug-lines help editors identify and keep track of stories that are being prepared for publication. They also provide a quick summary of each story's topic. A story that reports an increase in college tuition might be slugged "Tuition Increases"; a story about a fundraiser dance for charity might be slugged "Fundraising Dance." Slug-lines should not exceed three words and should be as specific as possible. Vague slug-lines, such as "dance" or "fundraiser" or "charity," might be used on more than one story, and the stories, their headlines and their placement in the paper might then become confused.

In devising a slug-line, journalists avoid jokes, sarcasm, insensitivity and statements of opinion that would cause embarrassment if the slug-line were accidentally published, as sometimes happens. A columnist opined on the religion of candidates for U.S. president. A new employee thought his slug-line was the headline. It was set in type, and the story the next morning bore the misspelled and insensitive heading "A Moron President?"

- Begin each story about one-third of the way down the first page. The space provides room for editors to comment and for instructors to evaluate students' work.

- Set the tab key to indent a half-inch at the beginning of each paragraph.

- Double-space and keyboard each story so that it is neat, uniform and easy to read.

- Editing should be placed clearly above the typed lines in the skipped spaces. The spacing should make editing easier to do and see. Do not leave any extra space between paragraphs.

- Use left justification, and avoid hyphenating words at the end of a line.

- Traditionally, journalists never divide a paragraph across pages. Keeping a paragraph together keeps its information together should following pages be misplaced. On computers, this means inserting a page break between paragraphs.

- If a story is continued on a second page, type the word "more" centred at the bottom of the first page to indicate to the editor and production staff that the story does not end on the first page; more information is on an additional page.

- Begin the second page and all later pages about one inch from the top of the page. Type your last name, the slug-line and the page number of the story in the upper left-hand corner:

    Ruvinsky

    Girl Hero

    Page 2

- At the end of the story, type an end mark to show that the story is complete. The most common symbols are "30," "###" or the journalist's initials. Telegraphers used the Roman numerals "XXX" to indicate the end of a message. Eventually, editors put it at the end of a story indicating its completion, and the Roman numerals were ultimately changed into the Arabic "30." Traditional end marks to Linotype operators were "-30-" or three pound signs ("###"). Printers preferred "#" because it avoided confusion between "30" and "—3—" or "3-em," a sign that called for the insertion of a dash to separate parts of a story.

The news business has its jargon, and some of the terms have unusual spellings. Instead of using the word "paragraph," some journalists call it a "graph" or "graf." Other journalists refer to a page of a story as an "add" or a "take." Sometimes reporters use the word "copy" instead of "story" to refer to the written version of a news report. The first sentence of a story is often referred to as a "lead" or "lede."

News organizations also vary on the use of datelines (also called placelines), which indicate the place where the event occurred. Datelines are placed at the beginning of the story and normally include the name of the city, printed in capital letters and followed by a comma, the abbreviation for the province in upper and lowercase letters, and a dash (for example: BRANTFORD, Ont.—). Names of major cities that have large populations and are synonymous with a province or nation (Montreal, New York or Tokyo) are used without the name of the province or country. Most news organizations do not use datelines for stories that originate within their own communities. When they use the names of other cities within their own province, they omit the name of the province.

Datelines routinely used to include the date the story was written. Because communication was slower in the nineteenth century, the dates in datelines helped readers know how fresh the news was. Now, many stories are published the day they are written or the day after. In the rapidly expanding world of online news, publication is nearly instantaneous and updating is continual.

News organizations also have different policies about when to use datelines. Some organizations tell their reporters to use datelines to indicate where the basic information in the story came from even if the writer of the story was in another city. A more rigorous standard, and the one followed by the Canadian Press, says datelines should be used only when the principal reporter of the story is in the city named in the dateline.

COPY-EDITING SYMBOLS

Reporters should edit their stories and correct all errors before giving the final version to an editor. If the editor finds a problem, the story is often returned to the reporter for revisions. Correcting stories is called editing; symbols used to edit are called copy-editing symbols.

Stories written for reporting classes should be neat and easy to read. To edit a story on paper, use a pencil to insert the copy-editing symbols shown in the following paragraphs. Ink cannot be erased, and the original markings might be confused with revised editing. Editing online obviously does not allow for this sort of traditional editing, but learning the copy-editing symbols and how to apply them is still the best way to become proficient (and good editors are still in high demand, regardless of medium).

If several errors appear within one word, draw one line through the word, and place the correct spelling above it. Make these copy-editing symbols and corrections plain and obvious. If several major errors appear in a paragraph or section of a story, retype that section. If corrections become too numerous and messy, retype the entire story so that it is easy to read. The following is an example of copy-editing for print publications. Copy-editing symbols for broadcast are discussed in Chapter 17. Copy-editing symbols are on the inside front cover.

```
     Double-space your story. Indent every paragraph in a news

story, and mark the beginning of each paragraph with the proper

copy-editing symbol:|_____ If you want to mark a para-

graph to be divided into two shorter paragraphs, you can use ei-

ther the same copy-editing symbol or this one: ¶ .

     If you indent a line and then decide that you do not want to

start a new paragraph, link the lines together with a pencil, as

shown here.

     The same symbol is used to link the remaining parts of a sen-

tence or paragraph after a major deletion, involving the elimina-

tion of a great many words and more than one line of type, or even

a complete sentence or two, as shown here.

     Always use a pencil, not a pen, to correct any errors that

appear in your stories.  If you make a mistake in correcting your

story with a pen, the correction will be difficult to change.
```

Write "OK" above facts or spellings that are so unusual that your editors are likely to question their accuracy, and circle the letters. (For example, you might need to check again the spelling of Suzanne Schlovitkowitz, when writing that she became a millionaire at the age of 13.) The notation "OK" indicates that the information is correct, regardless of how odd, unlikely or bizarre it may appear to be.

If you accidentally type an extra word or letter, cross out with one line the word or or letter, then draw an arc above it to link the remaining portions of the sentence. An arc drawn above a deletion indicates that the remaining segments of the sentence or paragraph should be moved closer together, but a space should be left between them. To eliminate a space within a word, draw an arc both above and below i t. To eliminate an unnecessary letter, draw an arc both above and below itt, plus a *vertical* line through it. To delete a letter or punctuation at the end of a word, you can draw a symbol through it like this.

When two words or letters are inverted, use symbol this to indicate that they should be transposed. If you want to move an entire paragraph, retype that portion of the story. Particularly if the transposed paragraphs are on different pages, several errors are likely to occur if you fail to retype them.

draw three lines under a letter to indicate that it should be capitalized. If a letter is capitalized, but should not be, draw a *slanted* line through it. If two words are incorrectly run together, draw a *straight*, vertical line between them to indicate that a space should be added.

If you make a correction and then decide that the correction is unnecessary or mistaken, write the word "stet" (from the Latin word "stare," meaning "let it stand") alongside the correction to indicate that you want to retain the original version.

If you want to add or change a letter, word or phrase, write or type the change above the line, then use a caret to indicate where it fits into the sentence. Many punctuation marks, including colons, semicolons, exclamation points and question marks, are added in the same manner (for example: When will he have dinner ready?). Make certain that your caret is legible by inserting it in the space above or below the text line.

To add a comma, draw a comma in the proper place and put a caret over it (for example: The dog is big, black and furry.). If you add an apostrophe or quotation mark, place a caret under it (for example: He said, "I'm going to the store."). To add a period, draw either a dot or a small "x" and circle it. A hyphen is indicated by the symbol =, and a dash by the symbol)—(.

Never type or write over a letter or word. Also, place all corrections above (never below) the typed line and error. Otherwise, an editor won't know if your correction goes with the line above or below it.

As you examine various newspapers, you will see that they never underline because typesetters do not have a key to underline. However, you can use the symbol shown here to indicate that a word needs to be set in italics, and you can use the symbol shown here to indicate that a word needs to be set in boldface. You can use this symbol to center a line on the page:

]By Gordon Elliott[

⌐ This symbol means flush left.   This symbol means flush right.⌐

Spell out most numbers below 10 and use numerals for the number 10 and most larger numbers.   Consult The Associated Press
Stylebook and Libel Manual for more exact guidelines.   If you type
a numeral, but want it spelled out, circle it (for example: She
has ④ dogs.).   If you spell out a number, but want to use the numeral, circle it (for example: She has (twelve) horses.).   Similarly, circle words that are spelled out, but should be
abbreviated (for example: He is from Madison, (Wisconsin)), and
words that are abbreviated but should be spelled out (for example: Her dad is from(Tex.) .   Do not use a circle to indicate that
a letter should or should not be capitalized.

Below the last line of each news story, in the center of the
page, place one of these "end marks":

-30-
-0-
###

THE CANADIAN PRESS STYLEBOOK

Most Canadian news organizations have adopted *The Canadian Press Stylebook.* The stylebook contains a briefing on Canadian media law and lists hundreds of rules, presented in alphabetical order, for abbreviations, capitalization, punctuation, grammar, spelling and word usage. A summary of the stylebook appears in Appendix B of this book, and students should study it and learn all its rules. The complete stylebook is available at most campus and community bookstores.

The stylebook helps journalists avoid misspellings and errors in grammar and word usage. In addition, the stylebook saves journalists time, because in a single volume it answers most of the questions they are likely to ask about the proper use of the language. Thus journalists seldom must search through several reference books or interrupt more experienced colleagues with questions. Further, news organizations have found it less expensive and much easier to follow a nationally accepted stylebook.

News organizations large and small rely on consistent standards. By specifying a single set of rules for everyone to follow, *The Canadian Press Stylebook* encourages consistency. Without a single set of rules, news organizations would publish more errors, which could be both costly and embarrassing. For example, four reporters within the same news organization might write the same phrase in four different ways. One reporter might spell "per cent" as two words (17 per cent); another might use one word (17 percent); a third might use the percentage sign (17%); and a fourth might spell out the number 17 (seventeen per cent). The first version (17 per cent) is correct. Reading newspapers is also easier if the style is consistent.

Over the years, the stylebook has grown to include information necessary for journalists, such as guidelines for the Internet, sports and business, media law, and photo captions. In addition to its other uses, the stylebook helps students prepare for their first jobs. If beginning journalists learn the book's basic rules while enrolled in college or university, they can easily begin writing for the media—and move from one employer to another. Because most news organizations have adopted *The Canadian Press Stylebook*, reporters do not have to learn a new set of rules each time they move to another newsroom.

A couple of large newspapers, such as the *Globe and Mail* and the *National Post*, have published stylebooks of their own. Other large news organizations publish books that specify the rules for handling stylistic problems particular to their fields or disciplines. Similarly, some college and university newspapers specify a standardized set of rules for common usage.

ACCURACY OF NAMES AND FACTS

Editors, instructors and the public do not tolerate sloppiness, and they are particularly critical of errors in spelling, names and facts because there is rarely any excuse for them.

Be especially careful to check the spelling of people's names. Most misspellings are the result of carelessness, and they anger two sets of people—those whom the reporter intended to name as well as those who were inadvertently named. Most editors require their reporters to consult a second source, usually a telephone book or city directory (hard-copy or online) to verify the way names are spelled. Always confirm the spelling of a source's name and title before ending an interview.

In the real newsroom, of course, you would check the spelling in the appropriate directory. For the exercises in this textbook, assume that a name is spelled correctly the first time it is used in the story, and make subsequent references conform to that spelling. To avoid inconsistent spelling of names, check a name every time it appears in a news story, not just the first time it is used.

Journalists understand the importance of double-checking the accuracy of every fact in every news story. Any factual error will damage a news organization's reputation and could seriously harm people mentioned in the stories. Because of the serious consequences of inaccuracies, an instructor is likely to lower grades significantly for a factual error. Students are also penalized for errors in diction, grammar and style. If an instructor accepts late assignments (most do not), grades may be lowered because of a missed deadline. All media organizations must meet rigid deadlines, and editors expect work to be turned in on time.

The Writing Coach

RUSSELL'S RULES FOR GOOD WRITING

By Nicholas Russell, journalist and author, Victoria, B.C.

1. Editing. Good copy editors polish, without imposing on a piece. They make good copy even better. But brilliant copy editors draw out the possibilities of the story, the possibilities of the writer; they identify the fine writer's style, discreetly refining it, so the writer sees the piece in the paper and says to herself: "Yeah, that's what I meant to say," or "Good, they never touched it."

2. Sentence length. There is no iron rule, and no ideal length. But we need to wonder why the average sentence in daily papers is generally 50 per cent longer than in popular American bestsellers. A sentence in a news story can be immensely long—if it's for some deliberate effect. Short, staccato sentences can add speed and excitement to a story, but they don't work all the time. Best is a mix. And if your lead sentence is more than 20 words long, it had better be damn good!

3. Verbs. The most important word in most sentences is the verb. Verbs need to be strong, vivid, clear, and ACTIVE. It follows that the verb in the lead is likely the most important word in the entire story. The second-weakest verb in the journalist's vocabulary is "is." The weakest verb is "'s," as in, "There's a new yadda yadda."

4. Vocabulary. Words are our tools. The fine cabinet-maker never uses all her tools, but they are there when she needs them, shining and sharp. They need TLC: cleaning, polishing, careful storage for quick retrieval. Journalists should not be the first to use a new word, nor the last to use an old word. Every word needs to communicate clearly and instantly exactly what the writer wants it to communicate.

5. Loaded language. Some words carry a burden of emotion—words such as censor, reform, admit, disabled. They are effective, powerful weapons in our arsenal, but they must be used very carefully; a loaded word is an editorial opinion.

6. Bafflegab. We're not just in the reporting business—we are in the translation business. As the world gets more complex, each specialist develops special vocabulary, and it's up to us to make these fields accessible, without getting sucked into the techno-babble of the experts we cover—the computer geeks, the sewage engineers, the rocket scientists.

7. Syntax. The rules of English grammar are often arcane and illogical. But if you break them unknowingly, you'll probably confuse the reader to the point of irritation and turn-off. If you know the rules, you can break them—occasionally—with great effect.

8. Style. Good writing will be tight, clear, crisp, and accurate, drawing vivid word-pictures for the reader. But VERY good writing will also have flair: a sensitive, crafted use of pace and rhythm and mood. And the best copy editor looks at that with enthusiasm and respect, thinking, "I wish I'd written that," and leaves it alone.

CHECKLIST FOR COPY PREPARATION

1. Devise a slug-line (no more than three words) that specifically describes the story's content. Type your name, the date and the slug in the upper left-hand corner of the document.
2. Begin keyboarding the story one-third of the way down the first page and one inch from the top of all following pages.
3. Double-space each story.
4. Indent each paragraph.
5. Use a pencil and the proper copy-editing symbols to correct errors on hard copy.
6. Make certain no words are divided and hyphenated at the end of a line and no paragraphs are divided across pages.
7. Print separate stories on separate pages, and do not use the back of pages.
8. If the story continues on a second page, type "more" at the bottom of the first page; type your name, the page number and the slug-line at the top of the second and subsequent pages; and type an end mark at the end of the story.
9. If the story originated outside your community, add the proper dateline.
10. Consult the appropriate directory to verify the spelling of all names used in the story; check these names every time they are used.

SUGGESTED READINGS AND USEFUL WEBSITES

Barber, Katherine. 2007. *Only in Canada, You Say: A Treasury of Canadian Language.* Don Mills, ON: Oxford University Press.

The Canadian Press Caps and Spelling. 2009. 19th edn. Patti Tasko, ed. Toronto: The Canadian Press.

The Canadian Press Stylebook: A Guide for Writers and Editors. 15th edn. 2008. Toronto: The Canadian Press.

Canadian Writer's Handbook. 5th edn. 2008. William E. Messenger et al., eds. Don Mills, ON: Oxford University Press.

Cook, Claire Kehrwald. 1985. *Line by Line: How to Edit Your Own Writing.* The Modern Language Association of America. Boston: Houghton Mifflin.

Editing Canadian English: The Essential Canadian Guide Revised and Updated. 2000. 2nd edn. Toronto: Editors' Association of Canada. (First published by Macfarlane Walter and Ross in 2000; second printing published by McClelland and Stewart in 2003).

Paperback Oxford Canadian Dictionary. 2006. 2nd edn. Katherine Barber, Heather Fitzgerald, Tom Howell, and Robert Pontisso, eds. Don Mills, ON: Oxford University Press.

Truss, Lynne. 2003. *Eats, Shoots & Leaves: The Zero Tolerance Approach to Punctuation.* New York: Penguin.

The Canadian Press:
http://www.thecanadianpress.com

Editors' Association of Canada:
http://www.editors.ca/index.htm

Sources for Students:
http://www.sources.com/students.htm

EXERCISE 1   Format and Copy-Editing Symbols

Using the proper copy-editing symbols, correct the errors in the following stories. Use the reference chart for copy-editing symbols on the inside of the front cover to help you. Use Appendix B for matters of CP style and Appendix C for help with possessives.

1. Background Investigations

for $150, threee retirde detective s will Help you investigate a potential date roommmate, emploeye or anyone else you are curous about.

one year ago, the detectivrs openedBackgroundds Unlimited and, for $150, will conduct a basic background investigation. The investigation includes on an examinatino of an Indi-viduals criminal record, driving record, employment history credit historyy and educational background

"People have started coming to us, askingus to on check there spouses, tenants nannies—anyone you nac can imagin," said Roger datolla, retired who after wworking 26 years for the city s police department,. HIS partners, Betsy Aaron and Myron Hansen, retired after 20years "We re friendds, and this seemed like a natural for us," Datolla said. "Were all familiar with the routnie, and its catching on faster than we expected. Of coarse, some people want us condcutt more detailed investigations, and we chagre more for that."

Lar ge corporations ask bBackgrounds Unlimited to investigate potential employes. "They want to find out about soneone before they hire the person, before its two late,"" Datolli continued "A charming personality isn't enough these days for someone loking for a good job. People in personnel offices realizze they can't rely on instinct, refences, or even diplomas or written employment histories. Its too easy to fake all that.plus, small businessses, especially, don"t have the contacts or know-how to conduct good background checks."

Aaronadded: "WE started fo off thinking almost all our worlk would be from businesses, mainly checking on ojb applicamnts, possibly employee thefts and that type of thing. Sudenly, we re getting other people, and that part of our business is mushrooming, almost half ofwhatdo we now. We ve had mothers comein,checking on guys their daughterss are dating, and couples checking onneighbors. We even had a colllege teacher ask u s to cheCk on a student he thought was dangereous.

2. Jury Award

A judge Monday ordered the cityy to pay $2.8 million too Caleb Draia, a thieve from Calgary shot in the back

A polic officer fired threee shotsat Dr aia, and one hit him, paralyzing him for live.

Draia admitted that he grabed a purse from 74 year old Celia Favata as she as was returning to hwrher car in parking lot at cColonial Mall. He pleaded guilty to a charge of robbary and was sentenced to five yearns in prison, a ternm he;s now serving.

Draias lawyer argued that the police were not justified in shooting, his client in the bcak as he fled. A judge agree, ruling that Draia was the victim of excessive, deadly policcpolice force.

Favata testified tht she was nearly chokked todeath. "I tried to holler for help, and he threatened to choke me to death if I didn't shut up," she said Her glassses were broken her dress torn, her nose bloodied and her left arm broken when Draia through her to tHE ground.

"Thiis wasn't just a mugigng," city atorney Allen Farci argud."This was really a case of attempted murder."

After Judge Marilyn PIcot annnounced her verdict, FAvata said: "Its not right. I never got 10 centts, and now this thug gets nearly $3 million. He deserved to be hurt,."

Police officer George Oldaker was shoppiing at the hall heard Favatas cries, and asw her lying injued on the ground. "Officer Oldaker was justified in shooting Draia because he was preventing the flight of a violent felon," the citey attorney argued. "Theirwas no other way to stop Draia, to keep from him escaping. N o one know who he was, so if he got away, chances were he'd never be CAUGHT."

Farci said hewill apppeal the judges decison. "Its ludicrous," he siad said. "This verdict sends a message to people that you can be rewarded if anything happens to you, even iff you're hurt while connitting a very serious crime. HE could've killed thtat poorold woman.

EXERCISE 2   Format and Copy-Editing Symbols

Using the proper copy-editing symbols, correct the errors in the following stories. Use the reference chart for copy-editing symbols on the inside of the front cover to help you.

1. Truancy

REGINA -- premier Brad wall is looking to change labour legislatiion on underage workers.

Earlier th is week, 20 15-yeearr-old Dairy Queen employees wer laid off in northwes Regina, becccause they were undreage according to Saskatchewan labour standard's legislation.

The legislation, which has been in effect since 1971, states: "you have to be at least 16 years old tO work in hotels, restaurants, educational institutions, hospitls and nursing homes."

The controversy around the ississue has Pemier Brad Wall and Advanced Eddducattion, Employment and Labour Minister Rob Norris talking abouttrying to change the legislation.

"It doesn't make a lot of sense that you CAN maybe pump gas and sell a person a muffin across a counter at a certain age, but you couldn't go acccross the street and hand a person a wrapped cheeseburge at a fAst food Place," said Wall, who was in White City discussing saskatchewan's role in thaNational Job Fair in Toronto.

Wall anndd Norris both ssaidd that safetyand ecudation for childrem is important, but that "commoonsense" is needed in labor legislation.

"As we look at the job market as it evolves in Ssaskchewan in the twenty-first century, its time that WE take a sensible appraoch," said Norris. "What that includes is having an iinfoormed approach, taking a look acrossjurisdictions... and common sense is goingg to prevail on this."

According to Wall, the Government was already looking at The legislaton before the layoffs happened, but the labour standards officer haad no choice But to followthe law.

"When a complaint is recieved and its the law of the province, I think there's a duty there to enforce that. But it doesn't Channge the fact that we need to find somme answers," Wallsaid.

However, Larry Hubich, president of the Saskatchewan Federation ofLabour, said that the soluution is more complex than justchanging Legislation.

"Why not change it in the Ohter direction and say, in odrder for you to work in any occupation in Saskatchewan, you need to be at least 16," hubich said.

"I would be very intersted in having a respectfuull and comprehensssive consultation on what is an apropriate age (to work) and to take into consideration What our inetrnational obligations are wiht respect to the minimum age for Child lbour."

He also said that truancy laws in the Province exist that reqiure childrem to be in shool until Thye turn 16.

2. Police Sting

tHe policehavearrested 114 people who thought they inherited $14,000.

"Most evrey criminal i s greedy," PoliceChief Barry Kopp errud said, "and we appealed to their greed."

THe police created a fictitious law firm, then spent $1,100 for a fake sign and for pprinting and postage send to letters to 441 peeple wanted on warrants issued in the past three year. Each leterletter was mailed to the persons last known a ddress and said the recipient had inherited $14,200 from a distaant relative. The letter set An appointment time for each person to come to the firm and pick up acheck.

Fourteen officers posing as lawyers and their asistants were assigned to donated space and workeed from there 8 a.m.to 9 p.m monday through Friday last week. Recipients who appeared to collect their money were led to a back room and quietly arrested.

Koperrud siad offficers are often unable to find people wanted on w arrants. "When we go to tyhere homes and try to pick these peopl up, we often mis s them, and that warnz them we're after them.They disappear, staying with friends or relatives or moving toother cities."

DetectiveManuel Cortez added: "Ths was a good tactic. I dont have any qualms about tell-ing a little white lie to criminls trying to ezcape the law. Be sides, it saved a tonn of money. Normally, too make these arrests would take hundreds of hoUrs of our time, and some of these people would commit new crimes before we caught hemthem, if we caught them at all."

MOst of the people policc arrested weer wanted for probation violations drunken driving writing bad checks failure to pay child support and other nonviolent crimes. However, seven were wanted for burglary, thee for car theft, thre for robbery and one for aiding an escape

EXERCISE 3   CP Style

Circle the correct CP style within the parentheses. Use the condensed *Canadian Press Stylebook* in Appendix B for help with your answers. Use Appendix C for help with possessives.

1. Sooyoung ran a red light at the intersection of Brown and Grant (Streets/streets).

2. The (prime minister/Prime Minister) will return to the (Parliament Buildings/parliament buildings) at 3 p.m.

3. The ophthalmologist's office is at (nine/9) Westwind (Avenue/avenue/Ave./ave.).

4. Emily is taking a course in the (Sociology/sociology) and (English/english) (Departments/departments).

5. Copy-editing symbols have not changed much since the (1920s/1920's).

6. Only (three/3) (%/per cent/percent) of the U.S. population in 2003 bought duct tape and plastic for their windows when (President/president) Bush put the country on high alert for terrorist attacks.

7. (Mrs. Fred Greene/Josephine Greene) won the (womans/womens/woman's/women's) (golf/Golf) (Tournament/tournament).

8. The (winter's/Winter's) lowest temperature was (minus/−) (fourty/forty/40) (degree's/degrees/°).

9. One of the (potato/potatoe) sacks weighted (4/four) (lbs./pounds), and the other weighed (11/eleven) (oz./ounces).

10. The Italian flag is (red, white, and green/red; white; and green/red, white and green/red, white & green).

11. Many people in Canada and the (US/U.S./United States/united states) are worried about the SARS (Virus/virus).

12. The textbook cost (forty dollars/40 dollars/$40).

EXERCISE 4   cp **Style**

Circle the correct cp style within the parentheses. Use the condensed *Canadian Press Stylebook* in Appendix B for help with your answers. Use Appendix C for help with possessives. Answer Key provided; see Appendix D.

1. The (priest/Priest) (said/celebrated) (Mass/mass) during their marriage ceremony.

2. Morgan's new book is (entitled/titled) ("Rachael's New Glasses"/*Rachael's New Glasses*).

3. Her (dad/Dad) celebrates his birthday in (August/Aug.).

4. The jury found him (not guilty/innocent).

5. The miniature ponies were (reared/raised) in Elliott (county/County).

6. The mayor lives at (forty-nine/fourty-nine/49) Morning Glory (Street/St.).

7. Seven of the (people/persons) in the room were reading newspapers.

8. (Jean and Diane's/Jean's and Diane's) room was in a mess.

9. Neither Jason nor his friends (was/were) going to the party.

10. The wine was bottled in (October 2002/Oct. 2002/October, 2002).

11. Most news organizations want a reporter with a (Bachelor's degree/Bachelor degree/bachelor degree/bachelor's degree) in journalism.

12. The (Police/police) clocked the (mayor/Mayor) going (thirty/30) (km/h/k.m.h/kilometres per hour) over the speed limit.

13. The address is (twenty-one/21) Merryweather (Road/Rd.)

14. She will remember (September 11, 2001/Sept. 11, 2001,) always.

15. Manuel (Middlebrooks, Jr./Middlebrooks Jr.) works for the (Canadian Security Intelligence Service/C.S.I.S./CSIS).

EXERCISE 5   cp **Style and Copy Editing**

Use the proper copy-editing symbols to correct the mechanical, spelling and stylistic errors in the following sentences. Refer to *The Canadian Press Stylebook* in Appendix B, the common writing errors on the inside of the book's back cover, and the copy-editing symbols on the inside of the front cover to help you.

Remember that none of the possessives has been formed for you. If you need help in forming the possessives, see the guidelines in Appendix C.

1. Next Summer, Maurice Reimer, an accountant with an office on Bender Ave., wants to buy a 4-door toyota avalon that costs about 29000 dollars.

2. Atty. Miguel Acevedo, who lives on Bell Ave. said his seven-yr.-old son received serious injuries when hit by the drunk driver in a ford van.

3. Canadian Senator Connie Mack, a conservative from Alberta, said the social security system is bankrupt and, in ten years, the Federal Government will slash its benefits.

4. Prof. Denise Bealle, a member of the History Dept., estimated that one third of her students will seek a Masters Degree within 5 years.

5. Fire totally destroyed the Dries Manufacturing Company at 3130 River Rd., and the damage is estimated at 4,000,000 to 5,000,000 dollars.

6. The boy, an 18 year old College Freshman, arrived in Flin Flon Man.at 12 noon and will stay until February 14th.

7. 50 youths met in the YMCA at 3010 1st Avenue yesterday and agreed to return at 7:00PM October 4 to view the film titled Sports.

8. Irregardless of the investigations outcome, the thirty two White youths at Colonial high school want Mr. Tony Guarinno to continue as their Coach.

9. During the 1920s, the Federal Government allocated 820000 dollars for the project, and Mrs. Mildred Berg, who has a Ph.D. in Sociology, said 8% of the money was wasted.

10. On February 14 1996 the temperature fell to 0 in Moosejaw Saskatchewan and on February 15th it fell to -14.

11. Yesterday the United States President promised that the United States Congress would help the flood victims in Miss., Ala., Ga., and La.

12. He wants to duplicate copies of the e mail he received last Spring and to mail copies to 8 members of the Eastwind Homeowners Assn.

13. The jury reached their verdict at 12 midnight November 4th, finding Kevin Blohm, age 41, not guilty of the 3 charges.

14. Doctor Rachael Rosolowski, of Toronto, said the X rays taken yesterday reveal that the Popes cancer is spreading.

15. Police said the ford mustang driven by Anne Capiello of 8210 University Boulevard was traveling sixty mph when it collided with a tree at the corner of Wilson and Hampshire Avenues.

16. The building on Grand Av. was totally demolished during the 1990s, and the state legislature yesterday voted 120-14 to spend 14,300,000 million dollars to rebuild it.

17. Four fifths of the hispanic medical students said they watched the television program entitled "ER" at 10:00PM last Thur. night.

18. 24 women, led by Prof. Maxine Cessarini, met at 9:00p.m. last night and concluded that their childrens 3rd grade teacher lacks a Bachelors Degree and lied at the P.T.A. meeting held last Aug. 29th.

EXERCISE 6   CP **Style and Copy Editing**

Use the proper copy-editing symbols to correct mechanical, spelling and stylistic errors in the following sentences. For help, refer to *The Canadian Press Stylebook* in Appendix B and to the common writing errors on inside of the book's back cover.

Remember that none of the possessives has been formed for you. If you need help in forming the possessives, see the guidelines in Appendix C.

1. After earning her Masters Degree the Mayor of Lethbridge Alberta resigned and, on January 1st, established the Alberto Corporation at 8192 South Hawkins Dr.

2. On September 27 2005 Haitian born Michaelle Jean made history by becoming the 1st black Governor General of Canada and the 2nd immigrant in a row named to be Canada's titular head of state.

3. Ms. Delta Comanche, the Companys Number 1 choice for the job of Head of Purchasing, estimated that 80% of the Department Heads favor the new Plan.

4. In January as the Priest celebrated a high mass at St. Margaret Mary Church on Park Ave., Ronal Sheppard, Junior, age 3, fell asleep.

5. The Canadian Civil Liberties Association (C.C.L.A.) was founded in Toronto Ontario in 1964 to defend civil rights country-wide and uphold the constitution.

6. The ford mustang driven by a white male in his 20s sped South on Pennsylvania Av., then turned left onto Franklin Dr. at speeds up to 80 m.p.h.

7. Chapter 20 in the book entitled Wasteful Solutions charges that in May, 2004 the parliamentary committee wasted 2 to 2.3 million dollars sightseeing in the gaspésie and the Queen Charlotte islands.

8. James Eastland, III, a Lieutenant Colonel in the Canadian forces, received an M.A. in Business Administration and will speak at 2:00pm Sunday afternoon to the Small Business Owners Assn. at 626 North 3rd Street.

9. Reverend Audrey Van Pelt, of 420 North Wilkes Rd., arrived October 20th at 6:00 p.m. in a white Cadillac he bought last Summer.

10. The twelve youths from Montreal Quebec said yesterday that their number one fear is the rising cost of College tuition.

11. The President of People's Gas Company said the new building at 1840 North Hampton Rd. will cost $12,400,000 dollars and be completed in 2 years.

12. Two teenagers saw the 8 year old boy in a car and said the driver was about 30, 6 ft. tall, and weighed 180 lbs.

13. The conference started at 12 noon yesterday and, ten minutes later, the groups President introduced the 3 MPs from Ont.

CHAPTER 21

14. Prof. Mayerline Valderama of Kelowna British Columbia arrived for work on February 23 2004 when two college Freshmen, both majoring in Political science, stepped towards her and demanded her resignation.

15. The clubs Vice-President said his seven year old son found a wallet containing $1434, and that 7 persons have claimed it.

16. Afterwards, the Sask. Premier estimated that 1/4 the teenagers and 80% of their parents favor tougher standards, but implementing them would cost $1,000,000,000 a year.

17. The woman was born in the town of Cache Creek in January 1986 and is minoring in german. At 8:00pm Tuesday night, she attended a meeting of the German Friendship Assn. with 3 friends.

18. After leaving the official residence on Sussex Drive, Prime Min. Stephen Harper retired from the Federal Government and moved to southern British Columbia but continued to meet with conservative leaders.

22 | Becoming a Professional

All media work us over completely. They are so pervasive in their personal, political, economic, aesthetic, psychological, moral, ethical and social consequences that they leave no part of us untouched, unaffected, unaltered. The medium is the message. Any understanding of social and cultural change is impossible without a knowledge of the way media work as environments.

— Marshall McLuhan, *The Medium Is the Message*, 1967

Journalists are passionate about their work. They find their jobs varied, creative, important and challenging. Perhaps more than people in any other profession, journalists witness the kaleidoscope of the life within their communities: the good and the bad, the joyous and the tragic, the significant and the mundane.

Longtime investigator and journalistic trailblazer Stevie Cameron once commented on the basic purpose of good journalism and in that comment indicated a touchstone of the craft: "I've always figured my job is simple: to tell people what I know—within the laws of good taste and libel. Readers should know what the insiders know, and that's what I have tried to do here." Even earlier, writer and journalist Robertson Davies insisted that good journalism requires rather more than craft; it requires a sense of mission: "A journalist is not something which just happens. Like poets, they are born. They are marked by a kind of altruistic nosiness."

Journalists represent the public when they cover a story. They ask questions as members of society. By providing citizens with the information they need to be well informed, journalists perform a vital function for a democratic society.

In addition to obtaining information to make events and issues understandable for the public, journalists get to do something else inspiring and fun: they get to write and tell stories. And telling a good story—selecting the important facts, the correct words, the proper organization—is a highly creative process. It is also challenging. Always working to deadlines, journalists often have to summarize complex topics in clear, accurate stories that will interest, inform and enlighten the public. Once the story is released, it may be read, heard or seen by thousands of people. Since the advent of online communications and the profusion of social media sites, those same readers, listeners and viewers, in ever greater numbers, are also now able to respond and interact not only with the news media who originate the story but also, and more radically, with each other.

Students who major in journalism learn how to write well, communicate clearly and do research. Even more foundational, they come to understand the concept of "objectivity"— a concept much contested by the upstart "underground" journalists of the 1960s—as a yardstick not of elitist non-involvement and dissimulation but of basic fairness and as an antidote to the use of the privileged platform journalists enjoy for self-promotion or promotion of particular points of view. Aspiring journalists learn, in other words, to understand the importance of the search for truth (without fear or favour) and of the balanced reporting that is its trademark. Balanced reporting fully represents the issues and treasures a diversity of voices (as opposed to rounding up the usual suspects and "speechifiers"). Objectivity means asking (lots of) questions before proposing to provide answers, and it implicitly recognizes that there are always more than two sides to a story. What objectivity doesn't mean is the kind of detachment from a story that amounts to "playing it safe" rather than seeking the truth.

In *The Pickton File*, Stevie Cameron departed from her usual areas of expertise to document and shed light on the largest criminal investigation in Canadian history (over the disappearances and, as it would turn out, murders of dozens of women from Vancouver's stricken Downtown Eastside). In the opening chapter of the book, she explained why:

> And though I knew people would ask why I was moving away from politics and white-collar crime, I was quite frankly sick of the same old frauds, the same corrupt politicians trying the same old scams, almost always successfully—and when they were caught and charged, they almost always emerged with very few penalties because of political interference and incompetent policing. What particularly concerned me was the bland assumption that there was a big difference between white-collar and blue-collar crime and that a slap on the wrist—a couple of months in jail or a big fine—would be enough for a crook in a suit, regardless of how much he had stolen or how many lives he'd ruined. For a long time, I have believed that the criminal mind is the same whether the perpetrator is a politician or another well-educated professional, or a drug smuggler, gang member or killer. In both groups there are psychopaths with no regard for the law. In fact, both white-collar criminals and violent criminals delight in breaking the law. Getting away with it is half the thrill.

Lindsay Kines, the reporter who broke the story of the missing women for the *Vancouver Sun*, believes that mastering the craft of journalism has everything to do with developing sources (by showing them that you are a trustworthy reporter) and digging for the truth:

> I've never called myself an investigative reporter. I'm just a reporter. But I believe that any good reporting, by definition, should be investigative. Covering the police beat improved my reporting immensely, because that's where I first learned how to develop and work with sources.... If I hadn't been covering the police for six years, I don't believe officers would have trusted me enough to tell me about the myriad problems with the original missing-women investigation.

The strengths of communicating well are critically important in all areas of human endeavour, from engineering to fine art. And knowing how to write well has one great payoff: journalists can switch their careers and still remain within the communication arena, using the skills they learned as students and practitioners of journalism. Print reporters often become public relations practitioners; broadcast journalists move into print reporting; and magazine writers produce stories online. Hard-news reporters who no longer want the stress of quick deadlines can become wonderful feature writers; reporters who have developed expertise in given subjects and hard-earned style often author books. As well, in this age of convergence and digital/multimedia journalism, professional reporters might write a story for the newspaper, layer it with video for the web, and tell it in a stand-up to TV audiences.

Being able to think clearly and write concisely are advantages in almost any industry, not just journalism. One journalism graduate who enjoyed art landed a job in a metropolitan museum. Her ability to capture an artist's work in a few words was of great benefit when writing captions for creative works on display. A First Nations student who graduated with a journalism degree went on to found her own aboriginal communications company.

A JOURNALIST'S ATTRIBUTES

News executives want job applicants who are intelligent and well informed and who have a sense of the news—what is happening in the community and what people want to know. They want talented writers: good grammarians who can spell and write clearly and accurately. They also want applicants who are prepared to report, write or edit.

The news industry seeks applicants who are honest, curious, aggressive, self-starting and dedicated. The best applicants are also clearly committed to careers in journalism, willing to sacrifice and likely to stay in their jobs for several years. Editors and news directors look for applicants who show a long-term interest in journalism. They want applicants who have demonstrated their desire to be journalists, perhaps by working for student media, freelancing or working at an internship. Kim Bolan, famed for her courageous coverage over decades of the 1985 Air India bombing and its aftermath, is the author of *Loss of Faith: How the Air India Bombers Got Away with Murder* (McClelland and Stewart, 2005). She epitomizes the sense of social obligation and dedication that characterize the best journalists:

> I call it my *sewa* because that's what the Sikhs have always told me: It's your *sewa*. In Sikhism, *sewa* is a tenet of the religion; you have to serve selflessly, without any gain coming back to you, and that's your service—your *sewa*. ... So I use *sewa* to describe it, regardless of whether it's a Sikh story or not. I do have a sense of service toward my community.

Editors interviewing prospective new hires look for energy, for commitment to the news business, and for a willingness to take work home. After that, they looked for knowledge, ability and judgment. Most publishers and editors agree that applicants should have imagination, energy, a flair for risks, a passion for long hours and demanding deadlines, and that indefinable sense of service and relevance known as a "nose for news."

Applicants should also be familiar with how government works at all levels; be able to cope with deadline pressures; and possess an adequate general background in economics, history, literature, philosophy, science and math.

About 75 per cent of all newcomers to the field come directly from college or university journalism programs. Editors are impressed by graduates who have developed an added expertise in some area of specialization, such as medicine, science, the arts or the environment. Partly for that reason, many of the students who major in journalism also minor in another field.

Smaller newspapers, broadcasting stations and public relations firms often hire applicants who can operate a video or digital camera, can work with information in spreadsheet or database programs, or can demonstrate proficiency in online/Internet communications. Knowing how to do more than one job is always an advantage. Good copy editors, for instance, are in perpetual demand in the newspaper industry; students who excel at copy editing should highlight that expertise in their applications. Learning and practising many skills while in school also gives students the chance to learn from their mistakes in an environment where learning is emphasized and penalties generally include second chances. Mistakes "out in the world," on the other hand, can lead to a firing, not just to a bad mark or a teacher's reprimand.

BE THE APPLICANT WHO GETS HIRED

William Ruehlmann, author of *Stalking the Feature Story*, tells of one of his first attempts at finding a newspaper job. He arrived in town a couple of days ahead of his scheduled interview, wrote three feature stories and submitted them to the paper as freelance pieces. The day he went in for the interview, the paper had already published one of his stories. He got the job.

Lori Culbert also got the job she was seeking at a major big-city daily through passionate perseverance and by unconventional means:

> I guess I ended up in Vancouver [at the *Vancouver Sun*] because I irritated the deputy managing editor so much. I was emailing and faxing him story ideas every day

for about three months, and he finally said to me, "If I give you a job for three months will you stop writing to me?" . . . I was determined to get onto a broadsheet. And it was at a time when there weren't a lot of newspapers hiring. So I just kept sending them story ideas and I would critique the paper every day and then send them followup ideas for the stories.

Culbert added: "That's not necessarily good advice. I'm sure there are editors who would just tell you to go away." Still, Culbert's strategy does reflect the kind of determination required not only to land the job but also to do the job.

Internships

Successful journalism students obtain some experience while still in school. Many students start by working for campus publications. As their skills mature, they may freelance or work part-time for a local public relations firm, Internet company or news organization. Internships enable students to acquire more job experience and become better acquainted with the editors who hire regular staff members. Such experience provides a variety of benefits: it demonstrates a student's commitment to journalism, improves professional skills and provides the clips, tapes or online stories that students need to obtain jobs when they graduate. Nearly three-fourths of the journalism graduates who find media-related jobs have worked somewhere as interns.

One news editor explained the value of internships this way: "It's just not enough to have a degree. We look for someone who has interned, worked for the school newspaper and who has a pile of clips so we don't have to play journalism school." Another news executive added: "Somehow, some way, the real gutsy students will find a summer newspaper job. We are impressed with them. They show us that they are actively pursuing a journalism career. And they can offer us something other than a journalism degree: experience."

The media employ thousands of interns every summer. Many news organizations have internship programs in which a recruiter schedules a day at a college or university to see all applicants who want an interview. Large organizations often set an early application deadline, such as November or December, for the following summer's internships. Unfortunately, many students do not interview with national or metropolitan news organizations because they assume they are not good enough to be chosen. This is not always the case. Sometimes, students who sign up with recruiters to practise their interviewing skills win a job because they are at ease in the meeting.

Many students work as interns for smaller news organizations or their hometown newspaper, radio or TV station, or website. Motivated students simply visit the business and ask for an internship. Managers might provide internships because they feel an obligation to support journalism education or because they want to help students get ahead in the field. Editors also use internships to observe talented young journalists whom they might want to employ after graduation.

Bert Freeman/Alamy

For journalists working abroad, an international press card can be useful. For example, the international press card offered by the International Federation of Journalists confirms that the cardholder is a working journalist and can help journalists gain access to media events and official meetings.

Where to Look for a Job

Metropolitan news organizations look for people with several years of solid professional experience, but students who have had an internship at the news organization often have a good chance of being hired, since the internship is the traditional way into the business.

New graduates should consider working at smaller news organizations. Smaller media receive fewer applications and are more likely to accept applicants with less experience. Also, jobs at smaller news operations often provide better experience because they offer journalists a variety of assignments and greater responsibilities. The experience that young journalists gain working in a smaller market enables them to find jobs at metropolitan news organizations later. Many award-winning Canadian journalists who rose to the top of their profession began their careers at small media organizations; as well, many fine journalists happily spend their whole careers at smaller, community media papers and still manage to write stories that win them well-deserved recognition. Another avenue for gaining valuable and marketable experience and skills is to work for a newsletter or other specialized publication that focuses on a specific topic such as criminal justice, oil spills or aerospace.

Graduates seeking journalism jobs should consult professional magazines and websites that cover specialized areas of the industry and often feature announcements of job openings. Students also should check for job listings or consider posting their resumés on the websites of professional organizations such as the Canadian Association of Journalists (www.caj.ca), the Canadian Science Writers' Association (www.sciencewriters.ca), and the Canadian Public Relations Society (www.cprs.ca). Students who attend conventions of these professional groups also can make valuable contacts for jobs.

The Cover Letter, Resumé and Portfolio

A resumé is an opportunity for an applicant to highlight and summarize his or her work experience and skills to a prospective employer. If candidates apply for a position through traditional or electronic mail, they send their resumé with a cover letter and work samples. If candidates apply for the position in person, they submit the resumé and work samples when they fill out and turn in the company's job application form.

The cover letter should be addressed to the specific individual at a news organization who is responsible for hiring and focus on the particular position for which the candidate is applying. A cover letter may include information supplemental to the applicant's resumé, or it may highlight important points about the applicant for the editor to note. Successful applicants stress their particular strengths that can help the company. A good cover letter begins as would a news story, with a lead that will capture the attention of the reader. It often ends with the applicant's displaying initiative by promising to call the editor in a few days to schedule an appointment. Wording for the cover letter should be specific, concise and direct. After all, applicants who cannot present a well-written cover letter may be advertising that they lack journalistic skills as well.

Resumé formats vary, but the layout and content of the resumé is designed to give a prospective employer a good understanding of the applicant within 30 seconds. Readability is a key ingredient. A cluttered resumé is too hard to read quickly, and one with too much space wastes time. Too many underscores and bold characters lose their purpose of making a few important points stand out.

Work samples are duplicated legibly and pertain to the job position. They represent the strongest examples of an applicant's work. Applicants may use their cover letters to direct a prospective editor's attention to important points about their stories. For example, the applicant might write that the story was written within a 30-minute deadline or describe the lengths the writer went to in finding a crucial fact. The best way to manage a portfolio of work samples is to regularly scan published clippings to an electronic format such as Portable Document Format (PDF). Electronic storage makes it easy to sort and arrange stories, choosing the best work to be attached to each email application or printed out for a hard-copy application. Just as with old-style paper clippings (or "clips"), the scanned documents should include the publication's name, page number, and date of publication—preferably scanned from the top of the actual page in the newspaper. Providing this information makes it easy for a prospective employer to confirm that the applicant wrote the piece for publication.

The Job Interview

When an applicant's cover letter, resumé and clips impress an editor, the applicant may be invited for an interview, a critical step in obtaining a job. When applicants appear for an interview, they bring evidence of commitment and experience, such as additional clips or other samples of their work.

An applicant's appearance in an interview is important. Studies show that most employers of new journalism graduates say that a candidate's overall appearance influences their opinion about the candidate. Non-traditional attire—body piercings, obvious tattoos, unusual hair colour and unusual hairstyles—negatively influence potential employers. Every applicant should appear clean, neat and in appropriate business attire. An applicant's appearance should not detract from what an applicant has to say.

During a typical interview, an applicant is likely to meet managers and editors and other members of a news organization's staff. Successful applicants are enthusiastic, honest, confident, consistent and positive. They use the person's name and speak in a relaxed yet assertive voice.

The editors will want to learn more about the applicant: strengths, personality, interests and intelligence. They will want to know about an applicant's expectations and understanding of journalism. Is the applicant realistic about the salary range and aware that work might include evenings, weekends and holidays? If the applicant wants to be a columnist, editorial writer or parliamentary correspondent, it could take several years to achieve that goal. If the applicant wants to be a foreign correspondent, the ability to speak foreign languages is an advantage.

During an interview, editors might ask questions like the following:

- What can you tell me about yourself?

- What books and magazines have you read during the last month or two?

- Why do you want to be a journalist?

- Why should I hire you?

- What are your short- and long-range goals?

- What is it that you like about this particular company?

- What would you like to know about us (the news organization and company that owns it)?

Kent University in Britain offers additional questions commonly asked during an interview and tips for handling the responses at http://www.kent.ac.uk/careers/interviews/ivjournalism.htm. Employers look for answers that provide evidence of an applicant's commitment, intelligence and initiative.

Applicants ask questions too. Questions that are thoughtful and informed impress interviewers. Applicants ask about assignments or opportunities for advancement. They are prepared to talk intelligently about the news industry generally and media organizations specifically. Successful candidates will have studied the company and the area before the interview. They also will have examined recent editions of the newspaper (printed or online), newsletter, newscast or website publication they are applying to.

Applicants should be ready to give three references who are previous employers, professors or other individuals knowledgeable about the applicant's accomplishments and work ethic.

After the interview, applicants write a letter or email thanking the editors and expressing a continued interest in the job. If they are not hired immediately, they continue to write to the editors every few months, submitting fresh clips or other samples of work.

When offered a job, it is important to understand the offer. Is it a full-time position? Does it begin with a probation period? If so, how long is that probation, and will the salary increase when probation is over? What do company benefits include, such as insurance coverage? Also, will the company provide a car for reporters and photographers? If not, will the company pay mileage and other expenses?

Job Testing

Increasingly, news organizations test job applicants. Some also test current employees who want a promotion. The tests range from simple typing exams to more elaborate tests of an applicant's personality, mental ability, management skills and knowledge of current events. News organizations everywhere are also testing applicants for drugs. Almost all news organizations that give entry-level tests want to learn more about applicants' ability to spell and knowledge of grammar and punctuation. Most also test writing ability, and others check reporting and copy-editing skills. To test their writing skills, applicants might be asked to write a story summarizing information from rough notes.

Starting Salaries

Generally, people with better education and more experience earn higher salaries. Earnings for entry-level journalists depend on the type of job and the size, location and type of news organization. Many new reporters double their salaries in five years, especially if they move to larger markets. However, many journalists decide to stay where they are because they like their particular job, news organization or community.

The news industry is undergoing rapid change at the time of writing, making current and reliable figures hard to come by, but updated data on journalists' salaries can be found by consulting Statistics Canada labour force surveys and sites like the one sponsored by the Canadian Journalism Foundation (see Suggested Readings and Useful Websites at the end of this chapter).

Newsroom Organization and Procedure

Most journalism graduates who work for print or broadcast news organizations begin as reporters. As new reporters, they might spend the first several weeks in their offices, completing minor assignments that enable them to become better acquainted with their employers' policies while enabling supervisors to evaluate their work more closely. Or, to become better acquainted with a city, newcomers might follow experienced reporters on their beats. Each beat involves a topic that is especially newsworthy or a location where news is likely to happen.

More experienced reporters have beats, often a specific building such as the city hall, the local courthouse, or federal building. Other beats involve broader topics rather than a geographical location. Some of the most common of these beats are local politics (city hall), business, education, religion and features. Larger news organizations establish dozens of more specialized beats, covering such topics as agriculture, environment, art, medicine, science and consumer affairs. This system promotes efficiency because reporters become experts on the topics they cover and cultivate important sources of information. Reporters often remain on the same beats for several years, become well acquainted with their sources, and obtain information from them more easily than they could from strangers.

On a typical day, the reporter assigned to cover, say, the city hall for a medium-sized morning daily or TV station will arrive at the office at about 9 a.m. The reporter might write minor stories left from the previous day, scan other newspapers, TV newscasts, or websites covering the area, rewrite minor news releases, or study issues in the news. He or she is likely to confer with an editor about major stories expected to arise that day and then go to the city hall about 10 a.m. During the next hour or two, the reporter will stop in all the major offices in the city hall, especially those of the mayor, council members, city clerk, city treasurer and city attorney. He or she will return to the newsroom and quickly write all the day's stories. Other reporters, meanwhile, will be gathering information from their respective beats. A few reporters might not

CP PHOTO/Edmonton Sun–Darryl Dyck

Alberta NDP Leader Brian Mason responds to questions from journalism students at Grant MacEwan College in Edmonton. Mason was a guest speaker at their class and then allowed the students to scrum him in small groups to ask questions.

even begin work until 3 or 4 p.m. The time that journalists report to work depends on the news organization's deadline. TV stations usually have several newscasts: early morning, noon, evening and night. Most newspapers have morning editions (in the days before computers, many newspapers published afternoon editions or even multiple editions). Some newspapers with morning editions have their copy to the printers by midnight. However, new technologies and digital transmission mean reporters no longer have just one deadline; they may be constantly updating and revising stories for the web or for broadcast as they develop new information. Copy editors at morning newspapers typically come to work in the afternoon and work until the final edition is published, which could be after midnight. At an afternoon daily, copy editors might start their shift at 6 a.m. and finish about 3 p.m.

The Industry Needs More Women and Minorities

Traditionally, white men have made up the work force in media organizations. As organizational experts have found in businesses around the world, managers hire and promote people most like themselves. This situation has made it difficult for women and minorities to be hired and promoted. A goal for some news organizations is to have the same percentage of women and of racial and ethnic minorities as is found in the community or the Canadian population.

FREELANCE WRITING

Students often dream of becoming freelance writers. As freelancers, the students imagine, they will be able to set their own hours, write only about topics that interest them, pursue those topics in greater depth, sell their stories to prestigious national magazines, and live comfortably on their earnings.

Getting a start as a freelancer is sometimes difficult. It takes time to understand what editors want. Once editors accept a freelancer's work for the first time, however, they will often accept it many more times because they have become familiar with the freelancer's writing and reliability. Once a relationship has begun, editors sometimes ask freelancers they already know to write special articles. As well, magazine editors generally consult other magazine editors in the search for reliable writers (especially when an assignment given to a freelancer has failed to work out—in a pinch, in other words).

Freelance writing can also be an enjoyable hobby or part-time pursuit. It provides another outlet for people who like to write and enables them to supplement their income from other jobs. Beginners are most likely to sell their articles to smaller publications, such as special-interest or city magazines. These publications might not pay as much as *Chatelaine*, but they receive fewer manuscripts and are much less demanding. A freelancer's indispensable tool is a book titled *The Canadian Writer's Market*. This guide, updated frequently, lists hundreds of markets for freelance writers and describes the types of articles each publication wants to buy and the fees it pays. Because the Canadian magazine market is relatively small, those wishing to pursue a full-time freelance writing career should also consult the *American Writer's Market*, updated annually, to avail themselves of a larger potential market for their work.

CHECKLIST FOR FINDING THE RIGHT JOURNALISM JOB

1. In what type of atmosphere can you work best—an online news organization where new technology skills are used every day; a magazine, which has longer deadlines; a television station where talent for oral presentation is valued; a small newspaper that uses its entry-level reporters to do just about everything? Decide also where you want to live and work.

2. Working in a professional newsroom increases your experience, your work samples, your references, and your ability to ask good questions during an interview. Also, internships might help you decide where you do not want to work, instead of finding out too late at your first professional job.

3. Your cover letter should be one page, creative (not cutesy) and error-free. Use the name of the recruiter. The cover letter is the first part of your first impression.

4. Your application is the opportunity to tell someone about yourself—work experience, awards, special skills such as computer-assisted reporting, travel and foreign languages.

5. Some recruiters skip the resumé and go straight to the work samples. Send a variety that will let an employer know what you can do. Add a short explanation of your work to every sample.

6. Include the names, titles and telephone numbers of three or four people who know your work. Former employers are best; professors are fine. Make sure your references can speak to your abilities as a journalist.

7. Learn what you can about the news organization where you'll interview. Go to its website; read several issues of the newspaper; watch several broadcasts; and look it up in directories for objective information on the media outlet you're targeting.

8. Dress in business attire. Bring several sets of the same or additional work samples. Ask recruiters questions that make them think, such as questions about competitive pressures or the news organization's long-term goals. Show enthusiasm for being a journalist. Before leaving, obtain the recruiter's email address or telephone number.

9. Send a thank-you note within five days of the interview. Briefly review your skills and touch on something the recruiter said in the interview. Call or email the recruiter if you haven't heard anything by the deadline given you. Remember to respect publication deadline cycles when making calls.

10. If you don't get the job, still thank the recruiter and ask what can be done to better your chances. You might consider reapplying to the same organization later.

SUGGESTED READINGS AND USEFUL WEBSITES

Bly, Robert W. 2006. *Secrets of a Freelance Writer: How to Make $100,000 a Year or More*. New York: Owl Books.

Brewer, Robert Lee. 2009. *2010 Writer's Market*. Cincinnati: Writers Digest Books.

Cormack, Paul G., and Murphy O. Shewchuk, eds. 2002. *The Canadian Writer's Guide*. 13th edn. Markham, ON: Fitzhenry and Whiteside.

Formichelli, Linda, and Diana Burrell. 2005. *The Renegade Writer: A Totally Unconventional Guide to Freelance Writing Success*. 2nd edn. Portland, OR: Marion Street Press.

Tooze, Sandra. 2007. *The Canadian Writer's Market*. 17th edn. Toronto: McClelland and Stewart.

Wylie, Betty Jane. 2003. *The Write Track: How to Succeed as a Freelance Writer in Canada*. 2nd edn. Toronto: Dundurn Press.

The Future of Journalism as a Career: http://thelinknewspaper.ca/articles/1694

Canadian Association of Journalists National Conference 2003: http://www.chrysalisgroup.com/knowledgeNE1.htm

Discussions on Charging for Web Access: http://www.nowtoronto.com/news/webjam.cfm?content=168424&archive=28,28,2009

Free Speech: http://thetyee.ca/Views/2006/10/23/FreeSpeech

Copy-Editing Practice

Using copy-editing symbols and a pencil, and referring to your *Canadian Press Stylebook, Caps and Spelling* and *Oxford Canadian Dictionary*, make all the necessary corrections to the news stories that follow. Look for errors in grammar, spelling, punctuation and CP style. There are three review tests (with three stories in Test A, two stories in Test B, and one story in Test C). When you've completed each test, check your work against the original versions of these stories (you'll find stories A1 and A2 in Chapter 12, story A3 in Chapter 10, and stories B2, B3 and C1 in Chapter 7). Each test contains a total of 100 errors, so you can count the errors you've found and corrected and so gauge your progress in terms of a percentage grade. If capital letters are needed for terms such as "House of Commons," capitalizing the "h" in "house" and the "c" in "commons" counts as one error/correction (not two).

COPY EDITING REVIEW TEST A

A1 12 January 1998

SAINT JOHN, N.B.— After a bitterly cold nite in eastern Ontario and Quebec, the largest military and civilian disaster effort in canadian history continues today in an effort to bring releif to hundreds of thousand's of people struggling without light and heat.

Quebec premier Lucien Bouchard appealled to Montrealers to stay home from work today, leaving roads clear for hydro crews and there military helpers.

He also urged people suffering without electricity to leave their homes and move in with friends and relatives—or join the estimated 100,000 Quebeckers already living in emergency shelters.

"I'm appealing to all Quebeckers who have electricity to get in touch with relatives and friends in difficulty to invite them, even persuade them, to come to they're house," Bouchard said. "People must realize they can't stay at home without heat if, as we expect, tempertures start dropping."

Bouchard said the condition's at emergency shelters are barely adaquate.

"They're are 1200 to 1500 people in the same room sleeping side by side," he said. "They are often depending on generators which supply the mininum power. The best solution is to go to live with friends or family.

Shelters in both provinces were getting mixed reviews.

"I feel like I can cry," said 78-year-old Eleanor Mott, who has been in an emegency shelter in Vankleek Hill, Ont., midway between Ottawa and Montreal, for 3 days. "Its like World

War Two. But its good here. They have done very well and deserve credit. The army, to. They

couldn't of been better."

Elsewhere, overcrowding and lack of supplies was fraying tempers. A woman clutching her

baby at a shelter in St-Jean-sur-Richelieu, Que., described the emergency acommodation as "hell."

"I'd rather go to be with the Devil than stay here any longer," she said. "I just can't take it

anymore."

Hundreds of people at another shelter in Ste. Julie, Que., were happier after dining yester-

day on donated filet mignon, lobster tails and shrimp.

Robberies and break-ins have been rare in the effected areas. About 600 police cars are

patrolling darkened Montreal streets and 1,300 officers—three times the usual number—are

on duty. City police arrested seventeen people for robbery and car theft Saturday night—fewer

than usual—and detained others for attempting to smuggle beer into shelters.

A2 7 November 1991

MONTREAL (CP)—For years, critics of orthodox cancer treatments have charged that a multi-

billion-dollar cancer industry suppresses alternative therapies.

Many believe the controversy owes it's persistance to the "failure" of orthodox

treatments.

"What's fueling the whole debate is that orthodox methods have failed miserably ... in

terms of treatment, its a stalemate situation at best," said Ralph Moss, author of *The Cancer

Industry* and former assistant director of public affairs for the Memorial Sloan-Kettering cancer

center in new York.

"After all, you don't see too many unorthodox treatments for polio."

Many alternative therapies are based on strenghening the body's immune system rather than

destroying malignant tissue. They are sometimes used in Mexico, the Bahamas and alternative

clinics in the United States.

However, radiation, chemotherapy and surgery remain the only "proven" treatments and

the only one's covered under government and private health-care insurance plans.

"With chemotherapies, which are given to the vast majority of people with cancer, we clearly have no evidence of survival benefit for 80 percent of people taking them," said Frank Wiewel, Executive Director of People Against Cancer.

"Chemotherapy is the snake oil of the '90s," said Wiewel, whose Iowa-based patient advocate group distributes information about alternative treatments to thousands of members around the world. "It is for all practical purposes an unproven therapy used for profit—the US Senate's own definition of quackery."

Doctor Shocked

"Thats incredible," said Dr. Jack Laidlaw, medical director of the Canadian Cancer society, referring to Wiewel's assessment of chemotherapy as quackery.

"I don't have in my head the information which would tell me if the 80-per-cent figure is correct, but I'd be very surprised if the situation were that bad."

Laidlaw said chemotherapy has proved highly affective against some cancers, including testicular, Hodgkins (cancer of the lymph glands) and acute childhood luekemia, which today has a 5-year survival rate of 73 per cent compared with five per cent in the 1960's.

Yet even some mainstream medical practitioners concede traditional treatments have not been as successful as hoped in treating all patients diagnosed with the more common cancer's, among them lung, colon, breast and prostrate.

Over-all cancer statistics paint a grim picture: 50 percent of patients won't survive beyond 5 years, said Laidlaw, noting that cancer is "increasing faster than any other disease," with 110,000 new cases a year in Canada.

But Laidlaw doesn't believe alternative therapies are suppressed: "I have no evidence that that's so in Canada ... and I can't believe the same isn't true in the States.

"Its very rare that people touting these new kinds of therapies are studying them in ways recognised by authoriteis."

But obtaining government approval for a new drug is a lengthy and costly process, taking up to ten years and costing $200 million to $500 million.

"It's all based on an evaluation procedure that can only be undertaken by (the largest) five or six pharmaceutical companies (in the United States)," Wiewel said.

Meanwhile, numerous alternatives languish untested on the American Cancer Societys Unproven Methods of Cancer Management list.

Case study evidence siting the effectiveness of alternative therapies are often rejected as "anecdotal."

"When you hear about an unproven treatment, all that could mean—and usually does mean—is that no one has attempted to prove it," said Harris Coulter, an expert and author on alternative medicine. "So it's a self-fulfilling prophesy: no one will ever get the money to test them."

Some critics say the public is mislead by selectively cited statistics that underplay the failures of orthodox treatments.

Epidemiologist John Bailar, formerly with the National Cancer Institute in Washington and now at McGill University, says the statistics "from NCI and other official agencies are acurate.

"The problem is their used selectively by people who have a stake in coming to one or another conclusion."

Bailar, former editor of the NCIs professional journal, still advocates "the earliest possible conventional treatment. There is no doubt that their has been major progress against certain kinds of cancer.

"At the same time, there have been some real losses—the death rates and incidence rates are going up."

He believes that despite billions of dollars spent over decades seeking a cure, the war on cancer has been lost.

"For a long time we beleived treatment was the way to solve this problem; it hasn't worked," he said.

"It's time to take a whole new approach—and start getting serious about prevention."

A3 23 May 2009

WOODSTOCK, ONT.—There is a hollow look to the young addicts who wander Woodstocks main street.

Their cheeks are pulled tight, their limbs gaunt, their eyes dull and vacant. They have followed a high to it's logical end and are now trying to scrape themselves back off the bottom.

They gather daily at the bustling methadone clinic across from the city square for there medicine, a Narcotic cocktail called "the drink" made palatable by fruit flavoring. In a city of 35,000, 300 people are on the patient roles.

"I've lost my whole family pretty much," says Casey, a 25-year-old OxyContin addict. "I'm not your normal street feind. I've been raised by a good family. My parent's both work at toyota. I was in the interview process to get a job there too, but the drugs were more important so I lost that shot."

This is the unseemly side of Woodstock, a side that has been thrust into public view with the abduction and slaying of 8-year-old Victoria Stafford. The girl's mother, Tara McDonald, confessed to an addiction to OxyContin, and the woman accused in her daughter's homicide, Terri-Lynne McClintic, is also a user, according to neighbors.

Although their's no suggestion that OxyContin contributed to Victoria's killing, the incident has focussed public attention on a scourge that is ripping through this blue-collar town—one of many in North America, usually small and suffering economically, where the drug has cut a swath.

Surounded by some of the most fertile soil in Canada, Woodstock was the hinterland of Upper Canada when it was settled at the turn of the 19th century by Loyalists fleeing the United States. It has always been at the centre of a farm belt, famous for its statue of a prized cow, but from its origins to the present day the "dairy capital" has wagered it's own future on manufacturing.

Throughout the 20 century, that strategy helped Woodstock prosper: This was Ontario's heart-land, with ready access to rail and roads linking auto parts and machinery destined for detroit and textiles and furniture for Southern Ontario. In the citys musuem, a 1983 promotional film proclaims "industry chooses Woodstock," over a stream of pictures of molten metal and moving machinery.

But while other Southwestern Ontario cities such as Waterloo, Guelph, and London have gained from the research hubs of there universities, and from the influx of immigration and creativity that those institutions attracts, Woodstock has stuck to what it know's.

As the town's Mayor, Michael Harding, said this week, "We've always done good with our hands."

That approach has created a remarkably stable population, but one less inclined to education. Two-thirds of the town has lived in Canada 3 generations or more, according to the 2006 Census. But just 10 per cent have a university degree and 29 percent never graduated from high school. Only 4 per cent of its population belong to a visble minority. Compare that with nearby Waterloo, where 31 per cent have a university degree, only 16 per cent didn't graduate from high school, 29 percent are first-generation Canadians and 17 per cent visible minorities.

"We are what we are," Mr. Harding said. "Were a slow-growth community, always have been."

COPY EDITING REVIEW TEST B

B1 3 July 2009

TORONTO—On a still but rainy nite, the black Nissan Sentra had to thread two needles before plunging into the Rideau canal just North of Kingston, leaving local detectivs bafflled.

The 4-door car carrying 3 Montreal sisters' and an aunt to there graves' likly turned north off Kingston Mills road, where it had to skirt a locked green gate baring vehicle acces to the Canal.

The rocky ground nex to the gate would had given the nissan a bump, but the 1.7-meter-wide compact could probaby have squezed past. Its unlikely the manouver was a simple wrong turn.

The next obstacle was the Canal itself, with stone moorings spaced a few meters a part and the ancient black iron control wheel standing about a meter above the canals edge.

If the car went strait from the road into the water, the driver would have had to make a quick left turn into the canal. Witnessses and police say there are no skid marks in the green grass next to the canal, no tell-tale signs of sudden braking, turning or aceleration.

It would have been a smooth turn made at a reasonable speed. The stone edge of the canal shows just a few scrapes from the car sliding in.

"The area is fairly level, there are rocky areas, but you'd still have to do some maneuvring to get out to this spot," said Constable Mike Menor of Kingston Police.

The car was disscovered at 9 o clock a.m. Tuesday in three metres of water right next to the lock gates. Nearby residents had heard a noise some 6 hours earlier. The three sisters, aged 13, 17, and 19, and their 50-year-old aunt were found inside.

Investigators say the condition of the bodies suggest they'd gone into the water overnight. Police were witholding they're identities yesterday at the request of the family.

Police are left to sort through a myried of theories, each with glaring probems and unlikely probabilites.

"We're still trying to acertain the why, the why, the why," said Constable Menor, a 20-year veteran of the force. "Its the unknowns. I can't recall anything like it. It was their for a reason, it didn't drop out of the sky."

Without revealing details, police say the foursome had spent the earlier part of the evening in Kingston.

"We peiced together that they did have a bit of a family vacation West of us on the other side of Toronto and we're returning to Quebec," said Staff Sergeant Chris Scott of the Kingston police criminal investigations division.

With picknic tables along the canal shore, the tourists from Montreal may have stopped for a moment before the plunge. But 3:00 a.m. would be an unusal time for a picnic in the secluded spot.

Perhaps the driver didn't know the canal was their, or perhaps she didn't care. Police have not excluded a suicide pact, murder-suicide or something as simple as the bad luck of a mis-guided U-turn or mistaking "drive" for "reverse."

Another possibility is that the passenger's were all ready dead and someone else pushed the Nissan into the canal, with the four females inside.

Montreal police said they were asked by Kingston police to locate a 2nd vehicle in Monteal that may have been seen with the Nissan. Late yesterday, Kingston police denied they we're looking for another vehicle.

Autopsies were preformed yesterday but results could take weeks, investigators said.

Kingston police have refused to reveal if there was signs of violence on the bodies.

B2 20 September 2003

VANCOUVER—It's just after daybreak and rays of early sunlight make golden pillars where they slant through the canopy far overhead, plunging between the gray tree trunks to disapear into the glossy green salal and the whispering sword ferns.

From the salmonberry thickets and among the thimbleberry canes crowding the fence line of the University of BC's experimental farm here at Oyster River, about midway between Courtenay and Campbell river on the East Coast of Vancouver Island, a choir of songbirds raise a boistrous hymn of praise for the morning.

There is a cathedral-like quality to this small corner of forest at the estaury of the river that was doubtless what first attracted the tough First World War chaplan from Vancouvers east side who sought solace and solitude here with his fly rod and who the riverside trail comemorates.

Watching a big cut-throat trout as long as my fore-arm hang motionless in the swift, clear current, I'm reminded of that long-dead angler and his pastorel meditations. He msut have been an optomist. He may have fished for souls on east Hastings but for his own sense of peace and salvation he returned to this temple of Nature soo often that he finaly becume part of the geogaphy.

If this seems an unusual place to begin a contemplation of the trail by fire through which British Columbia has just past, perhap's its not.

For this rich Oasis of tranguility, throbbing with life, is the future of all the devastation around Kelowna, Kamloops and Cranbrook that so shocked our urban official's—and those television news directors who bring little historic memory to there coverage but have an insatable appetite for the dramatic. Those ravaged landscapes might also serve as images from the past of this place of present abundance.

Lieutenant-Govenor Iona Campagnolo described the summers losses as "agony." Premier Gordon Campbell, after flying over the burns in the southern interior that are expected to cost the province $500 million in fire suppression, said the desolation seemed "endless."

Almost everyone who owned a television could not help but be mesmerised by the image's of flaming forests menacing suburban neighborhoods and the steady mantra intoning British Columbia's worst summer of fire in 50 years. And who could not feel the deepest of pangs for the suddenly homeless.

COPY EDITING REVIEW TEST C

C1 6 August 2008

TORONTO—Punitive damages in Canda and the United States are under haevy fire, evident by recent decisions of the two countries Supreme Courts that drastically slashed such awards and limited the extent too which they should be granted.

That bode well for corporations that are found to have breeched the law, but not so well four those who suffer harm.

Punative damages is granted by courts to adress egregiuos conduct between parties. In Canada, they are relatively rare and seldom exeed six figures. In the United States, however, they can reach into the hundreds of millions of dollars and can form the bulk of the damage's awarded to injured parties'.

"Punitive damages may be alive in Canada, but their not very well," says Alf Kwinter of Singer Kwinter, a member of the plaintiffs bar. "The supreme court keeps raising the standard, saying conduct isn't bad enough to warrant punatives even after trial judges condem corporate behavior."

Thats not an unfair description of the recent supreme court of Canada decision in *Keays v. Honda*, which originated with an employees poor attendence record over 2 years, supported only by very summery doctors' notes. When Keays refused to meet with the companys dr., Honda terminated him.

The Ontario Superior Court concluded that Honda had engaged in a conspiracy to avoid accomodating Keays, and awarded $500,000 dollars in punitive damages. The Ontario court of appeal cut that to $100,000 dollars. That didn't satisfy the High Court. It ruled that Hondas conduct was not the type of "malicoius" or "outragous" conduct that deserved punishment on it's own, and voided the puntives.

The reasoning mirrored that of the court in it's 2006 decision in *Fidler v. Sun Life*.

In that case, pain and fatigue left Connie Fidler, a middle-aged receptionist with Royal Bank of Canada in Burnaby, BC, unable to work. A unanimus Supreme Court found that Sun Life Assurance Co. of Canada was libel for the mental distress Fidler sufferred when the insurer wrongfuly withheld disability benifits for five years—but not for the $100,000 in punitive damages that the BC court of appeal had ordered.

"The supreme court has been making the criteria for punitives almost unattainable," Kwinter says. "It refused to award punitives in *Keays* even though the Court called Hondas conduct 'ill-advised' and 'unecessarily harsh,' and even though it called the conduct in *Fidler* 'outrageous' and 'troubling.' "

Chris Paliare of Paliare Roland Rosenberg Rothstein LLP, who represented NE/FM Action Network, an intervenor in *Keays*, says the case is a big win for employers' in particular.

"The ruling is totaly antithetical and contradict everything the supreme court has said about employment law for the last decad," he says. "As far as I'm concerned, it demonstrate a lack of understanding and sensitivity on the court's part about the nature of the employment relationship, because it means that employer's can get off the hook on punatives for pretty well anything they do, as long as they write nice letters about it to the employee."

In the United States, ten year's of litigation that begun with the *Exxon Valdez* oil spill ended with a June decision from the Supreme Court slashing a U.S.$2-billion punitive award to U.S.$500 million. That left Native Alaskans and local fisherman and landowners with just twenty percent of the amount awarded by a Federal appeal's court.

Justice David Souter, writing for the majority in a split court, said the punitives should not have exceeded the compensatory damage award of US$507.5 million.

"Were seeing a backlash to what the public and the business community percieved as extreme and disproportionate punitive awards," says Peter Simmons, a litigator at Fried Frank's New york office. "Conseguently, federal and state courts and legislaters have been trying to eliminate the 'outlier' awards, as opposed to punitive damages in general."

Indeed, Judge Souters criticism of punitive damages focussed on the ocasional blockbuster awards, saying they introduced "stark unpredictibility" into litgation.

"Theres no question that their are cases where puntives are right and reasonnable," Simmons say. "But the chance of an outlier award make's it hard for anyone to predict what there downside risk is. Litigation isnt suppossed to be a game of chance or roullette or a lotterry."

Meanwhile, in Canada, Kwinter says the solution for plaintives is to elect trial by jury.

"Juries will be the last bastion of punitive damages, because judges don't get so shocked by egregous corporate conduct," he says.

Fortunately for the denisens of Bay Street and their counsel, however, high-profile corporate–commercial litigation almost always end up before a judge alone. However, other stakeholders in the justice system, like the insurance industry, may find the Supreme Court's distaste for punitives increasingly leaves them subject to the wims of their peers.

The Canadian Press Stylebook

The following pages summarize the most commonly used rules in *The Canadian Press Stylebook* (15th edition, 2008) and *The Canadian Press Caps and Spelling* (19th edition, 2009). Section and subsection numbers have been added. These selected rules have been reprinted with the permission of the Canadian Press. Most newspapers in Canada follow the rules it recommends. Both national papers (the *Globe and Mail* and the *National Post*) have their own in-house stylebooks. For the style rules applicable to writing scripts for broadcast news, see Chapter 17 Writing for Broadcast. For fuller treatment and individual listings, consult the appropriate chapter in the *The Canadian Press Stylebook* or section in *The Canadian Press Caps and Spelling*. Complete copies of both books can be ordered from most bookstores or directly from the national wire service (36 King St. E., Toronto, ON M5C 2L9; 416-364-0321; www.thecanadianpress.com).

SECTION 1: ABBREVIATIONS AND ACRONYMS

1.1 GENERAL. Use only abbreviations and acronyms (abbreviations pronounced as words) familiar to ordinary readers. Except for abbreviations that have become household terms, provide the full name on first reference; if the abbreviated form is used in the lead, provide the full name later. Do not put a bracketed abbreviation after the name of an organization: World Health Organization (WHO). Do not spell out common abbreviations if the full term is not in general use or if it is hard to pronounce (e.g., deoxyribonucleic acid for DNA); instead, provide a brief general description (DNA, the carrier of genetic information). Finally, abbreviations that are suitable in one context may not work in another. For example, the abbreviation MLA (for member of the legislative assembly) should be spelled out for readers in Newfoundland and Labrador, Quebec, and Ontario. Similarly, the following abbreviations should be spelled out for readers in other provinces: MHA (member of the house of assembly, Newfoundland and Labrador); MNA (member of the national assembly, Quebec); and MPP (member of the provincial parliament, Ontario).

1.2 STYLE FOR ABBREVIATIONS. All-capital abbreviations are written without periods (YMCA, CN, MP, URL) unless the abbreviation is geographical (B.C., U.K., U.S., P.E.I., T.O.), refers to a person (J.R. Ewing), or is a single letter (E. for 36 King St. E.). Most lowercase and mixed abbreviations take periods (f.o.b., Jr., Ont.). Mixed abbreviations that begin and end with a capital letter do not take periods (PhD, POW, U of T). Note that metric symbols are not abbreviations and do not take periods (m, l, kW). Most abbreviations are written without spaces (U.K., U.S.), but those written without periods are spaced (U of T).

1.3 STYLE FOR ACRONYMS. Acronyms formed from only the first letter of each principal word are all capitals: AIDS (acquired immune deficiency syndrome), NATO (North Atlantic Treaty Organization). Usually, acronyms formed from initial and other letters are upper and lowercase: Norad (North American Aerospace Defence Command), but some exceptions have crept into common use (BMO, for Bank of Montreal). Acronyms that have become common words are not capitalized: laser (light amplification by stimulated emission of radiation), radar (radio detection and ranging).

1.4 ACADEMIC DEGREES AND HONOURS. In general, prefer an explanatory phrase to the abbreviation (Jane Wong, who has a doctorate in literature). If using an explanatory phrase is awkward and the abbreviation is well-known, use the abbreviation, following the rules for abbreviations noted in section 1.2 (BA for a bachelor of arts degree; MA for master of arts; B.Sc. for bachelor of science; PhD for doctor of philosophy).

1.5 DATES AND TIMES. For months used with a specific date, abbreviate only Jan., Feb., Aug., Sept., Oct., Nov. and Dec. Spell out standing alone or with a year alone (Oct. 1, 1999; June 5, 2006; August 2009). Do not abbreviate a month spelled out in the name of an organization (the November 17 terrorist group). In tabular matter, use abbreviated forms without periods (Jan, Feb, Mar, Apr, May, Jun, Jul, Aug, Sep, Oct, Nov, Dec). Days of the week are abbreviated only in tabular matter and without periods (Sun, Mon, Tue, Wed, Thu, Fri, Sat). The term AD is acceptable in all references for anno Domini and BC for before Christ. AD precedes the year; BC follows it (AD 410, 55 BC), but write 12th century AD. Write 10 a.m., 3:30 p.m., EDT (eastern daylight time), AST (Atlantic standard time).

1.6 MEASUREMENTS. In general, spell out such terms as kilogram, metre, and minute (a five-kilogram packet costs $2). A few common terms—km/h, mm, m.p.h., c.c.—are acceptable when used with figures (70 km/h, 105-mm cannon, the 30-m.p.h. speed limit, 2,000-c.c. engine). Terms may be abbreviated in tabular matter and if used repeatedly (kg, c.w.t., l). Use this style for imperial abbreviations, both singular and plural, in tabulations: in., ft., yd., mi.; oz., lb., cwt.; sq. ft. Similarly: sec., min., hr.

1.7 ORGANIZATIONS. Use Bros., Co., Corp., Inc., and Ltd. with corporate names and without commas. (Texaco Inc. has announced a new development.) Spell out company, etc., in the names of entertainment groups unless the group name includes an abbreviation (Canadian Opera Company, Blues Brothers). Do not abbreviate other terms (association, department, division, organization, and so on) in corporate and government names (Reader's Digest Association, Justice Department). An ampersand is acceptable in corporate names if the organization uses it (AT&T, S&P). Spell out compound nouns like United Nations when used as a noun; the abbreviation (UN) is acceptable when used as an adjective with well-known organizations.

1.8 PLACES. For Canadian provinces and territories, use these abbreviations after the name of a community: Alta., B.C., Man., N.B., N.L., N.W.T., N.S., Ont., P.E.I., Que., Sask. After the name of a community, use Yukon rather than Y.T. When standing alone, make it the Yukon. An abbreviation has not yet been established for Nunavut, so it should be written out in all references. For American states, use these abbreviations after the name of a community: Ala., Ariz., Ark., Calif., Colo., Conn., Del., Fla., Ga., Ill., Ind., Kan., Ky., La., Md., Mass., Mich., Minn., Miss., Mo., Mont., Neb., Nev., N.H., N.J., N.M., N.Y., N.C., N.D., Okla., Ore., Pa., R.I., S.C., S.D., Tenn., Vt., Va., Wash., W.Va., Wis., Wyo. Do not abbreviate the following: Alaska, Hawaii, Idaho, Iowa, Maine, Ohio, Texas, Utah; Puerto Rico, Virgin Islands. In general, do not abbreviate the names of countries, provinces or states when standing alone or used adjectivally (the Nova Scotia cabinet, not the N.S. cabinet), but the following exceptions may be used adjectivally: U.K., U.S., B.C., and P.E.I. (the U.S. team, the B.C. legislature). In Quebec place names, use a hyphen instead of a period after St and Ste (Ste-Agathe, St-Eustache). Generally, abbreviate Saint and Sainte in place names: St. John's, N.L., Sault Ste. Marie, but note the exception: Saint John, N.B. Do not abbreviate the following words when they are part of a proper name: county, fort, mount, point, and port (Fort McMurray, Mount Everest).

1.9 TITLES. Abbreviate Gov. Gen. and Lt.-Gov. before names on first reference; lowercase with "former," "late" or "then" (former governors general Georges Vanier and Adrienne Clarkson; the late lieutenant-governor Pat Filippo; the then-president John Redway). Do not abbreviate the following titles: attorney general, auditor general, district attorney, postmaster general, representative, secretary, secretary general, senator and treasurer. Do abbreviate titles such as the following before full names on first reference: Dr., Msgr., Prof., Rev., Sgt.

1.10 MISCELLANEOUS USAGES. In general, prefer a descriptive phrase to bracketed style, but in parliamentary and legislature copy, use the following style for bracketed political affiliations: Tom Arlee (NDP–Edmonton East), Senator Mary Atkins (Con–Man.), Myron Martin (Lib–Snowy River), Representative John Whyte (R–Pa.), Senator Obie Black (Ind.–Va.), state Senator Darleen Healey (D–Queens). Abbreviate ship and plane designations (USS Johnson, SST), but spell out on first reference (supersonic transport). Do not abbreviate books of the Bible (Genesis, Leviticus). Do not use periods when letters designate persons or things (exhibit A, the mysterious Madame X), but use a period if the letter is an abbreviation (Mrs. G. as a short form for Mrs. Gamp). Do not use shortenings such as the following: Peterboro (for Peterborough), Xmas (for Christmas), Soo (for Sault Ste. Marie).

SECTION 2: ADDRESSES

2.1   ADDRESSES.   In numbered addresses use abbreviations (36 King St. E.); spell out general locations (on King Street, the Fort Street metro station). Do not abbreviate official residences (24 Sussex Drive, 10 Downing Street).

2.2   DIRECTIONS.   Abbreviate compass points used to indicate directional ends of a street or quadrants of a city in a numbered address: 562 W. 43rd St., 600 King St. N.W. Do not abbreviate if the address number is omitted: West 43rd Street, King Street Northwest.

SECTION 3: CAPITALIZATION

In general, avoid unnecessary capitals. The Canadian Press follows a modified down style: Capitalize all proper names, the names of departments and agencies of national and provincial governments, trade names, names of associations, companies, clubs, religions, languages, races, places and addresses. Otherwise, lowercase is favoured where a reasonable option exists.

3.1   COMMON NOUNS.   Common nouns such as church and league are capitalized when they are part of a proper name (Catholic Church, National Hockey League). They are lowercased when standing alone (the church, the league, the church's position, a league spokesperson).

3.2   PLURAL USES.   The common-noun elements of proper nouns are normally lowercase in plural uses (the United and Anglican churches, the National and American leagues).

3.3   FORMAL TITLES.   Capitalize formal titles directly preceding a name, but not when the title follows the name (Prime Minister Stephen Harper / Stephen Harper, the prime minister). Lowercase formal titles when they stand alone and in plural uses (the prime minister, premiers Jean Charest and Gordon Campbell).

3.4   JOB DESCRIPTIONS.   Lowercase job descriptions (managing editor Anne Davies, Acme Corp. chairman Joseph Schultz). Long and cumbersome titles and job descriptions should be set off with commas (an internationally known Canadian architect, Arthur Erickson; the energy, mines and resources minister, Jean Dubois).

3.5   TITLES OF NOBILITY AND RELIGION.   All references to the current Pope, Canada's reigning monarch, and the current Governor General are capitalized. Titles of nobility and religion that are commonly used instead of the personal name are capitalized: Duke of Kent, Anglican Primate of Canada (but: the duke, the primate).

3.6   NATIONAL LEGISLATIVE BODIES.   The names of national legislative bodies, including some short forms, are capitalized: House of Commons, the House, the Commons; U.S. Senate; Knesset. Provincial legislatures and local councils are lowercased: Quebec national assembly, Toronto city council.

3.7   NATIONAL AND PROVINCIAL GOVERNMENT DEPARTMENTS.   National and provincial government departments and agencies are capitalized: Health Canada, Defence Department, Ministry of Natural Resources, U.S. Secret Service. Local government departments and boards are lowercased: parks and property department, Halifax welfare department.

3.8   COURTS AND CONSTITUTIONS.   Upper courts are capitalized (B.C. Supreme Court, Appeal Court). Lower courts are lowercased (juvenile court, magistrate's court). The proper names of constitutions are capitalized (the French Constitution); when the word is used as a common noun, it is lowercased (the constitution); but note that all references to the Canadian Constitution are capitalized (the Constitution).

3.9   MILITARY FORCES.   Canada's military forces are capitalized (Canadian Forces, the Forces). For other forces, army, navy, and air force are lowercased when preceded by the name of the country (the Greek air force, the U.S. army). This style is intended for consistency, since the proper name is not always a combination of country and force (the Royal Navy, the British navy; the Royal Air Force, the British air force).

3.10   HISTORICAL PERIODS, EVENTS AND HOLIDAYS.   Historical periods, historic events, holidays and other special times are capitalized (Middle Ages, First World War, Prohibition, Christmas Eve, Ramadan, Earth Day, October Crisis).

3.11   GEOGRAPHICAL REGIONS AND FEATURES.   Specific geographical regions and features are capitalized (Western Canada, Far North, Lake Superior). But northern, southern, eastern and western in terms derived from regions are lowercased (a western Canadian, a southerner, northern customs).

3.12 SACRED PROPER NAMES.   Sacred names and the proper names and nicknames of the devil are capitalized (the Almighty, Redeemer, Holy Spirit, Allah, Mother of God, Vishnu, Beelzebub, Father of Lies), but devil, hell and heaven are lowercased.

3.13 NAMES OF RACES AND NATIONS.   Names of races, nations and the like are capitalized (Aboriginal Peoples, Asian, Arab, French-Canadian). But white and black are lowercased.

3.14 PRINCIPAL WORDS OF TITLES.   The principal words in the titles of books, plays, movies, paintings and the like are capitalized (*Gone With the Wind*; *A Dictionary of Usage and Style*). Principal words are nouns, pronouns, adjectives, adverbs, verbs, and the first and last word of the title, as well as prepositions and conjunctions of four letters or more. For infinitives, use "to Go", "to Be". In titles, both words of compound adjectives are capitalized (Well-Meaning).

3.15 NICKNAMES AND FANCIFUL NAMES.   Nicknames and fanciful names are capitalized (Third World, Group of Seven, Mack the Knife).

3.16 AWARDS AND DECORATIONS.   Awards and decorations are capitalized (Order of Canada, OC; Victoria Cross, VC). University degrees are lowercased except when abbreviated (master of arts, a master's degree, MA; doctor of philosophy, PhD).

3.17 ONCE-PROPER NOUNS AND ADJECTIVES.   Proper nouns and adjectives now regarded as common nouns are lowercased: brussels sprouts, french fries).

3.18 CORPORATE AND PROMOTIONAL NAMES.   Except in the cases of all-lowercase or all-uppercase names, follow the capitalization of the organization or person unless it hampers readability (eBay, k.d. lang). Note: Capitalize at the beginning of a sentence (EBay). If a corporate or promotional name is all lowercase, capitalize the first letter for clarity (Adidas). If the name is all uppercase, capitalize only the first letter for readability (Band-Aid, not BAND-AID).

SECTION 4: NUMBERS

4.1 GENERAL RULE.   Spell out whole numbers below 10; use figures for 10 and above (nine contestants, 10 candidates, the fifth inning, the 22nd day). In a series, there will be a mixture (there are 20 trees: two elms, 10 beeches, and eight maples). Follow the organization's spelling style for numbers in official names, even if these differ from Canadian Press style (7Up, the film *7 Fathers*). Do not use commas with dimensions, measurements and weights of two or more elements (a man five feet 10 inches tall; in two hours 21 minutes 45 seconds). To avoid ambiguity when citing percentages, write "increased to 15 per cent from 10 per cent" (not "increased from 10 to 15 per cent"). Percentage losses or gains should always be accompanied by base figures (sales fell 10 per cent to $10,000).

4.2 WHEN TO USE FIGURES.   Use figures in the following cases:
Addresses (10 Clark Ave.), but spell out First through Ninth as street names (25 Fifth Ave., 42 10th St.)
Ages standing alone after a name (Melissa, 4, has two brothers)
When the context does not require "years" or "years old" (she was 3)
Dates and years (Dec. 5, the Dirty '30s, the 20th century)
Decimals and fractions (a .30-calibre rifle, 3½-year-old), but two-thirds
Decisions, rulings, scores, votes and odds (a 6–3 ruling; the team won by a 3–1 margin; the vote was 35–6 with one abstention)
Heights expressed informally (he stands 6-11)
Highlights at the start of an item ($1.5 billion for new equipment)
Military and paramilitary terms (1st Canadian Division, Petty Officer 3rd Class)
Monetary units preceded by a symbol ($2, but two dollars)
Designations of aircraft, ships, spacecraft and vehicles (Dash 7, Apollo 8)
Sequential designations (Act 1, Room 4)
Temperatures (5 C, −6 C); in times (1 a.m., 10:30 p.m.)
Latitude and longitude (59 degrees 30 minutes north)
Lists that include both whole numbers and fractions or decimals (7.25 per cent for five years and 7.00 per cent for four years).

4.3   WHEN TO SPELL OUT:
At the beginning of a sentence that starts with a number: Thirty adults and 12 children came. When numbers 21 through 99 must be written out, use a hyphen: Fifty-five or 56 participated.
In informal or casual usage: Get-well wishes poured in by the hundreds.
In figures of speech (a ten-gallon hat, wouldn't touch it with a ten-foot pole, the Big Ten)
In common fractions below 1 standing alone (one-half, one-quarter inch)

4.4   LARGE NUMBERS
Round numbers in the thousands are usually given in figures (2,000 prisoners, 375,000 francs).
Spell out for casual usage (there were thousands of mosquitoes).
Express large numbers in millions and billions instead of the less familiar terms trillion, quadrillion and the like (a million billion instead of quadrillion, a billion billion instead of quintillion). Note that in Canada and the United States, a billion is a thousand million; in the United Kingdom and some other places, it is a million million.
Except for monetary units preceded by a symbol, round numbers in the millions and billions generally follow the rule of spelling out below 10 (two million bushels, 10 billion cubic metres, $1 billion). Spell out for casual usage (a million times).
In expressing a range, repeat million or billion (20 million to 30 million).
Hyphenate adjectival forms before nouns (the 2.2-million-member group, a two-million-bushel crop).
Use commas to set off numbers of four or more figures except for house, telephone, page, year and other serial numbers (2,500; 100,000 million; 1250 Sherbrooke St.; 1-800-268-9233; the year 2010; p. 1005).
Use figures for numbers up to 999,999. Above that, switch to words if absolute precision is not required (a $1.2-million project; a profit of $100,000).

4.5   ROMAN NUMERALS
Use roman numerals to indicate sequence for people and animals and in proper names when that is the widely accepted style; otherwise, avoid them (Queen Elizabeth II, Henry Ford III).
In particular, paraphrase large numbers (the 36th Super Bowl, not Super Bowl XXXVI).
For the ship, write Queen Elizabeth 2 or QE2.
Write SALT II and Vatican II and the like to conform to widespread practice.

SECTION 5: PUNCTUATION

5.1   COMMA
5.1.1 AGE.   An individual's age is set off by commas: Phil Taylor, 11, is here.
5.1.2 CITY-PROVINCE.   Place a comma between the name of the city and the name of the province (a woman from Montreal, Quebec). Put a comma after the abbreviated name of the province, unless it ends the sentence: He was travelling from Montreal, Que., to Vancouver, B.C.
5.1.3 WORDS AND NUMBERS.   Use a comma to set off parenthetical words and numbers. For example, use a comma to set off a person's age, degrees, awards and affiliations (Lee, 39; Anne Gagnon, PhD); to set off the year from the month and day (March 14, 2010); and to set off thousands, except in years, street addresses, or page, phone and serial numbers (13,500 kilometres, serial number 77435). Finally, use a comma to mark the omission of words that are understood from the context (one received $5; another, $4; a third, nothing at all).
5.1.4 QUOTATION.   Use a comma to introduce a complete, one-sentence quotation within a paragraph: Wallace said, "She spent six months in Argentina." Do not use a comma at the start of an indirect or partial quotation: The water was "cold as ice" before the sun came out, the lifeguard said. When the attribution follows the quotation, change the period at the end of the quotation to a comma: "I will oppose the measure," the politician said. Always place commas and periods inside quotation marks. "The journey must end," she

said. "We cannot go on." For broadcast, avoid direct quotations in stories. Use paraphrases or tape instead. Where a direct quotation is central to a story, punctuate it as for print, but use a phrase that would make clear to listeners that the words are those of the source, not the reporter: In the actor's words, "He can run, but he can't hide."

5.1.5 SERIES.   Use commas to separate elements in a series, but do not put a comma before the conjunction that precedes the last item in the series: The wallpaper is white, yellow and blue. He said he would nominate Tom, Dick or Harry. However, retain the final comma if necessary to avoid confusion or ambiguity: The centre offers courses in broadcasting, newswriting, and public relations. (Without the last comma, readers could misconstrue "newswriting and public relations" as a single course.) Use a comma as well to separate consecutive co-ordinate adjectives that modify the same noun. Co-ordinate adjectives are those that equally modify the same noun; they could be reversed in order or separated by the conjunction "and" (a sincere, honest, hardworking woman). Omit the commas if the adjectives are not co-ordinate (her old brown winter coat).

5.2   COLON

5.2.1 LISTS.   The most frequent use of a colon is at the end of a sentence to introduce lists, tabulations and the like. (There were three considerations: expense, time and feasibility.)

5.2.2 QUOTATIONS.   Use a colon to introduce direct quotations longer than one sentence within a paragraph (Winston Churchill said in 1942: "This is not the end. It is not even the beginning of the end. But it is, perhaps, the end of the beginning.") and to end all paragraphs that introduce a paragraph of quoted material.

5.3   POSSESSIVES.   Appendix C contains the rules for forming possessives.

5.4   SEMICOLON.   Use semicolons (instead of commas) to separate elements of a series when individual segments contain material that also must be set off by commas: He leaves three daughters, Jane Smith of Belleville, Ont., Mary Smith of Toronto and Susan Kingsbury of Vancouver; a son, John Smith of Montreal; and a sister, Martha Warren of Kelowna, B.C. Note that the semicolon is used before the final "and" in such a series.

5.5   IN GENERAL FOR BROADCAST COPY.   Punctuation should help a newscaster understand and read a story. Most of the rules for punctuating print copy apply to broadcast copy.

5.6   EXCLAMATION MARK.   The exclamation mark shows strong feeling, surprise, emphasis or a command (Never! Fire!). Use an exclamation mark rather than a question mark with questions in exclamatory form ("Are you serious!").

5.7   HYPHEN.   Use the hyphen to ease reading, avoid ambiguity, and join compound modifiers, as follows: to join words that when used together form a separate concept (a light-year); to join compound modifiers preceding a noun (dirty-blond hair); to join certain word combinations even when standing alone (hard-earned, fire-resistant); to indicate joint titles and to join conflicting or repetitive elements (secretary-treasurer, drip-drop, walkie-talkie); to join well-known compounds of three or more words (mother-in-law, happy-go-lucky); with certain compounds containing an apostrophe (bull's-eye, cat's-paw); to avoid doubling a vowel, tripling a consonant or duplicating a prefix (co-ordinate, doll-like, sub-subcommittee); to join prefixes to proper names (anti-Harper, pro-democracy); to join an initial capital with a word (T-shirt, X-ray); with fractions standing alone and with the written numbers 21 to 99 (three-quarters, ninety-nine); and with a successive compound adjective (18th- and 19th-century fashions).

SECTION 6: PREFERRED SPELLINGS

6.1   CANADIAN OXFORD DICTIONARY.   The *Canadian Oxford Dictionary* is the authority for Canadian Press spelling, with specific exceptions noted in *The Canadian Press Stylebook* and *The Canadian Press Caps and Spelling*.

6.2   EXCEPTIONS.   When the spelling of a common-noun element of a proper name differs from CP style (Lincoln Center), use the spelling favoured by the subject. One exception applies to the names of government departments and agencies. Use U.S. Defence (not Defense) Department and U.S. Labour (not Labor) Department to avoid inconsistency with other words likely to be found in the story, such as defence secretary and labour laws.

6.3   SYMBOLS.   Ignore symbols and unnecessary punctuation in corporate or other names, or translate them into accepted punctuation if necessary (the Bravo TV channel, not Bravo!).

6.4   CANADIAN SPELLING: CP style is –our, not –or, for labour, honour, and other such words of more than one syllable in which the "u" is not pronounced (including armour, behaviour, colour, favour, harbour, humour, neighbour, rumour, saviour, tumour and vigour). In some forms, however, the "u" is dropped, especially where an –ous ending is added (laborious, rancorous, honorary).

6.5   CANADIAN SPELLINGS VERSUS AMERICAN SPELLINGS.   Other Canadian spellings also differ from American spellings, including the following (with American spellings in parentheses): axe (ax), centre (center), cheque (check), enrol (enroll), grey (gray), licence, as a noun (license), litre (liter), offence (offense), skilful (skillful), theatre (theater), and pyjamas (pajamas). As well, Canadian Press and Canadian style is usually to double the "l" when adding endings to words such as label and signal (labelling, signalling). American spelling tends to use a single "l" (labeling, signaling).

6.6   DIPHTHONGS.   For words in common use, Canadian Press style is simple "e" rather than the diphthongs "ae" and "oe" (archeologist, ecumenical, encyclopedia, esthetic, fetus, gynecologist, hemorrhage, pedagogy and pediatrician). Generally, proper names retain the diphthong (Caesar, Oedipus, Phoebe), as do some common nouns (hors d'oeuvre, manoeuvre, subpoena). The "ae" in words such as aerate and aerial is considered normal spelling.

6.7   UMLAUT.   The umlaut—ä, ö and ü—in German names is indicated by the letter "e" after the letter affected (thus: Goering for Göring).

6.8   RUSSIAN NAMES.   The –ov and –ev endings for Russian names are used instead of –off and –eff. Exceptions include such familiar names as Rachmaninoff and Smirnoff, where the spelling is established.

6.9   FIRST NATIONS NAMES.   Canadian Press style for First Nations names is to follow the preference of the band. For a current list of bands and their preferred spellings, check the Publications and Research page (community profiles) on the website of the Department of Indian and Northern Affairs (www.inac.gc.ca).

6.10   ARABIC NAMES.   For Arabic names, use an English spelling that approximates the way a name sounds in Arabic. If an individual has a preferred spelling in English, use it.

6.11   UKRAINIAN NAMES.   Use the Ukrainian, not the Russian, transliteration for Ukrainian place names (Chornobyl, not Chernobyl; Kyiv, not Kiev).

SECTION 7: TIME

7.1   HOURS AND MINUTES.   Use figures except for noon and midnight (do not put a 12 before noon or midnight). Use a colon to separate hours from minutes: 11:15 a.m., 1:45 p.m., 3:30 p.m. Avoid such redundancies as 10 a.m. this morning or 10 p.m. Monday night. Use 10 a.m. today or 10 p.m. Monday. The hour is placed before the day; a.m. and p.m. are lowercase, with periods.

7.2   DAYS.   The Canadian Press does not use "yesterday" or "tomorrow" in stories for print use; CP uses "today" only if needed in QuickHits—urgent copy intended for broadcast or online use. These items are updated later, with the day of the week added, for newspaper and other print media. Otherwise, to avoid confusion, the day is always named. Use the terms today, yesterday and tomorrow only in direct quotations and in phrases that do not refer to a specific day.

7.3   DAYS/DATES.   Use Monday, Tuesday, etc., for days of the week within seven days before or after the current date: The council will meet Wednesday. Use the month and a figure for dates beyond this range: The council will meet May 27. Avoid such redundancies as last Tuesday or next Tuesday.

7.4   MONTHS.   Follow the rules of abbreviation for months set out in Section 1. Spell out the names of all months when using them alone or with a year alone (June, September 1945). When a phrase lists only a month and a year, do not separate the month from the year with a comma (January 1978 was a cold month). When a phrase refers to a month, day and year, set off the year with commas: Feb. 14, 1976, was the target date. For broadcast, never abbreviate the names of months.

SECTION 8: TITLES

8.1   GENERAL.   With few exceptions, a person's given name is used with surname on first reference. Famous authors, composers and the like may be referred to by surname only (Beethoven's Fifth, Darwin's theory of evolution). Use titles on first reference but seldom in subsequent references; when a story is long or filled with names, however, repeat a title rather than risk losing a reader. Use chairman or chairwoman and spokesman or spokeswoman as appropriate. Chairperson and spokesperson can be used if the sex of the person is not known, but use substitutes for awkward constructions (councillor instead of alderperson) whenever possible.

8.2   COURTESY TITLES.   In general, do not use the courtesy titles Mr., Mrs., Miss, or Ms. If appropriate, refer to a couple on first reference by their first names and their common last name (William and James Wallace). If their relationship is not that of husband and wife, explain (Wayne Gretzky and his sister, Kim).

8.3   PROFESSIONAL TITLES.   In general, use Dr. for licensed health care professionals, and where pertinent, specify (Dr. Sonya Chong, a chiropractor). Do not use Dr. for people with doctorates outside the health-care field. If pertinent, say a person has earned a doctorate, and specify the discipline.

8.4   RELIGIOUS TITLES.   Use a religious title before a person's name on first reference; subsequently, use either the surname alone or a general description. Write "Rev." (not "the Rev."). All popes and some Eastern Orthodox archbishops and bishops, as well as some Roman Catholic and Anglican nuns and brothers, are known by a title and given name only (Pope Benedict, Sister Agatha, Brother James). The name of the office is preferred as the title before the name (Archbishop John Somers), but such forms as Most Rev. John Somers, Archbishop of New Westminster, B.C., are acceptable on occasion. Write John Cardinal Brown, not Cardinal John Brown. Some religions lack a formal hierarchy; in such cases, use descriptive terms such as holy man or priest. Forms of address familiar to the clergy but not to others should be avoided except when in direct quotation, and unfamiliar titles should be explained. Do not use "Rev." as a noun meaning clergyman (the reverend reads novels).

8.5   HEREDITARY, HONORARY TITLES.   The honorary titles right honourable and honourable are used only when they appear in direct quotations. The term Right Hon. applies for life to the Governor General, prime minister, chief justice of Canada, and members of the British Privy Council. Hon. is applied for life to members of the Canadian Privy Council and lieutenant-governors. The rules regarding the use of hereditary titles are complex and vary from country to country. In general, use the title as it is commonly used in the country of origin.

8.6   NEWSPAPERS AND MAGAZINES.   Lowercase "the" in the names of newspapers (the *Toronto Star*, the *Star*). For French-language papers, write "Montreal *La Presse*" rather than "the Montreal *La Presse*" in first reference. In subsequent references, avoid sentence constructions that juxtapose "the" and "le" or "la" (for example, "an editorial in *La Presse*" rather than "the *La Presse* editorial"). Capitalize the word "magazine" only when it is part of the title (*Maclean's* magazine, *Harper's Magazine*).

8.7   ITALICS IN COMPOSITIONS.   Normally, the titles of full-length works (books, films, TV programs, computer games, etc.) are given in italic type; parts of works (a chapter in a book, for instance) are distinguished with quotation marks ("Criminalizing Dissent" is the fifth chapter in *Investigative Reporting in Canada*). For technical reasons, however, the Canadian Press cannot deliver material in italics to all its customers. Follow this general rule for titles: If technically possible, use italics for the titles of full-length works; if not, use quotation marks.

Rules for Forming Possessives

1. To form the possessive case of nouns (whether singular or plural), add an apostrophe and an *s*. For example:

SINGULAR	man	child	Johnson	Microsoft
SINGULAR POSSESSIVE	man's	child's	Johnson's	Microsoft's
PLURAL	men	children	alumni	
PLURAL POSSESSIVE	men's	children's	alumni's	

2. To form the possessive case of plural nouns that already end in *s*, add an apostrophe alone.

   the doctors' patients
   the churches' association
   the two nations' leaders
   the Williamses' children

3. Singular nouns and names ending in *s* or an *s* sound (such as *ce*, *z* and *x*) usually take an *'s*.

   the witness's testimony
   Marliss's sandwich
   the prince's life
   Butz's policies
   Marx's theories

   But names ending with an *–iz* sound and classical or biblical names ending in *s* normally take the apostrophe only.

   Hercules' labours
   Moses' laws

4. Names that end in a silent *s* or *x* take an apostrophe and an *s* (*'s*).

   Duplessis's cabinet
   Malraux's paintings

5. For proper names of companies and institutions, follow the use preferred by the organization.

   Canadian Forces Headquarters
   British Columbia Teachers' Federation

6. Do not add an apostrophe to descriptive phrases ending in *s*: citizens band radio; teachers college. The phrase is descriptive rather than possessive if *for* or *by* rather than *of* would be appropriate in a longer form of the phrase: a radio band for citizens; a college for teachers. An *'s* is required, however, when the term in the descriptive phrase is a plural that does not end in an *s*: women's clinic; people's government (see #1).

7. If an object is jointly possessed by two or more people or entities, make only the last noun possessive.

   Mary and Fred's entry won a prize.
   Acme Co. and Smith Corp.'s joint business is profitable.
   My mother and father's home was destroyed by fire.

8. If the objects are not jointly owned—if they are separate objects owned or possessed by different people—make both nouns possessive.

   Mary's and Fred's entries won prizes.
   The Smiths' and the Browns' luggage was lost.

9. Some special expressions that do not end in *s* but have an *s* sound use only an apostrophe: for conscience' sake; for goodness' sake. In other expressions, especially those of time and measure, use *'s* even though there is no actual ownership: a stone's throw; one week's pay.

10. To form the possessive of indefinite pronouns such as *everyone*, *each other*, and *others*, follow the rules for nouns (*everyone's* business, *each other's* feelings, *others'* opinions). The possessives of personal pronouns have special forms that never use apostrophes (for example, *mine*, *yours*, *his*, *hers*, *its*, *ours*, *yours*, *theirs* and *whose*).

11. Note that the possessive form of the personal pronoun *it* (*its*) does not contain an apostrophe. The word *it's* (a contraction of the words *it is*) does contain an apostrophe. To avoid this exceedingly common error, commit to memory the difference between *its* (the possessive form of the third-person singular pronoun *it*) and *it's* (a contraction of *it is*, with the apostrophe representing the missing *i* in *is*).

    WRONG: Its higher than I thought.
    RIGHT: It's higher than I thought OR It is higher than I thought.

    WRONG: It's height scares me.
    RIGHT: Its height scares me.

Note that the same holds true for the difference between the possessive form of the pronoun *who* (*whose*) and the contraction of *who is* (*who's*).

    WRONG: Who's coat is that?
    RIGHT: Whose coat is that?

    WRONG: Whose coming to dinner?
    RIGHT: Who's coming to dinner?

12. If a term is hyphenated, make only the last word possessive.

SINGULAR	mother-in-law	She is my mother-in-law.
SINGULAR POSSESSIVE	mother-in-law's	It is my mother-in-law's car.
PLURAL	mothers-in-law	The program featured mothers-in-law.
PLURAL POSSESSIVE	mothers-in-law's	The mothers-in-law's cars were damaged.

13. Generally, avoid making inanimate objects possessives. Instead, try to rewrite the passage, either dropping the possessive or converting the passage to an "of" phrase.

    AWKWARD: the table's leg
    BETTER: the table leg OR the leg of the table

    AWKWARD: the book's chapter
    BETTER: the book chapter OR the chapter of the book

14. Compound nouns containing apostrophes are normally singular: baker's dozen, farmer's market, traveller's cheques.

Answer Key

Chapter 2: Newswriting Style

Quiz

1. She was in a ~~quick~~ hurry and warned that, ~~in the future~~, she will seek ~~out~~ textbooks that are sexist and demand ~~that~~ they be ~~totally~~ banned.
2. ~~As it now stands~~, three ~~separate~~ members of the committee said they will try to prevent the city from closing ~~down~~ the park during the winter ~~months~~.
3. His convertible was ~~totally~~ destroyed, and ~~in order~~ to obtain the money necessary to buy a new car, he ~~now~~ plans to ask a ~~personal~~ friend for a loan ~~to help him along~~.
4. After police found the ~~lifeless~~ body, the ~~medical~~ doctor conducted an autopsy ~~to determine the cause of death~~ and concluded ~~that~~ the youth had been strangled ~~to death~~.
5. ~~In the past~~, he often met ~~up with~~ the students at the computer lab and, because of their ~~future~~ potential, invited them to ~~attend~~ the convention.
6. Based upon her ~~previous~~ experience as an architect, she warned the committee ~~members~~ that constructing the ~~new~~ hospital ~~facility~~ will be ~~pretty~~ expensive and suggested ~~that~~ they ~~step in and~~ seek more donors.
7. The two men were hunting in a ~~wooded~~ forest ~~a total of~~ 12 kilometres away from the nearest hospital ~~in the region~~ when both suffered severe ~~bodily~~ injuries.
8. Based upon several studies ~~conducted in the past~~, he ~~firmly~~ believes that, when ~~first~~ started next year, the two programs should be ~~very~~ selective, similar ~~in nature~~ and conducted only in the morning ~~hours~~.

Exercise 4

SECTION I: REMAINING OBJECTIVE

1. The speaker will discuss the relationship of economics and poverty at tonight's presentation.
2. Police have identified the man who attacked the 65-year-old woman.
3. The man was presented with an award for his efforts on behalf of the agency.
4. Tickets for the community theatre production of *Cats* cost $20.
5. The board ended its water service contract with the company.

SECTION II: AVOIDING REDUNDANT PHRASES

1. small
2. join
3. public
4. truth
5. crisis
6. fell
7. lag
8. protrude
9. resume
10. custom

SECTION III: AVOIDING WORDY PHRASES

1. raze
2. contact
3. conclude
4. rarely
5. because
6. escaped
7. encourage
8. sue
9. investigated
10. called for (or summoned)

SECTION IV: AVOIDING UNNECESSARY WORDS

1. The professor said she ~~was acquainted with~~ (knew) the author ~~of the book on account of the fact~~ (because) they had made contact ~~with each other~~ years ago.
2. The university's board of directors wanted to postpone ~~until later~~ a decision on the project until the board received ~~concrete~~ proposals from the contractors.
3. The mayor said the ~~physical~~ size of the new development was not that large but it would have the maximum ~~possible~~ impact on the city's ~~future~~ plans.
4. Police ~~have the belief~~ (believe) that it was a(n) ~~freak~~ accident that allowed the ~~deadly~~ poison to seep out of the tanker truck and cause the worst ~~ever~~ chemical spill in the country's history.
5. Firefighters responding to ~~the scene of~~ the house fire were confronted with a(n) ~~blazing~~ inferno and succeeded in ~~doing their best to~~ contain(ing) the flames.

SECTION V: TESTING ALL YOUR SKILLS

1. Mike Deacosti, his wife, and their two children, Mark and Amy, were invited to the representative's reception along with several other local residents.
2. The police officer explained to the motorist that he had been exceeding the speed limit and would face the maximum fine if he could not locate his driver's licence.
3. Before children can begin school, they must be able to read and write their name. (NOTE: The word "child" is singular, and the pronoun "they" is plural. Nouns and pronouns must agree. It is easier to make "child" plural ["children"] than to make "they" singular [he or she]. Avoid using the masculine "he" when you are referring to any or every child, both male and female.)
4. The information was presented at this time because all the members of the board, including Chairman Maggy Baille, were present and could vote to increase contributions to the employees' retirement accounts. (NOTE: The word "employees'" is a plural possessive.)
5. Candidate Donna Moronesi has raised more than $1 million before the campaign has begun. (NOTE: Are the woman's attractiveness and hair colour relevant to the story? Would you mention such things if you were writing about a male candidate? You might want to discuss this problem with your instructor and classmates.)
6. The politician thanked his supporters, whose collaboration helped win the election.
7. He suffered a broken leg and was blinded in his right eye as a result of the accident.
8. The mayor said she considered the attorney's proposal to settle the suit filed by the man over the death of his dog in the city pound but decided the settlement was not in the best interests of the city and its residents. (NOTE: Attribution is important in this sentence to avoid the possibility that it will sound like the writer's opinion.)
9. The attorney possessed evidence that helped the jury decide. (NOTE: You can substitute the word "had" for "possessed.")
10. Chairwoman Jane Abbott believed the offer by the company would hinder negotiations for an equitable contract with her employees because the increase would create a crisis of confidence among the employees and change the rules of the negotiations. (NOTE: Be careful of sexist language. Change "chairman" to "chairwoman." You might want to discuss the use of chairman, chairwoman and chairperson with your instructor.)

Chapter 3: The Language of News

Exercise 4

SECTION I: AVOIDING SLANG AND CLICHÉS

1. The employees ignored the company president's plea to support the restructuring plan.
2. People became violent when the club doors were closed, leaving them outside.
3. The premier said the election results favoured his party.
4. The students believed the program would fail because few supported it.
5. Soldiers fought a group of guerrilla fighters.

SECTION II: IMPROVING VERBS AND SENTENCE STRUCTURE

1. It is hoped that university officials will soon decide to postpone construction of the building.
2. The man, dressed in a green hoodie and black hat and sitting across from me at the café, ordered an espresso from the waitress.
3. More than 10 student residences have been burglarized in the last two weeks.
4. Paramedics are required to take patients in need of medical treatment to the nearest hospital.
5. A bystander, who witnessed the three-vehicle accident that closed Main Street for two hours so authorities could investigate, called police to the scene.

SECTION III: KEEPING RELATED WORDS AND IDEAS TOGETHER

1. The city needed more than $5 million to begin construction of the new arts centre.
2. The letter Mary wrote to her husband stationed in Afghanistan with the Canadian Forces was filled with news from their neighbourhood.
3. The proposal to increase the gas tax to raise $1 billion to improve the province's roads is expected to be vetoed by the premier.
4. Detectives questioned the suspect in the Thursday night burglary of the Main Street Restaurant for two hours.
5. The accident victim was found trapped under the motorcycle with cuts on his arms and legs.

SECTION IV: TESTING ALL YOUR SKILLS

1. The committee said the program is beneficial because students can get class credit for all they do at an internship.
2. Realizing what a beautiful day it was, she lay on the beach from 8 a.m. until 3 p.m.
3. The police officer told the jury members during the trial they needed to understand police investigations to understand how the robbery occurred.
4. Workshop participants agreed that the nurses should get a 15 per cent to 20 per cent pay raise.
5. The woman said her son, whom she considered quite intelligent, is anxious to get to college next year.
6. The author implies in the book titled *It's a Great Day in MY Neighbourhood* that people can have a good life if they want to.
7. The city council worked late into the night before voting 6–1 to spend $50,000 a year for three years on a consulting expert for the construction job.
8. The director said the clothing display features adult and children's clothing from the archive's 1930s collection.

SECTION V: AVOIDING JOURNALESE

1. She incurred $30,000 in medical expenses. OR Her medical expenses reached $30,000.
2. He approved spending $26,000 for the car.
3. The program will help high school students.
4. The new building will cost about $6 million.
5. Three council members opposed the proposal.

SECTION VI: AVOIDING JARGON

1. Police said the burglary suspects would be arraigned later in the week.
2. Teresa Phillips, who also uses the name Marie Phillips, testified that she helped the defendant steal jewelry from the store around the 9th of last month.
3. The company said it would use every department to overcome the budget crisis.
4. The mayor said he would order other city workers to drive the trash trucks if sanitation workers went on strike.
5. Brown's lawsuit says that he suffered physical and mental injuries and aggravated a previous condition, as well as lost his ability to earn a living, because of the accident.

Chapter 8: Quotations and Attribution

Exercise 2

1. "Our goal is peace," the prime minister said. (Use a comma, not a period, before the attribution, and place the punctuation mark inside the quotation mark. Transpose the attribution's wording so the subject appears before the verb. Avoid using "claimed" as a word of attribution.)

2. Benjamin Franklin said, "Death takes no bribes." (Use a comma, not a colon, before the one-sentence quotation. Because it is a complete sentence, capitalize the first word of the quotation. Place the final period inside the quotation mark.)

3. She said her son calls her literary endeavours "mom's writing thing." (Condense the attribution, and place the period inside the quotation mark. Normally, you do not need a comma before a partial quote.)

4. He is a scuba diver and pilot. He also enjoys skydiving and explains, "I like challenge, something exciting." (Clearly attribute the direct quotation.)

5. The Mideast crisis is likely to last indefinitely, the prime minister said. (The quotation can be paraphrased more clearly and simply. Place the paraphrase before the attribution.)

6. Albert Camus wrote: "A free press can of course be good or bad, but, most certainly, without freedom it will never be anything but bad.... Freedom is nothing else but a chance to be better, whereas enslavement is a certainty of the worse." (Place the attribution at the beginning, not the end, of a long quotation, and use a colon to introduce the quotation. Quotation marks do not have to be placed around every sentence in a continuing quotation. Use normal word order in the attribution.)

7. "I think that America has become too athletic," Jesse Owens said. "From Little League to the pro leagues, sports are no longer recreation. They are big business, and they're drudgery." (The attribution "expressed the opinion that" is wordy. Do not place quotation marks around every sentence in a continuing quotation. If it remains at the beginning of the quotation, the attribution should be followed by a colon. Attribute a continuing direct quotation only once.)

8. The man smiled and said: "It's a great deal for me. I expect to double my money." (Because the quotation contains more than one sentence, "said" should be followed by a colon, not a comma. Do not use "smiled" as a word of attribution. Place quotation marks at the beginning and end of the direct quotation, not at the beginning and end of every sentence. Attribute a continuing direct quotation only once.)

9. The woman said she likes her job as a newspaper reporter and explained: "I'm not paid much, but the work is important. And it's varied and exciting. Also, I like seeing my byline in the paper." (Reporters should stress their source's answer to a question, not the question. Attribute a continuing quote only once. Avoid "grinned" as a word of attribution. The attribution "responded by saying" is wordy.)

10. The librarian said the new building will cost about $4.6 million. (The attribution can be condensed, and by paraphrasing, you can simplify the quotation. Also, virtually all the news published in newspapers is given to reporters. You do not have to mention that routine detail in every story.)

11. "Thousands of the poor in Canada die every year of diseases we can easily cure," the professor said. "It's a crime, but no one ever is punished for their deaths." (Use the normal word order: "the professor said." Place the attribution at the beginning or end of a sentence or at a natural break in a sentence. Attribute a direct quotation only once, and place quotation marks at the beginning and end of the quotation, not at the beginning and end of every sentence.)

12. Thomas said students should never be spanked. "A young boy or girl who gets spanked in front of peers becomes embarrassed and the object of ridicule," he said. (Clearly attribute the direct quotation.)

13. The lawyer said: "He ripped the life-sustaining respirator tubes from his throat three times in an effort to die. He is simply a man who rejects medical treatment regardless of the consequences. He wants to die and has a constitutional right to do so." (Because the quotation

includes more than one sentence, use a colon, not a comma, after "said." Attribute a direct quotation only once.)

14. Bobby Knight, the basketball coach at the University, said: "Everyone has the will to win. Few have the will to prepare. It is the preparation that counts." (Use a colon, not a comma, after "said" because the quotation includes more than one sentence. Attribute a continuing quotation only once. Place quotation marks at the beginning and end of a direct quotation, not at the beginning and end of every sentence.)

15. She said the federal government must do more to help cities support and retrain the chronically unemployed. (Condense the attribution and avoid orphan quotes—quotation marks placed around one or two words.)

Chapter 20: Grammar and Spelling

Exercise 1

SECTION I: AGREEMENT

1. The committee submits its data this weekend and expects the data to help the church.
2. She said the company failed to earn enough to repay its loans, and she does not expect it to reopen.
3. The jury reached its verdict at 1 a.m., concluding that the media were guilty of libelling the restaurant and its 22 employees.
4. The decision allowed the city council to postpone its vote for a week, and council members suggested that the site's developer design a plan to save more trees.
5. A representative for the organization said it helps people who are on welfare obtain some job training and raise their self-esteem.

SECTION II: PLURALS AND POSSESSIVES

1. The women's car was parked nearby, and sheriff's deputies asked to see the owner's driver's licence.
2. The woman said she opposes assisted suicide "because a doctor's job is to save people's lives, not end them."
3. Last year's outstanding teacher insisted that people's complaints about the school's problems are mistaken.
4. Manvel Jones's parents said their younger children's teacher earned her bachelor's degree in philosophy and her master's degree in education.
5. Everyone's money was stolen, and the neighbourhood association's president warned that the police are no longer able to guarantee people's safety in the city's poorest neighbourhoods.

SECTION III: PLACEMENT

1. The Board of Trustees voted 8–1 during an emergency meeting Thursday morning to fire the college president for his sexual misconduct.
2. When the guests arrived, the hotel manager took their bags to their rooms.
3. At the Unitarian church on Sunday, the union representative urged Canadians to support better working conditions for the country's immigrant workers.
4. As Zena jogged around campus, a thorn bush ripped a hole in her shirt.
5. A suspect in the burglary case involving two lawn mowers stolen from a hardware store was arrested after a high-speed chase.

SECTION IV: PERSONIFICATION

1. Slamming on the brakes, the driver turned the car to the left, narrowly missing the dog.
2. The city officials said they cannot help the three businesses whose owners asked for better lighting.

3. After detecting the outbreak, the hospital administrators admitted that seven babies born this month were infected, including one who died.
4. Firefighters treated the child for smoke inhalation, then transported her to Mercy Hospital, where her broken legs were treated.
5. The corporation officers, who denied any responsibility for the deaths, will appear in court next month.

SECTION V: PARALLEL FORM

1. He was charged with driving drunk and having an expired driver's licence.
2. Karen Kim was a full-time student and Air Force reservist and part-time worker for a veterinarian.
3. To join the club, one must be a sophomore, junior or senior; study journalism; be in good academic standing; and have demonstrated professional journalistic ability.
4. The mayor warned that the neighbourhood's high crime rate causes residents to flee, contributes to more unemployment for workers, deprives the city of tax revenue, and lowers everyone's property values.
5. She said the other advantages of owning her own business include being independent, not having a boss, having flexible hours, and enduring less stress.

SECTION VI: MULTIPLE ERRORS

1. A sheriff's deputy arrested the driver after he saw the teenager pull the Chevrolet out of the alley and drive recklessly without headlights.
2. City officials also said that they cannot silence Sooyoung Li, the woman who fears pollution is likely to affect the neighbourhood's 300 residents.
3. Seeking more money, publicity and help for the poor, the church's members said they want the city to help them by providing food and housing for the homeless.
4. A spokesman said the Public Works Department could pave the development's road itself for less than $1.2 million. The Roess Company submitted a bid of $2.74 million.
5. A jury awarded almost $10.5 million to the operators of an abortion clinic who charged that picketers tormented them and their clients. The clinic's operators praised the jury's verdict, saying the jurors' courage and understanding set a needed precedent.

Chapter 21: Format, Copy Editing and CP style

Exercise 4

1. The priest celebrated mass during their marriage ceremony.
2. Morgan's new book is titled *Rachael's New Glasses.*
3. Her dad celebrates his birthday in August.
4. The jury found him not guilty.
5. The miniature ponies were raised in Elliott County.
6. The mayor lives at 49 Morning Glory St.
7. Seven of the people in the room were reading newspapers.
8. Jean and Diane's room was in a mess.
9. Neither Jason nor his friends were going to the party.
10. The wine was bottled in October 2002.
11. Most news organizations want a reporter with a bachelor's degree in journalism.
12. The police clocked the mayor going 30 km/h over the speed limit.
13. The address is 21 Merryweather Rd.
14. She will remember Sept. 11, 2001, always.
15. Manuel Middlebrooks Jr. works for CSIS.

Credits

Pages 264–5: Excerpt from "'I Couldn't Believe What I Saw': Canadians Working in New York City React with Shock to the Carnage at the World Trade Center [Final Edition]," by Rick Ouston and William Boei, with a file from Michael McCullough, *The Vancouver Sun*, September 11, 2001. Material reprinted with the express permission of: "Pacific Newspaper Group Inc.," a Postmedi Network Partnership.

Page 265: Excerpt from "It Started with a Scream: A Special Report on the Effect of the Terrorist Attacks on Ordinary People Around the Globe," by Jonathon Gatehouse and Charlie Gillis, *National Post*, September 12, 2001. Material reprinted with the express permission of: "The National Post Company," a division of Postmedia Network Inc.

Pages 265–6: Excerpt from "Former P.G. Man Watched as Plane Hit World Trade Center [Final Edition]," by Gordon Hoekstra, *Prince George Citizen,* September 13, 2001, Canadian Newsstand Pacific. Article courtesy of *The Prince George Citizen*–Gordon Hoekstra.

Pages 267–8: Excerpt from "Sidebar, Your Honour," and "Character Sketch," by Paul Benedetti, in *The Bigger Picture,* Ivor Shapiro, ed. (Toronto: Emond Montgomery, 2009), pp. 230–1 and 168–9.

Pages 317–18: Excerpt from "Government Violated Khadr's Rights," *Niagara Falls Review,* January 29, 2010. QMI Agency.

Page 318: Excerpt from CSIS "Celebrating 25 Years of Service," by Richard B. Fadden, www.csis.gc.ca/cmmn/dr_mssg_25-eng.asp.

Page 324 box: Adapted from Gregg McLachlan "Q.U.O.T.E.," www.newscollege.ca.

Pages 377–8: Excerpt from "Ron Meyers: A Song in His Heart and Law by His Side," by Kevin Rollason, *Winnipeg Free Press,* January 16, 2010, p. B1.

Page 379: Excerpt from "'Accidental' artist set the bar high," by Juan Rodriguez, *Vancouver Sun,* January 20, 2010, p. E4. Material reprinted with the express premission of: "CANWEST NEWS SERVICE," a division of Postmedia Network Inc.

Page 379–80: Excerpt from "Sweet harmony: Kate McGarrigle gave the world some memorable folk-pop music," *Ottawa Citizen,* January 20, 2010, p. C7. © The Times (London) and 20th January 2010/ nisyndication.com.

Pages 381–2: Excerpt from "Former Reporter Believed in 'Service to Mankind':; Citizen 'Woman's Page Writer' Was Caring and Adventurous," by Steven Mazey, *Ottawa Citizen,* January 7, 2010, p. C6. Material reprinted with the express permission of: "Ottawa Citizen Group Inc.," a division of Postmedia Network Inc.

Pages 382–3: Excerpt from "Talented Poet 'Left the World a Brighter Place,'" by Grania Litwin, *Ottawa Citizen,* January 16, 2010, p. G8. Material reprinted with the express premission of: "CANWEST NEWS SERVICE," a division of Postmedia Network Inc.

Pages 383–4: Excerpt from "Internet Map Zooms in on Fallen Soldiers: Memorial features photos, hometowns and obituaries of soldiers who have died in Afghanistan and Iraq," by Raveena Aulakh, *Toronto Star*, June 6, 2009, p. A12. Reprinted with permission of TorStar Syndication Service.

Page 409 box: Adapted from *The Canadian Press Stylebook,* 15th ed., pp. 183–93.

Page 420: Adapted from *The Canadian Press Stylebook,* 15th ed., p. 57.

Pages 422–3: Excerpt from "The SCOOTER Store Donates Power Mobility Scooter to World's Tallest Teenager," www.prnewswire.com/news-releases/paralyzed-pennsylvania-teenager-regains-hope-and-mobility-with-special-gift-from-the-scooter-store-58252017.html. Gift of Mobility, Registered Trademark of The Scooter Store.

Page 423–4: Excerpt from "Canada's first-ever astrobiology training program actually is rocket science," University of Western Ontario, Monday, November 23, 2009. Jeff Renaud, The University of Western Ontario.

Page 426: Excerpt from "Beef fuels Olympic Calibar Athletes," http://albertabeef.org/res/Fuel%20for%20Gold%20release%202008.pdf. Courtesy of Alberta Beef.

Pages 431–2: Excerpt from Megan Walde Manlove, Specialist, Science Communications & Marketing Office of Strategic Services, Penn State Hershey Medical Center. Megan Walde Manlove is a former journalist who currently serves as manager of media relations and public affairs for Penn State Milton S. Hershey Medical Center in Hershey, PA.

Page 454: Excerpt from *Investigative Reporting in Canada,* by Maxine Ruvinsky, Oxford University Press Canada, 2008, p. 128. Reprinted with permission of TorStar Syndication Service.

Pages 456–61 box: Excerpt from Canadian Association Journalists Code of Ethics. Courtesy of the Canadian Association of Journalists.

Pages 462–4: Adapted from "Some Thoughts on Plagiarism," published in August 1992 in *The Write Stuff,* an in-house publication of the *Houston Chronicle.* Reproduced with permission of HOUSTON CHRONICLE PUBLISHING COMPANY.

Page 504 box: Adapted from "Russell's Rules For Good Writing," by Nicholas Russell, Ph.D.

Pages 508–9: Exercise 2: "Gov't May Change Rules for Underage Workers," by *The StarPhoenix* (Saskatoon), September 27, 2008. Material reprinted with the express permission of: "Saskatoon Star Phoenix Group Inc.," a CanWest Partnership.

Pages 536–43: Appendix B adapted from *The Canadian Press Stylebook*, 15th ed., 2008, and *The Canadian Press Caps and Spelling*, 19th ed., 2009. Published by The Canadian Press.

Index

Note: Page numbers in italics refer to photographs.